ECCLESIASTICAL LORDSHIP, SEIGNEURIAL POWER AND THE COMMERCIALIZATION OF MILLING IN MEDIEVAL ENGLAND

For Emma Quartermaine, with all my love.

Ecclesiastical Lordship, Seigneurial Power and the Commercialization of Milling in Medieval England

ADAM LUCAS
University of Wollongong, Australia

Routledge
Taylor & Francis Group

LONDON AND NEW YORK

First published 2014 by Ashgate Publishing

2 Park Square, Milton Park, Abingdon, Oxfordshire OX14 4RN
52 Vanderbilt Avenue, New York, NY 10017

Routledge is an imprint of the Taylor & Francis Group, an informa business

First issued in paperback 2020

British Library Cataloguing in Publication Data
A catalogue record for this book is available from the British Library

Library of Congress Cataloging-in-Publication Data
Lucas, Adam.
  Ecclesiastical lordship, seigneurial power, and the commercialization of milling in medieval England / by Adam Lucas.
    pages cm
  Includes bibliographical references and index.
  ISBN 978-1-4094-2196-2 (hardcover : alk. paper)
  1. Monasticism and religious orders—Economic aspects—England—History. 2. Monasteries—Economic aspects—England—History. 3. Monastic and religious life—England—History. 4. Mills and mill-work—England—History. I. Title.
  BX2462.L83 2014
  338.4'766472009420902—dc 3
                                                                    2014008231
ISBN 978-1-4094-2196-2 (hbk)
ISBN 978-0-367-60033-4 (pbk)

Contents

Acknowledgements

This book is built on the groundbreaking research of Richard Holt and John Langdon, who have been mentors and friends for more than 15 years. The research which forms the basis for this book could not have been started, let alone completed, without their patient guidance. I nevertheless take full responsibility for any errors of fact or interpretation which it might contain.

Over the last several years, Marjorie Chibnall and Rosamond Faith have read and commented on parts of the manuscript that were relevant to their own research. Nicholas Brooks, Christopher Dyer, Bill Day, Jens Röhrkasten and Robert Swanson all took the time to discuss my research with me during my brief sojourn at the Centre for Medieval Studies at the University of Birmingham in 2000 while still conducting my doctoral research. Professors Brooks and Dyer have also provided occasional guidance since then, for which I am most grateful. I would also like to thank archaeologist Stephen Moorhouse for drawing my attention to the remains of a number of horizontal-wheeled watermills dating to the post-Conquest period in northern England, and to Colin Rynne, Pamela Long, Kevin Greene, John Schuster and Steven Walton for their intellectual and moral support over many years. The former Faculty of Arts at the University of Wollongong provided me with study leave in 2011 and a book completion grant in 2012 to finalise my research and write up the first draft of the book manuscript, providing me with valuable time to re-familiarise myself with my own research and that of my predecessors and contemporaries.

My son, Conrad, my wife, Emma, and many other friends and family members have been gracious and loving in allowing me the time to spend writing and doing research for the book when I would often have preferred to have spent it with them. They have also been subjected to many a long account of the problems and obstacles I have faced along the way; for all your attentiveness and helpful comments and suggestions, thank you.

Thanks also to my graphic artist and friend, Carlos Agamez, my commissioning editor, Emily Yates, and the anonymous readers and editors at Ashgate for having been so patient and supportive of this project from its inception.

Abbreviations

DM   *Domesday Monachorum*
IPM   *Inquisitiones Post Mortem*

IRMA industrial revolution of the Middle Ages

MI   monastic innovation

VCH   Victoria County Histories

Table Abbreviations (unless otherwise indicated in notes to table)

admin administrator

c   customary tenant

f   free tenant

kt   knight

lb   pound (weight)

n   *nativi*

n/a   not applicable

n.d.   no data

p.a.   *per annum*

Y   yes

<   after

>   before

Note on Currency

aureus	gold coin (esp. bezant)
kronna/cronna	crannock; dry measure of (esp. Welsh and Irish)
gallina/galo	gallon; gallon measure (usu. of wine or beer)
mark	a unit of account; 1 oz. of silver; 13s 4d or 2/3 of a pound sterling, or 160 pennies
mancus	a gold or silver coin worth 12-1/2 pennies
pound (*libre*)	20 shillings, or 240 pennies
shilling	12 pennies

Glossary of Medieval Terms

advocate	lay protector of a religious house
advowson	the right to present a clerk to a vacant ecclesiastical benefice or living; patronage of an ecclesiastical office and obligation to defend its rights as advocate
alien priory	religious house dependent on a continental monastery
amercement	fine
appropriation	transfer of the endowments and income of a parish church to a religious house in return for the provision of pastoral care
assart	a piece of woodland or other land cleared for cultivation
assign	the beneficiary of a deceased estate who was not an heir
assize	'rent of assize' is a fixed rent
banlieu	an area of approximately three miles' radius around an abbey which delineated its precincts; all the lands within it were permanently freed from the payment of geld and other services
benefice	ecclesiastical living
bondsman	a **villein**; the name is probably derived from Icelandic *bondi* = a husbandman
bovate	a unit of land in the **Danelaw**, subdivision of a **carucate**; as much land as one ox could plough in one year; 1/8 carucate; 10 to 18 acres depending on the tillage system
capital messuage	portion of land occupied by the owner of a property containing several **messuage**s
cartulary	a volume containing a collection of charters, title deeds and other legal documents giving title to property
carucate	a unit of land in the **Danelaw** corresponding to the Anglo-Saxon **hide**; as much land as could be tilled by one plough in a year; in the three-field system 180 acres, in the two-field system 160 acres, but only plough land reckoned generally; therefore, a Norman carucate constituted 120 acres or 80 acres, and an English carucate 144 acres or 96 acres, but could be up to 240 acres
castle-guard	form of heritable tenure which required the tenant to perform castle guard duty for a specified number of days per year
chapter	(1) as prescribed in the Rule of St Benedict, the daily meeting of a community, which took place in the chapter house, for the reading of a chapter of the Rule, confessions of faults and imposition of penance, etc.; (2) body of clergy or monks/regular canons serving a cathedral church

charter	contract or title deed relating to conveyance of landed property
close	enclosed place, precincts (of monastery, etc.)
corrody	a pension, usually in the form of lodging, food and/or clothing, at a religious house, granted to a lay person in return for a lump sum payment
cottager	one who lives in a cottage (usu. same as **cottar**)
cottar	a farm labourer having free use of a cottage; the owner of a cottage, courtyard, and generally five acres of arable land; a superior type of **villein**, corresponding to the modern agricultural labourer
croft	homestead, site of house and its outbuildings
cultura	a furlong in the open field
curtilage	house with stables and/or outbuildings, surrounded by a hedge or enclosure
customary	a written collection of the 'house rules' or code of practice of a single religious house
customary tenure	property held outside the **demesne** in exchange for feudal services, sometimes commuted to a nominal cash rent in the twelfth and thirteenth centuries and subsequently
custumal	a written collection or abstract of the customs of a **manor**, city, province, etc.; a manual of feudal rules
Danegeld	the land-tax developed and administered by the Anglo-Saxon kings and applied to the English **Danelaw**, which provided part of the basis for the tax assessment of **Domesday Book**
Danelaw	the north-eastern region of England, subject to Scandinavian settlement and retaining distinctive customs and nomenclature
demesne	home farm of an individual estate; alternatively land or estates kept in the possession of, and worked on behalf of, the landlord, and not leased to tenants
Domesday Book	the great inquest undertaken throughout England by the tax assessors of William I in 1085–1086 with the object of assessing through local inquiry how much land-tax was due from each estate, as well as a basis for possible revision
dredge	a mixture of barley and oats
dreng	an Anglo-Saxon soldier or warrior who held land in free tenure directly from the king
drengage	the land held by an Anglo-Saxon **dreng**, roughly equivalent to the later knight's fee
ealdorman	the highest Anglo-Saxon magnate
enfeoffment	the granting of land in return for military service

escheator	the king's officer who oversees the process whereby property passes into the hands of the government in circumstances in which an owner dies intestate and without heirs, or has their property confiscated for some other reason
estover	right to cut firewood
fee	see **knight's fee**
fee-farm	right to collect and retain revenues in return for a fixed rent
feodary	(1) an office in the Court of Wards, appointed to receive all the rents of the Ward's lands within his circuit; (2) the ***Inquisitiones Post Mortem*** taken by escheators and feodaries; (3) one who holds lands of an overlord on condition of homage and service; a feudal tenant, a vassal; (4) a subject, dependant, retainer, servant
fief	see **knight's fee**
forinsec service	'foreign service' (or 'knight's service'); a service not belonging to the chief lord, but the king, whereby tenants-in-chief are required to supply a knight for foreign service
frankalmoin	literally 'in free alms'; ecclesiastical tenure in return for which prayers alone were due
frankpledge	the compulsory mutual pledging of the tithing; members of the local tithing (i.e., the local area in which tithes were due) acted as sureties for each other if any were unable to pay fines or **amercement**s.
freeman	a free peasant, one who is not subject to labour services
gage	a pledge, or property held as security
gavelkind	partible inheritance whereby all sons (and daughters?) would receive an equal share of their father's estate (Kentish)
gavelswen	the lord's right to the third largest pig belonging to a tenant
geld	the Anglo-Saxon royal tax levied on a territorial basis
***gersum* (or gressum)**	a premium or fine, esp. **merchet**
general chapter	annual meeting of the heads of all houses of an order (Cistercian, etc.)
grand serjeanty	feudal tenure by which land was held in return for a specific (non-military) personal service to the Crown
grange	farm estate, worked by hired labour and supervised by lay brethren; a system of farming, created by the Cistercians and followed by others, which existed outside the manorial system
hereditary tenure	property held outside the demesne by a tenant in heredity, i.e., his or her heirs or assigns would inherit the tenure, which may or may not have involved an increase in the rental paid (a.k.a. free tenure)

heriot	death duty
hide	a unit of land varying in acreage according to locality, c. 100 acres; often under-recorded when cited in taxation records
holm	meadow
hundred	a subdivision of a county or shire with its own court
Inquisitiones Post Mortem	royal inquiries into the tax payable on the deceased estates of tenants-in-chief, first instituted by Henry II
knight's fee	the holding which supported a knight and in return for which he owed military service, generally consisting of anything from one to five hides (80 to 600 acres), the size of the holding being determined by the status of the fighting man concerned; although normally part of a **manor** or **vill**, some fees attained the status of manors during the late eleventh and twelfth century (in York in early thirteenth century worth between £3 and £6 per annum)[1]
leuga	same as *banlieu*
liturgy	public, as opposed to private, prayer
manor	the territory around a lord's residence within which he or she had rights over the land and men; during Anglo-Saxon times, a house and its associated territory against which **geld** was charged
marl	right to improve the soil
mensa	a formal separation between a bishop's activities and possessions and those of his priesthood or monks; instituted partially as a means of preventing the monks or canons from appropriating episcopal and archiepiscopal property upon the deaths of bishops and archbishops, but also to prevent the latter from having to contribute materially to the living costs of the cathedral clergy
merchet	payment to a lord on the marriage of a daughter or son
messuage	portion of land occupied by (or site for) a dwelling house and its appurtenances (usually including outbuildings)
miles	a knight or military retainer of a lord, who could be of varying wealth and status
Mortmain, Statute of	law passed by Edward I in 1279 which forbade all lords from granting or selling land to an ecclesiastical body without the written authorisation of the king
nativi	persons who were unfree by birth; slaves (also *servi*, *ancille*, *mulieres serviles*)
obedientiary	monk, canon or nun to whom has been assigned particular administrative responsibilities
pannage	right to feed pigs on acorns and beech mast

---

[1] Between 8 and 12 carucates made a fee in York, with 1 carucate worth 9s. per annum; 3 carucates 23s. 4d. per annum. See *Cal. IPM Edw. II*, Vol. 5, pp. 317–18.

pasture	right to graze stock
pightes/pightles	means the same as **croft**
pingles	as above
pittance	small dishes of food and drink allowed to members of a community on special occasions, for example, on the anniversary of a founder
ploughland	the acreage which an eight-oxen team could plough; might be artificial when cited in taxation records
possessory assize	legal action based upon possession rather than fundamental right
prebend	the stipend of a canon or member of a chapter; the portion of land or tithe from which this is drawn
purpresture	reclamation either by clearance or drainage
register	an official list of names, items, attendances, etc.; the book or other documents in which this is kept
relief	a fee paid by an outgoing tenant upon a change of tenure
sac	the privilege of exclusive jurisdiction over an estate, which included the power to fine or punish those who were found guilty by law and to collect a proportion of the revenues of justice
scutage	a cash payment in lieu of military service
serjeanty	see **grand serjeanty**
serf	a labourer who could not be removed (except by manumission) from his lord's land on which he worked, and was transferred with it when it passed to another owner; free, he was restricted in his movements and in the disposal of his property, and was inferior in status to a free tenant
seisin	possession
selion	strip of ploughland
soc **(soke)**	the territory over which a right of local jurisdiction extended, which included the collection of taxes and the exercise of justice
socage	the tenure of land by certain determinate services other than knight's service (Norman)
sokeland	land held freely under the jurisdiction of a lord owing military service, bridge and fortification work (Anglo-Saxon); a form of dependent or **villein** tenure (Norman)
sokeman	a free peasant with a small holding owing military and public services (Anglo-Saxon); another term for a **villein** (Norman)

spirituality	church property (churches, glebe [church land], tithes, burial dues, etc.) from which income is derived
subinfeudated land	land that has been granted by a **tenant-in-chief** to a knightly vassal in return for military service or to a religious house in return for a cash rent or other service which has been in turn let to other tenants for cash or labour services, sometimes leading to the alienation of that property
suit of court	obligation of all free holders to attend manorial court sessions as a condition of tenure
tallage	annual aid paid to the lord by a **villein**
temporality	church possessions such as land, rent, mills, etc., from which revenue is derived
tenmentale	provision of 10 men to keep the public peace as tribute to the king (Anglo-Saxon); also a payment due from these men of six shillings per plough
tenant-in-chief	one who holds land directly of the king
thegn	a member of the Anglo-Saxon aristocracy who held land from the king or other superior in return for performing military service
thegnage	the land belonging to an Anglo-Saxon **thegn**
tithe	a tenth part of produce, given to the Church
toft	same as **croft**, although 'toft' can mean the garden and 'croft' the holding itself; 'toft and croft' denotes a house and its arable land (Old Norse)
turbary	right to cut peat and turves
vill	village
villein	a feudal tenant entirely subject to a lord or attached to a **manor**; status of villein changed gradually from free at **Domesday** to unfree by the thirteenth century, mainly due to royal writs which protected freeholders, but surrendered villeins to their lords [Hilton 1965]
virgate	a subdivision of a **hide**, corresponding to the **Danelaw bovate** but divided decimally rather than duodecimally; long, narrow ploughland, averaging 30 acres; generally four virgates to a hide, but may be as much as six per hide; may be 20, 24, or 30 acres, even 40 acres.
wapentake	a **Danelaw** subdivision of the county corresponding to the Anglo-Saxon **hundred**
wist	a measure of land in Sussex of 1–4 **virgates**

Sources:

Janet Burton, *Monastic and Religious Orders in Britain 1000–1300*, Cambridge University Press, 1994.

Ephraim Chambers, *Cyclopedia, or, An universal dictionary or arts and sceinces*, 2 vols. J. & J. Knapton, London, 1728.

Rosamond Faith, *The English Peasantry and the Growth of Lordship*, Leicester University Press, London, 1999 (1st pub. 1997).

Sally Harvey, 'The Knight and the Knight's Fee in England', *Past and Present* 49, 1970, pp. 3–43.

Rodney H. Hilton, 'Freedom and Villeinage in England', *Past and Present* 31, July 1965, pp. 3–19.

R.E. Latham, *Revised Medieval Latin Word-List*, Oxford University Press, London, 1999 (1st pub. 1965).

F.W. Maitland, *Domesday Book and Beyond: Three Essays in the Early History of England*, Cambridge University Press, Cambridge (1st pub. 1897), 1987.

Oxford English Dictionary, 1st & 2nd edns.

Sandra Raban, *The Estates of Thorney and Crowland: A Study in Medieval Monastic Land Tenure*, University of Cambridge, Department of Land Economy, 1977.

Eleanor Searle, *Lordship and Community: Battle Abbey and Its Banlieu, 1066–1538*, Pontifical Institute of Medieval Studies, Toronto, 1974.

List of Figures

List of Charts

List of Tables

Introduction
The History and Historiography of Medieval Milling

This book is the first detailed study of the role of the Church in the commercialization of milling in medieval England, a process which began as early as the tenth century and reached its medieval zenith in the early fourteenth century.[1] Drawing on theoretical approaches and research methodologies developed in medieval social and economic history, it seeks to determine how religious houses first acquired their property, including their mills, and how changing notions of social status, landholding and tenure under the Anglo-Saxons, Normans and their successors shaped the involvement of the Church in medieval milling, as well as its role in the development of both seigneurial and non-seigneurial forms of milling activity.

Focusing on the period from the late eleventh to the mid-sixteenth centuries, the book examines the estate management practices of more than 30 English religious houses, with an emphasis on the role played by mills and milling in the establishment and development of a range of different sized episcopal and conventual foundations. Contrary to the views espoused by a number of prominent historians of technology since the 1930s, the book seeks to demonstrate that patterns of mill acquisition, innovation and exploitation were shaped not only by the size, value and distribution of a house's estates, but also by environmental and demographic factors; changing cultural attitudes and legal conventions; prevailing and emergent technical traditions; the personal relations of a house with its patrons, tenants, servants and neighbours; and the entrepreneurial and administrative flair of bishops, abbots, priors and other ecclesiastical officials.

Although a sophisticated understanding of mills and milling during the Middle Ages has emerged from the work of medieval historians and archaeologists over the last few decades, the topic has remained relatively peripheral within both the history of technology and medieval history. There are, however, a number of reasons why it should be accorded a more important role. The first is that it has already provided scholars with some significant insights into the transition from post-classical times to feudalism and capitalism in Western Europe,[2] illuminating a number of processes which have preoccupied scholars since the mid-nineteenth century.[3] The second is that historians of technology have contended for decades that medieval milling was not only profoundly innovative, it provided the foundations for the development of modern industry.[4] The two main theories which have generally been relied upon to explain why this was supposedly the case (the industrial revolution of the Middle Ages (IRMA) thesis and the monastic innovation [MI] thesis) continue to enjoy some cachet within the field,[5] even though both theories have proven to be inadequate to the task in a number of respects.[6]

For social and economic historians, and particularly those of a Marxist persuasion, the primary motivation for the ownership of mills by lords during the medieval and early modern periods was their ability to provide them with a significant source of cash or grain revenue. As I have argued in my earlier work on the subject,

---

[1]   The term 'commercialization' is used throughout this book in both the weak and strong senses first articulated by Britnell (1996), to refer to both a simple increase in commercial activity during the period from roughly 1000 to 1300, as well as an increase in commercial activity which outstripped population growth from roughly 1000 to 1500.

[2]   Through the work of scholars such as Colin Rynne and Niall Brady on Ireland, Paolo Squatriti and John Muendel on Italy, Thomas Glick on Spain, and Richard Holt and John Langdon on England, all of whose research will be discussed in more detail in the chapters to follow.

[3]   See Hilton (1976) and Aston and Philpin (1987), respectively, for the Dobb-Sweezy and Brenner debates between the 1940s and 1980s, and Epstein (2007) on Rodney Hilton's contribution to these debates. Cf. Langdon (2004), pp. 296–305, for his reflections on how recent mill scholarship might help recast the bases for these debates.

[4]   The most prominent exponents of this position were Mumford (1963), pp. 112–18, Gille (1954) and White (1964), p. 88. Later exponents include Blaine (1966), Gimpel (1988) (1st pub. 1976) and Reynolds (1983).

[5]   For example, both theories garner a surprisingly affirmative mention in George Ovitt's recent entry on medieval technology in Lindberg and Shank (2013), pp. 631–44.

[6]   See Lucas (2005), (2006a), (2006b), (2010).

even though Marc Bloch's famous article of 1935, "Avènement et Conquêtes du Moulin à Eau" can be seen as having been one of two key works responsible for initiating both the MI and IRMA theses,[7] medievalists have tended to focus more on Bloch's contention that ecclesiastical elites imposed the 'advanced technology' of the watermill on peasants and townsfolk as a means of surplus extraction, as their tenants preferred to use the cheaper and simpler technology of the handmill, or rotary quern. And while there is ample evidence from France and England that lords sought to maximize the revenues from their mills through the creation or maintenance of seigneurial monopolies on their estates – what Bloch called *banalités*[8] – just as the received wisdom of an earlier generation of historians of technology does not sit favourably with the empirical evidence, we now know that a lord's ability to impose seigneurial monopolies on his or her tenants, and milling monopolies in particular, varied considerably throughout feudal Europe. For example, in England, France and Italy, the existence of mills outside seigneurial control was far more common than earlier scholars were prepared to accept.[9] Indeed, as I will argue in the pages to follow, some of the forms of non-seigneurial tenure that existed in England from the twelfth and thirteenth centuries onward have their origins in pre-Norman forms of land tenure, and provide important precedents and models for the forms of freehold tenure that emerged at the beginning of the modern period.

A third important, but related, reason for studying the development of medieval milling is that it is one of the earliest sectors of the medieval economy in which cash rents were paid on leases as a substitute for labour rents and rents in kind. Although in some cases the mill rents recorded in Domesday Book are in sticks of eels caught in the ponds and watercourses appurtenant to these mills, and sometimes also in measures of grain, iron, salt, honey and malt, most of them are in cash.[10] By the late fourteenth century, when lords were divesting themselves of any direct responsibility for demesne agriculture, mill rents were paid almost exclusively in cash.[11] Because there is a wealth of mill-related legal documents from various parts of Europe dating back as far as the sixth and seventh centuries, it is possible to use these documents to trace the transition from an Iron Age economic system based on tribute, to one of feudal obligations and the beginnings of a cash economy from the eighth or ninth century, and on to a more consumer- and market-driven economy (albeit still largely grounded in feudal obligations) from the twelfth and thirteenth century onward.

Milling is also one of the earliest forms of work to be mechanized and partially automated, largely because of the extraordinary amount of manual labour required to grind grain to make flour. Watermills for grinding grain were in widespread use from at least the first century CE throughout the Roman Empire, including Roman Britain,[12] strongly suggesting that there was some continuity of classical milling traditions into the medieval period. However, although the use of water power for purposes other than grinding grain also originates during the Roman period,[13] it does not appear to have occurred in England until the late

---

[7]   The other being Lewis Mumford's *Technics and Civilization* (1934). See Lucas (2005), pp. 1–2; (2006b), pp. 89–90.

[8]   See Bloch (1935), (1967).

[9]   Such 'non-seigneurial' mills have been documented by Holt (1987), (1988), (1990), (1996); Langdon (1991), (1994), 2004); Bois (2002); Squatriti (1997), (1998); Lucas (2006b).

[10]   For example, in Worcestershire, the mills of Kyre Magna, Salop and Ryton paid their rents in grain, while another at Cleeve Prior paid in honey, whereas the Wasperton mill in Warwickshire paid in salt, the Bledlow mill in Buckinghamshire paid in malt, and two mills at Lexworthy in Somersetshire paid in blooms of iron (*ii molini reddentes ii plumbas ferri*) (see Darby [1979], p. 270). Lynn White's contention that these latter renders in blooms of iron indicate that the mills concerned were water-powered forges is not sustainable on the basis of this flimsy evidence (see White [1980], p. 84). As Colin Rynne has rightly pointed out, "the mill renders recorded in Domesday only reflect the activities of those who controlled the mills and *not* the actual industrial activities of the mills" (see Rynne [1988], Vol. II, p. 161). However, it should be added that the cash rents listed for Domesday mills may in some cases have indicated the conversion of the value of tollcorn consumed on the manor into a cash sum (see Holt (1987), p. 13). For more information on honey rents, see Darby and Welldon Finn (2009), p. 27; Seebohm (1915), p. 185. Beaulieu Abbey's mill of Kyndlewere on the Thames in Berkshire is recorded as rendering six gallons of honey in Hockey (1975), p. 75.

[11]   Holt (1988), p. 71. All of this evidence is in accord with the argument of Britnell (1996), that large sectors of the English economy were well and truly monetized by the early fourteenth century.

[12]   Recent studies include: Spain (1984), (1992); Trovò (1996); Wikander (1984), (2000a) (2000b); Wilson (2002a), (2002b); Bennett, Riddler and Sparey-Green (2010).

[13]   Wikander (2000b); Wilson (2002a), (2008); Greene (2012).

twelfth century onwards for fulling cloth and forging iron.[14] And even though English mills were being turned to a number of different tasks by the middle of the thirteenth century, including grinding malted grain for brewing beer, grinding bark to extract the tannin for curing leather, and powering grinding wheels for tool sharpening, there is nowhere near as much evidence for industrial uses of mills in medieval England as there is for medieval France and Italy.[15] The lower rents and revenues from English industrial mills as compared to grain mills appears to have acted as a disincentive to lordly investment until the late fourteenth century, when grain mills struggling for custom in the wake of successive plague epidemics were increasingly converted to mills for fulling cloth.[16] Furthermore, the manuscript evidence suggests that although it was lay lords and in some cases, ecclesiastical lords, who were early investors in industrial applications of water power in the late twelfth and thirteenth centuries, it was 'small men', e.g. millers, carpenters and members of the lesser gentry, who were the main investors from the late fourteenth century onwards.[17]

Finally, because grain milling was a focus for lordly profit-making, it was also a source of conflict over such issues as land and water rights, who had the right to own and operate mills, the proportion of milled grain paid to millers, and the obligation of manorial tenants to mill their grain at the lord's mill. Of the more than 50 religious houses discussed in this book, Bury St Edmunds, Christ Church Canterbury, Cirencester, St Albans and Worcester Cathedral Priory were all involved in disputes over who had the right to own and operate mills within their demesnes, while Bury St Edmunds, Chichester, Lacock, Old Wardon, Sibton, St Denys's and St Peter's York were just some of those houses engaged in disputes with tenants and neighbours over water rights. Cirencester, Halesowen and St Albans were also famously involved in the breaking and/or confiscation of tenants' handmills, as Bloch and many others scholars have noted.[18] Such activities engendered much resentment and ultimately violence against those houses from their disgruntled tenants. And yet it would appear from the court rolls and the religious houses' own records that such authoritarian and even oppressive behaviour was not universal, or even very common.[19] As we will see in the pages to follow, even amongst those houses that diligently exercised their feudal rights, concessions were made, liberties were granted, and loyal servants, retainers and tenants were rewarded.

Because the Church was one of the largest and wealthiest landowners in Christendom, an analysis of its role in the social and economic development of medieval milling can provide important insights into the long transition towards a market-based economy and the transformation of work practices, property relations and social roles which accompanied those changes. It can also reveal just how inadequate have been previous efforts by most historians of technology to describe the social and economic significance of medieval milling, especially with regard to the role of the religious houses and monastic orders in that process.

The Historiography of Medieval Milling

Since the mid-1930s, there have been two dominant approaches to the study of mills and milling in the Middle Ages. Although both appeared at around the same time, they came from completely different theoretical perspectives. One was primarily informed by an empirical, materialist historiography that focussed on social, economic and environmental factors, while the other was primarily informed by a liberal idealist historiography that took a more interpretative approach and drew on a wide range of sources and types of evidence. These two approaches did not, on the whole, cross-fertilize, and generally remained on divergent

---

[14]   Holt (1990), pp. 56–7; Langdon (1994), pp. 13–17. On the English and Welsh fulling industries see: Scott (1931–32); Carus-Wilson (1941), (1944) (1950); Lennard (1947), (1951); Miller (1965); Donkin (1978), pp. 53, 135–8, 172–3, 188–90; Jack (1981); Beamish (1983); Holt (1988), Ch. 9; Langdon (1991), pp. 434–6; Lucas (2005), (2006), Ch. 6–9.

[15]   Lucas (2006a), Ch. 6–8 and Appendix A. See also Langdon (1997).

[16]   Holt (1988), pp. 155–8; Langdon (1994), pp. 13–15, (2004), pp. 40–54; Lucas (2005), pp. 24–5, (2006a), pp. 248, 254–5, 261, 270–71.

[17]   Langdon (2004), pp. 40–54, 176–235; Lucas (2006a), Ch. 8, (2006b), pp. 103–6.

[18]   See, for example, Bennett (1937), pp. 129–33; Bloch (1967); Razi (1983); Holt (1988), pp. 40–45.

[19]   The lack of English evidence for lordly compulsion in relation to medieval milling is most clearly demonstrated by Langdon (2004), pp. 259–95. Cf. Bennett (1937), pp. 130–32 and Holt (1988), pp. 38–40. I will take up this issue in more detail in Chapter 3.

paths for many decades, with occasional examples of the former approach sometimes informing debates in the latter, although seldom the other way around.

Generally speaking, the two approaches arose within two different disciplines with very different origins: medieval social and economic history and the history of technology. Medieval social and economic history emerged from nineteenth-century philology and local and national historical traditions with a firm basis in academia, whereas the history of technology had a far more eclectic genesis. Its earliest exponents were either self-trained amateurs, often with backgrounds in engineering or the sciences, or were academically trained historians, economists or sociologists who had decided to focus their academic studies on 'the history of techniques'. Most tended to focus on a few key pieces of scholarship from medieval studies to make a number of broad generalizations about the role of different social groups in the development of medieval technology. One of the main theses advanced by these scholars was that the Latin Church played a fundamental role in the development of wind- and water power in the Middle Ages, and consequently, in the transition from medieval to modern societies.

The question of why Western European societies underwent the transition from agrarian feudalism to mercantile and industrial capitalism as the result of their own internal dynamics, when similar societies amongst their contemporaries in North Africa and Asia did not, has preoccupied scholars in the humanities for more than a century, serving as it does to bolster broader conceptions of Western cultural and technological superiority.[20] In the history of technology, the answer that received the most widespread support until the 1980s was that medieval Western Europeans were not only a remarkably inventive people compared to any of their historical predecessors, they were enthusiastic assimilators of technological innovation. They acquired this psychological orientation through the widespread dissemination of Latin Church doctrine, which sanctified manual labour and the practical arts, and encouraged a willingness to engage in technical activity. The vehicle for the dissemination of these attitudes was the monastic system. Christian attitudes towards labour, the practical arts and the natural world were exemplified by the Benedictines' and Cistercians' contagious enthusiasm for building watermills and windmills, activities which freed the monks' time for more spiritual pursuits.

This received wisdom was espoused by earlier historians of technology independently of their ideological and methodological commitments. Whether we look at the work of internalist historians of technology such as Robert Forbes and Friedrich Klemm, or those who followed the roughly parallel post-war American and French 'contextualist' traditions such as Lewis Mumford, Lynn White and Bertrand Gille, all of them subscribe to the narrative that medieval Western Christianity acted as a nurturing 'cultural climate' for the development of science and technology.[21] While a range of social and technological developments in the Middle Ages were supposed to have been stimulated by this new cultural climate, foremost amongst them was the spread of watermill and windmill technologies. Milling has for decades been deployed as the exemplar of medieval technological development. It is supposed to have been *the* main focus for technological innovation and diffusion in the European Middle Ages, laying the foundations for the widespread automation of industry which came with the steam engine.

Mumford, White, Forbes and Gille were perhaps the most prominent scholars to argue that the large number of manuscript references to water- and wind-powered machines from the early to later Middle Ages in the civilizations of Western Christendom, Islam and Confucian China indicated a rapid increase in the numbers and kinds of power machines deployed during this period, and that the increase was most pronounced in Western Europe during the later Middle Ages. They consequently believed that these developments were an important sign of the West's autochthonic transition to modernity, in contrast to Islamic countries and Confucian China, which they assumed had stagnated technologically, or even regressed during the same

---

[20]   See Ovitt (1986), pp. 477–86, for an overview of the debate. See also Adas (1989).

[21]   See, for example: Forbes (1956), pp. 605–6; Klemm (1959), p. 85; Mumford (1967), Ch. 12; White (1978), pp. 89–90, 221, 231–53; Gille (1969), pp. 559–62. Although all of these scholars came from nominally Christian backgrounds, it would seem that White was the only active church-goer amongst them. Why they should have all adopted what might be interpreted as a Christian idealist thesis of technological development is therefore unclear. The notion of a nurturing 'cultural climate' is one used by White in his 1971 essay, "Cultural Climates and Technological Advance in the Middle Ages", an essay in which he fully develops his thesis that the monasteries and Christian doctrine played a central role in the scientific and technological developments of the Middle Ages. See Staudenmaier (1985), Roland (2003) and Lucas (2010) for historiographical discussions of these trends.

period. Medieval European technical prowess was deemed so significant by White, Gille and Jean Gimpel that they felt it constituted 'an industrial revolution of the Middle Ages'.[22]

As I have argued at length elsewhere,[23] this latter thesis has its genesis in the writings of Mumford, Bloch and White between the 1930s and 1970s,[24] although Mumford and White were part of a larger group of scholars who shared similar conceptions of a unique medieval mentality that had its roots in Western Church theology.[25] According to these scholars, the positive attitude towards labour and technology held by medieval Europeans was fundamentally different to any that had existed previously.

Until the late 1980s, most of the debate about medieval technological development within the history of technology was preoccupied with discussions of the views of the aforementioned scholars and a few other notable figures, but paid little attention to research that had come from outside the discipline. The IRMA and MI theses remained largely unchallenged and consequently attained the status of the conventional view. Although there was excellent work in medieval social and economic history, archaeology, and social and economic geography that could be drawn upon and used as a guide for further study, only in a handful of instances did scholars within the discipline take such an approach.[26]

Nevertheless, there are some elements of both the IRMA and MI theses which do require further investigation, including the claim that by the eleventh or twelfth century, the number of watermills in medieval Europe can be regarded as having attained an industrial scale. While there are a number of reasons for questioning such a conclusion,[27] it is a claim that has found some sympathy in medieval social and economic history circles, and therefore warrants further discussion.[28]

Amongst those medievalists who touched upon the subject of milling in the context of broader discussions about the histories of particular estates, and in general histories of particular regions or nations, are N. Neilson, Marc Bloch, H.S. Bennett, Margaret Hodgen, Eleanora Carus-Wilson, H.P.R. Finberg, E.A. Kosminsky, Ann-Marie Bautier, H.M. Colvin, Rodney Hilton, Georges Duby, H.C. Darby and Barbara Harvey.[29] While all of these scholars clearly recognized that mills and milling were integral aspects of life on the medieval manor, they were conscious of mills' symbolic role as emblems of lordly power as well as their more tangible role as suppliers of milled grain and cash revenue for lordly and peasant households. Bloch, Kosminsky, Hilton and Duby saw mills as important tools of revenue-raising for lords and a focal point for class conflict, whereas Carus-Wilson, Margaret Hodgen and Ann-Marie Bautier tended to share at least some of the assumptions about medieval technological development embraced by their contemporaries in the history of technology.[30] Given their shared orientations, it is perhaps unsurprising that it should be the work of these three medievalists that is most often cited in the history of technology literature before 1990.[31] Bloch is the only other medievalist of note who appears in the pre-1990 history of technology literature, although he is only rarely cited or quoted.

---

[22]   See note 4 above.

[23]   Lucas (2005), (2006a), (2010).

[24]   See Mumford (1963) [1st pub. 1934], (1967), Bloch (1967), and White (1964) [1st pub. 1962], (1975), (1978).

[25]   This larger group of scholars were most active between the 1940s and 1990s, and includes Samuel Lilley, Robert Forbes, W.H.G. Armytage, Bertrand Gille, Bradford Blaine, Jean Gimpel, Edward Kealey, George Basalla and J. Kenneth Major.

[26]   Amongst these notable exceptions are Muendel (1972), (1974), 1981), (1991), Reynolds (1983), (1984) and Kealey (1987). More recently, Pamela Long has done some excellent work bridging the disciplinary divide between history of technology and social and economic history, e.g. Long (1997), (2000), (2001).

[27]   See note 6 above.

[28]   For example, in the work of Eleanora Carus-Wilson, and more recently, John Langdon. See: Carus-Wilson (1941), (1959); Langdon (1994), (2004). I will take up this issue again in Chapter 3 and in the book's concluding chapter.

[29]   See, for example, Neilson (1910), Bloch (1935), Bennett (1937), Hodgen (1939), Carus-Wilson (1941), (1959), Finberg (1951), Kosminsky (1956), Bautier (1960), Colvin (1963), Hilton (1965), Duby (1968), Darby (1977), and Harvey (1977).

[30]   See Carus-Wilson (1941), Hodgen (1939), Bautier (1960).

[31]   A brief perusal of any number of pre-1990 texts on the subject of medieval milling will soon reveal the sometimes heavy reliance of past historians of technology on the work of these three authors, not infrequently with inadequate or no citation. See, for example: White (1964), pp. 84 and 89; Reynolds (1983), pp. 52, 64, 71, 82, 83, 107, 111 and 114; Gimpel (1988), Ch. 1.

The fact that a passage from Bloch's classic paper about the seigneurial control of mills by medieval lords is included in a collection of contemporary essays on the history and sociology of technology from the mid-1980s attests more to the paucity of research on the topic during the intervening period than a serious attempt to come to grips with the contradictions between Bloch's views and those of White, Gille, Gimpel and other prominent historians of technology.[32] Although their work was subjected to critical scrutiny within medieval studies, such criticisms did not find their way into the history of technology literature, resulting in the frequent repetition of errors that had already been corrected elsewhere.[33]

One of the few indications that any notable contact between the history of technology and medieval studies ever occurred during this period was Rodney Hilton and Peter Sawyer's scathing review of Lynn White's *Medieval Technology and Social Change* in *Past and Present* in 1963.[34] However, while the Birmingham University medievalists took White to task on a number of issues relating to agrarian technology, weapons and metallurgy, they did not engage with him on the issue of mills and milling, perhaps because it was, at that stage, a relatively under-theorized subject.[35] Such an engagement would have to wait until the late 1980s and 1990s with the work of Richard Holt and John Langdon.

Focussing on such questions as the continuities and discontinuities between milling practices in the Roman Empire and early medieval Europe, the extent to which lords were able to secure a monopoly on milling during various periods of the Middle Ages, and whether industrial mills were a significant part of the later medieval economy, the work of Holt and Langdon has provided a sound basis for both reassessing our understanding of the subject and conducting further research. Together with the work of scholars such as Colin Rynne and Niall Brady on medieval Ireland, John Muendel and Paolo Squatriti on medieval Italy, Thomas Glick and Miquel Barcelo on medieval Spain, and Paul Benoit and Catherine Verna on medieval France, the subject of medieval milling started to take on the characteristics of a research program within medieval studies in the mid- to late 1990s.[36]

Largely as a result of this recent scholarship, medievalists now generally acknowledge that medieval milling has not received the scholarly attention it warrants, and that there remain many avenues for further exploration. Furthermore, the quality of mill research that has been produced in recent decades on medieval England, Wales, Ireland, France, Spain and Italy has inspired a younger generation of medievalists to explore the topic in greater depth in these and other countries.[37]

The doctoral dissertation upon which this book is based was stimulated by the pioneering work of Holt and Langdon, who acted as mentors throughout my doctoral research. It explored in detail the role of the Church as a major player in, and contributor to, the commercialization of milling in England in the second half of the Middle Ages: a role which both Holt and Langdon had touched on, but not examined in depth.

My first book, *Wind, Water, Work* (Brill, 2006) arose out of preliminary research for the doctorate. It provides a critical overview of the development of milling technology from ancient to medieval times. It also elaborates on several case studies that were orthogonal to my main thesis in the doctorate, such as the structure and profitability of the Welsh fulling industry, and the extent to which industrial milling was pursued in different parts of medieval Europe. This latter topic was developed into a paper for *Technology and Culture* ('Industrial Milling in the Ancient and Medieval Worlds: A Survey of the Evidence for an Industrial Revolution in Medieval Europe', 2005), as well as a book chapter for *Wind, Water, Work*.

In Chapter 6 of *Wind, Water, Work*, as well as an article titled, 'The Role of the Monasteries in the Development of Medieval Milling', published in a collection of essays on medieval milling edited by Steven A. Walton (*Wind and Water in the Middle Ages: Fluid Technologies from Antiquity to the Renaissance*, 2006),

---

[32]   See Mackenzie and Wacjman (1985), pp. 141–55.

[33]   One of the most frequently repeated pieces of erroneous information is Hodgen's calculation of 5,632 watermills throughout England at Domesday, a topic that will be discussed in more detail in Chapter 3.

[34]   See Hilton and Sawyer (1963). Cf. Lucas (2010) for a critical discussion of the relevant literature.

[35]   The most extensive piece of scholarship on the subject by that date was Bennett and Elton's wide-ranging but flawed four-volume *History of Cornmilling* (1898–1904), some of whose flaws are discussed by Holt (1988), pp. 37–8, 41, 52, 81.

[36]   See: Holt (1987), (1988), (1989), (1996), (1990), (2000); Langdon (1991), (1992), (1994), (1996), (1997), (2004); Rynne (1988), (1989a), (1989b), (2000); Brady (2006); Muendel (1972), (1974), (1981), (1991); Squatriti (1997), (1998), (2000); Barceló and Sigaut (2004); Glick and Kirchner (2000); Benoit and Rouillard (2000); Verna (1995), (2002).

[37]   See, for example, Hammer (2008), van der Beek (2010), (2010a).

a number of themes and conclusions are summarized about the role of the Church in English milling that were first broached in the doctoral thesis upon which this book is based. In this book, I attempt to consolidate a number of strands of research from the doctorate that were previously unpublished. I have also pursued several lines of inquiry that required more detailed research, some of which has led me to rethink a number of conclusions that informed my earlier work.

For example, one of the more significant findings of the thesis was that the largest and wealthiest religious houses tended to be the most extractive and litigious with respect to the enforcement of their seigneurial milling rights, whereas a number of small and medium houses (especially from the Augustinian order) appear to have offered cheaper milling services from non-seigneurial mills that were analogous to the 'independent' or 'tenant' mills described by Holt and Langdon in their earlier research.[38] What I initially found was that, although historians of technology were correct to note that the religious order to which a house belonged had a significant impact on their behaviour as lords and the management of their estates (including their mills), this appears to have been less important overall than their level of wealth and the structure and distribution of their holdings. However, the question of the origins and status of the non-seigneurial mills acquired by the Augustinians in particular was not able to be satisfactorily resolved during my doctoral research, even though it was clear from the manuscript evidence that virtually all of these mills had been acquired from knights and other free men. One of the reasons for this lack of resolution was my own inadequate conception of the complexities of medieval land tenure, inadequacies which require a far better understanding of the Anglo-Saxon period than is generally considered necessary by researchers working on the period after the Conquest.

One of my subsidiary claims in the pages to follow is that Robin Fleming's *Kings and Lord in Conquest England* (1991) and Rosamond Faith's *The English Peasantry and the Growth of Lordship* (1999) provide a number of critical insights into several unresolved controversies about the development of feudal patronage, fealty and lordship in Norman England which are directly relevant to the resolution of some of the problems I encountered in my doctoral research. In particular, it would appear that some of what passes today as conventional wisdom about the Anglo-Norman manorial system and its continuity with Anglo-Saxon forms of land tenure does not take sufficient account of how it actually came into being, and tends to minimize or ignore the importance of discontinuities that were first brought to light more than a century ago by Maitland, Vinogradoff, Stenton and Seebohm.[39] If medieval scholars are prepared to acknowledge that the system of villeinage associated with the 'classic' manorial system was not as all-pervasive at the time of the Conquest as we are often led to believe, that the Normans were in fact responsible for a massive manorial reorganization of the country,[40] and that some kinds of free tenure that existed under the Anglo-Saxons persisted in one form or another for decades and even centuries after the Conquest, a number of otherwise inexplicable features of the ecclesiastical acquisition and management of mills begin to make far more sense.

Primary Sources for the Study of Ecclesiastical Mills in Medieval England

Scholars interested in pursuing research into medieval milling have at their disposal a rich body of primary and secondary historical literature, as well as a growing body of archaeological evidence from which to draw. When studying the role of the Church in that development three main sources of primary evidence can be drawn upon: material remains, texts and illustrations. To follow is a brief outline of the types of evidence available within each category, together with an explanation of which specific sources will be drawn upon in this study.

The graphic evidence from illuminated manuscripts, stained glass windows, graffiti and mechanical treatises is possibly the least informative of the three categories, primarily because medieval artists were not particularly concerned with the technical details of the machines they illustrated until the late fifteenth and sixteenth centuries. Most of the graphic evidence is religious in intent, if not content, but there have been few attempts to systematically examine it or compile any comprehensive record of where it is and of what it consists, a notable exception being John Salmon's 'The Windmill in English Medieval Art' (1941).

---

[38] Holt's and Langdon's research on this topic, and how my own relates to the various arguments they have made, will be discussed in more detail in Chapters 2 and 3, and in the book's conclusion.

[39] Maitland (1987) (1st pub. 1897); Vinogradoff (1892), (1932) (1st pub. 1904), (1908); Stenton (1910); Seebohm (1915).

[40] Fleming (2004), p. 124.

The archaeological evidence consists of the physical remains of mills, millhouses, waterworks, mill-stones, quarries and other related structures, providing important insights into chronologies of design and construction materials. The most comprehensive work of this kind has been done in the British Isles, although French archaeologists have recently begun to show a strong interest in the field.[41] Several dozen British and Irish mill sites have been excavated over the last hundred years or so, many of which have been documented in a variety of more or less accessible historical and archaeological journals, along with a handful of books, some of which will be drawn upon in this study. Archaeological fieldwork has not, however, generally shed a great deal of light upon the internal workings and mechanisms of mills, for the simple reason that their mostly wooden parts are seldom well-preserved. Because this study is primarily focused on issues of ecclesiastical management, it makes relatively little use of archaeological research, although readers may be interested in consulting some of the relevant literature.[42]

The most abundant and possibly the most informative type of evidence pertaining to mills in the medieval period consists of religious, literary, and historical texts on the one hand, and a number of varieties of official records on the other. The religious, literary, and historical works consist of ecclesiastical and popular histories, narratives in verse form, poems and folk songs. For medieval Europe, the official records consist of papal, royal and ecclesiastical surveys, taxation records, ministers' accounts, court records, treatises on estate management, and lay and ecclesiastical account books, custumals, charters and cartularies, the latter recording grants, sales, deeds, inquisitions, memoranda, letters and legal agreements, amongst other things. Such official records formed the basis for account keeping, taxation collection and the settlement of legal disputes, as well as the sale, leasing and transfer of property, and the assessment of labour and cash rentals. The papal and royal machineries of government and the regional feudal systems which they coordinated and directed were in part constituted and regulated by these various literary technologies, which were in turn carefully created and maintained by a veritable army of secular and ecclesiastical officials.[43]

England is a particularly good source of manuscript evidence for the medieval and early modern periods, as it is the only country in Europe fortunate enough to avoid having most of its medieval records destroyed in successive wars.[44] With respect to the source material relating to mills in particular, there are literally tens of thousands of entries pertaining to mills and milling in a wide variety of English medieval documents, the largest and most comprehensive of which are Domesday Book, the Hundred Rolls, and the many and various *Inquisitiones Post Mortem* (IPM).

Domesday Book and the Hundred Rolls are royal surveys of property holdings in England, dating to 1086 and 1279 respectively, and cover both lay and ecclesiastical holdings. But whereas Domesday Book encompasses most of England in considerable detail, the Hundred Rolls cover only five counties, i.e., Bedfordshire, Buckinghamshire, Cambridgeshire, Huntingdonshire and Oxfordshire.

Listing its information county by county, Domesday Book includes detailed assessments of manors and other holdings, including the amount of arable land, meadow, pasture, woodland and marshland held by each lord, as well as tenants bond and free, ploughlands, ploughteams, the number of head of cattle and other farm animals, and other assets such as mills, saltpans, quarries and fisheries. It also records the payments and services due from each and every estate, and in what kind of tenure each of them was held. For each manor and vill that held a demesne mill, it lists that mill's location, its rental value, the name of the lord or lords and the name of the tenant or tenants. Both Domesday and the Hundred Rolls record only those holdings that were in demesne, i.e., directly held and managed by the lords concerned, but not those in customary or hereditary tenure.[45]

---

[41]   See, for example, Levesque, Bessonet and Boureau (2002); Buchsenschutz, et al. (2011).

[42]   For overviews of the archaeology of monastic sites, which include discussions of grain mills and industrial mills, see: Astill (1989); Bond (1989) (2000); Moorhouse (1989). For specific digs on windmills see, for example: Bellairs (1905); Westell (1934); Posnansky (1956); Pierce (1966); Zeepvat (1980). For specific digs on watermills, see: Beckwith (1971); Greenhow (1979); Bedwin (1980); Bennett, Jones and Vyner (1980); Rahtz (1981), p. 7; Graham (1986); Boucher (1987–88); Moorhouse (2003). On industrial sites, see: Bedwin (1976); Crossley (1981), pp. 35–8; Astill (1989); Moorhouse (1989), p. 54.

[43]   See Fuller (2000), pp. 55–8, for an interesting discussion of the historical and sociological significance of these developments.

[44]   Jens Röhrkasten, personal communication, October 2000.

[45]   See Chapter 3 for a summary of some of the mill-related data in these two sources as found by Holt, Langdon and Ambler.

The IPMs are royal inquisitions into the property holdings of deceased lay tenants-in-chief, covering the period from 1236 to 1422. By definition the IPMs do not include ecclesiastical holdings and will therefore not be considered in any detail in this study, although relevant data and findings produced by other scholars who have used the IPM material will be drawn upon for comparative purposes.[46]

The published and unpublished medieval manuscript sources provide a wealth of empirical data that can be subjected to statistical analysis. While Richard Holt, John Langdon and some other scholars have already done extensive research on medieval milling in England drawing on Domesday Book, the Hundred Rolls and the IPMs, useful comparative material for ecclesiastical estates can be found in the papal survey the *Taxatio Nicholai IV* of 1291 and the *Valor Ecclesiasticus* of 1535, commissioned by Henry VIII and Thomas Cromwell just prior to the Dissolution of the monasteries. There are also numerous ecclesiastical charters and cartularies from the period, along with court rolls, rentals, extents, property surveys and account-books, all of which provide useful insights into the growth and development of the ecclesiastical milling sector, and will therefore be drawn upon extensively in this study.[47]

Although there is a clear evidential bias toward ecclesiastical estates in the medieval records, these biases are not universally reflected in all of the surviving records from the period, the notable exceptions being Domesday Book, the Hundred Rolls and the IPMs. The disproportionate amount of primary source material relating to medieval ecclesiastical authorities has meant that their estates and affairs are far better known and understood than those of lay lords or commoners. Nevertheless, while the mill management practices of individual religious houses and episcopal authorities have been fairly well studied, there have been no systematic attempts made prior to this study to gain an overview of the subject for the whole of England, even though Langdon's recent book on English milling covering the period from 1300 to 1540 drew heavily on ecclesiastical material.[48]

Sampling Rationale and Key Data for the Selected Religious Houses

In his *Medieval Cartularies of Great Britain* (1958), G.R.C. Davis recorded 1,109 known cartularies and registers relating to ecclesiastical estates throughout England and Wales, some of which are different copies of the same house's documents, others which are fragments of a larger collection, and a handful of which have been lost or destroyed. These manuscripts were compiled by 438 different religious institutions, ranging from abbeys, priories and cathedral churches to chapels, parish churches, colleges, cells and hospitals.[49] Because there were between 1,000 and 1,200 religious houses throughout England and Wales at the height of the monastic movement, the surviving manuscripts provide documentation for between 37 per cent and 44 per cent of the total. Around 10 per cent to 14 per cent of these documents have been published, mostly by local county history societies. By way of contrast, there are only 158 cartularies and registers which relate to lay estates in England and Wales. These manuscripts were compiled by 120 families and individuals.[50] Less than 20 have been published at the time of writing, i.e., around the same proportion as for ecclesiastical estates.

In setting the parameters for the scope of primary source material covered in this book, a desire to comprehensively document the management practices of a proportionally representative sample of different religious orders and different sized religious houses were the main considerations. Mill-related charters from the cartularies of 21 religious houses form the basis for the study, as well as extents, rentals and surveys for three of those houses and seven others.

In categorizing the various types of religious house, I have followed a convention outlined by Bruce Campbell, which distinguishes between secular ecclesiastics, i.e. archbishops, bishops, deans, rectors and so on, whose associated houses are classified as 'episcopal', and those of regular ecclesiastics, which included

---

[46] For a discussion of the history of the use of IPMs by medieval scholars, and their general reliability as historical sources, see Campbell, Galloway and Murphy (1992), pp. 3–6. For their use as a source of information on the English milling industry, see Langdon (1994), pp. 7–9.

[47] On the shortcomings of the documentary evidence regarding monastic estates, see Moorhouse (1989), pp. 29–32.

[48] See Langdon (2004), Appendix 2, for a list of the ecclesiastical estates' records from which his manorial survey primarily drew.

[49] See Davis (1958), pp. 2–128.

[50] See ibid., pp. 140–57.

monks, nuns, most canons, friars, members of the military orders and scholars at universities. With respect to the university colleges of Oxford and Cambridge, for example, the associated houses are classified as 'collegiate', while the houses associated with the other regular ecclesiastics are classified as 'conventual'.[51]

Of the 28 house's estates examined in the sample, 5 were episcopal and 23 were conventual. The exclusion of collegiate estates was a function of the published sources available. Of the 23 conventual houses examined in some detail, four were Benedictine, nine were Augustinian, five were Cistercian, and five were from minor religious orders. In compiling data on the Benedictine houses, existing research conducted by Richard Holt in *The Mills of Medieval England* (1988) on the mill holdings of Glastonbury Abbey has been incorporated, while the estate management practices of a dozen or more (mostly Benedictine) religious houses not contained in the sample are discussed in the introductory chapters. I should also note that during my doctoral research I systematically examined the charters of seven other Benedictine houses (Daventry, Eye, Luffield, Ramsey, Reading, Shrewsbury and Stoke-by-Clare), two other Augustinian houses (Edington and Missenden), and one other Cistercian house (Rufford). The houses focused upon in the book were chosen to provide a suitable mix with respect to their levels of wealth and geographical location, or because their extant mill records lent themselves better to analysis.

The number of religious houses sampled in the book constitutes around 2.3 per cent of the 1,200 or so that existed throughout England and Wales during the Middle Ages, and 4.3 per cent of the approximately 650 houses that survived to the Dissolution.[52] Of the 17 episcopal houses that survived to the Dissolution, the sample constitutes 29.4 per cent of the total. Because Langdon drew on the accounts of six episcopal houses for his 2004 computer program, only two of which are covered in this sample, some useful insights can be gained from comparing some of his findings with my own, as more than half of all the dioceses are covered by our research. Of the conventual houses that survived to the Dissolution, the sample constitutes 5.1 per cent of the total if the M\mendicant orders are excluded, none of which held mills (Table I.1). Depending on whether one uses the figures from the Dissolution or the cumulative figures for the monastic movement throughout its history, the number of houses of each monastic order that are examined in the case studies constitute the following percentages of their totals: Either 3.5 per cent of those Benedictine houses that survived to the Dissolution, or 1 per cent of all those that existed in England and Wales throughout the movement's history; 5.3 per cent or 3.6 per cent of the Augustinian houses; 6.6 per cent of the Cistercian houses (the order suffered no diminution in the number of its houses over the centuries); and 1.9 per cent of the 260 other religious houses that survived to the Dissolution, or between 1.3 per cent and 2.6 per cent of all those houses from other religious orders that existed throughout England and Wales during the Middle Ages. With regard to this last figure, however, if the mendicant orders are excluded, the sample size for the other religious orders is substantially increased to around 8.3 per cent of those that survived to the Dissolution.

The Dissolution-related percentages of the conventual houses' sample are set out below in Table I.2, indicating that it is somewhat biased in favour of the minor orders and to a lesser extent the Cistercians. The sample of Benedictine houses was reduced due to the extent to which the Benedictines have already received detailed attention from Holt and Langdon in their previous research on the subject.[53]

Table I.1   Types of English ecclesiastical estates sampled expressed as a percentage of their numbers at the Dissolution

Type	No. sampled	No. at Dissolution	Proportion of total
Episcopal	5	17	29.4%
Conventual	23	c. 447	5.1%
Collegiate	0	2	0%

---

[51]   Campbell (2000), p. 33.

[52]   Cook (1961), p. 15.

[53]   Holt (1988); Langdon (1991), (2004). In his 1988 book, Holt studied the Benedictine estates of Glastonbury, Ramsey, Peterborough and Bury St Edmunds. In his 1991 paper, Langdon studied the Benedictine estates of Westminster and Gloucester abbeys, and in his 2004 book, Battle, Bury St Edmunds, Glastonbury and Westminster, constituting seven houses in total.

Table I.2   English conventual houses sampled by order expressed as a percentage of their numbers at the Dissolution

Order	No. sampled	No. at Dissolution	Proportion of total
Benedictine	4	142	2.8%
Augustinian	9	170	5.3%
Cistercian	5	75	6.6%
Other orders	5	262 (c. 60 non-friar)	2.0% (8.3%)

Although the sample size for the Augustinians is slightly smaller than that for the minor orders and the Cistercians, it is sufficiently large to give some insight into the diversity of Augustinian estate management practices with respect to mills, a topic which has, hitherto, received very little attention.

The names of those houses whose rentals and surveys have been examined in detail, along with the time periods and counties covered, are listed in Table I.3. Most of the relevant records pertain to the last quarter of the thirteenth century and the first quarter of the fourteenth century (for Canterbury, Hereford, Battle, Bec and Holy Trinity), but there are also records from the late twelfth and early thirteenth centuries (Durham and Holy Trinity), for the third quarter of the thirteenth century (Hereford and Bec), for the third (Sibton) and last (Durham, Ramsey and Bolton) quarters of the fourteenth century, and for the fifteenth century (Ramsey and Sibton).

The same data for those houses whose mill-related charters have been analysed are set out in Table I.4. A simplified map (Figure I.1) showing a single cross for each county in which any single set of documents lists a holding provides an indication of the coverage of the sample of the houses studied in detail. The properties represented by the crosses in Figure I.1 are documented in 20,000 to 25,000 charters, of which more than 1,000 make reference to one or more mills.

Table I.3   English ecclesiastical estates: Extents, rentals and surveys

Name	Years covered	Counties over which estates extend
Canterbury Cathedral Priory (Episcopal)	1285, 1305–6	KENT, SUSS, SURR, HERTS, OXON, BUCKS, MIDDS, SUFF, NORF, DEVON.
Cathedral Priory of Durham (Episcopal)	1183, 1197, 1208–13, 1377–80	DURHAM, DERBS, CUMB, YORKS, T&W, LANCS, RUTLAND.
Cathedral Church of Hereford (Episcopal)	1253–70, 1285, <1288	HEREF, GLOUCS, WORCS, ESSEX, SHROPS.
Battle Abbey (Benedictine)	1283–1312	SUSS, KENT, BERKS, WILTS, HANTS, OXON, ESSEX.
Abbey of Bec (Benedictine)	1272–73, 1276–77, 1281–82, 1283–84, 1287–88	DORS, WILTS, HANTS, NORTHANTS, BUCKS, OXON, BERKS, WARKS, SUFF, NORF, SUSS.
Ramsey Abbey* (Benedictine)	1398–1401, 1409–14, 1422–26, 1432–34, 1438–41, 1443–44, 1447–50	HUNTS, CAMBS, BEDS, HERTS, NORTHANTS.
Bolton Priory (Augustinian)	1287–1324, 1377–78	YORKS.
Sibton Abbey (Cistercian)	1325, 1328, 1363–72, 1484, 1508–9	NORF, SUFF.
Holy Trinity Abbey, Caen (Ducal family foundation)	c. 1170, c. 1306–c. 1320	ESSEX, DORS, GLOUCS, WILTS, NORF.
Grove Priory (Alien Priory)	?1318, 1341–42	BEDS, BUCKS.

* Because Ramsey Abbey's mill holdings have already been discussed in detail by Holt (1988), the discussion here is restricted to an analysis of its post-plague mill revenues in Chapters 1 and 2 and its level of involvement in the fulling industry and building new mills in Chapter 10.

Table I.4   English ecclesiastical estates: Cartularies and charters

Name	Religious Order	Counties over which estates extend
Cathedral Priory of Chichester	Episcopal	SUSS.
Treasury of York Minster	Episcopal	YORKS, HANTS, MIDDS.
Battle Abbey	Benedictine	SUSS, SURR, MIDDS, KENT, BERKS, SUFF, NORF, WILTS, HANTS, OXON, ESSEX.
Lancaster Cathedral Priory	Benedictine	LANCS. +
Blythburgh Priory	Augustinian	SUFF, NORF.
Bradenstoke Priory	Augustinian	WILTS, GLOUCS, DORS, SOMS. +
Burscough Priory	Augustinian	LANCS.
Butley Priory	Augustinian	SUFF, NORF, LINCS, YORKS, MIDDS.
Cirencester Abbey	Augustinian	GLOUCS, WILTS, SOMS, DORS, BERKS, NORTHANTS, BUCKS, OXON.
Lacock Abbey	Augustinian	WILTS, GLOUCS.
St. Denys Priory	Augustinian	HANTS, DORS, WILTS.
St. Gregory's Priory	Augustinian	KENT, SUSS, BUCKS.
Beaulieu Abbey	Cistercian	HANTS, BERKS, CORN, DEVON, GLOUCS, OXON, WILTS, SUFF.
Furness Abbey	Cistercian	LANCS, CUMB, YORKS, LINCS.
Kirkstall Abbey	Cistercian	YORKS, LANCS.
Old Wardon Abbey	Cistercian	BEDS, BUCKS, CAMBS, HERTS,HUNTS, MIDDS, NORF, NORTHANTS.
Sibton Abbey	Cistercian	SUFF, NORF, SUSS.
Cockersand Abbey	Premonstratensian	LANCS.
Leiston Abbey	Premonstratensian	BEDS, BUCKS, CAMBS, HERTS, HUNTS, MIDDS, NORF, NORTHANTS.
Holy Trinity Abbey, Caen	Ducal family foundation	ESSEX, DORS, GLOUCS, WILTS, NORF, MIDDS.
Wakebridge Chantries at Crich	Aristocratic family foundation	DERBS, NOTTS.

While the manuscript sources in general do tend to be more plentiful for certain regions, such as the south, east and Midlands, Yorkshire is also well documented. The main gaps tend to be the areas around Lancashire and Cumberland, as well as the extreme south-west, and most notably, Cornwall. The same kinds of gaps also tend to be reflected in the ecclesiastical charter evidence. Some of these inadequacies in the sources have been addressed by focussing on four Lancashire houses, i.e., Burscough, Cockersand, Furness and Lancaster, as well as the counties of the south-west for which medieval mill records are otherwise fairly scarce. Figure I.1 reveals a dense cluster of holdings stretching from East Anglia to Wiltshire and Dorset, reflecting the overall density of religious settlements in that part of England, but noticeable gaps in Northumberland, Staffordshire, Leicestershire and Cheshire.

Other gaps in the sample relate to an absence of urban records, and the fact that most of the cartularies studied do not contain systematic records of the relevant houses' mill holdings. This means that the involvement of many of the houses in milling has had to be reconstructed from the extant records of grants, sales, agreements, disputes and leases, for which there are undoubtedly some omissions, including those relating to the records of industrial mills held by the various houses concerned.[54] However, where it has been possible to check the tables of mill holdings compiled from the charters against those contained in rentals, surveys and account books, the level of accuracy appears to be sufficiently high to justify the conclusions drawn. In those cases where there is uncertainty about the mill documentation available, I have drawn attention to the limitations of the sample in the relevant chapters and their related conclusions.

Because E.A. Kosminsky and Richard Holt have already discussed the mill holdings of the large East Anglian Benedictine houses of Bury St Edmunds, Norwich, Ely, Ramsey and St Albans in some detail,[55] the

---

[54]   This issue has already been discussed in detail in Lucas (2006a), Ch. 8.

[55]   Kosminsky (1956); Holt (1988).

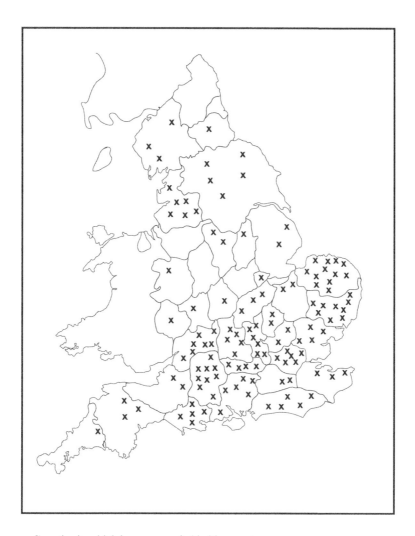

Fig. I.1   Counties in which houses sampled held property

chapters to follow examine a number of religious houses in the region that have received relatively little attention from medievalists in recent comparative studies, i.e. the Cistercian house of Sibton, the Augustinian houses of Blythburgh and Butley, and the Premonstratensian house of Leiston. Drawing on Tim Pestell's six-fold typology of monastic foundations in East Anglia, i.e. urban sites, reused sites, sites in isolated locations, sites twinned with castles, sites twinned with other manorial centres, and 'removed' monasteries,[56] none of the eastern houses studied in the chapters to follow were located on urban sites or twinned with castles or manorial centres, whereas Blythburgh and Butley had Anglo-Saxon antecedents that were regularized around 1120 and 1170, respectively. In other words, both houses were established at the sites of former minster churches,[57] whereas both Sibton and Leiston were 'removed' monasteries located in fairly remote sites. While Butley and Sibton were mid-ranking religious houses in terms of their wealth and possessions,[58] the other two houses

---

[56]   Pestell (2004), p, 192.
[57]   Ibid., p, 194. Archaeological excavations in the 1980s have apparently revealed evidence of a high-status Anglo-Saxon site less than 2 kilometres from the priory at Burrow Hill.
[58]   The *Taxatio* values Butley's holdings at £280 in 1291, while Sibton's holdings were valued at more than £250 in 1535 after suffering a severe decline in its fortunes in the wake of the Black Death.

were relatively poor. Leiston's possessions were valued at £147 in 1291, whereas Blythburgh's were only valued at around £62, making it one of the poorest houses sampled.

One notable feature of the mill-related documents pertaining to the Augustinian and Premonstratensian houses sampled are the many examples of clerks, stewards, lawyers and other curial and royal administrators who were involved in granting, leasing and selling windmills and watermills to the religious houses concerned, most of which date to the thirteenth and fourteenth centuries. In some cases, it is clear that the men in question had some kind of fiduciary relationship with the house concerned, but in others it would appear that the relationship was simply that of a donor or patron to a preferred order. For reasons that will be outlined in more detail in Chapters 2 and 3, these documents are significant because they reveal a category of non-seigneurial mill that was not identified by Holt and Langdon in their earlier research on the topic.

Through a detailed study of these sources, combined with the findings of earlier research by other scholars, it is possible to build a relatively comprehensive picture of the nature of ecclesiastical involvement in the commercialization of milling in medieval England.

Outline of the Book's Structure and Chapter Contents

In order to provide the reader with sufficient context to grasp the relevant historiographical issues, the first three chapters of the book provide an overview of the growth and development of both the Church and the milling industry in medieval England. They also outline several major themes and findings that inform the analysis in the remaining case studies, including the conceptual and evidentiary problems which I attempt to tackle in the rest of the book.

Chapter 1 provides an outline of the social and economic foundations of English monasticism from around the time that the first Benedictine and Celtic missionaries arrived in England around 600, to the Dissolution of the monasteries in 1540. It provides a summary of the wealth and histories of the various orders, along with some explanation of how they acquired that wealth and why their management practices changed over the centuries in response to various political, economic, cultural and environmental factors, using what is known of their mill management practices to illustrate the relevant issues where possible.

Chapter 2 seeks to explain some of the complexities of feudal land tenure, with a focus upon the means by which various sectors of medieval society acquired their property, and under what terms and conditions they were able to exploit it. It also examines how the patronage of religious houses evolved over the centuries, including the changing role and status of patrons. It concludes with a discussion of the role of seigneurial monopolies in the management practices of secular and ecclesiastical lords, and how mills and milling fitted into those practices.

Chapter 3 provides an outline of the changing structure and profitability of English milling during the latter half of the Middle Ages. It seeks to explain just how important was milling to the medieval economy overall, and how milling became a focus for renegotiating the extent and limits of lordly power by the lower orders of medieval society, as well as a site of economic activity in which new forms of non-seigneurial tenure were established.

The detailed analyses of the religious houses chosen for the sample are organized by type and order in Chapters 4 to 8, and consist of a series of profiles of the land acquisitions, mill holdings and changing management practices of 28 religious houses. The mill holdings of the five bishoprics and archbishoprics which form the episcopal part of the sample are discussed in Chapter 4. It includes Canterbury Cathedral Priory, the Cathedral Church of Hereford, the Cathedral Priory of Chichester, the Treasury of St Peter's York and Durham Cathedral Priory. Chapter 5 on the Benedictines includes Glastonbury Abbey, the English lands of the Abbey of Bec-Hellouin, Battle Abbey and Lancaster Priory. Chapter 6 on the Augustinians includes the priories of St Gregory's, St Denys's, Bradenstoke, Blythburgh, Butley, Bolton and Burscough, and the abbeys of Lacock and Cirencester. Chapter 7 on the Cistercians includes the abbeys of Beaulieu, Sibton, Old Wardon, Furness and Kirkstall. Chapter 8 on the minor orders includes the alien Priory of Grove, Leiston Abbey, the English lands of the Abbey of the Holy Trinity Caen, the Wakebridge Chantries at Crich and Cockersand Abbey. Each chapter opens with summaries of the financial positions of each of the religious houses covered, and concludes with summaries of their mill holdings as a means of orientating readers within the later discussion, and to flag subsequent points of interest.

Chapter 9 is organized thematically. It begins with a discussion of the possible origins of the customary obligation of suit of mill and the extent to which tenurial status affected a tenant's obligation to do suit. It then moves onto an analysis of the mill-related legal agreements and disputes in which the various houses were involved. These include such issues as how illicitly built mills were treated by ecclesiastical lords, the means by which legal recognition was conferred to non-seigneurial mills, and disputes and agreements concerning mill tithes, mill seisin and water flow to and from watermills.

The concluding chapter, Chapter 10, attempts to summarize the findings of the previous chapters and draw some broader conclusions. It discusses the differences found between the episcopal and conventual houses and between the various houses of different orders with respect to their estate management practices, and how mills and milling fitted into those practices. In the process, it seeks to identify those houses and individuals that displayed skill or entrepreneurial flair with respect to mill acquisition and management, and the role which non-seigneurial and industrial mills appear to have played in the various houses' milling activities. It also discusses the technological and management innovations which they deployed, and assesses the extent to which the monastic innovation thesis, the IRMA thesis and the seigneurial monopoly model find support in the evidence which the book has canvassed. In the process of examining these issues, it also looks at how the relative profitability of watermills versus windmills, and grain mills versus industrial mills affected ecclesiastical mill management. This will necessitate the examination of a third issue in turn, i.e., the manner in which ecclesiastical lords exercised their lordship with respect to mills, and how milling figured in their social and economic relations.

In order to test the evidence for regional differences in lay and ecclesiastical lordship, and the claim that the wealthier religious houses tended to be harsher landlords than wealthy lay lords, the book pays particular attention to the social status and wealth of founding donors and later patrons, and how mills and milling fitted into the initial foundation and subsequent development of individual houses. This will include some discussion of the strategies deployed by different houses to sustain or build their mill holdings, including grants, sales, purchases, maintenance, conversions and new constructions. It also examines whether there were stronger commonalities in those strategies between particular orders, or whether the approaches of individual houses to estate management may perhaps have been more dependent upon such factors as the relative age, wealth and geographical location of the house concerned, as well as the backgrounds of donors, the managerial acumen of individual bishops, canons, abbots and chapters, or some other contingent factors.

By drawing attention to the diversity of mill management practices amongst ecclesiastical lords, and the changing roles of custom and tradition in the forms of feudal patronage and tenure that developed in England during the post-Conquest period, it is hoped that those who read this book will acquire a richer understanding of the contribution of religious houses and their benefactors to the commercialization of milling during the late medieval and early modern periods. In particular, I hope to demonstrate that non-seigneurial forms of mill tenure were not simply the outcome of lay and ecclesiastical lords relinquishing control of what were temporarily regarded as expensive-to-maintain assets but were also a legacy of pre-Norman forms of land tenure, as well as an outcome of the development of conceptions of royal, ecclesiastical and public service that enabled low- and mid-ranking laymen and women to rise to the status not only of religious patrons, but of owners in their own right, patrons and owners who were very much aware of the practical and symbolic value of possessing mills.

Sydney
November 2013

Chapter 1
The Social and Economic Foundations of English Monasticism, c.600–1450

It is difficult for those living today to fully appreciate the power and wealth of the Latin Church in the Middle Ages. Controlling vast areas of land and other property throughout most of Continental Europe and Britain, church authorities exercised an extensive and enduring influence over the spiritual, economic and cultural lives of medieval people. Foremost amongst the wealthy church landowners were the great Benedictine monasteries, of which there were hundreds throughout Europe by the eleventh century and more than a dozen in England alone. These houses had already amassed enormous wealth by the time William of Normandy crossed the English Channel, and as we will see in the pages to follow, many of them were able to further expand and consolidate that wealth over the subsequent four centuries.

As many as 20 religious orders were involved in the ecclesiastical affairs of England and Wales during the Middle Ages. The largest and best-documented of them were the Benedictines, Augustinians and Cistercians. We have records for the existence of at least 485 Benedictine abbeys, priories and nunneries; 251 Augustinian houses; and 76 Cistercian houses.[1] Distribution maps of their geographical coverage in the late fifteenth century reveal a cluster of Benedictine houses in south central England, and of Augustinian houses in eastern England, with Cistercian houses scattered across most of the country.[2]

At the height of English monasticism in the thirteenth century, there were more than a thousand religious houses throughout the country.[3] By the time of the Dissolution of the monasteries in 1540 there were only about 650 still functioning, many of which had survived the intervening period with far fewer monks and reduced revenues.[4] Of those which survived to the Dissolution, 142 were Benedictine,[5] 170 were Augustinian,[6] and 76 were Cistercian,[7] constituting respectively about 30 per cent, 70 per cent and 100 per cent of their numbers at their peak. Even though the Benedictines had fared worst of the major religious orders during the intervening period, at the time of the Dissolution, the 10 largest religious houses in England were all Benedictine. In order of wealth, they were Glastonbury, St Peter's in Gloucester, Westminster, Christ Church (Canterbury), St Albans, Reading, the Priory of St John of Jerusalem, Abingdon, Bury St Edmunds, and Ramsey.[8] The annual income of each of these establishments was in the order of several thousand pounds. The richest of the houses only numbered two or three dozen, while many nunneries and friaries spent much of their existence on the verge of poverty.[9] According to A.N. Savine, the net total of annual monastic incomes for the year 1535 was more than £103,132, and of this, a little over 80 per cent was derived from temporalities, at approximately £80,084.[10] David Robinson points out that considering Augustinian houses derived 40 per cent or more of their income from spiritualities, the other orders must have derived significantly more than 80

---

[1] The sources for these figures are, respectively, Dickinson (1961), p. 75, Robinson (1980), p. 25, and Knowles and Hadcock (1953), p. 490 (c.f. Knowles [1940], pp. 707–11). Donkin (1978), p. 29, gives a figure of 75 Cistercian monasteries at the Dissolution. Cook (1961), p. 15, gives figures of 245, 212, and 108 respectively for each order for the whole period, although these seem wildly inaccurate.

[2] See Knowles (1940), Burton (1994).

[3] Dickinson (1961), p. 4.

[4] Cook (1961), p. 15.

[5] Stockdale (1980c), p. 82.

[6] Cook (1961), p. 177.

[7] Knowles and Hadcock (1953), p. 490.

[8] The net annual value of seventh-ranking Abingdon's spiritualities and temporalities was £1,876 10s 9d, whereas those for Beaulieu Abbey, a mid-ranking Cistercian Abbey, were £475 11 1/2d.

[9] Dickinson (1961), p. 4.

[10] Savine (1909), p. 99.

per cent of their income from temporalities, which is not, perhaps, what most people who are unfamiliar with this subject would expect.[11] Such wealth ensured that the monks of the larger houses enjoyed a pampered and lavish existence, and one which was not frequently interrupted by the general poverty of the peasantry surrounding them.

Perhaps unsurprisingly, an enduring concern of those who dealt with the clergy as a matter of course was the extent to which they demonstrated the Christian virtues of mercy, charity, compassion and generosity. Although few religious houses were obligated by custom to distribute any significant proportion of their wealth to the poor or needy within their estates, or to provide anything but moral guidance in support of the less privileged members of medieval society, the evidence discussed in the pages to follow suggests that those houses that were considered the most virtuous tended to attract the most patronage, while those which demonstrated concern for the well-being of their tenants, servants and retainers generally had the least acrimonious relations with them.

Nevertheless, the extent to which any religious house was considered virtuous or venal, benign or malign, varied greatly according to the size, wealth and location of the house concerned, as well as the character of those who occupied it. Many religious houses provided alms and legal defence for the poor, board and lodging for the disenfranchised and destitute, care for the sick and aged, and hospitality for travellers and pilgrims, but any examination of an ecclesiastical account book will soon reveal the relatively small sums generally devoted to such activities, even amongst the wealthier houses.[12]

One of the services which religious houses provided for their own households, servants, retainers and tenants were watermills and windmills to grind their grain. Traditionally, most households had ground their grain at home using a handmill. However, one of the outcomes of the extension of feudal services and obligations throughout medieval Europe between the ninth and thirteenth centuries was the creation of a demesne milling sector in which the lower orders were required to grind their grain at their lord's mill.[13] This obligation, known as 'suit of mill', generated significant revenues for lords throughout the latter half of the Middle Ages.

Contrary to the assertions of an earlier generation of historians of technology who claimed these mills were built to relieve tenants from the drudgery of grinding their own grain, medievalists have long argued that watermills and windmills were primarily acquired and built by religious houses to provide them with a reliable source of cash income, and were therefore considered valuable assets throughout the Middle Ages and well into the modern period.[14] As we will see in the pages to follow, these observations are supported by a close examination of the surviving manuscript evidence from the best documented country: England. This evidence also reveals just how significant was the contribution made by mills and milling to medieval social and economic life.

In order to gain an adequate understanding of the role of English religious houses in the development of commercial milling in medieval England, it is necessary to be familiar with the histories of the more important religious orders, and their different and changing estate management practices. This chapter therefore begins with a brief outline of the origins and diffusion of the religious orders sent from Rome and elsewhere to convert the English after the collapse of the Roman Empire. It then examines the role of the religious orders in the development of England's political, legal and religious institutions from Anglo-Saxon times to the late fourteenth century, and how religious orders and individual houses responded to the shifting mix of social, economic, political, demographic and environmental pressures which characterised the period. Where appropriate, the mill holdings and revenues of individual religious houses are cited to illustrate relevant points. This background provides a set of conceptual themes through which ecclesiastical involvement in milling will be examined in more detail in later chapters.

---

[11]   Robinson (1980), p. 172.

[12]   See Knowles (1940), pp. 479–81, Wood (1955), pp. 101–7, Cook (1961), pp. 17–20, 75–7, Turner (1980b), pp. 54–6, and Burton (1994), pp. 178–80, on the sometimes onerous obligations for hospitality that were expected of some houses and the arrangements that were made for them; Cook (1961), pp. 21–3 on the monastic obligation to give sanctuary for criminals.

[13]   Langdon (1994), pp. 36–7; Langdon (2004), pp. 15–20, 257–8.

[14]   See Lucas (2006b) for a critical discussion of these issues.

Pre-Conquest Foundations

Although organised Christianity arrived in Britain as early as the first half of the second century under Roman rule, the Roman and Celtic Churches, each with its own distinct forms of monasticism, sent their first missionaries into England almost simultaneously at the turn of the sixth and seventh centuries.[15] Within a few decades, a number of churches and religious houses had been established throughout the country, from Kent to the Severn and Northumbria. By the end of the seventh century, the whole of the Anglo-Saxon kingdom of Sussex had been converted. Further growth was to be slow, however, until the tenth century and the monastic revival which took place throughout Europe.[16]

The Benedictines were the first order of monks to establish themselves in England, arriving in the person of St Augustine of Rome (d. 604–609) with a small group of monks in 597.[17] Augustine and his monks had been sent to evangelize England by St Gregory the Great, pope from 590 to 604. Augustine's success was limited, however, leading to the foundation of only two monasteries for certain, the first in Canterbury in 597 at the site of the present cathedral of Christ Church, which was under the patronage of St Gregory (known as St Andrew's), and another nearby, dedicated to Sts Peter and Paul (later St Augustine's) about a year later.[18] These were followed by a number of other foundations, including Rochester (604) and Sheppey (670).[19] The first 'true' Benedictine monastery was founded by St Wilfred (d. 709) at Ripon around 661, followed soon afterwards by his foundation of Hexham in 674.[20] Wilfred's friend St Benedict Biscop (d. 689) was also inspired to follow his example at Wearmouth (674) and Jarrow (685) in Northumbria.

Known as the 'black monks' owing to the colour of their habits, the order was founded by St Benedict of Nursia around 499 in Subiaco.[21] Benedict (b. *circa* 480) had never been trained as a priest, founding his order as a community of laymen dedicated to the search for God. While priests and clerics had been welcome to join the order, his 'Rule' specified that there was to be no distinction between their status as monks and those of laymen. The monks' status as priests gradually developed over the subsequent period, and was completed by around the middle of the twelfth century. Decisive in this process was the monastic engagement in pastoral work, which led to a distinction being made between a superior class of ordained brothers (*monachi*), who were fully engaged in liturgical life and the administration of the monastery, and those of lay brothers (*conversi*) whose liturgical life was limited. The latter had no say in matters of governance, their work for the monastery being exclusively manual.[22]

Around the middle of the seventh century, a number of Celtic religious houses which had originated in Ireland established themselves in England, including Lindisfarne in Northumbria, Whitby in Yorkshire and Wimborne in Dorset. Although the origins of the Irish orders are obscure, it seems likely that they derived from Egypt, either from seafaring Egyptian monks or by way of Gallic monasteries.[23] Their survival as Celtic houses was to be short lived, however. In 664 the Synod of Whitby decreed that all of the English houses should come under the same Benedictine Rule,[24] even though the extent to which this was actually achieved remained limited until the tenth and eleventh centuries.[25] By the time of the coming of the Danes and Norsemen at the end of the eighth century and the sacking of Lindisfarne in 793, monastic activity in the north was in a state of neglect and the first wave of Benedictine monasticism had largely spent itself. The Viking raids and colonisation of the north and east appear to have simply hastened a process which was already underway.

---

[15]   Knowles (1940), p. 21.

[16]   Burton (1994), pp. 1–20.

[17]   Dickinson (1961), p. 61; Burton (1994), pp. 1–3.

[18]   Ibid. Turner (1980a), p. 15 gives a date for the latter as c. 605.

[19]   Dickinson (1961), p. 61.

[20]   Ibid., p. 62.

[21]   Turner (1980a), p. 10.

[22]   Ibid., p. 14.

[23]   See Dickinson (1961), p. 57 for the conventional view, and White (1978), p. 243, n. 102, for some provocative suggestions as to how such direct Egyptian influence may have taken place.

[24]   Cook (1961), p. 40; Dickinson (1961), p. 59; Burton (1994), p. 2.

[25]   Burton (1994), pp. 3–5.

Over the same period that the Benedictines sought to extend their influence throughout England, a number of secular houses and colleges were also established. Known as 'monasteries' (*monasterium*), or 'minsters' by the people, they were communities of clergy attached to local churches not generally bound by a Rule. The secular canons who oversaw the minsters were not monks who lived a cloistered life separate from the population, but were priests who went amongst the people to perform their various duties. Also unlike monks, these secular canons were allowed to acquire personal property, including their own houses and prebends, and to marry. According to Bede, many of the smaller minsters were established by local ruling families as a means of establishing their perpetual possession of land by charter (*bocland* or 'bookland'),[26] land that had previously been subject to the claims of kinship. These 'family monasteries' also provided a cultural milieu in which the education of children and aristocratic women could take place.[27]

Although the minster churches were very popular during the ninth and tenth centuries, the attitude of later monastic chroniclers from the reformist orders was to ignore or denigrate their significance.[28] By the tenth and eleventh centuries, minster churches constituted the vast majority of religious institutions throughout England, and predated the establishment of the parochial system between the tenth century and the end of the twelfth century. At the time of the Conquest, there were more than 50 secular colleges extending as far as Durham in the north, Dover in the east, Oswestry in the west, and St Germans and Selsey in the south.[29]

Meanwhile, on the European continent, the Benedictine reform movement was rapidly gaining ground. The Capitula of Aachen issued by the Carolingian emperor Louis the Pious and his spiritual mentor St Benedict of Aniane (d. 821) on 10 July 817 was a series of edicts to monks based firmly upon the Rule of St Benedict. With the foundations of the monasteries of Cluny in 910, Gorze (refounded c. 933) and Brogne c. 920, the Benedictines established a basis for extending their influence throughout Europe.[30]

One of the main proponents of Benedictine reform in England was Dunstan (909–988), who quickly rose from the abbacy of Glastonbury to become archbishop of Canterbury and counsellor and minister to King Edgar (959–975). Edgar had described the monasteries in his kingdom as 'worm-eaten', 'rotten' and 'devoid of divine service'. Dunstan brought uniformity to the practices of a more or less disorderly monastic culture through his insistence that the Benedictine Rule be observed by monasteries throughout the kingdom. The *Regularis Concordia* issued at Winchester sometime between 965 and 970 was primarily intended to provide the basis of an ethical code for monks, although it also included provisions for the royal confirmation of abbots and abbesses, as well as confirmation of the liberties and privileges enjoyed by each monastery. It thus served to formalize the legal bond between the monarch and religious houses, establishing royal protection for all of them, and a powerful form of legitimation for the kings' authority and position as monarch.

By the end of the tenth century, the Benedictines had been successful in bringing some of the larger of the minsters in southern England under their rule, while the poorer ones were left to become parish churches within the new parochial system.[31]

Thirty or more Benedictine abbeys and six nunneries were founded or restored south of the Trent, including Bath (944), Westminster (958), Abingdon (c. 964), Peterborough (966), St Albans and Ramsey (969).[32] Benedictinism subsequently remained the norm of monastic life in Britain from the time of the *Concordia* until the end of the eleventh century.[33] The newly resurgent order was, however, significantly different from that of

---

[26]   See Bede's letter to Egbert, in Haddan and Stubbs (1871), pp. 314–25. 'Bookland', or land held by charter, came with the threefold obligation (*trinoda necessitas*) to provide military service and bridge and fortification work. See Maitland (1987), pp. 226–58, 293–318 and Faith (1999), Ch. 4 and 5, for a detailed discussion of these obligations and what they entailed.

[27]   Faith (1999), pp. 159–60.

[28]   Hill (1981), p. 150.

[29]   Ibid., p. 153.

[30]   Turner (1980a), p. 18, Burton (1994), p. 4.

[31]   Burton (1994), p. 176.

[32]   Cook (1961), p. 41; Dickinson (1961), p. 64; Burton (1994), pp. 3–5.

[33]   Turner (1980a), pp. 19–21. Due to the religious zeal of later Benedictine chroniclers, there has been some confusion in scholarly circles until fairly recently about the number of Benedictine houses established in England before the eleventh century. According to this older view, by the end of the eighth century, several dozen Benedictine monasteries

its founder at Monte Cassino. The monks were expected to become more involved in liturgical and intellectual activities to the virtual exclusion of manual labour, and the monasteries themselves became centres of learning and civilization, as opposed to retreats from worldliness, as the founding father had intended.

At the time of the Norman Conquest, there were more than 60 Benedictine monasteries throughout the country, including 12 nunneries, with a combined value that amounted to around one sixth of the nation's wealth south of the Humber at Domesday.[34] Such wealth was unevenly distributed throughout the country, however, as almost all of the English monasteries lay 'east of the Severn and south of a line from Burton-on-Trent to the Wash'.[35]

The annual incomes of Benedictine monasteries at Domesday ranged from less than £20 in the case of the six smallest houses (i.e., Tewkesbury, Buckfast, Horton, Selby, York and Swavesey), up to high three-figure sums for giants such as Glastonbury (£828) and Ely (£769). Four monasteries enjoyed an income of between £600 and £700 (i.e., Christ Church, Bury St Edmunds, St Augustine's, Old Minster Winchester); two had an income of between £400 and £600 (i.e., Westminster and Abingdon); six had an income between £200 and £400 (i.e., New Minster Winchester, Ramsey, Peterborough, St Albans, Wilton, Shaftesbury) and another seven earned between £100 and £200 *per annum* (i.e., Chertsey, Malmesbury, Barking, Cerne, Coventry, Romsey, Evesham).[36] In other words, more than one-third of the English monasteries in 1086 enjoyed earnings of over £100 annually, at a time when the average annual wage for an 'unskilled' worker was around £1.[37] By the time of the Dissolution four and a half centuries later, well over half of the Benedictine monasteries were earning over this sum.[38]

Ecclesiastical Reform and Economy under William I

In the aftermath of his victory at the Battle of Hastings, William of Normandy not only sought to impose a new political and administrative system upon his newly conquered lands; he also sought to reform and reinvent the institutions and practices of the Anglo-Saxon Church, including the monasteries. Like the Carolingian and Anglo-Saxon kings before him, William cultivated these changes as a means of providing a cultural and religious base for his political authority. Inevitably, his efforts faced considerable opposition, not the least of which was related to the two very different styles and orientations of the old and new orders.

Whereas the Anglo-Saxon Church had revered tradition and the past, being grounded in an essentially rural and somewhat parochial view of its obligations to the faithful and to God, Norman and French clerics were raised in a far more cosmopolitan and progressive atmosphere; an atmosphere in which the virtues of novelty and innovation were emphasized. The Norman clerics brought to England by William to oversee his reforms were suspicious of the claims to holiness represented by the Anglo-Saxon Church, whose representatives they regarded as vulgar yokels lacking in education and sophistication. Of course, their snobbery conveniently ignored their own relatively rapid elevation in status within less than two generations as a result of Normandy's own rise to power.

---

of a substantial size and an unknown number of smaller ones had sprung up throughout England and Wales, especially in Kent and the region around the lower Severn. However, it now seems certain that these were all, in fact, minster churches, and that although many of them did follow a pattern of existence at least partially shaped by Benedict's Rule, local custom and tradition tended to guide most Anglo-Saxon religious houses. Benedictine monks of the eleventh century manipulated the evidence to claim earlier Benedictine origins for these houses than were justified. With the exceptions of Glastonbury, Bath, Westminster, Abingdon, Peterborough, Winchester, St Albans and Ramsey, which were converted to Benedictine Rule by Dunstan in the tenth century, most of the others were not converted until the middle of the eleventh century. See Burton (1994), Ch. 1; also, Richard Holt, personal communication.

[34] Burton (1994), p. 9. The combined value of these holdings was around £11,000.

[35] Dickinson (1961), p. 65.

[36] Knowles (1940), p. 702.

[37] See Dyer (1989a), p. 226; Langdon (1996), pp. 41–3. By the middle of the thirteenth century, the annual wage for ordinary labourers was somewhere in the order of £1.5–£2.

[38] Dickinson (1961), p. 124. The survey of monastic wealth conducted by Thomas Cromwell in 1535, the *Valor Ecclesiasticus*, provides the following statistics in comparison to those of Domesday: proportion of houses with an income under £20: 9 per cent, £20–£100: 35 per cent, £100–£300: 35 per cent, £300–£1000: 16 per cent, over £1000: 4 per cent.

Despite their conviction that English religious houses were in dire need of reform, the initial loyalty of the invaders remained to Normandy, ensuring a continued flow of endowments to the homeland rather than England. Nor were Norman monks initially interested in establishing new houses in England, as such moves were regarded as potential taxes on their resources that would render few or no returns. Furthermore, they were poor seafarers, disliked the crossing, and feared the social disorder that had erupted in the wake of William's victory. Being fond of peace and tranquillity, they were also convinced that their lives would be far more difficult in the new and smaller communities in which they would be forced to establish themselves. Indeed, it was only at the importuning of wealthy and powerful patrons, together with the lure of well-established and sometimes well-endowed English churches, that French and Norman houses were persuaded to extend their influence across the Channel, invariably with a substantial endowment of land and liberties.[39]

The architect of William's reforms was Lanfranc, archbishop of Canterbury from 1070 to 1089. An Italian by birth, Lanfranc had been trained as a lawyer and joined the preeminent Norman abbey of Bec around 1040, followed by a brief stint as abbot of St Stephen's, Caen. His major contribution to English monastic life was his formulation of the Monastic Constitutions, specifically designed for the Rule of his own house of Christ Church, but clearly intended as a model for other houses to follow. Derived from the Rule governing Cluny, Lanfranc said that his constitution was compiled 'from the customs of those monasteries which in his day have the greatest prestige'.[40]

In order to better achieve his social, political and economic ambitions, William I created a powerful means of colonizing England which at once satisfied the need for military security, financial prosperity and religious conformity. Functionally inter-related units of castles, towns and priories were built at strategic locations across the country. The new priories were intended to also serve as parish churches in the new boroughs. As the Normans persuaded an ever larger number of French and Norman houses to take over the responsibilities of administering the new priories, the need for those houses to protect and exploit their new possessions provided the appropriate incentive for them to establish new communities of monks in England. But it was not only in the new boroughs and manors that colonization was taking place; it was also happening in cases where Norman monastic houses had been endowed with English churches that had formerly belonged to Anglo-Saxon landowners. In those cases in which a Norman house held a number of English churches, it made sense for them to establish a local headquarters.[41]

There were several quite specific reasons why these new and often small priories were made dependent on French and Norman religious houses. Firstly, there was a strong desire on the part of great noblemen with French and English possessions to bring French monks across the Channel to serve their own chapels in order to enhance their social status and prestige. Secondly, there was a desire amongst the lesser gentry to establish their own communities on freshly acquired estates at less cost to themselves than were they to attempt to start a new house or order from scratch. Finally, it was a means by which the religious houses could secure their lands outside of France and Normandy from the depredations of noble families and sometimes even those families which had founded their alien priories.[42] All in all, the initial establishment of these new foundations had little to do with the spiritual well-being of the people which they served, and more to do with the political and economic interests of the Norman aristocracy and monasteries. As Colin Platt has shrewdly observed, '[t]heir purpose lay in the collection of revenues, not in the instruction and cure of souls.'[43]

A good example of the political, rather than economic, role which such endowments served was William's establishment of Battle Abbey at Hastings shortly after the Conquest. William famously insisted that the abbey's altar be the site at which Harold Godwinson was slain, despite it being nowhere near water and inconvenient for the monks in other ways. Obviously, the abbey's role was more of a war memorial than a monastery; its primary function being the settlement of political debts to his faithful soldiers (who served as knightly retainers to the monastery in various capacities) rather than any initial effort at religious reform.

---

[39]   Platt (1984), pp. 3–5.

[40]   Turner (1980a), p. 22.

[41]   Platt (1984), p. 5.

[42]   Ibid., p. 6. See Fleming (2004), Ch. 5–6, on the lengths to which religious houses went within England to secure their properties from appropriation and theft by their new rulers.

[43]   Ibid., p. 7.

Indeed, it was not until the late 1070s that any genuine efforts at introducing a reformist agenda with regard to the establishment of religious houses took place in England. Between 1078 and 1081, William de Warennes, with the assistance of the king, established the first Cluniac house in England at St Pancras in Lewes, but even this initiative required persistent entreaties by both men to persuade Abbot Hugh of Cluny to agree. The Cluniacs were the first wave of reformed Benedictines, taking their example from the abbey of Cluny in Burgundy, founded in 910 by the Duke of Aquitaine.[44] Throughout the late eleventh and early twelfth centuries, the order quickly spread its foundations across England, having attracted a succession of wealthy patrons. The most successful of these were Much Wenlock (c. 1080) in Shropshire, Castle Acre (c. 1089) and Thetford in Norfolk, Bermondsey (c. 1089) in Surrey, Pontefract (1090) in Yorkshire, Reading (1125) in Berkshire, and Faversham (1148) in Kent.[45]

Despite this surge in power and influence, only about one-third of the Cluniac houses established during this initial colonization survived, the most successful of the earlier foundations being Lewes, Bermondsey, Castle Acre, Thetford and Pontefract, with Daventry in Northamptonshire, Lenton in Nottinghamshire and Montacute in Somerset coming to rival them in later years. Lewes, however, laid out as a replica of Cluny, never lost its pre-eminence. Most of these houses, with the important exception of Wenlock, were built from nothing.[46]

For all of his reforming zeal, William I tended towards conservatism, although he never missed an opportunity to replace an Anglo-Saxon abbot with a Frenchman or a Norman when the opportunity arose; the appointment to a vacant abbacy being one of the heritable rights of the Wessex kings which William was keen to maintain.[47] Not all such appointments were successful, however. For example, Turold's 28-year abbacy of Peterborough resulted in the loss of half of the abbey's possessions, which had been valued at £1,050 upon his arrival in 1070, and scarcely £500 upon his departure. He was reputed to have given most of it to his kinsfolk and the knights who came with him. Within a century, however, the abbey's fortunes had fully recovered.[48]

But such troubles were not just associated with 'bad abbots'.[49] They were also related to a lack of enforcement of the law by those in power, or the abuse of power by or under weak or unpopular monarchs. Glastonbury, Ramsey and Abingdon abbeys, for example, had both lost lands that had been leased out before the Conquest, but which were not returned after it.[50] Similarly, during Stephen's reign, a number of monasteries had land taken from them by unscrupulous friends and enemies of the king. On the other hand, King John and Richard II were two monarchs who felt justified in appropriating monastic lands when they thought it convenient.

These successive periods of despoliation, theft and rapine by first the Danes, then corrupt royal officials and tax collectors under the Anglo-Saxons and finally under the Normans provided a strong incentive for the religious houses to keep scrupulous records of their estates.[51] It is, ironically, partially as a result of social disorder and the victimisation of the ecclesiastical authorities by powerful lay lords that we now possess such extensive collections of charters, rentals and accounts relating to their holdings.

Having disenfranchised and marginalised the Anglo-Saxon clergy and nobility during the first few decades of their rule, the Normans set upon an ambitious building programme, partially as a means to reconciliation, but also as further demonstration of their power and authority. Through the construction of such impressive monuments as Durham, Norwich and St Paul's cathedrals, all begun in the 1090s, the Anglo-Norman clergy sought to surpass in scale (if not in beauty) that which had existed previously.[52]

The Augustinians were one of the new orders which benefited from the change in power, although support for it was generally drawn from an association between the regular canons and the administrative or curial

[44]   Dickinson (1961), p. 71.

[45]   Platt (1984), p. 10; Dickinson (1961), p. 72; Cook (1961), p. 127; Knowles (1940), p. 152.

[46]   See *Reading Abbey Cartularies, Berkshire*, Vols. I and II, and *The Cartulary of Daventry Priory*.

[47]   Platt (1984), p. 15.

[48]   Ibid., p. 18.

[49]   Of which we will learn more in later chapters.

[50]   Platt (1984), p. 18. See *Two Cartularies of Abingdon Abbey*, Vols. I and II.

[51]   Ibid., p. 19.

[52]   Ibid., pp. 19–21.

classes, rather than the nobility.[53] Formally constituted only a short time before the Conquest, the order claimed to derive its Rule from Augustine of Hippo (392–430), who in the early fifth century had founded a monastery in that city, insisting that the clergy there live under a common Rule.

There is some controversy over the source of the Augustinian Rule, with some arguing that his followers managed to piece one together from a letter he had written to the nuns at Hippo in 423, which was 'basically a booklet of precepts which were to be read weekly', while there are others who argue that it derives from a sixth century document.[54] In the case of Augustine's letter, the precepts which he set out did not form a systematic whole, giving only general guidance about such issues as 'simple points of obedience ... property holding ... and the designation of fixed hours of prayer'.[55] Consequently, the ownership of private property was forbidden, and all common property was to be distributed to each monk or nun according to his or her needs.

Robinson points out that the brevity and vagueness of Augustine's Rule made the transfer of allegiance of a variety of older foundations and related groups more attractive, including groups of hermits and some of the ancient Celtic communities, as well as the secular canons of the ancient collegiate churches.[56] Such a lack of detail also gave Augustinians considerable latitude in their interpretation of the Rule, from 'broad' to 'severe' schools of thought.[57]

Although some secular canons in Italy and southern France had already begun to adapt to the Rule of St Augustine earlier in the eleventh century, it was not until the Lateran synods of 1059 and 1063 that the process of bringing the secular canons under Augustinian Rule was formalized.[58] This also involved official recognition of the Augustinian community of clerics. After the Conquest, a number of those minster churches which had not yet adopted Augustinian Rule were suppressed, while most of the others were refounded as Augustinian houses.[59]

Growth and Expansion in the Twelfth Century

By the end of the twelfth century, the Augustinian community of clerics consisted of three orders: the Augustinians, Premonstratensians and Gilbertines. The first of these had several offshoots, including the Arrouaisians, a contemplative branch of Augustinians founded at Arrouaise in northern France in the eleventh century, and the Augustinian or Austin Friars, who were originally congregations of hermits that were brought together under the Rule of St Augustine by Pope Alexander IV in 1256.[60] Papal intervention also allowed the Austin Friars to be Mendicants, i.e. to live like the Franciscans and Dominicans on alms alone.[61] Also known as the Hermit Friars of St Augustine, the Austin Friars were heavily influenced by the Dominicans and quickly adopted an urban and intellectual way of life.[62] The Austin Canons first arrived in England c. 1100 with the founding of St Botolph at Colchester in Essex,[63] the Arrouaisians in 1133 with the founding of Missenden in Buckinghamshire,[64] and the Austin Friars in 1248 with the founding of Clare in Suffolk.[65]

---

[53]   Ibid., p. 31. There were, however, some notable exceptions, such as Burscough Priory, whose patrons and donors were almost invariably local knights and gentry, as well as some smallholders (see Chapter 6). See also Janet Burton's discussion of this issue with respect to the Augustinian houses of Yorkshire, in Burton (1999), pp. 94–5, in which she points out that many of these houses were established by local magnates or barons.

[54]   Robinson (1980), p. 5.

[55]   Platt (1984), p. 31.

[56]   Robinson (1980), p. 9.

[57]   Platt (1984), p. 31.

[58]   Robinson (1980), p. 6.

[59]   Cook (1961), p. 176.

[60]   Ibid., p. 213. See Burton (1994), Ch. 3, for a more detailed discussion of the history of the Regular Canons.

[61]   Dickinson (1961), p. 92.

[62]   Ibid.

[63]   Cook (1961), p. 177. However, St Gregory's Priory in Canterbury, founded in 1184–85 by Archbishop Lanfranc could just as easily be accorded this status. See the detailed discussion of St Gregory's in Chapter 6.

[64]   Dickinson (1961), p. 82. See *The Cartulary of Missenden Abbey*, Pts. I, II and III.

[65]   Ibid., pp. 92–3.

The Premonstratensians followed the Rule of St Augustine but under a stricter moral code. Founded by St Norbert in 1120 at Prémontré in a forest near Laon, the order first arrived in England in 1143 with the founding of Newhouse Abbey in Lincolnshire.[66] Its brethren were also known as the 'white canons', again for the colour of their habits. Although stricter in its observances than most Benedictines – emphasizing uniformity in dress, diet and religious exercises – it was not as ascetic as the Cistercians and tended to locate its foundations in remote areas, such as Leiston Abbey in Sussex and Cockersand Abbey in Lancashire. Nearly all of its houses were moderate in size.[67] Although the early members of the order followed their founder's example as missionaries, this trend did not last, with the monastic life prevailing in later times. Within a little over 120 years of the establishment of their first foundation in England at Newhouse Abbey in 1143, the Premonstratensians had 31 abbeys and three nunneries throughout the country, nearly all of which had been established in the twelfth century.

With the exception of the Premonstratensians, the Augustinians were moderates and no lovers of asceticism, running hospitals, leper and aged retreats. Their clerics became school-teachers, chaplains, and confessors, and, from the second half of the twelfth century onwards, the order assumed responsibility for an increasingly large number of parish churches as lay owners were pressured by church reformers to divest themselves of such property.[68]

By the end of Henry I's reign (1135), 43 Augustinian houses had been established in England and Norman-held Wales. Most of them had been created in the period from 1120–35. Three-quarters of them were associated in some way or other with the king and his circle.

Such noble patronage did not necessarily guarantee popular support, however. For example, St Denys Priory in Southampton was established by Henry I in 1127, but was not successful in gaining the support of its immediate neighbours, especially the burgesses of Southampton. Although local landowners were more generous, many of whom had connections at court, it was primarily royal curialists and administrators who maintained the existence of this small community.[69]

By the end of the twelfth century, there were 140 Augustinian houses in England and Wales, most of these being in the Midlands and East Anglia.[70] The order was still rapidly growing at this stage, however, as 40 more English houses had been built by 1216. While most of the houses run by the Augustinians were priories, they also held around 13 abbeys at one time or another.[71]

It was around this time that the appeal to asceticism began. A number of new monastic orders emerged, including the Tironensians and Grandmontines,[72] as well as the Cistercians, Savigniacs and Carthusians. The earliest of these was St Dogmael's Abbey in Pembrokeshire, founded c. 1115 as a Tironensian house,[73] while Furness Abbey was established in Lancashire in 1127 as a Savigniac house.[74] These were followed by Grosmont in Yorkshire as the first of only three Grandmontine houses ever to be established in England,[75] Waverley Abbey in Surrey in 1128 as the first Cistercian house,[76] and Witham Priory in Somerset c. 1179 as the first Carthusian house.[77] In 1147, the Cistercians absorbed the Savigniac order, which by then had about 20

---

[66]   Burton (1994), p. 57. See also ibid., pp. 100–101, on the histories of the associated nunneries. The case study chapters later in this book treat the Premonstratensians as a separate order to the Augustinians due to their asceticism and monastic orientations, as outlined below.

[67]   Dickinson (1961), p. 83. The estates and mill holdings of Cockersand and Leiston are discussed in detail in Chapter 8.

[68]   Platt (1984), p. 32.

[69]   Ibid., p. 38. See, *The Cartulary of St Denys Priory*, as well as the detailed discussion of this house in Chapter 6.

[70]   Cook (1961), p. 177.

[71]   Dickinson (1961), p. 82.

[72]   See Knowles (1940), pp. 201–2, 227, on the Tironensians, pp. 203–4, on the Grandmontines; also Cook (1961), p. 46, on both.

[73]   Knowles (1940), p. 227.

[74]   Platt (1984), p. 39.

[75]   Cook (1961), p. 46.

[76]   Ibid., p. 45.

[77]   Dickinson (1961), p. 71.

houses in England, the most important of which was Furness.[78] All of these monasteries were located in remote and isolated areas, supported disinterestedly by magnate patrons.

The new orders borrowed precepts from one another, and were somewhat fickle in their doctrinal commitments, although they all shared a commitment to an ascetic adherence to their respective Rules and to isolating themselves from the wider society.[79] The most successful of them were the Cistercians, who, according to Platt, 'owed more ... to Bernard of Clairvaux (1090–1153) than to Robert of Molesme, their founding father, or even to Stephen Harding, their original legislator'.[80] He also says that for many years 'confusion between the emergent orders was extreme.'[81]

Perhaps as a result of this confusion, their founding benefactors seemed unsure as to which order they should direct their benevolence, and frequently changed their minds, redirecting their largesse to a second order after first directing their preferences elsewhere. It would seem that what determined a patron's choice was his or her perception of the sincerity of the community concerned, a factor which appears to have been independent of their rank.[82] For example, King Stephen, on whose land Furness was located, supported the Savigniacs, Gilbertines and Cistercians.[83] In Suffolk, Ranulf de Glanville founded Butley Priory in 1171 and Leiston Abbey in 1183 as Augustinian and Premonstratensian foundations respectively.[84] If the house in question was considered insufficiently prestigious, or lacking in some other way, it was abandoned in favour of another.

Constituting the second wave of Benedictine reform, the Cistercians exercised a profound and far-reaching influence upon English monasticism. Established at Cîteaux in 1098 by Robert of Molesme, the order was greatly expanded under the leadership of Bernard of Clairvaux in the first half of the twelfth century. Bernard was the main instigator of Cistercian ingress into England, first at Rievaulx in Yorkshire, then at Melrose in Roxburghshire (Scotland) and Old Wardon in Bedfordshire.[85]

Perhaps due to its remote and wild location, Rievaulx was established with two-thirds of its brethren as lay brothers, recruited as labourers, thus emphasizing 'the spiritual advantage of hard manual work, giving both dignity and holy profit to labour'.[86] Because the normal sources of monastic revenue were initially deemed by them as inappropriate for the maintenance of monastic purity, intensive cultivation of their lands was the only path open for their economic survival. Platt observes that Fountains became 'the hub of a complex network of estates, the most important of which were organised as home farms or "granges" at which the role of the lay brethren was crucial'.[87]

The main period of patronage for the Cistercians was from the 1120s to the 1160s, a period of general monastic expansion which does not appear to have been hindered by the internecine wars of Stephen and Matilda from 1135–54. The Cistercians' major patrons were the king and such tenants-in-chief as Bishop Alexander of Lincoln (1123–48); Ranulf, earl of Chester (d. 1153); his half-brother, William, earl of Lincoln and Cambridge (d. c.1161); Robert, earl of Leicester (d. 1168); and his twin brother Waleran, count of Meulan.[88] Interestingly, traitors and rebels such as Ranulf and William saw it in their best interests to give generously to the Cistercians and Savigniacs, Ranulf having founded five houses for both orders, and patronising another six Cistercian houses.[89] Presumably, they felt that their largesse may protect them if the political winds changed

---

[78]   Ibid., p. 75. See the detailed discussion of Furness Abbey in Chapter 7.

[79]   Platt (1984), p. 26.

[80]   Ibid.

[81]   Ibid.

[82]   Ibid., p. 27.

[83]   Ibid., p. 40.

[84]   See *The Coucher Book of Furness Abbey*, (Vol. I), Pts. I–III, *Leiston Abbey Cartulary & Butley Priory Charters*. All three of these foundations will be examined in more detail in later chapters.

[85]   See *The Cartulary of the Cistercian Abbey of Old Wardon, Bedfordshire*. Old Wardon is another of the abbeys whose mill holdings are examined in detail in Chapter 7.

[86]   Platt (1984), pp. 48–9.

[87]   Ibid.

[88]   Ibid., p. 28.

[89]   Ibid., pp. 43–4, citing B.D. Hill, *English Cistercian Monasteries and their Patrons in the Twelfth Century*, 1968, pp. 30–36. Ranulf also played a role in the endowments of Lancaster Priory, on which see Chapter 5.

against their favour. Nevertheless, support for the Cistercians was not just an English lordly fashion, as the order was also rapidly spreading throughout continental Europe at this time. Donkin records that over 740 houses were established throughout Europe during the order's lifetime.[90]

Within a few decades of the establishment of the earliest foundations in England, the Cistercians had attracted thousands of lay brethren to their monasteries, transforming the early poverty of the order into substantial wealth. The large numbers of Cistercian *conversi*, combined with their exemption from paying tithes on lands which they had themselves cultivated, both made considerable contributions to their wealth. By the late thirteenth century, the order had become instrumental in the development of the English wool trade, and was also involved in the development of the English iron industry.[91]

Following the anarchy of 1135–54, Henry II supported a number of different orders, including the Cistercians, Victorines, Augustinians, Carthusians and Gilbertines. Like many of his contemporaries, Henry was attracted to asceticism, but he was also a snob, and upon his death was buried with Eleanor of Aquitaine and his son Richard at Fontevrault nunnery, a monastery famed for its wealth and the nobility of its nuns.

One of the major reforms achieved by the new orders was the divestment by lay owners of parish churches to monastic houses from the second half of the twelfth century onwards. The reformers had denounced lay proprietary rights in churches and their tithes, as well as a lord's entitlement in some circumstances to give away the tithes on demesne lands to those he or she favoured. The Cistercians took the most radical stance on the issue, completely renouncing any ownership of tithes, including: 'churches, altar-dues, burial rights, the tithes from the work of nourishment of other men, manors, dependent labourers, land rents, revenues from ovens and mills and [similar] property which is not in accord with monastic purity'.[92] However, these prohibitions had been largely overturned by the 1250s, and by 1300, the Cistercians possessed extensive holdings of these and other kinds, collecting revenues from all of them.[93] The Benedictines, on the other hand, were unconcerned with such prohibitions, as were the Augustinians, who, to the contrary, were keen to take over the care of churches hitherto neglected by their lay owners and to recover misappropriated tithes.[94]

As a consequence of such pressure from the reformers, lay lords became much more scrupulous about to whom they gave their tithes and under what conditions, realizing they could no longer keep them for themselves in good faith. However, founding patrons were able to achieve considerable concessions on their families' behalves for making such donations, including the following rights and obligations:

- ongoing obligations to the founder's kin, heirs and assigns for community prayers;
- the right to enjoy the hospitality of those communities with which they were associated;
- the right to keep horses and hounds in the priory stables, and valuables and heirlooms within the monastery;
- the right to lodge elderly relatives or servants in the guest-house;
- the right to supply benefices for a clerk or provision for a dependent;
- the right to appoint relatives to vacancies within appropriated churches or associated communities.[95]

A founding patron was also able to extract loans from his or her foundation, and financial support for their own or their patrons' business and military ventures.[96]

---

[90]   Donkin (1978), p. 28.

[91]   Dickinson (1961), p. 74. See *The Chartulary of Cockersand Abbey of the Premonstratensian Order,* Vol. I, Pts. I and II, Vol. II, Pts. I and II, and *The Coucher Book of Furness Abbey,* (Vol. I), Pts. I–III, as well as Donkin (1979), Ch. 3 and 5, and the more detailed discussion of both houses in Chapters 7 and 8.

[92]   Constable (1964), p. 138.

[93]   Donkin (1978), p. 17. As we will see in Chapter 7, Beaulieu Abbey had come into seisin of the tithes of three churches and the suit of at least three mills by 1233.

[94]   Platt (1984), p. 32.

[95]   See Wood (1955), pp. 107–10, 113–16; Cook (1961), pp. 20, 23–5.

[96]   See Wood (1955), pp. 116–20, for more details on the kinds of transactions that took place, or which were expected to be provided, and Chapter 2 for more details on ecclesiastical patronage in general.

For the orders that were the beneficiaries of aristocratic endowments the arrangement was equally beneficial. By the thirteenth and fourteenth centuries, revenues from the spiritualities of Augustinian houses had come to equal or exceed those from their temporalities, which was true not just of the large houses, but also of the medium-sized and small ones. For example, Butley Priory, which at its foundation in 1171 held the advowsons of as many as six churches, held 29 by the time of the Dissolution, with interests in another five. By the late thirteenth century, or possibly even a little earlier, the priory's spiritualities were its most important source of revenue, although this did not remain the case throughout the remainder of its existence. On the other hand, Burscough Priory in Lancashire was a small Augustinian foundation with little wealth which had to maintain a leper hospital from its revenues. The three parish churches granted to it at its foundation in the late twelfth century brought in the vast majority of its income, although none of them were very valuable.[97]

Burscough's founder, Robert son of Henry of Lathom, had a number of motivations for making the foundation, including the enclosure and development of his own lands. This was a well-documented reason for the foundation of many religious houses in Lancashire, as well as other remote and poorly developed areas of the north-west. The monasteries played an important role in the drainage of fenland, the construction of ferries and the ongoing maintenance of causeways, fords and bridges.[98] Abbeys such as Furness and Cockersand in Lancashire, being Cistercian and Premonstratensian houses respectively, also made a significant contribution to the development of mining and fishing resources in the region.[99]

Three very important events took place in the middle of the twelfth century which had an enduring effect upon the development of the Cistercian order. The first was their union with the Savigniac order, which was ratified by the Cistercian General Chapter in 1147, and immediately recognized by Pope Ignatius III, who had himself formerly been a Cistercian monk. The second was a formal acknowledgement by the order in 1152 that its expansion had been too rapid, and that there were to be no more new houses founded or monks from other orders admitted. The third was the death of St Bernard of Clairvaux. These events had a major flow-on effect. The absorption of the Savigniacs had led to a relaxation of the Cistercian Rule, with the consequence that any differences between them and the Benedictines seemed to have been further diminished. This appears to have had an immediate and significant impact upon the aristocracy's perception of the moral standing of the order.

Whereas Stephen's reign had seen the foundation of an additional 36 monasteries to the order, there were only five founded under Henry II (r. 1154–89), and only two of those were of any significance. In the second half of the twelfth century, the preferences of founding patrons had shifted primarily towards the Augustinians. However, even though the Cistercians were no longer being granted large tracts of land during this period, they were acquiring property in smaller parcels via exchange or sale, primarily from members of the local gentry and wealthier peasants.

The Cistercians' successful attempts at consolidating their properties in the second half of the twelfth century generated more wealth and status for the order, both of which were further enhanced by royal patronage in the thirteenth century as Beaulieu in Hampshire (1203–4), Hailes in Gloucestershire (1246), and Vale Royal in Cheshire (1274) were all established as royal foundations. The order further benefited from the patronage of other powerful figures such as the Bishop of Winchester, Peter des Roches (1205–38). Largely as a result of their aggressive land acquisitions, it was during this period that the Cistercians began to be regarded as avaricious within court circles, while many of their neighbours began to look upon them with envy and hatred owing to their successful farming practices.[100]

Although the Cistercians did not begin acquiring many parish churches until the later fourteenth century, they had already begun the process in the second half of the twelfth century. By the sixteenth century, a number of Cistercian houses in Wales were drawing as much as 30 per cent of their income from spiritualities, although the proportion was lower in England.[101] While the growth of the Cistercian order tailed off after 1152, the

---

[97]   See *Leiston Abbey Cartulary and Butley Priory Charters* and *An Edition of the Cartulary of Burscough Priory*. All three houses will be examined with respect to their mill holdings in later chapters.

[98]   Platt (1984), pp. 34–5.

[99]   See the detailed discussion of both houses in Chapters 7 and 8.

[100]   Platt (1984), pp. 51–2. See Knowles (1940), Ch. 39, for a detailed discussion of Gerald of Wales and his criticisms of the Cistercians and Cluniacs, as well as some other critics of the monks.

[101]   Wagstaff (1970); Williams (1962), pp. 164–5, 348. According to the *Taxatio Nicholai IV* of 1291, Beaulieu Abbey, for example, drew about 17 per cent of its income from spiritualities within the manor of Faringdon. See Hockey (1976), p. 218.

greater popularity of the Augustinians did not translate into a greater number of foundations. With their heyday in the early 1130s, the growth of the Augustinians was steady at 10 to 15 houses per decade until around the middle of the thirteenth century, when it abruptly ended. One of the main attractions for potential patrons to Augustinian foundations was their relative economy. A modest endowment might be sufficient for establishing a hospital or hostel, but at the same time made any expansion difficult, and could be the cause of later failure.[102]

With the exception of the establishment of the mendicant orders in England in the thirteenth century, the arrival of the Premonstratensians in 1142 constituted the last wave of monastic renewal in England. The order accepted advowsons, but rarely served them, and took no part in caring for the sick or in the construction of public works. Such a withdrawal from practical affairs no doubt contributed to its popularity amongst the wealthy and pious. Nevertheless, it took some years for the Premonstratensians to benefit from the declining patronage of the Cistercians and Augustinians, as the order did not begin its expansion until the second half of the twelfth century.

Because the families of the great magnates or tenants-in-chief had tended to support the great Norman abbeys and Cluniacs in the first decades after the Conquest, and later switched their patronage to the Cistercians, by the time the Premonstratensians had arrived in England, such families had already acquired a sufficient number of foundations to satisfy their spiritual and temporal needs. Intermarriage between the great families had further compounded this situation, whereby multiple foundations had come under the control of a single family. This usually meant that the house which received favour was the one which a patron knew personally.

Like the Augustinians, therefore, the Premonstratensians had to appeal to the administrative classes for support, a class of men which had grown in number and stature under Henry II and his sons. In the words of H.M. Colvin, these men constituted 'the last generation which took it for granted that the foundation of religious houses was among its spiritual obligations'.[103] One of the most prominent in late twelfth century England was Ranulf de Glanville. His foundation of Leiston Abbey in 1183–85 as a Premonstratensian house reflected the status he had recently gained as chief justiciar of England, and ensured the best protection for his soul that was then available, i.e. the prayers of the blameless and pure monks of Premontré. Ranulf died in 1189, however, before Leiston could attain the wealth and status of his earlier Augustinian foundation at Butley, but his family later involved themselves in the foundation of other Premonstratensian houses in other parts of the country, including Cockersand in Lancashire.

By the end of the twelfth century, the various foundations were already jostling one another for space and patronage in the more densely populated parts of the country. This resulted in the relocation of many houses as the relevant communities (sometimes of the same order) came into conflict with one another. Both Dickinson and Burton have recorded that as many as 30 per cent of English religious houses changed their location at one time or another during their lives. This was invariably because they were poorly located for one of several reasons, including inadequate water supplies, inclement climate and conflict with or proximity to other religious houses or urban centres.[104]

While most houses preferred to accumulate property close to their foundations, the late arrival of any order in a region meant that it often had to accept grants over scattered areas. The newer orders therefore tended to avoid accumulating land in areas already dominated by another house. Many of the Augustinian and Cistercian houses were recipients of scattered holdings, although it was the latter order on the whole that was most successful at later consolidation. This was primarily because it had established its foundations in what were then remote areas such as Hampshire, Yorkshire, Northumbria and Lancashire, whereas the later Premonstratensians were disproportionately represented in counties like Sussex, Suffolk and Derbyshire, 'where the new monasticism had remained, until that date, comparatively thinly spread'.[105]

---

[102] Platt (1984), pp. 56–7.

[103] Colvin (1951), p. 30.

[104] See: Dickinson (1961), pp. 6–9; Donkin (1978), pp. 31–6; Burton (1994), pp. 131–5. One such example was Beaulieu Abbey in Hampshire, which was originally intended to be built in the royal manor of Faringdon in Oxfordshire but was moved even before construction began, probably due to lack of water and the close proximity of other religious houses. Another was Kirkstall Abbey, which was moved from Barnoldswick to Headingley due to the continual rains and raids by bandits. See Chapter 7.

[105] Platt (1984), pp. 61–2.

Land Acquisition and Direct Management, 1180–1315

The extraordinary growth of monasticism in England and Wales during the twelfth century is well borne out by the following figures. At the time of the Conquest, there were about 60 religious houses and 1,000 monks throughout both countries. By 1216, there were nearly 700 houses and 13,000 monks and nuns, constituting a more than 10-fold increase in 150 years. This observation would appear to put to rest any doubts about when the major period of monastic expansion took place in England.

While the spirit of reform of the twelfth century had directly contributed to the spread of the reformist orders throughout England, the winds of change had yet to blow through the great Benedictine monasteries. Perhaps the most well-known example of the parlous state in which some Benedictine houses found themselves at the end of the twelfth century is Bury St Edmunds, as famously described in *The Chronicle of Jocelin of Brakelond*.

Most of the *Chronicle* was written while Jocelin was a monk at the abbey, probably between 1194 and his death in 1211, but it also features later interpolations by other monks from the early thirteenth century. The beginning of the *Chronicle* describes the ruin into which Bury St Edmunds had fallen in the last years of Hugh's abbacy from 1157–80, which Jocelin attributes to the trust which the abbot had placed in his obedientiaries, or monastic officials, to handle the abbey's financial and legal affairs: 'The townships of the Abbot and all the hundreds were given out to farm; the woods were destroyed, and the houses of the manors threatened to fall in ruin, and day by day all things went from bad to worse.'[106]

While Jocelin is here clearly associating the ruinous conditions of the abbey's holdings with its policy of letting all of its property out to farm, and on many occasions in his *Chronicle* draws attention to the mismanagement of the abbey by various abbots and obedientiaries, Platt has observed that the farming out of manors that was characteristic of the twelfth century 'did not imperil monastic finances to the degree that some historians have since argued'.[107] But although direct management of estates also had its drawbacks, these were certainly not financial, as both Richard Holt and John Langdon have clearly demonstrated with respect to mill holdings, and for which I will present more evidence in later chapters.

Hugh's successor, Abbot Samson (1182–1211), was one of many prelates of the time who saw that the leasing out of demesne land from father to son might result in tenants acquiring hereditary rights in the land concerned and thereby falling out of the abbey's hands altogether. He therefore refused the renewal of such a grant to Adam de Cockfield after it had been held by his grandfather and father, although the latter had never made any hereditary claim over the disputed land. Another concern of prelates like Samson was that if such a tenant or his wife held any land from the king in chief, once that tenant died, the Crown could seize the entire holding, including any land that had previously been leased from the abbey.[108]

Samson's abbacy exactly corresponded with a period of inflation from the 1180s to the early 1200s, which had resulted in pressure on every landowner to resume control of leased out lands. Not only did long-term fixed rentals mean a relatively lower revenue from rented properties during a time of inflation, but also higher revenues from the sale of produce from which the tenant also benefited, meaning that the lord missed out twice over.

Battle Abbey was one of the houses that had been especially adversely affected by the granting out of lands on long-term and generous leases to tenants ranging in status from the more prominent of their patrons and lay officials to servants and retainers who had served them well. During the twelfth century, these grants had gradually acquired the status of hereditary tenancies, resulting in a concerted effort by the abbey to resume its alienated lands. The monks went so far as forging a foundation charter of William I, while forbidding the

---

[106]   *The Chronicle of Jocelin of Brakelond*, p. 1.

[107]   Platt (1984), p. 65, citing A.R. Bridbury, 'The Farming Out of Manors', *Economic History Review* 31 (1978), pp. 503–20. Cf. Faith (1999), pp. 180–82, who argues that leasing out large estates at fixed rents had been 'an accepted management strategy since the eighth century', and that 'Domesday Book shows that leasing was widespread and routine in the eleventh century.'

[108]   *The Chronicle of Jocelin of Brakelond*, pp. 58–9. Cf. Chibnall (1986), p. 181, who notes that the knights who bore witness in the king's court to Bury's claim that the manors of Semer and Groton had been granted to it by Robert of Cockfield would not recognize the validity of the relevant charter, maintaining that both were held in hereditary fee farm by Adam of Cockfield's family going back more than a century.

granting out of hereditary leases within the abbey's *banlieu* (an area of three miles diameter around the abbey), or any significant proportion of this area to lay servants.[109]

Subsequently, Battle sought to consolidate its holdings in the area, purchasing land adjoining its demesne as it became vacant and clearing, enclosing and draining its existing forests and wastelands. Between 1240 and 1305 the abbey had quadrupled its holdings in the town of Battle alone.[110]

Peterborough Abbey similarly benefited from such practices. Between 1170 and 1200, the abbey went from having all its manors let out to farm, to having them all in hand, in the process more than doubling their income.[111] Westminster Abbey also managed to double its income over a similar period, partly through the acquisition of new lands, but more importantly through the recovery of estates formerly let out to farm, as well as the implementation of direct management practices.[112] But as Platt observes, more direct and assertive management was not restricted to land let out to farm for the monks of Westminster:

> Thus whereas the produce of their home farms was certainly to result in increasing profits for the Westminster monks, it is probably the case that they benefited still more from the perquisites of their courts, and from such other incidental dues as the receipts to be expected at their mills. Strong lordship, at all times in the middle ages, was quite as likely to be the source of profit on the estates as any improvement in agricultural techniques.[113]

For many religious houses, the thirteenth century was the first time that any of them had exercised direct control of their own main assets. It was also a period during which the process of land acquisition had been reversed from one of continual sales of land to neighbours during the twelfth century, to one of enlargement and consolidation of monastic demesnes in the thirteenth century.

The buying power and land acquisitions of the larger monasteries contributed to inflation in the land market and resulted in the impoverishment of some members of the lesser gentry in those areas where competition for land was particularly fierce. But even small foundations benefited from the change-over to direct management.[114]

The greatest purchasers of land were also the most enthusiastic at clearing, fencing and reclaiming wooded, uncultivated and waste land. Situated in the Cambridgeshire Fens, Ramsey Abbey spent a great deal of money on draining and clearing its lands, especially during the thirteenth century. Following the example of the Cistercians, other rich Benedictine abbeys such as Spalding and Crowland established arable granges in the Lincolnshire fens during the same period.[115] Such efforts at reclamation made these areas substantially more productive and therefore valuable, not only in terms of produce, but in potential rental or sale values.

During the same period, the Benedictines of Glastonbury and Christ Church, Canterbury, were reclaiming the Somerset Levels and the north coast of Kent, respectively, while Battle Abbey built sea defences at Pevensey, and Peterborough in the north-east of Northamptonshire reclaimed the fens adjoining the forests which they had already cleared, supposedly relieving its human inhabitants of the vexatious assaults of foresters and beasts.[116] Meaux Abbey in Yorkshire had also instituted 'ambitious drainage schemes in the flat country east of Beverley', while Missenden in Buckinghamshire was clearing and reclaiming the Chilterns.[117]

Platt makes the telling observation that 'each of the three principal regions of growth during the period coincided strikingly with areas of known monastic investments.' The first he describes as a 'scatter of former marchlands and forest' throughout England, which was the work of laymen as much as monks, while the

---

[109]   Searle (1974), pp. 104–5.

[110]   Ibid., pp. 151–2.

[111]   King (1973), pp. 144–5.

[112]   Harvey (1977), pp. 83–4.

[113]   Platt (1984), pp. 65–6.

[114]   Ibid., pp. 71–2.

[115]   Hallam (1965), p. 218.

[116]   King (1973), p. 74. The 50 years from 1175 to 1225 were an intense period of forest clearing throughout England which continued at a lesser pace for another 25 years.

[117]   Platt (1984), pp. 73–4.

second, the Lincolnshire silt fens, was primarily the work of the Benedictines, while the third area in Northern England was mostly cleared by 'the Cistercians and their imitators'.[118]

Because large land grants to monasteries had basically ceased since the mid-thirteenth century, any further growth had to be achieved through land purchases, building and land improvements, or allowing neighbours to lease and improve the land themselves. It was during this time that many religious houses began investing in mills, either through purchase or construction.

For example, between the 1230s and the 1340s, Westminster Abbey acquired seven mills via purchase and litigation. Around 1235–36, it purchased from Laurence, son of William le Petit, the 'island' of Eye in Middlesex, which was a share of the manor of 'La Neyte' that included a mill, with the grantee paid £10 annually in perpetuity.[119] Such purchases became especially frequent during the first half of the fourteenth century, when a fulling mill and two grain mills at Pershore were acquired, probably through litigation.[120] Birdbrook mill in Essex was purchased by the wardens of the abbey in 1341–42 from William Lengleys and Michael de Birdbrook, who received £20 payment.[121] Moulsham and Wandsworth mills were also bought outright or through reversion at around this time.[122] Similar patterns of investment in mills by other houses will be noted in later chapters.

The new affluence of the monasteries was reflected in impressive and ambitious building programmes, many of which were self-financed. But not all such programmes were wholly successful. Some of the craftsmen employed to construct these fine new edifices overstretched their own skills, leading to some spectacular failures, such as the collapse of the south aisle of St Albans Church in 1323, while other monasteries simply lacked the finances to complete projects which they had begun, such as St Dogmael's, Talley and Cymer in Wales, all of which were unable to complete the construction of their conventual buildings.[123]

These ambitions generated significant debts for even some of the largest abbeys and priories. By the 1290s, Lewes, Reading, Rievaulx, Fountains, Kirkham, Dunstable and Guisborough were all in trouble, although none faced ruin or insolvency as their basic financial situations were still sound. Christ Church, Canterbury, is one of the best-documented of the larger monasteries during this period. Although most of the priory's problems were due to poor management, litigation in Rome to protect their ancient privileges had cost the priory dearly, especially archiepiscopal elections, as had the payment of papal and royal taxes. By 1285 – the same year that Henry of Eastry was elevated to the priorate – the priory owed almost £300,000 to the merchants of Florence and over £100,000 to the merchants of Pistoia. At the end of his 46-year priorship, Christ Church was free of debt, primarily due to Henry's sound management practices, which included clearing the debt to the merchants of Pistoia within four years, meaning that he must have repaid them an average of £25,000 *per annum* – no mean feat by any standards.[124] Holt records that Prior Henry's investment policies not only encompassed agricultural improvements but also urban land and mills. At the end of his priorship, he reported having built eight and a half mills which brought an extra £20 *per annum* into the priory's coffers, including a new windmill at Milton Hall, Essex, and a reconstructed tide mill at Lydden on the Isle of Thanet in Kent.[125]

The Cistercians attempted to remedy problems of maladministration of their houses by setting up their own Paris school of studies to train better quality administrators, but also to combat heresy. Another reform which they pursued was the institution of standard account-keeping practices, especially from the early

---

[118] Ibid., p. 74.

[119] Harvey (1977), p. 414, citing PRO, CP 25 (1) 146/10/144.

[120] Ibid., p. 169. On Pershore see also Flete (1909), pp. 104–5.

[121] Harvey (1977), p. 417, citing *CPR* 1343–5, p. 136. The sale was amortized on 24 October 1343. Although Harvey notes that the £20 payment 'may have only been part of the purchase price', given the costs of construction of new watermills, this was probably the full price. See Lucas (2006a), Ch. 4.

[122] Ibid., p. 169.

[123] Platt (1984), pp. 90–91, citing: L.F. Salzman, *Building in England down to 1540*, 1967 (2nd edn.), pp. 369–75; C.A. Ralegh Radford, *St Dogmael's Abbey*, 1962, p. 17; J.B. Smith and B.H. St J. O'Neil, *Talley Abbey*, 1967, pp. 11–15; C.A. Ralegh Radford, *Cymmer Abbey*, 1946.

[124] Ibid., p. 93, citing Mavis Mate, 'The Indebtedness of Canterbury Cathedral Priory 1215–95', *Economic History Review* 26 (1973), p. 192.

[125] Holt (1988), p. 88. See also pp. 136–7, on the history and fate of the tide mill.

thirteenth century. As we will see in Chapter 7, the Cistercian houses of Beaulieu and Sibton had adopted such practices by the second half of the thirteenth century.

Within a few years, a number of Benedictine houses were already following suit, with annual audits required by the pope. Jocelin of Brakelond records in his *Chronicle* how diligent was Abbot Samson of Bury St Edmunds at pursuing this course, compiling extensive and detailed records of all payments due to the abbey, 'so that within four years from his election there was not one who could deceive him concerning the revenues of the Abbey to a single pennyworth', even though no such records had previously existed.[126] By the end of the thirteenth century, it was very unusual for any house large or small not to have some kind of accounting system in place. Platt observes that '[a]t the greater houses, certainly, sophisticated calculations of profit and loss were beginning, for the first time, to influence policy decisions on the demesnes.'[127]

The relatively poorly endowed nunneries were particularly at risk of financial ruin, a situation that was compounded for many of them by the poor training and education of many of the nuns. Although Lacock Abbey, for example, had been well endowed by its founder, Ela, Countess of Salisbury, and continued to recruit the daughters of county aristocrats, it still had financial difficulties throughout the thirteenth and fourteenth centuries.[128]

The interference of patrons in monastic affairs was also on the increase during the thirteenth century, especially in its closing decades. Edward I's second Statute of Westminster (1285) protected patrons' interests in their various foundations by stating the founder's right to reclaim land or rents that had been misapplied or alienated by the grantee. The statute also allowed the founder and his or her heirs to summarily resume church lands if the patron felt seriously aggrieved for whatever reason.[129] A case in point was the resumption of lands and customs in the wealthy dependency of Osbourne St George in Wiltshire by the patrons of the alien Abbey of Bec after Pope Clement V (1305–14) had granted it to his nephew, Raymond de Got. The manor included a mill that had been drawing an average rent of £4 13s 4d in the late thirteenth century.[130] The patrons justified their action by arguing that the dependency had been granted for the souls of their families, as well as for the provision of hospitality and alms to the poor of the locality; granting it to an individual would remove these obligations. The great magnate Gilbert de Clare had already taken into his own hands another Bec dependency at Goldcliff in Monmouthshire in 1289, because he felt that the abbey had abused the privilege to his detriment.[131]

Such practices were relatively unusual, however. It was more usual for a monastery and its patron to cooperate and compromise to their mutual advantage. For the monasteries, there were certainly many advantages to be had by staying on good terms with a wealthy and powerful patron, and as far as the latter was concerned, such good relations were also to be fostered for the benefit of their own souls and those of their heirs. Platt describes in some detail the efforts of a number of patrons to have their heraldic crests, tombs and other dedications integrated into the designs of the many new conventual buildings constructed during the thirteenth century with their assistance, and how such families became more or less permanently identified with their foundations.[132]

However, even the wealthy monasteries had to secure outside sources of finance for their ambitious building projects. An important source of additional revenue for the Augustinians and Benedictines was the appropriation of nearby churches, which often had valuable property attached to them. For example, St Mary's Church, which was probably one of nine churches bestowed on Battle Abbey by William II, had three

---

[126] *The Chronicle of Jocelin of Brakelond*, p. 29.

[127] Platt (1984), p. 95.

[128] See *Lacock Abbey Charters*, p. 20, and the more detailed discussion of the abbey's affairs in Chapter 6.

[129] Platt (1984), p. 98. See also the discussion of patron's rights and privileges in Chapter 2.

[130] See the analysis of the rentals from Bec's computus rolls in Chapter 5.

[131] Morgan (1968), pp. 31–2, 29.

[132] Platt (1984), pp. 99–113. For example, Guisborough Abbey was able to rebuild the east end of its church after the fire of 1289 with the help of the Brus patrons, while Tintern Abbey rebuilt its church around 1300 with the help of its new patron, Roger Bigod, earl of Norfolk (1270–1306). Both houses celebrated the generosity of their patrons in conventual dedications of various kinds. See Platt (1984), p. 108, citing: R. Gilyard-Beer, *Guisborough Priory*, 1955, p. 5; O.E. Craster, *Tintern Abbey*, 1956, pp. 8–10.

mills in demesne, 'two within the *leuga*, namely one below Loxbeech, the other farther down the valley'. The third lay outside the *leuga*, and had been acquired through exchange with the lord of Catsfield for 'a tiny meadow' near Bulverhythe.[133] This was consistent with Battle's early policy of concentrating upon exploiting and extending its holdings in the immediate surrounds of the abbey.[134] By the fourteenth century, like many other Benedictine houses of the time, Battle had split its manors into a home group, which provided for the material needs of the abbey, and an income group, which provided the abbey with a cash income.[135] The latter were those properties which lay outside easy droving or carting distance. They included the pensions from eight unappropriated churches, three rent-rolls (two of which included mills) and 10 manors.[136] Amongst these were four appropriated churches from East Anglia, described by Searle as 'fully manors, with demesne lands (much enlarged after appropriation), dairies, flocks, occasionally a mill and seignorial rights'. Two of these church-manors, Ixning and Aylsham, with net valuations of £66 and £69 in 1346–47, were amongst Battle's most valuable revenue holdings.[137]

Although the process of appropriating churches was expensive and time-consuming, it was ultimately worthwhile. In 1279, Edward I had issued the Statute of Mortmain, which forbade any person, lay or cleric, to give lands or rents to a monastery or other such body without royal license. The reason for this was that when property passed into the control of a religious house, it never again fell vacant, and the king, therefore, lost all rights in such property. Hence, after 1279, both the Augustinians and Benedictines needed royal permission to acquire any further churches or advowsons.[138]

The statute also forbade monastic houses from recovering lands of their own which had been alienated without going through the same process, a sanction which placed some houses in a rather invidious position, as they had then to expend sometimes considerable amounts of money to recover their lands.[139] Nevertheless, some houses continued such appropriations without going through the appropriate channels. For example, Westminster Abbey appropriated Mordern Rectory in Surrey in 1301, including its tithes of hay and a mill, but was fined £40 in 1319 for failing to obtain a royal license.[140]

Another means of raising additional revenue for construction work involved a levy on the income of obedientiaries. For example, St Augustine's, Canterbury, raised £277 4s 8d over eight years from such a levy for the construction of its new chapter house,[141] while at Ely, the reconstruction of the central tower after its collapse in 1322 was financed by the prior and his obedientiaries, a levy on the monks' pittances, and subsidies from John Salmon, the bishop of Norwich (1299–1325), and John Hotham, bishop of Ely (1316–37).[142]

Platt lists several other strategies that were available to the monasteries in order to raise revenues for their building programmes, including better administrative oversight of leased properties in order to recover lost rents, the sale of corrodies to wealthy lay folk, and the manumission (or emancipation) of serfs in return for cash payments. Worcester and Dunstable priories were two religious houses which instituted these and the aforementioned policies during the late thirteenth and early fourteenth centuries.[143]

---

[133] *The Chronicle of Battle Abbey*, pp. 62–3.

[134] Searle (1974), pp. 36–7.

[135] Ibid., p. 251. See the detailed discussion of Battle's estates in Chapter 5.

[136] One of these mills, at Southwark, paid £3 rent *per annum* in 1351–52, an amount which does not appear to have varied over the subsequent 30 years. See ibid., p. 454.

[137] Ibid., p. 252.

[138] Robinson (1980), p. 185.

[139] Finberg (1951), p. 260. In 1366, Urban V passed a similar law decreeing that papal consent was also needed for such appropriations to take place anywhere within Latin Christendom (see ibid., p. 186).

[140] Harvey (1977), p. 411.

[141] Platt (1984), p. 113, citing A.H. Davis (ed.), *William Thorne's Chronicle of Saint Augustine's Abbey, Canterbury*, 1934, pp. 439–40.

[142] Ibid., citing F.R. Chapman (ed.), *Sacrist Rolls of Ely*, 1907, II: 50–51.

[143] Ibid., pp. 120–22, citing R.M. Haines (ed.), *A Calendar of the Register of Wolstan de Bransford, Bishop of Worcester 1339–49*, Worcs. Hist. Soc., Vol. 4, 1966, pp. ix–x; Harry Rothwell (ed.), *English Historical Documents 1189–1327*, 1975, p. 773.

Another process which directly benefited religious houses was the gradual loss of legal freedom of villeins during the thirteenth century, a process which had been initiated by William in the late eleventh century, but which was strengthened and furthered by the strategy of both lay and ecclesiastical lords to resume leased-out lands in the thirteenth century and impose additional feudal services on villeins. While labour services had been due from villeins in the twelfth century, many had avoided them by making cash payments to their lords. By the thirteenth century, such payments were widely interpreted as an indication of free status, and serious efforts were made by many lords to determine not only the status of smallholders paying cash rents, but the status of properties for which cash rents were paid, and whether labour services were being avoided thereby.[144]

This situation had been exacerbated by the inflation of the late twelfth and early thirteenth centuries, when many of the additional costs of production and administration were passed by lords onto the lowest orders. Consequently, the 1190s saw the initiation of many prolonged lawsuits by smallholders in the lay courts to win free status. Because the justiciars were drawn from the ruling élites, it is, perhaps, not very surprising that they demonstrated a remarkable bias towards the interests of lords, and almost invariably found against the smallholders. It should also be noted that great church estates such as Cirencester, Glastonbury, Bury St Edmunds, Evesham and Ramsey all played a significant role in this process.[145]

By the late thirteenth century, lay patronage of the monasteries was almost at an end. In an interesting anticipation of Protestantism, changing fashions in religion had promoted the concept of a more direct relationship between the faithful and God, a relationship which made the role of the monks somewhat redundant. At the same time, the success of the mendicant orders in the towns was partially the result of a popular perception that their stricter rules regarding the ownership of property had preserved their holiness, and therefore offered a more attractive alternative to those seeking salvation in the Afterlife.[146] This sometimes led to direct competition between the monks of urban houses and the newly arrived friars. For example, the monks of Walsingham appealed to their benefactress, Elizabeth de Clare (daughter of Gilbert), to disallow the Franciscans from building a hospice in the town, a request that was denied. The Walsingham monks were justifiably afraid that as the friars expanded their property holdings within the parish, the friars' exemption from tithes would reduce the priory's income.[147] Such fears were well summarised by the Benedictine monk, Matthew Paris, who accused the friars of setting themselves before the monastic orders in holiness, of publicly vilifying the monks in their sermons, and of interposing themselves between the faithful and the monks with regard to deaths, marriages and the holding of counsel.[148]

By 1300, the mendicant orders had reached their maximum point of expansion in England, which happened to coincide with the economic downturn of the late thirteenth and early fourteenth centuries. This also meant that competition between the monks and friars became particularly intense during this period due to the scarcity of resources, with the monks usually coming off worse. For example, at the turn of the century, the Priory of St Denys in Southampton, which, as noted earlier, had never been popular with the burgesses of Southampton, was no longer winning donations from its traditional patrons in the administrative classes, whereas the Franciscans of Southampton were popular with the burgesses and continued to be for at least another 200 years. The fourteenth century was a bad time for St Denys, and although its situation improved slightly in the fifteenth century, by the Dissolution it was one of the poorer houses in the country.[149]

One monastic house whose fortunes proved particularly volatile during the thirteenth century was Tavistock Abbey in Devon. Although the twelfth century had been a time of relative prosperity for the abbey, it had experienced a series of crises during the thirteenth century, not least of which were due to the negligence and/or incompetence of its abbots. In 1262, the abbey was nearly bankrupt, and although its

---

[144] Hilton (1965), pp. 5–13.

[145] Ibid., pp. 11–19.

[146] Platt (1984), p. 123.

[147] Ibid., pp. 124–5, citing: Rothwell, op. cit., pp. 686–7, 771; Henry Richard Luard (ed.), *Annales Monastici*, Rolls Series, 1869, IV: 537; James Lee-Warner, 'Petition of the Prior and Canons of Walsingham, Norfolk, to Elizabeth, Lady of Clare. Circa A.D. 1345', *Archaeological Journal* 26 (1869), pp. 166–73. Also Richard Holt, personal communication.

[148] Platt (1984), pp. 125–6, citing Rothwell, op.cit., pp. 685–6.

[149] See *The Cartulary of the Priory of St. Denys near Southampton*, Vol. I, pp. xxxviii–xxxix, 1, and the more detailed discussion of St Denys in Chapter 6.

fortunes recovered slowly under the abbacy of Robert Colbern (1280–85), the Statute of Mortmain placed further financial strains upon the house as it sought to recover alienated properties. Colbern's successor, Robert Champeaux (1285–1324), proved himself a fine administrator and a keen builder, and managed to restore the abbey's fortunes to an unprecedented level,[150] although his replacement, Bonus of Aquitaine, was a papal appointee with none of the flair of his predecessor, and again left the abbey nearly bankrupt in 1333 when he was eventually deposed by Bishop Grandisson. Grandisson replaced Bonus with his own cousin, John de Courtenay, who proved no better than Bonus, running up £1,300 of debts with London and Florentine merchant bankers. The bishop was subsequently forced to appoint a receiver-general to manage the abbey's affairs, although its fortunes remained poor until the death of Courtenay during the Black Death, when rents were raised, and a flexible system of land leasing was introduced, both of which contributed to its improved condition in the decades leading up to the fifteenth century.[151]

Tavistock's fortunes had been further compromised by climatic variations in the period after 1250, following a century-long respite from prevailing conditions which had allowed the farming of marginal uplands in both the south-west and the north of the country. The adverse change in climate had also had a detrimental effect upon other monasteries with marginal arable such as Egglestone and Coverham in North Yorkshire,[152] a situation that was further aggravated by the Scottish Wars at the turn of the century and subsequently.

The Impact of the Agrarian Crisis on the Monastic Economy, 1315–21

Poor administration, climate change, hostile incursions by the Scots and crop failure were not the only problems facing ecclesiastical estates in the fourteenth century. According to Michael Postan's famous thesis, by the early fourteenth century, the English population was outstripping its ability to feed itself. A succession of bad seasons in 1315–16 and again in 1320–21 precipitated a crisis, imposing a Malthusian check on any further growth, and leading to a reversal in both agricultural production and population growth.[153] Postan argued that because of a general scarcity of pasture for grazing livestock in relation to arable land, a shortage of manure on many estates resulted in a gradual impoverishment of the soil, leading to poorer than average harvests and the abandonment of marginal arable. Combined with a general increase in the rural population during the thirteenth century, a supposed lack of any significant progress in agricultural techniques, and rising prices for meadows and pasture,[154] by the time of the crop failures and livestock murrains of 1315–21, the agricultural system throughout the country was in serious crisis. However, Postan's thesis has been criticised from a number of different perspectives. For example, J.C. Russell has argued that the famines and epidemics which accompanied the poor harvests of 1315–21 were not sufficient to have any significant downward impact upon the population, and that England remained prosperous throughout all but the worst years of the crisis.[155] Barbara Harvey has argued not only that population trends remained fairly stable during the early fourteenth century until the Black Death, but that land values generally remained buoyant, and that soil exhaustion was a relatively minor problem.[156] More recently, research conducted by several scholars, including Bruce Campbell and his colleagues who worked on the 'Feeding the Cities' project, has revealed that urban consumption in London and several leading provincial towns during the thirteenth and the first half of the fourteenth centuries encouraged agricultural specialization in the surrounding hinterlands.[157] Such urban patterns of consumption

---

[150] See Finberg (1951), pp. 259–61.

[151] Ibid., pp. 261–2.

[152] Parry (1978), pp. 65–6, 97–100, 103–5, 124–5. Kershaw's scepticism that climatic change was responsible for the period of cooler and wetter weather in England at the beginning of the fourteenth century is no longer credible given the weight of evidence subsequently gathered by Parry and other researchers. See Kershaw (1973a), pp. 7–8, and n. 22.

[153] See, for example, Postan (1950), p. 235, (1966a), pp. 552–9.

[154] According to Campbell, Galloway, and Murphy (1992), p. 14, the difference between the two is that meadow is mowable, whereas pasture is not.

[155] Russell (1966).

[156] Harvey (1966).

[157] See, for example, Campbell, Galloway and Murphy (1992).

generated zones of specialized land usage and more dynamic and adaptable agricultural practices, including progressive and intensive systems of cultivation, thus calling into question Postan's essentially static view of agricultural technology in the thirteenth and fourteenth centuries, as well as his conclusion that '[h]igh prices and valuations of meadow and pasture are ... evidence of the scarcity of these resources rather than the returns contingent upon their productive and profitable use.'[158]

Ian Kershaw has noted that there were some other important events that preceded the crop failures of the second and third decades of the fourteenth century, and which contributed to the subsequent crisis. First of these was the inflation of the English currency from 1304–14, which was primarily due to 'currency depreciation and the large influx of foreign silver coined into sterling'.[159] This led to rises in the price of livestock, dairy produce and most other foodstuffs. By 1308, many prices were as much as 25 per cent higher than they had been only a decade earlier, whereas the price of grain had dropped significantly over the same period due to a series of favourable harvests. Poor harvests from 1308–10, however, resulted in a rapid increase in prices, leading to grain shortages in some parts of the country, while in Scotland, the problem reached famine proportions.[160]

In the spring of 1315, prices for livestock, meat and other victuals were stabilized by an Act of Parliament, but no attempt was made to regulate grain prices, which would have been practically impossible anyway due to the poor harvest of 1314 as well as subsequent crop failures. Torrential rain throughout the summer of 1315 caused widespread flooding and the destruction of hay and cereal crops. The archbishop of Canterbury responded by ordering penitential processions by the clergy 'in the hope of encouraging the people to atone for their sins and appease the wrath of God by prayer, fasting, alms-giving, and other charitable works'.[161]

In 1316, grain prices soared. During the first decade of the fourteenth century, the average price for a quarter of grain had been 5s 7 1/4d. The year after the crop failure, prices went as high as 44 shillings in some parts of southern England, with 30 shillings being a commonly paid sum. In the West Country, however, the price increases were more modest, with prices of 16 shillings a quarter recorded at Chepstow in Monmouthshire, while Cornwall appears to have been relatively unaffected. The result was a sudden expansion in the long-distance grain trade, with merchants and manorial officials travelling far and wide to both buy and sell grain. Kershaw records that in the same year there were also extreme price increases in the costs of salt, dairy produce, and many other victuals, including horse-meat.[162]

In February 1316, the price cap on livestock and meat was abandoned due to the dearth of animals. The harvest of the same year was as bad, if not worse, than the previous year, with torrential rains once more destroying crops. This was accompanied in many parts of England by what may have been typhoid, an epidemic which claimed the lives of at least 10 per cent of the population. The mortality rate in the larger towns and cities may well have been higher.[163]

But while some of the wealthier lay and ecclesiastical estates had managed relatively well during the period of inflation, and even appear to have gained the upper hand in buying out the livestock of small-holders in the wake of the first harvest failures, their situation gradually worsened over the subsequent years. Christ Church, for example, was forced to introduce stringent economies on its already well-managed estates in order to stay solvent. Kershaw reports that many lay and ecclesiastical lords reduced their expenditure during this period by decreasing the sizes of their households and withdrawing customary alms, a case in point being John of Laund, prior of Bolton in North Yorkshire.[164]

---

[158] Ibid., p. 2. See Campbell (2000), for a more detailed exposition of his thesis for the whole of England.

[159] Kershaw (1973a), p. 6.

[160] Ibid.

[161] Ibid., pp. 6–7.

[162] Ibid., pp. 8–9. In Marjorie Chibnall's analysis of the English possessions of the Abbey of Bec, she briefly discusses the fluctuations in grain prices which Bec's possessions had been experiencing as early as the 1270s and 1280s in southern and eastern England, with the lowest point being the years 1287–89, when the average price was only 2s 10 1/2d. See Chibnall (1987), p. 9.

[163] Kershaw (1973a), pp. 10–13.

[164] Ibid., pp. 10–11. See the analysis of Bolton's fourteenth-century mill holdings in Chapter 6.

Laund was an exemplary administrator who had managed to double the priory's income during the inflation of 1305 to 1315, but could do nothing to alleviate the effects of the first crop failure. The priory's fortunes improved in 1318 with the plentiful harvests of that year. However, the Scots invaded and plundered Yorkshire soon afterwards, repeating the incursion during the following harvest season. These ravages were followed by the second harvest failure of 1320–21.[165] By then the priory's income was down by one-third, as were its receipts from tithes and spiritualities, leading to the dismissal of half of the priory's servants and retainers.[166]

By 1318, the worst of the famine had passed, with grain prices dropping to as low as one-seventh of what they had been the previous year. But the crisis was not yet over, as a series of livestock epidemics had also afflicted most parts of the country during this period. While sheep had been the worst affected during the years from 1315–17, cattle and oxen were struck by a new epidemic that had begun in Essex during the Easter of 1319 which had probably been introduced from France. By 1321 it had reached Scotland and Ireland, with similarly devastating consequences.[167]

Kershaw records that losses of half of an estate's flocks were not unusual during the sheep murrain, with one house, i.e., Crowland Abbey, losing more than 80 per cent of its flock between 1315–21, while wool exports across the country declined during the decade 1315–25 by around 30 per cent, although some areas were more badly affected than others.[168] The cattle murrains were even more devastating, with Ramsey Abbey recording losses of between 84 per cent and 95 per cent of its cattle on three Huntingdonshire manors in the accounting year of 1319–20, with the consequence that the abbey was no longer able to till its own lands.[169] Such heavy losses of cattle and oxen across the country resulted in the widespread adoption of horses for ploughing.[170] Kershaw concludes that the extent and degree of the devastation were far worse than anything which had occurred since Norman colonization.

The second harvest failure of 1320–21 was also caused by inclement weather, leading to a similar escalation in grain prices as that seen between 1315 and 1317. The smaller religious houses were particularly badly affected by the successive crises. Prittlewell Priory in Essex, for example, was taken into royal protection due to its sorry state, while the nunnery of Elstow in Bedfordshire was made a grant of royal alms in order to support its household. The canons of Rocester Priory in Staffordshire were forced to solicit their friends for food, while the canons of Bolton Priory were forced to temporarily disband.[171]

Those of the larger estates with significant areas of grain cultivation actually benefited from the crisis, however, despite the low yields, being able to profit handsomely from the high grain prices. In the accounting year of 1316–17, for example, the Winchester estates enjoyed one of their most profitable years of the thirteenth and fourteenth centuries, while both Christ Church Canterbury and Ely also enjoyed some of their most profitable years during the crisis.[172] Chertsey Abbey in Surrey was another house that did well during this time, its 'high farming' abbot, John of Rutherwick (1307–47) 'raising his house ... to a position of economic importance without parallel in its history, before or after', during the first half of the fourteenth century.[173]

While most parts of England were recovering by 1322, south-eastern England was hit by drought in the summers of 1325–26, as well as severe storms and another livestock epidemic, as the result of which Christ Church Canterbury lost over 1,200 acres to the sea from flooding and more than 5,000 head of sheep and cattle, the latter valued at almost £800.[174] God's House, Southampton, was also more badly affected by this

---

[165] The Scots were themselves suffering from the effects of the famine, and had done so since as early as 1310.

[166] See Kershaw (1973b), pp. 13–14, 23, 25, 52, 77, 113–17, 137, 141–3.

[167] Kershaw (1973a), pp. 13–14. See also pp. 20–29 for details of the livestock murrains, in which pigs, horses and goats were also affected.

[168] Ibid., pp. 20–22. Interestingly, London's wool exports were little affected during this period, while Southampton's actually rose slightly, neither area being seriously affected by the murrain until 1324–28.

[169] Ibid., pp. 24–5.

[170] Ibid., p. 26. See also Langdon (1989).

[171] Kershaw (1973a), p. 30; *VCH York* Vol. 3, pp. 195–99.

[172] Ibid., p. 34.

[173] Knowles (1948), p. 47.

[174] Kershaw (1973a), p. 15.

drought than by the earlier crises. Although its mainly urban tenants had managed to settle their rent arrears in the late thirteenth century and appear to have suffered little in the famine years, rent arrears for 1325–26 skyrocketed, with many debts having to be written off and tenements taken back into the demesne due to the impoverishment or death of tenants.[175]

Nevertheless, landless peasants and smallholders were the worst affected, some of whom simply starved to death, while many others were forced to sell what little they had and become vagrants or beggars. Many of those smallholders who were able to hold on to their land in the medium- to long-term were unable to cultivate it due to livestock losses or insufficient funds to buy seed. The evidence from land sales of this period suggest that what was sold was bought out by those with more substantial holdings, and the capital to make such acquisitions.[176]

Although soil exhaustion may have been exaggerated by Postan as an effect on the abandonment of marginal arable, Kershaw has demonstrated that the worst land on many estates was taken out of cultivation in the wake of the agrarian crisis, especially those in demesne cultivation, an observation supported by J.Z. Titow.[177] He concludes that the causes of the extensive tenant vacancies which followed the crisis included the depredations of the Scots (in the North), the continued inundation of the land in some areas, a drastic shortage of plough-teams due to the livestock murrains, poor or exhausted soils, shortages of seed corn, and 'a lack of tenants who had abandoned their holdings through poverty'.[178] Neither Russell's nor Harvey's earlier cited criticisms of Postan's thesis can therefore be sustained, although Kershaw's findings and those of subsequent scholars such as Campbell, et al., require Postan's thesis to be modified and qualified with respect to local and regional variations, as well as the reinterpretation of some of the evidence along the lines already suggested.

Ecclesiastical Responses to Civil Disorder, Plague and Popular Protests, 1310–1450

While crime levels and civil unrest had increased during the famines,[179] there had already been trouble during the last years of Edward II's reign. For example, Colvin reports that '[i]n 1312–13 the burgesses [of Bristol] revolted against the ruling oligarchy in the town, and when the sheriff attempted to restore order the townspeople besieged him in the castle, draining the moat, destroying the castle mill, and digging a ditch in front of the gate.'[180]

By the late 1320s, popular resentment towards the clergy had reached an unprecedented level. In 1327 there were major riots in St Albans, Bury St Edmunds and Abingdon, all of which involved armed assaults and the burning of conventual buildings by angry tenants. However, all of these disputes had their roots in the thirteenth century.

In the vicinity of such wealthy pre-Norman houses as Abingdon, Bury St Edmunds, Canterbury, Glastonbury, Peterborough, St Albans, Westminster and Worcester, there were a number of planned settlements that eventually developed into prosperous towns. These towns were essentially controlled by the monasteries and cathedrals whose lands they occupied, with the latter taking the responsibility for the maintenance of roads and bridges, the appointment of civic officers, and the administration of trade and justice.[181]

During the twelfth and thirteenth centuries, many towns throughout England were seeking liberties from their lords, including self-government, as a consequence of their size and wealth. This included towns under

---

[175]   Ibid., p. 16. See also *Cartulary of God's House, Southampton*, Vols. I and II.

[176]   Kershaw (1973a), pp. 36–43.

[177]   See ibid., pp. 32–4.

[178]   Ibid., pp. 36–46.

[179]   See, for example, ibid., pp. 12–13.

[180]   Colvin (1963), p. 580.

[181]   Such houses nevertheless often sought to avoid what they obviously considered to be some of the more onerous of their feudal obligations, such as bridgeworks. See Cooper (2006), pp. 70–75, on the efforts of St Albans, Glastonbury, Peterborough, Westminster and Worcester during the twelfth century to forge charters claiming ancient privileges and liberties, including exemptions from bridgework.

abbatial domination, which sought, amongst other things, freedom from tolls and suit of mill, and the liberty to run their own markets and courts. It would appear that those who were aggrieved consisted of a coalition of members of the civic patrician class (i.e. urban aristocrats and large land-holders, some of whom also had mercantile interests, as well as 'newly made men' such as merchant venturers and master craftsmen),[182] artisans, smallholders of urban property and landless urban peasants.[183] There is no doubt that ecclesiastical lords were regarded as especially oppressive and overbearing by medieval townspeople, primarily because they refused to negotiate such liberties with their townspeople. The previously cited example of riots in Bristol was exceptional, as the town was under royal control until 1373, and was autocratically ruled by the constable of the castle.[184]

Although some towns were on good terms with their lords,[185] many had a history of antagonism, which was particularly true of those controlled by ecclesiastical lords. Many ecclesiastical lords were reluctant to grant any kind of concessions to their tenants, and even after having done so, tended to treat them as they had in the past. For example, Hilton reports that 'the abbey of Halesowen, having given the burgesses of the town the privileges of the borough of Hereford sometime in the 1260s, was still trying to treat the burgesses as servile villeins at the beginning of the fourteenth century.'[186]

The bad feeling which such behaviour elicited from tenants sometimes led to open hostility and violence, and it is significant to note that much of the violence was directed at the wealthier religious houses. At Christ Church Canterbury in the late thirteenth century, for example, the tenants fought with their lords over 'meadows, mills and markets, sometimes before the courts, and sometimes with bows and arrows',[187] while at Norwich in 1272, the priory was set on fire, leading to the excommunication of the townsfolk, the hanging of the ringleaders, and a fine of 3,000 marks imposed for the restoration of the priory.[188]

At St Albans, the disputes between the abbey and townsfolk had persisted for more than a hundred years. In 1274 there had been a dispute over the use of handmills by tenants, with the abbot insisting on the townspeople's obligation to mill their grain at his mill, while in 1326, the event which precipitated open revolt was the abbey's rejection of a town charter of freedom. The townsfolk subsequently laid siege to the abbey and cut off its supplies. Royal intervention and a court of arbitration gave the case to the townsfolk, leading to the granting of a liberty charter to them, but not the right to own their own mills. A few years later, the attempted arrest of a townsman for using a handmill provoked a riot, during which the same man was killed. The following inquiry in 1331 ruled against the townsfolk, leading to the revoking of the charter of liberty and the confiscation of about 80 illegal handmills, which were subsequently used by the abbot to pave the monks' parlour.

Such simmering tensions continued well after the Black Death. During the Peasants' Revolt of 1381, the abbey was stormed and the same handmills that had been used to pave the floor of the parlour were dug up by the rioters and distributed amongst themselves as they would the holy sacrament. The appearance of Richard II and the chief justice put an end to the troubles, with the ringleaders executed.[189]

It is important to note with regard to this unrest that the townspeople's insistence upon their right to use handmills was a pretext for wider grievances about the oppressive rule of the abbey, not because they were averse to using water- and windmills, as Marc Bloch and his followers have claimed.[190] Unlike lay magnates and the Crown, the wealthiest of the religious houses were far from willing to renounce the profits and

---

[182]   See Hibbert (1978), for a pan-European survey of the different constituencies from which this class was formed in different cities and regions; also Hilton (1985), pp. 15–22, on the situation in various parts of England.

[183]   See Hilton (1985), pp. 4–13, for a discussion of the different kinds of small-scale producers and consumers in medieval English market towns.

[184]   Richard Holt, personal communication.

[185]   See Hilton (1985), p. 14, where the lordship of Pershore and the borough of Stratford-upon-Avon are described as being 'relatively free' of interference by their episcopal overlords.

[186]   Ibid.

[187]   Cook (1961), p. 30.

[188]   Ibid., pp. 30–31.

[189]   See Bloch (1967), pp. 157–8, for the classic, but somewhat erroneous, statement on St Albans. C.f. Holt (1988),pp. 40–41.

[190]   See Bloch (1967), and the more detailed discussion of this issue in Chapter 2.

privileges of the towns under their control for any kind of short-term financial gain. It was for this reason that the burgesses of St Albans and other ecclesiastically ruled towns sought symbolic foci for their dissatisfaction, for which suit of mill and the prohibition of handmills served admirably.

Even more extreme than the behaviour of the townsfolk of St Albans was that of the people of Bury St Edmunds. On the 13 January 1327, 3,000 rioters broke into and looted the abbey. Later in the same year they repeated their felony on the abbot's house, vandalized the church, and cut off the abbey's water supply. In October 1327, the outer court was burned down, including the 'almonry, guesthouse, brewery, bakehouse and granary, stables and mill, and various buildings occupied by officers and obedientiaries'. Prolonged litigation resulted in the abbey being awarded the extraordinary sum of £140,000, but Edward III remitted the whole except for a 2,000-mark fine.[191] During the Peasant's Revolt of 1381, the burgesses of the town lynched the prior.[192]

Because salaries and pensions in the monasteries stayed fixed, when a period of deflation hit in the 1330s and 1340s, the monasteries were left with 'barns ... full of unsaleable foodstuffs ... [and] markets crowded with unwanted goods'.[193] At the same time, a number of houses that had begun ambitious building projects in the early fourteenth century never completed them, or took over a century to complete, e.g., Sempringham Priory (Lincs.) and Milton Priory (Dorset).[194]

The Black Death hit England late in 1348, although the spring and summer of 1349 was the period during which it was at its most virulent. The plague took the abbot and most of the monks of St Albans and half of the brethren of Westminster, while Wothorpe in Northamptonshire was completely extinguished, and Sandleford in Berkshire and Ivy Church in Wiltshire temporarily ceased functioning. Manorial tenants were similarly afflicted. For example, on the Premonstratensian estates of Titchfield in Hampshire, almost 60 per cent of the tenants were killed by plague, while another 40 per cent were taken in the subsequent plague of 1361–62. At Crowland Abbey in Cambridgeshire from 1348–50, 57 per cent of Cottenham tenants, 70 per cent of Oakington tenants and 48 per cent of Dry Drayton tenants died.[195]

Although there may be some doubt that the first wave of bubonic plague that hit England between 1348 and 1350 was as severe in its immediate impact as is often claimed, the country was subjected to a series of successive plagues at least once per decade for the next 140 years. According to John Hatcher, the overall mortality from the Black Death was in the order of 30 to 45 per cent, with a multiplicity of regional outbreaks characterizing the period after 1362, compounded by a number of other disease epidemics in the late fourteenth and fifteenth centuries.[196]

Christ Church, Canterbury, which was one of the houses least affected by the first plague outbreak, suffered during every decade of the fifteenth century, except the 1490s.[197] Finberg records that Tavistock Abbey's revenues after the Black Death in 1352 were about half of their former value, but had recovered by the end of the fourteenth century, while Searle reports that Battle Abbey lost between one-third and one-quarter of its income following the plague and never recovered.[198] The nunneries were particularly badly affected, as most were marginal and poorly endowed. With the dearth of male labourers following the plague they were in a parlous state, although most survived to the Dissolution.[199]

After 1349, labour had become scarce and costly, and the monasteries again began letting out their demesnes. Restless, discontented and rebellious peasants were able to recover some economic ground from their lords, as the latter half of the fourteenth century was a period during which leases freed up and the status

[191] Cook (1961), p. 31.

[192] Richard Holt, personal communication.

[193] Bridbury (1977).

[194] Platt (1984), pp. 130–32, citing Rose Graham, 'Excavations on the Site of Sempringham Priory', *Journal Brit. Archaeo. Assoc.* 5 (1940), pp. 86–90, and *Royal Commission on Historical Monuments Dorset*, 1970, III: 183–9.

[195] Knowles (1948), pp. 10–11; Dugdale (1846), IV, pp. 226–8; Dickinson (1950), pp. 65–6; Page (1934), pp. 120–1.

[196] Hatcher (1977).

[197] Ibid., pp. 17–18.

[198] Finberg (1951), p. 262; Searle (1974), pp. 261–2.

[199] Platt (1984), pp. 133–5, citing Eileen Power, *Medieval English Nunneries c. 1275 to 1535*, 1922, p. 219.

of peasants improved generally, with somewhat of a return to freedom from feudal services. But not all lords were compliant, the Revolt of 1381 being the most extreme example of peasant dissatisfaction with any continuation of autocratic rule.

Westminster Abbey's fortunes following the Black Death were somewhat mixed, but perhaps give some indication of the general climate for the larger ecclesiastical estates. While annual dues on some of the abbey's demesne lands had increased from those agreed just after the first plague, the dues on others were lower. Even though the abbey's patterns of investment had shifted from agricultural land to semi-urbanized and even urban property during the fourteenth century, their investment in mills continued.[200] For example, the abbey spent £60 in 1364–65 to acquire Stratford mill in Essex from Robert Aleyn, a London fishmonger. In 1375–76, the abbey repurchased the mill with 12 acres of meadow from the same man for £66 13s 4d. As Harvey points out, neither purchase appears to have been amortized, as in 1392 the mill was regranted to the abbey by Richard and his wife Matilda in return for a corrody of 14 loaves and 14 gallons of ale per week and £6 13s 4d annually.[201] Considering the sums paid, the custom to it must have been very substantial indeed, and is probably the main reason why the monks felt it worthwhile to invest in such a mill.

Christopher Dyer's study of the bishopric of Worcester estates has revealed similar trends in the West Midlands at the same time, with mill profitability and therefore investment in mill repairs continuing until the late 1370s, after which revenues appear to have collapsed due to low grain prices and the growing reluctance of manorial tenants to patronise their lord's mill, with the result that at least 40 per cent of seigneurial mills were allowed to fall into ruin by the early fifteenth century.[202] Dyer records that there were 31 mills held by the bishop in the 1290s, at least 12 of which had decayed by the early fifteenth century. However, a number of those that survived were drawing as much as, or more than they had in the thirteenth century. Interestingly, the number of mills held by Worcester between Domesday and 1300 appears to have hardly varied, with 30 mills recorded in 1086.[203] This is consistent with Holt's and Langdon's analyses of the Worcester estates, and provides support for their contention that the established religious houses had largely exploited their available waterways for mills by Domesday.

By the middle of the fifteenth century, the rents on many of Westminster Abbey's leased-out demesnes were lower than they had been in the decades following the Black Death, and in some cases had been losing ground for several decades. For example, the abbey's demesne at Launton had been rented at £12 *per annum* in 1410, a rental which probably included the local mill along with a virgate of land that had previously been rented for £1 6s 8d *per annum*. However, by the 1420s, the same land was being rented for £6 annually, and soon afterwards, for only £4.[204]

A similar pattern of reduced rentals can be seen over the same period at Ramsey Abbey, where the Warboys windmill, which had been rented for 40 shillings *per annum* during four periods from 1400 to 1439, was rented for 30 shillings in the year of 1443–44, and only 26s 8d for the year 1448–49. The fortunes of Wistow windmill were even more volatile. In 1409–10, it was rented for 20 shillings, but only 8 shillings in 1413–14, after which it increased to 13s 4d in 1433–34, 20 shillings in 1439–40, and 22 shillings in 1443–44. However, only five years later, its rent had been reduced once again to 20 shillings.[205]

As the plague years wore on, the monasteries had to lower their standards of induction in order to recruit more monks; this included those untrained in Latin and perhaps in temperament unsuited; morale that had already been low at the turn of the century was at rock bottom after the plague – many monks felt their ideals thoroughly tarnished. But certainly by the middle of the fifteenth century, a new spirit of optimism and celebration of what we might now call 'progress' was apparent in the writings of the monks, despite the sometimes violent fluctuations in many houses' economic fortunes.

---

[200] Harvey (1977), pp. 157, 168.

[201] Ibid., p. 424, citing Westminster Abbey Muniments 19859, 19867, and *Liber Niger Quaternus*, 88.

[202] Dyer (1980), pp. 144 and 172. As Jan Titow has argued, Hatcher's (1977) claim that there was a late fourteenth-century boom in the English economy is based on limited and misleading evidence. See Titow (1978).

[203] Ibid., p. 37.

[204] Harvey (1977), p. 156.

[205] See *The* Liber Gersumarum *of Ramsey Abbey*, pp. 42, 91, 99, 115, 165, 229, 261, 268, 295, 328–9, 336. See also Appendix B for the rental list extracted from this document.

Conclusion

The previous discussion has identified several notable trends in the growth and development of the Church in medieval England that provide a useful framework for analysing the changing role of mills and milling in the temporal affairs of English religious houses. These trends include:

- shifting patterns of royal, baronial and knightly patronage of religious orders and houses between the ninth and fourteenth centuries;
- changing management practices, methods of revenue raising and styles of lordship between the twelfth and fifteenth centuries;
- the abandonment by some orders of commitments to not collect revenue from certain sources (e.g. the Cistercians in relation to mill tithes by the latter half of the thirteenth century);
- the resistance of urban and rural tenants to the imposition of higher cash and labour rents in the thirteenth century, leading in some cases to open rebellion in the fourteenth and fifteenth centuries in response to ecclesiastical lords' refusal to grant liberties and other concessions; and
- the ongoing social and economic impacts of the plague, which lasted well into the middle of the fifteenth century, and included the freeing up of land tenure and a measure of liberty for peasants freed from (often recently imposed) lordly obligations.

In the chapters to follow, the social and economic dimensions of the milling activities of individual houses and orders will be explored through the prism of shifting patterns of patronage and estate management. Through this analysis, I hope to demonstrate the variety of approaches to mill management in the temporal affairs of religious houses, a number of which have previously eluded the attention of medievalists.

Chapter 2
Feudal Land Tenure, Ecclesiastical Patronage and Milling Monopolies

Feudal power relations were based primarily on the bestowal of property rights by rulers and magnates upon their subjects, which in turn conferred a range of privileges and obligations upon the beneficiary. These privileges and obligations determined how revenue, produce and services were drawn and distributed from land and other fixed assets. It has long been argued that one of the most significant of the privileges of feudal lordship was the seigneurial monopoly, or *banalité*, which was the right of the lord to exercise private justice or *ban* over any manorial holding granted to him by his monarch.[1] These seigneurial monopolies could extend over a number of activities, including brewing beer, baking bread, fulling cloth and grinding grain, and reserved the right of the lord to be the sole provider of these services to his or her tenants.

Amongst the most lucrative of lordly monopolies was suit of mill, which obliged manorial tenants to grind their grain at the lord's mill and pay a proportion as tollcorn.[2] Marc Bloch and his followers argued that it was this particular privilege of lordship which most rankled with tenants, who preferred the domestic handmill over the authoritarian imposition of the watermill. Bloch argued on the basis of the confiscation and destruction of handmills which he found documented in the records of St Albans, Peterborough and Cirencester that religious houses were particularly oppressive lords, and that their enthusiasm for exploiting their seigneurial privileges and dominating the lower orders was exemplified by their involvement in milling.[3] Turning Marx's famous thesis on its head, Bloch argued that in the case of the watermill, social relations (i.e. the feudal relationship between lord and vassal) determined the mode of production, and that the Church was a more exacting landlord than most laymen. Bloch's thesis has had a mixed reception in scholarly circles, being widely accepted by medievalists until fairly recently, but largely ignored by historians of technology.

The most influential scholarly tradition within the history of technology was first articulated by Lewis Mumford, Lynn White Jr. and Bertrand Gille between the 1930s and 1960s. It contends that the ethical basis for monastic life required that religious houses treat their tenants with care and consideration, and that this manifested itself in various forms of technological innovation, including the provision of watermills and windmills for their tenants to save them from the drudgery of milling at home using handmills.[4] Historians of technology appear to have remained almost universally oblivious to the historical examples of antagonism and open conflict around suit of mill that preoccupied Bloch and other neo-Marxist scholars, whereas those medievalists who shared the technological historians' idealized view of the Church tended to argue that such incidents were exceptions rather than the rule.[5] For Bloch and his followers, these 'exceptions' were, to the contrary, emblematic of the oppressive nature of ecclesiastical lordship, which was built on the foundations of pervasive seigneurial privilege.[6]

---

[1] Marc Bloch's famous 1935 paper, 'Avènement et Conquêtes du Moulin à Eau', in the seventh volume of *Annales Économique, Sociale et Culturelle* was the first to make a cogent argument in support of this claim with respect to medieval France and England (see Bloch [1967], pp. 151–3, 156). Bloch observed that such *banalités* sometimes extended even beyond the bounds of the manor to 'neighbouring lordships whose lords were too feeble or too unskilful to succeed in winning this privilege on their own account'. He also speculated that suit of mill was probably the most ancient of these privileges, a claim that will be explored later in this chapter and in Chapter 9.

[2] The extent to which suit of mill applied to the free tenants of a manor will be taken up in more detail later in this chapter and in Chapter 9.

[3] Bloch (1967), pp. 153, 157–8.

[4] See, for example, Mumford (1967), pp. 263–71; White (1968), pp. 63–6; Gille (1969), pp. 559–62.

[5] Cook (1961), pp. 27–31, is one example of a medievalist who espouses such a view.

[6] See Bloch (1935), (1967), Dockès (1982), Razi (1983).

Scholarly debate about the role of the Church in medieval milling has tended to revolve around these twin poles of ecclesiastical tyranny and benevolence,[7] although they share some important presuppositions, such as their attribution of a key role to the Church in the widespread dissemination of Roman watermilling technology throughout Western Europe during the latter half of the Middle Ages, and their contention that the monks embodied a revolutionary new attitude toward nature and technology. However, whereas the claims made by Mumford, White, Gille and their followers have tended to have relatively little impact on medieval scholarship,[8] those made by Bloch have been very influential indeed.

And while it is certainly true that the empirical evidence does not support most of the claims made by previous generations of historians of technology, it also provides challenges to many aspects of Bloch's position.[9]

Although Bloch took what might be described as a 'maximalist' position on seigneurial monopolies, and especially suit of mill, subsequent research on medieval England indicates that such monopolies were exercised to different extents in different parts of the country. For example, Holt has demonstrated through an analysis of the Hundred Rolls that the many free tenants in the eastern and central counties covered by the survey were not obliged to do suit of mill and that as many as half of the demesne mills on some manors had slipped out of seigneurial control between Domesday and the late twelfth century as a result of having been let on generous leases during the first three quarters of the twelfth century. What is more, some remained outside seigneurial control permanently, even after concerted efforts by the houses concerned to regain seisin during the thirteenth century.[10]

The fact that there are many examples from the manorial court records of tenants being fined for taking their grain to be milled at another lord's mill because that lord charged a lower rate of tollcorn, or because the manorial mill had a backlog of custom which required the tenant to wait longer than was customary to have his or her grain ground, clearly indicates that it was not the technology of the watermill to which tenants objected, but having to pay high rates of tollcorn, being punished for not obeying suit of mill and being made to wait for hours to have their grain ground.[11] John Langdon has argued that peasant demand for milling services was ultimately a far more significant driver of the development of medieval milling than lordly coercion,[12] while Holt and Langdon have both argued that lords were more concerned with restricting competition to their seigneurial milling monopolies by controlling who could build mills within their manors and where their servile (and even free) tenants took their grain to be milled, rather than trying to completely eradicate the practice of handmilling at home.[13] By the end of the thirteenth century, the primary objective of most lords was to secure as many of the profits of milling as they could reasonably (and legally) retain.[14]

Some of the great Benedictine houses were prepared to enforce suit of mill on recalcitrant tenants, and to severely punish tenants for refusing to comply, but such incidents are only part of a much more complex story. Bloch's tendency to generalize from what would at first appear to be compelling evidence has tended to skew the subsequent debate. There nevertheless remain several aspects of the issue which require further debate, including the origins of seigneurial monopolies, under what conditions suit of mill could be legally enforced, and the extent to which suit of mill was primarily a function of a tenant's status or the territory in which he or she held grain-growing land. All three issues will be explored in the pages to follow, but for the moment, I wish to focus on the issue of origins.

---

[7]   Ricardo-Malthusians of the post-war era such as Michael Postan remained detached from this debate. They believed that medieval technology was not a significant contributor to improvements in medieval social and economic conditions and consequently tended to minimize its role as a causal factor. See Epstein (2007), pp. 253–4, 255, 262–3.

[8]   Hilton and Sawyer (1963); Holt (1988), pp. 145–7; Holt (1990), pp, 51–3, 55–7; Langdon (2004), pp. 3–4.

[9]   See Lucas (2006b), (2010), and the argument concerning the origins of suit of mill in Chapter 9.

[10]   Holt (1988), pp. 52–69. We will look at some of the examples discussed by Holt, along with several others found through my own research, in the case study chapters to follow. On the general issue of ecclesiastical estates losing property as a result of leasing it out in the twelfth century, see Faith (1999), pp. 161–3.

[11]   Bennett (1937), pp. 130–2; Holt (1988), pp. 43–9.

[12]   Langdon (1994), (2004).

[13]   Holt (1988), pp. 44–5, 65; Langdon (2004), pp. 258, 265–72, 275, 290. Indeed, Holt found several cases of handmills being licensed to tenants from the 1330s onward.

[14]   As Holt (1988) argues with respect to Glastonbury Abbey (p. 66), and for lords more generally (p. 84).

The notion that lords had the right to enforce on manorial tenants their exclusive use of lordly equipment such as mills, ovens and breweries undoubtedly arose from custom, but it is the origins of the custom which remain controversial. Maitland points out that although Anglo-Saxon land tenure was a combination of personal, tenurial and justiciary bonds to one's lord in the form of *commendatio* (personal dedication), *consuetudo* (customary services) and *sac* and *soc* (justiciary rights), these three bonds might be separable from the land held by a tenant, depending on their status.[15] We know that freemen and women in straightened circumstances voluntarily put themselves under the protection of a lord, which meant giving up their freedom and submitting themselves to a form of servitude commonly known as serfdom. The lord would give them housing and land in exchange for renders of food and labour. This kind of dependent tenurial relationship was a feature of the demesne holdings of kings, religious houses and great magnates, but probably originated as a form of service due to royalty on their inland estates, which were properties that directly provided for the needs of itinerant kings and their households as they moved about the countryside.[16] With the granting out of such royal demesnes to the Benedictines and various episcopal houses from the mid- to late seventh century onward, the obligations of the bonded tenants who farmed the inland were transferred to religious houses, and by the ninth century, to any lay or ecclesiastical lord who held a former royal manor or vill.[17] As I will argue in the pages to follow, although suit of mill appears to have been one of the customary services associated with these royal and formerly royal demesne holdings, the number of people who were obliged to perform suit increased dramatically in the wake of the Norman's massive manorial reorganization of the country.[18] William's newly enriched followers could not possibly accommodate, let alone adopt, the extraordinarily complex network of rights and obligations associated with the Anglo-Saxon lands they had confiscated, and so negotiated a range of new services that were required of unfree tenants, the ranks of whom had considerably swelled since the great dispossession. Suit of mill appears to have been one of these services. Nevertheless, there is strong evidence that the power and even the desire of lay and ecclesiastical lords after the Conquest to enforce (and possibly to create) milling monopolies on their estates varied greatly, both historically and regionally.

The Benedictines were almost undoubtedly the first monastic order to acquire mills in Britain, and did so shortly after they were first granted former royal estates by various Anglo-Saxon kings.[19] The ancient Benedictine and episcopal houses were, therefore, probably the first landlords apart from the king to acquire seigneurial monopoly rights on their estates. By the tenth century, they had become major landowners throughout southern England, holding between 1/3 and 2/5 of the demesne mills throughout the country by Domesday.[20] What this meant in practice was that the ancient ecclesiastical houses were largely responsible for establishing the customary patterns of seigneurial milling in the latter half of the Middle Ages, but were themselves limited in the extent to which they could enforce monopoly rights by customs which have their origins in Anglo-Saxon times.

---

[15] See Maitland (1987), pp. 67–75, 102, 104, 326. Cf. Vinogradoff (1908), pp. 346–8, 423; Faith (1999), pp. 120, 178–9. These issues will be taken up in greater depth in Chapter 9.

[16] See Faith (1999), Ch. 2–3.

[17] See Maitland (1987), pp. 267–77 (esp. 276), 320–1. Bloch argued this process was the result of the degeneration of the machinery of state, which 'enabled lords to establish monopoly rights over a range of communally used facilities, of which the village wine-press, the bread-oven and above all the mill were the most profitable' (Holt [1988], p. 37). However, it seems more likely that they were, to the contrary, a result of the extension of the rights and privileges acquired by kings over the land to those to whom he directly bestowed his land, in which case they were more the result of the creation of a new kind of machinery of state, i.e. feudal vassalage.

[18] On this latter issue, see Fleming (2004).

[19] Such a chronology is consistent with the evidence from early medieval Ireland, in which monastic involvement in mill construction and ownership dates back to the seventh century and possibly earlier. See Rynne (2000); Rynne (2011), pp. 94–5; Hardy, Watts and Goodburn (2011). The earliest archaeological evidence for watermills in England dates to between the second and fourth centuries under Roman rule, and to the late seventh and early eighth centuries under the Anglo-Saxons. The earliest manuscript evidence consists of charter references to around 50 mills from the mid-eighth to early eleventh centuries. See Lucas (2006a), pp. 74–7, and Hooke (2007), pp. 42–4, for summaries of the relevant evidence with sources.

[20] See Lucas (2006a), pp. 94–5, and the more detailed discussion of this issue in Chapter 10.

Insofar as the debate about suit of mill has tended to focus on the better documented Anglo-Norman period, it has tended to overlook some crucial discontinuities in the development of property rights and the manorial system in the immediate aftermath of the Conquest, and has not given sufficient attention to the complexities of ecclesiastical patronage, both of which had profound implications for the ways in which religious houses and other lords acquired, managed and drew revenue and services from mills. The following two sections of this chapter therefore provide some appropriate background. These are followed by a third section, which discusses the evidence for seigneurial monopolies on milling in Anglo-Norman England. As we will see as the discussion progresses, a number of different forms of mill tenure were tolerated by English lords: forms of tenure which conferred a variety of rights to the tenants concerned. The groundbreaking research of Rosamond Faith and Robin Fleming provides the evidential framework for discussion in the section to follow.

Land Tenure in Early Medieval England

The development of feudal land tenure under the Anglo-Saxons and Anglo-Normans was a complex process shaped by customary patterns of land settlement, the political and economic needs of lords and rulers, and processes of colonization and militarization which persisted in various forms from the collapse of the Roman Empire until a century or more after the Conquest. The resultant regional particularities tended to constrain or enable certain kinds of property acquisition and management by both lay and ecclesiastical lords.

The forms of private property ownership with which we are now familiar did not exist in any recognizable form until the late Middle Ages in England. Some idea of property rights with cash exchange value had existed in some parts of Britain under Roman rule. But the growing number of purchases and exchanges of land that we see in England from the ninth century onward were not only at the will of the chief lord, and ultimately, the king, but carried with them obligations to provide the lord with renders of food and other resources, as well as labour services. In other words, whoever held land was ultimately responsible for providing the feudal services, renders and fines attached to it. This was the meaning of *nulle terre sans seigneur*: 'no land without a lord', or more explicitly, no fixed property could be held by a vassal without owing fealty to a liege, the ultimate fealty being to the sovereign. Furthermore, any ruler or magnate who granted land, or allowed it to be sold for a cash sum or exchanged for other property, could take it back in certain circumstances.[21]

By way of contrast, late Iron Age land tenure in Britain was based on extended clan groups with historical connections to particular tracts of territory which they held freely, from which tribute and gifts were drawn by ruling families in the form of food, provisions and fighting men. Under this system of tribute, the land was neither directly exploited nor owned by rulers; it constituted the subordinate territory which belonged to the people they ruled and protected. Iron Age hillforts were the consumption sites at which rulers reaped their harvest of warriors and rewarded them with feasts.[22]

In those parts of Britain subsequently subject to Roman rule, tribute and gifts were replaced by taxes, subordinate territories were replaced by villa estates and towns, and customary or clan-based land tenure was at least in part replaced by transferable property rights protected by law. Faith has argued that although the Romans introduced to Britain notions of transferable property rights, the old bonds of kinship which tied extended families to particular tracts of land persisted and remained important.[23]

After the collapse of the empire, members of the former Romano-British nobility and local ruling families were able to secure dominion over significant tracts of land, while the peasantry remained largely self-sufficient in scattered settlements which practiced mixed forms of subsistence agriculture.[24] There is some evidence that former villa estates and Roman towns continued to draw taxation as tribute from the territories that had previously been under their jurisdiction, thereby recreating important aspects of the economic basis for late Iron Age society.[25]

---

[21]   For example, if the vassal who held it failed to meet his or her feudal obligations, such as falling behind on cash or labour rents, or if he or she fell out of favour with the lord.

[22]   Faith (1999), pp. 1–3.

[23]   Ibid., p. 3.

[24]   Ibid.

[25]   Ibid., pp. 3–5. Cf. Seebohm (1915), pp. 322–4; Vinogradoff (1932), pp. 37–87.

Under the Anglo-Saxons, the pre-Roman obligations to provide ruling elites with food, provisions and fighting men were further extended to include labour and hunting services, along with cash payments in lieu of one or more of these obligations. It was also during this period that the Anglo-Saxon kings began rewarding their male relatives and most faithful warriors with gifts of territory from which they could raise their own wealth. In this way, political and military authority was delegated and dispersed, along with the power to extract surpluses and command loyalty. Nevertheless, local dominant families in some parts of Britain appear to have continued to exercise their power independently of any king for many, many years.[26] Drawing on the work of G.W.S. Barrow, Faith has described this era as one of 'extensive lordship', in which '[t]he dominance of considerably developed local political authorities over a society based on a still relatively undeveloped agrarian economy took the form of a complex of rights to services and renders of a given territory.'[27]

The kinds of obligations owed by tenants from different holdings depended on a variety of factors, the most important of which were the tenant's social status and level of favour with his or her lord, but also included the previous history of tenure of that holding and the strength of one's lord. As the Anglo-Saxon state became more efficient at documenting these obligations,[28] and at collecting and enforcing them, the complexity of these arrangements became increasingly difficult for lords to monitor and sustain. In the tenth and eleventh centuries, many obligations, some of which had existed for centuries, were converted to cash rents. However, the right to commute various services and renders to payments of cash – some of which were commutations of food renders, and others of labour, hunting and military services – was at least initially restricted to free men.[29]

The territorial units which became the basis of the manorial system under the Anglo-Normans were based on several different sources: tribal areas under the jurisdiction of a dominant clan, minster estates under the jurisdiction of a bishop or senior cleric, sokelands under the jurisdiction of a noble family or military retainer of a king, and hundreds (of hides) under direct royal supervision. In each case, the physical boundaries of these territories were determined by their ability to provide for the survival of their inhabitants, along with a modest surplus which was transferred annually to their lords.[30]

Della Hooke has dubbed those tribal areas dominated by a single clan, 'folk-areas', which combined 'developed regions, usually located in riverine situations, linked to areas of outlying woodland surviving along major watersheds in a pattern of seasonal transhumance'.[31] Faith has argued that the dual basis for the Anglo-Saxon territorial unit of the hide was the minimum tract of land deemed sufficient to feed, clothe and house a family, and from which a single fighting man was to be provided. It was also, and perhaps most importantly, an assessment of the value of the holding in terms of the public obligations that it owed, and was therefore a mark of freedom. She also points out that a single hide continued to be the basis for provisioning the so-called 'rustic knights' and 'riding knights' (*radcnihts*) of the late Anglo-Saxon and Anglo-Norman periods.[32] As we will see in later chapters, many of these holdings appear to have included, or at some stage acquired, watermills, from which knights of the twelfth and thirteenth centuries often donated rents and sold or granted whole windmills and watermills to Augustinian, Cistercian and Premonstratensian religious houses.

Faith has described the bipartite distinction between the inner and outer core of these Anglo-Saxon territorial units centred on former villa estates, minster churches, monasteries, towns and the seats of ruling families, as the 'inland' and the 'outland', or 'warland'. The inland was directly managed to provide for the immediate needs of the religious house or noble family, and was worked by dependent peasants, servants and slaves, whereas the outland was held freely by peasants in kin-based groups in return for military and public service to the king or thegn: a mark of liberty and citizenship, as well as the basis for sokelands and for tax

---

[26]   Ibid., pp. 5–8.

[27]   Ibid., p. 4.

[28]   For example, through the creation of 'bookland' for superior and lesser thegns from the late eighth century onward, i.e. land held freely by *bocriht* or charter with the rents and services specified.

[29]   Faith (1999), pp. 175–6, 206–9.

[30]   Ibid., pp. 8–9.

[31]   Ibid., p. 9, citing D. Hooke, *Anglo-Saxon Settlements of the West Midlands: The Charter Evidence*, BAR British Series 95, 1981, Ch. 3 at 48.

[32]   Ibid., pp. 91–2, 98–9. And also some of the wealthier sokemen who acted as *fyrd* soldiers for Peterborough Abbey identified by Hollister (1962).

liability under the Anglo-Norman kings.[33] Faith argues that this estate structure can be found in many parts of southern, central and eastern England, such as Glastonbury Abbey which provides one of the case studies in Chapter 5. The division between inland and warland provided a model for the later manorial system, with its division between demesne holdings under direct management close to an estate centre, and leasehold properties in more distant locations.[34] This division also determined the social status and feudal obligations of those who lived and/or held land in these areas, although most sokemen's holdings were appropriated by the Normans within decades of the Conquest and converted to demesne inland, with a consequent loss of status for those who had customarily occupied that land.[35] This had important implications for the extension of seigneurial monopolies to territory that had not formerly been subject to them.

In seventh-century Wessex, the core or inland of the holding was known as the 'worthy' and was surrounded by an outer ring of hamlets, all of which was managed by a single ecclesiastical lord. This inner core was free of geld, unlike the outer territories or warland.[36] William I emulated this structure after the Conquest in the many new manors he created throughout England to reward his retainers.[37] Around William's own foundation, Battle Abbey, the core holding was called the *banlieu*, or the *leuga*, which was geld-free, and surrounded by manors consisting of newly settled taxpaying tenants.[38] Many of the Benedictine houses sampled in the case studies to follow adopted (or inherited) this form of estate structure.

The system of obligations in return for defence developed by the Anglo-Saxon kings required a growing number of officials to administer its burgeoning responsibilities, which in turn resulted in a growing number of royal grants of land in heredity to these public officials, particularly from the ninth and tenth century onward. Faith argues that it was primarily through the process of splitting former royal estates to endow such officials that most of the territorial units called 'manors' first came into being. At the centre was a minster church or a town, or one or more village communities and scattered farms, which was in turn surrounded by cultivated land and meadows, along with tracts of forest, woodland and marshes. These newly created manors usually preserved the mixed topographies and natural resource bases of the larger estates from which they had been created, with the obvious intention of making each unit as self-sufficient as possible.[39]

The so-called 'multiple estates' that kings granted to their favoured vassals from the ninth century onward were usually of a significant size, as they had to be sufficiently large and prosperous to generate a surplus for dozens and sometimes hundreds of more or less unproductive individuals. Most of these grants were of one or more whole manors or vills, and may have consisted of anything from a hundred or more acres of land to several thousand, often spread over many counties, and known as an 'honour'.[40] Although it may well be true that the whole of England fell under some form of land tenure by the eleventh century, and that even if the land in question was not directly occupied, it was exploited in some way,[41] Faith has pointed out that not all of England was 'manorialized' by the time of the Conquest, and that there are suggestions in Domesday Book and elsewhere that many areas of warland and sokeland had not been incorporated into a vill or manor at this relatively late stage.[42]

[33]   Ibid., Ch. 2–4. Cf. Vinogradoff (1908), pp. 193–6; Stenton (1910), pp. 30–31. These observations, together with those about the origins of the hide, help to explain some of the complexities of military tenure first identified by Hollister (1962) and Harvey (1970), and will provide the basis for some of the arguments made in later chapters about the feudal status of some of the non-seigneurial mills acquired by religious houses.

[34]   Wickham (2006), pp. 401–3, notes similar patterns of estate structure in the Paris basin in the early eighth century which similarly provided a model for the structure of later feudal holdings.

[35]   Faith (1999), Ch. 2–6 and 8, esp. pp. 215–20; Fleming (2004), Ch. 4 and 5.

[36]   Faith (1999), pp. 33–4.

[37]   Ibid., Ch. 7.

[38]   Most of these tenants were former military retainers of the king. For more information, see the detailed discussion of Battle's estates and mill holdings in Chapter 5.

[39]   Faith (1999), Ch. 6. See, for example, the reproduction in Fig. 18, p. 158, of the division of the Shapwick estate in Somerset which follows this model. See also Seebohm (1915), p. 83.

[40]   See Vinogradoff (1908), pp. 348–50.

[41]   Aston (2000), pp. 20–23; Bond (2000).

[42]   Faith (1999), pp. 123, 140–43, 207–9. Cf. Seebohm (1915), Ch. 3, who argued that although there were manors 'everywhere' by Domesday, land that was 'extra-manorial or belonged to no township was probably royal forest or waste'

Nevertheless, after the Conquest, all of the fixed property throughout England, i.e., forests, wastes, developed lands and buildings, were deemed the property of the Crown. All the king's subjects therefore held land as tenants at his will, which meant that they could have that land taken from them if they failed to meet their obligations or had somehow displeased him. Both lay and ecclesiastical tenants could be subject to such revocations.

In return for oaths and duties of fealty, the king granted estates of various sizes and value to lay and ecclesiastical tenants-in-chief who then had leave to grant portions of those estates to their own vassals, relatives, associates and minions. Regardless of where a man or woman was positioned in the feudal hierarchy, all but the king had a lord, and he or she must serve their lord by meeting those obligations specific to their rank or which they had customarily held and could prove by charter. In return for their loyal service, even the unfree had access to certain privileges and liberties.

Lay tenants-in-chief were generally the heads of prominent families and the military retainers of the king, whereas ecclesiastical tenants-in-chief were the bishops, abbots and priors of the great religious houses. Tenants-in-chief had legal, political and economic jurisdiction over those on whom they bestowed property as sub-tenants, whether those sub-tenants were gentry or peasants, free or servile. The jurisdiction of tenants-in-chief was supported by royal documentation and backed up with the power to impose legal sanctions through manorial, borough, hundred, wapentake and county courts.

Many of the feudal obligations imposed on tenants by the Anglo-Norman kings had their roots in Anglo-Saxon and even pre-Roman times. They could be solely or primarily to provide fighting men and public works for the king or a tenant-in-chief (forms of military tenure), or they might require the payment of food, resources, labour and/or cash rents (forms of non-military tenure).

There were four main types of military tenure that developed under the Norman kings, all of which were heritable and of potentially indefinite length. Tenants-in-chief held their property in barony, which obligated them to provide military and even parliamentary services for the king. Sub-tenants holding by knight service provided military service either directly for the king *in capite* or as a 'mesne' (i.e., intermediate) tenant for a tenant-in-chief. This obligation was at the king's pleasure, but was virtually defunct by 1350.[43] At the lower end of the *miles* scale were tenants holding by castle-guard, who, as the name implies, provided castle guard duty for a specified number of days per year. Finally, scutage was a cash payment in lieu of military service that became increasingly common from the thirteenth century onward.

While there were many more types of non-military land tenure, only six of them appear in the manuscript evidence examined in later chapters. Tenures in serjeanty, frankalmoin and to some extent copyhold were both indeterminate and heritable, whereas tenures in socage, fee-farm and quit-rent were non-heritable and for fixed terms. Tenancies under serjeanty were relatively unusual as they involved acting in some form of non-military capacity as servant to the king, whereas tenancies in frankalmoin (literally in 'free alms') were generally restricted to clerics, whose only obligation for the tenancy was to provide prayer services to the grantor. Tenure by copyhold was a late medieval concession by lords to growing peasant discontent at their servile status. Copyhold tenure effectively erased any reference to serfdom and allowed peasants who were not freeholders to record their holdings in the manorial court rolls upon the payment of an entry fine, which then granted hereditary rights over that property, albeit on a servile basis at the will of the lord.[44]

Tenure by socage was a legacy of the Anglo-Saxon period. It was initially a form of free tenure with obligations to perform military service in the *fyrd* and contribute to the maintenance of fortifications and bridgeworks.[45] Within 20 years of Norman occupation, however, the number of sokemen holding tenure by socage had diminished significantly or completely disappeared throughout many parts of England. Those

---

(p. 83), the former being described as *terra regis* and part of the royal demesne. Land that had been settled within such forests, or in other areas of 'waste' remote from existing settlements at Domesday, were not included in manorial estates or vills.

[43] Bean (1991), p. 547.

[44] Fryde and Fryde (1991), pp. 813–19. They note that on the Cambridgeshire manor of Wilburton held by the bishop of Ely, Maitland found the earliest instance of a grant in heredity combined with servile wording was from 1389, after which the examples multiplied.

[45] These services formed the *trinoda necessitas*, or 'three-knotted obligation' required of freemen in Anglo-Saxon times. See Faith (1999), pp. 95–9. Cf. Albertoni (2010), p. 418, for similar obligations on freemen in Carolingian Italy. See Maitland (1987), pp. 271–4, concerning religious houses being exempted from and included in this obligation by various Anglo-Saxon kings.

that remained in the east of England were relegated to the lowest form of feudal tenure, their former warland obligations combined with servile duties and payments to indicate their reduced status.[46] Faith cites the computer-aided analysis of post-Conquest land settlement patterns undertaken by Robin Fleming as strong evidence for William I's 'massive manorial reorganization' of the kingdom.[47] This process was especially focused on the creation and expansion of manorial demesnes from land which had formerly been held in socage by free peasants, who were subsequently reduced to servitude as dependent retainers or *villani*.[48]

Two other forms of non-military tenure were fee-farm, which appears to have been practiced since at least the eighth century[49] and involved conferring to the lessee the right to collect and retain all of the revenues from a leased property in return for a fixed rent, and quit-rent, which emerged in the late twelfth and thirteenth centuries as a means of commuting all feudal obligations to an annual fee. Both of these latter forms of tenure became more commonplace in the thirteenth and fourteenth centuries as lords sought to rationalize and simplify the dues owed them from their holdings.

With respect to tenure by barony, up until the twelfth century and the Statute of Mortmain, feudal barons, abbots, priors and bishops could exercise the right to grant at will the land which they held from the king. After the Statute was introduced, they needed the king's permission before proceeding, and could be brought before the courts for failure to comply. Likewise, higher-status mesne tenants – who were usually knights, senior clerics and various kinds of official – were allowed to grant or lease property which they held of the chief lord if he or she was able to obtain royal permission. The situation was modified further, however, with the Statute of *Quia Emptores* (1290), which abolished subinfeudation, while effectively allowing tenants freedom to alienate land in fee simple if 'the donee was substituted for the donor in the latter's tenure from his feudal lord.'[50] The practical effect of this legislation was that from henceforward, land transfers became more of a commercial than a feudal transaction. The situation with respect to tenants-in-chief was settled in 1327, whereby royal permission was required, and if undertaken without permission, was subject to royal fine.[51]

Land granted to a knight or military retainer was called a 'fief' or 'fee'. It generally consisted of anything from one to five hides (about 80 to 600 acres) carved out of a larger manor, the size of the holding being determined by the status of the fighting man concerned.[52] Some of these fees attained the status of manors during the late eleventh and twelfth centuries.[53] Land granted to a religious house could be a whole manor or vill, or a part of a manor or vill, or a whole or part of a knight's fee, depending on the wealth and status of the donor. Generally speaking, it was the Benedictines who were the main beneficiaries of grants of whole manors and vills from various kings and great magnates between the ninth and eleventh centuries, placing them in a strong social and financial position by the time of the Conquest.[54]

Although freehold tenure tended to be a privilege of barons, bishops and their administrative and military retainers under the Normans and their successors, in East Anglia, Kent and some other parts of England, significant parcels of land were held freely by a mixture of great lords, peasants of varying status and royal officials and their retainers.[55] In the Danelaw and some other parts of southern England subject to ecclesiastical

---

[46]   Faith (1999), p. 216. Faith notes several examples of the decline in the number of sokemen and 'free men' between 1066 and 1086 in the eastern and northern counties, citing Darby (1977), pp. 62–3 and Appendix 3, Maitland (1987), pp. 63–6; Kapelle (1979), p. 176. For example, she cites Maitland's argument that the decline in status of such sokemen can be seen in microcosm on the manor of Meldreth in Cambridgeshire, where a small group of 15 sokemen who held three and a quarter hides of the abbot of Ely and Earl Aelfgar before the Conquest were transformed into 15 bordars working half a hide of inland on the same manor in 1086. See Maitland (1987), pp. 62–3. Cf. Fumagilli (1976), who traces the initial loss of status of small allod holders in Carolingian Italy to the first half of the ninth century.

[47]   Fleming (2004), esp. Ch. 4–7.

[48]   Faith (1999), pp. 216–17, citing Fleming (2004). Cf. Maitland (1987), pp. 36–79.

[49]   Ibid., pp. 180–81.

[50]   Bean (1991), p. 549.

[51]   Ibid.

[52]   See Harvey (1970).

[53]   Faith (1999), pp. 168–79. One example of a knight's fee attaining the status of a manor is cited in *The Chartulary of Cockersand Abbey*, which records that the fee of Garstang held the suit of its tenants for milling and fulling (pp. 357–8).

[54]   Seebohm (1915), p. 106.

[55]   See, for example, Homans (1953), (1969), Hallam (1988a).

control, a system of land purchases had existed since as early as the ninth century, which placed some limits on the extent to which feudal power was exercised by chief lords in these territories under the Normans.[56]

It now seems clear that the expansion of manorial demesnes and the consequent decline in the numbers of freemen, sokemen and *servi* (slaves) is primarily a phenomenon of the Anglo-Norman period.[57] The new common law category of the villein tenant was a means of stripping many formerly free peasants of their status, while legitimating a number of feudal obligations that were increasingly being imposed on peasants of varied status as the population grew and the pressure to expand territory under cultivation presented lords with new opportunities to extract additional obligations and/or surpluses from their tenants as they partitioned the land into smaller and smaller parcels, and allowed more and more common land and 'waste' to be brought into cultivation.[58] There can be little doubt that amongst the additional obligations imposed on tenants as a consequence of the tenurial reorganization of the country in the decades after the Conquest, including the creation of new manorial demesnes from the late eleventh to the late thirteenth centuries, was the imposition of suit of mill.[59]

Although tenants who felt they had been wronged could officially air their grievances in court, the dominance of the medieval legal system by men of the ruling elite meant that the interests of lords were generally the most likely to be upheld.[60] There were, as a consequence, a growing number of disputes throughout the thirteenth and fourteenth centuries between peasants, townspeople, religious houses, lords and barons about how far the king's and lords' dominion extended vis-à-vis their own rights, privileges and freedoms. The ultimate outcome was a freer peasantry with more rights and privileges than they had probably enjoyed since Anglo-Saxon times.[61]

Feudal Patronage and the Status of Ecclesiastical Possessions

It is important to state from the outset that the granting of land and other property to a religious house at its foundation by patrons of any rank entailed certain rights and obligations on both the donor and the donee. Foundation grants did not confer automatic lordship to the abbey or priory upon which they were bestowed; founding patrons exercised a variety of limited forms of lordship over their foundations, and this included even those religious orders that had been given specific exemptions from certain kinds of feudal obligation. A patron's rights of lordship were not only heritable but transferable to other parties by commendation or royal grant. If the patron had granted land which was held by his or her own chief lord, the patron was required to either seek formal legal approval of the chief lord for the grant, or the two parties might share patronage, with the chief lord later acquiring sole patronage.

Under the Anglo-Saxon kings, minster churches were the property of individual lords and could be bought and sold.[62] Possession of these churches included the right to draw any of the associated tithes from the parishes' lands, stock and traded goods.[63] The monasteries, on the other hand, which had been subject to royal domination during the ninth century, established with the Benedictine reforms encapsuled in the *Regularis Concordia* of c. 970 that the king and queen would henceforth act as protector, lord and sole patron of all the

---

[56]   See Maitland (1987), pp. 46–50, on who could, and could not, sell their land and/or leave their lord, and under what conditions; also Bois (2002), pp. 44–9, for his observation of how similar processes of monetization of the land from the middle of the tenth century in France brought about a loss of status for many free peasants.

[57]   See Fleming (2004), Ch. 5–6.

[58]   Faith (1999), pp. Ch. 5–8.

[59]   Fleming (2004) has described in detail the condition under which such new settlements came about, esp. in Ch. 6.

[60]   This was true from as early as the late 1060s and 1070s when low- and medium-ranking Anglo-Saxon freeholders sought in vain to have their cases heard by unsympathetic royal vice-regents after their own lords had been summarily dispossessed. See Fleming (2004), pp. 187–8.

[61]   Fryde and Fryde (1991).

[62]   Faith (1999), p. 165–7. The priests associated with these churches were also the 'property' of the lord, and as inland residents could be bequeathed in the same manner as slaves.

[63]   See Blackstone (1832), for a detailed discussion of the origins of tithing in England.

monasteries throughout England.[64] Most of the property subsequently granted to the Benedictines by various English kings therefore consisted of former royal manors and shared the rights and obligations which that entailed, including, as I have already suggested, suit of mill. After the Conquest, however, anyone from a member of the lesser gentry or royal administration to a great magnate or bishop could establish their own religious house and become a patron; the generosity of their endowment being an indication of the status and wealth of the patron concerned.

More than a hundred religious houses were founded or re-founded by English kings and queens up to the time of the Dissolution. Around 27 were founded by bishops, while the rest were primarily established by magnates.[65] There were exceptions, however, such as Cockersand Abbey, nominally founded by Hugh the Hermit in the late twelfth century, and the Wakebridge Chantries at Crich, founded by the legal commissioner and justice, William of Wakebridge, in the mid-fourteenth century.[66] Although there is clear evidence in the chapters to follow that the status of patrons to different religious houses and orders varied substantially between the twelfth and fourteenth centuries, Karen Stöber's recent study of late medieval patronage has found that it was the king and a handful of powerful nobles such as the Duke of Norfolk who assumed the patronage of multiple monasteries in the century or so leading up to the Dissolution, with as many as half of the monasteries passing into the hands of the peerage and crown by 1540.[67]

Janet Burton argues that the Benedictines and Augustinians enjoyed much wider powers of patronage than did the Cistercians, Premonstratensians and Carthusians, who from their time of foundation sought to avoid external interventions in their affairs.[68] However, it is apparent from the analysis of the Cistercian and Premonstratensian houses to follow that, while they may not have enjoyed the initial levels of generous royal patronage that characterized the ancient Benedictine houses, they were the beneficiaries of substantial donations from members of the knightly and administrative classes, including in many cases mills or the rents from mills.

Lordship via patronage was still a relatively fluid concept in the twelfth century. By the thirteenth century, it was far more clearly defined,[69] and could be exercised in any of several different ways.[70] The granting of tithes from mills within parishes subject to ecclesiastical jurisdiction was a common practice, and one from which the majority of houses studied in the sample benefited. Rights to grind grain free of multure were also quite common, as were mill revenues dedicated to various liturgical functions.[71] The granting of whole manors and whole mills was understandably far less common, primarily because patrons with that level of wealth were in the minority. In those instances in which such generous donations were made, however, it is quite common to see the descendants of the original donor seeking to regain possession of mills which they felt had been unjustly alienated.[72] Nevertheless, any exploitative urges which a patron-as-lord (or a descendant of the patron) may have felt towards his or her foundation were nevertheless moderated by the fear of purgatory or excommunication, as well as the prestige which patronage entailed.

The proprietary claims of patrons were gradually tempered by feudal and canon law, so that in England, they became treated as a form of feudal lordship with specific characteristics. Essentially, this involved a kind of legal fiction whereby lay ownership was transformed into a privilege conferred by the Church to the founder and his heirs: 'it was in effect the feudal relation, not denied but limited and charged with obligations of defence.'[73]

---

[64]   *Regularis Concordia*, pp. 6–7; Birch (1965), vol. 1, no. 312; Brooks (1984), pp. 175–206.

[65]   Burton (1994), p. 212.

[66]   See the detailed discussion of both houses in Chapter 8.

[67]   Stöber (2007).

[68]   Burton (1994), p. 212.

[69]   Ibid.

[70]   Wood (1955), p. 1.

[71]   For example, William le Botiler granted the tithes of Bispham mills and one bovate of land in the same vill to the Church of St Mary in return for the right to build a chantry in the church for the sole use of his family. See *Materials for the History of the Church of Lancaster*, pp. 436–7. The Augustinian abbey of Cirencester reserved the right of free multure for its own grain when it leased the mill of Milborne to Thomas the Mercer in the mid-thirteenth century. See *The Cartulary of Cirencester Abbey*, ms. 590. Both documents are discussed in more detail in Chapters 5 and 6.

[72]   See Chapter 9, in which several such examples are examined in detail.

[73]   Wood (1955), p. 16.

The success of Church reformers in gaining control of the advowsons on churches from lay lords during the twelfth and thirteenth centuries has already been discussed; the Statute of Mortmain of 1279 subjected all such future transactions to royal approval. Those rights conferred to the founder and his heirs varied widely depending on the location of the religious house and the nature of its holdings, as well as the order to which it belonged and the idiosyncrasies of its abbots, priors, obedientiaries, prebendaries and chapters. For example, while the Benedictines, Augustinians and most nuns recognized the patron's right to custody in vacancies, and licence and assent in elections, the exempt orders were free of such impositions as part of their tenure in frankalmoin.[74] The rights of frankalmoin were sometimes extended to ecclesiastical exemptions from knight's service or scutage, and in the fourteenth century 'from attendance at parliament and certain other services, in contrast to tenure by barony',[75] the latter being a common form of episcopal tenure. The patron was nevertheless still able to exercise a certain amount of control over exempt orders with regard to the disposition of property and claims for feudal services.[76] The situation was further complicated in the case of dependent houses and alien priories, with regard to which the mother house, patron and local bishop may all have had some rights of lordship over the house in question, sometimes leading to acrimonious disputes.[77]

Because of the nature of the relationship between patrons and their foundations, there was an ongoing tension between the two with regard to how they exercised their respective rights. A possessive patron might regard his foundation as 'a fief held of him, over which he kept a hold, and which in some circumstances he might recover', while an independently minded prelate might regard it as 'a gift to God, inalienable and sacrosanct'.[78] Disputes over whose rights should be decisive were tested in the lay courts.

An indication of the kinds of agreements that were negotiated between a patron, the dependent house to which he or she made a grant and the bishopric which oversaw it are well illustrated by the following example from the cartulary of the bishopric of Chichester. On 18 January 1322–23, Robert Alard of Wynchelsee, a patron of the Church of St Thomas the Martyr at Wynchelsee, granted to the Abbot and Convent of Battle a considerable number of landholdings – including a watermill – in West Greenwich and Lewisham in Kent, as well as some other properties in Surrey and Sussex, that were worth £20 a year. In return, Robert and his heirs had the right to appoint four priests to the Church of St Thomas with the Bishop of Chichester's approval, while the priests were to be provided for from the rents of £20. The bishop was given the right to remove any priest who proved delinquent, as well as the right to appoint priests to the chantry and appropriate these rents if Robert or his heirs failed to replace any of them within 40 days.[79]

Even in instances such as this in which the abbot or prior and patron were in accord, a patron's heirs – or one of several patrons, where patronage was shared by several family members – may have felt dissatisfied with their lot and made legal suit for amends. A number of instances of such disputes relating to the ownership of mills and/or tithes and other obligations on mills are analysed in Chapter 9.

The ultimate fate of lands endowed to ecclesiastical estates was also of concern to the king. According to Susan Wood, although the Statute of Mortmain was not introduced until 1279, the alienation of land by the king's tenants without royal permission had been foreseen as a problem earlier in the century. The statute had been anticipated in the Provisions of Westminster and to some extent in the Magna Carta, while in 1227 'Henry III had ordered all sheriffs not to let tenants-in-chief alienate anything to a religious house or ecclesiastical person without his license, and more than once he gave orders to prevent religious men acquiring land of particular fiefs in his hand.'[80]

Following the introduction of Mortmain, disgruntled heirs of patrons sometimes sought to use it to recover lands which they felt had been unjustly granted away, and which in some instances a monastery itself might

---

[74] As stated previously, 'frankalmoin' literally means 'in free alms' indicating a form of ecclesiastical tenure in return for which prayers alone were due.

[75] Wood (1955), p. 13.

[76] Ibid., pp. 2–4.

[77] One such dispute between the Abbot of Reading and the Bishop of Coventry and Lichfield over possession of a grain mill and fulling mill in Sheffield during the late thirteenth century is discussed in some detail in Chapter 9.

[78] Wood (1955), p. 33.

[79] *Chartulary of the High Church of Chichester*, ms. 909.

[80] Wood (1955), pp. 35–6.

have attempted to alienate through grant or sale. The aim of this law fitted into the general land legislation, the objective of which was to instil into lords the desire to keep a firm grip upon the lands and services of their tenants, whether lay or monastic.[81]

Although a monarch or patron had well-defined rights and privileges with respect to the religious house he or she founded, the patron was still expected to respect the house's customs and liberties, and usually did so. The person who was most likely to be prevailed upon by a patron who wished to exercise his or her lordly rights was, of course, the abbot or prior, as it was he who held ultimate authority over the brethren within his community. But it was also the abbot who was expected to defend the customs and liberties of the house, and often did so successfully. Although the role of patron was almost invariably eclipsed by that of the abbot, it should also be noted that the lords of founding patrons were sometimes called upon to act as lay advocates for the religious houses of their vassals, such as Newhouse Abbey, whose founder was Peter of Goxhill, but whose advocate was Peter's lord, Rannulf of Bayeux.[82]

As previously noted, the range of people enabled to practice monastic patronage diversified as the feudal system developed. At the same time, the status of abbatial office underwent a process of feudalization. As the monastic orders grew in wealth and stature, particularly from the tenth century onwards, they began to take on many of the characteristics of other large feudal landholders, including a more hierarchical and less democratic internal organisation within the wealthiest houses, with abbots and priors assuming the mantle of great landlords.

It was the abbot who made the day-to-day decisions about the running of the monastery, including its financial transactions, and although the position was subject to various attempts at reform, by the thirteenth century, an abbot was essentially regarded by the common law as an absolute monarch. From both a theological and an administrative perspective, this was far from an ideal situation. Because an abbot was appointed for life and controlled both the monastic revenue and the household, there were ample opportunities for the abuse of power.

Up until the late twelfth century, there had been no effective constraints on the way in which an abbot or prior wielded his power, meaning that a house could be ruined by an unscrupulous or incompetent abbot before his misdeeds became more widely known. The papal Curia under Innocent III and his near successors sought to curb the abbot's power by subjecting him to the same kind of scrutiny and financial control as that placed on monastic officials, as well as attempting to bring the abbot back into the monastery's life in common, rather than continuing to live a separate life in a separate household, a trend which had begun in the twelfth century.[83]

However, these reforms of the abbot's office only met with limited success, as the Benedictine Rule had stipulated that monks of the order should subject themselves totally to the abbot's will, and this proved a particularly difficult notion to dislodge. Over the course of many legal disputes regarding abbatial rights and jurisdiction during the eleventh and twelfth centuries, the supremacy of the abbot gradually became enshrined in common law, with the courts even going so far as to reinterpret what had been the notion of the abbot as head of a corporation aggregate to casting him as the sole corporate authority of the monastery. Thus was the 'absolute, unlimited power of the abbot' exalted by both church and state, 'and against them no constitutional movement could make any headway.'[84]

Because of the abbot's position as a major landlord, he was obliged to seek technical advice on various points of law, whether feudal, common or ecclesiastical. For this purpose, a group of advisers was employed on an annual retainer and 'bound by oath to advance the interests of their employer'.[85] Although this was most likely an informal procedure in smaller houses, it acquired formal status in medium and larger houses by the second half of the thirteenth century, and continued to be followed to the middle of the fifteenth century.

This permanent group of counsellors consisted of four different elements: 'a small group of permanent officials, including the abbot's steward and perhaps one or two monks; a number of neighbouring landowners, whose local knowledge and social influence would be of value; a small number of professional lawyers, civil

---

[81]   Ibid., p. 38.

[82]   Burton (1994), p. 212.

[83]   Knowles (1940a), p. 270.

[84]   Ibid., p. 271.

[85]   Ibid.

and ecclesiastical; and, finally, one or two of the leading judges or itinerant justices of the day'.[86] Knowles explains that the first and third of these groups were easy to assemble and frequently accompanied the abbot or prior when travelling, while the second consisted of neighbours and friends whose advice was sought on particular issues, and the fourth contained men of eminence who could monitor the house's interests at Westminster, or assist in securing favourable outcomes for the monastery in the courts. He also points out that the first and third groups tended to be the most cautious and hidebound, and were sometimes regarded by monastic tenants and townsfolk as needlessly repressive and authoritarian, becoming the focus for their anger and frustration when a serious dispute arose, such as at St Albans in 1381 at the start of the Peasants' Revolt.[87]

The cartulary of Cirencester Abbey contains several charters recording the employment of individuals on such an abbot's council, and in relation to which their remuneration or patronage involved mills or mill revenues. The first such charter involved the lease for one mark a year of the canons' mill of Medford to Robert, son of William of Blewbury, sometime between 1166 and 1176. The grant also obliged Robert to ride with the abbot or his deputy at the abbot's expense whenever he needed Robert to assist in his pleas, indicating that Robert was a lawyer who acted on the abbey's behalf.[88] Between 1197 and 1213, Robert was also granted a lease of the canons' mill in Hagbourne, Berkshire, for £1 annually.[89]

At the end of the thirteenth century, the abbey acquired *Clerkesmill* for £20 from the rector of Ampney St Mary, Walter of Cheltenham, who was presumably the grandson of Richard the clerk who had originally built the mill. Prior to taking on the position of agent for the abbot on several property transactions and joining the abbot's council, Walter was able to lease the mill back from the abbey for life, with reversion to the abbot and convent upon his death.[90]

Although there were several efforts made during the thirteenth century by ordinary monks and the papal Curia to curb the powers of the abbots and make the monasteries more democratic in their modes of governance and decision making, most of these attempts failed. This left the abbot to exercise the same kinds of powers and privileges that he had enjoyed since the eleventh century.

Despite any moral or administrative shortcomings which individual abbots or priors may have had, there were nevertheless significant overall differences in the ways in which ecclesiastical lords managed their estates as compared to lay lords. Perhaps most importantly, the institutional imperative of having to maintain a religious house for a long period of time (more than 800 years in some instances) meant that, generally speaking, monastic lords had a very different outlook upon the past and future than their lay counterparts. Whereas most aristocratic dynasties seldom survived intact for more than two or three generations, a well-endowed monastery could expect a life of three or four centuries or more, and had to plan and make decisions accordingly.

As a consequence, religious houses and church authorities generally displayed greater caution than lay lords when managing their spiritual and temporal affairs, a caution that was exercised either autocratically by the abbot and his obedientiaries, or more properly but less commonly through the collective decision-making process which was supposedly a mark of the monastic orders, and which, according to their various Rules, required the majority support of those entitled to vote (i.e. ordained monks, and, as we have just seen, sometimes a patron and/or mother-house). Furthermore, due to the life-long involvement of ecclesiastical members in the affairs of a particular religious house, it was relatively easy for them to preserve an institutional memory, which in turn ensured that there was a greater sense of shared responsibility towards the aims and objectives of the order.

Nevertheless, almost every religious house experienced alternate phases of relaxation, laziness, incompetence and even corruption in the management of its affairs, followed by periods of energy, care and attention; the latter occasionally resulting in economic and even technological innovation. One interesting example of a Benedictine prior who was undoubtedly a technological innovator was Henry of Eastry, prior

---

[86] Ibid., pp. 271–2.

[87] Ibid., p. 272.

[88] *The Cartulary of Cirencester Abbey*, ms. 540.

[89] Ibid., ms. 541. A mill in *Hacheborne* is listed in Domesday Book as rendering 12 shillings a year. See Bennett and Elton (1899), p. 138.

[90] Ibid., ms. 195 with note, and ms. 307.

of Christ Church, Canterbury, from 1285–1331. Although some management reforms had been implemented over the previous century, including the establishment of a central treasury in the 1160s and regular audits from 1225,[91] Henry inherited a priory with £5,000 in debts, which was more than twice the priory's annual income. Reducing wasteful and unnecessary expenditure, he took personal control of the management of the priory and its estates:

> He developed the existing treasury of the monastery and overhauled the auditing system. He pursued a 'scientific' farming policy, suiting the crop to each type of land and selling the produce with an eye to the advantages of the market. His methods were recorded in the varied content of the memorandum-book: detailed taxation records, notes on administrative procedure, inventories, a catalogue of books in the library, lists of animals and crops, household requisites, accounts, copies of charters and statutes affecting Christ Church and its possessions, notes of new building projects undertaken by himself and lands which he acquired. The result of his efforts could be seen in the golden age of prosperity enjoyed by Christ Church, which raised it even above the great Cistercian houses whose names were synonymous with sound economy.[92]

Such entrepreneurial ecclesiastical officials were generally a rarity amongst English religious houses until the thirteenth and fourteenth centuries, when a transformation took place in the management of monastic estates.[93] Although we will come across more shrewd monks and canons in the case studies to follow, we should keep in mind that it was not until the reforms of monastic administration previously outlined that such improved management practices became possible. Even so, any tendency amongst the various orders towards innovation was obviously tempered by a generally conservative and tradition-oriented outlook. Physical and/or social isolation, as well as the cosseted nature of a religious house, could all contribute to a lack of enterprise, as its location, doctrines or privileges cushioned its members from the pressures and influences of the outside world.

Seigneurial Monopolies on Milling in Anglo-Norman England

As we have already seen, Marc Bloch is largely responsible for disseminating the idea within medieval studies that 'suit of mill' or 'mill soken' (multure or *mulctura* in Latin) was characteristic of milling in medieval France and England, and applied to all tenants, whether free or unfree. Bloch argued that suit of mill was one of the most important and jealously guarded of seigneurial privileges, and extended over most forms of milling. Only high-ranking townsfolk escaped suit of mill, although it was more difficult to enforce in rural areas.[94] Largely due to Bloch's influence, it had until recently been generally assumed within medieval social and economic history circles that the ownership of mills was exclusively a privilege of lordship, and that the obligation to perform suit of mill was a mark of serfdom. Commoners were prohibited from owning or building watermills or windmills, and were required to procure a license and pay a fee to their lord if they used their own handmills or owned a horse mill.[95] Suit of mill was a privilege that ensured handsome profits for the lords concerned.[96]

One of the crucial arguments advanced by Bloch was that seigneurial milling monopolies were ubiquitous throughout medieval England and France, and were greatly resented by the general population. Describing a

---

[91]   Burton (1995), pp. 251–2.

[92]   Stockdale (1980a), pp. 34–5. For more information see Knowles (1948), Ch. 5, devoted to Henry of Eastry, who was also responsible for initiating the rental survey of Canterbury's Sussex manors in 1285, which is analysed in Chapter 4 with respect to Canterbury's mill holdings in the county.

[93]   See, for example, the case studies of Battle Abbey in Chapter 5 and Bolton Priory in Chapter 6.

[94]   Bloch (1967), pp. 151–3, 156.

[95]   Ibid., p. 156. Although Bloch does not specifically mention this fact, it was also the case that if tenants built mills without permission, they could be lawfully destroyed by the lord, or taken into the possession of the lord. See Chapter 9 for a discussion of some of the relevant manuscript evidence.

[96]   Ibid., p. 152.

number of disputes between English peasants and their lords over handmilling in the thirteenth and fourteenth centuries, Bloch argued that these were emblematic of peasant resistance to the imposition of suit of mill and the obligation which that entailed to use the lord's mill rather than the household handmill, which of course incurred no tax. Such disputes were, furthermore, supposedly indicative of the more widespread phenomenon of peasant resistance to new technologies generally.[97]

However, we now know that many of Bloch's observations and arguments were based on limited evidence from which he tended to over-generalize.[98] Most of his sources covered areas of strong lordship in northern France and England, and almost invariably focused on the estates of great lords. A number of other sources which have been examined in detail more recently indicate that mixed forms of land tenure and weak lordship existed in some parts of medieval England, including Kent, Sussex, the former Danelaw and other pockets of the south with strong traditions of customary and hereditary tenure.[99] The French, Spanish and Italian allodial systems provided similar ownership rights and protections to free peasants and others in medieval France, Spain and Italy, and can be traced back to pre-feudal times.[100]

According to Bloch, seigneurial monopolies were first introduced in France during the tenth century, and slightly later in England in the late eleventh and early twelfth centuries.[101] However, the large number of mills that were undoubtedly built well before they were first recorded in Domesday Book strongly suggests that seigneurial milling monopolies had already been established in England during the late Anglo-Saxon period.[102] As Maitland was one of the first scholars to note, some of the great English ecclesiastical lords were acquiring seigneurial rights as early as the ninth century. In *Domesday Book and Beyond* (1897), he cites an example, in which Edward the Elder (r. 899–924) granted in perpetuity the estate of Taunton (Soms.) to the bishop of Winchester: 'I have granted to Christ that the men of the bishop, noble as well as non-noble, living on the said land shall be worthy of the same right that is enjoyed by those who dwell on the demesnes of the crown, and that jurisdiction in all secular causes shall be exercised to the use of the bishops in the same manner as that in which jurisdiction is exercised in matters pertaining to the king.' Of course these rights also came with obligations, which included the customary obligations of the demesne. [103] As I will argue at greater length in Chapter 9, although seigneurial monopolies almost undoubtedly originated in this way, the reason why they had become widespread throughout England by Domesday was primarily due to them having been imposed on the many tenants who had recently been made unfree by their new Norman overlords.[104]

---

[97]   Ibid., pp. 154–60.

[98]   For a critical overview of Bloch's claims, see: Holt (1987), pp. 4–6, (1988), Ch. 3; Langdon (1994), pp. 22–7, (2004), pp. 2, 19, 237, 257; Lucas (2006b).

[99]   See, for example, Kosminsky (1956), pp. 198–206; Holt (1988), Ch. 4; Hallam (1988a); Faith (1999), pp. 87–8, 121–4, 207. See also the case studies of the estates of Canterbury, Glastonbury and Holy Trinity examined in Chapters 4, 5 and 8.

[100]   Bois (2002), pp. 36–44; Jarrett (2010), pp. 332–3, 338, 340–41; Albertoni (2010), pp. 418–19. See also Vinogradoff (1908), p. 221, for a reference to the manor of Spersold in Berkshire which the shire testified was held of the king in allod by one Edric before the Conquest.

[101]   Bloch (1967), pp. 151–3, 156. In France, there were also 'monopolies concerning the use of the baking-oven, the wine-press, the breeding-boar or bull, the sale of wine or beer ... [and] the supply of horses for treading out corn'. Of these, Bloch argued that the seigneurial monopoly on milling was 'probably the most ancient and certainly the most widespread'. He also noted that in Canada, such monopolies lasted until as late as 1854. Other scholars have noted that even in England, milling monopolies on some estates, such as the manor of Otterton in Devon, continued until the early twentieth century [see Greenhow (1979), pp. 315–7]. Similarly, a milling monopoly in the Wakefield district in West Yorkshire was not abolished until 1853 (see Norman [1970], p. 176).

[102]   Holt (1988), pp. 37–8; Langdon (1994), pp. 36–7; Langdon (2004), pp. 16–17.

[103]   Maitland (1987), p. 276. Cf. Bennett and Elton (1899), pp. 122–3; (1900), pp. 206–7. The latter citation includes references to the monastery of Sts Peter and Paul which held soke rights over half the town of Hythe through its mill of Cert Dover in 762, and the tenants of Sutton Coldfield (Warks.), who in 940 'were said to be bound to the mill of that manor'. They also cite a Welsh law code which 'declared a lord to own the toll of his mills'. Although Holt (1988), pp. 37–8, notes that Bennett and Elton contradict themselves on this issue between volumes I and III, his own observations on the issue are not particularly satisfactory either, as I will argue at greater length in Chapter 9.

[104]   The most illuminating discussions of the extension of seigneurial monopolies before and after the Conquest can be found in Maitland (1987), pp. 318–40; Faith (1999), Ch. 6–9.

During the Anglo-Saxon period, manorial employees and household slaves were the main caretakers of mills on behalf of lords, suggesting that most of the mills concerned were in the manor's inland and under direct control of the lord. Holt has argued that there is no reason to believe that the vast majority of the 6,000 watermills recorded in Domesday Book did not have monopoly milling rights over their manorial tenants.[105] Within 20 years of the Conquest, however, a large number of mills were held at will from lay and ecclesiastical lords by tenants paying cash rents.[106]

Even though lords probably controlled virtually all of the watermills recorded in Domesday Book, and all of them were probably of the Roman or Vitruvian type,[107] John Langdon has estimated that up to half of all the milling being conducted throughout England in the late eleventh century was being done within the domestic setting of the household using handmills and the occasional horse mill.[108] This was at least partially due to the higher concentration of mills in areas of higher population density on major waterways in the south-east of England, which meant that manors in counties outside this region were significantly lacking in powered milling capacity.[109] While there is some archaeological evidence for the existence of horizontal-wheeled watermills in northern England from the late Anglo-Saxon and early Anglo-Norman periods, it is still not clear whether any were recorded in Domesday Book. However, the post-Conquest dating of some of these sites indicates that they were at least tolerated by lords and allowed to continue to exist in some contexts.[110]

Furthermore, contrary to Bloch's claim that the twelfth century was the period during which seigneurial privilege became entrenched in England, there is strong evidence that many lords throughout the country actually abandoned their claims to such privileges during this period. While French lords continued to jealously guard their ownership of mills and the seigneurial monopolies that went with them throughout the twelfth century and subsequently (despite fluctuations in their profitability),[111] many English lords appear to have come to the conclusion by the middle of the twelfth century that mills were not particularly valuable assets.[112]

From the time most French and Norman lords were granted their English possessions, they sought to retain them in direct control, managing them personally or through a steward and collecting revenues for their own benefit without leasing them out. Faith argues that this was primarily because the small sizes of most of their holdings required intense cultivation and management in order to maximize the returns from them.[113] If a mill was held by a lord within the demesne of the manor and was directly managed, the lord collected all of the revenue from the mill, but was also responsible for all the costs of maintenance and repairs. Typically, the maintenance costs for a watermill averaged around 12 per cent to 20 per cent of the mill's income over its lifetime.[114] However, if a mill needed to be partially or totally rebuilt, such costs could significantly reduce lordly profits during a time of low grain revenues. In order to minimize their financial exposure, lords allowed those mills that had in the previous century been held on tenancies-at-will to fall into hereditary or customary tenure, or granted them out to religious institutions. The surviving records suggest that seigneurial milling monopolies in southern England were relaxed by lords during the second half of the twelfth and the first quarter of the thirteenth century through the farming out of demesne mills on hereditary and customary leases, a phenomenon which is consistent with Michael Postan's thesis that demesne agriculture in the early part of the twelfth century experienced a period of substantially reduced profitability due to a combination of political

---

[105] Holt (1987), pp. 11–13; (1988), p. 38. While Holt may be correct, his statement is informed speculation.

[106] Holt (1988), pp. 68, 70.

[107] That is, vertical-wheeled watermills with right-angled gearing.

[108] Langdon (1994), p. 37.

[109] Ibid., pp. 44–6. Langdon notes that only 10 per cent of 'fringe' communities had mills, compared to 38 per cent of communities in the south-eastern 'core' (p. 46).

[110] See: Holt (1988), pp. 4–5, 118–22; Langdon (2004), p. 72; Lucas (2006a), pp. 76–7. Some of the archaeological evidence for the survival of horizontal-wheeled watermills in northern England after the Conquest is canvassed in Moorhouse (2003a), (2003b), (2003c).

[111] Bloch (1967), pp. 153–6.

[112] The first scholar to draw attention to this phenomenon was Holt (1987).

[113] Faith (1999), Ch. 7. She comments that none of the estates granted by William I to his vassals were anywhere near as large as some of the former Anglo-Saxon estates (p. 179).

[114] Lucas (2006a), pp. 133–41, 153. Cf. Holt (1988), pp. 86–7. Windmills do not appear in the records until the 1180s.

turmoil, disruption of local trade and stagnation in commodity prices.[115] As we will see in the later case studies, the main beneficiaries of these changed management practices were free peasants and artisans, the curial and administrative classes, the military retainers of lay and ecclesiastical lords, and the minor gentry.

The rationale for letting such expensive-to-maintain enterprises as watermills to free or customary tenants for a life, or even for two or three lives, was that it allowed the lord to diminish his or her ongoing costs by shifting those costs onto tenants, or in the case of donations to religious houses, almost completely relinquishing responsibility for them.[116] This practice also meant, however, that the amount of rent charged for the mill remained fixed, despite any fluctuations in grain prices or other costs. The tenant may have had to pay all the costs, but they also accrued all the benefits when custom improved. An unforeseen consequence was that during the twelfth century and again in the wake of the Black Death, a significant number of mills effectively fell out of seigneurial control.[117] The only redress for lords who wished to recover such mills when their profitability improved was to sue their tenants or others who had illegally disseised them.[118] According to Holt, by the mid- to late thirteenth century, between a third and a half of the mills in many parts of southern England were held in customary and hereditary tenure.[119] Holt's findings are to some extent supported by Langdon's studies of mill ownership between 1086 and 1540, although the levels of customary and hereditary tenure he found never exceeded 18 per cent.[120] What could be described as periods of 'relaxed lordship' provided opportunities for smaller land holders to enter the milling trade and gain control of a significant proportion of the watermills and windmills in many parts of the south and east during the twelfth and thirteenth centuries, and again in the latter half of the fourteenth century and subsequently. All of this evidence undermines the main thrust of Bloch's seigneurial monopoly model of English feudal relations.

Grants of mills and other property to religious houses for the perpetual prayers of monks and canons, or to build family chantries or provide other liturgical services, were very common in the twelfth and thirteenth centuries, although many of these seemingly generous gifts involved some form of purchase by the houses concerned, particularly when the donations were in areas where the house already held property. Grants and leases of mills by both lay and ecclesiastical lords included the mill 'with its appurtenances'. In the case of a watermill, this included the wheel, millhouse and other associated buildings, as well as its 'waters and lands', which might include roads and footpaths to and from the mill, as well as leets, ponds, dams, trenches and other waterworks such as sluices and gates, along with the meadows in which the whole complex was located. In the case of windmills, the lease was usually restricted to the postmill itself and the mound and meadow in which it was located. In a reasonably large number of instances, however, the lease on either a wind- or watermill might also include a messuage or croft, as well as a significant parcel of land. Occasionally, long-term leases might include suit of mill, although this appears to have been fairly unusual.[121]

---

[115]   See Holt (1987), pp. 13–16, and p. 7, n. 15, for a bibliography of the debate between Michael Postan and Reginald Lennard and their followers on the changing fortunes of the English economy during the twelfth century, as well as Edward Miller's comments on the subject in Miller (1971).

[116]   Holt (1988), pp. 57, 59; Lucas (2006a), pp. 129–33; Langdon (2004), pp. 193–8. Property held in customary tenure was held outside the demesne in exchange for feudal services, sometimes commuted to a nominal cash rent in the twelfth and thirteenth centuries and subsequently.

[117]   Holt (1987), pp. 7–8, 13–14; Holt (1988), Ch. 4; Langdon (1994), pp. 5–6, n. 3.

[118]   That is, taken the mill from their lawful possession. This issue is discussed in detail in Chapter 9.

[119]   Holt (1988), Ch. 4.

[120]   Langdon (1991), (1994). The later case studies reveal some ecclesiastical estates had considerably higher proportions of mills in customary and hereditary tenure than any of those found by Holt or Langdon.

[121]   See Lucas (2006a), pp. 131 and 132, the latter case referring to a fulling mill granted to Cockersand Abbey, which is also discussed in Chapter 8. See also Langdon (1994), p. 6; Langdon (1992), pp. 56–7, in which he describes how the tenant of the watermill of Turweston was granted suit of mill by his lord in the thirteenth century, a privilege that was not able to be overturned when a demesne windmill was subsequently built on the manor. A somewhat different situation pertained to an acquisition by Blythburgh Priory, which was granted the watermill of Henham with the suit of the men of Henham in the early thirteenth century, but soon afterward leased it back to the donor's son on a hereditary lease for only four shillings a year, with suit, presumably because the father's generous grant had engendered some resentment in his son. See *Blythburgh Priory Cartulary*, Pt. I, mss. 304 and 314, and the longer discussion in Chapter 6. Other cases of donors' families attempting to renege on their ancestors' generosity can be seen in Chapter 9.

While customary and hereditary leases on mills varied somewhat in their conditions, most transferred rights of multure (i.e. the right to take toll-corn, or a percentage of the corn milled by its clientele) to the lessee. In exchange, the lessee was expected to pay for the maintenance of the mill, the cost of which was usually offset by the lord through the ongoing provision of timber for maintenance, and/or the provision of extra land from which to draw this and other resources, such as fruit from orchards, or fish and eels from the mills' ponds and leets. One of the defining characteristics of these mills is that they were usually let for a nominal rent, which might range from the proverbial peppercorn or a pound of cumin to a cash sum that was significantly lower than the rent charged on a demesne mill.

Because such mills were effectively outside lordly control, i.e. both maintenance costs and profits were born by the lessee, who paid a nominal rent, Holt coined the term 'independent mill' to describe them. For similar reasons, Langdon coined the term 'tenant mill', as a means of distinguishing them from demesne mills let at farm. Jack used the terms 'free mill' and 'private mill' in his papers on the medieval Welsh fulling industry to describe mills with similar tenurial status.[122] Of all these terms, perhaps 'independent' and 'private' capture the different senses of tenure the best, but the fact that such mills were essentially being licensed to tenants to operate independently of the lord by paying a nominal rent suggests a combination of terms might be appropriate in different circumstances: 'independent tenant' for instances when a former demesne mill was leased to a tenant on a customary or hereditary basis, and 'private tenant' or 'licensed tenant' for instances when a tenant built or inherited a mill without suit and was allowed to own and operate it by paying an annual rent of cash, produce and/or services.[123] In this latter case, the party who built the mill was an 'owner-operator', whereas in the former case, the mill was acquired by the tenant from another party and run on their behalf, even if the status of that tenure and ownership may have later been in dispute. I propose to use a combination of Holt's, Jack's and Langdon's terminology as outlined above, along with the broader term 'non-seigneurial', to designate such mills.[124] Two other sectors of milling activity described by Langdon that were outside seigneurial control were domestic mills, which were generally handmills (and occasionally horse mills) used by a household, and borough mills, which enjoyed feudal exemptions under town charters of liberty.[125]

Of the four milling sectors identified by Langdon, the demesne sector was the one that was routinely subject to seigneurial monopoly control. Although some independent tenant mills could have suit of mill attached to them, this was fairly rare, and would only have applied to former demesne mills, such as those identified by Holt on Glastonbury Abbey's estates as recounted in Chapter 5 and by Langdon on the manor of Turweston mentioned in the note above. Langdon argues that domestic mills were subject to seigneurial control inasmuch as they were illegal but generally tolerated, while borough mills only existed in towns with charters of liberty, and although they were undoubtedly profitable, they are not generally well documented.

In addition to the four different kinds of non-seigneurial mills already identified by Holt and Langdon, the ecclesiastical manuscript evidence reveals that there was a fifth category of mill which had a similar status to independent tenant and private tenant mills. These mills were donated to religious houses by knights of varying rank. They did not hold suit and had invariably been held by knights on fees within existing manors which they held in turn from their own lords or tenants-in-chief. As we will see in the pages to follow, many of these mills were granted (or sold) to Augustinian and Cistercian houses in the latter half of the twelfth century and throughout the thirteenth century. At the end of the thirteenth century, more than 60 per cent of the mills held by the Augustinian houses sampled had this type of status, i.e. they were donated by knights or purchased from knights as mills without suit and tended to be let out to third parties on very long and/or inexpensive leases. The social status of the donors generally ranged from the military retainers of lords, to royal, juridical and ecclesiastical officials.[126] I propose to call this category of non-seigneurial mills 'fee mills' because they appear to have been primarily carved out of knights' fees, and had a similar status to French allodial mills in that they were largely free from feudal obligations. Like private tenant mills and independent tenant mills,

---

[122]   Holt (1987), pp. 7–8, 13–14; (1988), Ch. 4; Langdon (1994), pp. 5–6; Jack (1983).

[123]   Holt identified four fulling mills held on such terms of the abbot of Glastonbury and the bishop of Bath and Wells in the fourteenth century: Holt (1988), p. 157.

[124]   Holt coined the term 'non-seigneurial mill' in his 1987 paper, 'Whose Were the Profits of Corn Milling?', p. 13.

[125]   See Langdon (1994), p. 6, 28–31; Langdon (2004), pp. 16–20, and the more detailed discussion of Langdon's mill sectors in Chapter 3.

[126]   These issues will be discussed in more detail in Chapters 6 to 10.

their status within the manorial system is ambiguous, whereas Langdon's category of independent 'borough mills' is explicable in the context of charters of liberties.[127]

As we will see in the pages to follow, there is clear evidence throughout most of England from the twelfth to sixteenth centuries of a growing number of private tenant mills, independent tenant mills, borough mills and fee mills, especially during the twelfth and thirteenth centuries, and in the wake of the Black Death. However, the proliferation of such non-seigneurial mills during these two periods can only be adequately explained if it is acknowledged that the extent to which suit of mill applied to, and was enforced upon, the tenants of a manor or vill varied considerably throughout England. Holt argued that independent tenant mills could only be financially viable if the free tenants of a manor were not bound by suit of mill, and could draw custom from such tenants either within or outside the manor. He saw the large number of independent tenant mills in regions such as East Anglia as a function of the large number of free tenants in those counties.[128] Because Holt was aware of evidence from other parts of England, particularly the north, where free and villein tenants were both obliged to perform suit of mill,[129] his statement that 'certainly by the thirteenth century suit of the lord's mill was occasioned only by a tenant's villein status' should probably only be seen as applying to the region south of the Humber.[130] It is therefore no coincidence – as we will see in the chapters to follow – that the evidence for non-seigneurial mills in the north is substantially less than it is for the south.

Many of the English lords who had let their demesne mills fall into non-seigneurial tenure in the twelfth and early thirteenth centuries sought to renegotiate such leases when economic conditions improved in the late twelfth and thirteenth centuries. By the early fourteenth century, they had been largely successful in drawing such mills back into the demesne.[131] Indeed, Holt argues with respect to Glastonbury Abbey's mill holdings, that 'the enforcement of suit of mill must have been universal' after 1300 in the wake of the 'almost complete victory of the demesne mill'.[132] However, there were clearly some parts of England where this victory was anything but complete, including Glastonbury Abbey's own estates, as Holt also notes that at least 14 out of 40 mills on 31 of the abbey's manors in the early fourteenth century remained in independent tenant hands.[133]

Furthermore, as we will see in later chapters, lords often had to take their tenants to court in order to regain seisin of mills that had fallen out of the demesne, which frequently involved the payment of large sums of money to compensate the disenfranchised tenant for lost future revenue. Many of the smaller religious houses and those which administered their property from afar had neither the financial resources nor the will to pursue such cases through the courts. This meant that such houses might never recover direct control of what had once been profitable demesne mills, and had to remain content with drawing a fixed and relatively low income from those mills. St Denys Priory in Hampshire is one example of a smaller house whose mills were appropriated by the descendants of the knights who originally leased them from the Priory and which had neither the skill nor the will to win them back, whereas the Abbey of the Holy Trinity, Caen, is an example of a much wealthier religious house administering property from afar which similarly lost control of a large number of its mills, but which also appears to have been reluctant to seek legal redress to recover them.[134]

At the same time that the larger and more powerful lay and ecclesiastical lords were attempting to bring hereditary and customary tenancies back into the demesne, many of them sought to re-impose or even to increase the labour services paid them by their bonded tenants, while imposing entry fines on new tenants in an attempt to recover some of the profits previously lost to the demesne.[135] In response, those villeins who

---

[127] See, for example, Hilton's discussion of what these urban liberties constituted in Hilton (1984), (1992), pp. 127–8.

[128] Holt (1988), pp. 52–3. Cf. Langdon (2004), pp. 257–8.

[129] Cf. ibid., pp. 50–51 and 80–82. Stackhouse mill in Lancashire, in which Furness Abbey acquired an interest at the end of the twelfth century, was one such mill (see Chapter 7).

[130] Ibid., p. 52. Cf. Holt (1988), pp. 43–4, 80–81.

[131] See Holt (1987), pp. 11–13, 17–18, and Holt (1988), p. 14.

[132] Holt (1987), p. 17.

[133] Holt (1988), pp. 114–15.

[134] See Chapters 5 and 7, in which the two houses' mill holdings are discussed in detail.

[135] Holt (1987), p. 11; Holt (1988), pp. 57 n. 10, 60 and 66. Langdon argues that entry fines are theoretically only found in relation to hereditary leases, although he found some examples of temporary leases including such fines, on which see Langdon (2004), p. 190. However, as mentioned earlier, entry fines are also associated with the securing of copyhold titles by villeins in the late fourteenth and fifteenth centuries. See Fryde and Fryde (1991), pp. 813–19.

had held property under customary tenure on cash rents during the previous period sought to argue a case for their free status, although in most cases they appear to have been unsuccessful.[136] Knightly families, on the other hand, were far more successful at retaining mills in hereditary tenure, probably because they had more financial resources behind them to maintain their mills in working order and defend their possession against legal challenges.[137]

Holt has demonstrated, however, that despite these lordly efforts at 'turning back the clock', non-seigneurial mills remained relatively common throughout southern England, and particularly East Anglia, even after their general decline in numbers post-1300. Furthermore, in the wake of the plague, a significant number of demesne mills once again reverted or were converted to customary tenure on many English estates.[138] Overall, more than 80 per cent of the mills held by the four Benedictine houses examined in the sample held suit in the late thirteenth and early fourteenth centuries,[139] a figure that is around twice as high as that found by Holt for the Oxfordshire and Cambridgeshire estates he examined from the Hundred Rolls,[140] but consistent with his general observation that there were far fewer of these mills by the early fourteenth century. The Benedictines overall had a far higher average number of mills with suit than the other orders, simply because most Benedictine houses were granted many more whole manors and vills with seigneurial rights by their founding lords when first established, rather than piecemeal holdings which had then to be consolidated, as was the case with the other orders.

Conclusion

Although Bloch argued milling monopolies were first established in England between the late eleventh and twelfth centuries, it now seems most likely that such monopolies actually originated on royal and ecclesiastical estates in the ninth century, but became far more widespread in the wake of William I's transformation of property relations throughout the country in the decades immediately after the Conquest. However, the economic downturn of the first half of the twelfth century resulted in lords largely abandoning demesne agriculture (and therefore, suit of mill) in favour of customary and hereditary tenancies in the second half of the twelfth and first quarter of the thirteenth centuries. As a consequence, manorial monopolies on milling were not re-established in many parts of southern England until the late thirteenth and early fourteenth centuries, after which these feudal rights were allowed to lapse again in many places during the late fourteenth and fifteenth centuries in the wake of the Black Death. As we will see in the next chapter, what could be described as periods of 'relaxed lordship' provided opportunities for 'small men' to enter the trade and gain control of up to half or more of the watermills and windmills in many parts of the south and east during the twelfth and thirteenth centuries, and again in the fifteenth century and subsequently.

It is this phenomenon of English lords allowing mills to fall out of seigneurial control, a phenomenon first articulated in detail by Holt, which provides one of the fundamental challenges to Bloch's model of a universal seigneurial monopoly on milling in post-Conquest England.[141] Furthermore, as we will see in later chapters, the Augustinians and even the Cistercians played a significant role in providing non-seigneurial milling alternatives to manorial tenants and others through their acquisition of mills and land from knights of varying status, while some of the older Benedictine houses seem to have never recovered seisin of mills that had been alienated from their possession in the twelfth and thirteenth centuries and possibly even earlier. This ensured the continuous survival in some parts of southern England of non-seigneurial mills for centuries.

---

[136] See Hilton (1965), pp. 13–19; Holt (1988), p. 60.

[137] Holt (1988), pp. 61, 63.

[138] Holt (1987), p. 14. We will see more evidence for this in the case studies of Furness in Chapter 7.

[139] See Table 10.2 in Chapter 10.

[140] Holt (1988), pp. 54–5.

[141] See, in particular, Holt (1988), Ch. 3, for an effective rebuttal of this and most other aspects of Bloch's thesis. Another challenge to Bloch's model will emerge from my case studies of Augustinian and Cistercian mill holdings in Chapters 6 and 7.

Holt's and Langdon's research suggests that the size and wealth of a religious house largely determined its mill management practices, but that cultural and geographical factors also played a significant role in determining the extent to which both lay and ecclesiastical lords could exercise seigneurial control over mills which they held or which impinged on their seigneurial rights. The fact that some religious houses directly held non-seigneurial mills on manors with seigneurial mills suggests that, like the free peasants discovered by Holt who managed independent tenant mills in East Anglia and the south-west, these houses were involved in providing a milling service to locals without feudal compulsion, i.e. they were providing a commercial milling service. The fact that there was some diversity in the mill management practices of religious houses indicates that the same kind of complexity seen in the industry as a whole is also evident in the forms of ecclesiastical tenure of mills and how they operated.

Chapter 3
The Commercialization of English Milling, 1086–1450

The previous two chapters provided a summary of the development of the religious orders in England, and how their involvement in the growth of medieval milling was emblematic of their different and changing administrative practices, practices which were in turn shaped by each house's internal politics and its relationships with its patrons, retainers, neighbours, tenants and the land. In this chapter, we will examine just how important was milling to the medieval economy overall, and how milling became a focus for renegotiating the extent and limits of lordly power in the latter half of the Middle Ages. We will also look at how milling became a site of economic activity in which new forms of consumption, investment and entrepreneurship were established, and the role played by religious houses in these processes.

The most detailed analyses to date of the history of milling in medieval England have been undertaken by Richard Holt on the whole of England from Domesday to the fifteenth century, and by John Langdon for the West Midlands over the same period and for the whole of England from the period between 1300 and 1540.[1] Langdon has supplemented this research with a country-wide study of lay lords' involvement in milling during the early fourteenth century using the IPMs for the reign of Edward II, while he and John Ambler have drawn some tentative conclusions about the economics of milling at Domesday based on an analysis of the proportion of mill rentals to manorial incomes in 30 counties.[2]

Until Holt and Langdon began their temporal analyses of mill-related data, most medievalists had restricted their comments on mills to generic observations about suit of mill and the value of mills to the revenues of lay and ecclesiastical estates. With the exceptions of Marc Bloch, H.S. Bennett and E.A. Kosminsky,[3] most of the relevant discussions revolved around the mill holdings of well-documented religious houses, conceptualizing changing mill management practices as one aspect of broader developments in farming, assarting and leasing from the twelfth to fourteenth centuries.[4]

On the basis of their analysis of the mill holdings of such wealthy episcopal and Benedictine houses as Bury St Edmunds, Christ Church Canterbury, Durham, Glastonbury, Peterborough, Ramsey and Worcester, Holt and Langdon have argued that, generally speaking, the abbots and priors of the larger religious houses were harsher landlords than their lay counterparts, and quicker and more determined to exploit their seigneurial privileges.[5] While some of these factors related to being the dominant landlords in a county (e.g. Huntingdonshire), others were related to their position at one of the frontiers of lordship (e.g. Durham, Northumberland).[6]

The case studies to follow demonstrate that the estate management techniques and overall styles of the Augustinian houses and many of the smaller and medium houses of the minor orders were quite different to those adopted by the ancient bishoprics and Benedictine houses which were the main foci of Holt's and Langdon's analyses.[7] The smaller houses displayed some interesting and novel perspectives on ownership, technological innovation, employment and philanthropy. Some of these differences in outlook and management style were related to the kinds of tenure in which the houses concerned held and acquired property, some to

[1]   See Holt (1987), (1988); Langdon (1991), (2004).

[2]   See Langdon (1994); Ambler (1994).

[3]   Bloch (1935), (1967); Bennett (1937); Kosminsky (1956).

[4]   See, for example, Finberg (1951), Searle (1974), Hockey (1976), Harvey (1977).

[5]   Holt (1988), pp. 58, 61–3; Langdon (1991), pp. 431, 441; Langdon (1994). pp. 17, 28, esp. n. 69

[6]   Langdon (1994). pp. 33–5; Ambler (1994), pp. 43–4.

[7]   The episcopal and conventual houses which Holt and Langdon have examined in detail were as follows: Holt (1987) – Glastonbury; Holt (1988) – Bury St Edmunds, Christ Church Canterbury, Durham, Ely, Glastonbury, Holy Trinity Caen, Norwich, Peterborough, Ramsey, Winchester, Worcester; Langdon (1991) – Holy Trinity Caen, Gloucester, Westminster, Worcester; Langdon (2004) – Battle, Bury St Edmunds, Canterbury, Durham, Ely, Glastonbury, Holy Trinity Caen, Norwich, Westminster, Winchester, Worcester.

the order to which they belonged, some to the values, interests, skills and competence of their ecclesiastical and lay officials, and others to their geographical location and relationships with patrons, neighbours and tenants. Drawing primarily from my own and the aforementioned research of Holt, Langdon and Ambler, the discussion to follow seeks to locate ecclesiastical ownership of mills in the broader context of milling as an increasingly commercialized activity throughout England from Domesday to the mid-fifteenth century.

Mill Possession at Domesday

Richard Bennett and John Elton were the first scholars to conduct an analysis of the mill-related information in Domesday, from which they compiled county-by-county lists of Domesday mills in the late nineteenth century.[8] Margaret Hodgen was the first to attempt to tally all the mill references in the late 1930s, coming up with a total of 5,632 mills in her oft-quoted paper, 'Domesday Watermills'.[9] It was not until the work of Henry Darby and his colleagues in the late 1970s that the more accurate figure of 6,082 mills was calculated, or around one mill for every 50 recorded households.[10]

Although there are several hundred 'missing mills' in Hodgen's sample, the distribution map which she plotted on the basis of her findings is still useful, as are some of the other maps which she made of mill numbers per county and their distribution along major river courses in the south and east. The maps reveal Domesday mill concentrations in eastern and southern England: Lincolnshire, Northamptonshire, Norfolk, Suffolk, Essex, Kent, the Cotswolds, Wiltshire, Hampshire and parts of Somerset and Dorset had the highest concentrations of mill numbers. Cornwall, Devon and Dorset west of the Exe, as well as the Fenland to the west of East Anglia and the Weald, had the lowest concentrations. On the basis of these findings, Hodgen proposed that the areas in England in which watermills were longest established were the counties of Lincolnshire, Norfolk and Wiltshire, while their earliest concentrations were in Lincolnshire, Norfolk and Kent. Her conclusion was that there had been a steady diffusion of watermill technology into the rest of England from these centres 'in the period just antecedent to the Norman Conquest'.[11]

Holt's analysis of Hodgen's findings is worth briefly summarizing.[12] With regard to the virtual absence of mill references west of the Exe, he proposes a number of explanations. The first is the carelessness of the Domesday surveyors, which appears unlikely given their rigour with regard to settlements in the region. The second is that Cornish mills were held freely, outside the demesne, although there is no evidence for this. The third and most likely explanation is that watermills really were rare in Cornwall due to the locals' custom of eating porridge rather than bread.[13]

With regard to the uneven distribution of watermills in other regions of England, Holt makes the following observations. The highest densities of watermills in the east and south-west are explicable with respect to the high population density in the east, and the high rainfall and hilly terrain of the south-west. The relative absence of watermills in the Fens, Somerset Levels and Norfolk Broads is explicable on the basis that these areas were simply not suitable for watermills, lacking sufficient watercourses to site them. The lack of references to mills in the Weald, on the other hand, is probably the result of inadequacies in the survey results.[14]

As a result of this uneven distribution of English water resources relative to the population density throughout the latter half of the Middle Ages, Holt notes that the watermill would never be able to sufficiently meet the demand for ground grain required by its people.[15] It was not until the invention of the windmill in the late twelfth century that this latent demand could be met.

---

[8] Bennett and Elton (1899), pp. 150–80.

[9] Hodgen (1939).

[10] See Darby (1977), p. 361; Miller and Hatcher (1978), pp. 12–13.

[11] Hodgen (1939), p. 276.

[12] Holt (1988), pp. 7–13.

[13] Ibid., p. 10.

[14] Ibid., pp. 10–11.

[15] Ibid., pp. 13–16.

A detailed analysis of Domesday mill rentals for 30 counties undertaken by John Ambler is also worth briefly summarizing. Ambler found that Huntingdonshire possessed by far the highest earning mills in the country, an artefact of the two large rivers running through it and the domination of its economy by large ecclesiastical estates.[16] The fact that the county's economy was dominated by large ecclesiastical estates that extracted high mill revenues from their tenants places somewhat of a cloud over the rhetoric of monastic beneficence, and provides further support for Holt's and Langdon's earlier observations about the authoritarian management styles of most of the wealthy religious houses. Ambler's analysis of the 10 counties with the highest average mill values per year is reproduced below in Table 3.1.

Table 3.1   Ten Domesday counties with the highest average mill values *per annum*

	County	Average mill value *per annum*
1.	Huntingdonshire	£1 2s 5d
2.	Surrey	16s 4d
3.	Middlesex	15s 10d
4.	Bedfordshire	15s 7d
5.	Berkshire	13s 4d
6.	Cambridgeshire	13s 8 1/2d
7.	Kent	11s 5d
8.	Buckinghamshire	10s 11d
9.	Oxfordshire	10s 10d
10.	Wiltshire	10s 6d

Source: Ambler (1994)

As we can see, the counties of the south-east contained the highest value mills, which appear to accord with their population density and the amount of arable land in this region.[17] By way of contrast, the lower population density in the north and south-west was reflected in a much lower mill density and relatively low mill values. While 38 per cent of communities in the south-east had mills to service them at Domesday, only 10 per cent of communities in the so-called 'fringe' areas had them; an area that stretched from Yorkshire through to the western marches and down to Devon and Cornwall.[18]

As in Huntingdonshire, most of the high value mills in other counties were concentrated on the larger watercourses. Those that were sited on navigable rivers appear to have been the most profitable, as they were able to draw custom from outside their localities, possibly from some distance away, unlike those mills sited on smaller rivers in comparatively larger and more populated manors. It is also clear that peasants who were not adequately serviced by manorial watermills were carrying their corn to other lordships to have it milled.

Ambler's analysis has clearly revealed a direct correlation between the distribution of mill values at Domesday, and the distribution of both the population and arable land at that time, i.e. the larger the population and amount of arable land in a given county, the higher the mill values. Like Langdon, Ambler concluded that the south-eastern counties had by this stage already exploited most of the suitable waterways in the area for the siting of watermills.[19] He suggested that around 35 per cent of the total millable grain during this period was being processed by demesne mills, although Langdon argued this figure is probably too low given that the proportion of demesne mill values to total manorial values in the south was around the same at Domesday as it was during the reign of Edward II a little over two centuries later. This would then give a figure of around 50 per cent of millable grains going to the demesne sector, with the rest being milled in what Langdon has called the 'domestic sector', i.e., household handmills and possibly some horse mills,[20] although

[16]   Ambler (1994), p. 44.

[17]   Ibid.

[18]   Ibid., p. 45.

[19]   Ibid., p. 44.

[20]   Langdon (1994), p. 37, n. 93.

it is also possible that some knight- and peasant-owned horizontal-wheeled and vertical-wheeled watermills were also involved.[21] By the early fourteenth century, the percentage of grain being ground by the demesne sector had dropped to about 40 per cent across the country, despite the efforts of many lords to draw mills in customary and hereditary tenure back into the demesne, while the domestic sector had declined to about 20 per cent.[22] Langdon also notes that the late Anglo-Saxon period 'probably signalled the first major shift from a family- or household-oriented activity to a commercialized industry, as lords sought to tap into the demand for milling'.[23] It is clear that by Domesday, lords – especially ecclesiastical lords – had been successful in gaining a significant share of what had previously been a largely domestic activity performed by the women of the household. But what exactly was that share?

When the Domesday survey was undertaken, William I and his relatives directly held around 20 per cent of all the land in the counties recorded, while the Church held around 25 per cent of the land with the approval of the king, and a dozen leading tenants-in-chief held another 25 per cent.[24] The remaining 30 per cent was held by a diverse mixture of greater and lesser nobles, and even by free peasants in Kent, the south-west, and those regions of eastern and north-eastern England described as the Danelaw.[25] In other words, almost half of the land in England at Domesday was held in demesne by the royal family and tenants-in-chief, with another quarter held by ecclesiastical estates (i.e., 70 per cent in total).

A reasonable idea of the structure of English mill ownership in the late eleventh century can be gleaned from comparing the evidence of the different proportions of overall property ownership from Domesday Book with Langdon's and Ambler's estimates of the amount of grain being milled in the demesne sector at the same time. If we accept Langdon's estimate that half of all the grain throughout England at Domesday was being ground by demesne mills, all of which were presumably held by the royal family, Church and tenants-in-chief,[26] the Crown would have controlled over 14 per cent, and the Church and tenants-in-chief about 18 per cent each of total milling custom in the late eleventh century. This would translate into the ecclesiastical sector and lay tenants-in-chief controlling together about 72 per cent of the watermills in the country, or a little over a third of the total number of demesne mills each.[27]

However, based on the evidence that there was an unusually high density of demesne watermills on the estates of religious houses in the south of England at Domesday, it would seem that they had already exploited

---

[21]   On the basis of archaeological finds of horizontal-wheeled watermills in the north (Moorhouse 2003b and 2003c) and the increasing frequency with which fee mills became objects of donation and purchase between the twelfth and fourteenth centuries (see Chapters 6 to 8), it seems reasonable to surmise that there were dozens and perhaps hundreds of non-seigneurial watermills, held on former sokeland or warland, but which were seldom documented in manorial surveys or other *inspeximi*.

[22]   Langdon (1994), p. 37.

[23]   Ibid., pp. 36–7.

[24]   Hallam (1986), p. 19; Goody (1983), pp. 125–7; Hudson (1994), p. 230. According to Goody, the percentage of land held by the Church in England at this time was roughly the same as in most other parts of Europe.

[25]   See Kosminsky (1956), pp. 198–206; Holt (1988), Ch. 4; Hallam (1988a); Faith (1999), pp. 87–8, 121–4, 207, as well as the case studies of the estates of Canterbury, Glastonbury and Holy Trinity examined in Chapters 4, 5 and 8. Historically speaking, these areas had a significantly larger free peasantry than most of the rest of England. In East Anglia, this was a legacy of Danish settlement from the ninth century onwards, while in Kent, the peasantry remained similarly free of lordly domination largely because of the significant movements of goods through that county to and from the Continent, providing the population with numerous opportunities to exploit the passing trade and secure independent incomes. The Kentish practiced customs throughout the Middle Ages which appear to have their origins in Dark Age Friesia, and constituted one of the early waves of 'Anglo-Saxon' migration. See Homans (1953), (1969). These areas are also those which tended to have the highest rate of non-seigneurial mills over the subsequent period.

[26]   Langdon (1994), p. 37.

[27]   Also of relevance is evidence for growth in the number of English watermills in the two to three decades after the Conquest. One of William I's major strategies in the colonization and subjugation of Anglo-Saxon England was the construction throughout the country of functionally inter-related complexes of castles, priories and towns. Mills were usually attached to all three units, with the castle mills serving the garrison, the priory mill serving the monks or canons, and the town mill, the townsfolk. It is hard to imagine that the mills attached to these complexes were anything but new mills, but the numbers built between 1066 and 1086 cannot have been many more than several hundred, and those that were built by or associated with new monasteries, cathedrals and priories, were probably no more than one third of those.

most of the suitable waterways within their manors for the siting of watermills.[28] The lay sector, on the other hand, spent the subsequent two centuries catching up to their religious brethren. This evidence suggests that ecclesiastical lords were quicker at exploiting their demesne privileges than their lay counterparts, in which case it is possible that the Church controlled as much as 40 per cent of the demesne watermills in England by the late eleventh century. It would therefore appear that while the Church was but one of three élite social groups that was initially responsible for developing the demesne sector of English milling, religious houses almost undoubtedly dominated this sector between the tenth and thirteenth centuries, and were responsible for either building or acquiring from laymen a significant number of mills during this period.

On the basis of this evidence, as well as the charter and archaeological evidence which I have summarized in my earlier work on the subject,[29] it would appear that the first major phase of monastic mill acquisition in medieval England occurred during the tenth and eleventh centuries.[30] While there are good reasons for believing that ecclesiastical authorities were enthusiastic about *acquiring* mills during this period, it remains to be determined *how* the monasteries and cathedrals acquired them, because the sparse charter evidence provides few indications. If the French and Italian evidence is at all indicative of what happened in England, the appropriation of allodial and communally held mills from free peasants by religious houses was not uncommon.[31] Because minster churches appear to have had few mills attached to their estates at Domesday, it was almost exclusively the Benedictine and episcopal houses that held these ecclesiastical mills. As we will see in the pages to follow, their primary motivations for acquiring mills appears to have been the provisioning of flour and bread for their own chapters, demesne servants and retainers, along with the desire to secure a reliable source of cash (or grain) revenue. While there is some evidence of ecclesiastical interest in technological development, there is little or none that they had any interest in relieving their tenants from the drudgery of handmilling at home, as some historians of technology have claimed. There is, however, strong evidence that tenants' growing desire to rid their households of that drudgery and to consume finer grades of flour and bread were major drivers for lordly investment in powered milling in the latter half of the Middle Ages.

The Twelfth and Thirteenth Centuries

John Langdon's temporal analysis of the milling industry in the West Midlands from 1086 to 1500 has revealed that there was stagnation or even a decline in mill numbers in this region during the 1100s, a trend which has been noted in other parts of England over the same period. Overall mill numbers did not recover until the first decades of the thirteenth century.[32] Considering that this was the period of the greatest growth of monasticism in England during the Middle Ages, Langdon's findings are particularly interesting and significant, because if the contention by early historians of technology is correct that the monasteries were largely responsible for building watermills in, and introducing watermill technology to, Western Europe during the Middle Ages, one might consequently expect a growth in mill numbers during the twelfth century which directly corresponds with the third phase in the growth of European monasticism and the proliferation of religious houses throughout England. But at least as far as the West Midlands were concerned, this was clearly not the case.

Although the general economic decline and political instability of the twelfth century may partially account for this downward trend in mill numbers, as we have already seen, there is some evidence that the Benedictine and episcopal houses had exploited as much of their own capacity for siting watermills as they

---

[28]   See Langdon (1991), pp. 431–2; Langdon (1994), p. 8, n. 17; Ambler (1994), p. 44.

[29]   Lucas (2006a), pp. 74–7.

[30]   Based on the charter and archaeological evidence available to them at that date, Rahtz and Bullough (1977), p. 29, proposed that it was during 'the tenth century ... [that] mills multiplied rapidly in England'. Cf. Astill (1997), pp. 198–9.

[31]   See, for example, Bois (2002), pp. 112–13, where he notes that a network of watermills preceded the arrival of the monks of Cluny in the early tenth century, who then went about doing their best to secure possession of all of them. See also Squatriti (1998), pp. 142–5.

[32]   Langdon (1991), p. 430, esp. Table 1.

could by the end of the eleventh century, so that any existing and new religious houses were unable to make further headway on this score in the twelfth. As we will see in the chapters to follow, the vast majority of the new monasteries had to rely on donations of existing watermills from lay benefactors, but lacked either the water resources or capital to build more mills. The largest number of acquisitions of new mills by both the Augustinians and Cistercians, for example, was in the thirteenth and early fourteenth centuries, after they had already established themselves in their respective localities.

Around 70 per cent of the sample of West Midlands manors studied by Langdon were ecclesiastical, i.e., 72 of 104.[33] While lay manors are under-represented by a factor of two to one in the surviving records, Langdon's survey provides a good overview of the mill management practices of the bishoprics, military religious orders and larger monasteries in the region.

In contrast to the twelfth century, which as we have seen was a period of economic stagnation, decline and even anarchy during which many lords abandoned responsibility for their demesne holdings, the thirteenth century was a period of both managerial and technological innovation for lay and ecclesiastical lords. By the end of the century, these innovations, which included advances in book-keeping, estate management, and the new technology of the windmill, had been enthusiastically embraced by most of the larger religious houses and great lords, although the reasons behind such enthusiasm varied. As we saw in Chapter 1, one of the main reasons for these innovations within the Church was a desire to minimize the opportunities for clerical officials and lay servants to misappropriate or mismanage property and funds – a common problem in the twelfth century – and the consequent need to increase manorial revenues in order to reduce or clear debts.

A common strategy pursued by both lay and ecclesiastical lords was increased investment in, and attempts to create and consolidate, new manorial holdings, combined with a much higher degree of direct control than had been the norm in the twelfth century. There was a sharp rise in the number of new watermills and windmills built during the thirteenth century by both ecclesiastical and lay lords, most of which were either leased out on fixed terms, or directly run as demesne operations by miller employees.[34] Those responsible for building most of these mills were, however, the larger religious houses and wealthier lay lords, much of which involved the construction of windmills in areas that had previously been inadequately served by watermills.

On the basis of his studies of the eastern and south-western counties, Holt has argued that the most rapid growth in the number of windmills (mostly in eastern England) was in the 1230s and 1240s, with their numbers only growing marginally over the subsequent decades. Langdon's study of the West Midlands showed that the highest level of growth there occurred in the last decades of the thirteenth century, most of which also consisted of windmills.[35] In eastern England, the rapid early growth in the number of windmills was a direct result of the limited number of waterways in those counties which were suitable for operating watermills, whereas in the case of the West Midlands, the peak at the end of the century would appear to be related to increased consumer demand resulting from the dual processes of population growth and urbanization, which is the case put forward by Langdon with regard to growth in mill numbers generally.[36] However, it should also be noted that lords' apparent preference for windmills over watermills in the West Midlands was related at least partially to their significantly lower costs of construction and the relative ease with which they could be located in a range of different settings.[37]

---

[33]   Ibid., pp. 427, 429, 442. The 72 manors were held by five ecclesiastical estates, i.e. the Bishopric of Worcester, the Priory of Worcester and the abbeys of Westminster, Caen and Gloucester.

[34]   Holt (1988), p. 71.

[35]   See ibid., pp. 54–5, Langdon (1991), pp. 430–31.

[36]   Langdon (1991), p. 433; Langdon (1994), pp. 26, 36, 41–2. With regard to the 'lag' between the periods of greatest growth in the number of windmills and their earliest appearance in the 1180s, this was probably due to caution on the part of lords over inadequacies in the design of the earliest postmills. Once these 'reverse salients' – to use a term coined by Thomas Hughes – were ironed out, the technology had proven itself sufficiently to encourage its more widespread adoption. For a general discussion of reverse salients in the development of new technologies, see Hughes (1988) and Langdon (2004), p. 134, on the postmill.

[37]   Langdon (1994), pp. 16, 26, 33, 36.

By the end of the thirteenth century, milling capacity in the eastern counties had increased by 300 per cent or more on Domesday.[38] In the West Midlands, that growth represented at least a 60–80 per cent increase on Domesday, although it was probably more like 100 per cent when documentary biases are taken into account.[39] Langdon also found that lay estates in the West Midlands displayed the most rapid growth in mill numbers from Domesday to 1350, which supported his observation that ecclesiastical lords had been quicker than lay lords at establishing powered mills on their estates, and had done so by Domesday.[40] Langdon's research also tends to support Holt's on the overall increase in mill numbers over this period,[41] and adds further weight to Holt's contention that seigneurial monopolies on milling were already established in England before the Norman Conquest, *contra* Bloch, who as we saw in Chapter 2 argued that they had first been introduced to England in the twelfth and thirteenth centuries.[42]

Holt notes that in East Anglia by 1300, between two-thirds and three-quarters of the mills on lay and ecclesiastical estates were windmills.[43] Langdon's study of lay estates in the early fourteenth century found that around 56 per cent of all mills on 372 manors in the East Anglian and East Midlands counties were windmills, which was by far the highest proportion in the country.[44] As noted previously, he had already found evidence for a sharp increase in the number of windmills during the late thirteenth century from his West Midlands study.[45] A comparison of Holt's and Langdon's findings for East Anglia clearly indicates that ecclesiastical lords were responsible for building far more windmills than were lay lords in this region during the late twelfth and thirteenth centuries. The reverse appears to have been true in the West Midlands, however, where Langdon found that there was a 10.6 per cent increase in windmill numbers on both lay and ecclesiastical estates between 1276 and 1300, and a 12.6 per cent increase between 1301 and 1325, compared with a whopping 20.5 per cent increase on lay estates alone which was revealed by the IPM material for the reign of Edward II (r. 1307–27).[46]

Nevertheless, the inexorable growth in the number of windmills throughout England during the thirteenth century was to be short-lived. With the second economic downturn of the early fourteenth century, the windmill's fortunes took a turn for the worse. In those situations where the geography enabled them to do so, lords began to favour watermills over windmills because of the higher revenues from watermills, but equal costs of maintenance for both types of mill.[47]

The growing trend towards the payment of cash rents to lords by tenants during the twelfth and thirteenth centuries was more advantageous to tenants than it was to lords, as it allowed tenants, and particularly villeins, to free themselves from irksome labour services through the payment of a small sum of money in lieu of the

---

[38]   Holt (1988), p. 116.

[39]   Langdon (1991), p. 430. As Langdon notes on p. 432, taking into account the ecclesiastical bias of the sample, the real growth in the region was probably double over this period, i.e. due to the much greater relative growth in the number of mills built by lay lords.

[40]   Ibid., pp. 431–2. This observation is also borne out by the mill numbers cited by Dyer in his study of the Bishopric of Worcester estates between 1086 and c. 1300, where the number of mills increased only marginally from 30 mills at Domesday, to 31 in the 1290s. See Dyer (1980), pp. 37 and 172.

[41]   Holt (1988), p. 116.

[42]   Ibid., p. 36.

[43]   Ibid., p. 55. Similar ratios were found for individual religious houses in the sample. For example, Blythburgh Priory, where two out of the five or so mills directly held by the priory in the mid-thirteenth century were windmills (see in Chapter 6). Chichester Cathedral Priory in Sussex also held four windmills out of the six mills it directly held in the early fourteenth century (see Chapter 4).

[44]   Langdon (1994), p. 12, Table 1.

[45]   Langdon (1991), pp. 430, 433–4.

[46]   Ibid., pp. 433–4, Table 2 and n. 23. Langdon thought at the time that this was a problem with his sample, but it is in fact consistent with some of his other findings about lay lords 'catching up' to ecclesiastical lords with respect to mill construction in some regions of the country.

[47]   Holt (1988), pp. 55, 57; Langdon (1991), pp. 434, 435, 436–7; Langdon (1994), pp. 9–13; Lucas (2006a), pp. 136–40, 145–51. I should note, however, that Langdon has more recently argued that gross investment rates for windmills and watermills were about the same, which suggests that maintenance costs of windmills were about half those of watermills. See Langdon (2004), pp. 179, 181. I will return to this issue in Chapter 10.

labour service. It also allowed tenants the opportunity to sell their surplus produce in the markets that were rapidly emerging around urban centres throughout the country, which in turn stimulated changes to farming practices in response to market demand.[48]

In the late thirteenth and early fourteenth centuries, however, there appears to have been no clear preference for rents in cash or in kind. Generally speaking, the advantage of leasing mills for rents in kind was that their value increased as the cost of grain increased, an advantage noted by many large landholders who began to shift their rental policies accordingly, particularly during the last decades of the thirteenth century, although this shift appears to have been the result of *ad hoc* rather than systematic observations of the changing fortunes of their mills.[49] During the inflation, crop failures and famines of the early fourteenth century, grain rents proved to be particularly lucrative as the cost of grain soared to record heights, fetching as much as 10 times its pre-inflation price.[50]

The Early Fourteenth Century

Holt and Langdon have both argued that the peak in English mill numbers occurred during the first half of the fourteenth century,[51] which is in accordance with more widespread economic trends that have been noted in other large-scale empirical studies of the Greater London region in the fourteenth century by Bruce Campbell and his colleagues, and more recently by Campbell in his temporal analysis of English seigneurial agriculture from 1250 to 1450.[52] Based on his extensive survey of English lay and ecclesiastical estates across four centuries, Holt has argued that there were at least 10,000 English mills by 1300, and possibly as many as 12,000. Based on his own extensive work on the subject, Langdon initially estimated 10–15,000 mills c. 1300, the higher overall estimate relating to the marked increase in the number of watermills in the south-west after 1086.[53] However, in his most recent research on the subject, he concedes that Holt's lower estimate is probably the more accurate.[54]

---

[48]　See Hilton (1965), (1985); Dyer (1989), (2002), pp. 163–78. According to Hilton (1985), the social structure of the larger towns, especially from the twelfth century onwards, had been characterized by corporate control of an urban ruling élite, some of whom were merchants who had made their wealth through long-distance wholesale trade:

> On the whole, the commercial activity of their ruling elites was geared to commodities for at least national, often international, exchange. The buyers of their commodities, luxuries especially, were persons whose incomes ultimately came from the revenues of their landed property – that is, gentry and noblemen among the laity; bishops, abbots, other higher clergy and monks among the ecclesiastics; high ranking servants of church and state. (p. 4)

Hilton argued that the merchants who traded these goods were able to accumulate significant money capital which then enabled them to become money-lenders to the Crown and aristocracy, and that they had little interest in productive investment in either agriculture or industry. The economies of these towns were thus primarily based on long-distance wholesale trade, local retail trade and the tolls and dues therefrom.

From the thirteenth century onwards, however, a number of smaller market towns proliferated throughout the country. Those that were able to free themselves from lordly control were more diverse than the larger provincial towns in their corporate structure, usually being controlled by the richer burgesses through the manorial and borough courts (p. 16. See also Britnell [1981], [1996]) and characterized by local retail trade, although they tended to be more strictly policed by local lords (p. 22).

Hilton proposed that the growth of the local retail trade in smaller regional centres may well have been the predominant cause of the development of capitalism in England, as '[m]erchant capital derived from foreign trade had been prominent in the medieval economy for hundreds of years without significantly transforming it' (ibid.). Merchants did invest in industry at the same time as wage labour developed, but this could not have happened without the sound basis of already developed simple commodity production throughout the country, as seen in the small market towns.

[49]　See Holt (1988), pp. 71–7, for the changing policies of the religious houses of Ely, Ramsey, Peterborough, Westminster, Syon, Tavistock and Glastonbury, as well as the bishops of Norwich, Durham, Worcester, Bath and Wells, the duke of Cornwall, the de Lacy and Beauchamp families, and the earls of Norfolk, Lancaster, and Devon.

[50]　See Kershaw (1973a), pp. 6–9.

[51]　Holt (1988), p. 116; Langdon (1991), pp. 430–31; Langdon (1994), pp. 7, 26.

[52]　Cf. Campbell, Galloway and Murphy (1992); Campbell, Galloway, Keene and Murphy (1993); Campbell (2000). These observations are also consistent with the evidence discussed in the later case studies.

[53]　See Holt (1988), p. 116; Langdon (1991), pp. 440–41; Langdon (1994), p. 5.

[54]　Langdon (2004). pp. 14–15.

Langdon's 'Lordship and Peasant Consumerism in the Milling Industry of Early Fourteenth-Century England' (1994) is an in-depth analysis of English milling in the early fourteenth century. As stated previously, the paper draws on the IPM material for the reign of Edward II, which provides information on 1,592 mills on just over 1,200 manors.[55] He also draws on his own earlier work and that of Holt to highlight the inadequacies of previous efforts to characterize milling as an economic sector that was dominated by lordly monopoly: what he calls 'the Bloch model' of seigneurial authority.[56] The paper provides an excellent point of entry into the problems with Bloch's description of how medieval milling was organised, as well as the extent to which mills and milling were commercialized in late medieval England, and whether it is appropriate to use the term 'milling industry' to describe the commercialization of milling in the second half of the Middle Ages.

Langdon states his aim as being to encourage a reconceptualization of the nature of economic activity in the later Middle Ages. He argues that medieval milling had become a major service industry by the early fourteenth century, its material and labour requirements extending far beyond the boundaries of individual manors and estates.[57] One of his key concerns is 'the nature of investment and how it affected the structure of the industry', and 'whether ... the main driving force behind the establishment of the industry ... was dominated by the power of lordship, as Bloch claimed, or whether other economic forces, especially consumer demand, determined its future'.[58] His main point is that the contributions of non-élite social groups to economic development in the Middle Ages need to be given more weight, a contribution that is often overlooked when focusing upon the activities of the relatively well-documented élites. Obviously, this argument has some bearing on the role played by ecclesiastical authorities in the development of English milling.

In outlining the structure of milling activity in the fourteenth century, Langdon discusses the varying rates of profitability from agricultural and industrial milling throughout the country, the relative numbers and locations of windmills to watermills, who was investing in milling in the fourteenth century, the extent to which suit of mill violations were prosecuted and why there should have been such strong variations in milling practices between the northern and southern counties.[59] Contextualizing his argument by pointing out that the debate in general has revolved around whether it is class relations or economic relations which were dominant throughout the Middle Ages, he points out that, with regard to agriculture, the tendency has been to see that activity as dominated by feudal relations, whereas trade, particularly urban trade, is supposed to have been much freer.[60] The commonality between both approaches, however, is that royal governments, lords and merchants have been seen as the main players, with the lower classes excluded from playing any major economic role. This is also true of past analyses of the social and economic role played by milling, the trend having been begun in 1935 by Bloch.[61]

As we have already seen, Bloch argued that lords, and especially ecclesiastical lords, were instrumental in the diffusion of the watermill from the tenth century onwards, and dominated the feudal economy in general. Although milling was seen by Bloch as an important economic activity, he believed that it was fragmented and localized along manorial and estate lines, with the lower orders of society generally playing a passive role in the whole process, preferring the use of the handmill to the watermill, which he claimed they saw as an authoritarian imposition.[62] However, we have already seen some evidence that the real situation was far more complicated.

---

[55]   Langdon (1994), p. 9.

[56]   Ibid., pp. 4–7.

[57]   Ibid., p. 5.

[58]   Ibid., p. 7.

[59]   Ibid., pp. 8–33.

[60]   Ibid., pp. 3–4.

[61]   Ibid. As one of Britain's leading Marxist historians, it is interesting to see how Rodney Hilton's views on this issue changed over time, whereby he began to see the role of the lower classes in urban trade as increasingly important from the fourteenth century onward. See Hilton (1965), (1984), (1985), (1992). However, Hilton rarely commented on technological development, some of the exceptions being Hilton and Sawyer (1963) and Hilton (1976), pp. 20–2, 26–9, 151–7.

[62]   See Bloch (1967), pp. 151–60. This is a theme that was subsequently picked up by Pierre Dockès. See Dockès (1982), pp. 24, 28, 178, 182–96, and Holt (1988), pp. 48–53, in response.

At the end of Chapter 2, I briefly summarized Langdon's argument that the structure of medieval mill ownership was far more complex than most earlier scholars had realized. According to Langdon, by the beginning of the fourteenth century there were at least four different categories of mills which constituted four distinct sectors of milling activity. He describes them as demesne mills, tenant mills, domestic mills and borough mills.[63] The first category obviously included those mills held in demesne under lordly control, whether operated directly by the lord or leased on fixed terms to other parties. This is the category to which Bloch was referring when he used the term, 'seigneurial mills'.[64] These were mills that drew 'suit of mill': the compulsory milling custom of all the (villein?) tenants of the vill or manor in which they were located. Although most of the mills in most counties were demesne mills, they did not constitute a complete lordly monopoly on all milling, despite Bloch's assertions to the contrary.

The main challenge to any lordly monopoly came from what Holt has called 'independent mills', and Langdon, 'tenant mills'. This second category of mills included those that had been leased out on customary or hereditary leases, and were as a consequence outside of demesne control.[65] Holt has found that between 26 per cent and 55 per cent of the watermills and windmills in Oxfordshire and Cambridgeshire were run along such lines in the late thirteenth century,[66] although the maximum percentage found by Langdon from 1279 to 1540 was only 18 per cent.[67] As a consequence, he estimates that less than 20 per cent of millable grains were being processed by tenant mills in the early fourteenth century.[68] My own studies have revealed that in the late thirteenth and early fourteenth centuries, 93 per cent of the archbishop of Canterbury's Sussex mills and 86 per cent of the bishop of Hereford's mills in Hereford were in customary or hereditary tenure, as were significant numbers of mills held by other ancient houses such as Glastonbury.[69] The significance of these and other relevant findings will be canvassed in the conclusions to the case study chapters and in the book's conclusion. Taken together, this evidence seriously undermines any attempt to apply a universal model of seigneurial monopoly to milling in medieval England.

The third category Langdon identified as 'domestic mills' (after Bloch). These were mills that were not only outside demesne control but also the system of feudal land tenure, the most common type being, of course, the handmill, which was usually a rotary quern of the Roman type, but could also be a horse mill. Such mills were held by a single peasant or lordly household and used for domestic purposes. Langdon has estimated that as much as half of the milled grain at Domesday was being handled by domestic mills, although this proportion had probably dropped to as low as 20 per cent by the early fourteenth century.[70] The tenants of some manors and boroughs sought and attained from their lords licenses for these handmills,[71] but most were illegal, as the records of fines in the manorial courts and confiscation of handmills in famous cases such as Cirencester, St Albans and Bury St Edmunds testify.[72] Holt and Langdon have both found evidence that some were clearly operating on a commercial basis, which appears to have particularly offended lords as

---

[63]   Langdon (1994), p. 5.

[64]   Ibid.

[65]   Ibid., pp. 5–6.

[66]   See Holt (1988), pp. 54–5, for his calculations of the proportion of independent mills in the two counties based on data contained in the Hundred Rolls.

[67]   Langdon (1991), pp. 437–8, found evidence of around 14–18 per cent of mills in customary or hereditary tenure on two hundreds recorded in the Warwickshire Hundred Rolls and on the bishop of Worcester's estates in 1299. In his more detailed study of 333 manors, the percentage of tenant mills ranged from only 9.1 per cent in the 1360s to 16.2 per cent in the 1530s, although it should be said that the post-1300 period is generally acknowledged to be the period during which demesne agriculture was re-established throughout most of England. See Langdon (2004), p. 220.

[68]   Langdon (1994), p. 31.

[69]   See Chapter 5, Table 5.2, which shows that although the proportion of Glastonbury's mills in customary and hereditary tenure was 97 per cent in 1189, it was still as high as 23 per cent in 1307.

[70]   Langdon (1994), pp. 6, 31, 37.

[71]   Holt (1988), p. 38; Langdon (1994), p. 24.

[72]   Holt (1988), pp. 38–42, 44–5, 64; Langdon (1991), pp. 439–40; Langdon (1994), pp. 23–4. Most of the fines imposed for breaking suit of mill appear in the court rolls from the latter half of the thirteenth century. Holt found that sixpence appears to have been the usual fine, which was around a week's wages for a labourer at the time, and Langdon between threepence and sixpence.

they provided cheaper competition for demesne mills.[73] To this category should possibly also be added what appears to have been a significant number of watermills and windmills which did not operate on a commercial basis when originally built, but served the needs of large households of middling wealth, notwithstanding the fact that they did not meet Langdon's criterion of 'movable pieces of machinery'. A number of such mills that were acquired by religious houses from knights and local gentry during the late twelfth and thirteenth centuries are identified in later chapters.

Langdon's fourth category of mills is what he has called borough mills, which were mills built or held in independent boroughs (and usually in centres of population density) that fell outside the seigneurial system of land tenure that covered the rest of England. Due to strong lordship in most boroughs, which would have generally prevented the development of such mills, Langdon argues there were probably relatively few of them, although he does speculate that they were processing as much as 20 per cent of millable grains throughout England by the early fourteenth century. Because most of them were in centres of population density, their revenues would have been significant.[74] To give some indication of how high such revenues could be, H.M. Colvin and Ian Jack record the following extraordinarily high revenues from the royal mills of Chester between the late thirteenth and early sixteenth centuries, i.e., £180 in 1278–89, £200 in 1315, £190 in 1356, £240 in 1377, and £74 in 1504–27.[75] Similarly high sums were received from the Darlington mills in the See of Durham in the late fourteenth century, i.e., £93 6s 8d in 1377–80.[76]

Lords in the south invested in new mills at a high rate during the thirteenth and fourteenth centuries, and were able to extract high revenues from their mills in urban centres.[77] The new technology of the windmill made a significant contribution within this overall growth in the trade. Langdon estimates there were as many as 4,000 windmills throughout England by the early fourteenth century,[78] which is quite extraordinary considering that their earliest appearance can only be firmly dated to the 1180s, and could on this basis be interpreted as a revolutionary development in milling technology.[79] As noted previously, the vast majority of these new mills were built in areas that lacked sufficient water resources to build enough watermills to meet the existing demand for milled grain in those areas. The windmill-building 'craze' of the thirteenth century was therefore largely attributable to wealthy lords seeking to exploit unmet demand for milled grain on their own manors,[80] although as we will see in later chapters, some ecclesiastical lords, such as the bishops of Chichester in Sussex and the canons of Burscough in Lancashire, displayed a precocious enthusiasm for windmill building which appears to have been independent of any perception of pecuniary gain.[81]

Langdon also found that 42 per cent of all the mills listed in the Edward II IPMs were in clusters of two or more per manor, some of which were housed in one building (sometimes called 'multiple mills'),[82] or

---

[73] Holt (1988), pp. 39–40, 42–3; Langdon (1994), pp. 29–30, 32–3; Langdon (2004), pp. 24–5, 268. These issues will be discussed in more detail in Chapters 9 and 10.

[74] Langdon (1994), pp. 26, 28 n. 71, 31.

[75] Colvin (1963), II, p. 468; Jack (1981), pp. 98–9.

[76] See Appendix C.

[77] Langdon (1994), pp. 24–6, 34. See also Holt (1988), p. 12.

[78] Ibid., p. 9, n. 23; Langdon (1992), p. 55.

[79] This is, in fact, one of the few areas in which the IRMA thesis might have some leverage, but even here the 'revolution' had well and truly ended by the beginning of the fourteenth century.

[80] Holt (1988), pp. 115–16; Langdon (1994), pp. 9–12.

[81] See Chapters 4 and 6.

[82] Langdon (1994), p. 9. The practice of building more than one watermill at the one site was begun by the Romans at sites such as Barbegal, but also appears to have been common in ancient China and in some of the larger Islamic cities of the early Middle Ages (see Lucas (2006a), Ch. 1–2). The construction of multiple mills was also common in England, particularly from the thirteenth century onwards. One of the earliest English references in the manuscript sources is from the *Chronicle of Abingdon Abbey*, in which it is mentioned that 'the double mill below the curia, and the mill-stream were constructed in Ethelwold's time', i.e., 653–c.663 AD. See J. Stevenson (ed.), *Chronicon Monasterii de Abingdon*, Vol. II, Rolls Series, 1858, p. 285. At the royal site of Old Windsor in Berkshire, Phase III of its history revealed evidence of 'a large and sophisticated mill with three vertical waterwheels', dated post 700–750 AD. See *Medieval Archaeology* 2 (1958), pp. 183–213. This multiple mill and its surrounds were destroyed by fire in the late ninth or early tenth century, after which a horizontal-wheeled watermill was constructed on the same site that apparently fell into disuse early in the eleventh

within the same system of ponds, moats and leets, constituting a mill complex. Furthermore, windmills and watermills often appear next door to one another in the same manor, sometimes with the windmill extracting suit of mill in instances where a former demesne watermill had slipped permanently out of lordly control, or vice versa.[83] This is a phenomenon that we also find amongst some of the houses in the later case studies.

Although several thousand windmills were built in England in little more than a century, the English evidence clearly demonstrates that such mills were on average only half as profitable as watermills, but cost just as much to maintain.[84] Generally speaking, windmills were only sited in places where the watercourses were inadequate or it was too dangerous or costly to site watermills. For obvious reasons, East Anglia and the East Midlands contained the main centres of windmill development, where windmills outnumbered watermills.[85] However, windmills also appear to have been built in significant numbers in the predominantly flat, windswept counties of Sussex and Lancashire, as we will see on the estates of Chichester and Burscough in later chapters.

Langdon's research confirmed what he and Holt had tentatively suggested earlier, i.e. that by the early fourteenth century, seigneurial control of the milling industry had been firmly re-established. They consequently argued that it was lords who were therefore largely responsible for steering the development of milling over the next century or so. Langdon also found, again in support of earlier research by Holt, that lords between the late eleventh and early fourteenth centuries were relatively uninterested in using watermills and windmills for non-agricultural purposes, i.e. industrial mills. This was mainly due to their relatively low revenue-raising potential when compared with grain mills, which both of them have shown was as little as one-third or less than that obtained from grain mills.[86]

In his study of lay lords' estates in the early fourteenth century, Langdon found that only 55 mills of the 1,592 recorded were listed as fulling mills, or 3.5 per cent of the total, although he points out that there is some under-recording of such mills in the IPM accounts.[87] More than 80 per cent of these fulling mills were located on manors with other watermills.[88] In his study of the West Midlands, however, he found a much greater proportion of fulling mills, although their numbers 'never exceeded 10 per cent of all mills in the pre-plague period'.[89] Other industrial mills did not exceed 1 per cent of the total.[90] Given the ecclesiastical bias in the sources for the West Midlands study (i.e. 75 per cent of all manors surveyed), Langdon's findings again suggest that ecclesiastical lords were more enthusiastic than lay lords about building industrial mills and converting grain mills to industrial applications during the thirteenth and early fourteenth centuries. But even though these findings were confirmed by Langdon in his 2004 study with respect to ecclesiastical versus lay estates in the period after the Black Death,[91] he does not appear to have noticed that he had uncovered a similar trend in the thirteenth and early fourteenth centuries.

---

century (ibid., p. 185). A more recent example was excavated at Dixton in Monmouthshire, where Newton Mill on the Mally Brook was thought to have had five watermills. One of them was found and excavated with a leet, millrace and final ditch to return water to the brook; thought to date from the period of the fourteenth century to 1640–80 when it was abandoned. A hoard of thirteenth-century pottery was also found on the site. See *Med. Arch.* 8 (1964), p. 299 (map reference SO/519144). For more detailed discussions of multiple mills, see: Tann (1967); Holt (1988), pp. 113, 131–2; Wikander (2000a), pp. 393–4.

[83]   Holt (1988), p. 68; Langdon (1992), pp. 56–7; Langdon (1994), p. 6 n. 12, 15–16. Daventry Priory's demesne mills illustrate this kind of arrangement, on which see *The Cartulary of Daventry Priory*, mss. 8, 9, 11, 12, 18, 25, 47, 55 and 76.

[84]   Langdon (1991), pp. 436–7; (1994), pp. 12–13, esp. Table 2. On the West Midlands estates studied by Langdon, he found that watermills were on average two-and-a-half times as profitable as windmills. See Langdon (1991), p. 434. The higher profitability of watermills here may have been partially due to the relative lack of steady winds when compared with the east, providing less millable hours of work.

[85]   See Holt (1990), pp. 54–5; Langdon (1994), Table 1.

[86]   Holt (1988), pp. 155–8; Langdon (1994), pp. 13–15. See also Lucas (2005), Ch. 4, for additional evidence in support of Holt's and Langdon's initial findings. These findings are further borne out by some of the later case studies.

[87]   Langdon (1994), pp. 12–14.

[88]   Ibid., p. 15. Muendel has similarly found that 75 per cent of fulling mills recorded in the registers of the province of Firenze between 1407 and 1416 were located next to other fulling mills (see Muendel (1981), p. 98).

[89]   Langdon (1994), p. 14, and Langdon (1991), pp. 434–5 and Table 2.2.

[90]   Langdon (1991), p. 436.

[91]   Langdon (2004), pp. 47–8.

Langdon does note, however, that there is no evidence that either windmills or horse mills were used by English lords to free up water resources for industrial purposes, as was the case in England in the post-medieval period, and has been claimed by Robert Philippe with regard to medieval France.[92] My own previous research tends to support these conclusions.[93]

Langdon also found in his IPM study that milling revenues in the early fourteenth century contributed to an average of around 8 per cent of lay lord's total manorial income across the country.[94] If the revenues from non-seigneurial wind and watermills were to be added to this, along with those from commercial horse- and handmills, it is clear that medieval milling was very important to the medieval economy. Based on the data available to him at the time, Langdon estimated that total profits from English mills c. 1300 were probably in the order of £30–45,000 *per annum*,[95] which compares favourably with the value of international trade between 1275 and 1500, which Dyer has placed at more than £250,000 *per annum* over this whole period.[96] Based on his later study of 333 manors between 1300 and 1540, Langdon estimated that the sector in 1300 employed 15,000 to 25,000 full-time workers, providing enough grain to feed five to eight million people for a population that was probably around four million.[97] If these estimates are accepted as relatively accurate, there was clearly over-capacity in the sector by the early fourteenth century, an observation that is supported by the evidence from the later fourteenth and fifteenth centuries, when many windmills and marginal watermills were allowed to fall into ruin, or in the case of watermills, converted to fulling mills.[98] The over-capacity which Langdon found in early fourteenth century milling conforms with Britnell's stronger definition of the commercialization of the late medieval economy, whereby commercial activity – in this case, the construction of mills - outstripped market demand.[99]

Economic Decline in the Fourteenth Century

A marked decline in mill revenues and in the incidence of derelict or damaged mills during the latter half of Edward II's reign was clearly indicated in the IPM material studied by Langdon. In the north, this can be partially explained by the raiding Scots, but in the south appears to be due more to a general economic downturn in the decades leading up to the Black Death.[100] This is consistent with the findings of other medieval social and economic historians such as Ian Kershaw, and appears to be closely linked to the crop failures and livestock murrains of the 1310s and 1320s that were discussed in Chapter 1.[101] I have found further evidence in support of these observations in an earlier published analysis of Welsh fulling mill revenues,[102] and in the analysis of Sibton Abbey's and Bolton Priory's post-plague mill revenues in Chapters 6 and 7.

---

[92] Langdon (1994), p. 15, citing Philippe (1982), and R.A. Pelham, 'Corn Milling and the Industrial Revolution in England in the Eighteenth Century', *University of Birmingham Historical Journal* 6 (1957–58), p. 175.

[93] See Lucas (2006a), Ch. 6–8.

[94] Langdon (1994), p. 13. Also Holt (1988), pp. 82–6. This is roughly consistent with the figure of 6.2 per cent of total revenues from lands in the king's custody outside Cheshire held by the Lacy constables of Chester in 1211–12. See Miller and Hatcher (1978), p. 179.

[95] Langdon (1994), p. 5.

[96] Dyer (1989), p. 305.

[97] Langdon (2004), pp. 9–11, 19. The English population estimate is based on the work of Campbell, Galloway, Keene and Murphy (1993), p. 146.

[98] Langdon (2004), pp. 28–9, 34–9, 47–8. Langdon comments that ecclesiastical estates were particularly enthusiastic about converting former grain mills to fulling mills in the wake of the plague (p. 47), a trend that has also been noted in the later case studies.

[99] Britnell (1996), p. 228.

[100] Langdon (1994), pp. 26–7. See McNamara (1997), Ch. 3, on the Scottish raids of northern England during the period 1311–22. Thanks to John Langdon for drawing my attention to this source.

[101] See Kershaw (1973a), (1973b).

[102] Lucas (2006a), Ch. 9.

According to Langdon, during the fourteenth century, 80–90 per cent of millable grain went through demesne mills in the north, whereas this figure was as low as 45–52 per cent in the south.[103] The data suggest that no more than half of the missing grain in the south can be accounted for by non-seigneurial mills, and that the other half was undoubtedly being illegally handmilled, a conclusion which is supported by the enormous numbers of hand millstones being imported into England at the time,[104] as well as the frequency with which handmills appear in archaeological digs of medieval peasant dwellings.[105] Langdon argues that much of this handmilling was commercial in its nature, and that it was this form of activity which was most frowned upon by lords, rather than the household milling of grain.[106]

Langdon's rough estimates of the four different milling sectors' contribution to the overall milling of grain in fourteenth century England is as follows: the demesne sector attracted on average around 40 per cent of custom, the borough (or town mill) sector around 20 per cent, the domestic sector more than 20 per cent, and the independent tenant sector less than 20 per cent, although these proportions undoubtedly varied somewhat from region to region.[107] Against Bloch, he argues that all of the data suggest that the marked growth in the numbers of watermills and windmills throughout the country was due more to consumer demand in a highly competitive market than it was to seigneurial pressure, and was, in fact, an attempt by lords to ensure that they gained a significant share of the profits from this increasing demand.[108]

Langdon concludes that the role of consumer demand in the growth of the milling industry needs to be given far more attention, and that the role which lords played in this process has been exaggerated, implying that theories which rely on seigneurial compulsion as the main cause of economic change in the Middle Ages generally need to be re-examined. In contrast to the received view, Langdon concludes that 'changes *within the peasant economy itself* provided the first necessary step before lords – in parasitic fashion – were able to establish their own patterns of exploitation ... Altogether, the seigneurial element in early medieval economic development needs to be balanced in a more realistic fashion against the economic aspirations of the lower classes.'[109] Langdon's observation about 'bottom up' economic development will also provide a focus for discussion in the chapter's conclusion.

The Late Fourteenth and Fifteenth Centuries

As we have already seen in Chapter 1, the Black Death of 1348–50 and the many subsequent plague outbreaks cut a swath through the English population and hence the number of people consuming milled grain. A brief discussion of trends in mill revenue and management practices in the wake of the Black Death provides some further context for some of the material covered in the chapters to follow, where the effects of the plague on the milling activities of half a dozen religious houses are discussed in some detail.[110]

---

[103] Langdon (1994), p. 28.

[104] Ibid., p. 29. With regard to the importation of handmills at this time, Langdon cites Sharon G. Uhler, *English Customs Ports, 1275–1343, with Special Reference to Trade and Transport in Hull, Boston, Yarmouth and Southampton*, Univ. of St Andrews B.Phil. thesis, 1977, pp. 78, 79, 82, 148.

[105] Personal communication from Dr Bill Day, University of Cambridge, and Professor Nicholas Brooks, University of Birmingham, during a seminar given by the author on 12 August, 2000, Centre for Medieval Studies, University of Birmingham.

[106] Langdon (1994), pp. 29–30. For example, the monks of Westminster warned their tenants of Launton (Oxon.) to desist from taking their grain to the apparently commercial handmills of some of their fellows, while in many of the court rolls a distinction is made between those breaking suit of mill and those who possessed handmills, seemingly implying that the former were purchasing the services of the latter. See also Holt (1988), pp. 39–42, which includes a discussion of the famous cases of St Albans and Cirencester.

[107] Langdon (1994), p. 31.

[108] Ibid., pp. 31–2, 36.

[109] Ibid., p. 42. Italics his. He also notes that Chris Dyer has made a similar point in Dyer (1989a), pp. 7–8.

[110] The effects of the plague on milling and mill revenues are discussed with respect to Durham in Chapter 4; Battle, Glastonbury and Lancaster in Chapter 5; Bolton in Chapter 6 and Sibton in Chapter 7.

According to Holt, mill numbers throughout England after the plague fell by around half from their peak in the early fourteenth century, and more than that in some areas. In the last decades of the fourteenth century there was a slight recovery which was cut short by a serious depression in milling activity from around 1400 in some places, the 1430s in others, and as late as the 1470s in Cornwall. He argues that with mill rentals falling to unprecedentedly low levels, lords simply abandoned any mill that required any major expenditure for its upkeep. The relatively high maintenance costs of windmills over watermills when compared with their revenue meant that they were more likely to be allowed to fall into ruin.[111]

A somewhat more nuanced picture of the changing fortunes of English milling between 1350 and 1500 is revealed by Langdon's large-scale milling surveys. In his 1991 study of 104 manors in the West Midlands between 1086 and 1500, Langdon found that the number of mills doubled between Domesday and the early fourteenth century, then declined by almost 30 per cent between the 1350s and 1440s, after which the numbers again began to recover, but only by 8 per cent up to 1500.[112] In his 2004 study, he found that between 1086 and the early fourteenth century, the overall number of mills on 197 manors in 31 counties increased by almost 30 per cent, which constitutes the peak of milling investment. Within a decade of the first plague outbreak, mill numbers had declined by 10 per cent and persisted at that level for a few decades as lords attempted to respond to the rapidly deteriorating conditions. English milling was at its lowest ebb between the 1440s and 1480s, during which time it had declined by more than 20 per cent below its peak between the 1300s and 1340s. By the 1530s it had recovered to only 10 per cent below the peak.[113]

These raw figures conceal some far more profound changes in the types of mill investment strategies being pursued by lords in response to the plague and other demographic shocks.[114] Perhaps the most significant change between 1300 and 1540 was a decline of up to 50 per cent in the number of windmills,[115] a finding that is consistent with Holt's overall assessment cited earlier and which was probably informed by his focus on estates with relatively large numbers of windmills. A decline in the number of watermills for grinding grain of 18–23 per cent was to some extent offset by a 130 per cent increase in the number of watermills turned to industrial applications throughout England by 1540, whereas the decline in the number of windmills was partially offset by an increase in the number of horse mills, which were both cheaper to build and far less subject to inclement weather.[116]

Throughout the fifteenth century, mill numbers in most parts of England continued to decline. There are strong indications that even the more powerful lords were not able to enforce suit of mill on their tenants during this period, including the large religious houses. Holt notes that many millers actively sought custom in their surrounding districts, and that although it is possible that a large number of households chose to grind at home using handmills during this period, there is no evidence for this.[117] While the general trend between the twelfth and early fourteenth centuries had been to pay either cash or grain rents on mill leases, in the post–Black Death era, cash rents became virtually ubiquitous as lords withdrew from any active involvement in agricultural production in favour of drawing rents.[118]

---

[111] Holt (1990), p. 57. Muendel has similarly found drastic reductions in mill numbers between 1350 and 1430 in Pistoia, where numbers dropped from 258 to 121, or by 53.2 per cent, whereas in the commune of Prato in Firenze, numbers declined from 67 in 1296 to 59 in 1425–27, or by only 12 per cent. Muendel checked the latter figures against statutes regulating the canals that fed these mills and found them to still be accurate. He accounted for the difference in the decline in the two regions by the fact that the dense population of the city and plain of Prato was not so adversely affected by the famines, plagues and wars of the intervening period as had been Pistoia with its more dispersed population and variable geography. See Muendel (1972), pp. 44–5; Muendel (1981), pp. 88–9, 109, n. 36.

[112] Langdon (1991), p. 431.

[113] Langdon (2004), pp. 12–13, 26–7.

[114] See, for example, Hatcher (1977), Britnell (1990), (1996), Campbell (2000), Dodds and Britnell (2008), on the broader social and economic changes that occurred during this period.

[115] Langdon (2004), pp. 36–7.

[116] Ibid., pp. 39–43. However, Langdon cautions that the small number of horse mills in the sample may have skewed his results.

[117] Holt (1990), pp. 57–8.

[118] Holt (1988), p. 71.

Holt notes reductions of between 40 per cent and 80 per cent in mill revenues on some manors held by the Bishop of Durham between 1307 and 1380, although it should also be noted that there is evidence for only 27 of the 51 mills recorded in 1380 having experienced any decline in their annual revenue, or slightly more than half of them. Furthermore, any reductions in mill revenues for Durham were against a background of extremely high earnings.[119] Even though some of the mills held by the bishop had disappeared by 1380, 14 or more new ones had been built or acquired to replace them, suggesting that the situation in the far north was probably not so dire as it was in the south,[120] an observation that is borne out by Langdon's analysis of mill numbers in the north between 1300 and 1540.[121]

For many houses in the south, the effects of the plague had been both more immediate and more dramatic. Not only did the plague affect the amount of custom a mill could expect and the terms under which tenants would lease mills, it also affected the costs of making mill repairs and the fees and wages paid to labourers and millers. For example, Ramsey Abbey allowed some of its windmills in Norfolk to stand idle in the 1350s and 1360s while it either sought new tenants or considered the financial viability of making expensive repairs.[122] Ramsey's mill revenues remained volatile and unpredictable right up to the late 1440s, which was a decade of low grain prices, followed by a slight recovery during the 1450s and 1460s.[123]

A common strategy which lords pursued to maintain watermilling capacity between 1300 and 1450 in the face of declining revenues was the conversion of water-powered grain mills to industrial uses (mostly for fulling cloth). Langdon found that there was a 50 per cent increase in the number of conversions during this period, and a further increase in the number of newly built industrial mills in the first few decades of the sixteenth century, as noted above. While excess watermilling capacity was to some extent turned to industrial uses, no such imagination was shown with respect to windmills.[124]

As with the widespread introduction of the vertical-wheeled watermill and the postmill, it appears to have been a desire to increase or maintain lordly revenues which dictated the move towards industrial mills and the use of horse mills, rather than any desire on the part of élites to minimize the burden of manual labour on their subjects. Such efforts were nevertheless part of a losing battle by lords throughout most of England in the later Middle Ages. While milling revenues had averaged between 5 per cent and 7 per cent of manorial incomes in the early fourteenth century, by the time of the Dissolution, they were as high as 17.7 per cent in the four northernmost counties, but as low as 2.25 per cent of the temporal incomes of religious houses.[125]

Langdon observes that mill developments in England followed a very different course from those that occurred on the Continent with respect to the technologies that were adopted and widely used. Mill investment by English lords tended to be conservative and tradition-bound. Although most of the growth in the construction and use of industrial mills before and after the Black Death was undertaken by ecclesiastical estates,[126] from the 1490s onward, it predominantly took place in what Langdon has called the 'tenant' sector, i.e., that sector of operators from the free peasantry, lesser gentry and towns who held their mills under hereditary or customary tenure.[127]

Langdon's explanations for these various developments are cogent and persuasive. He argues that watermills were more highly valued than other types of mills for legal, economic and cultural reasons. Legal precedent invested them with superior access to manorial water rights over other activities such as fishing, transport and the farming of meadows, as well as conferring monopoly rights to grind the grain of manorial tenants

---

[119]   Ibid., p. 161.

[120]   See the more detailed discussion of Durham's mill holdings in Chapter 4.

[121]   Langdon (2004), p. 32.

[122]   Holt (1988), p. 161.

[123]   Ibid., pp. 163–4. See also the brief discussion of Ramsey's fifteenth-century mill earnings in Chapter 1.

[124]   Langdon (2004), pp. 63–4; Langdon (1991), p. 15.

[125]   See Langdon (1994), pp. 5, 13, 18, 27 n. 67, 32, 34, 37 n. 93, and Holt (1988), p. 170, citing Alexander Savine, 'English Monasteries on the Eve of the Dissolution', in Paul Vinogradoff (ed.), *Oxford Studies in Social and Legal History*, Oxford, 1909, pp. 126–8.

[126]   A point made earlier in the chapter with respect to Langdon's unrecognized findings from his 1991 and 1994 studies, and confirmed with respect to the period from 1300 to 1540 in his 2004 study. See Langdon (2004), pp. 47–8.

[127]   Langdon (2004), pp. 55–6.

and to own and build seigneurial mills. The technology of watermills also enabled increases in their size and capacity during the latter half of the Middle Ages that were not then available to the alternative technologies of windmills and horse mills. While windmills were far less restricted with respect to where they could be sited and the economic conditions under which they operated, their reputation as reliable income generators appears to have been lower than that of watermills, even if that reputation was more a culturally conditioned perception than based on real returns on investment. Watermills were thus far better favoured than windmills in terms of ongoing investment in the wake of various social, economic and demographic shocks during the fourteenth and fifteenth centuries, even to the extent that landlords tolerated long periods of rental arrears and tenant vacancies in order to maintain watermilling capacity during extended periods of labour shortage.[128]

Holt has observed that the evidence for a marked decrease in the number of windmills and to a lesser extent watermills combined with a marked increase in the number of horse mills during the fifteenth and sixteenth centuries demonstrates that 'there was no inexorable increase in the use of water power and wind power in the Middle Ages.'[129] His comment is a thinly veiled jibe at the technologically deterministic narratives favoured by an earlier generation of historians of technology, which rather pointedly fail to acknowledge that climatic, political, financial and demographic shocks all had a profound effect on the fate of powered milling and the kinds of mills that were built and maintained. If we accept that Langdon's 2004 analysis constitutes a reasonably accurate representation of the real situation, by the end of Middle Ages, the numbers of watermills throughout England were still somewhat shy of those at their early-fourteenth-century peak, whereas the number of windmills had been reduced by half. The 'big winner', at least as far as the type of mill in which lords were investing, was the fulling mill, whose numbers more than doubled.

Conclusion

Numerous recent studies grounded in a range of theoretical perspectives have found abundant evidence of increased commercialization and consumption in post-Conquest England, especially from the late twelfth century up to 1350, and of significantly increased investment in urban and rural industries, combined with periods of sporadic growth and decline in consumption, in the wake of the Black Death up to 1540.[130] The evidence that has been canvassed in this chapter supports these observations. Mills and milling were widely recognized by lords as important contributors to the revenue-raising potential of vills and manors, and provided what proved to be an increasingly popular alternative for tenants to grinding grain at home using a handmill, despite the many demographic, environmental and political shocks which were a feature of the fourteenth and fifteenth centuries. The acquisition of watermills and windmills by lay and ecclesiastical lords made a significant contribution to their social and economic status, and as we will see in later chapters, those lords who did not yet possess them, whether lay or ecclesiastical, often went to considerable efforts to acquire and hold them, especially during the latter half of the twelfth century and throughout the thirteenth and fourteenth centuries. Furthermore, the evidence canvassed in the case studies to follow suggests that the role of religious houses in the commercialization of English milling has so far been under-estimated.

Clearly, there is sufficient evidence of lordly and tenant attention to milling profitability, investment and consumer preferences to warrant a reassessment of some of the commonly held views in both the history of technology and medieval studies about the relationship between medieval technological and economic development. However, the question of how appropriate it is to describe the development of commercial milling in the latter half of the Middle Ages as a 'major service industry' requires further discussion.

Langdon first coined the phrase 'the English milling industry' in his 1994 essay 'Lordship and Peasant Consumerism in the Milling Industry of Early Fourteenth-Century England', and used the term repeatedly throughout his 2004 book, *Mills in the Medieval Economy*. Although we have already seen some compelling

---

[128] Ibid., pp. 63–4.

[129] Holt (1988), pp. 168–70.

[130] See for example: Hatcher (1977); Miller and Hatcher (1978), (1994); Hilton (1985), (1992); Day (1987); Dyer (1989a), (1989b), (2002); Campbell, Galloway and Murphy (1992); Campbell, Galloway, Keene and Murphy (1993); Campbell (2000); Goddard (2007); Bell, Brooks and Dryburgh (2007).

evidence that milling had become an increasingly commercialized activity, especially from the mid- to late twelfth century, and Langdon has demonstrated that it drew on extensive networks for the supply of millstones, building materials, labour and technical expertise,[131] and was increasingly turning to industrial applications between 1300 and 1540,[132] he has never sought to explain or defend his assertion that milling had become an 'industry' by the twelfth or thirteenth centuries.

Questioning Langdon's use of this terminology may appear to be pedantic. However, Holt and I have in the past been very critical of the tendency amongst historians of technology to unproblematically claim that there was an 'industrial revolution in the Middle Ages' (IRMA), based primarily on waterpower, a thesis which we have convincingly demonstrated to be overblown and inaccurate.[133] While Langdon has also been somewhat critical of the IRMA thesis in his previous work, including the 1994 article in which he coins the term 'the medieval milling industry',[134] it would seem that the sheer number of watermills throughout England by Domesday constituted sufficient evidence to justify for him at least the assertion that they had attained an industrial scale by the late eleventh century. Nevertheless, if there was no 'industrial revolution in the Middle Ages', and English lords were particularly conservative in their investment in primarily agricultural mills until the fourteenth and fifteenth centuries,[135] it seems rather unhelpful to describe the many thousands of mills which primarily processed grains for household consumption as constituting a distinctive 'industry', in the same way that medievalists speak of a 'wool industry', for example.

Milling was undoubtedly a major economic activity in the latter half of the Middle Ages. As Langdon has rightly noted, it required a network of skilled craftsmen and workers with the requisite technical knowledge to build and maintain the thousands of mills that existed by Domesday, and relied upon a network of suppliers and customers for its survival. However, if contemporary scholars wish to use modern terms like 'industry' to describe a very specific set of circumstances in the pre-modern period that can only with hindsight be seen as precursors to modern industrial activities, surely they should be required to explain why it is appropriate to use such terminology. My main objection to its use with respect to medieval milling is that the contemporary usage of the term 'industry' is extremely broad: it encompasses everything from mining, agriculture and forestry to manufacturing, materials processing and services such as tourism, education and finance; indeed, many activities that even our nineteenth-century forebears would have difficulty imagining as industries. Because the specificity of the meaning of terms which historians use must surely take some consideration of how our subjects viewed their own situation, if we start using vague and all-encompassing modern terms such as 'service industry' to describe the commercialization of milling in the latter half of the Middle Ages, we arguably risk descending into Whiggism and occluding, rather than illuminating, the historical processes to which we wish to draw attention.

With these issues in mind, I suggest that the use of terms such as 'the medieval milling industry', or 'the medieval milling business' are misleading and anachronistic, because they imply a range of processes and attitudes which are characteristic of late capitalism, and thereby place undue emphasis on those processes and attitudes during a period in which they were, at best, embryonic and relatively undeveloped. Furthermore, if we want to use a term that encompasses the commercialization of milling as an economic activity with many of the features that are associated with industrialization in the seventeenth, eighteenth and nineteenth centuries, we might want to adopt a less semantically loaded term, such as 'the milling trade', which captures the commercial aspects of milling activity without implying more than is necessarily warranted by the evidence. I therefore propose from now on to use this term as an alternative to Langdon's where relevant.

Turning finally to the role played by ecclesiastical lords in the commercialization of the milling trade, earlier research by Holt and Langdon suggests that the mill management practices of the wealthy religious houses tended to retard the growth of a non-seigneurial milling sector. Contrary to the benign view of the monasteries promoted by an earlier generation of historians of technology, both scholars have argued that ecclesiastical lords generally sought to exploit their seigneurial privileges to the extent allowed by custom,

---

[131] Langdon (2004), pp. 158–75.

[132] Ibid., pp. 40–54.

[133] Holt (1988), Ch. 9; (1990), pp. 51–2, 56–7; (1997), (2000); Lucas (2005); (2006a), Ch. 6–9; (2010).

[134] Langdon (1991), pp. 434–6; Langdon (1994), pp. 13–15; Langdon (1997); Langdon (2004), 2–4, 46–7, 64.

[135] As Langdon has himself noted in Langdon (1997) and (2004).

the law, local politics and geography. When large ecclesiastical estates were able to dominate demesne milling in individual counties, or to impose their seigneurial rights on their tenants by strictly enforcing suit of mill, such as in Huntingdonshire at Domesday and in Durham during the thirteenth and fourteenth centuries, they extracted higher mill rents from their tenants than counties with more mixed ownership. Regions with mixed ownership enabled competition between seigneurial and non-seigneurial mills, even in areas with strictly enforced suit of mill, which lowered multure rates for customers and mill revenues for lords and lessees.

The mix of small and medium religious houses that form an important component of the sample for the case studies to follow was not captured in the mill studies undertaken by Holt and Langdon. Detailed analysis of this material has revealed that the Augustinians, Cistercians and minor orders provided non-seigneurial milling alternatives to tenants in many parts of England from the twelfth century onward that were in addition to the non-seigneurial mills held by customary and hereditary tenants first identified by Holt and Langdon.

However, we still do not know how many of the mills held by the Benedictine and episcopal houses in the late Anglo-Saxon and early Norman periods were built by them and how many were acquired from kings who had built them on former royal estates before the Conquest, or indeed if they were purchased or appropriated from free men, as Bois found in tenth-century France and Squatriti found in post-classical Italy. Nor has anyone to date conducted any comprehensive study of Domesday Book to determine whether any non-seigneurial mills managed to survive the Conquest. Even though the question of whether the Church was a major force in the spread of watermill technology between the ninth and eleventh centuries remains unsettled, Langdon's 1991, 1994 and 2004 studies provide compelling evidence that the large ecclesiastical estates (the vast majority of which were wealthy episcopal and Benedictine houses) were not only making far more significant investments in windmills than were lay lords in the thirteenth century, they were also investing far more heavily in converting water-powered grain mills to fulling mills and acquiring new fulling mills in the late thirteenth, fourteenth and fifteenth centuries.

The source material on which the analysis to follow is based consists of a systematic examination of charters as well as account books, surveys and so on from the late eleventh to the early sixteenth centuries. This material reveals important details about how ecclesiastical mills were acquired by all but the ancient Benedictine and episcopal houses. It suggests that rather than having built most of their own mills between the twelfth and fourteenth centuries, most were acquired through grant and purchase from kings, magnates and knights. Perhaps unsurprisingly, the proactive and even entrepreneurial mill investment strategies of the wealthy episcopal and conventual houses that were important foci of Holt's and Langdon's earlier studies were seldom emulated by the small and medium houses, or even by many of the wealthier Cistercian and Augustinian houses. While Holt and Langdon certainly did find evidence that the milling activities of ecclesiastical lords were eclipsed from the late fourteenth century onwards by lay lords, smallholders, artisans, tradesmen, gentry and merchants, their sources did not reveal the extent to which religious houses had themselves acquired both seigneurial and non-seigneurial mills from men and women of noble and middling rank from the twelfth century onwards. The implications of these findings will be discussed in the conclusions to Chapters 6 and 7, and in the book's concluding chapters.

Chapter 4
Bishoprics and Archbishoprics

Although the Normans transformed property relations and customary obligations throughout England within six or seven decades of the Conquest, they were not quite so radical in their treatment of the Church.[1] They nevertheless managed to create a new episcopal structure throughout England by 1133 that preserved most of the changes made by their Anglo-Saxon predecessors, and which persisted until the Dissolution.

The sees of six of the 15 Anglo-Saxon dioceses that existed in 1066 were moved to fortified urban centres over the subsequent few decades, their number increasing to 17 through the addition of Ely in 1109 and Carlisle in 1133 (Table 4.1). Fifteen of these dioceses were under the supervision of bishops, which in turn fell under the jurisdiction of the archbishops of the Province (or archdiocese) of York (3 dioceses) and the Province of Canterbury (14 dioceses).[2]

Table 4.1   Medieval English dioceses and archdioceses

Dioceses	Date of erection	Last documented bishop+	Province
Bath and Wells (fmr Wells/Bath)	c. 909/1090/1245	1569 d.	Canterbury
Carlisle	1133	1559 d.	York
Chichester (fmr Selsey)	706/1075	1558 d.	Canterbury
Coventry and Lichfield (fmr Lichfield/Chester/Coventry)	c. 6 69/c. 1075/1102/1121	1559 r.	Canterbury
Durham (fmr Chester-le-Street)	883/995	1552 r.	York
Ely	1109	1559 r.	Canterbury
Exeter	1050	1559 r.	Canterbury
Hereford	676	1557 d.	Canterbury
Lincoln (fmr Lindine/Dorchester)	678/886/1072	1559 r./1584	Canterbury
London	4th c./604	1549 r.	Canterbury
Norwich (fmr Elmham/Thetford)	672/1072/1094	1558 d.	Canterbury
Rochester	604	1558 d.	Canterbury
Salisbury (fmr Sherborne/Sarum)	c. 705/c. 1075/1219	1559 d.	Canterbury
Winchester	c. 669	1560 d.	Canterbury
Worcester	680	1559 r.	Canterbury
Archdioceses			
York	735	1559 r.	York
Canterbury	597	1558 d.	Canterbury

Source: Podmore (2008)

* See Hill (1900), pp. 11–12, on an even earlier reference to 'Colonia Lindi'.

+ A letter 'd' next to the final date indicates the bishop concerned died, whereas 'r' indicates he resigned.

According to nineteenth-century antiquarian Geoffry Hill, most dioceses shared territorial boundaries with shires (or counties), groups of shires, or kingdoms, whereas parishes shared boundaries with manors or groups of manors. Hill points out that although county boundaries appear to have remained largely unaltered from Domesday to 1900, manors and parishes sometimes shifted counties but remained in their original dioceses, and less frequently, shifted dioceses but remained in their original counties.[3] However, given that

---

[1]   See Fleming (2004), Ch. 6.

[2]   Podmore (2008), pp. 19–20.

[3]   Hill (1900), pp. v–vii. Cf. Faith (1999).

Hill appears to endorse the view that the boundaries of manors remained largely unchanged from the ninth or tenth century (which, as we saw in Chapter 2 is clearly not correct), his observations about diocesan boundaries should be treated with some caution.

This chapter examines the mill management practices of five episcopal houses under the jurisdiction of three bishops and two archbishops. The estates covered include those of Canterbury, Chichester, Durham and Hereford Cathedral Priories, and the dignity of an archiepiscopal prebendary, i.e., the treasury of the minster church of St Peter's, York. Both Chichester and St Peter's York were former minster churches, and all were established before or soon after the Conquest. In chronological order from their dates of establishment, the five houses were held by the archbishops of Canterbury (598) and York (late eleventh century), and the bishops of Hereford (<1056?), Durham (1083) and Chichester (eleventh century). They were located respectively in Kent, Yorkshire, Herefordshire, Durham and Sussex.

Because the sample covers five of 17 episcopal houses, it forms a substantial statistical base from which to draw conclusions about their contribution to the commercialization of medieval milling. The names, dates of establishment, dates of documented bishops and archbishops, and their associated provinces are outlined in Table 4.1, with the diocesan boundaries reproduced in Figure 4.1. As we can see, the vast majority of the dioceses which survived the Dissolution were suppressed by Elizabeth I within two years of her ascendancy to the throne.

With respect to the extents of the estates of the episcopal houses examined, Canterbury's were spread across 10 counties in southern and eastern England, whereas Hereford's were mostly located in the Midlands, Chichester's in Sussex, Durham's in the north-east, and St Peter's in Yorkshire. Canterbury and Hereford were granted large parcels of ancient demesne at their foundation, while Durham and Chichester acquired numerous vills and/or parish churches due to their elevation in status as bishoprics within a century of their foundation. Most of the Treasurer of York's endowments came from the archbishopric or the ancient pre-Conquest patrimony of the cathedral church of York.

At the end of the eleventh century, the Archbishop of Canterbury's temporal holdings encompassed 25 or more ancient manors, most of which were in Kent, but also in nine other counties, namely Sussex, Surrey, Hertfordshire, Oxfordshire, Buckinghamshire, Middlesex, Suffolk, Norfolk and Devon. By the early fourteenth century, it had considerably extended its holdings. However, it is only the Sussex manors of the archbishop that are examined here. At the end of the thirteenth century, the bishops of Hereford held more than 100 hides in the five counties of Herefordshire, Gloucestershire, Worcestershire, Essex and Shropshire, about half of which were in Shropshire. At the same time, Chichester was collecting revenues from 50 churches and eight vicarages. Its temporalities consisted of 11 manors and property in seven other locations, all of which appear to have been in Sussex. Durham held at least 39 manors in the early fourteenth century, most of which were in Durham, but also in North Yorkshire and Rutland. At the same time, the Treasury of York Minster held nine or more manors and vills in Yorkshire and one in Hampshire, along with properties in half a dozen or more locations close to or inside the archiepiscopal demesne.

This chapter provides an overview of each episcopal house's foundation, location, wealth and holdings. It also examines how its milling activities fit into the broader picture of its estate management practices. As in the later case study chapters, there are six main issues that will be a focus for analysis and discussion:

1. how many mills and what types of mills each house held at the date of its foundation, as well as in the late thirteenth and early fourteenth centuries;
2. how each house acquired its mills, as well as the identities and status of those from whom it acquired those mills;
3. in what kinds of tenure were each house's mills held and leased to and from other parties;
4. the profitability of milling for each house from its date of foundation to the early fourteenth century (and where possible, until the Dissolution), as well as the factors which shaped that profitability;
5. the role of the different types of ecclesiastical estate and religious order in providing non-seigneurial milling alternatives to tenants, along with the origins of those mills; and
6. the overall proportion of mills that each house is likely to have built, and whether there were any significant differences in the relative proportions of grain mills, windmills and industrial mills held and built by the different religious orders.

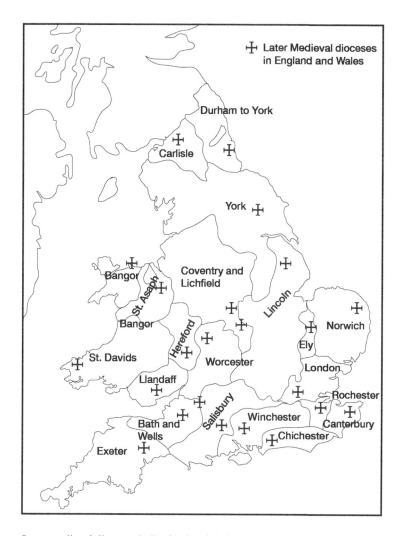

Fig. 4.1   Later medieval dioceses in England and Wales

Canterbury Cathedral Priory/Archbishopric of Canterbury

The church of Canterbury was founded by St Augustine in 598, marking the arrival of Latin Christianity in England. Canterbury Cathedral Priory (also known as Christ Church Cathedral) was the seat of ecclesiastical power in England, being the place from which the more senior of the two English archbishops wielded his secular and spiritual authority.[4] The cathedral monastery of Christ Church was amongst the largest and most influential of the religious houses in England throughout its history, holding a special relationship to the archbishop which was the cause of ongoing tension between the cathedral chapter, bishops, kings, magnates and popes for several centuries.[5]

---

[4] The other place being York.

[5] Du Boulay (1966), Brooks (1984).

Nicholas Brooks suggests that Christ Church was established on the site of a Romano-British church.[6] A community of monks was established there soon after Augustine's first mission, with the archbishop and monks adopting a 'quasi-regular' life with non-monastic clerks. This arrangement persisted in one form or another over the subsequent 150 years, after which the monastic component of the community declined to the point of non-existence for more than three centuries.

It was only in the late tenth century that monasticism was reintroduced to Christ Church by Archbishop Aelfric. Reconstituted under the Rule of St Benedict, the monks' chapter gradually grew in power and influence over the subsequent centuries.[7] A separation between the activities and possessions of the archbishop and his household, and those of the monks and their chapter was also probably formalized around this time. This separation of jurisdiction and property is known as the *mensa* division, and in the case of Canterbury Cathedral Priory has been traced by Brooks to the ninth century.[8] The division was instituted partially as a means of preventing the Canterbury monks from appropriating episcopal and archiepiscopal property upon the deaths of bishops and archbishops, but also to prevent either from having to contribute materially to the living costs of the cathedral clergy.[9] The archiepiscopal entries for both Domesday Book and the *Domesday Monachorum* (DM) make it very clear that this division was already well established by the late eleventh century.

At Domesday, Christ Church was one of the four highest earning religious houses in the country. The survey divides Canterbury's estates into those controlled by the archbishop, those controlled by his knights and those controlled by the monks. Sixty-three manors and 24 churches are listed, 25 manors being under the jurisdiction of the archbishop, 22 under that of the monks, and 16 controlled by knights, or 25 per cent of the total. Most of Canterbury's estates were in Kent, although it also held a number of properties in Sussex and Surrey, and one or two in each of the counties of Hertfordshire, Oxfordshire, Buckinghamshire, Middlesex, Suffolk, Norfolk and Devonshire (Figures 4.1 and 4.2).

The DM simply divides Canterbury's estates into those of the archbishop and those of the monks, allocating 26 to the former and 37 to the latter. Around half of the archiepiscopal estates had already been subinfeudated by the time that the DM had been completed (probably during the last decade of the eleventh century), and of these, knights' fees occupied 17 per cent of the whole Canterbury estate.[10] Many of these fees remained outside of archiepiscopal control for centuries, but not all of them were in the hands of prominent magnates and lordly families,[11] as Du Boulay found that the average fee was only one or two ploughs in demesne with a dozen or so tenants.[12]

The twelfth and thirteenth centuries saw a number of major reforms and setbacks for both the monastery and the archiepiscopate. Put simply, the monks were allowed to develop their own independent administration from the archiepiscopate during the twelfth century, but realized by the middle of the century that they were insufficiently experienced to run them on their own, so handed them over to Archbishop Theobald, who occupied the see from 1139 to 1161. Thirty years later, they again took over the job for themselves, and continued with the same kinds of reformist policies as those pursued by their mentor, i.e. replacing long-term with short-term leases, and bringing rented properties under direct management. By the late thirteenth century, however, the brethren had fallen into moral turpitude, and were poorly managing their estates. This led to royal intervention and possession on two occasions, in 1284 and again in 1297. In the former year, the monks were involved in 20 lawsuits, two of which were disputes with the prior, and another two with the king. In the early fourteenth century, from which time much of the data below is sourced, the new archbishop, Robert Winchelsey (1293–1313), reaffirmed the independence of the prior and convent, and issued a number of letters stating that the monastic lands were separate from those of the archbishopric, and included the church of Canterbury.[13] In 1291, the temporalities within the diocese of Canterbury alone were valued at £1,066 8s 1d, and at the Dissolution, £2,349 8s 5 1/2d.[14]

---

6   Brooks (1984).
7   Smith (1969), Ch. 1. See also Crosby (1994), pp. 66–7.
8   Brooks (1984), p. 158.
9   Crosby (1994), p. 21.
10   Du Boulay (1966).
11   *VCH Kent*, Vol. II, pp. 114–15; Crosby (1994), pp. 66–70.
12   Du Boulay (1966).
13   Crosby (1994), pp. 101–5.
14   Ibid., p. 115.

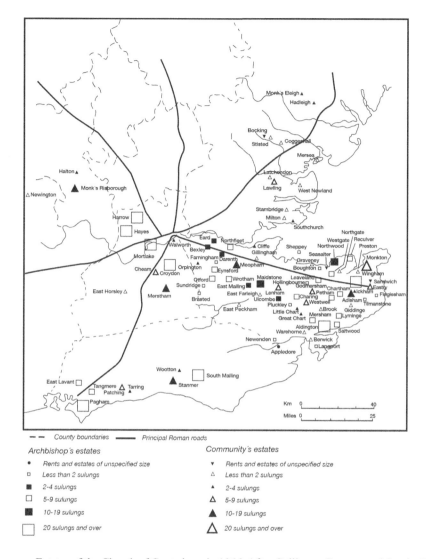

Fig. 4.2   Estates of the Church of Canterbury in 1066. After Collinson, Ramsay and Sparks (1995)

The following discussion is restricted to the Sussex manors of the Archbishop of Canterbury as recorded in a survey of 1285 and a rental of 1305. It does not cover all of the archbishop's lands in Sussex, as some had been let out as knights' fees to mesne tenants, while the estates of Wootton and Patching were held by Christ Church Priory. The survey of 1285 was undertaken under the archbishopric of John Pecham following an archiepiscopal vacancy between 1270 and 1273, during which time the King's escheator and the bailiff of Pagham appropriated significant amounts of money from the archiepiscopal estates. The vacancy had arisen because the Pope had refused to confirm the royal nominee, while the civil wars that were a feature of the latter part of Henry III's reign (d. 1272) had also taken their toll on the archbishopric's finances. The survey of 1285 was regarded as an urgent step towards restoring the financial situation of the archbishopric.

In 1285 there were seven bailiwicks for the administration of the archbishop's estates, two of which were in Sussex, i.e., South Malling (or Mellinges), which extended from the Kent boundary to the border of Lewes, and Pagham (or Pageham), about seven kilometres south of Chichester on the Sussex coast (Figure 4.2).[15] Each of these bailiwicks consisted of a number of smaller estates, as well as parks, gardens and woodlands. The bailiwick of Pagham consisted of the five manors of Loventon (Lavant), Pagham, Slindon, Tangmere and West Tarring, whereas the 80-hide bailiwick of South Malling, even though it consisted of a number of properties, was regarded as a single estate or manor and was also known as the hundred of Loxfield throughout the Middle Ages, suggesting that it was originally granted to Canterbury by one of the Wessex kings in the ninth century.[16]

Each of Canterbury's smaller estates was managed by a local official accountable to the receivers of the archbishop, who was usually either a local landholder or a clergyman living on an episcopal benefice. Each of the bailiwicks' accounts was annually audited by the receivers and an auditor, with the former then forwarding the year's revenues to the archbishop's household.[17]

Of the two bailiwicks recorded in the Sussex custumal of 1285, only South Malling appears to have contained any mills. South Malling was also the manor in which one of the two principal courts of the archbishop's barony was located, the other being the palace at Canterbury.[18] Whereas details of the rents, lands, labour services and tenants for 14 mills are listed in South Malling (including two fulling mills), there is only one reference to a single mill in the entries for the whole bailiwick of Pagham, although even this is a reference to a mill in the other bailiwick (Table 4.2). Presumably, none of the watercourses that ran through Pagham were sufficiently strong or reliable to run watermills, and none of the archbishops or their officials had ever considered windmills as an alternative.

Table 4.2   Fourteen mills in Canterbury's manor of South Malling, 1285

Name and Manor	Number of grain mills	Number of fulling mills
South Malling *'Borghs without the wood'*		
Aston	millsite only	0
Gote	0	0
Middleham	0	0
Southerham	0	0
Wellingham	3	0
South Malling *'Borghs within the wood'*		
Grenhurst	3	0
Framfield	0	0
Mayfield	0	0
Uckfield	1	2
Wadhurst	5	0
TOTAL	**12**	**2**

The entries in the custumal are divided between South Malling's borghs 'within the wood' and those 'without the wood'. The former consisted of Grenherst, Framfield, Mayfield, Uckfield and Wadhurst. These were in turn broken up into hamlets, the customary land of which was generally assessed at a single virgate, which averaged around 80 acres but was often more than 100 acres. A significant number of customary tenants held fractions of a virgate within the wood, such as John Marscal of Tangmere (a.k.a. Marescall or Marestall), who held of the archbishop Salkingham mill and half a virgate in the late thirteenth century.[19]

15   On the early history of this manor and how it came into Canterbury's possession, see Hill (1900), p. viii, n. 2.

16   *Custumals of the Sussex Manors of the Archbishop of Canterbury*, pp. xxxi–xxxii. See *Cartularium Saxonicum*, ms. 422, for a copy of the confirmation charter to Archbishop Ceolneth.

17   Ibid., pp. xxviii–xxix.

18   Smith (1969), p. 92, n. 2.

19   See Table 4.3 and the discussion below.

Table 4.3   Fourteen Sussex mills held by Canterbury Cathedral Priory, 1285

Name and Manor	Associated holding	Rent (s/d)	Tenant
South Malling *'Borghs without the wood'*			
Aston millsite	-	1/2d	John Marscal (aka Marestall) (f)
Mellinke mill, Wellingham	14 acres	10s + grinding services	Sir Richard le Waleys (f)
Salkingham mill, Wellingham (aka Framfield mill)	1/2 virgate	£2+ customary services	John Marestall (aka Marscal) (n)
Wellingham mill	1 1/2 virgates and 1 ferling	£1 1s 4d+ customary services	Peter de Molend' (f)
South Malling *'Borghs within the wood'*			
Grenhurst mill	93 acres	15s 6 1/2d + 6 d. for watercourse only	Sir Thomas de Marinis (f)
Plottesbreg mill, Grenhurst	-	-	In hand
Woburn mill, Grenhurst	100 acres	11s 11d	Philip de Woburn (f)
Uckefeud (Uckfield) mill	30 acres	15s 3d	Sir Thomas de Marinis (f)
Andrew's fulling mill, Uckfield	n/a	4s	Andrew de Luddesham (f)
Helwis' fulling mill, Uckfield	n/a	4s 2d	Helwis' de Fullestr' (f)
Bercle mill, Wadhurst	40 acres	customary services	John de Bercle (n)
Bocherst mill, Wadhurst (half share)	130 acres	8s 2d+ customary services	John de Botesfeud (f)
Crowherst mill, Wadhurst	1/2 share	2s	Simon at Breglonde (f)
	1/2 share	2s	Robert de Crowherst (f)
Curtehope mill, Wadhurst	80 acres	suit of court every 3 weeks	Sir Peter de Scotenay (f)
Pelle? mill, Wadhurst	7 acres	1s 5d	Adam at Pelle (f)

f = free tenants

n = neif or *nativi*, a cottar owing regular week- and boon-works

The borghs 'without the wood' were not broken up into hamlets, but rather into virgates which varied in size from Aston and Southerham at only 10 or 12 acres, to Gote and Middleham at 20, and Wellingham at 30 acres. Redwood and Wilson note that the size of the Sussex virgate and hide 'were clearly terms of convenience, connected with the services due therefrom, and not areal measures'.[20]

Of those borghs 'without the wood', Aston contained only a single mill site, and Wellingham three mills, one of which presumably served Framfield, as it was known as Salkingham or Framfield mill.[21] Of those borghs 'within the wood', Grenhurst contained three mills, Uckfield had one grain mill and two fulling mills, and Wadhurst five mills. Wadhurst may possibly have contained another grain mill and a fulling mill in customary or hereditary tenure, as Gilbert the miller held four acres there for two ploughshares annually, and William the fuller 16 acres for 16d and all services.[22] Neither appears as tenants elsewhere in the survey, although it is possible they were both demesne servants and these leases were rewards for service, or that they worked for others in the bailiwick.

The cash rents, tenants and associated holdings of the 14 mills of South Malling are listed in Table 4.3. Of these 14 mills, 11 paid cash rents, four of which also owed labour services. Of the other three, one was in the archbishop's hand (*Plottesbreg* mill in Grenhurst), one paid only labour services to the archbishop (Bercle

---

[20]   *Custumals of the Sussex Manors of the Archbishop of Canterbury*, p. xxxii.

[21]   Ibid., 'Borgh of Wellyngham [free tenants]', pp. 86–7.

[22]   Ibid., 'Wadhurst [free tenants]', p. 32.

mill in Wadhurst) and the other performed only grinding services for the archbishop for a month annually (Mellinke mill in Wellingham).[23] The tenants of these mills ranged widely in status, from knights such as Sir Thomas de Marinis and Sir Peter de Scotenay, to *nativi* such as John Marscal. The knightly tenants appear to have held property on former warland or sokeland; their military obligations enabling them to retain the tenurial status of their Anglo-Saxon predecessors.

The single reference in the custumal to a mill with respect to the bailiwick of Pagham specifies that the *nativi* John Marscal had to carry corn to and from the mill of Framfield for his lord when the latter was in residence at either one of his manors of Slindon or South Malling. Although South Malling was only a few hours' journey from Framfield, Slindon was a day's journey distant. This was just one of the 100 labour services that John was obliged to perform for the mill and half virgate which he held.[24] These heavy feudal burdens and the size of John's holding suggest that he was one of South Malling's inland tenants, a member of that class of tenants named 'bordars' in Domesday Book.[25]

In the bailiwick of Aystone (Aston), John Marscal also held the mill site of Blakcroft for a halfpenny.[26] Like the free tenants who held the mills of Wellingham and Mellinke, John had the right to take timber from the archbishop's woods to mend the mill. But he also had to plough, sow and harrow an acre of land with oats, and grind a quarter of the lord's corn for 30 days a year, as well as for an annual feast called Gutfelling (presumably, gut-filling!). Like other customary tenants during this period, John had been permitted to commute his ploughservice in Aystone to an annual payment of twelvepence.[27]

Peter the miller held Wellingham mill with one and a half virgates and a ferling for the same services owed by John Marscal on Blakcroft millsite, plus £1 1s 4d a year, suggesting that he was another bordar. Sir Richard le Waleys held Mellinke mill and 14 acres for only 10 shillings, although he was obliged to grind twice as much corn for the lord as Peter the miller and John Marscal. The roll notes that the previous tenant had paid £2 annually for the same holding.[28] It seems likely, therefore, that Sir Richard was either a military retainer or a lay official of the archbishop, possibly the administrator for the borgh of Wellingham.

Sir Thomas de Marinis's mill in Grenhurst is described as 'his mill' in the custumal, and is bundled with 93 acres of land for which he paid only 15s 6 1/2d annually, although he did pay an additional sixpence for the millstream.[29] He was also allowed the right to take timber from the lord's forest for mill repairs.[30] Sir Thomas presumably held a similar status to Sir Richard in the affairs of the archiepiscopate.

Of the three mills that paid no cash rents within South Malling, the first was Curtehope mill in Wadhurst with 80 acres, held by Sir Peter de Scotenay. Sir Peter's only rent was 'suit [of court] at the hundred of Lockesfeud every three weeks', implying that he also served in some official capacity for the archbishop.[31] A second mill in Wadhurst, the mill of Bercle, was held with half a virgate by John de Bercle. The customary services for virgaters in the borgh were extremely heavy, suggesting that it too, was a former inland estate.[32] The third mill, called Plottesbreg in Grenhurst, was in the archbishop's hand. It was the only mill in the two bailiwicks which the archbishop directly held, and lay outside the liberty of Grenhurst within the Barony of Leicester. For that reason neither the free tenants nor the *nativi* of Grenhurst owed suit to it, nor did anyone else 'except at the tenants' will'.[33] Indeed, none of the archbishop's 14 mills in South Malling appears to have held suit.

The very low rents of four shillings paid for each the two fulling mills in Uckfield by Helwis the fuller and Andrew de Luddesham, as well as the rent of 1s 5d paid by Adam at Pelle for his mill in Wadhurst, probably

---

23   Ibid., pp. 37, 74, 83, 86.

24   Ibid., 'Custumal of Tangmere [land owing works]', pp. 11–12.

25   See Faith (1999), pp. 70–75.

26   *Custumals of the Sussex Manors of the Archbishop of Canterbury*, 'Aystone [free tenants]', p. 102.

27   Ibid., 'Borgh of Wellyngham [free tenants]', pp. 86–7.

28   Ibid., p. 86.

29   Ibid., 'Grenhurst (Borgh) [free tenants]', p. 61.

30   Ibid., 'Borgh of Uckefeud: Demises', p. 83.

31   Ibid., 'South Malling (Wadhurst) [free tenants]', p. 31, 'Mallinges: Summary', p. 118.

32   Ibid., pp. 35–7.

33   Ibid., 'Grenhurst (Borgh) [neif tenants]', p. 74, 'Borgh of Uckefeud: Demises', p. 83.

indicate that all three mills were built, owned and operated by their tenants, and were merely paying a license fee for them, as noted in Chapter 2.[34] We will see many other examples of such licensed tenant mills in the estates of other religious houses throughout this study.

The tenants of the 11 mills who paid cash rents appear to have been free men, except John Marscal, who as noted previously was required to perform customary services in addition to the rent he paid for Salkingham mill. The only other two mills which carried labour services apart from the three in the borgh of Wellingham already described were Bercle mill and Bocherst mill in Wadhurst, the latter owing suit of court, gavelswen if the tenant held three pigs, and 12 days at the lord's hunt as a supplier of bows and arrows.[35] The rents and services owed suggest Bocherst mill was located in a former Anglo-Saxon royal vill, as the associated services bear all the marks of royal tribute, or *feorm*.[36] Bercle mill was attached to a half virgate of 40 acres and had heavy customary services attached to it.[37]

The mills of Wellingham owing labour services paid far more rent than most of the others in both surveys, the mill of Mellinke having only recently had its rent lowered from £2 to 10 shillings, presumably due to the status of its new tenant, although Uckefeud mill held by Sir Thomas de Marinis paid more. However, it would seem that most of the others were paying very low rents compared to those that were typical in the late thirteenth century on most ecclesiastical estates. Eleven of the 12 mills were held freely (which is not the same as the tenants being freemen!), including John Marscal's mill at Salkingham, with the tenants taking full responsibility for their maintenance, except in the cases of Mellinke, Salkingham and Wellingham mills, for which timber for mending was available from the common wood by livery from the bailiff.[38]

The total rents from the 11 mills paying cash rents in 1285 amounted to £6 15s 9 1/2d, of which £3 11s 4d, or about 53 per cent, was from the three mills of Wellingham. The mills were bundled with over 550 acres of land, an average of 100 acres per mill. Interestingly, the two smallest acreages were held by freemen, one of whom was a knight who performed milling services for the archbishop. Twenty years later, the mills of Wellingham were drawing slightly less rent, at only £3 5s. Because Wellingham's total revenues for the financial year of 1305–6 were £8 5s 1 1/4d, about 40 per cent of the borgh's rents for that year were from its mills.[39] Even so, the average earnings of the three mills were only £1 1s 8d each. As we will see in Chapter 5, these kinds of revenues are comparable to those of nearby Battle for several of its mills in customary and free tenure at around the same time.

The average rental for the 11 mills drawing cash rents in 1285 was only 12s 5d, with the fulling mills averaging about a third of this amount. This is around one-sixth of the typical seigneurial revenues for mills seen amongst the large Benedictine and episcopal houses of the time, and suggests either an inability or unwillingness to impose demesne management on the part of successive archbishops and their officials. This becomes particularly clear when we consider that this average is only about 40 per cent higher than the average rentals for all of the mills in Sussex at Domesday.[40] Considering that some comparable religious houses were drawing more than eight times as much rent from their mills in the late thirteenth century as they had in 1086, the Sussex manors of the archbishop of Canterbury appear to have been amongst those ecclesiastical estates that remained outside the demesne for centuries, if not permanently.

Even though a number of archbishops and chapters of Christ Church during the second half of the twelfth and the thirteenth centuries did institute the kinds of strict management policies and efforts to bring alienated lands back into the demesne as many of its larger ecclesiastical counterparts, the archbishop's officials appear to have been unable to affect the transition in Sussex. This can be seen most strikingly if we compare the average mill revenues from Canterbury's Sussex manors with the average revenue for mills

---

[34]   Ibid., 'Borgh of Uckefeud [free tenants]', p. 75; 'South Malling (Wadhurst) [free tenants]', p. 35.

[35]   Ibid., 'South Malling (Wadhurst) [free tenants]', p. 32.

[36]   See Faith (1999), pp. 102–5.

[37]   Ibid., 'South Malling (Wadhurst) [virgaters owing works]', pp. 35–7.

[38]   Ibid., pp. 94, 119.

[39]   Ibid., 'Appendix I: Rental of the manor of South Malling, 1305–6', pp. 124–5. The cash rent paid by Peter de Molend had been reduced from £1 1s 4d in 1285 to 15s in 1305–6. The other two tenants remained the same as in 1285, as did their cash rents.

[40]   Ambler (1994), p. 43.

held by lay lords in the south as compiled by Langdon for the Edward II IPMs. In the period from 1307–27, the average value for all lay mills in the south was £2 10s 8d, or more than quadruple those of Canterbury's Sussex mills.[41]

Unlike Battle Abbey and the Abbey of the Holy Trinity, Caen, that will be examined in more detail in later chapters, there is no clear evidence that successive archbishops of Canterbury during the thirteenth century made any significant efforts to bring their Sussex properties back into the demesne and direct management. Although it is possible that the problem for the Archbishop, as it was for many ecclesiastical lords, was the threat of violent reprisal from powerful local magnates who may have illegally seized their property at some time in the past, it might also have been a lack of will to maintain protracted legal proceedings to regain seisin, as such disputes could go on for decades. A third possibility, however, is that the archbishopric allowed and even encouraged the leasing out of property under generous conditions as a means of focusing on spiritual affairs, while utilizing its temporal holdings as a means to ensure the loyalty and devotion of its tenants, servants and officials. Whatever the explanation, the leasing out of demesne properties on hereditary and customary terms during the twelfth century had cost the archiepiscopate financially.

Cathedral Priory of Chichester/High Church of Chichester

Chichester Cathedral Priory began life as a minster church during Anglo-Saxon times, and was converted to the Rule of St Augustine some time during the archbishopric of Lanfranc (1070–1089). The priory accumulated extensive holdings throughout Sussex between the twelfth and sixteenth centuries, including the seisin and tithes of a large number of windmills and watermills. It was also one of the first religious houses in England to invest in the new technology of the postmill, possessing at least two and possibly as many as three windmills that were built before 1200, with another probably built soon after 1204.[42]

Chichester's donors were a mixture of aristocrats, local gentry and small local landholders. By the end of the thirteenth century, the bishopric was collecting the revenues of 50 churches and eight vicarages, most of which were distributed to a dozen or more dependent abbeys and priories, totalling £1,367 6s 8d in annual revenue. It held spiritualities in the dioceses of Chichester, Southmallyng (or South Malling) and Pageham (or Pagham), as well as in the city of Chichester and the *commia* of Chichester. Although as we have just seen, South Malling and Pagham were under the jurisdiction of the Archbishop of Canterbury, their spiritual income was collected by Chichester. Its temporalities at the same time totalled £462 4s 7 3/4d on 11 manors and seven other locations, all of which appear to have been in Sussex. The grand total for Chichester's annual income was therefore £1,829 11s 3 3/4d.[43]

The extant documents amongst the bishopric's muniments were collated and edited in the early 1940s, and cover a period from around the middle of the twelfth century up to the middle of the fifteenth century, although most pertain to the thirteenth and fourteenth centuries, and include extracts from the papal *Taxatio Nicholai IV* of 1291. The records pertaining to the bishopric's mill holdings are particularly rich, and provide a neat compendium of the kinds of mill-related documents that can be found in the records of ecclesiastical estates. They also include a number of unusual documents that record the granting of mills as compensation for certain kinds of imposition by the grantor or for perpetual prayers for the grantor and his or her heirs; the granting of land as sites for building new mills or rebuilding existing mills; the granting of parts of mill rents as contributions towards ecclesiastical building programs; the granting of water rights in relation to mills in return for cash or other concessions; and the outright purchasing of mills.

Well over 30 mills are mentioned in Chichester's cartulary, of which it held at least six directly, as well as the tithes of at least 16 others. Although it is difficult to determine precisely how many parishes were paying mill tithes to Chichester Cathedral Priory at various stages following its foundation in the late eleventh

---

[41]   Langdon (1994), p. 13. This figure is double that given by Langdon because the IPM valuations given for mill revenues are about half of the manorial values.

[42]   *Chartulary of the High Church of Chichester*, mss. 177, 180, 182, 206, 331, 352–3, 903. In *Harvesting the Air*, Edward Kealey misses one of these mills and dates another one incorrectly. See Kealey (1987), pp. 256–8.

[43]   These figures are extracted from the *Taxatio Nicholai IV*, pp. 137–8. Cf. *Chartulary of the High Church of Chichester*, p. 323.

century, a number of those that were paid are mentioned in its charters. The earliest of these is recorded in an *inspeximus* of 1095–1140, in which Count Henry of Eu confirmed all of the grants made to the Church of St Mary of Hastings upon its foundation, including the tithes of Hou Castle mill and those of the mill in the prebend of Rorer Daniel.[44] Most of the other relevant documents record the granting of mill tithes by the bishop to the vicars of various appropriated parish churches. The money raised was to be used by each vicar for the upkeep of the churches and for wages.[45]

As stated earlier, the High Church of Chichester was one of the first ecclesiastical estates to invest heavily in windmill technology. It held at least two and possibly three windmills that were built before 1200, and another that was built soon after 1204. The earliest of these was Amberley windmill, built sometime between 1180 and 1185 by Bishop Seffrid II. In 1185 he granted the mill in free alms to the Church of the Holy Trinity in Chichester for the use of the canons there, along with the tithes of the hay from the bishop's demesne.[46]

Sometime before 1183, a free peasant named William de Vescy was granted in fee-farm a mill site at Ecclesdon by the Dean and Chapter of Chichester, wherein William was permitted to build a mill at his own expense. The proposed mill was to be held by him and his heirs, in return for one mark a year.[47] William does not appear to have survived to build this mill, as it is later recorded that between 1183 and 1197 Seffrid II had built a second windmill, this time at Ecclesdon Down, at his own expense. It was then granted to his steward, Thomas de Ferring, 'for his service to the church of Chichester and myself' at an annual rent of one pound of pepper. The grant included two acres of land by the road to the mill and 'the breadth of an acre all round outside the outer end of the beam (*forinsec' capud ligni*) by which the mill is turned round'. He also gave right of way to anyone from the surrounding area required to do suit of mill there.[48] The phrase describing 'the beam by which the mill is turned around' in this very early manuscript demonstrates that 'tailtrees' or 'tailpoles' were indeed a feature of postmills from their earliest inception, as Langdon has previously speculated.[49] Ecclesdon windmill was later sold by the Augustinian Priory of Tortington to the Dean and Chapter of Chichester for 25 marks (£16 13s 4d) sometime before 1197. The mill had been given to Tortington Priory by Thomas de Ferring, the steward of Seffrid II, at some indeterminate time previously.[50]

Sometime around 1199, what was presumably another windmill at Middelton was held by Robert de la Haye. He had already granted four shillings a year in rent to the church of Erlinton (one of Chichester's appropriations) for his mother's soul, while this grant involved the provision of an additional four shillings a year to the church for his own salvation. The fact that it was a windmill is suggested by Robert's comment that the rent was to be rendered 'wherever [the mill] may be' (*ubicumque situm fuerit*), and that if it ceased to exist he or his heirs would warrant the rent.[51] The bishopric still held the tithes of the manor of Middleton in 1444.[52]

Another windmill was built by Ranulf de Warham, Seffrid's successor, sometime between 1204 and 1222, within the manor of Bishopstone at a place called Werdon Down next to the already existing watermill. Ranulf records that he similarly built this mill at his own expense on the land granted the canons by Seffrid. The grant included the breadth of a rod of land 'outside the outer end of the beam by which the mill is turned round' (the same phrase that occurs in the charter for the Ecclesdon Down windmill), the suit of mill of the men of the manor and any others who chose to grind there, as well as free access to and from the mill, and 'pasture for a horse and other animals'. Ranulf reserved the right of free multure to himself and his successors.[53]

---

44 Ibid., ms. 945.

45 Ibid., mss. 915, 247, 432, 233, 717.

46 Ibid., ms. 177.

47 Ibid., ms. 362.

48 Ibid., ms. 180.

49 See Langdon (2004), p. 124.

50 *Chartulary of the High Church of Chichester*, ms. 182.

51 Ibid., ms. 331.

52 Ibid., ms. 1092.

53 Ibid., ms. 206. As Kealey points out, the construction of this mill was wrongly attributed to Seffrid II in a catalogue of the achievements of the various bishops of Chichester dated to c. 1375 (see Kealey [1987], p. 258, citing ms. 903). However, Kealey himself gets Ranulf's dates wrong and claims that this mill was built as late as 1217–22, although ms. 352 clearly indicates that it may have been built as early as 1204, when Ranulf first became bishop.

As there is no clear indication in any of Chichester's foundation charters as to whether it held any mills outright at its foundation, one must assume that it did not, although it was collecting tithes from the mills of Hou Castle and Rorer Daniel. Of the 13 mills recorded in its charters in which it had a clear interest, only six appear to have been directly held by it. Of these six, four were built by successive archbishops and bishops associated with the priory: the windmills of Amberley and Ecclesdon, and the windmill and watermill of Bishopstone. A fifth – La Hale mill – was purchased by Bishop John II as a gift to St Pancras Church. The rents of three other mills were granted to the canons, one of which, Fordres mill, was later fully acquired by them. At least two other mills paid tithes only.

The earliest of Chichester's mill-related documents refers to a watermill at Bishopstone which regularly reappears within the priory's cartulary over the subsequent hundred years or so. Bishopstone watermill was granted by Seffrid II to the Canons of Chichester sometime between 1189 and 1191 after the bishop had paid the former owners of the mill, Reynold de London and his wife, five marks (£3 6s 8d) for their rights in it. The bishop also granted the canons the tithes of a portion of land formerly held by Leffelm the miller and others, along with two brooks. The mill appears to have been earning 13s 4d a year for the previous bishop, John, and had been built by Pagan the clerk 'of good memory'. Reynold and his wife were Pagan's heirs. The mill was intended to provide for the distribution of annual benefactions to various obedientiaries upon the anniversary of Seffrid's death.[54] This arrangement was confirmed in a charter of 1189–97,[55] and again acknowledged in a charter dated to 1222 or later, in which it was stated that the dole established by Seffrid was now insufficient to its original purpose.[56]

Sometime after 1204, Pagan de Sueise brought a plea in the bishop's court against the Dean and Chapter of Chichester over seisin of Bishopstone watermill, which he accepted Seffrid II had bought from his ancestors and granted to the Dean and Chapter 'for his anniversary', and thereafter quitclaimed any rights in it. Presumably, Pagan de Sueise was a relative to Reynold of London and a descendant of Pagan the clerk. The Dean and Chapter had subsequently granted Pagan both this mill and a windmill built by Seffrid's successor, Ranulf, at an annual rent of four marks (£2 13s 4d), as well as an entry fee or premium of another four marks. The mills were warranted to Pagan and his heirs and they in turn were prohibited from demolishing or moving either mill without the canon's permission.[57] Soon afterwards, Pagan had sold his interest in the Bishopstone mills to Roger de Warham, who in turn sold them back to the Dean and Chapter of Chichester for 16 marks (£10 13s 4d) with their suit. Roger was also to be acquitted of an annual payment of sixpence to Pagan.[58]

Both mills appear to have still been held directly by the Dean and Chapter at the end of the thirteenth century, when a charter of 5 March 1293–94 records an agreement between them and the bishop to let the mills to the latter in perpetual fee farm at £4 a year. The document also records that the Dean and Chapter were to be released from paying an annual rent of 14s 4d, presumably to the bishop, and that during an episcopal vacancy if the full rent was not paid by the king's bailiffs, the succeeding bishop was to make amends. While the payment of 14s 4d to the bishop by the Dean and Chapter is not recorded elsewhere, the sum of this amount with the four marks a year charged earlier in the century to Pagan de Sueise adds up to £3 7s 8d, i.e., around 12 shillings less than the amount specified in this agreement of 1293–94.[59]

A share of the rent of another mill was granted to the priory by Franco de Bohun sometime before 1196. It amounted to 10 shillings a year from his mill of Fordres, the money being intended to go towards the construction of a new building within the priory's precincts. Once the building was finished, the same amount was to be included in the priory's common fund, and Franco warranted the grant should the mill fail. The grant was in exchange for prayers for his and his wife's salvation.[60] The mill was still operating in the first half of the fifteenth century and had presumably come into the priory's full possession some time during the intervening period.[61]

54   *Chartulary of the High Church of Chichester*, ms. 179.

55   Ibid., ms. 181.

56   Ibid., ms. 186.

57   Ibid., ms. 352. It should be noted that the first time this mill is clearly identified as a watermill is in this charter.

58   Ibid., ms. 353.

59   Ibid., ms. 458.

60   Ibid., ms. 323.

61   Ibid., ms. 1110, dated 20 May 1428.

A grant of a mill site was made by one Robert Marsh to the bishop between 1204 and 1207. The property in question was located under the cliff between Amberley and Recham (Rackham), and included a pond. The charter records the grant was for the construction of a watermill 'or other improvement'.[62] As there remained only one mill in Amberley at the time of a papal confirmation of 1261–64, it would appear that the proposed watermill was never built.[63]

Between 1239 and 1256, 'a site with buildings ... in which once was a millpond' was granted by the Dean of Chichester to one Serlo le Tapiner and his wife Richolda for 3s 2d annually. It is not clear from the description of the land whether this was the same site mentioned in the previous charter, although this seems unlikely, as this one appears to have been close to Chichester, whereas the previously described site was at least 20 kilometres away.[64] Either way, both charters provide further evidence of the bishops' and canons' enthusiasm for mill building.

Another series of documents from the same period records the granting of various shares of the mill of Fitelworth to the Bishop of Chichester. The first share was from William de la Lee, who warranted annual payments of 8s 4d to the Abbot of Fécamp, and 16 pence to the Parson of Fitelworth, in return for which the bishop 'renounced all covenants in existing writings'.[65] The second share was from William de Bykewell, with no other details provided,[66] while the third was from Isabella de Grafham, similarly with no other details.[67] The last was from Lucy de Grofham for the remaining share of the mill, for which she received a fee of £1. Lucy was presumably the sister, sister-in-law, daughter or mother of Isabella.[68]

Two other documents from c. 1375[69] and 1407–8[70] make oblique references to the Fitelworth mill. The only other detailed entry about it relates to an agreement of 1288 to 1305 between the bishop and Henry Fizderay for the bishop 'to stop the watercourse on [Henry's] land, east of Fiteleworth mill, provided that his meadows are not damaged'. In exchange, Henry and his heirs were given free suit of the mill, as well as the right to grind their corn as soon as they arrived there, unless the bishop's corn was already waiting to be ground.[71] Whoever served as the miller was also bound to swear his fealty on this agreement, and Henry and his heirs were given the right to 'restore the watercourse to its former state' if the bishop or his successors broke this contract.[72]

Between 1253 and 1256, Bishop John II granted to the church of St Pancras in Erlinton the mill of La Hale, which Bishop John had bought from one John Gulafr'. The grant of the mill to St Pancras was in compensation for the bishop having reassigned the tithes of Ratton to the vicarage of Pevensey.[73] Another charter dated to c. 1253 records a grant from Eustace de Sessingham of a seam of barley to the prebendary of Erlinton and his successors. This had been formerly paid to Eustace for the right of way to the mill of La Hale, although it is not clear from the grant who had been paying this sum. In exchange, Eustace was given £1 by the prebendary.[74]

---

[62]   Ibid., ms. 338.

[63]   Ibid., ms. 658.

[64]   Ibid., ms. 426. This site is described as being 'between the land of Philip de Newtona on the east and the Lavant on the west'. The vills of Nyton and Norton are about eight kilometres east of Chichester.

[65]   Ibid., ms. 827.

[66]   Ibid., ms. 828.

[67]   Ibid.

[68]   Ibid., ms. 861.

[69]   Ibid., ms. 903.

[70]   Ibid., ms. 860.

[71]   The right to grind grain 'hopper free', i.e. to jump to the head of the queue, was a special privilege that was usually only reserved to lords and their greater free tenants, while others generally had to pay for the privilege. Holt (1988), p. 49, records an instance of two people on the manor of East Brent (Soms.) who paid threepence each in the 1330s to grind their grain 'next after the corn which is in the hopper'. See also Langdon (2004), pp. 274, 277, who cites an instance from Durham Cathedral Priory in which the tenants living on the manor were given priority over outsiders.

[72]   *Chartulary of the High Church of Chichester*, ms. 862.

[73]   Ibid., ms. 620.

[74]   Ibid., ms. 1073.

Table 4.4   Thirteen mills in which Chichester Cathedral Priory held an interest before 1340

Name	Year acquired	Grantor	Grantee	Annual revenue
Hou Castle mill	<1095–1140	?	Bishop of Chichester	tithes only
Rorer Daniel mill	<1095–1140	?	Bishop of Chichester	tithes only
Amberley windmill	1180–85	Bishop Seffrid II [built by priory]	Church of the Holy Trinity, Chichester	?
Ecclesdon windmill (with suit)	1183–97	Bishop Seffrid II [built by priory]	Thomas de Ferring (steward)	1 lb pepper
		Thomas de Ferring (steward)	Tortington Priory	
		Tortington Priory [sale]	Dean and Chapter of Chichester	
Bishopstone watermill (with suit)	1189–91	Reynold de London and wife [sale]	Bishop Seffrid II	16s 8d
		Bishop Seffrid II	Dean and Chapter of Chichester	
		Dean and Chapter of Chichester	Pagan de Sueise	
		Pagan de Sueise	Roger de Warham	
		Roger de Warham	Dean and Chapter of Chichester	
		Dean and Chapter of Chichester	Bishop of Chichester	
Bishopstone windmill (with suit)	1204–22	Bishop Ranulf [built by priory]	Dean and Chapter of Chichester	£3 6s 8d (<1204 for wind and watermills)
		Dean and Chapter of Chichester	Pagan de Sueise	£2 13s 4d (1293/4 for wind and watermills)
		Pagan de Sueise	Roger de Warham	£10 13s 4d (purchase price for wind and watermills)
		Roger de Warham	Dean and Chapter of Chichester	£4 (farm of wind and watermill)
	1294–94	Dean and Chapter of Chichester	Bishop of Chichester	
Fordres mill	<1196	Franco de Bohun (kt.)	Bishop of Chichester	10s (rent only)
Middelton mill	c. 1199	Robert de la Haye	Bishop of Chichester	4s (rent only)
Horsham mill	<1231	?	Bishop of Chichester	tithes only
Bigneur (?) watermill	1244–53	Hugh Saunzaver (kt.)	Chapel of St Cross, Bigneur (Bishop of Chichester)	£1 10s (rent only)
Fitelworth mill (with suit)	mid-13th c.	William de la Lee	Richard de Wych, Bishop of Chichester	9s 8d
		William de Bykewell	Richard, Bishop of Chichester	?
		Isabella de Grafham	Richard, Bishop of Chichester	?
		Lucy de Grofham (incl. £1 fee)	Richard, Bishop of Chichester	?
La Hale mill	<1253–56	John Gulafr' [sale] Bishop John II	Bishop John II Church of St Pancras, Erlinton	?
Launcyngge mill	<1334–35	?	Bishop of Chichester	tithes only

The details of all of Chichester's mill acquisitions are set out in Table 4.4. Chichester is the only episcopal house in the sample to have displayed any enthusiasm for mill building, being one of the pioneer windmill-builders in England. The geography of the area played an important role in this regard; being relatively flat and close to the sea, it enjoys a reliable source of wind power. Interestingly, all the mills built by the bishops of Chichester were constructed between c. 1180 and c. 1222, which is considerably earlier than the period during which most other lay and ecclesiastical lords entered their most intensive mill-building phases, i.e., the 1230s to 1280s. It would seem, therefore, that this early enthusiasm for mill building had much to do with the personalities of Bishop Seffrid II and his successor, Ranulf, who both presumably had a personal interest in mill technology. Chichester was unusual amongst the southern houses examined in this and the other case study chapters in that more than half of the mills that it directly held were windmills. Some of these issues will be explored in more detail in Chapter 10.

With regard to those who donated or sold the priory mills or mill rents, two of the donors were men of the knightly class, one was a cleric and three were local burgesses. Chichester thus appears to have been fairly unusual amongst the episcopal houses examined in the sample in that it appears to have acquired half of its donor interests in mills from burgesses. What is also interesting about the bishop's mills is that of the six that came into his full possession (i.e. Amberley, Ecclesdon and Bishopstone windmills, and the watermills of Bishopstone, Fitelworth and La Hale), he appears to have retained only three of them (i.e. the two Bishopstone mills and the mill of Fitelworth). All of these mills held suit, as did the windmill of Ecclesdon, which ultimately found its way back into the hands of the Dean and Chapter of Chichester after passing through the hands of the bishop's steward, Thomas de Ferring, and Tortington Priory.

With regard to the revenues that Chichester was collecting from its mills, only the Bishopstone and Fitelworth mills and those held by nearby Shulbrede Priory as recorded in the *Taxatio Nicholai IV* appear to have been drawing anything approaching the seigneurial mill rents enjoyed by the Benedictine and Cistercian houses studied, for the simple reason that these are the only mills with suit which they directly held.

Cathedral Church of Hereford/Bishopric of Hereford

Situated within the fortified town of Hereford near the Welsh border, the Church of Hereford was established as the seat of the diocese of Hereford by Archbishop Theodore of Tarsus in 676, although no record of its foundation survives as Hereford was taken by the Welsh in 1055 and the cathedral burnt.[75] Between 1057 and 1060, Edward the Confessor issued a writ on behalf of the priests of the church, confirming they had *sac* and *soc* over the lands and people within the borough and their other holdings. The writ suggests that the *mensa* division between the bishop's possessions and those of the priesthood had occurred sometime before the Conquest, although it is possible that it may simply have been an extension of royal protection to the Hereford chapter when the bishopric was vacant, rather than a formal division of the *mensa*. There is no question that by Domesday, however, such a separation had been made, at least in theory.[76]

The Domesday entry for the bishopric of Hereford reads, 'In all there are in the bishopric [of Hereford] 300 hides, although of 33 hides the bishop's men have given no account,' indicating that they did not perform a comprehensive survey of the bishop's estates.[77] The bishop held land in six counties, including 12 hides in Herefordshire; 28 hides in Worcestershire (eight at Bockleton, 15 and a half at Inberrow, and two at Kyre); 30 hides in Gloucestershire (including Sevenhampton and the large estate of Prestbury), parts of which had been subinfeudated; two hides in Essex (the much reduced estate of Writtle); and the manor of Onibury and 53 hides in Shropshire, of which two-thirds was waste.[78]

Domesday reveals that the value of the possessions of the bishop had been reduced by as much as 50 per cent compared to what they had been before the Conquest, while of the 48 properties assigned to the canons, 28 of them appear to have been under the bishop's control. Nineteen of these estates had been enfeoffed to local knights, and 13 let to clerks and chaplains. Six individuals held eight out of the total assessment of 12 hides. A number of these estates were alienated in whole or in part in the twelfth century, the main beneficiaries being a number of military tenants and the Clifford family.[79] Some of these tenures appear to have been held by military retainers of the bishop, while others were held as knights' fees by men of higher rank.[80]

Military tenures served a political role in the defence of the bishop and the border town of Hereford. The security of the bishopric and the town were a major concern, partially due to the proximity of the estates

---

[75] Podmore (2008), p. 18; 'Transcript of the Red Book', pp. vi–vii.

[76] Crosby (1994), pp. 278–81.

[77] GDB, 182v: *DB Hereford*, 2,57.

[78] Crosby (1994), p. 284.

[79] Ibid., p. 281.

[80] Ibid., pp. 283–4.

and town to the Welsh border, but also due to the somewhat unpredictable predatory activities of local lords and magnates. The bishop and canons had regular disputes with such individuals over property boundaries, tenancies and possession in the twelfth and thirteenth centuries, some of which will be discussed in further detail in Chapter 9.[81]

A survey of the bishopric's estates has survived as what the sixteenth century surveyor, Swithun Butterfield, described as 'The Redd Book'. Along with several *inspeximi*, the book contains the rentals of 20 manors held by the church in the second half of the thirteenth century, all of which were within the diocese of Hereford. These consisted of: Barton, Tupsley, Shelwick, Hampton, Eton, Ross, Upton, Bromyard, Whitbourne, Frome, Grendon, Ledbury, Eastnor, Cradley, Bosbury, Colwall, Prestbury, Sevenhampton, Bishop's Castle and Lydbury North.

The rentals are from three distinct periods, i.e., c. 1253 to 1270, 1285, and c. 1285 to 1288, although all of them are probably based on returns from earlier in the century, as the expression '*Facta collacione concordat cum veteri originali*' at the end of the returns for Colwall would suggest.[82] The returns from Ledbury are the latest, with those from Bishop's Castle and Prestbury being the next most recent (i.e., 1285). All of the other returns are from the earlier period. There is little reason to believe that the revenues drawn from these mills varied during the period from 1253 to 1288.

The rentals record the bishopric's ownership of 21 mills on the 20 manors, including two fulling mills and one windmill. In other words, there was an average of one mill per manor, although some of the manors had more than one mill, including Hampton (2), Ross (3), Upton (2), and Ledbury (3), while six others had none, i.e., Tupsley, Eton, Whitbourne, Cradley, Colwall and Prestbury. Of these mills, one was in the bishop's hand, 11 were held freely, seven customarily and two by employees of the church. Only the mill of Grendon is specifically said to have not held suit.

Most of the relevant data are set out in Table 4.5. The status of the various tenants is indicated by an (f) indicating holdings in free tenure, (c) indicating customary tenure, (s) indicating a servant of the church and (h) indicating in the bishop's hand.

As was the case on the manors of the abbots of Glastonbury, Battle, Holy Trinity and the Archbishop of Canterbury, the Bishop of Hereford let many of his mills with considerable parcels of land. The two watermills of Upton were let with more than seven virgates and a wood,[83] while the mill of Shelwick was held in heredity with five virgates and more than two acres of pasture.[84] Bromyard mill included a virgate and a perch containing the millpond,[85] Sevenhampton and Brocton mills each had a virgate attached to them,[86] Bishop's Castle mill two carucates,[87] and North Lydbury mill eight acres of ploughland and a meadow.[88] Wymondestre mill was let with the place beside the mill for an additional four marks (£2 13s 4d).[89]

As we can see from Table 4.5, the revenues from the bishop's mills varied considerably, despite almost all of them holding suit and 86 per cent of them being held in free or customary tenure. The three mills of Ross averaged more than £6 each, although one of them was a fulling mill, suggesting that the grain mills were earning more than £6 each. These three and six other mills were earning high revenues of over £3 annually, two of which were held freely, and four customarily. Another four mills rendered between £2 and £3 each, three rendered between £1 and £2, and five rendered less than £1. It would therefore appear that by the second half of the thirteenth century, the bishop had been able to secure high rents from at least some of the mills that had fallen out of his direct control earlier in the century.

---

[81]   Ibid., pp. 281–7.

[82]   'Transcript of the Red Book', p. vi.

[83]   Ibid., p. 11.

[84]   Ibid., pp. 6–7.

[85]   Ibid., p. 12.

[86]   Ibid., pp. 27 and 32.

[87]   Ibid., p. 29.

[88]   Ibid., p. 31.

[89]   Ibid., p. 19.

Table 4.5   Twenty-one mills on twenty manors held by the Cathedral Church of Hereford, c. 1253-88

	Name	Manor	Rental	Tenant
1.	*Shotemulle*	Barton	13s 4d	Prior of Hereford (f)
	Ibid.	"	11s	Ralph de la Burcote (f)
2.	Shelwick watermill	Shelwick	£10 8s	Ralph de la Burtone (f)
3.	Hampton grain mill	Hampton	£6 (for 3 & 4)	Not recorded (s)
4.	Hampton fulling mill	"	As above	"
5.	Ross grain mill I	Ross	£20 6s 8d (for 5,6,7)	Walter le Marescal (f)
6.	Ross grain mill II	"	As above	"
7.	Ross fulling mill	"	As above	"
8.	Upton watermill I	Upton	£4 4s (for 8 & 9)	Walter le Marescal (f)
9.	Upton watermill II	"	As above	"
10.	Bromyard mill	Bromyard	£6	Not recorded (c)
11.	Frome watermill	Frome	£4 0s 4d	Bishop of Hereford (h)
12.	Grendon watermill	Grendon	7s 6d	William de Wallecroft (f)
13.	Bishopstrete watermill	Ledbury	£2 14s 4d	Not recorded (f)
14.	Bishopstrete windmill	"	£1 6s 8d	"
15.	*Wymondestre* mill	"	£2 6s 8d	"
16.	Eastnor watermill	Eastnor	£3 6s 8d	"
17.	Bosbury watermill	Bosbury	£1 5s	William of the mill (c)
18.	Sevenhampton watermill	Sevenhampton	9s	Galfridus of the mill (c)
19.	Bishop's Castle mill	Bishop's Castle	£1 4s 8d	Lord Robert Blundel (f)
20.	Lydbury North mill	Lydbury North	20 *summas* tollcorn	"
21.	Brocton mill	Brocton	2s 6d	Philip Bode (c)

The low rents from Shotemulle and the mills of Grendon, Sevenhampton, North Lydbury and Brocton suggest that these five mills – two of which were held customarily, and three in free tenure – did not hold suit. However, the fact that 12 of the mills that were earning over £2 in annual rents for the bishop were held in free tenure or in the hands of church servants suggests that he had been charging entry fees and/or increasing the rents every time a new tenant took over each mill's lease. Although tenants are not recorded for the mills of Hampton, Bishopstrete, Bromyard, Wymondestre and Eastnor, it would appear that the only mill in the hand of the bishop when the surveys were taken was Frome watermill.

It would also seem that at least two of the 21 mills were farmed by millers, i.e., Bosbury and Sevenhampton. Although it is not possible to determine the separate rentals for the two fulling mills, if we average out the rentals for 20 of the mills (i.e., excluding North Lydbury mill with its grain rent of 20 *summas* of tollcorn), we get an average income for the late thirteenth century from Hereford's mills of £3 5s 3d. This sum is slightly less than the Abbey of Bec's average income from its English mills for 1272–89, at £3 13s 7d, and significantly less than the average income from Beaulieu Abbey's mills, at £5 for the financial year of 1269–70.

Langdon's earlier mill studies suggest that the West Midlands was the highest earning region for milling revenues in the south of England in the early fourteenth century.[90] Compared to the average mill value per year for lay lords in the region that was extracted from the IPMs for 1307–27 by Langdon, which was £2 12s 4d,[91] Hereford's average revenue from its mills was 13 shillings (or 25 per cent) higher. Most of the rentals here are from 20 or more years earlier than the IPM material compiled by Langdon. The bishop was therefore clearly drawing high average rents from his mills compared to lay lords in the West Midlands, with roughly a third of his mills earning over £4 annually, although five were earning very low rents of

---

[90]   Langdon (1994), p. 13, Table 2.

[91]   Ibid. The figure quoted is double that given by Langdon, due to the fact that the IPM mill valuations are about half of the manorial valuations (see Langdon [1994], p. 8, n. 20).

between 2s and 13s 4d, suggesting that these mills had somehow escaped being brought back under the full control of the bishopric.

Finally, by comparing the total income from Hereford's mill revenues to its total manorial income, we can determine what percentage of its total revenue was derived from its mills. The returns contained in the *Redd Book* give total revenues for a single year within the period covered by the book of £788 19s 4d. This sum is comparable to Bishop Adam Orleton's estimate of £744 worth of revenues from all of the bishopric's manors in 1317, but higher than that recorded in the *Taxatio Nicholai IV* of 1291, which renders total temporal incomes of £677 6s 3/4d.[92] However, the *Taxatio* figures are generally acknowledged to be under-estimates.

The total revenues of 20 of the 21 mills listed above was £65 6s 4d. Dividing this figure by the total income gives us a figure of 8.3 per cent of Hereford's total income being derived from its mills on 20 manors, which of course may not be an accurate figure as it does not include the revenues of North Lydbury mill or its revenues from mills outside the diocese of Hereford. However, the *Taxatio* of 1291 appears to confirm that these were indeed all of the mills in the bishop's possession at this time, because it provides the significantly higher total revenue of £79 8s 6 1/4d for 21 mills.[93] The average mill revenue based on the *Taxatio* figure is £3 14s 4d, a figure which is almost identical to that for Bec's English mills. With the lower annual temporal income given by the *Taxatio*, the proportion of Hereford's manorial income derived from mills was 11.5 per cent.

These two figures compare with an average percentage for the whole county of Herefordshire as determined by Langdon of 9.1 per cent for the period from 1307–27, and 6.8 per cent of manorial income for the same period for the whole of the West Midlands.[94] This can also be compared to the mill revenues of the bishops of Worcester, who were drawing 6 per cent of their total manorial income from mill rents in the late thirteenth century,[95] Norwich Cathedral Priory, which was drawing between 4.3 per cent and 5.7 per cent of its total manorial income from its mills and attached services, the Bishopric of Ely, which was drawing about 6 per cent of its estimated gross income of £3500 from its mills in 1298, and Durham Cathedral Priory, which was drawing around 10 per cent of its income from its mills in the early fourteenth century.[96]

It would seem, therefore, that the bishops of Hereford were among the most extractive of southern ecclesiastical lords in the late thirteenth century in terms of both their average mill revenues and the proportion of their mill revenues to manorial revenues. Both figures were significantly higher than most of their peers in the south, including most of their fellow lords in the West Midlands. However, despite the early episcopal practice of letting out large parcels of land to lay servants, knights, and local lords and magnates which resulted in 86 per cent of the bishopric's mills remaining in free and customary tenure at the end of the thirteenth century, it seems to have been able to secure high annual rents from all but a handful of these mills, which continued to remain outside seigneurial control. The difference between them in their earning capacity may have been because the maintenance costs for the higher earning mills were borne by the bishop, while those of the lower earning mills were borne by their tenants.[97]

Church of St Peter's York/Treasury of York Minster

Like all the other minster churches in England, that of St Peter of York had its origins in Anglo-Saxon times. The origins of the position of treasurer of the minster and the nature of its endowments remain obscure, but both appear to have been created during the latter half of the eleventh century by Archbishop Thomas I, when he divided the lands of the patrimony among various prebendaries and supplemented them with

---

[92]   *Taxatio Nicholai IV*, pp. 168–70.

[93]   Ibid.

[94]   Langdon (1994), pp. 13 and 34.

[95]   Dyer (1980), pp. 73–4.

[96]   Holt (1988), pp. 82–4.

[97]   See Langdon (2004), pp. 193–8 on maintenance cost agreements for mill leases and the different forms these could take.

archiepiscopal lands. It would also appear that most of the Treasurer's endowments were derived from the ancient pre-Conquest patrimony of the cathedral church of York, or from the archbishopric. These included the manor of Acomb and Alne with Tollerton, and the vills of Youlton, Tholthorpe, Skelton and Wigginton, all of which are recorded as amongst St Peter's Domesday holdings. It also included the manors of Ripon, Otley, Southwell in Yorkshire, Mottisfont in Hampshire, and other lands in Newthorpe, Wilton and Clifton in North and West Yorkshire that were part of the archiepiscopal demesne.[98]

Next to the deanery of York Minster, the treasurership was the richest of the four dignities of the church. The office was valued at £233 6s 8d in 1291, and £220 in 1535.[99] During the thirteenth century the treasury acquired a significant number of additional possessions around the city of York, including the vill of Holgate and lands in neighbouring Clifton, Acomb and Bootham. The treasurer also acquired the prebend of Newthorpe about 20 kilometres due east of Leeds, as well as its tithes of grain and vegetables along with those of eight other vills.[100] The patronage of the churches of Skelton and Wigginton, and a grant of a weekly market and annual fair at Tollerton, rounded out the Treasurer's holdings.[101] By 1300, the Treasurer appears to have acquired all of the lands of his endowment, the subsequent two centuries being witness to further consolidation rather than expansion.[102]

The surviving charters make reference to at least nine mills in which the Treasurer had some interest, including the mills of Alne,[103] Newthorpe,[104] Clifton,[105] Acomb, Mottisfont, Nether Wallop, Market Weighton and Grateley.[106] However, the mills of Acomb and Mottisfont manors are not mentioned in the surviving charters, and the Treasurer appears to have only collected tithes of the mills of Nether Wallop, Market Weighton and Grately. In other words, the charters suggest that the Treasurer directly held only six of these nine mills. It also seems likely that he held mills in places other than these based on the nature of the obedientiary's extensive possessions, although whatever property the Treasurer did acquire over the course of time appears to have been ultimately dependent upon the largesse of whoever was archbishop.

The earliest reference to any of the Treasurer's holdings is to the church of Alne in the mid-twelfth century, which records an agreement between St Mary's Abbey, York, and the then treasurer, John de Bellesmains, regarding the status of the chapel of Myton on Swale, which had been granted to the monks of St Mary's. The dispute had been over whether the chapel had been elevated to the status of an independent parish church, as the monks claimed, or whether it was still a dependant chapel of the church of Alne, which would have then brought it under the Treasurer's jurisdiction.[107] This situation was exacerbated by another dispute over the siting of one of the Treasurer's mills on the river Foss in the manor of Clifton, which was located on the same watercourse as the monks' mill on the boundary of the city of York, and was apparently interfering with the waterflow to the latter.[108]

---

[98]   *Cartulary of the Treasurer of York Minster*, pp. v–vi.

[99]   Ibid., p. v.

[100]   Ibid., pp. viii–ix.

[101]   Ibid., pp. ix–x.

[102]   Ibid., p. xii.

[103]   Ibid., pp. vi–vii and ms. 45.

[104]   Although there appear to have been at least two mills in Newthorpe when the Archbishop of York separated the offices of Treasurer of York from the Archdeacon of East Riding (mss. 23 and 24), by the end of the century, there only appears to have been one mill in the vill (ms. 45).

[105]   The mill in Clifton was the so-called Fosse mill discussed below.

[106]   That there was a mill or mills in each of the manors of Nether Wallop, Market Weighton and/or Grateley is confirmed by a grant of Henry I to York Minster of the churches of Nether Wallop and Market Weighton and the chapel of Grately, in which tithes of mills are included as part of the holding. See *Cartulary of the Treasurer of York Minster*, ms. 1.

[107]   Ibid., ms. 13.

[108]   Ibid., mss. 13–15. In her discussion of this dispute, Janet Burton speculates perfectly plausibly that these were the locations of the two mills, *contra* the suggestions made in the *Victoria County Histories* for North Riding (Vol. II, p. 159) and the City of York (p. 506). I see no reason for discounting her suggestion or continuing to accept those of the *VCH* historians. See *Cartulary of the Treasurer of York Minster*, pp. vi–vii. The dispute is discussed in more detail in Chapter 9.

Table 4.6   Nine mills in which the Treasurer of York Minster held an interest before the Dissolution

Name	Year acquired	Grantor	Annual revenue
Alne watermill	c. 1066–87	Archbishop Thomas I	£8 6s 8d (1292)
Acomb mill	"	"	?
Mottisfont mill	"	"	?
Newthorpe mill (incl. suit?)	13th c.		£4 (1292)
Clifton mill	"		?
Alne windmill	post-1292		£8 (1542 for watermill and windmill)
Nether Wallop mill	pre-1300		tithes only
Market Weighton mill	"		"
Grately mill	"		"

The names of the various mills in which the Treasurer held an interest, as well as their approximate dates of acquisition, the grantor and any revenues recorded are set out in Table 4.6. The only three mill rents that are mentioned in the cartulary are from a rental of the Treasurer's estates, compiled in 1292, a year after the *Taxatio Nicholai IV*, and from a lease dated 24 May 1542. The mills concerned were drawing very large amounts in comparison to many of the mills of the southern ecclesiastical estates that we have looked at, and are even high when compared to the most extractive of ecclesiastical and northern lords. The rental of 1292 shows that Alne mill was drawing 10 marks (£6 13s 4d) annually in rents, while Newthorpe mill was drawing £4 a year.[109] The lease of 1542 was for life to one Richard Thomson, miller, for a watermill and windmill in Alne, for which he paid £8 a year, as well as a tenement for 2s 4d, and tithes of Youlton (£2 13s 4d) and of Flawith (£1 6s 8d).[110] In other words, the two mills of Alne were drawing an average of £4 a year each, at a time when mill rents in other parts of the country were still well below their peaks. While it is clear that the mills of Alne and Acomb were seigneurial mills attached to ancient demesne, that of the prebend of Newthorpe, while perhaps not attached to a manorial holding, presumably came with suit seeing as it drew such a high income. It is not clear where the mill of Mottisfont was located, unless it was on the same manor in Hampshire in which Mottisfont Abbey was established in the twelfth century. Nor is it clear whether this mill or the mill of Clifton held suit.

As we have seen, at least three of the five mills directly managed by the Treasurer before 1300 almost certainly held suit, i.e. the manorial mills of Alne and Acomb, and possibly also the prebendary mill of Newthorpe. The mills of Alne, Acomb and Mottisfont had been granted to the Treasurer by the Archbishop when the lands of the patrimony were first divided amongst the prebendaries. The mills of Nether Wallop, Market Weighton and Grately paid tithes only. The average mill revenue for the seigneurial mills of Alne and Newthorpe was £6 3s 4d in 1292, a significant sum that is comparable to the high mill revenues enjoyed by other northern lords. Once again, we can see that it was not the order to which a house belonged or the type of house that primarily determined its mill revenues, but the tenurial status of its mill holdings, which was strongly correlated to the amount of custom which they could draw. Other crucial factors were the population density of the area in which the mill was located, and the extent to which monks, nuns and canons were prepared, or in this case, permitted, to be entrepreneurial and/or extractive in their estate management practices.

Durham Cathedral Priory/Bishopric of Durham

According to the early-nineteenth-century antiquarian, James Raine, the see of Durham was originally founded as the see of Lindisfarne in 635 by King Oswald of Northumberland at Holy Island. The body of St Cuthbert, one of the see's earliest bishops, was originally housed in the cathedral at Lindisfarne. After the second Viking

---

109   Ibid., ms. 45.

110   Ibid., ms. 92.

invasion of 875, the bishop and clergy wandered the countryside for several years with the body of the saint before moving to Cuncacestre (Chester-le-Street) in 882. After a third Viking assault in 995, the episcopate was again removed to what became known as 'the White Church on Dunholme'; the saint's body was re-housed in the newly built church, and four years later, in the recently completed cathedral dedicated by Bishop Aldhune (Aldwin). In 1083, the first cathedral was demolished and the Benedictine Priory of St Cuthbert at Durham erected on its ruins by Bishop William of St Carileph; most of the new cathedral was completed by 1104 under the bishopric of Flambard.[111]

Because the church and the surrounding countryside had been plundered and laid waste several times by the Danes over the previous decade or so, Bishop William saw the establishment of a monastery on the site as a means of re-establishing order in the region. The original body of secular clergy was driven out and replaced by monks from the newly restored monasteries of Wearmouth and Jarrow. The Bishop then divided the lands of the church between the bishopric and the monastery, both of which accumulated valuable estates over the subsequent centuries. Durham Cathedral Priory's annual gross income was estimated at £1,572 shortly before the Dissolution, and at £2,000 in yearly revenues a century earlier.[112]

Three manorial surveys are extant for the bishopric of Durham. The first, dated 1183, was undertaken during the bishopric of Hugh Pudsey and is known as *Boldon Buke*. The second is a damaged vacancy account from the reign of Edward I that was undertaken in the twenty-fifth year of the bishopric of Anthony Beck, and is dated to 1307. The third is dated to between 1377 and 1380, and was undertaken during the bishopric of Thomas Hatfield (1343–1381).[113] Because the estates of the bishop have been studied and described in detail by others scholars,[114] the following discussion restricts itself to a brief description of the scope of the three surveys and an analysis of the mill-related data contained in them (tabulated in Appendix C), with some reference to the earlier research on the bishopric's mills undertaken by Holt. Summaries of the data most relevant to the discussion are summarized in Tables 4.7 and 4.8.

Tables 4.7   Summary of mill-related data in three surveys of the bishopric of Durham, 1183, 1307, 1380

	1183	**1307**	**1380**
No. of manors/vills	39	39	39
No. of mills	43	38–9	43
Seigneurial mills	41	33–4	29
Non-seigneurial mills	2	5	14
Newly acquired mills	?	12	23
Ruined/not operating mills	1	10	19*
Windmills	0	1	7
Fulling mills	0	1	3
Average mill income per vill	£5–£6 14s	£14 4s	?
Multure rate	1/13	1/13	1/13
TOTAL MILL REVENUE	**£228 9s 4d**	**£554 9s 4d**	**?**
TOTAL ESTATE REVENUE	**?**	**£5,695 0s 3/4d**	**?**

* Including two fulling mills (North Aukland and Cornforth) and one windmill (Hertilpole).

The 1183 survey records at least 43 mills held by Bishop Pudsey in 39 vills, although he may have held as many as 50 mills or more at this early stage (Table 4.8). The revenues for about 10 of these mills are incorporated into the general income from whole vills, while those for at least 34 others are given as separate figures, normally in marks. The annual revenue from the latter amounted to a staggering £228 9s 4d: more

---

[111]   Raine (1833), pp. 1–12.

[112]   Dobson (1973), p. 250.

[113]   See Appendix C for a tabular representation of the data extracted from *Boldon Buke* and the other two surveys.

[114]   See for example, Fraser (1958), Scammell (1966), Blanchard (1973), Britnell (1990), Liddy (1990), Newman (2000), Arvanigian (2009).

than the total income of the vast majority of individual religious houses that existed throughout England in the latter half of the Middle Ages. If we assume that this income refers to between 34 and 46 mills, the average income from them was between £6 14s 4d and £4 19s 4d.[115] These were extremely high sums in the late twelfth century, and demonstrate that the bishops of Durham had already been able to establish high multure rates and widespread conformity to suit of mill by the end of the twelfth century.[116] Only two of the mills were paying low rents: Burdon, whose tenant paid 16s 8d, and Great Usworth, which paid 10 shillings.

The second survey of 1307 is known as the Great Roll of Durham, which is a fragment of the annual account which itemizes two sets of quarterly receipts – including mill farms – from more than 30 manors and townships belonging to Bishop Beck of Durham. The previous two quarterly receipts are missing from the account, as are the first two entries under the third quarterly receipt. Based on the sub-totals of receipts given in the account, including those for the bishop's mills, Holt surmised that 31 manors produced an annual mill rent of £554 9s 4d, or an average of almost £18 for each manor. Expenses amounted to £28 8s 11½d.[117] He argues that although the vacancy account gives no clear indication of how many mills were involved, the later survey of 1380 conducted during the episcopate of Bishop Hatfield reveals that most of these manors had only one mill.[118]

An analysis of the published version of the 1307 survey in the appendix of Greenwell's translation of *Boldon Buke* accords with Holt's in relation to the number of mills per manor and the total revenues, but differs with respect to the number of mills and manors. The Greenwell translation reveals 38 or 39 mills on 39 manors in 1307. The total mill income recorded for each of the two 1307 quarters is £138 12s 4d, exactly one quarter of that cited by Holt.[119] On the basis of the revised figures, the average income for Bishop Beck's mills is slightly lower than that calculated by Holt. However, at well over £14 per vill, it is still very significant, and far higher than that found on any other ecclesiastical estate in this study.[120] It is also between three and four times higher than Bishop Pudsey's average mill revenue from only 120 years earlier.

Five of the 39 mills in the early fourteenth century were paying low rents of between 3s 4d and 16s 8d.[121] Consistent with the evidence discussed earlier in this chapter and in previous chapters, it would seem reasonable to conclude that these five mills were held in non-seigneurial tenure, indicating that around 13 per cent of the bishop's mills were outside his direct control in 1307.

Bishop Hatfield's survey from 1380 records 43 mills and the moiety of another mill on 39 manors, indicating that the overall number of mills on the episcopal estates had remained essentially static over a period of two centuries. However, these figures are somewhat misleading, as 14 of the manors on which mills were located in the 1380 survey are different from those listed in the 1307 survey. Furthermore, 19 of the mills that are listed in 1307 are either not listed or explicitly stated to be ruined by 1380, meaning that half of those listed in 1307 were no longer operating in 1380. In their place, an additional 23 mills had been built or acquired during the intervening period, including eight windmills, one of which was ruined by the time of Hatfield's survey.

Of the 43 mills which the bishop held in 1380, only one was under direct management while 12 were paying very low rents of between 6d for Kyblesworth mill and 13s 7 1/4d for the recently erected Tunstall windmill. One other mill was paying the same rent as Tunstall (Burdon mill) and three others were paying 13s 4d. Two mills were paying nine shillings or so, and four others less than 3s 4d. The two fulling mills paid five shillings

---

[115]   This is based on the assumption that where 'mills' are referred to in relation to a vill or vills, this refers to at least two mills. In addition, if the revenue cited is more than £10 for more than a single mill, it is assumed that the figure given may represent the sum of revenues for more than two mills, assuming an average of £4 to £6 per mill.

[116]   The only exceptions to this were the burgesses of Wearmouth, who were allowed to operate their own handmills, and William, the tenant of Oxenhall, who was allowed to operate his own private horse mill for a fixed rent while being freed from suit. See *Boldon Buke*, pp. xli–xlii and 55.

[117]   Holt (1988), p. 79.

[118]   Ibid., pp. 79–80.

[119]   See Appendix C.

[120]   See *Boldon Buke*, pp. xxv and xxxii. If 35 mills are assumed, the average mill revenue for 1307 was £15 16s 10d. If 36 mills are assumed, the average mill revenue for 1307 was £15 8s 1/2d.

[121]   Hamsterley and one of Norton's mills paid 3s 4d, Lynesak paid 9s, Westow paid 15s 6d and Rouley paid 16s 8d. See Appendix C.

each. Total revenues for these 12 mills was £5 2s 5 1/2d, or around 8s 8d each. As with the five low-rent mills cited above, it would seem reasonable to conclude that all of these mills were held in customary, hereditary or private tenure. Given the fact that several of the mills were paying an identical rent, and those paid by the fulling mills are similarly identical or very similar to rents paid by other fulling mill tenants on some of the other estates examined in the sample, it seems likely that the two fulling mills and several of the grain mills were run as licensed owner-operator premises, whose tenants were fully responsible for the upkeep and maintenance of their mills.

The first record of a fulling mill (i.e. Auklandshire) on the bishop's estates occurs in the 1307 survey, whereas five are mentioned in the 1380 survey (North Auckland,[122] Cornforth,[123] South Bedburn[124] and Wolsingham[125]). By the time the later survey was taken, however, two fulling mills in Cornforth and North Auckland had already been allowed to fall into ruin, the income from the first having dropped from £1 a year to five shillings for the site only, while the other earned nothing. The evidence suggests that most of these mills had been built since the 1307 survey, with only the fulling mill at Wolsingham having been converted from a grain mill.

Although North Auckland and possibly the Wolsingham fulling mill were earning more than the others, the average earnings of these mills were significantly less than those for the grain mills on the bishopric's estates.[126] Ranging between £1 and £2 8s 4d in the two surveys, the fulling mills earnings matched those of the lower-earning grain mills. The marginal profitability of these ventures is clearly indicated by the fact that only two of the five mills were drawing any significant rents by the end of the fourteenth century. That the North Auckland fulling mill was no longer considered a viable enterprise by 1380 is further supported by the survey registering that its site had been put to pasture for the animals of the village.[127]

Although Durham did not record any windmills on its estates in either the 1183 or the 1307 surveys, the mill data is consistent with the general trend identified by Langdon in his 2004 study, which saw fairly steady numbers of windmills from 1300 until the first major plague outbreak, followed by a decline of 10–15 per cent up until the late 1380s, which essentially persisted until 1540 when the survey results end.[128] What is interesting about these data is that they indicate the bishopric was slow to adopt (or possibly allow?) the technology of the windmill on its estates, perhaps reflecting a certain conservatism in investment decisions borne of a complacency engendered by widespread seigneurial control. If the bishopric was bankrolling the windmills' construction, however, somtime between 1307 and 1377, its desire to maintain mill revenues had clearly overcome its reticence to this (relatively) new-fangled machine.

One quarter of Durham's rental income in 1307 was derived from its mills, and almost 10 per cent of its total revenues of £5,695 0s 3/4d, even when expenses are deducted.[129] This was a significant proportion of manorial income being derived from mill revenues. Although it was not common for such a large proportion of an ecclesiastical or lay estate's income to be so derived, for some of the great French and English Benedictine and episcopal houses, it was not at all unusual.

The main factors contributing to Durham's high mill revenues throughout the period of the three surveys appears to have been the high rate of multure charged to its customers, and the high proportion of manorial tenants compelled to do suit. The multure rate is recorded in the survey of 1380 and in several final concords for Durham and Northumberland between the late twelfth and late thirteenth centuries as 1/13.[130] It would seem, however, that even though 95 per cent of the bishop's mills were seigneurial in the late twelfth century, by the early fourteenth century, that number had fallen to 87 per cent of the total, and by the late fourteenth century, to only 74 per cent of the total. These figures make it clear that despite the highly extractive mill rents

[122] *Boldon Buke*, 'The Great Roll of Durham', pp. xxv; *Bishop Hatfield's Survey*, pp. 41, 45.

[123] *Bishop Hatfield's Survey*, p. 192.

[124] Ibid., p. 56.

[125] Ibid., p. 61.

[126] The fulling mill of Wolsingham may have earned over £3 a year in the late fourteenth century in a combined lease with a grain mill.

[127] *Bishop Hatfield's Survey*, p. 41.

[128] Langdon (2004), p. 36

[129] Ibid., pp. 82–3. Cf. *Boldon Buke*, pp. xxv, xxx, xxxii, xxxiv and xxxvi–xxxvii.

[130] Holt (1988), p. 80. See the more detailed discussion on rates of multure in Chapter 10.

that continued to be charged to Durham's lessors and tenants, by the late fourteenth century there were at least milling alternatives available to both groups of people.

It is also interesting to note that while the 1183 survey recorded 43 or more mills in 39 vills, the number of mills and vills is slightly lower in the 1307 survey, with between 35 and 36 mills recorded in 35 vills. With the exception of Bolton Priory, this situation appears to have been unique amongst all of the houses examined, and is probably the result of raids by the Scots, who torched and destroyed property throughout the north during the latter years of the reign of Edward I. Nevertheless, unlike most other English lords, the bishops of Durham appear to have been able to slightly increase not only the number of mills which they held after that temporary setback, but to also maintain their overall profitability in the wake of the Black Death, a feat that does not appear to have been repeated by any other ecclesiastical lord in this study.

Britnell argues that Bishop Hatfield took full advantage of the repressive legislative tools that were available to him after the first waves of the plague epidemic to extract as much revenue in cash and labour rents as the law permitted. Hatfield's strategy was executed in the context of a set of established customs that made it extremely difficult for tenants to resist the conditions imposed on them.[131]

The fact that average mill revenues in the far north of the country at Domesday were much lower than those in the south clearly demonstrates that the bishops of Durham managed to substantially increase their mill revenues within a century.[132] These observations are borne out by a comparison of some of the mill rentals given in the survey of 1183 with those of 1307 (Table 4.8). The overall increase from the mills listed in the table reveals that Durham had almost tripled its income from these mills over 124 years, some of which had experienced a five-fold revenue increase. It seems most likely that these increases in revenue were directly related to population growth in the vills concerned, but possibly also due to more rigorous enforcement of suit of mill. Successive bishops of Durham were able to increase their mill revenues at a similarly impressive rate to the abbots of Glastonbury and the bishops of Ely between Domesday and the early fourteenth century, who likewise experienced four-fold and six-fold increases in their respective revenues from their tenants over the same period.[133]

Table 4.8   Revenues for selected mills held by the Bishop of Durham, 1183 and 1307

Name	1183	1307	Revenue Growth
Easington and Shotton mills	£6 13s 4d	£34	510%
Stanhope and Wolsingham mills	£8 6s 8d	£41 13s 4d	500%
Sedgefield mills	£5	£19	380%
Darlington, Houghton and Ketton mills	£25	£75	300%
Middleham and Cornforth mill	£8 6s 8d	£20	240%
Lanchester mills	£6 13s 4d	£13 6s 8d	200%
Norton mills	£16 13s 4d	£27 6s 8d	164%
Urpath mill	£3 6s 0d	£4 13s 4d	140%
TOTAL	**£79 19s 2d**	**£235**	**294%**

It is clear from these data that mill revenue was an extremely lucrative source of income for the bishops of Durham throughout the second half of the Middle Ages. Not only did they secure a higher proportion of their total income from mills than most other lay and ecclesiastical lords – at around 10 per cent in the late fourteenth century – they drew more revenue from their mills than most religious houses earned from all of their possessions, and were able to increase their mill revenues in the wake of the Black Death.

In the late twelfth century, the bishops of Durham were already drawing very high incomes from their mills. By the early fourteenth century, they were extracting by far the highest average mill revenue of all the ecclesiastical lords in England, amounting to between three and four times as much as that rendered to the most extractive ecclesiastical lords in the south. Durham's average mill revenue was twice that of lay lords in

---

[131] See Britnell (1990).

[132] See Langdon (1994).

[133] Ibid.

Yorkshire, which had previously been regarded as the most extractive in high medieval England. Durham is therefore unique in the survey from a number of perspectives.

Conclusion

By the late thirteenth and early fourteenth centuries, the five conventual houses examined in this chapter held more than 78 mills between them on 77 manors and 13 or more other properties (Table 4.9). Of these 78 mills, at least 37 of them (i.e., 47.4 per cent) – or almost half – were held in free or customary tenure. This finding is somewhat consistent with the figures of 25–48 per cent calculated by Holt from the Hundred Rolls, but not at all consistent with the 14–18 per cent figure found by Langdon in his 1994 analysis of the bishopric of Worcester's estates and two hundreds in Warwickshire from around the same time.[134] However, it should be noted that the proportion of independent tenant mills amongst the northern episcopal houses, at 15 per cent, was far lower than in the south, at 83.7 per cent, most of which were on 24 ancient manors held by the archbishops of Canterbury and the bishops of Hereford.

Table 4.9   Mill holdings of five bishoprics and archbishoprics and their annual revenues in the late thirteenth/early fourteenth century

Name	No. of manors and/ or vills	Total no. of mills	Mills with suit	Mills in customary and hereditary tenure	Windmills	Industrial mills	Annual revenue#
Canterbury (Sussex manors only)	6	14	0	13	0	2	£3,000+
Chichester	11	3	3	0	1	0	£1,830
Hereford (Hereford manors only)	20	21	16 (?)	18	1	2	£3,230°
Durham	39	38–9	33+	5	0	1	£5,695 (1380)
St Peter's (treasury only)	10	5	4	1	1 (?)	0	£230
TOTAL	**77**	**78+**	**53**	**37**	**3**	**5**	**£13,985**

Annual revenues for Canterbury and Hereford are based on the valuations given in the *Taxatio Nicholai IV* of 1291. The others are taken from the contemporaneous surveys examined in each of the relevant case studies.
* This consists of £2,553 19s 6 3/4d for Hereford's spiritualities, and £677 6s 3/4d for its temporalities.

The archbishop of Canterbury held 14 mills on his Sussex manors in the late thirteenth century, two of which were fulling mills, or 14 per cent of the total number of mills it held in that county. The prelate held a much larger number of grain mills and fulling mills on his many other estates. Around the same time, the bishop of Hereford held 21 mills, including two fulling mills and a windmill; the number of mills dedicated to industrial purposes therefore being about 10 per cent. The bishop of Durham held 38 or more mills in the early fourteenth century, only one of which was a fulling mill (i.e., only 2.8 per cent of the total). The very wealthy treasurer of St Peter's York held five mills, none of which were industrial mills, although it may have held one windmill.

---

[134] Holt's calculations were for Cambridgeshire and Oxfordshire, respectively, on which see Holt (1987), pp. 20–21, Holt (1988), pp. 54–5. Langdon (1991), pp. 437–8, found evidence of only around 14–18 per cent of mills in customary or hereditary tenure on two hundreds recorded in the Warwickshire Hundred Rolls and on the bishop of Worcester's estates in 1299.

In terms of the acquisition dates of these mills and the kinds of revenues that they were drawing in the late thirteenth and early fourteenth centuries, Canterbury's Sussex mills were part of its ancient demesne lands, many of which had fallen into tenants' hands prior to or soon after the Conquest. Because the archbishops' officials seem to have been unable or unwilling to draw these properties back into the demesne, most of its Sussex mills were returning relatively low revenues in the late thirteenth century. Almost 80 per cent of Canterbury's Sussex mills remained in free or customary tenure on low rents until the end of the thirteenth century, when most other ancient houses had returned such holdings to the demesne.

The bishop of Hereford's mills were, like those of the archbishop of Canterbury's Sussex mills, located on ancient demesne lands. The bishop had similarly allowed a number of his mills to fall into tenants' hands during the eleventh and twelfth centuries. Nevertheless, around three-quarters of the bishop's mills were earning high annual revenues, even though most of these had fallen out of his direct control.

Chichester's benefactors were a mixture of nobles, local burgesses and small local landholders. What is most interesting about Chichester as a bishopric was that even though two of its bishops had built three of the first windmills in the country in the last decades of the twelfth century, they had soon given away two of them to clergy under their supervision. The bishop only held three mills by the late thirteenth century: the windmill and watermill of Bishopstone and Fitelworth watermill, all of which were owed suit and appear to have been directly managed from the dates they were acquired in the early to mid-thirteenth century.

Like the Abbey of Bec, Durham kept a tight rein on all of its possessions from the earliest times. Virtually all of its mills appear to have held suit, from which it drew the highest revenues in medieval England. Only five of its mills in the early fourteenth century appear to have been held in customary or hereditary tenure, whereas this number had radically increased to 14 by 1380, indicating a profound change in mill management practices during the interim that was most likely attributable to the plague. Virtually all of the bishop's mills were at farm throughout the whole period covered by the three surveys from 1183 to 1380.

Chichester, Durham and the Treasury of St Peter's York had the highest proportion of mills with suit. Durham and St Peter's were amongst the most extractive of all the houses sampled. In at least one instance the Treasurer was prepared to enter into a long and protracted legal dispute with another large religious house in order to gain the upper hand.[135] St Peter's also appears to have been the only former minster church to have benefited from minster endowments of seigneurial mills. In the late thirteenth century the Treasury was drawing over £8 a year from one of its four mills, and £4 a year from another mill. These rents are extremely high, even when compared with those of the bishop of Durham, and clearly reflect a regional variation in the rentals achieved by lords in Yorkshire and other northern counties that was undoubtedly related to the fact that most mills in the north were tied to a seigneurial system in which feudal obligations were strongly enforced. This included charging tenants higher rates of multure than they would generally have had to pay in the south.

Table 4.10   Average annual mill revenues and proportion of mills with suit of five episcopal houses in the late thirteenth/early fourteenth century

Name	Average annual mill revenues	Mills with suit	Mills in customary & hereditary tenure
Chichester	£2*	100%	0%
Durham	£14 4s	87%	13%
St Peter's (treasury only)	£6 3s 4d	80%	20%
Hereford (Hereford manors only)	£3 5s 2d	76%	86%
Canterbury (Sussex manors only)	12s 5d	0%	93%

* Based on £4 revenue for two out of its three mills in Bishopstone in 1293/4.

135   See Chapter 9.

Even though there is no relevant mill revenue data for Chichester, Table 4.9 reveals that there was a clear correlation between the number of mills with suit held by the other four houses and the average revenues they could expect from their mills. Although part of the explanation for this correlation can be linked to the regions in which the various houses were located, in the case of Hereford, it was able to secure seigneurial rents from its mostly free tenants, despite their tenurial status. Canterbury, on the other hand, appears to have been content to accept very low rents on those mills which it had allowed to fall into customary and hereditary tenure, possibly because it was earning more than 51 per cent of its total income from 1288 to 1400 from crop sales.[136]

As many other scholars before me have noted, the most financially successful houses in the long term were those prepared to actively involve themselves in the management of their estates by introducing new farming, investment and leasing practices, and by regularly auditing their obedientiaries and lay officials. The bishops of Durham and treasurers of York Minster appear to have always been committed to closely monitoring their estates, while the bishops of Hereford only appear to have entered into the reformist spirit in the second half of the thirteenth century. The archbishops of Canterbury appear to have never reformed their estate management practices with respect to their Sussex lands, possibly because they were regarded as relatively unimportant in the larger context of their holdings. The bishops of Chichester, on the other hand, appear to have been both entrepreneurial and generous to the clergy and houses that were under their jurisdiction, indicating an unusual sense of philanthropy not often seen amongst medieval religious houses, particularly those with episcopal responsibilities. The extent to which these different estate management practices were emulated by the conventual houses sampled will be explored in the chapters to follow.

---

[136] Miller and Hatcher (1978), pp. 201–3; Campbell (2000), pp. 184–5.

Chapter 5
The Benedictines

The Black Monks exercised their financial and political power along local and regional lines through a vast number of conventual sites sustained by extensive networks of spiritual and temporal properties. The Benedictines held more property throughout England than all the other religious orders combined, and although they suffered the greatest diminution in the number of their houses from the peak of the monastic movement in the early fourteenth century to the Dissolution (a reduction of about 70 per cent), the 10 wealthiest houses in 1535 were all Benedictine. The continued economic pre-eminence of the order in England indicates that although many of the smaller Benedictine houses had had difficulty surviving the post-plague era and the greatly reduced popularity of the order amongst donors, most of the larger and better established houses were able to reorganize and restructure their affairs during the thirteenth century and subsequently, thereby maintaining their status and positions.[1]

All of the Benedictine houses examined in this chapter were founded before 1100 and most had a strong influence on the development of monastic life during the latter half of the Middle Ages. Glastonbury Abbey was re-founded as a Benedictine house by Dunstan in 943. Bec was a French abbey founded in 1034 by a Norman knight named Herluin, and endowed by members of William's retinue with English holdings in the late eleventh century. Battle Abbey was established as a royal foundation by William in 1076, and Lancaster Cathedral Priory was an aristocratic foundation by Roger de Poitou as a dependent cell of the Norman abbey of Saint Martin of Sées in 1094. The four houses were located respectively in Somerset, Normandy, Sussex and Lancashire.

Glastonbury, Bec and Battle were wealthy and well resourced, with extensive properties across a number of counties. Given their locations and the dates of their foundations, it should not be surprising to learn that most of their possessions were in the south. Glastonbury Abbey held more than 700 hides on 58 estates at Domesday, most of which were in Somerset and Wiltshire, but also in Devon, Dorset, Gloucestershire, Berkshire and Hampshire. By the time of the Dissolution, Glastonbury had retained its position as the wealthiest religious house in England. At the end of the thirteenth century, the Abbey of Bec held 26 manors and other properties in 11 counties, i.e., Dorset, Wiltshire, Hampshire, Northamptonshire, Buckinghamshire, Oxfordshire, Berkshire, Warwickshire, Norfolk, Suffolk, and Sussex. Battle Abbey's holdings at this time consisted of 20 manors and seven other major holdings which extended across the 11 counties of Wiltshire, Hampshire, Oxfordshire, Berkshire, Middlesex, Essex, Suffolk, Norfolk, Kent, Surrey and Sussex. The least wealthy of the Benedictine houses in the sample, the alien priory of Lancaster, held virtually all of its property within a 40-kilometre radius of the priory within Lancashire. It consisted of two manors, one vill, shares of the town of Lancaster and another vill, and several other smaller possessions. The sample's coverage with respect to the Benedictines is thus quite comprehensive, covering the south-west, south-east, Southern and Western Midlands, East Anglia, north-west and north-east.

As the oldest and wealthiest of the major religious orders, the Benedictines were probably the first of the orders to become involved in milling in medieval England, and played an important but as yet difficult-to-specify role in the emergence of milling as a commercial activity. We have already seen evidence that they were among the first lords to exploit the seigneurial privileges extended to all English lords between the ninth and eleventh centuries, and held the largest number of mills of all the orders at both Domesday and the time of the Dissolution. Their pre-eminence in both the land market and milling was a direct result of the order having been able to establish itself in many parts of England without any competition from other religious orders or lay lords. As a consequence, they had built or acquired hundreds of seigneurial mills before the other orders had even arrived in the country.

---

[1] That is, a reduction from 485 to 142 Benedictine houses, as opposed to a reduction from 251 to 170 houses in the case of the Augustinians, and stable numbers in the case of the Cistercians. The reasons for the decline are examined in Burton (1994).

Glastonbury Abbey

Following its initial establishment in the mid-seventh century, Glastonbury Abbey was re-founded as a Benedictine monastery in 943. The abbey quickly rose to become the wealthiest and most powerful religious house in England, and maintained its pre-eminent position until the Dissolution. Its annual income at Domesday was the highest in England: a staggering £828; more than 40 times the earnings of such small Benedictine houses as Tewkesbury, Buckfast and Swavesey.[2] Four years before the Dissolution, its estates were valued at £3,311 7s 4d annually; this was increased to £4,085 6s 8d in 1539.[3] Amongst the last of the religious houses to be dissolved and plundered by Henry VIII, the king sent Thomas Cromwell to Glastonbury to arrest and try the last abbot, Richard Whyting, on charges of treason for having allegedly hidden some of the abbey's valuables from the king's commissioners. Whyting and two of his fellow monks who had acted as treasurers were subsequently hanged, drawn and quartered on Glastonbury Tor.

Glastonbury's wealth had drawn the avaricious attentions of monarchs since at least the time of the Conquest. William I imposed the heavy obligation of 40 knights' service on the abbey, beginning the process of subinfeudation which proceeded apace during the twelfth century. William also allowed members of his retinue, such as the Bishop of Coutances and William's half-brother, Robert, Count of Mortain, to appropriate valuable thegnland and manors from the abbey. At Domesday, the quantity of land lost to the abbey totalled more than 105 hides and 3 virgates, and was valued at £109 3s annually. Almost all of it was thegnland which had been held by tenants.[4]

In 1086, Glastonbury held property in the seven counties of Somerset, Wiltshire, Devon, Dorset, Gloucestershire, Berkshire and Hampshire, most of which appears to have been thegnland and could not be alienated (Figures 5.1–5.2). More than half of its land was in Somerset alone: out of 816 hides that it held in total in 1066, 443 were in Somerset and another 260 in Wiltshire. Of the Somerset hides, 12 were tax-exempt inland and another 14 were tax-exempt thegnland. In 1066, 244 of Glastonbury's Somerset hides were held by tenants, more than 80 of whom were retainers of some kind. More than 354 hides in total were held by tenants at this time: almost half of all Glastonbury's lands. Although this figure had decreased substantially to 266 hides by Domesday, it had forced the adoption of open-field agriculture on Glastonbury's estates to provide it with the additional productivity and revenue it required to meet the needs of a growing class of landed military retainers.[5]

The classic studies of Glastonbury's estates were undertaken by Reginald Lennard and Michael Postan in the 1950s and 1970s,[6] while more recent work on the archaeology and history of the abbey and its manuscripts has been undertaken by James Carley and Lesley Abrams.[7] However, none of these scholars have examined any of the abbey's extensive mill-related documents in any detail. The first historian to do this was Richard Holt, who used Glastonbury as one of his major case studies in a 1987 paper for *Past and Present*, and in *The Mills of Medieval England* (1988). The following discussion is based on Holt's research, which draws on the Longleat and British Library manuscripts relevant to Glastonbury, a survey known as the *Liber Henrici de Soliaco* (1189), a history of Glastonbury Abbey written by the monk, Adam de Damerham (<1291), and rentals, custumals and terriers from the early fourteenth and sixteenth centuries.

The two most notable features of Glastonbury's changing patterns of mill ownership and revenue were that it experienced 80 per cent growth in 200 years in the number of its mills between Domesday and the early fourteenth century, while its mill revenues quadrupled over the same period.[8] These changes are a direct

---

[2]   Knowles (1940a), pp. 101–2, 702. Based on the assumption that the average annual wage for an unskilled worker in the late eleventh century was around £1 10s. *per annum*, as opposed to around £12,000 *per annum* today, Glastonbury's annual income translates into £6.624 million.

[3]   *VCH Somerset*, Vol. II, pp. 82–99.

[4]   Abrams (1996), pp. 311, 317.

[5]   Ibid., pp. 316–7; Costen (1991), p. 54. See Harvey (1988), pp. 107–8, on Glastonbury's early interest in demesne agriculture.

[6]   See, for example, Postan (1953), (1956), (1975); Lennard (1956); Lennard, Harvey and Stone (1975).

[7]   Carley (1985); Abrams and Carley (1991); Abrams (1996).

[8]   Holt (1988), p. 116.

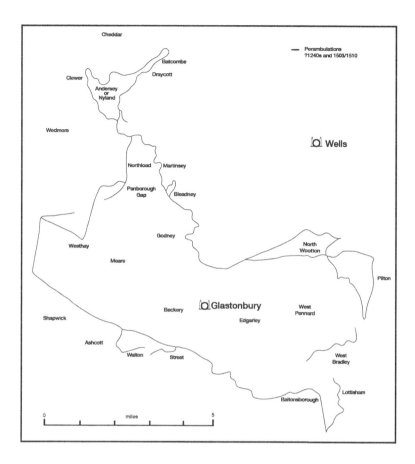

Fig. 5.1   The Twelve Hides of Glastonbury. After Abrams (1996)

consequence of Glastonbury's estate management practices, which were typical of the larger Benedictine houses in the latter half of the Middle Ages.

With respect to the growth of mill numbers, in 1086, Glastonbury held 21 mills on 32 of its manors. This had grown to 26 mills on the same manors by 1189, and 40 by the early fourteenth century (Table 5.1). Only 13 of these 40 mills were directly managed. Twenty-seven of Glastonbury's mills in the early fourteenth century were watermills, along with 13 windmills and one horse mill, clearly indicating that most of the gains in mill numbers post-1189 were windmills.[9] For example, Holt records that all four windmills in a sample of 28 of Glastonbury's Somerset manors in 1296 had been built by the abbey on the Levels. Many of these windmills appear to have been built by the reforming abbot, Michael of Amesbury, elected to the abbacy in 1234. Adam de Damerham credits Michael with having built or recovered 10 mills. However, the monks appear not to have been convinced by the efficacy of the technology of the windmill, as an unreliable windmill at Westonzoyland was replaced by a horse mill sometime after 1274, and even when it was rebuilt sometime after 1316, the horse mill was retained for grinding malt. It was still operating in 1335.[10] By 1307, Glastonbury also had interests in three fulling mills out of the 40 which it held, or 7.5 per cent of the total.[11]

---

[9]   Ibid., pp. 114–15.

[10]   Ibid., pp. 28–9 and 61.

[11]   Ibid., p.

Table 5.1   Growth in mill numbers on 32 manors held by Glastonbury Abbey, 1086–1307

	1086	1189	1307
No. of manors	32	32	32
No. of mills	21	26	40
Demesne mills	21	1	28
Watermills	21	26	27
Windmills	0	0	13
Industrial mills	0	0	3
Horse mills	0	0	1
TOTAL MILL REVENUES	**£10 19s**	**£19 1s 2d**	**<£80**

Compiled from data provided by Holt (1987), p. 18; Holt (1988), pp. 60–61, 70, 84–5, 114–15, 168–9.

With respect to the growth in mill revenues, in 1086, 28 mills in 23 of Glastonbury's West Country manors were receiving annually £10 19s (Table 5.2). The same manors were again surveyed in 1189, by which time there were 31 mills receiving £21 15s 4d annually, indicating the same upward trend in incomes over the century as that seen in Peterborough's East Midlands mills. A significant difference between the two houses is, however, the 10 per cent increase in Glastonbury's level of exploitation of waterways for milling during this period, something which was possible in the West Country, but not in East Anglia, where it would seem that all of those waterways available for milling had already been exploited by Domesday.[12]

Table 5.2   Growth in mill revenues on 23 West Country manors held by Glastonbury Abbey, 1086–1307

	1086	1189	1307
No. of manors	23	23	23
No. of mills	28	31	40
Mills in customary or hereditary tenure	0	30	9
Mills owing labour services & cash rents	0	15	4
TOTAL MILL REVENUES	**£10 19s**	**£21 15s 4d**	**<£80**

Compiled from data provided by Holt (1987), pp. 11–13; Holt (1988), pp. 14–16, 56–7.

By 1189, 30 out of 31 of Glastonbury's West Country mills had been let out under customary or hereditary tenure. A little over 100 years later, however, two-thirds of these non-seigneurial mills were back under seigneurial control, with their total revenues more than quadrupling over this period.[13] According to Holt, the four-fold increase in mill revenues which Glastonbury experienced after 1189 was entirely the result of the reforms instituted by Michael of Amesbury after 1235, with most of the gains occurring over the period from 1280 onwards.[14]

In the 1189 survey of Glastonbury's estates, only one of its mills was on a short-term lease or in direct management, while the rest were let to individuals either freely or customarily. Thirteen mills were let with holdings of between a half and one and a half virgates. Fifteen mills owed labour services as well as cash rents.[15] Similar trends have been uncovered in the case studies of the estates of the Archbishop of Canterbury, Battle Abbey, the Bishop of Hereford and the English lands of the Abbey of Holy Trinity, Caen. All of these houses had inherited or been granted ancient demesne lands during the eleventh century or earlier.

The status of those mills that had been let freely or customarily became of increasing concern during the inflationary periods of the late twelfth and early thirteenth centuries. On Glastonbury's manor of Wrington

---

12   Holt (1987), pp. 14–15.

13   Ibid., pp. 11–13, 18; Holt (1988), p. 14.

14   Holt (1988), p. 85.

15   Ibid., pp. 56–7.

in 1189, for example, its three mills were simply recorded as being held for cash rents. By 1239 it recorded four mills on the same manor, one of which was held freely, one in demesne and two in customary tenure.[16]

However, as Holt notes, there was a considerable difference between mills held freely or in heredity and those held customarily. Customary tenure was more advantageous to lords than free or hereditary tenure as it allowed renegotiation of rents and recovery of lost profits through entry fees for new lessees. The crunch came for the tenants of these mills when the lord began to try to reassert control of them. On the Glastonbury manors after 1234, for example, the abbot had simply to fail to enforce suit of mill on manorial tenants and thus starve the miller or tenant of income, a very effective strategy for ensuring that he handed over the property.[17]

Furthermore, only one such seigneurial mill needed to be recovered on a manor in order to prevent independent tenant mills from drawing custom owed to the lord. Holt cites one such example on Glastonbury's manor of Bridgeham in Norfolk, in which one mill held at will without suit in the 1220s gradually declined in income against the directly managed demesne mill over the subsequent few decades.[18] Similar strategies appear to have been pursued by Battle on its manor of Wye in Kent, by Bec on its manor of Weedon Bec, and by Holy Trinity Caen on its manor of Minchinhampton. Considering the costs involved in regaining seisin by litigation, such a strategy had much to recommend it.

The practice of letting property freely or in heredity was pursued by Glastonbury in relation to demesne servants and administrative officials as rewards for service possibly as early as the tenth century.[19] However, such practices generally did not take into account inflationary pressures and subsequent significant rises in property values, particularly during the thirteenth century. For example, although he had successfully regained seisin of a number of alienated mills following the lax abbacy of his predecessor Ralph, Abbot Samson of Bury St Edmunds granted out six mills in heredity, although he did go to some lengths to ensure that a number of grants for a lifetime did not fall into hereditary tenure.[20] Those mills granted in heredity almost invariably remained outside the demesne permanently.

Holt argues that it is on the whole difficult to determine what happened to Glastonbury's estates after the thirteenth century with respect to the number of independent tenant mills that it continued to tolerate due to the lack of detailed estate surveys from the fourteenth century. The evidence from Glastonbury is that the last two mills that it regained from villeinage were purchased in 1323, and that the other non-seigneurial mills on its manors were subsequently tolerated, some of which still existed in the early sixteenth century.[21] About a quarter of the Glastonbury manors whose milling histories Holt was able to trace had no demesne mills during the Middle Ages but probably did have independent tenant mills, some of which would have paid rent to the abbot.[22]

Holt notes that while Glastonbury experienced a four-fold increase in its mill revenues from Domesday to the early fourteenth century, successive Bishops of Ely were able to extract a six-fold increase in mill revenues from their tenants over the same period.[23] Despite the significant increases in revenue from its mills under direct management, Glastonbury suffered similar levels of volatility and reductions in its mill income to those of Ramsey and other great estates after the plague. This included a decline of 10–20 per cent in the number of its mills and reductions of up to 80 per cent in its mill revenues. By the late fifteenth and early sixteenth centuries there were, however, signs of recovery. Significantly, the overall reduction in grain milling revenues had made the construction of fulling mills a more attractive proposition by this time, with the number of such mills in which the abbey had an interest increasing from one to four, although three of these were run by owner-operators judging from the low rents paid for them.[24]

---

16   Ibid., p. 59.

17   Ibid., pp. 59–60.

18   Ibid., pp. 64–5.

19   Abrams (1996), pp. 271–2. C.f. Knowles (1940a), p. 441.

20   Holt (1988), pp. 56–7.

21   Ibid., pp. 65–6.

22   Ibid., p. 67.

23   Ibid.

24   Ibid., pp. 168–9. The fulling mills were paying 4s 4d, 2s, 1s and 8d. The relevant figures for mill numbers and mill revenues are drawn from two terriers dated 1516 and 1520.

If we compare Durham's mill holdings and average mill revenues with the evidence from the southern estates of Glastonbury, we see that 32 Glastonbury manors possessed 29 mills between them in 1189, all of which were watermills. These rendered a little over £20 in rent, but included some significant parcels of land. By the early fourteenth century, the same 32 manors possessed 40 mills between them, of which 26 were watermills, 13 were windmills and one was a horse mill. These rendered more than £80 in rent, most of the increase in revenue having occurred in the last quarter of the thirteenth century.[25] In other words, 40 of Glastonbury's mills were averaging only a little over £2 each in revenues in the early fourteenth century, as compared to Durham with its average of well over £15 per mill. Furthermore, whereas most of Durham's mills appear to have been let at farm on short-term leases in the early fourteenth century, 40 per cent of Glastonbury's mills at the end of the previous century were still independent tenant mills, although these only contributed 17 per cent of the total mill revenue.[26] Those mills that were still part of the demesne were therefore earning average revenues of a little over £2 15s each. Even when the many lower-income mills are taken from the equation, therefore, Glastonbury's revenues from its demesne mills were still only about one-sixth of those for Durham.

Finally, a comparison of mill numbers on 25 manors held by the abbey between the early fourteenth century and a terrier undertaken between 1516 and 1520 during the abbacy of Richard Beere reveals that there had been an 11.4 per cent increase in the total number of mills over that period, but this was primarily in the number of fulling mills and horse mills, as there had been a decrease in the number of water- and wind-powered grain mills during the intervening two centuries (Table 5.3).[27] These trends in Glastonbury's post-plague mill management are reflected at a national level in Langdon's sample of 330 lay and ecclesiastical manors between 1300 and 1540.[28]

Table 5.3   Growth in mill numbers on 25 manors held by Glastonbury Abbey, early fourteenth century and 1516–20

	Early 14th c.	**1516–20**
No. of manors	25	25
No. of mills	35	39
Water-powered grain mills	21	18
Windmills	12	10
Industrial mills	1	6
Horse mills	1	5

Compiled from data provided by Holt (1988), pp. 168–70.

The evidence from Glastonbury seems to indicate that the general attitude amongst successive abbots and chapters was to maximize the income from mills on their manors, rather than to ensure monopolistic control of them. While the main disadvantage of independent tenant mills for lords in the thirteenth century was that the tenants holding their mills paid a fixed rent while profits increased, in the fourteenth century, those mills that were in customary tenure could have their rents raised every time a new tenant took over the lease, while the lord avoided all the costs of maintenance and repair. What is most interesting about the evidence that Holt was able to uncover on the Glastonbury estates is that while a fair proportion of these independent tenant mills did not survive into the fifteenth century, a significant number of them did, suggesting that despite their lack of suit they were still viable business enterprises.[29]

---

[25] Ibid., p. 84.

[26] Ibid., p. 85. Only four of Durham's mills in 1307 appear to have been outside demesne control, i.e., the mills of Hamsterley, Lynesak, Rouley and Westow. See Appendix C.

[27] Ibid., pp. 168–70.

[28] Langdon (2004), pp. 26–52, esp. pp. 32–42.

[29] Ibid., pp. 66–68.

Abbey of Bec-Hellouin

The Norman Abbey of Bec-Hellouin was one of those alien houses that had been encouraged to establish a foothold in England during the time of William I. William's architect of ecclesiastical reform, Lanfranc, had first entered the brotherhood at Bec, while Herluin and Anselm were other notable figures to emerge from Bec at around the same time. The abbey was a spiritual and intellectual centre for the Latin Church in Western Christendom, training bishops and abbots and founding dependent priories throughout France and England.

Bec's influence on the development of English monasticism was founded upon the patronage of some of the most powerful men in William's retinue, including Hugh, earl of Chester, and Gilbert of Brionne, father of Richard, founder of the house of Clare.[30] A number of different branches of the Clare family were to subsequently donate significant estates to the abbey, although some of them, including Gilbert de Clare, were to later become dissatisfied with Bec's management and reappropriated their gifts.

By 1100, Bec had been endowed with three conventual priories and 12 or 13 manors, mostly in southern England. By the middle of the thirteenth century, it had virtually doubled its holdings. Four conventual and three non-conventual priories owed allegiance to it, while it collected the revenues from as many as 26 manors.[31] Bec's English lands were initially allocated to the use of various obedientiaries and administered by small cells of monks sent from Normandy, but the neglect of conventual life that resulted led to the suppression of some of these cells during the papacy of Innocent III (1198–1216).

By 1220, the abbey had established a General Chapter in England that oversaw its English dependencies and estates.[32] Part of its role included the recovery of property that had been alienated to laymen and clerks, and the enforcement of various papal bulls forbidding the granting of pensions, division of conventual property and the farming of tithes.[33]

By the middle of the thirteenth century, there were seven groups of manors, each of which was administered by a priory or grange at its centre. Such administrative arrangements were not necessarily logical with respect to their geographical locations, or convenient for the monks who oversaw them. Nevertheless, like most of the other large Benedictine houses throughout Europe, by the end of the century, Bec's dependencies and obedientiaries were rendering annual accounts of their financial affairs.[34]

By the late thirteenth century, Bec had interests in 27 mills on its 26 widely scattered manors and three appropriated parishes in southern and eastern England. Bec's possessions extended from Dorset to Norfolk, and Warwickshire to Sussex (Figure 5.2). Its mill holdings included a windmill at Ogbourne Major (now Ogbourne St Andrew) in Wiltshire and a fulling mill at Blakenham in Suffolk. Another of its mills at Ogbourne Minor (now Ogbourne St George) was resumed by its patrons – along with the manor – when Pope Clement V, a former abbot of Bec, gave it to his nephew.

A broken series of computus rolls for the abbey have survived, covering five rental years over the period from 1272 to 1289 (see Appendix A). These include most of the mill revenues over this period and the expenses for 14 of them, thus allowing some insight into the fluctuating fortunes of these mills and the changing management strategies used to extract income from them. They also demonstrate the development of more systematic methods of manorial accounting during this period, methods that had been adapted from the Royal Exchequer that had customarily run Bec's English estates whenever an abbatial vacancy arose.[35]

Of these 27 mills, Bec appears to have actually held the title on 23 and collected tithes on the other four. Of the 23 mills directly held by Bec, only two or possibly three were at farm in the 1270s. By the 1280s, this figure had increased to six, or a little over a quarter of them. It also seems that three of the mills may have been held in customary or hereditary tenure (see below). Ten of the 23 were collecting a mixture of cash and grain rents in the 1270s, and 11 in the 1280s. In terms of their earning capacities, however, some of them increased

[30]   Morgan (1946), pp. 10–11.

[31]   Ibid., p. 12.

[32]   Ibid., pp. 14–15.

[33]   Ibid., pp. 16–17.

[34]   Ibid., pp. 18–19.

[35]   See Marjorie Chibnall's discussion in the introduction to 'Computus Rolls of the English Lands of the Abbey of Bec (1272–1289)'.

Fig. 5.2   Locations of the English mills held by the Abbey of Bec-Hellouin.

their revenue, while others remained stable and some even went backwards. This was presumably related to lower grain prices in the late 1280s.[36]

For example, the tithes of the Hungerford mill fluctuated wildly over the 16-year period from 1272 to 1288, earning between 2s 3 1/2d and 10s 6d, with the lowest earnings in 1281–82 and the highest in 1272–73. A single figure for tithes from the mill at *Chelegrave* in 1287–88 rendered only 1s 6d, suggesting an annual revenue in that year of around 15 shillings. The low rent from another mill at Deverill may indicate that it was an independent tenant mill held in customary or hereditary tenure, as no information is recorded about expenses associated with it.[37]

Although complete rental records and expenses for all of these mills over the five rental years covered by the computus rolls have not survived, it is still possible to draw some meaningful data from the available information. Table 5.4 records the yearly averages of rentals for the 23 manorial mills recorded, incorporating grain rents as cash figures by averaging the prices received by the abbey for its own grain over the rental years concerned.[38] Also listed are averages of expenses for the same period for all of those mills for which expenses are recorded. The overall average of 18 per cent of revenue being spent on mill maintenance by Bec

---

[36]   Chibnall records the following price ranges for a quarter of wheat sold by Bec during this period: 1272–73, 4s 4d to 6s 8d; 1276–77, 5s to 9s; 1281–82, 4s to 7s 4d; 1283–84, 4s to 8s; 1287–89, 1s 9d to 4s. See ibid., p. 9.

[37]   That is, for Waddesdon, 4s 7 1/2d in 1276–77, and for Deverill, 2s in 1281–82.

[38]   I have omitted calculating the prices of bushels, however, and all fractions of a penny are rounded to the nearest quarter penny.

is somewhat higher than that paid out on some other watermills recorded by Holt, which were around 12 per cent, but is probably not untypical. The figure may also be artificially lowered by the number of mills at farm.

Table 5.4   Twenty-three mills on 26 English manors held by the Abbey of Bec, 1272–89

Mill name	Average earnings	Average expenses	Ratio of expenses to earnings (%)
Atherstone mill	£2 17s 4d	n.d.	n/a
Anna mill	£5 15s 10d	£1 13s 1 3/4d	28.6%
Blakenham watermill	£5 16s 3 1/2d	£2 2s 4d	29.8%
Blakenham fulling mill (comb. fig.)	£1 6s	(comb. exp.)	
Bledlow mill	£9 3s 3 3/4d	n.d.	n/a
Chisenbury mill	£6 0s 4d	16s 8 1/4d	13.9%
Combe mill	£2 3s 0 1/4d	7s 6d	17.5%
Cottisford mill	£1 4s 6d	n.d.	n/a
Deverill mill	2s	n.d.	n/a
Hooe mill	£1 9s	1s 3d	4.3%
Lessingham mill	£5 14s 1 1/2d	18s 8d	16.4%
Ogbourne Major watermill	£4 12s.	n.d.	n/a
Ogbourne Major windmill	£2 0s 1d	n.d.	n/a
Ogbourne Minor mill	£4 13s 4d	n.d.	n/a
Povington mill	£2 10s	n.d.	n/a
Preston mills I and II	£4 6s 4d (comb. rev.)	5s 7 1/2d (comb. exp.)	6.2% (comb. fig.)
Ruislip mill	14s 4d	n.d.	n/a
Swyncombe mill	£4 12s 8d	11s 2d	12.1%
Wantage mill	£7 13s 0 1/2d	2s	1.3%
Weedon Bec mills I	£4 6s	8s 6d (comb. exp.)	8.6% (comb. fig.)
(Stowe) II	12s 7 1/2d		
Wretham mill	£6 19s 11 1/2d	£1 8s 2 3/4d	20.2%
AVERAGE OVERALL	**£3 13s 7d**	**13s 2 3/4d**	**18%**

The average income from Bec's English mills from 1272 to 1289 was £3 13s 7d. This is considerably lower than the average revenue from northern mills compiled by Langdon for the early fourteenth century, which was around £5 14s, but considerably higher than the average revenue for mills in the south, which was around £2 10s 8d.[39] It is, however, on a par with the average revenues from the Bishop of Hereford's mills in the late thirteenth century, which was £3 5s 3d, but considerably less than the average income from Beaulieu Abbey's mills, at £5 for the financial year of 1269–70.

Discounting the very low figure of two shillings for the annual rent on Deverill mill, which was presumably held in customary or hereditary tenure and had been built and/or was being repaired and maintained by its tenant, Bec's mill revenues ranged from a low of 12s 7 1/2d for the Stowe mill in Weedon Bec, to a high of £9 3s 3 3/4d for Bledlow mill, both of which were in Buckinghamshire. The latter is certainly comparable to the high revenues drawn by many northern mills, and was presumably drawing upon the custom of a large manorial population.

It is also interesting to note that Stowe mill in Weedon Bec was the only mill for which there are any rental records dating to before 1272. In 1180 the mill was let at farm to the abbey by one David Darmenters for 12 shillings, which in turn let it out for £1, making an instant profit of eight shillings annually.[40] As Chibnall comments in her introduction to Bec's computus rolls, it is very clear that the abbey was running its English lands at a profit.[41]

---

[39] Langdon (1994), p. 13.

[40] See 'Computus Rolls of the English Lands of the Abbey of Bec (1272–1289)', p. 20, n. 15.

[41] Chibnall (1987), p. 6.

Comparing Bec's milling revenue with its overall manorial revenues for the single financial year of 1281–82 provides us with an indication of the relative contribution that milling made to Bec's English income. The Royal Exchequer received £148 5 1/4d from the abbey's English lands while it was *sede vacante*, while its mill revenues for the same year were only £11 6s 6d, or 7.7 per cent of its overall revenue (7.9 per cent is the nationwide average determined by Langdon). However, the rents of a number of mills are not included in the Exchequer's accounts.

Looking instead at the abbey's computus rolls for the same year, its mill revenues for that year were £37 9s 11d, plus 103 quarters and 2 bushels of tollcorn. If we assume a conservative average of 40d per quarter, this would give us a total mill revenue of £54 14s 1d for 1281–82, or almost five times as high as that given in the *Sede Vacante* Roll. Bec's total revenues from its English estates for that year were £1070 2s 10d (more than seven times the figure given in the *Sede Vacante* Roll), which is comparable to some of the highest earning English religious houses. This gives us the comparatively low figure of 5.1 per cent of Bec's English manorial income being drawn from its mills, which is lower than the country-wide average as determined by Langdon, but precisely the same as that of lay estates in the East Midlands, in which it held a considerable amount of property.

Thus, although its average earnings from its mills were considerably higher than those of most other southern lords, its milling income as a proportion of its overall income was fairly average when compared with other lords throughout the country. Bec was, nevertheless, one of the most extractive southern lords in the sample when it came to collecting rents and tolls from its mills. It would therefore seem that the romantic picture of benign Benedictine lordship promoted by supporters of the monastic innovation thesis does not stand up to empirical scrutiny, whereas the Bloch model of strict imposition of seigneurial privilege, à la northern France, seems well confirmed in this instance. While a few of Bec's mills were drawing comparatively low incomes, this was probably related to them having been alienated at some point during the twelfth century, following which the abbey had been unable to regain full seisin, as was the case with some of the other houses sampled in this chapter.

Battle Abbey

Battle Abbey was one of the larger Benedictine houses created and endowed by the Conqueror in commemoration of his victory over Harold Godwinson in 1066. At the insistence of the victorious king, the new monastery was built on the site where his vanquished rival had fallen. It was consequently located an inauspicious distance from running water and other conveniences, although the monks were able to commission the construction of a conduit sourced from a spring soon after the abbey was built.[42] Construction of the abbatial buildings was not completed until sometime after 1076, when the first abbot was appointed. It was not until 1095 that the abbey was consecrated.[43]

William's foundation grant to the abbey included the site of the abbey with a *banlieu*, six additional manors, and two churches in Collumpton (Devon) and Reading, all of which was valued at a little over £200 at Domesday.[44] William II added to this initial endowment the royal manor of Bromham in Wiltshire (worth £24 at Domesday), and more churches in Suffolk, Norfolk and Essex. During the reign of Henry I, Battle exchanged its church in Reading for the small manor of Appledram near Chichester, completing the properties granted to it by the Crown (Figures 5.3 and 5.4). Most of the property that it acquired subsequently was by purchase, apart from a number of small holdings in the locality of the abbey that were donated by new monks entering the abbey.[45] In 1291, the abbey's properties were valued at £528 10s, £211 of which came from its Sussex holdings. In 1535, the gross valuation of its properties was £987, with its net value being £880 14s 7 3/4d.[46] This placed the abbey within the wealthiest 10 per cent of religious houses in England at the

---

[42]   Magnusson (2001), pp. 116–7.

[43]   *VCH Sussex*, Vol. 2, p. 52.

[44]   Knowles (1940), p. 703. In Normandy and France, the *banlieu* was an area of special jurisdiction surrounding a castle. In this case, it surrounded the monastery as geld-free inland on which were housed dependent retainers. See Faith (1999), pp. 91 and 188.

[45]   Searle (1974), p. 36.

[46]   *VCH Sussex*, Vol. 2, p. 52.

Dissolution. Interestingly, none of Battle's temporal possessions were held by military service, even though it had been established as a means of commemorating William's victory over Harold.[47]

By the fourteenth century, most of Battle's holdings were within a 20-kilometre radius of the abbey, with a number of the closer properties within carting distance. The most distant holdings were the manors of Crowmarsh in Oxfordshire and *Hou* (Hoton) in Essex. The names of the various estates held by the abbey in the fourteenth century and the counties in which they were located are set out in Table 5.5. Unfortunately, Eleanor Searle's thorough research on the abbey does not include any systematic study of its mill holdings, although she did note some unusual features, such as its possession of a bark or tanning mill in the late fourteenth century and what appears to have been a tide mill that was later replaced by a windmill in the thirteenth century. It has therefore been necessary to cobble together whatever information could be gleaned from the published records relating to the abbey. An obvious source of valuable information is Domesday Book, which records a handful of references to the abbey's mills as set out below. A second source is *The Chronicle of Battle Abbey* (c. 1185?), while a third valuable source is a series of cellarer's accounts covering the period from 1275 to 1513. These have revealed a long series of rents and expenses for one of the *leuga* watermills from the early fourteenth to early sixteenth centuries, and the existence of a horse-driven cider mill. The richest source of information on the abbey's mills is, however, its published custumals.[48] The abbey's custumals clearly reveal the importance of customary services to its economy, as well as its practice of breaking up the holdings within individual manors into demesne lands and assized lands. The demesne lands were those reserved for the abbey's use and were mostly cultivated by abbatial servants, whereas the assized lands were let out to tenants for cash rents or a combination of cash and labour services, with the latter rendered as agricultural or other work for the demesne. Interestingly, a custumal of Henry VI (r. 1422–61) reveals that the services due on the abbey's estates hardly varied between the late thirteenth and mid-fifteenth centuries.[49]

Table 5.5   Estates held by Battle Abbey in the fourteenth century

Income Properties	Home Properties
1. Hoton, Essex	1. Battle leuga, E. Suss.
2. Appledram, W. Suss.	2. Westfield rectory, E. Suss.
3. Anstey, Hants. (rent-roll)	3. Iklesham rectory, E. Suss.
4. Crowmarsh, Oxon.	4. Barnhorn, E. Suss.
5. Brightwalton, Berks.	5. Marshals (rents), E. Suss.
6. Bromham, Wilts.	6. Berhurst (rents), E. Suss.
7. Wyke, Wilts.	7. Snape (rents), E. Suss.
8. Aylsham rectory, Norf.	8. Alciston, E. Suss.
9. Ixning rectory, Suff.	9. Lullington, E. Suss.
10. Samford and Hempstead rectories, Essex	10. Wye, Kent (manor, beadry)
11. Brampford rectory, Suff.	11. Kingsnorth and W. Kingsnorth, Kent
12. rents in Deptford and Greenwich	12. Wachindene, Kent
13. Southwark and Camberwell: rents and house	13. Dengemarsh, Kent
	14. Limpsfield & Brodeham, Surrey
manors: 10 rentals: 3	manors: 10 rentals: 4

[47]   Knowles (1940), p. 609.

[48]   See Scargill-Bird's comments in the introduction to *Custumals of Battle Abbey*, pp. i–iv. The custumals cover the period from around 1236 to 1351, and include the following items: some memoranda from around 1236; rentals and custumals for nine manors in Sussex, Essex, Berkshire, Oxfordshire, Kent, Hampshire and Wiltshire that are dated to around 1284; some rentals compiled in the time of Edward III that are probably from the late twelfth or early thirteenth century; some rentals for boroughs within the Hundred of Battle and for the manor of Merle or Marley in Sussex from the reign of Edward I; an extent of the manor of Barnhorn in Sussex from 1307; further extents for the manors of Limpsfield and Brodeham in Surrey and Wye in Kent dated to 1312; and some more rentals for the manors of Limpsfield and Anesty (Hampshire) from 1342 and 1351, respectively. The custumals include rentals on nine mills for 1236, 1307, 1312 and 1351, although the data are quite thin.

[49]   Ibid., pp. iii–v. The custumal for the reign of Henry VI can be found in *Augmentation Office, Misc. Books*, Vol. 56.

Like many other religious houses in the late thirteenth and early fourteenth centuries, the abbey further split its possessions into a group of home properties, which was dedicated to the subsistence of the monks, and another group of properties from which it primarily drew a cash income. Searle notes that 'the income properties were less valuable and had had considerably less investment put into them than had the home group of properties.'[50]

The woods and waste of each manor were usually included within its demesne, while cultivated areas of demesne often appear to have been intermingled with those of the tenants and scattered across the manor. Amongst some of the customary services due on the manor of Marley, for example, was the obligation of the tenants to undertake hedging work known as 'Gavelmerke', which probably involved separating the demesne from assized plots.[51] Hedging is also described as having been undertaken 'against the millpond for Park mill' in the cellarer's account for 1409–10, and was presumably done for the same reason.[52]

As in most of the rest of England, the tenants of the assized lands let out by Battle consisted of four classes of peasants: free tenants (*liberi tenentes*), villeins (*villani*), cottars (*cottarii* and *coterelli*) and landless peasants (*coteriaie*). As their name implies, free peasants held their land as freeholders, and could sell up on the manor and move elsewhere at any time. On Battle's manors they were what are called 'customary freeholders' (*custumarii*), who were bound to perform certain common services, as well as payment of heriot and reliefs on change of tenure. Most of them were probably smallholders who had been successful in commuting their labour services to cash rents over the course of the twelfth and thirteenth centuries, although some held their property in a mixture of villein and customary tenure and some were possibly the descendants of sokemen, knights and officials. They were able to acquire such property through the alienation of demesne land and the assarting of waste.[53]

Villeins consisted of those peasants who had been born on the manor, also known as *nativi*, as well as those who were from outside the manor but held land within it, or *forinseci*. Their rank and holdings were above those of cottars, but like *custumarii* or customary holders, they were still obliged to perform common services for the lord. The *villani* were serfs inasmuch as they were restricted from leaving the manor, marrying off their daughters to outsiders, selling their cattle or allowing their sons to become priests without the lord's permission. In some of Battle's documents, the only distinction that is made between the different classes of peasants is that of *liberi* and *nativi*.[54]

Generally speaking, *cottarii* or cottars rendered the same kinds of services as customary holders, and were under the same restrictions as *nativi*, but as a rule held only four acres of land, although as many as 15 acres are recorded for some cottars. *Coterelli* were cottars with smaller holdings of seldom more than one or two acres, while the *cotteria* appear to have been landless peasants. Both classes probably laboured for larger holders.[55]

The labour services obliged of Battle's tenants consisted of four kinds of work: daily or weekly labouring services (*opera diurna*); carrying services (*averagia*); occasional works such as mowing, clearing a millpond, sheep-shearing and so on; and special requests (*precariae*). All four classes of tenants performed some mill-related duties. Within Battle's *banlieu* or *leuga*, for example, 'each messuage not specifically exempted was to provide one man for one day for the mowing of Bodiam meadow, and one man for one day for the repair of the mill, receiving in return a loaf and a half of bread *et companagium*.'[56] By the thirteenth century, however, the duty of mill-repair had been dropped, along with that involving malt making.[57] As I will explain in more detail shortly, a number of the mills that were let to customary and hereditary tenants in the thirteenth and fourteenth centuries also carried with them obligations of labour services, as well as cash or grain rents and rents in kind.

Turning now to an analysis of the various mill-related entries in the published documents pertaining to the abbey, there are three entries listing watermills held by Battle at Domesday. The first entry lists a single

---

[50]   Searle (1974), p. 252.

[51]   Ibid., p. vi.

[52]   *Accounts of the Cellarers of Battle Abbey*, p. 103.

[53]   *Custumals of Battle Abbey*, pp. vi–vii.

[54]   Ibid., p. vii.

[55]   Ibid., p. viii.

[56]   Searle (1974), p. 84, citing *The Chronicle of Battle Abbey*, pp. 12, 16,

[57]   Ibid., p. 110.

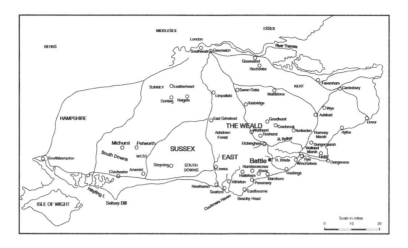

Fig. 5.3   Possessions of Battle Abbey. After Searle (1974)

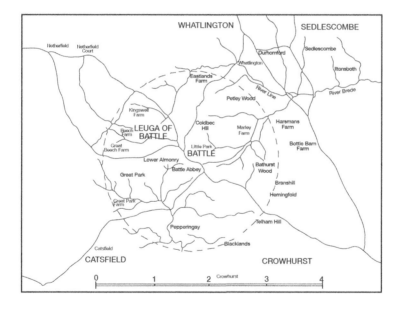

Fig. 5.4   Battle Abbey's *Leuga* possessions. After Searle (1974)

mill valued at seven shillings a year in the manor of Hoton in Essex. The second makes reference to two mills within the liberty of Battle that were not rented at Domesday, whereas the third lists four mills within the manor of Wye in Kent that were rented for £1 3s 8d.[58] Among some of the other early references to mills amongst the abbey's muniments is a document which lists three mills attached to the advowson of St Mary's Church that was one of nine such advowsons probably granted to the abbey by William II (r. 1087–1100). Two of these mills were within the abbey's *banlieu*, while the other was only a short distance away.[59] Presumably,

---

58   *VCH Sussex*, Vol. I, pp. 394–5; *VCH Kent*, Vol. III, p. 242.
59   *The Chronicle of Battle Abbey*, pp. 62–3.

the two mills within the *banlieu* were different from those two mills referred to as within the liberty of Battle in Domesday Book, which would have brought the number of mills within the *banlieu* to four. One of these would have been the watermill within the Great Park in the south-east of the *leuga* that is mentioned several times in the cellarer's accounts,[60] while another was the watermill of *Peperynghey* described in more detail below. Both mills were operated by the cellarer in the fourteenth and fifteenth centuries.

Like many other large estates of the period, Battle Abbey had been adversely affected by the granting out of demesne lands on generous conditions during the twelfth and early thirteenth centuries. The monks had, furthermore, been frequently disadvantaged by their neighbours and those lay lords and stewards who had been entrusted to care for their more distant estates. Possibly the worst of these situations related to the very large manor of Wye that lay just over the county border from Battle in Kent. A Kentish lord who had been given the responsibility to care for the manor had divided it up between himself and four other barons, and subsequently refused to relinquish it. Despite the intervention of Henry I, the monks were forced to allow some continuation of this arrangement, which explains how the demesne mills of Wye were held as shares by multiple tenants on customary and hereditary leases in the thirteenth and fourteenth centuries (see below).[61]

Although there is little in the way of documentary evidence from the twelfth century to enable the construction of a detailed picture of the abbey's management practices during this period, the available evidence indicates that the monks had been under pressure from local lords and knightly families who had sought to appropriate or encroach upon their lands. Through economizing on living expenses, saving money and making strategic purchases and exchanges, the monks were subsequently able to regain, enlarge or secure their possessions, a policy which they continued to pursue until the mid-fourteenth century.[62]

In 1230, Battle's customary tenants within the *leuga* paid as much as they had in 1100, meaning that revenues had remained stagnant while maintenance costs and the value of produce had increased.[63] In order to regain some of the ground they had lost in the twelfth and early thirteenth centuries, between 1240 and 1305, the monks made a concerted and fairly successful effort to draw what property they could back into the demesne. On the one hand, they tried to reverse the earlier process of alienation by forbidding any further grants of large parcels of land to lay servants or allowing hereditary leases within their *banlieu*. On the other, they sought to consolidate their holdings in the immediate vicinity of the abbey, purchasing land adjoining demesne holdings as it became vacant, and clearing, enclosing and draining their existing forests and wastelands. By the early fourteenth century, the monks had quadrupled their productive holdings within the *banlieu*.[64]

The earliest of those references to mills which appear in Battle Abbey's custumals are from a memorandum dated to 1236 (i.e., the twentieth year of the reign of Henry III). It describes the rentals for the shares of two mills in the manor of Wye.[65] The first of these records that Simon de Tuna held 1/8 of a share of the mill of Wye from Abbot Ralph of Battle for an annual fee of £2 6d, with the sixpence to go to the heirs of Ralph Saltbrede who had presumably held that share previously. The second records that a man named Richard held three shares of another mill in Wye, the first of which was 1/4 owing £5 6d a year to the heirs of Stephen de Rengesdune, the lease of which had been confirmed by Stephen's widow. The second share was 1/8 of the mill held by Richard of the heirs of Organ son of Stephen for a fee of one shilling and an annual rent of threepence. The third share held by Richard was 1/5 of the mill held of John de Bosco of the heirs of Walter of Wye and Alan Putac for one shilling a year. It is also recorded that another 1/5 of the mill was held by the abbey and convent, while the heirs of Walter held another three parts.

The reasons for the comparatively high rent of £5 6d paid to the heirs of Stephen de Rengesdune (as against the 1s 3d that he paid to four other parties for another two parts of the mill) is not clear, but this complicated arrangement almost certainly relates to the baronial appropriation of the manor of Wye in the twelfth century. Both of the mills of Wye had fallen out of demesne control during the twelfth century, following which the abbey appears to have only been able to recover shares of 1/8 and 1/5 respectively of the

60   See Searle (1974), p. 267, and *Accounts of the Cellarers of Battle Abbey*, pp. 53, 103, 121.

61   Searle (1974), 36–8.

62   Ibid., pp.158–9, 253.

63   Ibid., p. 157.

64   *Chronicle of Battle Abbey*, pp. 151–2.

65   *Custumals of Battle Abbey*, pp. 135–6.

two mills. Sometime between 1236 and 1351, however, it appears to have regained seisin of an additional 1/5 of the second watermill, bringing its total share to one quarter. What had happened to the other two mills in the manor that are recorded in Domesday Book is also unclear, although they may have been allowed to fall into ruin, or had become completely alienated from the abbey's possession during the baronial appropriation.

Searle notes that sometime before the rental of 1240 was completed, a windmill was built on the northern spur of the ridge on which the abbey was located.[66] The windmill is referred to in the cellarer's account of 1320–21 as Mountjoy (or Montjoy) windmill, and was leased out at this stage,[67] although it had presumably been initially built to serve the needs of the monks and save them the trouble of carting their own corn down to one of the *leuga* watermills and back up to the abbey.

Chronologically, the next references to any mills in the abbey's custumal are from the reign of Edward I (1272–1307). The first, dated 1307, simply records a rent of £1 a year from the windmill of Barnhorn,[68] while the second refers to a watermill held by Micheleham Priory in the manor of Alciston, Sussex, which paid 10 shillings a year to the abbey for the overflow from its mill, with a remittance of two shillings a year from this sum to be paid to a free peasant named Symon of Sternerse who held the land downstream from the mill. This sum would have been intended as a regular fee to compensate both the abbey and Symon for any flooding of their land and to discourage them from interfering with the water leading from the mill.[69] Such payments were common and can be found amongst the charters of a number of the other houses examined elsewhere and in detail in Chapter 9. The only other mill reference from this series is to a cottar named John who held an acre attached to Bromham mill in Wiltshire for sixpence.[70] As no reference is made anywhere in the custumal to any rent from Bromham mill, John may have been a demesne servant directly running the mill on behalf of the abbey while holding the attached land as a tenant for additional income from eels, honey, hay or pasturage.

In the same year of 1306–7, there is a reference in the cellarer's account to the purchase of 'a blind horse for the mill' for 13s 4d, and another eight shillings spent on purchasing another horse for the same mill in 1319–20.[71] Presumably, this horse mill was located within the conventual complex, and may have been built as a substitute for the windmill in order for the latter to be let out. The horse mill was still operating in 1373–74, as 40 shillings were spent on purchasing another horse for the mill, and in 1395–96, 22 shillings were spent on shoeing *stots* (riding horses?) and mill horses.[72] It was still operating in 1465–66, as four pence were spent on new halters for the mill horses in that year, and 13s 10d on various ironworks for the cellarer's holdings, including shoes for the mill horses.[73]

A few clues as to the kind of work to which this horse mill may have been turned in the late fourteenth, mid-fifteenth and early sixteenth centuries are given in the accounts of 1371–72, and 1438–39, 1440–41 and 1512–13. In the earliest account, 3s 4d was spent on repairs to the 'brewery mill'.[74] In the second and third accounts, 'the cellarer's mill' is described as having been dedicated to making cider. In the first of these second two accounts, 22s 4d was rendered to the cellarer for five 'pipes' of cider, and an additional 4s 3d from various outsiders for making cider in the same mill.[75] In the later entry, 3s 4d was spent on making two spindles (*spyndelys*) for the cider press, described in the account as a *molend' pomorum*.[76] This appellation is so far unique amongst medieval English documents, although it seems likely that Battle was not the only body to hold such a mill. That this mill was still operating in 1512–13 is revealed by two entries referring to eight pence in repairs that were undertaken on the cider mill, and sixpence paid for a lock and key for the

66   Searle (1974), pp. 72, 123–4.
67   *Accounts of the Cellarers of Battle Abbey*, p. 51.
68   *Custumals of Battle Abbey*, p. 17.
69   Ibid., p. 40.
70   Ibid., p. 76.
71   *Accounts of the Cellarers of Battle Abbey*, pp. 46, 51.
72   Ibid., pp. 70, 93.
73   Ibid., p. 144.
74   Ibid., p. 67.
75   Ibid., p. 119.
76   Ibid., p. 130.

same mill.[77] Given that two of the *leuga* watermills and one windmill are almost always referred to by their names (i.e., *Peperynghey* and Park watermills, and Mountjoy or the abbey windmill), and the location of this brewery mill (or mill of the cellarer's) inside the abbatial complex, it can only have been a horse mill: the same mill referred to in the previously cited documents.

Returning to the custumals, the next four entries refer to the watermill of Brodeham and to two watermills in the neighbouring home manor of Limpsfield (*Lemenesfeld*), both of which were in Surrey, almost 50 kilometres to the north-west of the abbey. An extent of 1312 records that Brodeham watermill with its watercourse were held by its tenant for 9 quarters of multure grain and 3s 4d at four terms for a total of £1 10s of cash rent a year.[78] This was, apparently, one of the watermills that Battle had managed to draw back into the demesne, and is one of three mills recorded in the extents of that year that paid a mixture of cash and grain rents. The other two mills paying grain rents were those at Limpsfield. They were valued at 18 quarters of multure grain and 3s 4d per quarter along with their watercourses, which could be paid as a cash sum of £3 a year in total, while another 4s 4d a year was to be paid for the farm of the millpond and fishpond. Both mills were held by freemen in the early fourteenth century.[79]

The first of two rentals for 1312 records that one of the mills of Limpsfield was held with one messuage and one acre of land for £1 8s 7d annually, as well as doing suit (of court), relief and heriot. The mill was held by a free tenant called Robert de Langenherst.[80] The second rental records that another free tenant named Hamo Broun held the other Limpsfield watermill with one messuage and 120 acres of ploughland, wood, meadow and pasture for £1 3s 8d a year, and also doing suit of court, relief and heriot.[81] Although these two cash amounts only add up to £2 12s 3d, the total of £3 given in the extent was probably a notional value based on a mixture of cash and grain as income. It is nevertheless clear that by the early fourteenth century, the free tenants of demesne mills were paying what might be considered commercial rates for their rent.

Although the following entry actually appears in the cartulary for the High Church of Chichester and is discussed in more detail in Chapter 6, it is worth noting that the abbey received a watermill in West Greenwich or Lewisham in Kent (now part of Greater London) in January 1322 or 1323 as part of a parcel of properties donated to them by Robert Alard of Wynchelsee, a patron of the Church of St Thomas the Martyr in Winchelsea, East Sussex. The donation was to provide for the upkeep of the church and its priests. A number of other landholdings from these two manors were granted to the monks, as well as other properties in Surrey and Sussex. Their total value was £20 a year.[82] Given the location of the watermill in a place of high population density, this must have been one of the more valuable assets included in the parcel.

Sometime before the financial year of 1346–47, the abbey acquired some additional properties in Southwark just outside of London which included a mill. In 1351–52, the mill was earning £3 a year. The other rents there were worth an additional £2 a year.[83] This investment was but one of many that Battle made in urban properties during the thirteenth and fourteenth centuries.[84] Searle also mentions that the abbey held a mill or two attached to one or more of its four church-manors in East Anglia, although no other information is supplied. She does point out, however, that two of these manors, Aylsham in Norfolk and Ixning (Exning) in Suffolk, were among the most valuable of its income properties in the mid-fourteenth century.[85]

The latest references to mills held by the abbey within the custumals relate to what were by then three watermills in the manor of Wye in Kent, two of which appear to have been described in the memorandum of 1236 described above. The first of these was the watermill of *Bolle*, which is recorded as paying £1 a year

[77]   Ibid., p. 158.

[78]   *Custumals of Battle Abbey*, p. 159.

[79]   Ibid., pp. 137, 141.

[80]   Ibid., p. 146.

[81]   Ibid., p. 147.

[82]   *Chartulary of the High Church of Chichester*, ms. 909. Apart from the watermill, the grant included three houses, 320 acres of land, four acres of meadow, eight acres of wood, five acres of alder grove and nine shillings rent.

[83]   Searle (1974), p. 454.

[84]   Ibid., pp, 134–51; Goddard (2007), pp. 150, 154–5, 158.

[85]   Searle (1974), p. 252. In n. 11 to this entry, she explains that '[t]he churches were Ixning in Suffolk, Aylsham in Norfolk, Sampford-and-Hampstead in Essex, and after 1350, Brampford in Suffolk.'

for all services, as well as 26d for multure and six sticks of eels from the millpond. This mill had either been built or rebuilt by the abbey since 1236 and was held in full by it (although the low rent suggests that it did not hold suit), or else it was one of the two mills that had been alienated during the baronial appropriation of the manor and had subsequently been regained. A quarter share of another watermill in Wye paid £1 12s for all services, 26d for multure and 10 sticks of eels, while a quarter share of the mill of *Holmthege* was rented at 11s 4d for all services and 26d for multure. Both of these mills were leased to one Richard Brun, who was almost undoubtedly an ancestor of Hamo Broun who was leasing one of the Limpsfield mills in 1312, and of Richard Brown who leased two of the mills of Wye in 1351–52 (see Table 5.6). Such multi-generational families of miller-lessees have also been identified by Langdon.[86] How Richard Brun's share of the mills was to be divided between his four sons upon his death is also stipulated, indicating that Richard held these two shares of the abbey in hereditary tenure. Furthermore, as John de Bosco is mentioned in this entry as having earlier had an interest in this mill of *Holmthege*, it can presumably be identified with the second watermill of Wye described in the 1236 extent.

However, this does not account for why John de Bosco's share of 1/5 as described in the 1236 extent was interpreted as only a 1/8 share in the rental from 1351. Nor do we know how what had been two 1/5 shares held by John and the abbey in 1236 had been converted into a 1/4 share by this stage. Nevertheless, if it is reasonable to assume that the two 1/4 shares held by the abbey of the two mills in 1351 constituted a quarter of the revenues from the two mills, Wye watermill was earning something like £6 8s a year for all services, as well as 8s 8d in multure and 40 sticks of eels, whereas *Holmthege* mill was earning £2 5s 4d in rent and 8s 8d in multure.[87] If these assumptions are correct, the two mills of Wye were earning less than half as much in 1351 as they had in 1236. Considering that the plague had hit the abbey a few years before, these figures roughly conform with Searle's finding that Battle's income was reduced by 1/4 to 1/3 after the Black Death and never recovered.[88]

If, on the other hand, we simply add the earnings from the two mills in 1236 (£7 2s 3d) and the three mills in 1351 (£3 19s 10d and 16 sticks of eels), and compare them to the earnings of four mills in the same manor at Domesday (£1 3s 8d), even discounting any additional earnings from the other shares, the three mills were drawing six times as much in 1236 (exactly 150 years later), and almost three-and-a-half times as much revenue in the wake of the Black Death, as they had at Domesday.

While the above figures for the mills of Wye are the only comparative pieces of evidence on mill rents that we have from the custumals and Domesday Book, as mentioned earlier, there is a long series of rents and expenses for the *leuga* watermill of *Peperynghey* that was held by the cellarer between the early fourteenth and early sixteenth centuries. These rents and expenses are mapped out below in Chart 5.1.

Although the time axis is somewhat truncated due to the lack of data for a number of the accounting years covered by the total sample, the graph still clearly indicates that there had been a significant loss of income from the mill after 1351, and that this continued to fluctuate at an average of around half of that peak for the next 150 years or so. These kinds of figures are fairly typical of earnings during this period, as both Holt and Langdon have shown.[89] That earnings were still high in the accounting year of 1351–52 is probably related to the fact that the plague did not hit the abbey until 1350, during which time it carried off the abbot. The largest number of monks were killed during a second plague in 1423, however, which was 10 years before the mill was taken out of commission to be extensively repaired and rebuilt, at a total cost of £6 19s 4d. It should also be noted that although earnings of 16s 8d are recorded for the mill in the accounting year of 1320–21, this figure is unreliable, as the earlier part of the entry is missing, and it included rent from Mountjoy windmill.[90] It is not clear, therefore, how much money the mill had been earning in the first half of the fourteenth century.

---

[86] Langdon (2004), pp. 238–43.

[87] *Custumals of Battle Abbey*, pp. 127–8. Although *Holmthege* mill was in Kent and not Surrey, it is possible that Richard Brun, being a free peasant, was a descendant of Hamo Broun who held one of the Limpsfield mills in 1312. The two mills are about 70 kilometers apart.

[88] Searle (1974), pp. 261–2.

[89] Holt (1988), Ch. 10, Langdon (1991).

[90] The information on the plague is taken from *VCH Sussex*, Vol. 2, p. 54, while the data in Chart 5.1 is from *Accounts of the Cellarers of Battle Abbey*, pp. 51, 53, 55, 57, 58, 61, 67, 68, 71, 73, 75–6, 78, 91–3, 95, 103, 104, 106, 109, 111, 115, 119, 121, 130, 132, 136–7, 142–4, 148–9, 156–8.

As mentioned earlier, the abbey also possessed a tanning mill. This was contained within its lucrative tannery about four kilometres to the north-east of the abbey 'beside the stream at Iltonsbath, next to Sedlescombe, in the meadow *Tannerywyssch*'. Although the abbey had been involved in leatherworking in the town of Battle since the late thirteenth or early fourteenth century, the mill and tannery appear to have been late fourteenth-century innovations. The monks were able to tap into an extensive and well-resourced local and regional market, and were able to draw profits as high as £20 a year from the tannery.[91] Like the tannery of Bolton Priory, this establishment appears to have been quite profitable when compared with mechanized fulling workshops.

Table 5.6   Twenty mills held on 20 manors by Battle Abbey, 1086–1385

Name	County	Date Recorded	Annual Revenue	Lessor	Lessee
Hoton watermill	Essex	1086	7s	Battle Abbey	n/a
Battle watermills I (x2)	Sussex	1086	In hand	Battle Abbey	n/a
Wye watermills (x4)	Kent	1086	23s 8d	Battle Abbey	?
Battle watermills II (x3)	Kent	<1100 (?)	In hand	Battle Abbey	n/a
Barnhorn (tide?) mill	Kent	1107–85	In hand	Battle Abbey	n/a
Wye watermill I	Kent	1236	£2 6d (1/8 share)	Battle Abbey	Simon de Tuna
Wye watermill II	Kent	1236	£5 6d (1/4 share)	Stephen de Rengesdune	Richard Brun
			3d (1/8 share)	Organ, son of Stephen's heirs	Ibid.
			? (3/5 share)	Walter of Wye's heirs	Ibid.
			1 s (1/5 share)	John de Bosco (tenant) Walter of Wye's and Alan Putac's heirs (tenants-in-chief)	Ibid.
			? (1/5 share)	Battle Abbey	n/a
Mountjoy windmill	Sussex	<1240 (?)	?	Battle Abbey	n/a
Battle horse mill	Sussex	1306–7	In hand (?)	Battle Abbey	n/a
Bernehorne (Barnhorn) windmill	Sussex	1307	£1	Battle Abbey	?
Bromham watermill	Wiltshire	1307	In hand (?)	Battle Abbey	?
Limpsfield watermills (x2)	Surrey	1312	£3 (18 quarters of grain @ 3s 4d per quarter + 4s 4d for millpond farm)	Battle Abbey	?
Limps. I (+ 1 mess, 1 a.)			£1 8s 7d	Battle Abbey	Robert de Langenhurst
Limps. II			£1 3s 8d	Battle Abbey	Hamo Broun
Brodeham watermill	Surrey	1312	£1 10s	Battle Abbey	?
West Greenwich/ Lewisham mill	Kent	1322–23	rented in 1340s	Battle Abbey	?
Southwark mill	Surrey	1351–52	rented in 1340s	Battle Abbey	?
Ixning/Aylsham mill/s?	East Anglia	1351–52	?	Battle Abbey	?
Bolle watermill, Wye	Kent	1351–52	£1 (+ 26d. multure + 6 sticks eels)	Battle Abbey	Simone de Brunesford
Wye watermill	Kent	1351–52	£1 12s	Battle Abbey	Richard Brown
Holmthege mill, Wye	Kent	1351–52	11s 4d (+ 26d multure for 1/4 share)	Battle Abbey	Richard Brown
Iltonsbath tanning mill	Surrey	1384–85		Battle Abbey	n/a

---

      91   Searle (1974), p. 301. See Searle's informative discussion of the tannery and the mill's place within it on pp. 299–303.

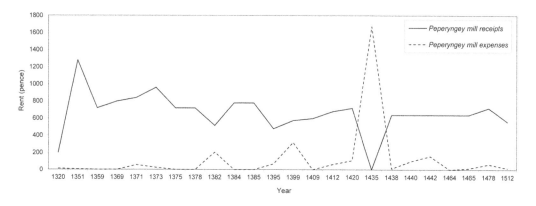

Chart 5.1   *Peperynghey* mill farm mapped against mill expenses, 1320–1513

Turning now to an overall assessment of these data, all of the material relating to the various mills held by the abbey is reproduced in Table 5.6. The abbey seems to have held at least 10 mills by the end of the eleventh century, four of which were within its *banlieu*, and one of which lay just outside. By the early 1350s, it held almost twice that number. There were at least 20 different mills in which the abbey had a direct interest between 1086 and 1385, including a possible tide mill, two windmills, a horse-driven cider mill, and a water-driven tanning mill. The abbey was also donated two mills in London between 1322 and 1352. At Domesday, the mills of Battle were in hand, and, with the exception of the mills of Wye in Kent, appear to have remained so until the early fourteenth century, when two of them begin to appear in the cellarer's accounts. Interestingly, only six or seven of the 13 estates that were part of Battle's income group appear to have included a mill, or roughly half of them.

In terms of the revenues being drawn from these mills, there is rental data on a mill in Hoton and four mills in Wye from 1086, two mills in Wye from 1236, a mill in Barnhorn from 1307, three mills in Limpsfield and Brodeham from 1312, and four mills in London and Wye from the early 1350s. The average revenue from the four mills for which rentals are recorded in the early fourteenth century was only £1 7s 6d.

Apart from the comparison of the various mills of Wye and the analysis of the series of rentals and expenses for *Peperynghey* mill just undertaken, these various entries will now be analysed in chronological order.

The rents drawn from the two shares of the mills of Wye in 1236 indicate that both were high-earning seigneurial mills that had been alienated to free tenants or servants of the abbey in the twelfth or early thirteenth century. Given that both of the larger sums entered were only 1/8 and 1/4 shares (i.e., £2 6d and £5 6d respectively),[92] these rents compare with some of the highest revenues for mills in medieval England. The rents which the monks drew from the mills of Wye, together with the high earnings from *Peperynghey* mill in 1351–52 of £5 6s 8d, clearly indicate that the monks of Battle were able to draw significant revenues from their seigneurial mills.

Turning now to four of Battle's other seigneurial mills, the picture is somewhat clarified when we compare the level of mill rents with the number of tenants and their arable holdings. For example, the windmill of Barnhorn in Sussex was earning £1 a year in 1307. The mill was drawing custom from 33 tenants who held 193 acres between them. Just under a quarter of the tenants were free, and one of them held 40 acres. Most of the land (132 acres) was held by *nativi*, however.[93] The abbey's windmill at Mountjoy was only earning slightly more than this in the cellarer's account of 1373–74 (24s),[94] although this had dropped to 13s 4d in 1375–76, and drew no rent between 1378 and 1383, 'since it is standing empty'.[95] Nor is it clear

---

92   *Custumals of Battle Abbey*, p. 135.

93   Ibid., p. xvi.

94   *Accounts of the Cellarers of Battle Abbey*, p. 68.

95   Ibid., pp. 71, 73.

how many tenants were bound to grind their grain at this mill. Nevertheless, an erratic income interspersed with vacant leases was evident across many estates in England in the wake of the plague. Westminster and Ramsey experienced similar volatility,[96] while Holt and Langdon have found similar fluctuations in the milling revenues of other large ecclesiastical and lay estates throughout England in the late fourteenth century and well into the fifteenth century, fluctuations that are graphically illustrated in my analysis of Ian Jack's Welsh fulling mill data in *Wind, Water, Work* (2006), and in the earnings of Battle's mill of *Peperynghey* (Chart 5.1).

The two demesne watermills of Limpsfield were drawing together £3 in rent in 1312, all of which was paid as toll corn worth 3s 4d per quarter. Both mills were let to free tenants of the manor. In Limpsfield, however, the number of free tenants far outnumbered the *nativi*, basically reversing the ratio of free to bonded tenants seen in Barnhorn, with between 50 and 60 people in the former group, and only 20 in the latter. Together, they held 663 acres. Of this total, a third (230 acres) was held by three men. There were also a handful of 'tenants at will' who held small portions of land for which they paid rent as a single sum, and an additional 14 free and customary tenants in the attached holding of *Prynkehamme* who held a total of 506 acres. In both cases, the free tenants of the manor held around two-thirds of the total acreage.[97] With a manorial population of around a hundred people, it seems fairly clear that most of the profits of these mills were going to their free tenants.

The watermill of Brodeham paid the same as the two mills of Limpsfield, at £1 10s, and was also paying its rent in grain. Twenty-two tenants in Brodeham held 92 acres between them, eight of whom were free and five who were tenants-at-will. Brodeham watermill earned 10 shillings more *per annum* than did Barnham's windmill with 33 tenants and 193 acres of arable. The relatively higher rent for the watermill can most likely be attributed to the windmill not being able to handle all of the grain grown by the abbey's tenants, presumably due to a lack of steady winds. It is also possible that the level of flour consumption in Barnham was lower than in Brodeham.

The single rent of £3 a year drawn from the Southwark mill in the middle of London in 1351–2 does not give us any indication of whether it had been affected by the plague, although the *leuga* mill of *Peperynghey* enjoyed its highest recorded rental income in that year (Chart 5.1). On the other hand, two of the mills of Wye that had existed in the early thirteenth century were drawing only about half of the income in 1351–52 that they had enjoyed at that time. Because the effects of the plague do not seem to have been fully felt by the abbey at this stage, the lower income from the two mills of Wye may have had something to do with the abbey's construction (or reacquisition) of a third mill on the manor, the mill of *Bolle*. It is also possible that because the abbey had been unable to regain full seisin on the other two mills in Wye, it had allowed the suit of those mills to lapse in order to pick up some of the custom from its newly built (or reacquired) mill.

All in all, therefore, while Battle does appear to have sought to maximize its revenues from all of its mills, it also seems to have been a reasonable lord. The monks and abbots were clearly willing to invest in new milling technology where it was deemed appropriate and/or profitable, i.e. the windmill of Barnhorn to replace what was probably a tide mill, an abbatial windmill built as a substitute for a more distant watermill, an abbatial horse-driven mill possibly built to substitute for the abbatial windmill and which was subsequently turned to making cider, and a tanning mill built within a new tanning complex. It also seems quite clear, however, that the monks were drawing substantial incomes from their mills by the 1240s. The incomes from shares of the mills of Wye, for example, compare favourably with the highly extractive rents being charged by northern lords and the wealthiest ecclesiastical lords, although there only seem to have been a limited number of mills that the monks could exploit in this way.

Finally, only two or three of the four to six mills in Battle's *leuga*, and two other mills on its income manors of Hoton (Essex) and Bromham (Wilts.), do not appear to have ever been let out by the monks, whereas the other 13 or more were. Furthermore, there does not appear to have been any radical change in policy on this score, even though the number of mills held by the abbey appears to have tripled between 1086 and 1385. Battle appears to have maintained a 'core' of directly managed mills throughout

---

[96]   See Chapter 1.

[97]   *Custumals of Battle Abbey*, pp. xliii–xlv.

the period from its foundation until the late fourteenth century, constituting around 20 per cent of the mills in its possession at the peak of its involvement in the medieval milling trade. Battle's mill management practices were, therefore, not atypical amongst large Benedictine houses, although its monks and abbots do seem to have been more capable administrators than most, as well as being more willing to explore new milling technologies.

Lancaster Priory/St Mary's Church

Situated on the highest hill overlooking the old town of Lancaster and the River Lune, the Church of St Mary, Lancaster, was established as an alien cathedral priory of the Benedictine order in 1094 by way of a foundation grant from Roger, the Earl of Poitou. Roger was the third son of Roger, earl of Shrewsbury, a cousin of William the Conqueror. The priory had originally been bestowed by Roger the younger upon the Abbey of Saint-Martin of Sées in Normandy. The town of Sées formed part of the inheritance of Roger's mother, the Countess Mabel, while the abbey had been re-founded by his father in 1060, and was the recipient of significant parcels of land in England from the house of Montgomery. Although Sées exercised titular authority over Lancaster, it appears to have rarely interfered in its affairs.[98]

The site of the priory had been occupied since at least the Roman period, during which time it had been a fortress and cavalry garrison. There is also some evidence that a Roman church had been built within its walls. A minster church was consecrated there sometime around 630, and subsequently operated as an Anglian monastery during the eighth and ninth centuries. A Saxon church also appears to have been built on the site in the late tenth century. Several other churches were built in the area during Anglo-Saxon times, although the majority of medieval establishments in the area were built after the Conquest.[99] It is therefore clear that the area not only had a long history of occupation, but also of Christian devotion.

Amongst Roger's endowments to the priory were the church of St Mary itself, 11 additional churches, part of the township of Lancaster, the two adjacent manors of Aldcliffe and Newton,[100] one-third of the vill of Heysham, the vill of Poulton-le-Fylde, the tithes of four parishes (including Preston and Bolton-le-Sands), and the small tithes of 19 townships. The right to collect these tithes was subsequently confirmed by the abbot of Sées and Pope Innocent II in 1133. All but four of Roger's donations were within what was to later become the county of Lancaster, and comprised virtually all of his demesne lands in the district. To this were added a tenth of all his hunting, pannage and fishing, as well as the third cast of every net belonging to the Church of Lancaster. Most of the churches were lost to the priory before the fourteenth century, however.[101] The most significant of its later acquisitions was a gift from Thomas of Capernwray, escheator of the county of Lancaster, of all his lands in Bolton and Gressingham that was made around the middle of the thirteenth century. The majority of its other post-foundation acquisitions were in the parishes of Lancaster and Poulton.[102]

In terms of the geographical spread of these properties, Heysham is eight kilometres to the west of Lancaster and Bolton-le-Sands about six kilometres to the north, both of which are within a kilometre or so of Morecambe Bay. Aldcliffe is a few kilometres south of Lancaster, while Poulton-le-Fylde, Bispham and

---

[98] *VCH Lancashire*, Vol. II, p. 167. According to the then administrators of the priory, Roger stipulated that up to 20 persons should be allowed to claim sanctuary in the priory until the end of their lives, if they were escaping from justice. Those concerned were to be supervised by a governor in a place specially set aside for the purpose. However, there is no evidence for this in the priory's foundation charter. See *Materials for the history of the Church of Lancaster*, pp. 8–12.

[99] This information was taken from the priory's former website at: www.priory.lancs.ac.uk/timeline.html, but has been removed from its current website.

[100] There is no extant place name recording the existence of the medieval manor of Newton, but it was to the south-east of Lancaster in what is now a largely uninhabited area.

[101] *Materials for the history of the Church of Lancaster*, pp. 103–4; *VCH Lancashire*, Vol. II, pp. 167–8, 172. The role played by Lancaster's possessions in Stephen's efforts to secure the goodwill of the earl of Chester and King David of Scotland during the Baronial Wars are detailed in *VCH Lancs*, Vol. I: 294–5, while its dispute with Shrewsbury Abbey over the advowsons of the Church of Kirkham is detailed in *VCH Lancs*, Vol. II, 11 and 168.

[102] *VCH Lancashire*, Vol. II, p. 172.

Carleton are about 30 kilometres to the south-east of the town between Fleetwood and Blackpool, south of the River Wyre. Preston is 34 kilometres due south. Those of Lancaster's properties that were nearest to it were also close to some of those held by the Cistercian abbey of Furness,[103] resulting in some conflict as outlined below, while its southern properties were very close to some of those held by the Premonstratensian house of Cockersand,[104] the same house which towards the end of the fourteenth century sought to take possession of all of Lancaster's property.

The priory was administered conventually from the earliest times, the convent consisting of the prior and five monks. Its income was administered by the convent, with an annual payment of 50 marks (£33 6s 8d) being made to Sées until the second quarter of the fourteenth century. During the war with the French, the priory was forbidden to forward this payment to Sées, and instead paid Edward III 100 marks a year.[105] However, it is not possible to accurately determine what its total annual revenues were during this period, as its temporalities in 1291 were taxed at £4, reduced to only 30 shillings after the Scottish raid of 1322. According to a tithe assessment of 1367, the priory's annual revenues were valued at a little over £80, although the Black Death had made a significant impact upon the priory's revenues, reducing its income to £26 13s 4d in 1349 after more than half of the population of the town of Lancaster had been wiped out. Given the hundred mark payment being made to Edward III in the years leading up to the Great Plague, one would imagine that its revenue must have exceeded this by at least 25 marks or so, simply for the prior and monks to survive and maintain their estates.

Lancaster's status as a dependent cell of an alien abbey meant that it was regarded increasingly unfavourably by Richard II during the war against the French, resulting in the farm of its possessions being granted to Cockersand Abbey in 1397 for 500 marks. Cockersand does not appear to have ever gained seisin, however, as Richard's grant was revoked by his successor Henry IV in 1399, and Cockersand was unable to recover either the fee it had paid or any profits pertaining to Lancaster's estates that had been owed to it in the interim.[106] Within a few years, however, Henry had decided to farm Lancaster's possessions for £100 a year.

Soon after ascending the throne, Henry V cut Lancaster's relations with Sées as part of his campaign to suppress alien priories. Lancaster then became a dependent house of the bishop of Durham. By 1413, the amount of rent extracted from it by the Crown was £110 annually, which is probably a reasonable indication of its pre-plague revenue. In 1414, the priory and its estates were handed over to the Bridgettine nunnery of Syon which Henry had just founded.[107]

Just before Syon gained full possession of Lancaster's estates in 1430, its gross income amounted to £326 2s 8d. After being turned into a perpetual vicarage in the same year by the archdeacon of Richmond, the vicar complained that his annual income was 'only' £77. Suppressed by Henry VIII in 1539, its possessions were valued at £216 13s 8d, although the bulk of its estates were sold in 1557 for £1,667.[108]

The history of the priory is filled with disputes with other religious houses over various issues, including tithes, advowsons, appropriations, parochial rights, mills and fisheries. Amongst those other northern houses that are dealt with in later case studies, Lancaster had a long-running dispute with Furness Abbey over fishing rights on the Lune, and with Cockersand Abbey over tithes and parochial rights in the parishes of Lancaster and Poulton.[109] The priory was also involved in a long-running dispute with the archdeacon of Richmond over the tithes of Bolton mill. These disputes are documented in detail in Chapter 9.

The earliest mention of any mills held by the priory is in a confirmation dated 27 July 1149, in which Ranulf, Earl of Chester, recognized its liberties, and gave the abbot a right to some multure from the mill of

---

[103]   See the section on Furness in Chapter 7.

[104]   See the section on Cockersand in Chapter 8.

[105]   *Materials for the history of the Church of Lancaster*, pp. 170–72. There are records of this payment being made to King Edward between the years of 1337 and 1343.

[106]   Ibid., pp. 155–6.

[107]   Ibid., pp. 35 and 171.

[108]   Ibid., p. 172.

[109]   Ibid., pp. 170–72.

Lancaster.[110] A simpler undated charter involving the same two parties confirms the priory's rights to 'waters and mills' amongst the tithes and rents owed to it.[111]

The same holdings were again confirmed by King John while he was still Count of Mortain, so can be roughly dated to between 1185 and 1199. However, this confirmation also includes in the priory's possessions 'the lands and meadows, and feedings, and ponds, and mills, and streams, and purprestures as far as the Lune' held by Amfridus de Montgomery of Roger of Poitou.[112] The mill or mills concerned were presumably part of a subinfeudated holding on the priory's lands in Aldcliffe and/or Lancaster that were then held by one of Amfridus's descendants. John is also supposed to have granted the priory the right to hold a market and fair in 1193, although there is again no evidence of this in the cartulary.[113] A charter of protection dated 26 March 1200 declares that John had taken the priory into 'our hand, custody, protection and maintenance'.[114] Only one mill is named as forming part of its foundation grants, i.e., the mill of the town of Lancaster, although it is not clear if the reference is to its possession of that mill. If there were other mills than these, none are mentioned in later charters, suggesting that either there were no other mills granted to it at its foundation, or if there were, they were directly managed throughout the priory's history.

A year later, the abbot and convent of Sées (Lancaster's mother house) granted one Gilbert the right to raise the causeway of his millpond on their land at Aldcliffe for a pound of pepper annually and the tithes of his mills and fishery on the pond.[115]

Lancaster also acquired one-third of a single fulling mill and grain mill in the same house in the manor of Caton (Lancs.) in the second half of the thirteenth century. A charter of December 1256 records a grant from Roger of Heysham to the priory of this share, including the mills, their site, the millpond and 'free water course to the said mills . . . free common in the wood of Caton for proper repairing and maintaining of the said mills without contradiction of any one [and] . . . all liberties and easements in land and in water pertaining to the said portion of the said mills'. Roger warranted the shares of these mills and their surrounds and stated that he or his heirs would exchange the mills for a portion of his land in Heysham if he or they failed to meet the conditions set out. As this grant was to ensure perpetual prayers for his own departed soul and that of his wife, his anxiety was perhaps understandable, as no money is mentioned in the grant, although this of course does not necessarily mean that none exchanged hands.[116]

Lancaster's surviving charters contain references to at least 11 mills in which it held an interest between the date of its foundation and the mid-fourteenth century. Amongst these was the aforementioned share of a single fulling mill. But as we have seen, there is insufficient information in its foundation charters to determine how many mills it held upon its foundation. Ranulf's confirmation of 1149 refers to the priory's right of multure from the mill of Lancaster, not its ownership of that mill. The only mills that the priory appears to have held outright at its foundation were those granted to it by Amfridus de Montgomery of Roger of Poitou, and there is no indication in the charter of how many there were, or where they were.

By the early fourteenth century, the prior and convent presumably held the mill or mills of Amfridus, and were collecting multure from the town mill of Lancaster and tithes from at least seven mills located in Aldcliffe, Bispham, Ashton, Stodday, Bolton, and the leper's hospital in Lancaster. They also held a third of two mills in Caton. The tithes for the mills in the manor and four vills, as well as the shares of the mills of Caton, were acquired by grants from four local knights during the thirteenth century, and the others probably as part of its foundation grant. It seems likely, however, given the generic mention of 'waters and mills' in its foundation grants and confirmations, that the priory had at least one other mill in the vill of Poulton.

---

[110] W. Farrer, *Lancashire Pipe Rolls*, Chetham Society, 1902, p. 298. I thank Phil Hudson for this reference.

[111] *Materials for the history of the Church of Lancaster*, pp. 18–20.

[112] Ibid., pp. 12–16.

[113] See the priory's earlier cited website.

[114] *Materials for the history of the Church of Lancaster*, pp. 16–17.

[115] See Hudson (1989), p. 12, citing *Lancaster Charters*, 37. These mills are not mentioned in the published volumes of the priory's charters.

[116] *Materials for the history of the Church of Lancaster*, pp. 166–8.

Only two pieces of direct information are available on the rents of any of these mills, i.e. for the significant revenues collected by two lay lords for the shares of the fulling mill and grain mill of Caton. Although Lancaster Priory does not appear to have owned many mills, it must have been drawing a reasonable income from the tithes and multure of its eight mills in an area (typical of the north) in which mills were with good reason regarded as very profitable pieces of machinery.

Table 5.7   Eleven or more mills in which Lancaster Priory held an interest before 1350

Name	Year acquired	Grantor	Grantee
Bolton mill, Lune River (tithes only?)	1094 (?)	Roger of Poitou (?)	Lancaster Priory
Lancaster mill (tithes only)	1149	Roger of Poitou	Lancaster Priory
Aldcliffe mills (x2?) (tithes only)	1150	Gilbert	Lancaster Priory
Bispham mills (x2?) + 1 bovate (tithes only)	1216–72	William le Botiler	Lancaster Priory
Ashton mill/s (tithes only)	>1241 (?)	Gilbert fitz Roger, son of R. fitz Reinfrid	Lancaster Priory
Stodday mill/s (tithes only)	>1241 (?)	Gilbert fitz Roger, son of R. fitz Reinfrid	Lancaster Priory
Stodday mill/s (12d part rent p.a. to priory)	1241–50	William of Lancaster	Lancaster Priory
Leper's mill, Lancaster + 5 a (1 m fee p.a. to priory)	mid-13th c.	Lancaster Priory	St Leonard's Hospital, Lancaster
Caton grain mill (1/3) + Caton fulling mill (1/3) (£2 p.a. to Roger 1251–59)	1256	Roger son of Vivian of Heysham	Lancaster Priory

The relevant information pertaining to the 11 or more mills in which Lancaster Priory held an interest before 1350 is set out in Table 5.7. Lancaster only appears to have held one mill of its own outright, i.e., the Leper's mill of Lancaster, plus the shares of two others, i.e., the fulling mill and grain mill of Caton. It only ever appears to have held the tithes of the other eight mills. The tithes of three or more of these mills were acquired around the middle of the twelfth century, and another four or more a century later, as were the shares of the mills of Caton, and the concession of tithes by Lancaster to St Leonard's Hospital. The donors of both the mill tithes and shares were local knights of various means, which is consistent with the findings of the other case study chapters, where mill donors to the other orders during the twelfth and thirteenth centuries came from the same social class. Despite having been granted the manors of Aldcliffe and Newton, Lancaster appears to have only ever drawn tithes from the mills of the manors, the donors presumably reserving for themselves the bulk of their revenues.

The only documents recording the acquisition of any of these tithes relate to the mills of Aldcliffe, Bispham, Ashton and Stodday. The tithes of Aldcliffe were provided in partial exchange for the raising of a causeway on the priory's land, whereas the tithes of the other three were granted in return for devotional rights.

Sometime between 1216 and 1272 (?), William le Botiler granted the tithes of Bispham mills and one bovate of land in the same vill to St Mary's in return for the right to build a chantry in the church for the sole use of his family. Although the charter is not dated, nor the name of the prior mentioned, the grant is made in perpetual alms 'for the souls of Kings Henry, Richard, and John', so is presumably dated to sometime during Henry III's reign (i.e., 1216–72).[117] This is the only reference in the charters to these mills. In an additional act of piety, the same William granted an acre of land in Layton to the priory which was located within a grange leading to Layton mill.[118]

[117]   Ibid., pp. 436–7.*VCH Lancashire*, Vol. II, p. 274, records that a William le Boteler granted all his leases at Warrington to a free tenant in 1305 'with the express stipulation that the tenant was to grind all his grain and malt at William le Boteler's mills of Warrington and Sankey'. In the *Calendar of Inquisitions Post Mortem, Edward II*, Vol. 6, p. 244, a Richard le Botyller of Lancaster held property near Marton of Nicholas, son of William le Botiller of Routhclif in 1323, as well as a horse mill and some other property of another William le Botiller of Werington (Warrington is about 25 kilometres east of Liverpool). This latter William is presumably the same man mentioned in the *VCH* entry. It seems likely that both men were descendants of the William who made these two grants to Lancaster Priory.

[118]   *Materials for the history of the Church of Lancaster*, pp. 438–9.

An undated charter from Gilbert, son of Roger fitz Reinfrid, records a second grant of mill tithes to the priory. In return for permission to form and raise the causeway of his millpond which was located on the priory's land in Aldcliffe, Gilbert granted the priory the tithes of his watermills and fisheries of Ashton and Stodday, as well as a rent of a pound of pepper annually.[119] This grant presumably predates the next one referring to a mill in Stodday, which names 'lord G.' as the prior, dating this document to Geoffrey's or Garner's priorship c. 1241 to 1250. It records a grant of twelvepence rent in perpetuity from the Stodday mill to the priory from William of Lancaster in return for William's right to 'have my chapel in my manor of Ashton'.[120]

A more unusual document from Lancaster's records concerns an undated grant from the priory to the leper brothers of Lancaster. As 'Sir G.' is cited as the prior at this time, this must have once again been either Geoffrey or Garner, and therefore dated to the mid-thirteenth century.[121] The grant gives the leper brothers the right to keep the tithes of their garden, beasts and mill, which were all presumably located on the five acres of land held by them, on the condition that they maintained an annual payment to the priory of one mark a year. A warranty clause guaranteed peaceful possession as long as the rent was paid as specified.[122] The leper brothers of Lancaster operated the Hospital of St Leonard, which stood outside the gate of St Leonard and had been founded by King John while Count of Mortain. Their property was bounded by that of Lancaster Priory.[123]

The annual payment to the prior of Lancaster of one mark would suggest that the tithes being collected by the brothers were far more than this, in which case the mill, garden, and sales of beasts must have been drawing significant revenues. This supposition is borne out by a survey taken of the hospital's temporalities in 1531, which then consisted of a ploughland in Skerton, and a manor and mill in Lancaster, which were valued at £6 13s 4d a year.[124] It should be kept in mind that this figure would be about 30 per cent less than what the brothers would have been receiving for the same properties in the early fourteenth century. Such considerations render a figure of about £9 annually for this period, at least half of which would probably have been drawn from the mill, suggesting that the mill had suit of part of the township, as per Roger of Poitou's foundation grant. This figure is also roughly consistent with the one mark fee paid to the priory being about a tenth of the brothers' revenues from their properties.

However, the only direct information on how much revenue these various mills were drawing is related to the fulling mill and grain mill of Caton in the mid-thirteenth century. The two mills appear to have been worth the considerable sum of £6 a year. On the basis of the previous discussion, it also seems likely that the leper brothers' mill of Lancaster was drawing £4 or more in annual revenues in the mid- to late thirteenth century. Both figures are in line with the mill rents being drawn by the de Lacys in southern Lancashire in the early fourteenth century, and with those from the earl of Lancaster's mill holdings throughout the county in 1322.

The De Lacy Inquisition of 1311 records rents of £6 13s 4d for Clitheroe watermill, £1 6s 8d for Downham mill, £5 6s 8d for two watermills and a fulling mill at Colne and Walverden, five shillings for a fulling mill at Burnley, £5 for Burnley grain mill, £2 for Padiham mill, £1 for Cliviger mill and 10 shillings for Haslingden mill. In terms of the mill revenues being secured by the de Lacys as a percentage of manorial income on eight manors in Lancashire, they were drawing a massive 26 per cent of their total revenues from these mills at this stage. Between 11 and 13 years later, the rent of the mill of Cliviger had increased from £1 to £2 14s a year, Clitheroe mill from £6 13s 4d to £12, the Colne grain mills from £5 to £12, and the Burnley watermill from £5 to £7 16s. Even the Colne fulling mill had increased in value from 6s 8d to 13s 6d in the intervening period.[125]

---

[119]   Ibid., pp. 37–8.

[120]   Ibid., pp. 38–9.

[121]   *VCH Lancashire*, Vol. II, p. 172.

[122]   *Materials for the history of the Church of Lancaster*, pp. 305–7.

[123]   Ibid., pp. 12–16, and p. 14, n. 2.

[124]   *VCH Lancashire*, Vol. II, p. 165.

[125]   *VCH Lancashire*, Vol. II, pp. 274–5.

The lands of the honour of Lancaster included a number of mills that were even more profitable. The IPM held in 1322 for the late earl's lands records that the Lune mill (near Lancaster Priory's mill on the same river) and *Brokemilne* were at farm for £14, while Salford mill was drawing £3, a horsemill and a watermill in Liverpool were drawing £4 6s 8d, and two watermills in Tottington were rented for £4 4s. The average revenue for these mills was £3 13s a year, which is almost identical to the figure calculated for Bec earlier in the chapter and for Hereford in Chapter 4.

Thus, while we cannot necessarily lump Lancaster Priory into the same category of extractive mill owners as some of the other houses studied in this and other chapters, this would appear to be simply because it held so few of its own mills outright, and of those which it did hold, we have little information on their revenues. The data just cited, however, clearly reveals that the mills in this area were drawing high incomes. Furthermore, judging by the frequency with which Lancaster engaged in litigation with its lay and ecclesiastical neighbours, we have some reason to believe that they were no different from most other English religious houses with respect to their willingness to turn to the courts in disputes with tenants and neighbours.

Conclusion

The mill holdings of each of the four Benedictine houses at the end of the thirteenth century, together with their total annual revenues, are set out below in Table 5.8. In the cases of Glastonbury and Battle, annual revenues are based on the valuations given in the *Taxatio Nicholai IV* of 1291. These figures are generally recognized to be under-valuations. In the case of Bec, the figures are derived from its accounts for the financial year of 1281–82, while those of Lancaster are inferred from a survey of the priory's estates in 1380. Only those mills that were directly held by the houses concerned are included in the tally. Mills for which rents only were paid by their donors, or which paid only tithes, are not included.

In the early fourteenth century, Glastonbury Abbey held more than 40 mills on 32 manors, 13 of which were windmills and three of which were industrial mills (7.5 per cent of the total). The Abbey of Bec held 23 mills on its 26 English manors, including a windmill and a fulling mill. Bec's English estates were, therefore, not engaged to any great extent in industrial milling (4.3 per cent of the total). Battle Abbey held 19 or more mills across its 20 manors by the early fourteenth century, including a possible tide mill, two windmills and a horse-driven cider mill. Only 5.2 per cent of its mills were used for purposes other than grinding grain by the time of the Black Death, although it had acquired a tanning mill at Iltonsbath by the 1380s. Finally, Lancaster Cathedral Priory had interests in as many as 11 mills at around the same time on its two manors and one-and-a-third vills, but appears to have only held outright two or three grain mills and a one-third share of a fulling mill. Only tithes were collected by the monks from the other seven mills. Nevertheless, their one-third portion of an industrial mill still constitutes roughly 10 per cent of the total number of mills that they directly held.

Table 5.8   Mill holdings of four Benedictine houses and their annual estate revenues in the late thirteenth/early fourteenth century

Name	No. of manors and/ or vills	Total no. of mills	Mills with suit	Mills in customary and hereditary tenure	Windmills	Industrial mills	Annual estate revenue
Glastonbury	32	40	30+	9	13	3	£1,406#
Bec*	26	23	20	3	1	1	£1,070
Battle	20	19+	17+	2	2	1	£528
Lancaster	3	2 1/3–3 1/3	2 1/3–3 1/3	0	0	1/3 share	<£80 (?)
TOTAL	**80**	**85+**	**69+**	**14**	**16**	**51/3 +**	**£3,084**

This consists of £51 for Glastonbury's spiritualities, and £1,355 for its temporalities.

* English estates only, 1281–2.

Like many other Benedictine houses between the eleventh and early thirteenth centuries, Glastonbury and Battle suffered from encroachment by neighbouring lay lords, as well as subinfeudation and alienation of a number of their properties. Bec, on the other hand, had not suffered in this way, although its manorial estates were scattered widely, while Lancaster, despite holding most of its properties in a fairly compact area, did not possess many manorial holdings, and therefore mills with suit. The geographical location of the various estates and the kinds of tenure in which the various houses held and let their property had a significant influence on each house's attitudes to mill investment and development, as well as the level of income that they were able to extract from their mills.

With respect to the types of property which they held, all four houses were established before or soon after the Norman Conquest. Like the sees of Canterbury and Hereford, the abbeys of Glastonbury and Battle were granted large parcels of ancient demesne at their foundation, while Bec and Lancaster received isolated manors and other holdings from knightly benefactors over a much longer period. Most of the property that the houses held consisted of manorial estates with clearly defined feudal rights attached to them, including in many cases suit of mill.

The abbot of Glastonbury's rich mill-holdings at Domesday were located on what was predominantly thegnland, around half of which was held by hereditary and free tenants, and much of which had suffered from the encroachments of powerful lords such as the Bishop of Coutances and Robert, Count of Mortain, in the decades after the Conquest. There is clear evidence that the number of mills held in hereditary and free tenure of the abbey remained fairly static from the late eleventh to the early fourteenth centuries, a significant number of them surviving until the fifteenth century, suggesting that the abbey was largely unsuccessful at denying its sokeland tenants and Norman retainers their claims to free tenure. In order to make up for its lack of success in regaining possession of its demesne mills, however, it engaged in an ambitious program of mill acquisition during the late thirteenth and fourteenth centuries, building or acquiring more than 20 mills over that period.

Like its sisters, most of Battle's mills were located on its ancient manors. But although it drew high revenues from some of its mills, the alienation of abbatial property to military and clerical retainers in the twelfth century had ensured that several mills remained in customary or hereditary tenure on relatively low rents throughout the thirteenth century. Where it could extract higher revenues, however, the abbey appears to have been more than willing and able to do so. It also appears to have been quite a keen mill builder, a strategy that may have been partially prompted by the loss of control of some of its mills in the twelfth and thirteenth centuries.

Of those Benedictine and episcopal houses in the sample that lost property between the eleventh and early thirteenth centuries, Battle appears to have been the most successful at recovering seisin. In the thirteenth and fourteenth centuries it was drawing reasonable levels of income from its demesne mills despite some of them having fallen out of their direct control in the twelfth and early thirteenth centuries. It should be noted, however, that the low average mill revenue calculated for Battle in the early thirteenth century (Table 5.9) is a function of the mills in question having been held in free tenure, rather than being a reflection of the level of its seigneurial mill rentals.

Bec was a different case altogether. Its English mills had been acquired gradually as portions of manorial grants by aristocratic benefactors in the twelfth century. However, even though Bec suffered from the same problem as many Augustinian houses of managing numerous properties across a wide geographical area, it was able to set up a relatively efficient system of estate management which allowed it to continue to draw significant revenues from its English manorial properties, unlike most of its Augustinian contemporaries who had in addition to an often wide scatter of properties the disadvantage of many of those properties being non-seigneurial and therefore earning low revenues. Only 13 per cent of Bec's mills were drawing less than 15 shillings a year in rents in the late thirteenth century, all three of which were held in customary or hereditary tenure. The vast majority of Bec's mills were valuable assets drawing high revenues, and Bec appears to have been loath to lose control of them.

Although there is insufficient rental data available for Lancaster's mills to draw any firm conclusions about its mill revenues, what information is available suggests that its northern mills were drawing similarly high revenues to other mills in the county and nearby. Its relatively modest holdings and income were, however, no great spur to mill investment or development.

Table 5.9   Average mill revenues and proportion of mills with suit and in customary and hereditary tenure of four Benedictine houses in the late thirteenth/early fourteenth century

Name	Average mill revenues	Mills with suit	Mills in customary and hereditary tenure
Glastonbury	£2	78%	22%
Bec*	£3 13s 7d	87%	13%
Battle	£1 7s 6d	89%	11%
Lancaster	£3 13s	100%	0%

* English manors only.

The most significant factor in terms of the revenues being drawn from these various mills appears to have been whether or not they were demesne mills with suit. The four houses held more than 85 mills between them on around 80 manors and vills by the late thirteenth and early fourteenth centuries. Of these 85 mills, at least 14 of them (16.5 per cent) appear to have been held in free or customary tenure, a finding which is consistent with the 14–18 per cent figure found by Langdon in his 1994 analysis of the bishopric of Worcester's estates and two hundreds in Warwickshire from the late thirteenth century, but somewhat lower than those found by Holt in the Hundred Rolls for Cambridgeshire and Oxfordshire.[126]

It is nevertheless clear that the Benedictine houses that were the most financially successful in the long term were those which were prepared to actively involve themselves in the management of their estates by introducing new farming and leasing arrangements, and regular auditing and accounting of the activities of obedientiaries and lay officials. Both Battle and Bec were engaged in such efforts in a systematic way in the latter half of the twelfth century and subsequently, as were Glastonbury and the East Anglian Benedictines. The priors of Lancaster, on the other hand, sought to make the best of their limited but locally concentrated possessions by jealously guarding them from encroachment and appropriation from more powerful lay and ecclesiastical neighbours.

---

[126] Holt calculated that 25 per cent of mills in Cambridgeshire and 48 per cent of mills in Oxfordshire were held in non-seigneurial tenure in 1279, on which see Holt (1987), pp. 20–21 and Holt (1988), pp. 54–5. Cf. Langdon (1991), pp. 437–8.

Chapter 6
The Augustinians

The Augustinians were the first major monastic order after the Benedictines to establish itself in England after the Conquest. Although seldom as wealthy as their predecessors, more Augustinian houses survived to the Dissolution than those of the Benedictines. Like the Benedictines, the order remained influential throughout the later Middle Ages. With regard to the order's mill holdings, however, very little work has been done on all but Cirencester Abbey, which is somewhat surprising given the extent of its property holdings throughout England.[1]

While one would expect age and wealth to be major indicators of the number of mills held by a religious house, this was not true of the Augustinian estates studied here. Unlike the great Benedictine houses, which inherited or were granted large parcels of ancient demesne which constituted coherent properties with clearly defined feudal rights attached to them – including in many cases suit of mill – the holdings acquired by Augustinian houses were complicated accretions of former minster estates, old feudal tenures and subinfeudated lands. Many of their holdings were scattered across wide geographical areas and had been donated in small parcels, making any systematic attempt at estate management extremely difficult. What is most interesting about the Augustinians' estates from our perspective, however, is the large number of non-seigneurial mills which were donated or sold to the canons between the twelfth and thirteenth centuries, and from whom those mills were acquired.

Seven of the nine Augustinian estates examined in the case studies to follow were established within 75 years of one another in the twelfth century: the period of greatest expansion for the order. St Gregory's Priory, Canterbury, was one of the first English houses to be founded under Augustinian Rule by Archbishop Lanfranc around 1084. Blythburgh Priory was built around 1116 on land in Suffolk provided by Henry I, while St Denys Priory in Southampton and Cirencester Abbey in Gloucestershire were royal foundations by Henry I in 1127 and 1133, respectively. Bradenstoke Priory was founded in Wiltshire by Walter 'le Eurus', father of Patrick, first earl of Salisbury in 1139. Bolton Priory was initially established at Embsay in North Yorkshire in 1120, but was moved to Bolton with the permission of its founding patron, the great northern magnate, Alice de Rumilly, in 1154. Butley Priory was founded in Suffolk by Ranulf de Glanville in 1171, and Burscough around 1190 by an ancient Lancastrian aristocratic family. The latest foundation in the sample was the small nunnery of Lacock, founded by Ela, Countess of Salisbury, around 1229.

With respect to the counties in which the various houses held most of their property, Burscough Priory's estates were located mainly in Lancashire, while those of Bolton Priory were mainly in Yorkshire. Cirencester Abbey's holdings extended across Gloucestershire, Oxfordshire, Northamptonshire and Berkshire, while those of Blythburgh and Butley priories were predominantly in East Anglia. Bradenstoke Priory's and Lacock Abbey's estates were mostly in Wiltshire, while those of St Denys' Priory were in Hampshire and Berkshire, and those of St Gregory's Priory, mainly in Kent.

With respect to their relative wealth, the houses in the sample ranged from small foundations such as Lacock in Wiltshire, to large foundations such as Cirencester in the southern Midlands. A few of them, such as Burscough, St Gregory's and St Denys's, were very small, with a dozen canons or less, and annual incomes in the late thirteenth century of under £40. Others, such as Butley and Cirencester, were earning well over £200. In between these two extremes of wealth were the houses of Blythburgh and Bradenstoke, both of which appear to have been quite successful with respect to their relations with patrons and the management and development of their estates.

---

[1]   The only Augustinian houses that have received any attention from earlier mill scholars are Cirencester Abbey, Nostell Priory and Newnham Priory by Holt (1988), pp. 41–3, 166, 175, and Wilsford Priory and Dunstable and Waltham abbeys by Langdon (2004), pp. 126, 264, 267. With the exception of Holt's treatment of Cirencester's dispute with its tenants over handmills, however, all the other references constitute passing mentions used to illustrate broader points.

Given the relatively modest means of many Augustinian houses when compared to those of the Benedictines and Cistercians, it would seem plausible to assume from the outset that the smaller houses of the order may have managed their properties in general and their mills in particular in a different fashion to the larger houses; some evidence for this has emerged from the analysis below. However, one thing is very clear from these documents: even though the Augustinians were very popular with kings and great magnates early in their histories, and with the knightly, administrative and curial classes as their reputations grew, it was almost invariably *milites* of varying status who donated mills to the Augustinians.

Knights who had acquired mills as part of their fiefs and prominent families who had held mills since before the Conquest were clearly convinced by the canons, or by their own reasoning, that the revenue from, or better still, the ownership of mills was a crucial component of the success of any religious house, and that because the Augustinians did not possess many whole manors, and therefore, seigneurial mills, their knightly patrons would be showing them a great kindness by donating or selling them mills or the tithes and rents from mills. The wording and content of many of the agreements between patrons and beneficiaries cited in the pages to follow indicate that there was considerable goodwill between the religious houses concerned and the knights and gentry who patronized them. However, because watermills and windmills were valuable assets and expensive to build and maintain, the Augustinians were donated relatively few mills at their foundation and most built few of their own. The majority of the mills held by the Augustinians in the early fourteenth century were acquired from knights through shrewd purchases, litigation and patronage.

Some other notable features of the mill records of the Augustinian houses sampled include an illegal horse mill built by one of Burscough's aristocratic neighbours which he was allowed to keep for an annual rent of one shilling, as well as the grant of a free borough to the burgesses of Ormskirk by the same canons, both in the late thirteenth century. These examples are interesting in the light of the general reluctance of most Benedictine and Cistercian houses to grant such liberties; the abbey of Cirencester being a counter-example to Burscough amongst the Augustinians.

As in previous chapters, the houses are organized by region, beginning in the south-east and working west and north, so that readers can gain a sense of some of the geographical and patronage relationships between the houses concerned.

St Gregory's Priory, Canterbury

Archbishop Lanfranc founded the priory of St Gregory in 1084 or early in 1085 as part of his ambitious program of reform of the English clergy. The priory is first mentioned in the *Annales Anglo-Saxonici*, where the relics of St Edburg and St Mildred are reported to have been moved from Lyminge to the new priory in 1085. However, Lanfranc's foundation charter was not set out until 1087, the same year that the priory is named in Christ Church Canterbury's *Domesday Monachorum*. While St Botolph's in Colchester is generally accepted to be the first Augustinian foundation in England, St Gregory's priority over St Botolph's as a house of regular canons appears likely, although it is difficult to determine when exactly the Augustinian Rule was specifically adopted.[2]

St Gregory's was founded in conjunction with the hospital of St John Northgate that was located on the other side of the road from it at Northgate in Canterbury. St John's was itself part of a twin foundation with a leper hospital at Harbledown not far from Canterbury. It does not appear as though St Gregory's was ever intended to be a hospital, although its canons were expected to minister to the poor and sick, and to take confession and see to the dead, as were other communities of regular canons. The priory also supervised a song and grammar school, but this appears to have disappeared by the early fourteenth century.[3]

Despite St Gregory's auspicious beginnings, and its continued status as a special foundation of the archbishops of Canterbury, it remained in relative obscurity throughout its existence. Amongst the uses to which it was put by the archbishops was a place of accommodation for visitors, a consistory court, and a repository for Christ Church's treasury and archives. Although the priory remained on good terms with Christ

---

2   *Cartulary of the Priory of St Gregory, Canterbury*, p. ix.

3   Ibid., pp. x–xi.

Church throughout its existence, the same was not true of its relationship with St Augustine's, with whom it had a centuries-long dispute over which house held the true remains of St Mildred.[4]

Most of the priory's original endowments were in a fairly compact area in and around Canterbury and in east Kent, while later acquisitions were mostly in Kent, apart from the Benedictine nunnery of Ramstede in Sussex. Its revenues were very modest compared to houses such as Chichester and Cirencester. The *Taxatio Nicholai IV* recorded its *temporalia* as worth £25 15s, and its *spiritualia* at £15. Its temporalities included six manors: the manor of Canterbury itself, as well as Thanington, Howfield and Chartham, all three of which were just outside Canterbury to its south-west, Natindone (Norton Barn?), and Harbledown, which was a kilometre or so west of Canterbury. It also collected tithes of the demesnes of Thanington, Lenham, Barham and Leaveland, all of which were in Kent, and held three appropriated churches with their tithes in Canterbury itself, as well as woodlands on the river Stour, and seven churches and four dependant chapels outside Canterbury. That St Gregory had acquired most of its possessions by the mid-thirteenth century is demonstrated by the fact that subsequent surveys revealed that it had virtually identical holdings right up until the mid-seventeenth century.[5]

Most of the grants made to the priory following its foundation were of small parcels of land and single messuages scattered over a large area. These ranged in size from half an acre to 50 acres. Few of them were of any great value, and were mostly granted to the priory by small freemen who held under gavelkind, a form of socage tenure unique to Kent.[6]

Because gavelkind involved the partition of inheritance, the end result was a large number of small tenements held by many different individuals. Consequently, cash rents and a money economy were early features of the county, as was the absence of customary tenure. The priory also purchased a reasonable amount of land by *gersum*, mostly during the first quarter of the thirteenth century, in order to consolidate its existing holdings. The fact that it was able to make such purchases at this time would seem to indicate that prudent management of its estates during the twelfth century had enabled it to accumulate enough capital to make these investments. It would also appear that a relatively large number of them were made from free men who were indebted to Jewish moneylenders. Nevertheless, the rents paid on many of these newly acquired lands were very small, and, unlike most of the other houses examined in the sample, the priory appears to have acted with genuine philanthropy towards those from whom it purchased property.[7]

Only five mills held by St Gregory's are mentioned in its charters, only three of which were part of its original endowment by Lanfranc, and all of which were in Kent. These were the mill of Tunford in Howfield and two mills at Fordwich (Kent).[8] Archbishop Theobald augmented St Gregory's holdings in the 1140s with additional lands in his manor of Westgate (now Westgate-on-Sea, Kent), which included a mill known as *Crienemelne*.[9] The four mills are specifically mentioned in general confirmations by subsequent archbishops dated to 1174–82, 1185–90, 1193–99, and two papal confirmations of 1146 and 1159–81.[10] Two anomalies are a general confirmation dated to c. 1227–32 by the prior and convent of Christ Church Canterbury of St Gregory's possessions, which only mentions the mills of Tunford and Fordwich,[11] while another papal confirmation by Lucius III dated to 13 July 1185 substitutes Tunford mill for a mill at Dover (*molendinum apud Douorum*).[12] It is likely, however, that this was a mill referred to elsewhere as Goldmill (*Goldmelna*) which was located on the riverbank at Dover (*Douore*) near two mills held by the archbishop and Christ

---

4   Ibid., pp. xi–xii.

5   Ibid., pp. xii–xv. By this time its holdings had become part of a lay estate but had nevertheless been kept intact after the Dissolution.

6   Gavelkind was partible inheritance whereby all sons (and daughters?) would receive an equal share of their father's estate (Kentish). On gavelkind and land tenure in Kent, see Homans (1969).

7   *Cartulary of the Priory of St Gregory, Canterbury*, pp. xvi–xviii.

8   Ibid., ms. 1, subsequently confirmed in 1108–9 by Archbishop Anselm (see ibid.., ms. 2).

9   Ibid., ms. 14, dated 1142–8.

10   Ibid., mss. 15, 16, 17, 25 and 26.

11   Ibid., ms. 18.

12   Ibid., ms. 27.

Church, respectively. The omission of the Tunford mill in the later confirmation appears to have been an oversight, as it was still in the priory's possession at this time.

Goldmill and its appurtenances were originally granted to the priory in the 1140s or 1150s by William de Albervilla, but only the confirmation of the grant, dated to 1195, appears to have survived. William made the grant on behalf of the souls of Henry II, Ralf de Glanville and his own family, with the priory to hold free of his jurisdiction.[13] William was presumably one of de Glanville's military retainers.

As no rents for any of St Gregory's mills are mentioned in any of its charters, or in the *Taxatio Nicholai IV*, it would appear that the priory directly managed all of its own mills throughout its history. The few details about these mills are set out in Table 6.1.

Table 6.1   Five mills in which St Gregory's Priory held an interest before 1200

Name	Year acquired	Grantor
Fordwich mills (x2)	1084–85	Archbishop Lanfranc
Tunford mill, Howfield	1084–85	Archbishop Lanfranc
Crienemelne, Westgate	1140s	Archbishop Theobald
Goldmill, Dover	<1185	William de Albervilla (kt.)

As we can see clearly, St Gregory's does not appear to have built any mills of its own, with the majority of them being granted to it at its foundation, and only one of the five being donated by a knight, with the rest being the gifts of two archbishops. It also acquired all of these mills within its first century of existence. While it is not possible to determine how much revenue it drew from these mills, evidence from its other charters would appear to suggest that it was, generally speaking, a relatively benign and generous landlord.

The only conclusion about revenues from its mills that can be inferred from the available data is based on the four marks which the canons paid to a local free man to use his land for a water diversion for their mill of Tunford (see Chapter 9), along with an annual rent of four shillings for himself and his heirs, which indicates an annual revenue well in excess of four shillings for the mill.[14] Nevertheless, even though the priory held seisin of six manors, suit of mill was not a privilege of lordship in Kent, so that high revenues from its mill of Tunford in Howfield were most likely the result of its location a few miles south-west of the town of Canterbury. The Kentish situation was of course the exception rather than the rule, however, and unfortunately there is no comparable information for any other religious house with mill holdings in Kent in any of the other case studies from which to draw any firmer conclusions.

St Denys' Priory

The priory of St Denys in Southampton was founded by Henry I on the banks of the river Itchen about five kilometres from the bar of Southampton in 1127. It seems likely that it was established on the site of a minster church which had already been dedicated to St Denys that was built by Edith, abbess of Wilton and daughter of King Edgar. Henry I's endowment consisted of two parcels of land, the first between Portswood and the river Itchen, valued at 11s 6d a year, and another in Portswood by the sea to the east of Southampton that was valued at £2 1s 6d. King Stephen later granted the priory his meadow in Portswood worth 10 shillings, and another 20 shillings worth of his demesne that was held by four villeins. By the end of Henry II's reign, the priory's estate of Portswood consisted of three ploughlands, three groves of wood, 100 acres of pasture, 40 acres of meadow and 40 acres of marsh: around the equivalent of one hide, or a small knight's fee. Richard I later added the wood known as Portswood, and, along with the services due from the priory's tenants, this appears to have constituted its manor of Portswood. The extent of the manor's demesne appears to have been around 400 acres of land, and this property remained its most profitable throughout

13   Ibid., ms. 104.

14   Ibid., ms. 129.

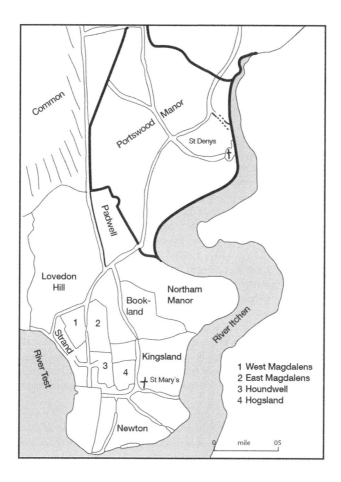

Fig. 6.1   Possessions of St Denys's Priory in Southampton and suburbs. After Blake (1981)

the priory's history.[15] Apart from Portswood, St Denys's held land and rents in Southampton (including two hospitals); some land in Winchester, Dorset and Wiltshire; and country estates in the manors of Lockerley, East Tytherley and Allington, all of which were in Hampshire.[16] It also held at least 20 churches and chapels by the early fifteenth century.[17] The priory's location with respect to its neighbouring holdings can be seen in Figure 6.1.

Aside from the aforementioned royal grants, most of St Denys' subsequent donations were derived from mid-ranking landed aristocrats, some of whom had a close association with the royal court. These included Humphrey de Bohun III, Geoffrey Hose senior, William Briwer senior, Michael de Columbers and his heirs, Robert son of Roger de Hamton, and Roger and his son, Nicholas de Sigillo. The first half of the thirteenth century was the period during which most of these grants were made to the priory.

With the exception of a handful of generous gifts in the fourteenth century, the end of the thirteenth century appears to have marked the end of St Denys's popularity as a preferred subject of benefaction. The burgesses of Southampton do not appear to have ever been amongst its benefactors, despite the large extent

---

15   *Cartulary of the Priory of St Denys*, pp. xxxv–xxxvii.

16   Ibid., pp. xxxvii and ix.

17   Ibid., p. xl.

of its holdings in the town, which were comparable to those of God's House Southampton.[18] In the *Taxatio Nicholai IV* of 1291, St Denys's total revenues were assessed at only £23 16s 8d, more than £21 of which was from its temporalities.[19] The *Valor Ecclesiasticus* of 1535 assessed its total revenues at £80 11s 6d.[20]

The priory's properties in and around Southampton were twice laid waste by French armies raiding along the south coast of England, first in 1338, and later in 1405. The intervening period between the two raids appears to have been a difficult one, both for St Denys and God's House, as both had to spend considerable sums of money repairing and rebuilding the damaged properties, and were unable to recover unpaid rents on many of them, a situation that was no doubt exacerbated by the Black Death. St Denys's financial problems in the wake of the first raid led the canons to seek leave to defer payments of a tenth, and following the second raid, an appeal to the bishop of Winchester for the right to appropriate three churches. St Denys was also expected to contribute in future to the defence of the town.

While the priory's abuses of the revenues and possessions of the leper hospital of St Mary Magdalene during this period may indicate that the priory had become greedy and oppressive during a time of general financial hardship, the prior and canons were at the same time over-cautious in prosecuting those who had disseised them of property or who had failed to pay their rents. Amongst these individuals were prominent burgesses. Either way, there is little evidence that the canons were scrupulous in the management of their properties.[21] During the 1390s and early 1400s a series of inquisitions and *inspeximi* were conducted to re-establish the extent of the priory's holdings and any rents that had been unjustly withheld.[22]

The priory appears to have been served by only six to 10 canons and as many staff throughout the period from the late thirteenth to early sixteenth centuries, and it is somewhat of an understatement to say that the quality of religious life in the priory was casual and informal. For example, amongst those on the payroll in 1426 were 'diverse minstrels and players' who were paid 6s 8d a year. A list of injunctions upon the canons' behaviour issued by Bishop Robert Foxe in the early fifteenth century further indicates that the canons had been illicitly involved in hunting and drinking in local taverns, and there is some suggestion that the ongoing presence of women within the priory had caused occasion for slander.[23] An earlier visitation by the bishop had resulted in two orders being issued to the canons to have 'certain suspect women' removed from the precincts between 1327 and 1328.[24]

As David Robinson has pointed out with regard to the declining fortunes of the Augustinian order in the fourteenth and fifteenth centuries, there is plenty of evidence that a 'loosening of discipline' and 'decline of standards' were the chief passive factors in the overall monastic decline of the later medieval period. He cites a number of damning orders being issued against various Augustinian houses by the bishop of Lincoln during the periods from 1420–49 and 1517–31 which point to the incompetence and misconduct of abbots, priors and members of the convents involved. Of 13 houses of varying sizes and reputations, the charges against abbots and priors included embezzling large sums of money, failure to render accounts, failure to attend services, keeping mistresses and fools at the expense of the convent, striking members of the convent and even incest. Of seven houses it was said that the canons had similarly been engaged in immoral behaviour, which included hunting, hawking, drinking at local taverns, sexual incontinence, violence, disobedience and leading younger canons astray.[25] It would seem, therefore, that the canons of St Denys's, being located close to a bustling port, were sorely tempted from an early date to break their vows on a regular basis, a situation which no doubt contributed to their financial woes and perhaps placed them in an invidious position when forced to bring their tenants to court for unpaid rents; tenants who may well have had resort to threats and acts of blackmail had any of the canons been so imprudent as to publicly reveal their misbehaviour.

---

[18]   Ibid., pp. xxxvii–xxxix.

[19]   Robinson (1980), Appendix 12.

[20]   Ibid., Appendix 14.

[21]   *Cartulary of the Priory of St Denys*, pp. xl–xliii.

[22]   Ibid., pp. xliii–xliv.

[23]   Ibid., pp. xlviii–l. E.O. Blake errs on the side of generosity in assessing the moral rectitude of the canons at this time.

[24]   Ibid., p. xlvi.

[25]   Robinson (1980), pp. 93–7.

By the end of the thirteenth century, St Denys's appears to have held interests in at least eight mills, one of which was a watermill close to the priory in Southampton, but also included, in order of their apparent acquisition, mills or rents from mills at Aldinton (Hampshire), Carhampton (Somerset), Stratford (presumably Stratford-upon-Avon in Warwickshire), and Lockerley, Winchester, Tytherley, and King's Sombourne, all of which are in Hampshire. The priory's charters reveal a long history of problems which it had with these mills, including tithe disputes (particularly with the church of St Mary's Southampton), and the failure of tenants or donors to pay the rents that were due to them. Perhaps the worst of these cases pertained to the priory's mill in King's Sombourne, which proved particularly difficult for the priory to hold, with a number of tenants withholding rents from it over several decades. This case, which will be discussed in more detail in Chapter 9, was symptomatic of St Denys's management of its estates.

The first of St Denys's charters to record any mention of a mill is dated to around 1204, in which William Alis and N. his mother granted St Denys a tenth of all his rent in Aldinton and 30 pigs in his wood free of pannage, as well as five shillings in rent from a mill in Aldinton.[26] This and other grants to the priory were confirmed by Godfrey de Lucy, Bishop of Winchester, in a document dated to 25 August 1204.[27] St Denys was later involved in a dispute with St Mary's Church Southampton over the tithes of this mill that was settled in favour of the priory in 1258.[28]

Around the same time that William and his mother granted the priory their rent from the Aldinton mill, Gilbert de Columbariis sold and quitclaimed to St Denys's a tenement in *Lokerleg'* (Lockerley) that was then held by the widow and two daughters of a former tenant named Sygar, for half a mark. He also granted the priory his interest in the mill of *Lokerleg'* and all the land which the deceased man had held of him. Five masses a year were also to be celebrated for Sygar's soul. Gilbert states that this transaction took place after the repeated entreaties of the tenant's widow and daughters.[29]

Gilbert's heir Thomas repeated part of the terms of this earlier grant some time before 1253, giving the priory a share of his mill called Basset (i.e., *Lokerleg'* mill), saving for himself and his heirs of *Lokerleg'* multure up to 40 quarters annually. The grant also included four acres of land near *Buriwal*, Thomas's part of the moor that had been held by Sygar, and some other land *Tristre*, with right of way for two of his men to draw water from the moor. Thomas also quitclaimed all his right in these lands as well as those which Sygar's widow, Leoviva Peche, had held of his fee.

It would appear that the share of the Basset mill held by the Columbariis family was a half share, as this same half was granted to Walter Basset at farm for life for a rent of 20 shillings annually, but subject to the usual distraining clauses.[30] The right of distraint seems to have been exercised by the priory within a relatively short period, however, as some time after 1253, the share of the same mill was granted back to the priory by Walter. The grant includes 'all my part of the mill at *Lockerl'* called Basset mill, half of which the priory held against me', as well as part of the moor by the millpond, and land four perches in length 'from the island in front of the mill and in width whatever there is between the two waters, saving the rest of my tenement of *Lokerl'* and free access to the rest of my moor'.[31] Walter had already granted the priory four parcels of land some years earlier for twelvepence a year, including part of the moor called *Sigar*, which he had subsequently released and quitclaimed to them.[32]

Sometime between 1228 and 1233, Adam de Cornhampton granted to St Denys all his lands and tenements in Corhampton, Hampshire. The grant included a mill (or mills), although the name and location is not specified, and was made for the souls of himself, his ancestors and successors and several of his lords.[33] The fact that Adam had several lords would suggest that he held property across a number of manors, and was therefore a man of means.

[26] *Cartulary of the Priory of St Denys*, p. 6, n. 1a. This place-name no longer exists, but it was almost certainly in Hampshire and relatively close to Southampton.

[27] Ibid., pp. 6–7, n. 1b.

[28] See Chapter 9.

[29] *Cartulary of the Priory of St Denys*, ms. 311.

[30] Ibid., ms. 319.

[31] Ibid., ms. 320.

[32] Ibid., mss. 317 and 321.

[33] Ibid., ms. 441.

A grant in fee-farm dated to 1252–58 by the priory to Richard le Bretun, a burgess of Southampton, consisted of six acres of land 'in the west field behind the house and garden of the lepers of St Mary Magdalene'. Part of the boundaries of this land included 'the ditch near the footpath that leads to the windmill'.[34] The windmill in question was undoubtedly the one after which Windmill Hill and Windmill (or Fulflood or Canshot) Lane was named in the area described as Abovebar Street West in the maps of St Denys's holdings in Southampton.[35] It appears to have been held by the church of St Mary's, Southampton, although a deed of 1225 records that there were two windmills on this site at that time, suggesting that one had been ruined in the interim.[36]

The Columbariis family appears to have been well disposed towards the priory, as another member of the family, Matthew de Columbariis, granted the priory £3 in rents, most of which was from a mill and land that was held of him by Adam de Bukesgate in *Okle* and *Tydderl'* (Tytherley) worth £2 13s 4d, as well some more land worth 6s 8d at an unspecified location, and an acre of land opposite the canons' court. In return, the priory was to provide a chaplain to celebrate in the church of St Peter at *Tydderl'* for the souls of the grantor and his ancestors and successors. Matthew made this grant some time before 25 May 1282.[37]

Matthew's brother and heir Michael confirmed all of the grants to the priory made by his predecessors sometime between 1282 and 1284. The confirmation included all their tithes of corn, an assart and a mill.[38] It should also be noted that Matthew's and Michael's grandfather Michael (who was Gilbert's father) granted the priory all the tithes of his assarts and newly broken land of *Tederleia* sometime between 1184 and 1235, although the land does not appear to have included a mill at this stage.[39] This land appears to have been one of the properties granted in fee to Michael the elder in the late twelfth or early thirteenth century by William son of William Marescallus de la Lade.[40] It would also appear that one of the other properties was a mill at *Mariscus* in the vill of *Kynessomburne* (King's Sombourne), as a plea in the county court from the beginning of the fourteenth century attests.[41] The difficulties which St Denys's had in maintaining possession of the rents from this property is discussed in Chapter 9.

Table 6.2   Eight mills in which St Denys's Priory held an interest before 1300

Name	Year acquired	Grantor	Annual revenue
Southampton/Portswood watermill	1127	Henry I	no data
Basset mill, Lockerley (1/2 share)	c. 1200	Gilbert de Columbariis (kt.)	20s (1253)
Aldinton mill	c. 1204	William and N. Alis	5s (rent only)
Carhampton mill	1228–33	Adam de Cornhampton (kt.?)	no data
Stratford mill	<1240	Built by priory?	no data
Postern mill, Winchester	<1278–79	Robert le Bal (burgess)	8s
Tytherley mill	<1282	Matthew de Columbariis (kt.)	£2 13s 4d
Brodesmede mill, King's Sombourne	<1301	Nicholas de Marisco (kt.)	20s (1301, 1333, 1410)

The last mill that appears to have been granted to the priory was the mill of the postern in Winchester some time before 1278–79 by Robert le Bal 'citizen of Winchester' (*civis Wint'*), a local burgess who was the guardian of the children of John Alwele. The site of the mill was at the southeast corner of Colebrook Street at the Cathedral Priory postern. The grant also included a tenement in Winchester and a *petrinum* (stone house) and cellar. The properties were the patrimony of John Alwele's son John, who had recently become a canon

---

[34]   Ibid., ms. 49.

[35]   Ibid., pp. lxxiv–lxxv.

[36]   See the section on mill tithes and tithe disputes in Chapter 9.

[37]   *Cartulary of the Priory of St Denys*, ms. 368.

[38]   Ibid., ms. 429.

[39]   Ibid., ms. 428. Blake suggests that the most likely identity of this Michael was the elder rather than the younger, which certainly fits the charter evidence more convincingly.

[40]   Ibid., ms. 430.

[41]   Ibid., ms. 338.

in the priory.[42] A list of rents in Winchester that were exchanged by St Denys's with the bishop of Winchester in 1278–79 for the rents in Southampton which the bishop held from Netley Abbey included eight shillings rent from the 'mill of the postern' (*de molendino posterne*), suggesting that the mill did not remain in St Denys's possession for very long.[43]

The details of St Denys's mill holdings as they appear in the charters are set out in Table 6.2. Of the eight mills in which St Denys's held an interest by the end of the thirteenth century, only one appears to have been held since its foundation. Although this mill in what was to become the manor of Portswood may well have acquired seigneurial status by the end of the twelfth century, it is not at all clear whether the tenants obeyed, or the canons enforced, suit of mill. The mill of Aldinton provided the priory with rents and tithes, but does not appear to have been held by it. Based on the rents and revenues recorded for Basset, Brodesmede and Tytherley mills, all three probably owed suit, but it would appear that St Denys did not necessarily benefit from it. As many as four of the seven mills held by the priory were donated to it by men of the knightly class, while a fifth was donated by a Winchester burgess and a sixth by a mother and son who appear to have been members of the local gentry. All of its mills other than its precinctual watermill were acquired by it during the thirteenth century, or a good 70 years or more after its foundation, while only one of these, i.e. the mill of Stratford, may have been built by the canons.

Only the mill of Tytherley appears to have been drawing anything approaching a high rent, and this was presumably because it had not been managed by the canons of St Denys in the interim! However, it is possible that the three urban mills in Portswood, Winchester and Stratford were earning decent incomes, even if they did not hold suit. It is very clear from the previous discussion and that relating to some of the disputes in which the canons were involved as set out in Chapter 9 that they were not competent estate managers, and were reluctant to prosecute recalcitrant tenants for back-rents to which they were legally entitled.

Bradenstoke Priory

Located on a hill overlooking the Avon Valley in the parish of Lyneham in Wiltshire near the township of Bradenstoke-cum-Clack, the house of St Mary at Bradenstoke was founded in 1139 by Walter 'le Eurus', who was the father of Patrick, the first earl of Salisbury. Established with a prior and 12 canons as a daughter house of Cirencester Abbey, Bradenstoke gained its independence in 1189 through the help of its patron, William Longspee, earl of Salisbury, and Richard I, patron of Cirencester.[44] Although the house grew sufficiently in size to be able to colonize the new foundation of Cartmel in 1194, it was never one of the more significant Augustinian houses, with an annual income of a little more than £140 in 1291, and around £212 in 1535.[45] The priory was suppressed on 17 January 1539.

Apart from the two cartularies that form the basis of the following review of Bradenstoke's mill holdings, none of its account books, extents or surveys have survived. Both cartularies cover roughly the same period, with little of the material extending beyond the late fourteenth century. The deeds for Chippenham, Wilton and several other places are missing altogether, while those for others such as Chitterne, Somerford and Stratton contain large lacunae. The basis for this latter assessment is two *inspeximi* of 1207 and 1232, which record 45 holdings not recorded in the cartularies.[46] About one-third of the extant charters are direct grants to the priory, while the remainder are a mixture of confirmations, quitclaims, inquisitions, fines, papal mandates, royal licenses and records of disputes with laypeople and other religious houses.[47] While priests are the main witnesses to most of the early deeds, their place is taken over subsequent decades by knights. Efforts to

---

[42] Ibid., ms. 457.

[43] Ibid., p. 282, n. a [PRO E326/9149].

[44] *Cartulary of Bradenstoke Priory*, pp. 1, 18–19.

[45] See Robinson (1980), Appendices 12 and 14. Although Blythburgh was amongst the top 17 per cent of Augustinian houses with respect to its earnings in 1291, its position had slipped significantly to being amongst the top 36 per cent in 1535.

[46] *Cartulary of Bradenstoke Priory*, pp. 1–2.

[47] Ibid., p. 9.

safeguard tenure through warranty clauses only begin to appear during the reign of Richard I, although the priory appears to have gone to great lengths throughout its history to ensure as many worthies as possible witnessed its transactions in order to better establish the security of its seisin of newly acquired properties.[48]

One of the priory's most important patrons was the aforementioned William Longspee and his various successors. William was the illegitimate son of Henry II, while his mother's identity had remained largely a mystery until the publication of Bradenstoke's charters. Two of William's charters specifically name his mother as *Comitissa Ida, mater mea*, or Countess Ida,[49] who may well have been King Stephen's grand-daughter by his daughter Mary, who married Matthew, count of Flanders. This would make her Ida, countess of Boulogne.[50]

Relatives, officers and tenants of the earls of Salisbury were other important donors to the priory, while a number of kings made small donations to it, including John, Henry III, and Edwards I–III, as well as the earls of Gloucester and Hertford, Essex and Hereford, and Pembroke. A number of small local landholders also made grants to the priory. Most of these were for the spiritual benefit of the families concerned, and occasionally for the lords of the donating party, while debt and economic pressure, particularly during the first half of the thirteenth century, appears to have been the motivation for a number of others. A relatively small number were intended for special purposes.[51] The thirteenth century saw a marked reduction in the number of grants received by the priory, as well as efforts by a number of the heirs of earlier donors to evade the obligations which they had inherited, although this is also the period during which the priory acquired a direct interest in at least 10 of 15 mills.[52]

While most of Bradenstoke's holdings were in Wiltshire, at one time they held property scattered across 12 counties, as well as in Wales and Normandy. Even its Wiltshire holdings were spread across 26 hundreds, although most were in the nearby hundreds of Kingsbridge, Chippenham and Swanborough. The canons' possessions were very diverse in nature, and included a number of appropriated churches and advowsons, franchises, fairs and markets, arable land, meadows, pastures, woods, moors, withy beds and crofts. They also held a number of rural and urban mills, a tannery, shops, stalls, burgages and plots of land in several towns, at least two quarries in Hazelbury (Wilts.), and a salt-pan on the Dorset coast. Clearly, the canons of Bradenstoke were enterprising men.

Although Bradenstoke held a substantial quantity of land, there were relatively few complete manors amongst its possessions. In her introduction to the priory's cartulary, Vera London lists Tockenham in Wiltshire and North Aston in Oxfordshire as the only complete manors which it held, whereas the *Victoria County Histories* (*VCH*) lists in addition to Tockenham, the manors of Chaddington, Seagry, Lyneham and Wilcot in Wiltshire; Limington in Somerset; and Canford Prior and Burton Bradstock in Dorset (the latter was later exchanged for Framptons in Berkshire).[53] Furthermore, whereas *VCH* makes Bradenstoke's possession of the manor of Tockenham seem fairly clear, it does not appear to have held the whole manor of North Aston until sometime after 1230.[54]

The manor of Tockenham was granted to Bradenstoke sometime between 1232 and 1265 by Thomas of Tockenham. However, the canons must have already held land on the manor by the late twelfth century, as they had built a mill in West Tockenham sometime between 1189 and 1194 which was involved in a dispute with a free tenant who held land adjacent. Additional plots of land in the manor were granted to the priory by Robert Russel and by Henry de Buntesdon and Robert Brut between 1302 and 1303, and in 1334 by Simon, Vicar of Seagry. The priory established its right to all tithes in the manor in 1364. Five years later, only 16 tenants owed service to the lord, suggesting that most of the tenants had freed themselves from villeinage or converted those

---

48 Ibid., pp. 10–11.

49 Ibid., mss. 481 and 646.

50 Ibid., pp. 8–9.

51 Ibid., pp. 11–12.

52 Ibid., p. 19. See Table 6.3.

53 *VCH Wiltshire*, Vol. III, pp. 275–88.

54 This assumption is based on the contents of charters 11 and 12 in the cartulary and later entries in the Hundred Rolls (see note 62 below).

obligations to cash rents by the late fourteenth century. No records appear to have survived about the revenues associated with the mill, although the manor was valued at £4 6s 8d in 1291, and £15 in 1535.[55]

Long before Bradenstoke acquired any interest in North Aston, Domesday recorded 25 inhabitants on the manor, including seven serfs, along with a fishery and mill valued at 30 shillings.[56] Bradenstoke was granted the church of North Aston and 50 acres of land by William de Eston in 1139 at its foundation, and soon after acquired an additional three houses and a virgate from Reynold St Paul. Appropriation of the church did not take place until 1227, however, when a vicarage worth 5 marks was ordained, which included the tithes of two mills. The priory was forced to enter into prolonged litigation to secure the tithes of the mills and of nearby Nethercote. The fact that it was successful is probably reflected in the increased value of the vicarage in 1291, which was then valued at £6 13s 4d.[57]

The manorial population of North Aston had increased to only 27 landholders in the intervening period to 1279, and at least 10 of these were freeholders.[58] The priory is recorded as holding two hides in the manor in 1279, by which time it also appears to have acquired full seisin of the mill and its holding of 1 1/2 yardlands, which together paid rent of 3 1/2 marks. The mill was held throughout most of the thirteenth century by the Gambon family, and retained the name Gambon mill until the late eighteenth century.[59]

The diversity of Bradenstoke's holdings made them difficult to administer, and it is clear from the charters that most of its revenues were from rents. The most active period in the priory's history appears to have been under Prior Simon (c. 1208–c. 1243), when most of its purchases, exchanges, leases, final concords and disputes are recorded.[60] From this period onwards, the priory appears to have pursued a policy of leasing out most of its property, especially in the towns of Cirencester, Chippenham, Calne, Bristol, Malmesbury and Marlborough. By the early sixteenth century, all of its revenues derived from rents and the farms of its rectories.

Despite this policy of renting out its properties, the only suggestion that it rented any of its mills relates to the mill of North Aston, held by the Gambon family throughout the thirteenth century, although there are no records of the terms under which it let the mill. The evidence from its other holdings does, however, indicate that the terms, rents and conditions of the priory's leases varied considerably, and the canons appear to have gone to considerable lengths to ensure that they were not disadvantaged.[61]

At least 18 mills are mentioned in Bradenstoke's cartulary, of which the priory appears to have had an interest in 14 by the late fourteenth century. At least five of these 14 mills were not held by the canons. Four paid rent to them as per the grants of a number of benefactors (two of which they held outright), and three paid tithes (see Table 6.3).[62] In other words, as many as nine of these 14 mills were directly held by the priory from the king, and of these only the mill of Christian Malford (Wiltshire) is explicitly stated to have held suit, although it is also likely that the canons held suit of a mill in East Chaddington.[63] Two of the mills from which it drew rents, i.e., Gambon mill in North Aston and Ewell mill, were held of the priory by free tenants in hereditary fee farm,[64] as was another not connected to Bradenstoke that was located on the boundary of

---

[55]   Ibid.

[56]   *VCH Oxford*, Vol. XI, pp. 6–21.

[57]   *VCH Wiltshire*, Vol. III, pp. 275–6.

[58]   *VCH Oxford*, Vol. XI, pp. 6–21.

[59]   Ibid., citing *Rot. Hund.* (Rec. Com.), ii. 860–1; *Oxon. Fines*, 193, 217; *VCH Oxford*, Vol. I, p. 420; *Wilts.* iii. 285; *Rot. Hund.* (Rec. Com.), ii. 860. The same mill is referred to as 'Gamondesmill' in 1452 and 'Cumon's mill' in 1785: *Oxon. Wills* (O.R.S. xxxix), 101; O.R.O., J VIII e/3. The later history of the mill is recorded in the same entry on North Aston.

[60]   *Cartulary of Bradenstoke Priory*, p. 19.

[61]   Ibid., pp. 15–17.

[62]   The four that paid rents only were the mills of Berwick, Amesbury, Stratford and Ewell.

[63]   Before 1189, Bradenstoke held a virgate in Christian Malford from Glastonbury Abbey, in return for knight's service, hidage and sheriff's aid. Glastonbury complained in that year that the canons were not fulfilling their feudal obligations for this land. The issue was not resolved until 1287, when the prior finally acknowledged those obligations. This was probably in return for the abbot's concession from a few days before that his tenants were obliged to do suit at the prior's mill in Christian Malford. See *Som. Rec. Soc.* xxvi, pp. xxii, 13; Aubrey, *Topog. Coll.* ed. Jackson 422. On the East Chaddington mill, see the discussion below.

[64]   The rent of 10s allocated to the priory from Ewell mill was to be used to pay for a lamp to burn before the altar of the Holy Trinity, the Virgin and All Saints in the priory church.

one of their other holdings, i.e., *Crookemill*. It seems likely on the basis of the rent it paid Bradenstoke in the late thirteenth century that Gambon mill also held suit. Unusually, no mills are mentioned in the priory's foundation charter, suggesting that all of its mill interests were acquired subsequent to its foundation, and only three or four during the twelfth century.

The earliest record of any mill in Bradenstoke Priory's charters is a notification dated 1144–91 by Rotrou III, count of Perche and Mortagne, of a grant to Bradenstoke of half a mark in rent from the mill of Berwick for the soul of his wife Maud and those of his ancestors.[65] This rent is not mentioned again in any of the priory's other documents, presumably because it ended when Rotrou expired, and it is not clear in which county the mill was located, as the placename no longer exists.

Between 1182 and 1193, Alexander of Seagry gave the canons a place called *Sechdewell* in Wiltshire in which there had once been a fishpond and a mill, with the priory given permission to rebuild either or both. Alexander also gave them permission to build a millhouse on the half acre of land adjoining the site, all of which were to be held freely with 'meadow, roads, footpaths, and all liberties'.[66] A royal confirmation by Henry III of a royal *inspeximus* by King John of 17 September 1207 demonstrates that the mill and fishpond had still not been rebuilt by that date, and there is no indication from any of the other charters that they ever were. The same *inspeximus* mentions only two other mills, i.e., that of Christian Malford (see below), and twelvepence worth of rent for the mill of Amesbury from Geoffrey le Veel.[67]

Sometime between 1196 and 1207, Adam Malherbe gave the priory his mill of Ekikeford, free of all exactions and royal service, for a rent of two spurs or sixpence annually, to be paid to the earl of Salisbury.[68] The mill had been granted by William Longspee, earl of Salisbury, to Adam his huntsman for his homage and service between 1168 and 1196 at the same rent that was stated in Adam's grant to the priory.[69] This grant and a number of others were confirmed by Earl William between 1197 and 1226.[70] The mill was later granted by Bradenstoke to the Carthusian house of Hinton Charterhouse.[71]

Ralph Lovel of Clive granted Bradenstoke the mill of Christian Malford, Wiltshire, sometime before 1207, with the consent of his wife, Juette, and son and heir, Silvester. The grant included the watercourses for the mill, a hamlet called Middlecombe and some additional land near the mill for building a house. The grant was to be held by the priors free from all services.[72] Ralph also gave the priory an annual rent of five shillings from some other land nearby, along with the homage and service of the villeins who held the land.[73] Between 1200 and 1220, Silvester twice confirmed his father's grant, in return for two gilt spurs or sixpence annually.[74] Some time before 1232, Silvester gave the canons some additional land pertaining to the mill as well as another mill that had been built on the original grant, including two small meadows and a reed bed, the watercourses and rights-of-way to both mills, and a messuage and land elsewhere. He also quitclaimed for himself and his heirs any rent or services due to them from the mills, but reserved the right of free passage over the land for his men to gain access to another of his meadows nearby.[75]

In April 1287, Abbot John of Glastonbury appointed Abbot William of Malmesbury as his attorney to 'put the prior of Bradenstoke into full seisin of the suit of mill of the abbot's men of Glastonbury to the prior's mill

---

[65]   *Cartulary of Bradenstoke Priory*, ms. 655. Rotrou le Grand (c. 1080–1144) was a well-known Crusader and participant in the re-conquest of eastern Spain.

[66]   Ibid., ms. 164.

[67]   Ibid., ms. 565. Henry II's confirmation is dated 20 July 1232. The latter was granted to the canons between 1168 and 1196 'for the soul of William, earl of Salisbury', Geoffrey's lord, 'for the sake of brotherly affection' (ms. 276).

[68]   Ibid., ms. 621.

[69]   Ibid., ms. 641.

[70]   Ibid., ms. 649.

[71]   Ibid., ms. 622. The relevant charter states that the mill was to be held in alms from the canons and is roughly dated to c. 1243 to 1260, or c. 1282–87. Hinton Charterhouse was founded between 1227 and 1232 by Earl William and the Countess Ela.

[72]   Ibid., ms. 150.

[73]   Ibid., ms. 151.

[74]   Ibid., mss. 152 and 153.

[75]   Ibid., ms. 149.

in Christian Malford, as before'.[76] A declaration by the abbot of around the same time lists 51 of his tenants who owed suit to the Christian Malford mill, eight of whom were women.[77] The dispute over suit of the mill appears to have arisen because W., the prior of Bradenstoke, had until then refused to swear fealty to the abbot of Glastonbury.[78] As noted in Chapter 5, Glastonbury held two mills on the same manor, but neither of them appear to have held suit, and one of them was already at farm for two lives by this time.[79] It seems clear, therefore, that it was the Lovel family, and subsequently Bradenstoke, that held suit on the manor, and not Glastonbury, although it would appear that the manor had earlier been alienated from Glastonbury's estates (see Chapter 5).

A charter dated to sometime between 1213 and 1241 records a 'grant' by Master Hugh clerk, son of Nicholas of the mill of Wroughton (Wiltshire), of all the land that he held in East Chaddington from the lords Walter de Dunstanville, Thomas Chamberlain and John Lovel. The canons were to hold of Hugh and his heirs by rendering customary services, and paid 55 marks (£36 13s 4d) consideration for the privilege.[80] The high purchase price strongly suggests that the property included the mill of Wroughton. The sale was confirmed via a quitclaim from the same period by one of the lords of the fee, Walter Dunstanville III, who released to the priors 'all suits and services due to him and his heirs for the tenements the canons hold in Chaddington, of the gift of Hugh the clerk, son of Nicholas of the mill of Wroughton'.[81] Unfortunately, there are no documents which make any specific references to the mill or its revenues, although it would appear from the wording of Walter's quitclaim that the purchase price included the suit of East Chaddington.

In 1249–50, Hilary de Godarville granted Bradenstoke all her land in Burton Latimer, Northamptonshire, which her brother Nicholas Malmains had given her as dower. This included all her rights in 'the rents, liberties, mills, and lands inside and outside the township, with free entrance and exit'. Based on the evidence from the next cited charter, Hilary's donation presumably amounted to a share of the mill on the manor. The grant was for the souls of her husband Walter, as well as her parents, relatives and ancestors who were buried in Bradenstoke's cemetery. In return she was to receive sixpence a year for all services and suit to her court and that of the hundred.[82]

Between 1260 and 1282, Geoffrey Gascelyn and his wife Joan granted the priory an additional three virgates of land in Burton Latimer, along with the villeins who held them and a third part of the mill in which the canons already had a share. In return, the canons were to render twelvepence a year to Geoffrey and his heirs 'for all services, suit of court and secular demands', but were also to perform any other services, including any repairs to the mill, and labour services.[83]

On 24 August 1290, William Wilegod of Joham quitclaimed his right in what was presumably the remaining one-third share of the same mill in Burton Latimer, and which is here called *Biggemulle*. In the process, William handed to the priors all of the documents which he held that concerned the mill.[84] If William's share constituted the only remaining share of the mill, this grant would have put Bradenstoke in full seisin, 40 years after they had acquired their first share of the mill from Hilary de Godarville.

Nine mills are mentioned in Bradenstoke's charters that were not held by it, several of which appear to have been independent tenant mills, but only one of which merits any discussion. In a grant dated to sometime around the middle of the thirteenth century, Hugh of St Martin, lord of Standen, provides Bradenstoke with a rent of 10 shillings a year from his mill of Ewell. This revenue was to provide a perpetual lamp in the priory's church. The mill was in the manor of Standen (Sussex) and held in hereditary fee-farm by Richard Wiard and his heirs. The rent was to be held by the canons free of all services, and they were given the right of distraint should the rent not be paid 'by whomever holds the mill'.[85]

---

76   Ibid., ms. 154.

77   Ibid. The wording of these documents suggests that only one of the mills on the manor was operating at this stage.

78   Ibid., p. 65, n. 1.

79   See Stacy (2001), pp. 18, 21, 28, 34, 38–39, 40–41, 62.

80   *Cartulary of Bradenstoke Priory*, ms. 61.

81   Ibid., ms. 63.

82   Ibid., ms. 510.

83   Ibid., ms. 512.

84   Ibid., ms. 516.

85   Ibid., ms. 268.

Table 6.3   Fourteen mills in which Bradenstoke Priory held an interest before 1300

Name	Year acquired	Grantor	Grantee	Annual revenue
Berwick mill	1144–91	Rotrou III, Count of Perche	Bradenstoke Priory	6s 8d (part rent)
Amesbury mill	1168–96	Geoffrey le Veel (kt.)	Bradenstoke Priory	12d (part rent)
West Tockenham mill	1189–94	Built by priory	n/a	3s (tithes only – 1341)
Ekikeford mill	1196–1207 c. 1243 to 1260, or c. 1282–87	Adam Malherbe William, Earl of Salisbury Bradenstoke Priory	Bradenstoke Priory Hinton Charterhouse	mill seisin with 6d to grantor free alms
Stratford mill	1168–79 1247	William, Earl of Salisbury Stanley Abbey	William ? Bradenstoke Priory	10s (rent to Church of St Mary, Stanley) 10s (rent only)
Christian Malford mill (incl. suit)	<1207	Lord Ralph Lovel of Clive	Bradenstoke Priory	mill seisin + 5s other rents
Christian Malford mills (x 2)	1229	Built by priory x 1	n/a	16s (for tithes only)
Wroughton mill, East Chaddington (incl. suit?)	1213–41	Master Hugh clerk (sale)	Bradenstoke Priory	mill seisin + tenements (55m purchase price)
Roger Tyrel's mill, Wells diocese*	1216–27	Papal confirmation	Bradenstoke Priory	tithes only
North Aston mill	1226–30 <1230	Bishop Hugh of Lincoln	Bradenstoke Priory (held in hereditary fee farm by Simon Gamboun and family)	initially tithes only, later came into full seisin. £2 10s 4d (rent in 1279)
Stratton St Margaret windmill	<1232?	Ralph or Everard de Arguges (?)	Bradenstoke Priory	mill seisin
Ewell mill	mid-13th c.	Hugh of St Martin, Lord of Standen	Bradenstoke Priory (held in hereditary fee farm by Richard Wiard)	10s (part rent only)
Burton Latimer mill (*Byggemull*) (share)	1249–50	Hilary de Godarville	Bradenstoke Priory	mill seisin + 6d to grantor
(1/3 share)	1260–82	Geoffrey and Joan Gascelyn	'	12d to grantor
(share)	1290	William Wilegod of Joham	'	?
Towcester mill (with houses and other rents)	1285	Exchange with St Wandrille Abbey	'	mill seisin + £2 17s 4d (annual rent)

Cartulary of Bradenstoke Priory, ms. 388.

The details of the grants pertaining to 14 mills made to Bradenstoke are set out in Table 6.3. Of the nine rents and considerations mentioned in the cartulary which pertain to eight different mills, the lords of Berwick, Amesbury, Stratford and Ewell mills simply paid the canons a proportion of their rents, whereas the other four were directly held by the priory (i.e. Ekikeford, North Aston, Burton Latimer and Towcester).[86] Although Bradenstoke held several manors, the only documents which refer to any of the mills on those manors holding suit refer to (what was by then) a single mill at Christian Malford.[87] However, the mill of Wroughton also presumably held suit based on the comparatively large sum of money which the canons paid

[86]   On the Stratford and Towcester mills, see *Cartulary of Bradenstoke Priory*, mss. 363, 505, 541, 557.

[87]   According to the entry on Bradenstoke in *VCH Wiltshire*, Vol. III, n. 98, one of the two mills on the manor was St John's mill by the 'High Bridge'. By the time of the Dissolution, one of the grain mills had been converted to a fulling mill. See BM Stowe 925, 65a–66a; E 315/446, f. 77.

for Master Hugh's lands in East Chaddington, as did North Aston mill, based on the rent the Gambon family were paying Bradenstoke in the late thirteenth century.

The fact that the two mills of Christian Malford paid 16 shillings for tithes only in 1229 (one of which was held at this stage by Bradenstoke and the other by Glastonbury) indicates that their revenues must have amounted to about £8, or £4 each, which is far higher than any of the rents recorded for any of its other mills, and twice the average earnings of Glastonbury's Somerset mills in the early fourteenth century, which no doubt explains why Glastonbury was so keen to claim that it was owed suit of the manor, rather than Bradenstoke.[88] Considering that the priory was involved in at least four mill-related tithe disputes in the first half of the thirteenth century (see Chapter 9), it was presumably drawing a reasonable income from these tithes as well.

As we can see, the social background of its mill donors varied considerably, from Rotrou III, tenant-in-chief, and lords such as Ralph Lovell and Hugh of St Martin, to the huntsman of a lord, i.e., Adam Malherbe, and a member of the administrative classes, Master Hugh clerk, as well as members of the local gentry and another religious house. It is also clear from this information that Bradenstoke acquired interests in the majority of its mills during the first half of the thirteenth century, which was the time during which the priory acquired most of its temporal property, mostly in places where it already held a manor and the value of pastures and meadows was high. It appears to have been able to achieve this through a combination of shrewd purchases, inducements of patronage, and litigation, most of which was undertaken during the priorship of the aforementioned Simon.[89]

The canons of Bradenstoke appear to have been canny estate managers throughout most of the priory's history, and entrepreneurial in their efforts to raise revenue, although the priory appears to have suffered at the hands of at least one unscrupulous prior in the early sixteenth century. The only evidence for any mill-building activity by the canons relates to the mills of Christian Malford, Tockenham and Stratton St Margaret, all of which were in Wiltshire. The original watermill of Christian Malford was rebuilt some 20 years or so after it was granted to the priory, together with a new watermill nearby. In this case, the incentive for construction was presumably the guaranteed revenue of mill soken. The canons also built a new watermill in their manor of Tockenham in the late twelfth century,[90] and a windmill in the hundred of Scipe at Stratton St Margaret.[91] Interestingly, the watermill site of *Sechdewell* granted to Bradenstoke by Alexander of Seagry in the late twelfth century appears to have never been built upon, presumably because reasonable revenues from it could not be guaranteed.

Lacock Abbey

Located about four kilometres south of the market town of Chippenham in Wiltshire, the Augustinian house of canonesses at Lacock was founded in 1229–30 by Ela, the countess of Salisbury, who was the widow of William Longspee, earl of Salisbury. As we have just seen, William and the later earls of Salisbury were major patrons of Bradenstoke Priory. Amongst the abbey's other major benefactors were the Crok family of Wick farm and the Bluets of Lackham, another branch of the latter family also having ongoing relationships with Cirencester Abbey, as we will see below.

Ela's original endowment included the manor of Bishopstrow near Warminster, half the manor of Heddington located just to the east of Lacock, the manor of Hatherop in Gloucestershire, and the advowson of Shrewton on Salisbury Plain. Bishopstrow and Heddington both possessed seigneurial mills, but neither appears to have drawn very high revenues, based on the evidence from the late thirteenth century. It is almost

---

[88] Holt (1988), p. 16, notes that the rents for two mills in Christian Malford that were held by Glastonbury Abbey in 1086 and 1189 were £2 and £2 15s respectively, suggesting that the earnings from Bradenstoke's mills on the same manor were considerably higher. This may have been because Glastonbury's mills had fallen out of the demesne during the twelfth century, as on p. 67, Holt records that one of these mills was at farm for two lives in 1289, but had disappeared by the time the same manor was surveyed in 1517.

[89] *VCH Wiltshire*, Vol. III, pp. 275–88.

[90] *Abbrev. Plac.* (Rec. Com.), 12.

[91] *Cat. Anct. D.* iii, A 4273, A 4718, A 5899; B.M. Stowe 925, 77*b*; *Tax. Eccl.* (Rec. Com.), 193.

certain that Hatherop also possessed a mill at this stage, although none is recorded in the abbey's cartulary.[92] Ela's son gave the abbey the manors of Chitterne on Salisbury Plain, and Aldbourne on the Marlborough Downs. Neither of these manors appears to have possessed mills.

Other early endowments included land in the manor of Woodmancote in Gloucestershire near Cirencester, and a former royal manor and tithes in the parish of Shorwell on the Isle of Wight. According to nineteenth-century antiquarian William Henry Davenport Adams, the manor of North Shorwell was granted to the abbey by Amicia, Countess of Devon, during the reign of Henry III, for which the abbess was later required by Edward III to provide three men-at-arms and a bowman.[93] It does not appear to have had any mills located on it. The great tithes of the manor went to the Abbey of Lyra, whereas those of a second manor in Shorwell (Woolverton) went to Lacock, including the tithes of the mill there.[94]

Between 30 and 40 kilometres to the north-east of the abbey, Lacock was donated other small parcels of land and rents, including some in Uffcott in Broad Hinton and Westlecott in Wroughton. It also acquired land in Slade in Box, about 10 kilometres due west of the abbey, and in the town of Amesbury, about 45 kilometres to its south-east, as well as a handful of urban properties in Bristol and the local market towns of Calne, Chippenham and Trowbridge.[95]

Lacock is one of only seven Wiltshire houses whose cartularies have survived into the present; the others being Bradenstoke Priory, Edington Chantry, Malmesbury Abbey, Vaux College (Salisbury), St Nicholas' Hospital (Salisbury) and Wilton Abbey. The house was surrendered to Henry VIII's men in 1539, its buildings being sold by the Crown to William Sharington in 1540, a descendant of whom was William Henry Fox Talbot, the inventor of the calotype process which provided the basis for modern photography. The abbey buildings, some of which survive, provided subject matter for many of Fox Talbot's earliest photographs, and more recently, for some locations featured in the *Harry Potter* films.

Apart from the charters upon which the study below is based, fragments of the abbey's annals have survived, as well as custumals and rentals from the mid-thirteenth century for Bishopstrow, Heddington, Hatherop and Lacock, and a number of miscellaneous documents. The custumals and rentals have also been analysed below.

Eleven mills are mentioned in the abbey's charters up to the early sixteenth century, five of which it had an interest in, but only four of which it held in full, and only two of those were in operation up to c. 1260. When the abbey was first founded in 1229–30, it only appears to have held a single watermill in the town of Lacock, as it did not acquire the mill in its manor of Bishopstrow until the second half of the thirteenth century, and only one mention is made in the abbey's customary of a half share in a mill which it held on its other manors, i.e., the mill of Heddington, in the mid-thirteenth century. This mill was earning only eight shillings a year in rents for the abbey c. 1260.[96]

There are a handful of indications amongst Lacock Abbey's charters of its sources of mill revenue, its policies towards leasing out mills and how much it was prepared to pay to purchase a mill. The first of the relevant documents is a lease from a lay lord to his tenant of two mills which, in its terms rather than its duration, is fairly typical of those of the mid-fourteenth century and subsequently.

An indication of Lacock's attempts to increase the revenues from its mills can be found in the series of documents relating to its acquisition of the mill of Bishopstrow in the manor held by the abbey which are discussed in detail in Chapter 9. A charter of the mid-thirteenth-century records that five shillings a year was one share of the rent from the mill of Bishopstrow,[97] while the customary of c. 1280 records that 20 shillings was the total due from the same mill with nine acres of land.[98] The various shares of the mill were granted to

---

    92   See Gloucestershire Archives, D540/T29 c.1540–1766.

    93   Amice de Clare (c. 1210–84) also founded Buckland Abbey in Devon using Cistercian monks from Quarr Abbey on the Isle of Wight.

    94   Davis (1958), pp. 154–5. Woolverton was assessed at one hide in the Hundred Rolls, with a value of 10 shillings, and the mill valued at 35 shillings. Shorwell was valued at £17 *per annum* in 1291. See *Taxatio Nicholai IV*, p. 214.

    95   *Lacock Abbey Charters*, pp. 1–2.

    96   'Customs of Four Manors of the Abbey of Lacock', p. 335.

    97   Ibid., ms. 225.

    98   Ibid., p. 333.

Lacock in 1259 by three related parties, with the grant confirmed and seisin transferred by the tenant-in-chief, Adam Sweyn of Westbury, sometime between 1259 and 1283 for six marks (£4).[99] This complicated network of grants and quitclaims had put the canonesses in full seisin of Bishopstrow mill by the end of the thirteenth century, at a cost of at least £4 (not counting legal fees) in return for £1 a year in rents. By 1533, the abbey held three mills in Bishopstrow in the one complex: a gig mill, a grist mill and a fulling mill.[100] Its tenants paid £2 3s 4d plus 20 quarters of wheat and 20 quarters of barley annually.[101] However, the 99-year lease on the property which was given the tenants was to be cut short only six years later when the abbey was dissolved. This document is of some interest in the light of Langdon's earlier findings that the number of industrial mills throughout England had increased by almost 125 per cent between 1300 and 1540.[102]

On 10 July 1340, Reynold de Paveley, lord of Brok, leased two watermills at Westbury to William de Grinstede with suit and pasture for a draught animal as well as timber from Reynold's woods for maintaining the mills and their waterworks, along with two additional pastures and other lands and tenements, for three years at £10 annually. Reynold also provided straw and thatching for roofing the millhouses, and William was expected to keep the heads of the ponds (*capita stagnorum*) properly maintained. He allocated nine shillings of the rent of *Colesmulle*, which was presumably the name of one of the Westbury mills, to the abbess of Lacock. While it is not clear exactly how much other land was involved, it would seem that the mills of Westbury were very profitable. William was also allowed to be quit of all service on the deed until 'next Lady Day' (1 January).[103]

The details of the various mills in which Lacock held an interest are set out in Table 6.4. Like many of the other Augustinian houses surveyed, Lacock does not appear to have built any of its own mills, acquiring two through its foundation grant from Ela, countess of Salisbury, and two others through the generosity of two local lords. Based on the evidence from elsewhere in England and Wales, although it is possible that the construction of the two industrial mills built in Bishopstrow between c. 1280 and 1533 was commissioned by the nuns, it is more likely they were built by tenants.

Table 6.4   Seven mills in which Lacock Abbey held an interest before 1540

Name	Year acquired	Grantor	Annual revenue
Lacock watermill	1229–30	Ela, countess of Salisbury	Precinctual mill
Heddington mill (half share)	1229–30	Ela, countess of Salisbury	8s (c. 1260)
Hatherop mill	?	?	?
Woolverton mill (Isle of Wight)	1216–72 (?)	Amicia, Countess of Devon (?)	tithes only
Bishopstrow mill	1259	Lord Adam Sweyn (tenant-in-chief) Emme Burgeys, Anastasia Serle, William de Smalebroke (tenants)	20s (c. 1280)
Colesmulle (Westbury)	1340	Reynold de Paveley, Lord of Brok	9s (rent only)
Bishopstrow mills (x3) (incl. 2 industrial mills)	1280–1533	Industrial mills built by tenants?	£2 3s 4d (1533)

[99]   The relevant charters are discussed in more detail in Chapter 9. Adam Sweyn was also a benefactor of Bradenstoke Priory.

[100]   A gig mill is a textile mill which employs rotating wire cylinders for napping cloth. A 'grist mill' is simply another name for a grain mill.

[101]   *Lacock Abbey Charters*, ms. 239. Robert Abathe and his wife Elizabeth were leased the property 'in consideration of the great charges Robert has incurred and will incur in repairing and rebuilding the farm, millhouse and tenement ... as William Cabell held them'. The property also included a wood, 320 sheep, two cottages, a curtilage and two pastures, for which separate rents totalling £6 8s were due. It would seem that the three mills had been held separately by one John George.

[102]   Langdon (2004), p. 41.

[103]   *Lacock Abbey Charters*, ms. 225. Lady Day was the traditional day on which year-long contracts between landowners and tenants would begin and end. Farmers were usually required to time their entry into new farms and onto new fields on Lady Day.

As we saw in the case of Bradenstoke's mill with suit in the manor of Christian Malford, it seems likely that because the mill of Bishopstrow was part of the original grant of the whole manor that it also held suit, while the rent paid for Heddington mill was presumably half of the suit owed to that seigneurial mill. As there were at least four other mills that existed on the boundaries of Lacock's Wiltshire properties, and there were many free tenants in Wiltshire, the low revenues which it drew from its seigneurial mills may well have been due to significant competition from non-seigneurial mills in the area. As we will see below, one of these mills was held by the Templars, and, judging from the series of disputes between the Bluet family and the abbess over the watercourse to her precinctual mill (see Chapter 9), the Bluets probably also held a mill in the area.

Four mills are mentioned as forming boundaries to parts of Lacock's holdings, two of which may have been independent tenant mills. One of these was the mill of Calne which is also mentioned in Bradenstoke's cartulary, while the other two were in the manor of Melksham and known as *Bibidmulle* and *Semannesmull*. The fourth was a mill held by the Templars in an unspecified location beside which Lacock received a grant of one acre of land by Hugh le Fronceis of Natton.[104] This was probably the mill of *Bradeshete* which was the subject of a case of novel disseisin in the Wiltshire county court in 1249. The case had been brought by Shaleburne Priory against Master Robert of Saunford, brother of the Knights Templar, and 15 other men, including Richard le Fraunceys (presumably a relation of Hugh le Fronceis), for having unjustly disseised the priory of the mill. The court found against Shaleburne, however, as the mill had been granted to it by one of Master Robert's tenants, a grant to which the latter had not agreed.[105]

Finally, an official perambulation of Lacock's estates dated to 10 June 1300 before Sir John de Berwyke and Walter de Gloucestre, escheator, by royal writ at Salisbury, confirmed the boundaries of the manor of Melksham, two of the borders of which were formed by the waters which fed the two mills of *Bibidmulle* and *Semannesmull*.[106] *Bibidmulle* is later mentioned as lying beside half an acre of land leased for life by the abbey in 1306 to John de Fifhide and his wife Joan, amongst a large number of small possessions making up a virgate of land in Lacock and Natton.[107] There is nothing in either charter to indicate who was in seisin of the two mills, although it seems likely that they were held by independent tenants. This observation is given further support by the large number of mills about which pleas were heard in the Wiltshire county court in 1249 that appear to have been held by independent tenants. Of the 14 mills recorded, two were held by religious houses, and one as part of a knight's fee, while the rest appear to have been held by customary and free tenants, or almost 80 per cent of them.[108]

Cirencester Abbey

Situated within the ancient town of Cirencester in Gloucestershire, the abbey of St Mary Cirencester was consecrated in 1131, although its foundation charter by Henry I is dated July 1133.[109] The house was almost undoubtedly established on the site of an Anglo-Saxon college of regular canons, as Henry's endowment is described as belonging to 'the whole tenure of Regenbald', who, apart from being a well-known early pluralist, had probably been the former dean of the college. While Cirencester's own canons came from Merton Priory, the only daughter-house that it appears to have produced was Bradenstoke Priory in Wiltshire, from which it was released through the intervention of Richard I in 1189. It also produced two illustrious clerics, Robert of Cricklade (twelfth century), who later became prior of St Frideswide, and Alexander Neckham (1157–1217), Cirencester's most distinguished abbot.[110]

---

[104]   Ibid., ms. 156. The charter is dated 1257–83.

[105]   *Civil Pleas of the Wiltshire Eyre, 1249*, ms. 74.

[106]   *Lacock Abbey Charters*, ms. 24.

[107]   Ibid., ms. 181.

[108]   *Civil Pleas of the Wiltshire Eyre, 1249*, mss. 9, 51, 74, 91, 102, 127, 147, 241, 258, 323, 344, 388, 397, 400 and 457.

[109]   *The Cartulary of Cirencester Abbey*, p. xix, ms. 28/1.

[110]   Ibid., p. xix.

In the early thirteenth century, Archbishop Hubert of Canterbury and Bishop Mauger of Worcester intervened in the affairs of the abbey, ruling that it was not being managed satisfactorily. A certain servant of the abbey named Jordan (of Cirencester or *Scotmodi*), along with the cellarer, appear to have been running the abbey's affairs to their own benefit. Amongst the reforms imposed on the canons was a centralized system of receipt and audit, the appointment of three treasurers to receive and disburse the abbey's revenues, as well as a quarterly accounting procedure that was to be supervised by two brethren who were appointed as examiners. The abbot was instructed not to conduct any business without the advice of the treasurers.[111]

These reforms were further strengthened shortly afterward during an episcopal visitation, possibly by Bishop William of Blois (1218–36). By the middle of the century, however, a compromise had been reached whereby the treasurers disbursed revenues to various obedientiaries (i.e. the cellarer, kitchener and abbot's chaplain), while others were allowed to handle their own income. Nevertheless, as late as 1352, the treasurers ordered officials to make daily reckonings of their expenditure in their presence, while in 1378, Bishop Wakefield ordered that all income was to be paid directly to the treasurers and to no other officers.[112]

Most of Cirencester's muniments have not survived. The material examined here derives from the two abbey registers known as A and B, while the other material mostly consists of fragments of the abbey's cartulary from the late twelfth century and from the fifteenth and early sixteenth centuries. Register A consists of material ranging from the early thirteenth to the fifteenth centuries, although most of it was written in the mid-thirteenth century. Register B appears to have been begun sometime after 1360. Apart from some obedientiary accounts from 1248–77 that are probably still in private hands, none of the house's account or court rolls have survived.[113]

By the time of the Dissolution, the abbey's annual income was valued at £1,046, making it by far the wealthiest house of regular canons other than Waltham and Leicester.[114] Although its wealth was exceeded by neighbouring Benedictine houses such as Gloucester and Tewkesbury, it was nevertheless wealthier than the venerable royal foundation of Winchcombe about 26 kilometres to its north.[115]

Cirencester was thus fairly unique amongst Austin houses in that its revenues were not only large, but were little augmented from the time of the abbey's foundation. Apart from the royal grants of the lordship of Cirencester and the Seven Hundreds in the late twelfth century,[116] there were few large-scale benefactions to the abbey after 1133, and none compared with Henry I's 'royal munificence', as the Hexham chronicler described them.[117] Fairs were granted to Cirencester by King John in 1215 and Henry III in 1253,[118] while Edward I gave the canons the privilege of administering their own affairs during abbatial vacancies.[119] Despite the lack of large-scale benefactions, as many as 16 of the mills in which the abbey held an interest were granted to it or purchased during the thirteenth century.

Cirencester's possessions lay mainly in four areas. The first was in Gloucestershire and north Wiltshire, where the abbey held six churches and lands in each associated vill (Preston, Driffield, Ampney St Mary, Cheltenham, Latton and Eisey), as well as in six other places (Cirencester, Norcote, Walle, Elmstone, Painswick and the borough of Cricklade). It also held two churches in central Somerset (Frome and Wellow), and two more on the Somerset-Dorset border (Milbourne Port and Pulham), each of which included land in their associated vills. The third area in which it held property was in central Wiltshire and Berkshire, and consisted of a number of scattered but valuable properties: churches and lands in Pewsey, Avebury and Shrivenham in the west, and Hagbourne, Cookham and Bray in the east. The fourth area was in Northamptonshire, some distance away from its other holdings, where it held churches and land in Rothwell and Brigstock. It also held

---

[111] Ibid., p. xx.

[112] Ibid., pp. xx–xxi.

[113] Ibid., pp. xi–xvii.

[114] Waltham's net revenue in 1539 was £900 4s 3d, and for Leicester, £951 14s 6d. See Robinson (1980), Appendix 14.

[115] Ibid. The net income of St Peter's Gloucester without its cells was £1,429 in 1539, while Tewkesbury with Deerhurst was valued at £1,598. Winchcombe, on the other hand, had a net income in 1539 of £759.

[116] *The Cartulary of Cirencester Abbey*, mss. 31, 32, 77 and 79.

[117] 'The Hexham Chronicle', p. 66.

[118] *The Cartulary of Cirencester Abbey*, mss. 43–4, 49, 51 and 115.

[119] For Edward I's grant, see ibid., ms. 93.

land in Boycott and the church of Passenham, both of which are in Buckinghamshire, and a small amount of property in London. Although the canons did not come into full possession of all of these holdings until the thirteenth and fourteenth centuries, those that did remained in their hands until the Dissolution.[120]

Like other Augustinian houses, the social rank of Cirencester's benefactors declined as the decades progressed. Apart from Henry I, the most prominent donors of magnate status which the abbey attracted were Roger, earl of Hereford, and Roger de Clare, earl of Hertford, although neither made major donations.[121] Roger's widow Matilda and her second husband, William d'Aubigny, also made minor grants to the abbey,[122] while Hugh de Chesney, whose family were patrons of Sibton Abbey and Blythburgh Priory, granted the canons land in Boycott, Northamptonshire, which had formerly been held by his father.[123] In a similar fashion, Henry I's grandson by Nesta, Meiler fitzHenry, endowed the abbey with land in county Kerry.[124]

Other than these more illustrious benefactors, most of those who donated property to Cirencester in the second half of the twelfth century were royal officials and members of the local nobility and gentry. Amongst the latter were families such as the Bassets, Damorys, Danvers and Courcelles.[125] For example, Jordan and Alice Basset sold the canons Black Mill in Berkshire in the late twelfth century.[126]

During the thirteenth century, the stream of donations dwindled, and Cirencester's benefactors tended to be men of more humble backgrounds. While several knights granted the abbey properties here and there, including four mills, most of its acquisitions in the thirteenth century were from modest landholders and even servants of the abbey such as Peter of Edgeworth.[127]

An unusual feature of the abbey's acquisitions in the towns of Bristol and Gloucester was that they were acquired predominantly through premiums paid to the canons for entry into the religious life at Cirencester. It would seem that the life of the canons was still sufficiently appealing to urban landowners and merchants in the late twelfth and early thirteenth centuries to warrant the dedication of their family members to the order.[128]

Nevertheless, in the light of the fewer gifts that were forthcoming from donors, lease, purchase and exchange were the primary means by which piecemeal acquisition of properties was pursued in the thirteenth century and subsequently. The price of some small donations was spiritual succour either in the form of a celebration of the donor's anniversary, or the inclusion of the donor in the canons' prayers, although unlike most of the other Augustinian houses studied in this book, such grants to Cirencester did not include mills or the shares of mills.[129] By the end of the thirteenth century, Cirencester was drawing £74 4s 6d from its spiritualities, less than a third of its total income of £242 6s 8d; the majority of these revenues came from its 18 churches and the pensions of 10 others.[130]

The abbey experienced a series of crises in the first half of the fourteenth century relating to whether it had the right to be exempted from the payment of tallage to the Crown, and whether the townsmen of Cirencester had burghal rights which the abbot had been illegitimately withholding from them. The Crown also placed excessive demands on the abbey for the provision of corrodies for former royal servants. While the dispute over tallage went on for 34 years, finally being resolved in 1357 to the canons' favour,[131] of more relevance to the abbey's milling history was the dispute over the burghal status of the town of Cirencester.

---

[120] Ibid., p. xxii. On Cirencester's London holdings, see *Taxatio Nicholai IV*, p. 12. The London properties were valued at £4 7d *per annum*.

[121] Ibid., mss. 31 and 669.

[122] Ibid., mss. 672, 673 and 678.

[123] Ibid., ms. 646.

[124] Ibid., ms. 634.

[125] Ibid., mss. 518–9, 652, 654, 73, 76, 184, 193, 597 and 615.

[126] Ibid., mss. 189 and 118/829. Another member of the family held the mill of Lockerley of St Denys's Priory in the mid-thirteenth century (see *Cartulary of St Denys' Priory*, ms. 319).

[127] *The Cartulary of Cirencester Abbey*, mss. 326, 396.

[128] Ibid., mss. 439–41, 445, 629, 630–31 and 633.

[129] See for example, ms. 269.

[130] See Robinson (1980), Appendix 12.

[131] *The Cartulary of Cirencester Abbey*, pp. xxxiv–xxxv.

More than 30 mills are mentioned in the abbey's charters, of which it appears to have directly held at least 19 by the end of the thirteenth century. It was, therefore, by far the largest mill owner of all the Augustinian estates studied in the sample, with mills in Gloucestershire, Oxfordshire, Northamptonshire and Berkshire. It also collected the tithes of mills in at least four parishes. Cirencester's mill holdings were no doubt a major source of income with respect to its temporalities, although this income is difficult to gauge because its list of mill revenues, while quite extensive, is also fragmented and inconsistent. An analysis of these revenues will nevertheless be undertaken below.

Cirencester probably held at least four mills at its foundation, but its foundation charter of July 1133 mentions only three: at Cheltenham in Gloucestershire, Boycott in Oxfordshire and Winton in Northamptonshire.[132] The mill of Winton is not mentioned in any of the abbey's subsequent charters, while the Boycott mill is mentioned only once. The only one of these mills that receives any significant attention in Cirencester's cartulary is Cheltenham mill, for which a handful of charters have survived. The other mill it acquired as part of its foundation was its own precinctual mill. The earliest references to it are in two documents dated to c. 1230 to 1250, the first of which is a grant of a share of land which lay between the abbot's street and the watercourse which led to the mill within the abbey. The grant was from Nicholas Pilet, son of Roger Pilet of Marlborough. The land concerned had formerly been held by Roscelin of Cirencester.[133] The other document is a quitclaim by Alice Mingnot, Nicholas' mother, of all her right in the same land.[134] The last mention of the mill is from a grant dated to the late thirteenth century from Walter Sturmy to the canons of a license to enclose a lane 'which lies between the court of the abbot and his mill'.[135]

As the abbey only held four mills at its foundation, but as many as 19 by the end of the thirteenth century, there was an almost five-fold increase in the number of its mills over that time. The majority of them appear to have been acquired through grants from knights; at least three of which were donated to it during the second half of the twelfth century, and the rest during the thirteenth century (see Table 6.5 below). Three mill purchases are recorded in the charters, the first being Blackmill in Berkshire which was bought by the canons in 1197 for £12 10s, the second being what was presumably a half share of Brain mill in Daglingworth (a few kilometres north of Cirencester), for £10, and the third being *Clerkesmill* near the abbot's barton in Cirencester, which the canons bought at the end of the thirteenth century for £20. All three figures are consistent with the prices paid by other houses for mills in the thirteenth and early fourteenth centuries. All of these mills were bought from local knights. The canons also built at least one watermill at Duntisbourne Nutbeam in Gloucestershire in the late thirteenth century, but no records of its construction are extant.

Some unusual features of the abbey's mill records include the leasing of two mills to a lawyer for relatively low rents in return for services rendered to the abbey in the second half of the twelfth century, and a document that releases a miller and his family from villeinage in the mid-thirteenth century. Both sets of documents are described in greater detail in Chapter 9.

The earliest grant of a mill to Cirencester is from a document dated to between 1147 and 1176, in which Hugh de Gunnovill, constable of William, earl of Gloucester, and his wife granted to the abbey all of their land in *Eastenest'*, along with a church and a mill there. Hugh stated that the grant was made with his lord's approval. It is not clear where this land and mill were located, however, as the inclusion of it under a heading for Cirencester's possessions in Aston Upthorpe in Berkshire appears doubtful because of the lack of any clear connection between it and either the Gunnovill family or the honour of Gloucester.[136] Nevertheless, it is possible that the location is as the abbey's scribes denoted, and that the property in question is simply not recorded elsewhere in the relevant families' documents. The grant was confirmed by William, earl of Gloucester, in a subsequent charter.[137]

---

[132] Ibid., ms. 28/1. The mill of Boycott is not mentioned in Domesday Book, so was presumably built between 1086 and 1133.

[133] Ibid., ms. 282/139.

[134] Ibid., ms. 283/140.

[135] Ibid., ms. 468.

[136] Ibid., ms. 808 and note.

[137] Ibid., ms. 809.

The canons granted Robert son of William of Blewbury a lease of their mill of Medford for one mark a year sometime between 1166 and 1176. The date of Cirencester's acquisition of this mill is not clear. Robert was also obliged to ride with the abbot or his deputy at the abbot's expense whenever the church needed Robert to assist in its pleas. This unusual charter indicates that Robert was a lawyer who acted on the abbey's behalf.[138] Sometime between 1187 and 1213, he was also granted a lease of the canons' mill known as Blackmill in Hagbourne (Berkshire) for £1 a year.[139] It would seem likely, however, based on the following documents, that the abbey's grant to Robert was later than 1197, as it does not appear to have gained (or regained?) seisin of the mill until then.

On 28 September 1195–97, a writ was issued by Hubert Walter, archbishop of Canterbury, to Peter Corbezun, commanding him to 'do right' to Jordan Basset in respect of a mill and six acres of meadow which pertained to it, as well as a free tenement in North Moreton, Berkshire. Jordan held both properties of Peter by feudal service and one knight's fee.[140] The mill concerned was undoubtedly Blackmill, as a final concord dated 23 April 1197 between Jordan and Alice Basset and Abbot Richard of Cirencester records that the latter paid the former 15 marks (£12 10s) for them to quitclaim all of their right in Black Mill with six acres of meadow.[141] As the mill was located in Hagbourne, it is sometimes also referred to as Hagbourne mill.

Sometime between c. 1230 and 1250, Nicholas Gulias granted the same mill (*Blakemelne*) to the canons and quitclaimed any right in it.[142] The charter mentions that the grant includes all of the mill's appurtenances, i.e., 'meadows, messuages, crofts, curtilages, roads and paths, waters and fisheries', but it should be kept in mind that the use of the plural in these charters does not necessarily mean that more than one of each item was being indicated. In 1255, the dean of Cirencester and four associates supplied a valuation of the abbey's temporal revenues in Hagbourne and Aston based on a statement supplied by Master Giles of Bridport. The total valuation was £18 4d, and an additional 36s for tithes, with the value of the mill of Hagbourne stated to be two marks (£1 13s 4d).[143]

A final concord dated 9 May 1219 between Adam of Cockfield and the abbot of Cirencester records that the abbot recognized the advowson of the church of Little Oakley in Northamptonshire to be the right of Adam, in return for which Adam and his heirs granted the abbot and his successors half a mark in rent from the farm of his mill in Little Oakley, which he held by feudal service.[144] The grant of the rent from the mill is also set out in a separate charter.[145] This Adam is the same man from whom the church of Corton was appropriated in the early thirteenth century by Leiston Abbey,[146] and to whom Abbot Samson spoke so harshly when the former tried to argue that his father and grandfather held some extremely lucrative property from Bury St Edmunds in heredity.[147]

The history of the acquisition and possession of two mills in Cirencester by the canons near the abbot's barton is somewhat circuitous and covers a number of grants and quitclaims over the course of about a century. Between 1197 and 1208, Eynsham Abbey gave a local knight named Geoffrey Marshall of Cirencester their mill of Wiggold in Cirencester, which was held of them by Hugh Mace, for an annual rent of £1 14s. The grant was confirmed to Geoffrey for an additional sum of three-and-a-half marks (£2 6s 8d).[148] The mill-race to the mill is described as forming part of the boundaries of some land granted by one layman to another that is recorded in one of Cirencester's charters.[149] In the early thirteenth century, the mill of Wiggold was also known as Maz or Mace mill, presumably after its tenant, Hugh Mace, who may also have built the mill.

---

[138]   Ibid., ms. 540.

[139]   Ibid., ms. 541. A mill in *Hacheborne* is listed in Domesday Book as rendering 12 shillings a year (see Bennett and Elton (1899), p. 138).

[140]   Ibid., ms. 189.

[141]   Ibid., ms. 118/829.

[142]   Ibid., mss. 538/827 and 539/828.

[143]   Ibid., ms. 461.

[144]   Ibid., ms. 194.

[145]   Ibid., ms. 725.

[146]   See the discussion of Leiston Abbey later in this chapter.

[147]   See Chapter 1.

[148]   *The Cartulary of Cirencester Abbey*, ms. 203.

[149]   Ibid., ms. 247, dated to the reign of King John (i.e., 1199–1216).

Sometime around 1240, Stephen of Harnhill gave the canons of Cirencester this same mill, called Maz in the charter. However, it is not at all clear how Stephen came into seisin, as Geoffrey Marshall's (eldest?) daughter Matilda had some claim in the mill, as recorded in three charters dated roughly from 1250 to 1266. Stephen was a local knight who attested several of the abbey's charters from the second to fifth decades of the thirteenth century, and was made local escheator in June 1246, although he was probably dead within another two years. It is therefore possible that Stephen had held the mill in wardship on behalf of Matilda, although there is no indication of this in any of the charters relating to her. The first of these records a grant of five acres of land in the field of Cirencester by Matilda, as well as a quitclaim of all her right in Mace Mill 'with all its lands, rents, and possessions' for a consideration of £3.[150] The same agreement was ratified by her attorney, Adam de Uley, on 3 June 1261 in Bristol. This final concord specifies that the mill was attached to a messuage and an acre of meadow.[151] Stephen of Harnhill's earlier grant to the canons specified that the mill's appurtenances included a meadow and two crofts, with the whole property drawing an annual rent of £1 14s a year. Stephen's grant says that the profits from the mill were to be spent celebrating the anniversary of his death, while 10 quarters of grain (five of wheat and five of barley) were to be distributed to paupers in the presence of the congregation on the same occasion. An amount of 20 shillings was to be allocated for the festivities of the day.[152]

At the end of the thirteenth century, the canons of Cirencester acquired a second mill next to the abbot's barton from Walter of Cheltenham for £20. This mill is described elsewhere as Richard the clerk's mill, *Clerkesmill*, or Barton Mill. The earliest mention of it is in a charter dated to some time before 1220, which records the grant of a tenement at Gildenbridge in Cirencester by Henry the clerk of Stratton to Basilia Holderness, part of the boundaries of which were the waters of the mill of Richard the clerk.[153] Henry had himself been given the tenement by his mother Emma earlier in the century.[154] The grant was confirmed by William son of John, who held the property in fee.[155] William also confirmed Henry's grant to Basilia Holderness at around the same time (i.e., c. 1220–30).[156] Based on references made to it in later documents, the mill was located just outside the abbot's barton, or inland, and the knight's fee in which it was located was presumably one of those that enabled Cirencester to meet its military service obligations to the Crown.

Walter of Cheltenham, the man who sold Richard the clerk's mill to the abbey, was the rector of Ampney St Mary, and the son of Alexander the clerk. He also appears to have been an agent for the abbot in some of his property dealings and was a member of the abbot's council in 1285, as well as a clerk to the abbot in the following year. Before attaining these positions, however, Walter was able to lease the mill for life from the abbey in a final concord of 8 July 1279. The mill and its appurtenances were to revert to the abbot and convent upon Walter's death. When Walter died in 1306, he was buried in the abbey's church, suggesting that the relations between the two parties had remained cordial throughout this period.[157] Sometime after this purchase had been made, Walter Springald, lord of Wiggold, quitclaimed any right to two mills called *Clerkenemulles* next to the abbot's barton in Cirencester, as well as the meadows adjoining the mills.[158] It is possible that Walter Springald was a descendant of William son of John who had held some of this property in fee.

Richard Bigod of Oldfield (Somerset?) quitclaimed his right in a quarter share of a virgate of land and a mill in Oldfield sometime between c. 1225 and 1233. The property was held by Alicia the daughter of Peter Paynel, who was to continue being responsible for the payment of foreign service, and four pounds of wax that was to be rendered yearly to the chapel of Langley.[159]

---

[150] Ibid., mss. 205 and 206.

[151] Ibid., ms. 207.

[152] Ibid., ms. 269/126.

[153] Ibid., ms. 297/154.

[154] Ibid., ms. 298/156.

[155] Ibid., ms. 299/157.

[156] Ibid., ms. 300/159. Two other charters relating to this same grant are mss. 301/160 and 302/161.

[157] Ibid., ms. 195 with note, and ms. 307.

[158] Ibid., ms. 202. Wiggold was about three kilometres to the north-east of Cirencester.

[159] Ibid., ms. 596.

Between 1230 and 1250, the canons granted and confirmed to Thomas the Mercer their mill of Milborne (Milborne Port, Somerset?) with all of its appurtenances for two marks (£1 13s 4d) a year. The appurtenances included a house with a curtilage, two acres of open field, and a portion of meadow (*hammo*). The abbey reserved the right of free multure for its own grain and obligated Thomas to make any necessary repairs to the mill. The grant also included standard warranty and distraining clauses.[160]

The canons leased all of their land in Boycott, Oxfordshire, to William of Stratford for life sometime between c. 1236 and 1240. The lease included woods, meadows and a mill with all of its appurtenances, for which William was to pay £5 a year. The lease also states that Walter the miller held half a virgate of land within Boycott of the lord for life, while Richard of Radcliff, miller, held the mill of Boycott for life. When Richard died, the land and mill were to be given over to William, and the total rent increased by half a mark. William was expected to preserve the liberties of the village of Boycott, and to maintain all of the buildings and structures in the vill, including the millpond. He was also expected to prevent any unlawful cutting of timber from the wood, and to bring to justice any of the men of the vill who were caught doing so.[161]

Cirencester held the tithes of the parish of Daglingworth (Gloucs.), although the property within the parish itself appears to have been held by Sir William Bluet of Daglingworth. But while the abbey collected the tithes of the mill there – known as Brain mill – and acquired several parcels of land around it, it does not appear to have acquired any interest in the mill itself until the mid-thirteenth century. Between 1230 and 1250, the canons acquired two acres of land next to the mill as part of an exchange of property with Robert and Matilda Barbast,[162] as well as another two acres next to *Cleiputtes* near Brain mill from Richard the carpenter of Baunton. This latter was amongst seven acres of land in the field of Cirencester which Richard had quitclaimed to the abbey.[163] Around the same time, Sir William Bluet gave the abbey the meadow of Resham 'on either side of the water of Churn above Brain's mill, and adjoining the meadow of Baunton on one side and the meadow of Stratton on the other.'[164]

Soon afterwards, the canons were granted a share of the mill of Robert Brain by Simon of Matson with the assent of his wife Alice, 'which Robert Brain formerly held in Cirencester of William Bluet of Daglingworth'. The charter calls the mill 'the mill of Gildenbridge'. In return for this 'grant', the husband and wife were paid 12 marks (£10).[165] A final concord between the two parties dated 8 July 1253 includes an acknowledgement on Simon's and Alice's part that the share of the mill which they had granted now belonged to the abbey, but requested in addition to the money which had already changed hands an additional one shilling annually to be paid to the Knights of the Hospital of St John of Jerusalem at their preceptory in Quenington.[166] These two documents make it fairly clear that the otherwise unidentifiable man named William who granted the abbey a share of the same mill between c. 1250 and 1260, with all its suit, customary services and secular demands, was none other than Sir William Bluet.[167]

Between 1266 and 1290, the canons granted to John de Briddesthorn and Simon his brother the whole of the abbot's share in the mill at Adderbury (Oxon.) with all of the multure of the abbot's men of Adderbury and Milton. In return, the brothers were to pay eight shillings annually, and an initial payment of one mark as surety.[168] Another charter of the same period makes the same grant to John with no mention of Simon.[169]

An agreement dated 13 April 1275 between Abbot Henry of Cirencester and Abbot Reginald of St Peter's, Gloucester, makes it clear that the canons were then in the process of constructing a mill, fishery and millpond at Duntisbourne Nutbeam in Gloucestershire. The agreement records that Abbot Reginald had withdrawn his claim to common of pasture in the place where the canons were building their watermill, and

---

[160] Ibid., ms. 590.

[161] Ibid., ms. 649.

[162] Ibid., ms. 335/290.

[163] Ibid., ms. 246/298.

[164] Ibid., ms. 191.

[165] Ibid., ms. 308.

[166] Ibid., ms. 309. The concord was drawn up at Westminster.

[167] Ibid., ms. 190. As this particular charter is incomplete, it is not possible to establish the full name of the grantor.

[168] Ibid., ms. 850.

[169] Ibid., ms. 851.

also granted the abbot of Cirencester the right to celebrate divine service in his oratory at Duntisbourne.[170] Between 1250 and 1275, John of Inglesham granted the canons some land in Duntisbourne Abbot, and also gave them permission to build a mill and fishery above their land in Duntisbourne Nutbeam.[171] Between 1267 and 1275, Helewyse, widow of Sir Henry le Rus, gave the canons similar permission.[172] The site for the mill and fishpond were granted to the canons by Philip of Matson in the late thirteenth century.[173] He had already granted them eight and a half acres of land nearby.[174] The site for the millpond was granted to the canons by Walter of Kingsbridge at around the same time.[175] Walter also granted the canons a piece of close with a dovecote, grange and surrounding walls in the same area.[176] All in all, the canons appear to have acquired significant holdings in the area during the last quarter of the thirteenth century.[177] The *Taxatio Nicholai IV* registers £1 2s in rents from Duntisbourne in 1291, but does not provide a separate rent from the mill, although it would seem likely that most of this revenue came from it and the fishery.[178]

The last three documents relate to the abbey's mill in Cheltenham (Gloucs.), and date to the late thirteenth and early fourteenth centuries. The first and second documents indicate that the abbey was still leasing at least some of its mills for life in the second half of the thirteenth century, while the final document involves the provision of a pension for the faithful service of a miller employee. On 14 July 1288, John son of Simon le Weke of Cheltenham quitclaimed to the canons all right in a mill, messuage and half a virgate of land in the town of Cheltenham which his father had held at farm of the abbey for the term of his life.[179] It would appear that the next tenant to hold the mill for life was one Thomas of the Mill of Cheltenham, who quitclaimed and surrendered the mill and messuage to the abbey, along with 10 and a half acres of land.[180] In return for his faithful service to the abbey, he was granted food and drink and a stipend 'appropriate to his service for the abbey'. The pension included three quarters and three bushels of wheat and three quarters and two bushels of rye per year from the abbey's granary, a robe valued at eight shillings, or cash in lieu, right of lodging to the value of four shillings, or cash in lieu, as well as a cartload of fodder.[181] Thomas was obviously a favoured servant! The dating of this charter to 1304, the year before the handmill breaking incident recounted in Chapter 9, is perhaps not coincidental.

Several charters make only the briefest mentions of mills held by the abbey. The earliest of these is dated to 1213–17, in which Abbot Alexander and the convent granted Martin of Latton the mill of Latton (Wilts.) on a lifelong lease for two marks a year (£1 13s 4d).[182] The second, dated between 1266 and 1307, records that the widow Sarra, daughter of Thomas Meysy of Ampney, quitclaimed to the canons all right in half a virgate and one mill in Up Ampney (Ampney Crucis, Gloucs.), which had once been held by her father of the abbot.[183] Clearly, the canons' granting of lifelong leases during this period required some vigilance once the lessee died. Finally, a memorandum of agreement dated 27 March 1320 between Sir John de Oddingseles and Cirencester records the terms for the settlement of a dispute between the two parties over rights of way, chace and warren in their manor of Broadwell in Oxfordshire. One right of way led to the canons' mill called *Cottemoresmulle* in the manor.[184]

---

[170] Ibid., ms. 367.

[171] Ibid., ms. 653.

[172] Ibid., ms. 655.

[173] Ibid., ms. 651.

[174] Ibid., ms. 650.

[175] Ibid., ms. 641.

[176] Ibid., ms. 640.

[177] See also mss. 639, 640, 642, 652, 654 and 656.

[178] *Taxatio Nicholai IV*, p. 235.

[179] *The Cartulary of Cirencester Abbey*, ms. 472.

[180] Ibid., ms. 482.

[181] Ibid., ms. 481.

[182] Ibid., ms. 465.

[183] Ibid., ms. 415.

[184] Ibid., ms. 220.

The details of all of the mills recorded in Cirencester's charters are set out in Table 6.5. Before analysing its contents, it should be pointed out that the Domesday rents for six additional mills in Frome and Fairford have not been included in the table as there is no indication in any of the extant documents that Cirencester could have drawn anything other than tithes from these mills. It is also unclear how many of these mills continued to operate up to the end of the thirteenth century. The three mills in Fairford paid £1 12s 4d a year at Domesday,[185] while the three mills in Frome paid £1 5s a year.[186]

One of the most striking features of the abbey's mill-related charters is the large number of mill rents recorded. Eighteen mill rents for 15 mills are listed. At least four of these mills were held on lifelong leases in the thirteenth century, including the mills of Robert the clerk, and those of Boycott, Cheltenham and Latton.

Table 6.5   Twenty-four mills in which Cirencester Abbey held an interest before 1320

Name	Year acquired	Grantor	Annual revenue
Cirencester (precinctual) mill	1131–33	Henry I	
Boycott mill	"	"	£5 (1236–40 incl. vill)
Winton mill	"	"	
Cheltenham mill (manorial)	"	"	11s 8d (1086 for 2 mills) £1 14s (1304 for 1 mill)
Eastenest' mill	1147–76	Hugh de Gunnovill and wife (kt.)	
Medford mill	<1166–76		13s 4d
Blackmill	1197	Jordan and Alice Basset (kt.) (£12 10s purchase price)	£1 (1187–1213) £1 13s 4d (1255)
Rothwell mill	early 13th c.		tithes only
Latton mill	<1213–17		£1 13s 4d
Little Oakley mill	1219	Adam of Cockfield (kt.)	6s 8d (rent only)
Oldfield mill	c. 1225–33	Richard Bigod of Oldfield (kt.)	
Milbourne Port mill	<1230–50		25d (1086) £1 13s 4d (c.1240)
Coates mill	< 235		tithes only
Shrivenham mills (incl. Merchant's mill)	<1236		tithes only 20s tithes from this mill
Maz mill, Cirencester	c. 1240	Stephen of Harnhill (kt.)	£1 14s (1197–1208, c.1240)
Brain mill, Daglingworth (share)	<1253	Simon and Alice Matson (£10 purchase price)	
(share incl. suit)	c. 1250–60	William Bluet (kt.)	
Sherston mill, Preston	<mid-13th c.	Thomas of Sherston	15s (1291)
Adderbury mill (incl. suit)	<1266–90		8s
Ampney Crucis mill	<1266–1307		
Winchester mill	<1291		£4 8s (1291)
Clerkesmill, Cirencester (a.k.a. Barton mill)	late 13th c.	Walter of Cheltenham (admin.) (£20 purchase price)	
Duntisbourne Nutbeam mill	"	Built by abbey	£1 2s (1291)
Cottemoresmulle	<1320		

Although there are three post-Domesday rents which are as low as those found on the other Augustinian estates, including Adderbury mill which held suit but only paid eight shillings a year in rent, most of the others were significantly higher, although still markedly less than the kinds of rents seen on Benedictine and Cistercian estates. The only exception to this appears to have been the abbey's mill in Winchester, which earned £4 8s in 1291, presumably due to its location in a densely populated urban centre, as it is unlikely that

---

[185] Ibid., ms. 354.

[186] Ibid., ms. 626. One of the mills included 25 acres of meadow and paid only five shillings annually.

it included suit. No record of this mill exists within the abbey's charters, although the *Taxatio Nicholai IV* records that £4 4s of this rent was paid to the abbey of Eynsham.[187]

Five rentals for five different mills are recorded for the end of the thirteenth century. These give an average rental of £1 13s 5d for Cirencester's mills at that time, which appears to be an accurate reflection of its mill revenues for that period when compared with some of the rentals recorded earlier in the century. This is, nevertheless, about half of the average rentals seen in comparable Benedictine and Cistercian houses, a fact which was presumably related to these mills being unable to draw custom from outside the manors in which they were located, although as we have seen, the low-rent paying mill of Adderbury did include suit, while the mill of Cheltenham was part of the abbey's manor. It would seem, therefore, that holding suit of mill in the Southern Midlands in the twelfth and thirteenth centuries was not necessarily a guarantee of a high income from one's mill.

While there are only four mills for which the rents recorded allow any comparison across time, the increases over the relevant periods are revealing. The first two rents are for the mill of Milborne (Milborne Port), which saw a huge 16-fold increase in its revenues over the 150-year period from 1086 to c. 1240, rising spectacularly from 25d to £1 13s 4d. A four-fold increase over a similar period on other ecclesiastical estates was not unusual. The second and third rents are for the mills of Cheltenham, two of which earned 11s 8d at Domesday, while a single mill in the same vill in 1304 earned 12s plus 3 quarters 3 bushels of wheat and 3 quarters 2 bushels of rye. While it is difficult to give an exact figure for the value of the grain rents for the Cheltenham mill, assuming a market price of 40d per quarter for both grains, it was earning the equivalent of £1 14s, which is very much comparable to the rents it was drawing from at least four of its other mills during the thirteenth century. This would indicate a far more modest three-fold increase in mill revenues over a period of more than two centuries on this single manor. On the other hand, Cirencester's revenues from Maz mill remained stable at £1 14s from c. 1200 to c. 1240, suggesting that the abbey was already extracting as much revenue as it could from its mills by the end of the twelfth century, although its mill rents do not appear to have been greatly increased subsequently.

Roughly a third of the abbey's mills were acquired during the twelfth century, with the vast majority of the others being acquired during the thirteenth century. At least three of the 19 mills that it held directly at the end of the thirteenth century were purchased, and at least nine were either donated or purchased from members of the knightly class. This pattern of knightly donations of mills is consistent with that found on most of the other Augustinian estates studied in the sample and will be discussed in more detail in the concluding chapter. The canons only appear to have built a single mill during the period covered by the charters, that of Duntisbourne Nutbeam.

Blythburgh Priory

Henry I granted the churches of Blythburgh and Stowmarket in Suffolk to Bishop Richard de Belmeis of the Augustinian priory of St Osyth sometime soon after 1116 while the king was overseas in Normandy.[188] It would seem that the grants were intended as the basis for a foundation, which became the priory of the Blessed Virgin Mary at Blythburgh. Blythburgh was one of the earliest Augustinian foundations in the diocese of Norwich in the twelfth and thirteenth centuries, which had hitherto been dominated by great Benedictine houses such as Bury St Edmunds, Eye and Stoke-by-Clare. Unlike the houses of the Black Monks, however, Blythburgh was, like most Augustinian houses, relatively small and poorly endowed.

Located about six kilometres west of Walberswick on the Suffolk coast, Blythburgh is recorded as having been a prosperous royal town and market in Domesday Book, its church holding two carucates and the dependent churches of Holy Trinity and Walberswick. This would appear to indicate that Blythburgh had been a minster church before the Conquest. It was also the burial site of Anna, the seventh century martyr-king, whose remains were still the site of pilgrimage in the twelfth century. While a small number of canons had probably been established at Blythburgh shortly after Henry's foundation grant, the first reference to a community of canons there is from a royal charter dated to before 1147 by King Stephen. Later in the

---

[187] *Taxatio Nicholai IV*, p 234.

[188] *Blythburgh Priory Cartulary*, Pt. I, mss. 7, 62.

century, Henry II gave the abbot of St Osyth the right to appoint and remove Blythburgh's prior, a privilege that was subsequently ratified by Pope Innocent III.[189] The pope also confirmed the abbot's right to dispose of the revenues of the priory, although it is clear from the cartulary that the priory acted as an independent corporation, holding its own common seal and being prevailed upon by the king in the fourteenth century to provide financial aid for his war efforts. The priory nevertheless paid St Osyth's an annual tribute to the Crown of 50 shillings, which was later reduced in the mid-thirteenth century to 40 shillings.[190]

The community at Blythburgh may have consisted of as many as a dozen canons in the late thirteenth century, although the only records of their numbers are from the fifteenth and early sixteenth centuries, in which figures of between four and seven are listed. The priory appears to have maintained at least four members throughout this period, as the official positions of cellarer, sacrist and almoner are recorded, the latter being the obedientiary to whom the prior formally leased lands for the provision of alms, and to whom were made a number of grants by laymen in the thirteenth century. The only two canons of note to emerge from Blythburgh were Gilbert the precentor, who was summoned to Butley to be its first prior, and John Valence, who was elevated in 1459 by Henry VI to act as suffragan to the bishop of Bath and Wells. The priory was suppressed in 1537, its holdings having been valued at £48 8s 10d only two years earlier.[191]

Most of the priory's holdings lay within Blything hundred and the neighbouring hundred of Wangford. By the end of the thirteenth century, after having acquired the churches of Blyford and Bramfield, the spiritual income of the priory was reckoned at £28 13s 4d annually, the income of its most recent acquisitions being £9. The *Taxatio Nicholai IV* valued its temporalities in Blythburgh and Walberswick at £20 19s 6 1/2d a year, including lands, rents, mills and foldage. Its other temporal holdings in neighbouring vills were valued at £12 7s 8d.[192] Even when room for under-reporting to the papal commissioners is taken into account, this is but a small fraction of some of the larger Augustinian houses, which were drawing 10 times or more from their temporal holdings.[193] Its possessions can be seen in Figure 6.2.

With respect to its donors, Blythburgh failed to attract many of high rank, its appeal being limited by its status as a dependent cell of St Osyth. A relatively large number of those granting lands to the priory in the twelfth and thirteenth century were peasants, including manumitted serfs, as well as members of the local gentry and knightly class, most of the latter being tenants of the earls of Norfolk and Richmond. The aristocratic families of the area had other, more prestigious foundations to attract their beneficence, such as Sibton for the Chesney family (which ended up acquiring three times the wealth of Blythburgh), Wangford for the Bigod family, Butley and Leiston for the de Glanvilles, and St Olave's Herringfleet for the fitz Osberts. In other words, the density of religious foundations in the area meant that competition for donations was fierce, a situation that was further aggravated by the arrival of the mendicant orders.

The earliest reference to any mills held by Blythburgh in its mill-related documents is from a royal confirmation of its foundation charter by Richard I. The charter lists all of the priory's grants and privileges, including its 'mills and ponds',[194] which at this stage presumably consisted only of Blythburgh watermill.

William de Chesney, second lord of Blythburgh and founder of Coxton and Sibton, made modest donations to the priory.[195] Upon his death in 1174, his property passed on to his daughter Margaret and her husband Hugh de Cressi, who confirmed her father's grants to the priory and gave in addition a quarter share of what appears to have been a watermill and two acres of meadow in Bulcamp at a rent of four shillings a year to be paid by Margaret to the priory. Margaret had purchased the share from Geoffrey Capra.[196] About a century later,

---

[189]   Ibid., mss. 63 and 64.

[190]   Ibid., pp. 2–3.

[191]   Ibid., pp. 3–4. Also Robinson (1980), Appendix 14.

[192]   Ibid., pp. 16–22. Webster's Dictionary (1913) defines foldage or faldage as the 'privilege of setting up, and moving about, folds for sheep, in any fields within manors, in order to manure them; often reserved to himself by the lord of the manor'.

[193]   For example, Leicester and Thornton in Lincolnshire were drawing around £332 and £347 respectively from their temporalities at the same time. See Robinson (1980), Appendix 12.

[194]   *Blythburgh Priory Cartulary*, Pt. II, ms. 485.

[195]   Ibid., Pt. I, ms. 42.

[196]   Ibid., Pt. I, ms. 87. Capra had been another of Blythburgh's donors, and was probably distantly related to the more prominent family of the same name in Essex, who were tenants of Walter fitz Robert (see ibid., p. 8).

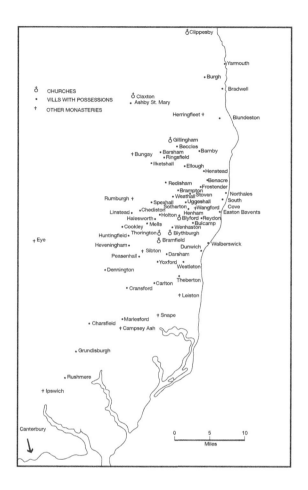

Fig. 6.2   Possessions of Blythburgh Priory. After Harper-Bill (1980)

Blythburgh was letting either this quarter share or the whole mill to Roger de Kerdistone, Lord of Bulcamp, for the same rent.[197] An agreement of 1324 records that the priory had remitted 32d of four shillings rent due from the mill and two acres of land, in return for which Roger was to defend the priory against all claims for lands held in the fee of Bulcamp, with the priory reserving the right of distraint for any rental arrears or other infringements of the priory's rights.[198]

Sometime before 1217, Osbert son of Walter de Henham granted the priory the watermill of Henham with the suit of the men of the manor of Henham (Essex), as well as an alder grove called *Melneholm* (lit. 'a river-meadow by the mill'), but exempted his own household from having to pay multure when grinding their grain at the mill. As Robert Fitz Walter is recorded as the tenant-in-chief of Henham in a document of 1199–1200, Osbert and Walter were probably mesne tenants of Henham.[199] Sometime soon after 1217, the priory granted Osbert's son Roger a hereditary lease of the mill 'with waters and pools and all its appurtenances' for four

---

[197]   Roger had originally held by serjeanty tenure in Claxton, owing service to Norwich castle. He was married to Ada, the daughter of Roger de Claxton who had granted Blythburgh the advowson of the church of Claxton in Norfolk (see ibid., p. 11).

[198]   *Blythburgh Priory Cartulary*, Pt. I, ms. 96.

[199]   Ibid., ms. 304; *Feet of Fines*, 1199–87 / 45 1199–1200 AD 1 John. Trinity Term.

shillings a year.[200] This kind of arrangement does not appear to have been particularly unusual, but unless the priory was taking toll-corn from the mill, or Roger was acting in some official capacity for the canons, the rent charged was particularly generous considering the mill included the suit of the men of Henham.

The last document recording a grant of a mill to Blythburgh is a charter from sometime before 1246. It records a grant from Roger de Cressi, a descendant of Margaret de Cressi, to the priory of 14 shillings of annual rent from his mill called *Crabbemille* in Burnham, Norfolk, which was then held by William de Gimingham. The grant was made in return for the maintenance of an altar candle for Roger's family by the priory.[201] Roger's son Hugh II and his brother Stephen confirmed the grants of their predecessors and made two more small grants and concessions to the priory.[202] A distant relative of the family, Roger de Chesney, granted the priory the windmill of Darsham in the early thirteenth century with the suit of the men of the vill.[203]

The priory had interests in at least 10 mills by the end of the thirteenth century, including a possible tide-mill at Blythburgh that was replaced with a windmill some time during the first half of the thirteenth century, and three or more other windmills at Claxton in Norfolk and Darsham in Suffolk. However, only five of these mills were directly held by the canons, as well as a share of another. The rents for four of the 10 mills are specified in charters from the first half of the thirteenth century, and all of them are for 14 shillings or less, suggesting that these low sums were all that the priory was able to extract from its tenants, even though one of these mills included suit, as did Darsham windmill, although no revenues for this latter mill are recorded (see Table 6.6 below).

It is worth noting that the two charters in Blythburgh's cartulary which refer to the Darsham windmill are roughly dated to the early thirteenth century. The first is a grant from Roger de Chesney to the canons of Darsham windmill with the suit of the men of Darsham plus 20 acres of arable in various small parcels and 15 perches of marshland.[204] The second is a grant from the priory to Turgild and Anastasia of the same mill with its suit as well as 15 acres of arable and 15 perches of marshland on a hereditary lease of 15d a year and half a mark 'consideration'.[205] Given the terms of the lease, Turgild was presumably acting on behalf of the priory in some official capacity, or was a relative or military retainer of Roger de Chesney.

The canons also replaced a marginal or ruinous watermill in Blythburgh sometime before 1240 with a windmill, a practice that was not at all uncommon in East Anglia at the time, as we saw in Chapter 3. Owing to the location of the priory on a prominent bluff close to the coast near mudflats that were only a metre or so above sea-level, the original watermill may well have been a tide mill, which would also explain why it was marginal and was replaced with a windmill.[206] The only two references to it occur in a grant and quitclaim by William the marshall to the priory of homage and rent from a tenement of two acres 'adjacent to the Canon's windmill and former watermill' (*iacentium ex parte aquilonis molendini ventilis dictorum canonicorum*), which he had previously held of them for eightpence a year.[207] While the canons' windmill was undoubtedly a relatively early example of this new technology, it was the priory's benefactor, Roger de Chesney, who appears to have built the first windmill in the area.

The details of those mills recorded in the priory's mill-related documents are set out below in Table 6.6. It is clear from the information contained in the table that while Blythburgh may have acquired a single watermill from the minster estates of its predecessor, it only built a single windmill to replace that mill during its existence, the rest of its mills being granted to it by donors of the knightly class. At least seven and possibly eight of the 10 mills in which it had an interest, or 70–80 per cent of those interests, were acquired from knights.

---

[200] Ibid., mss. 304 and 314.

[201] Ibid., ms. 169.

[202] Ibid., mss. 36, 279 and 40.

[203] Ibid., ms. 223.

[204] Ibid. These smaller parcels are also described in a number of other charters, for example, mss. 221, 222.

[205] Ibid., ms. 237.

[206] My thanks to Richard Holt for making this suggestion based on his knowledge of these features of the local geography.

[207] *Blythburgh Priory Cartulary*, Pt. II, mss. 15 and 16. William appears to have died before 1240. Cf. ms. 17.

Table 6.6   Ten mills in which Blythburgh Priory held an interest before 1250

Name	Year acquired	Grantor	Annual revenue
Blythburgh watermill	<1116	Henry I	no data
Claxton windmills and watermills	<1195	Roger de Claxton (kt.)	tithes only
Bulcamp mill (1/4 share)	1209–30	Margaret de Cressi (kt.)	4s
Darsham windmill*	early 13th c.	Roger de Chesney (kt.)	no data
Henham mill*	<1217	Osbert de Henham (kt.)	4s
Blythburgh windmill	<1240	built by priory	8d
Crabbemille	<1246	Roger de Cressi (kt.)	14s

* Mills with suit

It would also seem that suit of mill was no guarantee of a decent revenue from a mill in East Anglia in the first half of the thirteenth century, judging from the very low rent of four shillings from Henham mill. In stark contrast, the mill of Bulcamp may have been earning as much as 16 shillings, while *Crabbemille* earned 14 shillings. These were still not very high rentals for the period, however, and almost undoubtedly an outcome of the relatively large number of free peasants in East Anglia who were not obliged to do suit at the mills concerned (as previously noted by Holt), although it is also possible that at least some of the men who rented mills from the priory served it in some official capacity, as was the case with Bulcamp mill, and were charged low rents as part compensation for those services.

Butley Priory

Ranulf de Glanville founded Butley Priory in 1171, shortly after he had been deposed as sheriff of Yorkshire, and several years before his elevation to chief justiciar of England. The site that he chose for the priory was on land held by him as the marriage-portion of his wife, Bertha de Valeines. Its first prior, Gilbert, had been precentor of Blythburgh, who resigned from the former position in 1192, four years after the dedication of the church in late September 1188. The house was apparently founded for 36 canons, with its main functions being charity and hospitality. It would seem likely that most of its canons were drawn from St Osyth, rather than Blythburgh.[208] Gerald of Wales implies that both Butley and Ranulf's other foundation of Leiston were forbidden from acquiring new lands and rents through purchase, or from accumulating money for that purpose, but while Leiston's foundation charter does include such a clause, there is no such clause in Butley's.

Butley was one of the first of a number of Augustinian foundations in East Anglia, along with Ixworth and Walsingham, soon followed by Holy Trinity, Ipswich, Dodnash and Woodbridge, all of which were founded before 1200. Apart from Butley and Leiston, Ranulf also founded a modest leper hospital in West Somerton, Norfolk, whose guardian was the prior of Butley.[209] While Butley and Leiston appear to have generally been on reasonable terms with one another, as is witnessed by an early exchange of the church of Knodishall held by the latter for those of Leiston and Aldringham held by Butley, the two were subsequently engaged in a dispute related to this exchange over the tithes of Leiston's estate at Westhouse in what was now Butley's parish of Knodishall.[210] The dispute was settled by papal intervention.

Most of Butley's estates were in east Suffolk, but it also held some land just over the border in Norfolk, as well as a single holding in Lincolnshire and other property in Yorkshire and in London [Figure 6.3]. The largest and most profitable of its estates appear to have been the gifts of its founder or his daughters. One of the few surviving series of deeds for the priory relate to the vill of Weybread. These indicate that Butley was seeking to consolidate its possessions by purchase and exchange during the thirteenth century, while in the

[208] *Leiston Abbey Cartulary and Butley Priory Charters*, pp. 1–2.

[209] Ibid., p. 3.

[210] Ibid., mss. 6, 31, 90.

fourteenth century it was letting out its lands there. It would seem, therefore, like many other ecclesiastical estates at the same time, that Butley had begun to favour a policy of leasing over direct management of its estates after 1300.

By the time of the Dissolution, Butley held 36 churches, five vills with possessions, and a handful of other holdings. It was also the second wealthiest religious house in Suffolk. With annual revenue of £280 in 1291,[211] and £318 in 1535, it earned about twice as much as Leiston, although it was not nearly as wealthy as Bury St Edmunds.[212]

Evidence for Butley's mill holdings is extremely sparse, with only three of more than 150 of its surviving charters even mentioning what appear to have been only two mills. Even though the priory held a large number of churches and vills, none of them appear to have had mills attached to them, as the *Taxatio Nicholai IV* does not mention any. The first two charters which make any mention of mills are a royal charter of liberties from Henry II, dated to sometime between December 1184 and May 1185, which makes a generic reference to the 'waters and mills' of Butley, as does a royal confirmation by Richard I dated to 1 August 1190.[213] It is not clear, however, if this was just the repetition of standard legal phraseology in the absence of such assets, or whether there was one or more mills attached to the priory. Apart from these two generic references, there is a single grant from Prior William of Butley to Woodbridge Priory of the tithes of Woodbridge mill that is dated to 1192–1213. These tithes were to be collected by Woodbridge in exchange for an annual pension of a pound of cummin. The mill's tithes had been given to Butley at some earlier date by a man named Baldwin de Ufford about which nothing else is known, although he was presumably a free man and possibly a knight.

Table 6.7   Two mills in which Butley Priory held an interest before 1220

Name	Year acquired	Grantor	Annual revenue
Butley mill (?)	1184–85	Henry II	no data
Woodbridge mill	<1192–1213	Baldwin de Ufford (kt.?)	tithes only

These few fragments of information are set out in Table 6.7. Of all the nine Augustinian houses in the sample, Butley is the only one which has not revealed any firm evidence of having ever held any mills of its own. The generic reference to 'waters and mills' may be just that. It may well have been the case that Butley's tenants were frequenting non-seigneurial watermills or windmills held by other parties on the manor, mills on neighbouring manors, or their own or neighbours' handmills.

Bolton Priory

Bolton Priory was first established in 1120 as a house of regular canons at Embsay on the banks of the River Wharfe by two of the most powerful magnates in the north, William Meschines, lord of Copeland, and his wife, Cecily de Rumilly, lady of Skipton. The initial foundation grant consisted of the church of the Holy Trinity at Skipton, along with the chapel of Carleton and the vill of Embsay, while a later charter records Cecily's grants of the church of St Mary and St Cuthbert at Embsay, along with the vill and church of Kildwick, and the mills of Silsden and Harewood. The same charter includes a confirmation by her son-in-law William – nephew to the king of Scotland – and her daughter, Alice, of the church of All Saints of Broughton in Craven.[214]

---

[211]   Robinson (1980), Appendix 12. Mortimer gives a lower figure for its *Taxatio* assessment of £138 for its spiritualities and £100 for its temporalities. See *Leiston Abbey Cartulary and Butley Priory Charters*, p. 22.

[212]   *Leiston Abbey Cartulary and Butley Priory Charters*, pp. 22 and 27.

[213]   Ibid., mss. 121 and 122. This standard phrase of 'waters and mills' amongst the generic holdings of a religious house appears in many royal, papal and aristocratic confirmations of the twelfth and thirteenth centuries, and does not appear to have become less popular in the wake of the invention of the windmill, which in this case coincides with the date of the charter.

[214]   *VCH York*, Vol. III, pp. 195–9; Burton (1999), pp. 80–83.

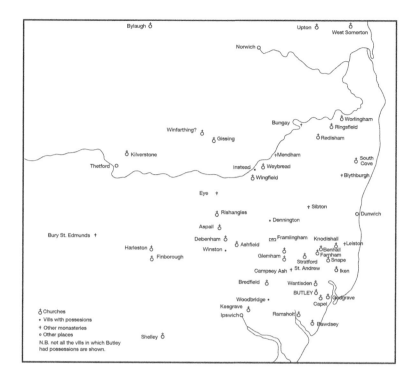

Fig. 6.3   Possessions of Butley Priory. After Mortimer (1979)

After she had inherited patronage of Embsay Priory some years later, Alice acquired the manor of Bolton about six kilometres to the east of Embsay, to which she relocated the priory in 1154 in exchange for the manors of Stirton and Skipton. The priory was not successful in winning patronage from many donors in the area, however, and the canons appear to have struggled financially for many years, not least because of the difficulties of farming in the area.

Although very few records have survived of the priory's first century of existence, there are several series of documents from the late thirteenth century onwards that are of particular significance: a 500-leaf manuscript consisting of the accounts of the priory's obedientiaries and lay officials covering the years from 1286 to 1325, a rental from 1473, extensive ministers' accounts of the priory's estates at the time of the suppression in 1538–39, and a Dissolution inventory of 1539. Ian Kershaw's well-known book, *Bolton Priory: The Economy of a Northern Monastery* (1973), is based on his research into these accounts, which he has also translated and published in two volumes as *Bolton Priory Rentals and Ministers' Accounts, 1473–1539* (1970), and *The Bolton Priory Compotus, 1286–1325: Together with a Priory Account Roll for 1377–1378* (2000). More material on the priory recently became available when Katrina Legg published a hitherto lost sixteenth-century copy of Bolton's cartulary.[215] Her book, *Bolton Priory: Its Patrons and Benefactors, 1120–1293* (2004) is the most recent scholarly interpretation of this evidence.

Because they cover in great detail an important period in medieval English social and economic history i.e., the height of demesne farming coinciding with one of the worst crop failures of the later Middle Ages, followed by a devastating cattle murrain and successive waves of Scottish depredation, Bolton's compotus from the late thirteenth and early fourteenth centuries provides invaluable insights into the response of a small religious house to a series of internal and external crises on the northern frontier. Because the changing fortunes of Bolton Priory have been discussed in detail by both Kershaw and Legg in their respective monographs on the subject, the following discussion restricts itself to an analysis of the priory's mill-related

---

[215]   *The Lost Cartulary of Bolton Priory* (2009).

income and expenditure relative to its overall expenditure as illustrative of some of John of Laund's most successful management practices in the decades before and after 1300.

During the decades leading up to the period covered by the compotus, the canons of Bolton had been the subject of repeated archiepiscopal visitations over various disciplinary issues and financial irregularities, including such seemingly minor infringements as canons taking walks on the moors and in the forests, to transgressions of canonical prohibitions on the possession of private money and the failure of obedientiaries to render accounts to the convent.[216] Apart from the prior, there were 15 canons and two *conversi*, along with several *armigeri* (retired knights?) dependent on the priory. The priory's immediate temporal needs were met by about 30 *liberi servientes* (free servants), which included the master carpenter and cook, brewer, baker, etc., along with more than a hundred *garciones* (villeins), many of whom were engaged in farming distant manors and granges for the priory.[217] However, due to the generally unfavourable conditions for pasturing and farming in the Yorkshire Dales, as well as the area's relative isolation and lack of easy transport options, the canons understandably had some difficulties in managing their estates in order to provide for their own subsistence.

By the 1270s, the priory was heavily in debt, and several wayward and non-compliant priors had been deposed before the election of the priory's most capable administrator, John of Laund. John worked hard to consolidate the priory's scattered holdings and completely overhauled its management and accounting systems. As mentioned in Chapter 1, he managed to double the priory's income during the inflation of 1305 to 1315, but was unable to alleviate the effects of the first crop failure and the later sheep and cattle murrains. While sheep had been the worst affected during the years from 1315–17, cattle and oxen were struck by a new epidemic that had begun in Essex during the Easter of 1319 and had probably been introduced from France.[218] Although the priory's fortunes improved in 1318 with the plentiful harvests of that year, the Scots' victory at Bannockburn had emboldened them to raid deep into Yorkshire, where they destroyed the priory's livestock and torched its property on several occasions.

These ravages were followed by the second harvest failure of 1320–21, leading to a similar escalation in grain prices as that seen between 1315 and 1317.[219] By then Bolton's income was down by 1/3, as were its receipts from tithes and spiritualities, leading to the dismissal of half of its servants and retainers.[220] This effect is clearly revealed in Bolton's receipts for grain and mills as recorded in the charts below.

By 1320, the priory's affairs were in ruins and the canons were dispersed to other houses. Only five years later, it appears to have recovered, however, as it records annual income to Michaelmas 1325 of £444 17s 4 3/4d, compared to only £302 9s 3d in 1535.[221] Although its income and possessions remained relatively stable until the Dissolution, it was never to regain the prosperity it had enjoyed only a few decades earlier.[222]

The three charts below draw on data contained in the priory's compotus rolls covering the period from 1287 to 1324, with an additional rental for the accounting year 1377–78.[223] They clearly reveal some important aspects of the strategy that Laund pursued. Chart 6.1 maps Bolton's total receipts (excluding grain receipts) against its mill farm and mill tithe receipts for the period from 1287 to 1324. Chart 6.2 maps Bolton's expenses for 15 mills over the same period. Chart 6.3 maps the Priory's tithe receipts from 10 mills over the period from 1300 to 1324, and Chart 6.4 maps receipts for all its mills at farm against its mill expenses and the associated profit margin, as well as its total mill tithe receipts for purposes of comparison.

Chart 6.1 reveals that Bolton's total cash receipts, including the revenues from its mills, went from an annual average of a little over £300 in the late 1280s, to an average of about £540 during the period of John's

---

216 *VCH York*, Vol. III, pp. 195–9.

217 Ibid.

218 Kershaw (1973a), pp. 13–14. See also pp. 20–29 for details of the livestock murrains, in which pigs, horses and goats were also affected.

219 The Scots were themselves suffering from the effects of the famine, and had done so since as early as 1310.

220 See Kershaw (1973a), pp. 13–14, 23, 25, 52, 77, 113–17, 137, 141–3.

221 Ibid.

222 See ibid., also Kershaw (1970).

223 See Kershaw and Smith (2000). This is the same material from which Kershaw drew to write his well-known study of the priory, now published, primarily due to his efforts.

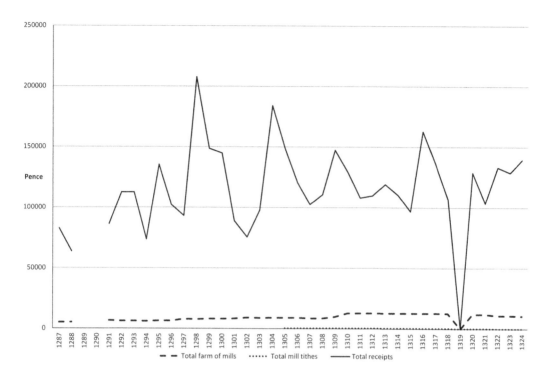

Chart 6.1   Bolton Priory total receipts mapped against total farm of mills and mill tithes, 1287–1324

administration (an 80 per cent increase). Not only were the total receipts higher, they were also more stable than they had been over the previous two decades, and were indeed one of Bolton's most stable sources of income. However, the large scale required to measure the fluctuating value of the total receipts to 1315 in this chart conceals an even more dramatic increase in the total revenue from mills at farm over the same period.

Chart 6.4 reveals that the average total revenue from eight or more mills at farm in the late 1280s amounted to around £21 a year, or £2 12s per mill. By the 1310s, the average total revenue had increased to more than £53 a year. However, the number of mills at farm by this stage had more than doubled, to at least 18, or £3 per mill. Subtracting overall mill expenses from overall mill receipts for the period 1300 to 1324 reveals that Bolton's profit margin was well over 80 per cent of total mill revenues, with mill expenses constituting 16.7 per cent of its mill income over the quarter century. There can, therefore, be little doubt that at least one of the contributing factors to John of Laund's success was the successful farming out of the priory's mills, which resulted in a 150 per cent increase in mill farm revenues over little more than 20 years. Even were we to take the average revenues between 1291 and 1309 as a more stable baseline, the increase from around £32 to £53 is still an increase of 65 per cent.

Turning now to Bolton's mill tithe revenues over the period from 1300 to 1324 as mapped out in Chart 6.3, it would appear that there was a 54 per cent drop in overall tithe revenues between 1300–1 and 1305, which recovered somewhat between 1310 and 1318, after which tithe revenues collapsed during the cattle murrains and floods of 1319, recovered again at a lower level in 1320 and 1321, but collapsed again in 1323 and 1324. Nevertheless, it would seem from the lack of data for mill tithes prior to John of Laund's priorship that it was he who was primarily responsible for ensuring that the canons collected these revenues.

Like other houses in the north, Bolton was able to take advantage of its position on the frontier of English sovereignty by extracting very high revenues from tenants on its seigneurial holdings. Were it not for Bolton's location and the number of seigneurial mills which it held, it would not have drawn such a lot of income from

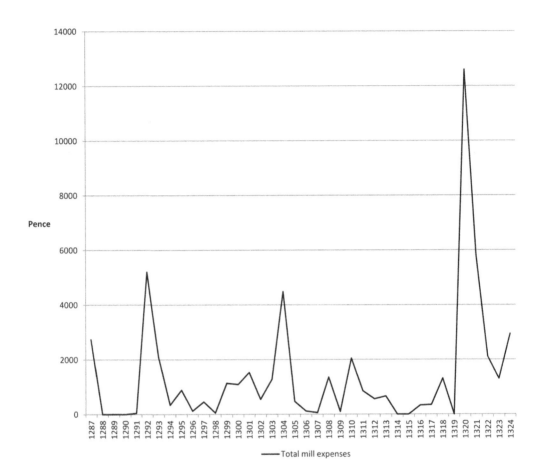

Chart 6.2   Bolton Priory – expenses for 15 mills, 1287–1324

its mills.[224] Nevertheless, judging from the low rents involved, at least nine of the 21 or more mills which the canons held during the period covered by the compotus rolls were let on customary or hereditary leases. In other words, almost half of the priory's mills appear to have been held by independent tenants. Given the previous findings of Holt and Langdon on northern lordship, this appears to have been quite an unusual situation, and was most likely connected to the tenurial status of the mills when they were first acquired by the priory. It seems likely, therefore, that Bolton had acquired a similar proportion of its mills from knights as other Augustinian houses in the sample.

Burscough Priory

The establishment of Burscough Priory in Lancashire was part of the second wave of Augustinian foundations in England that occurred during the period from around 1180 to 1200. Several other religious houses were established in the county at about the same time, including the Augustinian priories of Conishead and Cartmel, and the Premonstratensian foundations of Hornby and Cockersand. Burscough and these other foundations

---

[224] The only northern house examined in the sample that drew comparable revenues from any of its mills was the Church of St Peter's York, which was of course also located in Yorkshire.

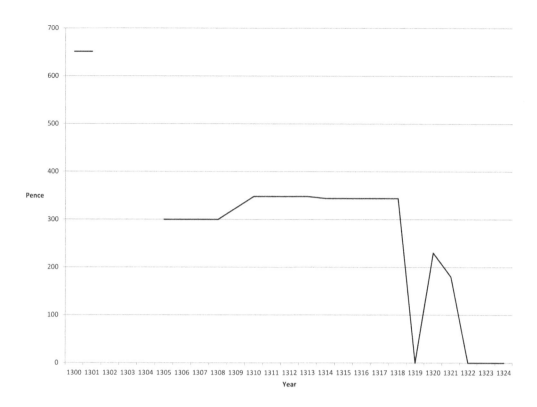

Chart 6.3   Bolton Priory, tithes from 10 mills, 1300–1324

represented the rapid emergence of a monastic presence in a county which had hitherto been sparsely endowed and which was still relatively undeveloped economically.

Lancashire south of the Ribble appears to have been one of the few parts of England that was not ravaged during William I's military expeditions into the North. While Norman military tenure was introduced into the county in the late eleventh century, large areas of it continued to be held under thegnage and drengage, while some of its pre-Conquest aristocratic families survived into the twelfth century. One of these was the family of Lathom which founded Burscough Priory.[225]

Located about 14 kilometres south of the Ribble and about 12 kilometres inland from Southport, the lands of Robert son of Henry of Lathom that were granted for the foundation of the priory sometime between 1189 and 1191 were at the head of the valley or wood of Burscough. The grant included land in and around Burscough, as well as the churches of Ormskirk a few kilometres to its south-west, Huyton on the outskirts of Liverpool and Flixton near Manchester. It also included the town of Ormskirk, which was made a free borough by the priory in the late thirteenth century.[226] The church of Huyton was later the subject of an episcopal appropriation.

Over the next century or so, the priory acquired additional lands in the area through grants, mostly during the first half of the thirteenth century. Some of these grants were from the relatives and descendants of Robert of Lathom, while other important donors included the Scarisbreck and Harleton families, both of which had originally been tenants of the Lathoms. Apart from some minor grants from the lord of Croston and Earl of Derby, a number of lesser tenants and smaller holders also made donations to the priory.[227] By the end of the fourteenth century, most of Burscough's possessions were within a 24-kilometre radius of the priory, with

---

[225]   *An Edition of the Cartulary of Burscough Priory*, p. 6.

[226]   Ibid., ms. 40.

[227]   Ibid., p. 10. The Lathom family also made land grants to Cockersand Abbey.

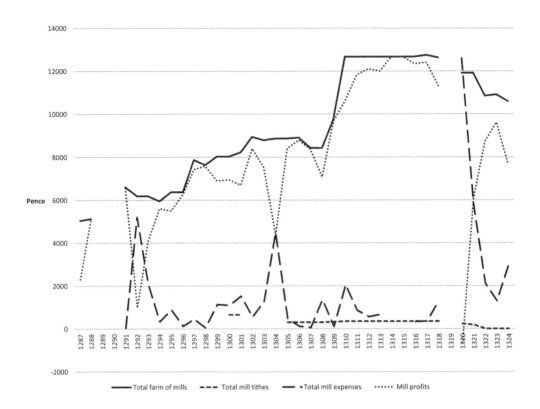

Chart 6.4   Bolton Priory, receipts from mill farms and mill tithes mapped against expenses, 1300–1324

a significant proportion of them within 10 kilometres or so. As mentioned briefly in Chapter 1, a primary motivation for the establishment of Burscough by Robert of Lathom was the enclosure and development of his own land.

While Burscough was nowhere near as large or wealthy as other Lancashire monasteries such as Whalley, Furness and Cockersand, it is the only Augustinian foundation in Lancashire for which a cartulary is known to survive. Probably compiled in the late fourteenth century, its charters date from between the late twelfth and the late fourteenth centuries, and consist of two parts, the first being a collection of lay grants to the priory which are arranged topographically and a few from the priory to lessees, while the second consists of confirmations and grants of privileges.[228]

Burscough's possessions appear to have been a mixed bag in terms of their agricultural potential, consisting of wooded slopes and low-lying marshes and meres, as well as pasture and arable land. By the early fourteenth century, the priory had interests in as many as 13 mills, all of which were in Lancashire, and a dozen of which it appears to have held outright, including four windmills and three watermills in the parish of Ormskirk alone, a horse mill at Cross Hall, and as many as five other watermills elsewhere (see Table 6.8 below). Only the mill of Lathom appears to have been part of its foundation grant. The four windmills were built before 1228, presumably by the priory, indicating that it was not only somewhat of a pioneer in adopting windmill technology in Lancashire, but a keen mill builder generally, with five or more of those mills which it held having been built by the priory.[229] However, the value of Burscough's temporal possessions as assessed by the *Taxatio Nicholai IV* (1291) were only a small fraction at £3 13s of those from its churches, being £13 6s 8d

228   Ibid., pp. 1–3.

229   The seven mills in Ormskirk are listed in a note from the fifteenth century referring to mills in the parish in 1228 and 1519. The mills in the earlier list include windmills in Quassam (Scarisbrick), Bykerstaff, Crosshall (aka Cross Hall), and Burscough, and watermills in Talde (Lathom), Scarisbrick, and Burscough. See ibid., pp. 226–7.

for Ormskirk and £10 for Huyton.[230] Nevertheless, considering how many mills were held by the priory, and that there is no indication that the granting of the free borough of Ormskirk included freedom from suit for its tenants, the canons must have been using whatever revenues they gained from their mills to feed themselves and their servants, a policy that was clearly pursued by Beaulieu and Sibton abbeys, as we will see in Chapter 7.

The small revenues from Burscough's holdings generally would seem to indicate that it did not develop an estate management system until the second quarter of the thirteenth century, like many of the other houses studied. What little evidence there is indicates that the priory was letting its possessions on long leases that were probably to its own disadvantage. One lease for two lives, another for the life of the lessee, and another for 12 years are recorded in relation to various land holdings,[231] while the mills of Lathom and Huyton were let for life in the first instance and for 30 years in the second.[232] Other leases from the thirteenth century required the tenants to make improvements to the leased property.[233] This evidence, combined with the very low revenues recorded from five of its mills, none of which appear to have been let for more than three shillings annually, would seem to indicate that the canons were farming out their possessions on similarly generous terms to those typically seen in the south in the first half of the twelfth century. Because there are no records of the revenues from the five mills it built in the second quarter of the thirteenth century, it would appear that it was directly managing them and diverting the revenues to the upkeep of canons and servants, as none are recorded.

The earliest mention of any of Burscough's mills is in its foundation grant of 1189 to 1191, which specifically mentions 'the mill of Lathom and all the mills of Robert's demesne built and to be built', implying that there was already more than one mill on the estates of Robert son of Henry of Lathom.[234] This document is followed by two confirmations made by Robert's son Richard that are dated to c. 1200 and c. 1232.[235] The priory's mills are also amongst the properties confirmed to it in two *inspeximi*, the first from between 1228 to 1238 by the dean and chapter of Lichfield of a confirmation by the bishop of Coventry and Lichfield dated 1198 to 1216, and the second from between 1360 and 1385 by the bishop of the same document and several others.[236]

The next reference to a mill or mills in the priory's charters is a grant and quitclaim in free alms of the site of a watermill in Burscough by Emma daughter of Siward of Burscough and dated 1199 to 1228. The site is in a river-meadow next to the land of Richard Smith, and includes all its waters and appurtenances. The grant is made in return for the prayers of the canons for the salvation of the soul of King John, as well as Emma's mother, father, ancestors and successors.[237] A quitclaim by Robert of Burscough dated to the first half of the thirteenth century would appear to be referring to this grant by Emma, who was Robert's mother.[238]

A quitclaim by Henry Travers of the mast of Tarlescough and Greetby and of the underwoods of Burscough dated to the early thirteenth century includes a grant with warranty of a river-meadow or river-islet (*holmus*) on the east side of the priory's mill in Burscough.[239] A further agreement between the priory and Henry repeating the terms of this quitclaim and grant record that the priory had in return given Henry the right to grind 10 measures of oats and barley, including one of winter corn, at their mill free of multure every year.[240] This would imply that by this stage the priory had either built or rebuilt a watermill on the site granted by Emma. This is confirmed by a list of seven mills held by the priory in the parish of Ormskirk in 1228

---

[230] Ibid., pp. 11–13. It would seem, however, that these figures were by no means exhaustive with respect to its temporal holdings, which were more than 40 per cent of its total revenues as recorded in the *Valor Ecclesiasticus*. See Robinson (1980), Appendix 14.

[231] Ibid., ms. 71 and Appendix I, mss. 36 and 34.

[232] Ibid., ms. 16 and p. 12. The former lease is from the second quarter of the thirteenth century, and the latter from the last quarter of the thirteenth century.

[233] Ibid., p. 12.

[234] Ibid., ms. 1.

[235] Ibid., mss. 2 and 3.

[236] Ibid., mss. 69 and 168.

[237] Ibid., ms. 64. A.N. Webb provides a range of 1199–1232 for this document, but the list of mills from 1228 mentioned below clearly indicates a watermill was operating in the vill at that date.

[238] Ibid., ms. 22.

[239] Ibid., ms. 19.

[240] Ibid., ms. 20.

and 1519, which includes in the earlier list a windmill and a watermill in Burscough.[241] Sometime around the middle of the century, Henry's son Henry granted the priory a water-course leading from their pool of the *Bayes* through his land to the nearby stream.[242]

Another grant of land by the priory to two brothers dated to 1238 specifically excludes the site of a watermill at Coppul and the water necessary for it.[243] There is no subsequent indication that a mill was built on this site, but it was anyway outside of Burscough's jurisdiction.

An acknowledgement by Richard of Tarbock from the early thirteenth century states that he was bound to pay an annual rent of three shillings from the mills of Tarbock which he held of the priory.[244] A similar agreement between the priory and Richard of Lathom dated to 1229 records that Richard held the mills of Lathom and Knowsley from the priory for life at two shillings annually. Lathom was located about three kilometres to the north-east of Burscough, and Tarbock and Knowsley 10 to 15 kilometres north-east of Liverpool. The mill of Lathom was sub-tenanted by Simon the miller. Richard also held land of the Cross for the same rent, but had not always paid this promptly, presumably because its two tenants had not been paying Richard as promptly as they should have. The agreement also records that the rent due from the land was in perpetuity, whereas the two mills were to revert to the priory upon Richard's death.[245] It would appear that Richard had prevailed upon the canons to allow him to take the mills into his own hands on a low rent at a time when he was most likely to benefit from their growing profitability.

This observation is supported by a writ of novel disseisin which was presented by the priory to Richard's successor, Robert of Lathom III, on 4 July 1287, concerning the same two mills of Lathom and Knowsley as well as some enclosures made by Robert in Ormskirk. The priory was prepared to grant Robert the two mills in fee and to let him build other mills on his land 'provided they are not sited upon Scakerdale Brook nor on the Burscough side of the field called Alton'. In exchange the canons were to be given permission to build mills wherever they wished on their own land, the right to enclose part of their waste at Ormskirk, and 40 acres in Lathom by the highway from Burscough to Wirples Moss which Robert would in turn enfeoff to them.[246] The fee for the farm of the mills is not specified, but the terms of this and the earlier agreement indicate that the canons of Burscough were effectively forced to allow Robert of Lathom's descendants to retain direct control of both mills and their profits in exchange for concessions that may not have ever benefited them.

A charter dated to sometime between c. 1275 and 1303 records a grant from Gilbert of Halsall to the canons of a watermill in Halsall on a 30-year lease, with its waters and lands, including two mill pools, for £1 10s annually.[247] Halsall is about eight kilometres due west of Burscough. This is only the third mill rental that is provided in the priory's charters, and indicates something approaching those seen on some of the larger Augustinian estates in the south, in contrast to the mills of Tarbock, Lathom and Knowsley, whose donor's descendants were only paying nominal rents of three shillings in the case of the Tarbock mills and two shillings for the other two in the late twelfth and early thirteenth centuries. In other words, the granting of these mills to the priory effectively amounted to grants of rents from them, rather than direct control of them and their profits.

The last charter in the priory's cartulary which makes any reference to a mill is a lease dated 1 June 1365, which grants Hugh of the Franter the lease of a mill in Shevington, which the priory must have acquired some time during the first half of the fourteenth century. Shevington is about 14 kilometres due east of Burscough. Hugh was apparently the great grandson of an earlier donor to the priory.[248] No information is provided about the amount to be paid.

---

[241] Ibid., pp. 226–7.

[242] Ibid., ms. 21.

[243] Ibid., Appendix I, ms. 34. Coppull is about 17 kilometres east of Burscough.

[244] Ibid., ms. 117. Richard was the son of Henry of Lathom. The manors of Tarbock and Huyton were held by Henry II before being granted to the Lathoms. This manuscript is the first indication in the charters that Burscough held mills in Tarbock.

[245] Ibid., ms. 16.

[246] Ibid., ms. 18.

[247] *An Edition of the Cartulary of Burscough Priory*, ms. 115.

[248] Ibid., pp. 69–70, of L.R.O. DDHe 40/8.

One of the most important and informative documents in Burscough's cartulary is its grant of a free borough to the people of Ormskirk, the only example discovered in all the manuscript evidence studied. Amongst other things, the grant specifies the concessionary multure rate to be paid by the townsmen. Sometime between 1280 and 1290, Prior Warin and the canons granted the burgesses of Ormskirk a free borough with rights, customs and liberties 'as in the king's charter'. It includes the right to an acre of land for each burgess at an annual rent of twelvepence, as well as the right to grind their corn at the priory's mill at a rate of 1/20, and the liberty to sell, give or assign their burgages as they pleased.[249]

This grant is significant for a number of reasons. From the twelfth to fourteenth centuries, multure rates in England varied from a high of 1/13 in Durham and Northumberland to a low of 1/32 in Devon and Hertfordshire. Obviously, if the concessionary rate for the burgesses of Ormskirk was 1/20, the normal rate must have been higher, perhaps 1/18 or 1/16, the latter figure being the average provided by Bennett and Elton for the whole of England. If we compare this with other northern lords, we can see examples of Lincolnshire, Derbyshire and Yorkshire lords charging a rate of 1/20, and in Yorkshire and Cheshire some who were charging 1/16. Other northern lords such as those in Durham were charging 1/16 as the concessionary rate for freemen. On the other hand, Ramsey Abbey paid 1/24 when having its grain ground at its own mill in Huntingdonshire.[250] Elsewhere in the north, the monks of Furness Abbey paid multure rates of 1/15, 1/18 and 1/20 for grain grown in granges in Cumbria and Yorkshire where they did not hold suit.[251] All of this would suggest that the concessionary rate granted by the priory was reasonable in the context of the more extractive multure rates that were typical of the North.

Table 6.8   Thirteen mills in which Burscough Priory held an interest before 1350

Name	Year acquired	Grantor	Lessee	Annual revenue
Lathom (*Talde*) watermill	1189–91	Robert son of Henry of Lathom	Richard of Lathom (1229) Simon the miller (sub-tenant)	2s (1229)
Knowsley mill	<1229	?	Richard of Lathom (1229)	2s (1229)
Tarbock mills	early 13th c.	?	Richard of Tarbock	3s
Burscough watermill site	1199–1232	Emma, daughter of Siward of Burscough	n/a	n/a
Burscough watermill	<1228	built by priory		no data
Burscough windmill	"	"		"
Scarisbrick watermill	"	Scarisbrek family?		"
Scarisbrick (Quassam) windmill	"	built by priory?		"
Bykerstaff windmill	"	"		"
Cross Hall windmill	"	"		"
Halsall watermill	c. 1275–1303	Gilbert of Halsall	Burscough Priory (30-year lease)	£1 10s to grantor
Cross Hall horse mill	<1290	Burscough Priory	Richard Waleys (kt.)	12d (license fee)
Shevington mill	<1365	?	Hugh the Franter	?

A summary of Burscough's mill holdings is set out in Table 6.8. The canons of Burscough appear to have gone through an intense mill-building phase before 1228. Four windmills and one watermill were built within the priory-held vill or parish of Ormskirk, well before the borough was granted free status. Because part of the charter of liberties included granting the burgesses of the vill a concessionary multure rate, the vill almost undoubtedly held suit of mill, providing a suitable incentive for their construction. The windmills were obviously built to take advantage of the flat geography and steady prevailing winds of the area. It also seems likely that they were built to take advantage of the growing numbers and wealth of the priory's tenants. While the revenues that were drawn from these mills remain a mystery, it seems likely that they were drawing at

---

[249]   Ibid., ms. 40.

[250]   See Holt (1988), pp. 80–82; c.f. Neilson (1910), p. 99, who cites a rate as high as 1/10.

[251]   See *Coucher Book of Furness Abbey*, Vol. II, Pt. III, pp. xxi–xxii, and the more detailed discussion in Chapter 7 of Furness's mill holdings.

least as much revenue as some of the town mills held by Cirencester, an observation that is supported by the relatively high rent paid by the canons to Gilbert of Halsall for seisin of Halsall watermill in the late thirteenth century (i.e., £1 10s a year), i.e. the total revenue was probably at least twice that amount.

Judging from the long leases on and low rents obtained for three of their watermills in the late twelfth and early thirteenth centuries, it was perhaps the low revenues of the priory's non-seigneurial mills which prompted them to build additional mills in a place where they did hold suit. The canons who managed Burscough's estates in the latter half of the thirteenth century appear to have directly managed their seigneurial mills at Burscough, Scarisbrick, Bykerstaff and Cross Hall, because there is no record of how much revenue they were collecting from any of their mills during this period. Of the 13 mills it held before 1350, four or five were receiving nominal rents from customary and knightly tenants (three of whom had donated the mills to the canons), one was being leased from a local freeholder, and six appear to have been in hand. Although they did grant away many of their feudal rights in the parish of Ormskirk to its citizens, there is no mention of the tenants having won freedom from suit of the seven mills there. Free status may have simply involved a reduced multure rate as stipulated in the charter.

Conclusion

The previous discussion has revealed that the Augustinians drew donations from a wide range of different landholders, from kings and tenants-in-chief to peasants with small holdings. Generally speaking, most Augustinian houses were established by donors from the ruling élite, and gradually became less fashionable and attracted less illustrious benefactors as the decades wore on. At the more rarefied end of the benefaction scale was Cirencester, whose donors were primarily a mixture of royal officials, local aristocrats and gentry, while the donors to St Denys's and Lacock were mainly mid-ranking nobles and gentry. At the medium level were Butley, whose donors were the daughters of its founding lord and his major tenants, Bradenstoke, whose benefactors were the earls of Salisbury and their relatives, officers and tenants, as well as some small local landholders, and Burscough, whose donors were the major tenants of its founding lord, as well as some of its patron's lesser tenants and small holders. At the lower end of the scale were Blythburgh, whose donors were a mixed bag of peasants, local gentry and knights; and St Gregory's, whose donors were mostly small freemen who granted their holdings to the priory under gavelkind.

Augustinian institutions were the recipients of the largesse of aristocratic and especially knightly benefactors in the form of mills to a very significant extent. Table 6.9 clearly indicates just how prevalent were knightly donations (and sales) of mills, mill rents and tithes to the Augustinians. The table contains data on eight of the nine houses sampled. Bolton Priory's mill holdings are not included as data pertaining to its mill acquisition were not analysed earlier in the chapter.

Eight Augustinian houses held 63 mills in whole or part at the peak of the medieval milling trade in the late thirteenth/early fourteenth century. Twenty-three of these mills were donated by knights, at 36.5 per cent of the total, along with four mill rents, one mill sale and tithes for two mills. Four houses were each donated four or more mills by knights. Seven of the 63 mills were donated by kings, four by archbishops, three by magnates and one each by a clerk, a burgess and a lord's huntsman. Three mills were sold to one of the houses (Cirencester) by a knight and members of the gentry and administrative classes. Ten mills were almost certainly built by the houses concerned and the sources of another 11 could not be identified.

Due to the fragmented nature of many of their holdings and the non-seigneurial status of roughly 60 per cent of their mills, the Augustinians were not able to take advantage of the same kinds of revenue streams from their mills that were available to the ancient episcopal and Benedictine houses with their captive markets of villein (and in the north, sometimes free) tenants. Nevertheless, it is clear from the evidence analysed in this chapter that the Augustinians were actively engaged in building and purchasing mills when they were not able to acquire them through donation. St Denys, for example, acquired one mill from Henry I, four from knights, one from a local burgess and built itself one other mill. In like fashion, Blythburgh acquired one mill from Henry I, four from knights and built itself one other mill. Burscough acquired five mills from knights and built itself another five mills, primarily because it did not have full seisin of the fee mills it had been granted. Due to its close association with the archbishopric of Canterbury, St Gregory's acquired four mills from two archbishops and a single mill from a knight. Bradenstoke was a little different, in that it acquired one mill from

Table 6.9   Patterns of mill acquisition and investment for eight Augustinian houses between 1084 and 1320

House/Patron	Sub-total	St Gregory's	St Denys'	Bradenstoke	Lacock	Cirencester	Blythburgh	Butley	Burscough
Kings	7		1			4	1	1	
Archbishops	4	4		1 T					
Magnates	3			1 R	2 T R				
Knights	23	1	4	2 2xR P	R P	4 R P	4 T	T	5
Gentry	1					P			
Admin. and curial	2			1		P			
Burgesses	1		1						
Huntsmen	1			1					
Built by house	10		1	2		1	1		5
Unknown	11			1		7			3
TOTAL MILLS	63	5	6 1/2	9	2 1/2	19	5 1/4	1	13

T = tithe donations
R = rent donations
P = purchases

an archbishop, one from a magnate, three from knights, two from middling men and built two of its own. Nevertheless, the obvious similarities in these patterns of mill acquisition suggest that a conscious strategy was being pursued by the canons of the houses concerned, who sought to emulate, as best they could, a pattern of mill acquisition which they saw in evidence at the earliest house of Augustinian canons to be established in England, St Gregory's. Even Cirencester, which acquired four mills from kings, four from knights, two by purchase and at least one through construction, fits this general pattern. The only houses which do not roughly conform are the nunnery of Lacock and Butley Priory.

While the Augustinian canons do not, on the whole, appear to have been especially entrepreneurial in the construction of mills, as we will see in Chapter 9, they did spend a great deal of time and sometimes considerable amounts of money securing the title of mills, as well as the lands and waters appurtenant to their mills, and in regaining or ensuring seisin of mills and the tithes of mills which they already held.

The manors, vills and mills held by each house, along with their total annual revenues as determined by the *Taxatio Nicholai IV*, are reproduced in Table 6.10. The houses are listed in order of their total annual estate revenue as recorded in the *Taxatio* to provide some idea of the relationship between their incomes, property holdings and the number of mills which they held. As with the Benedictines and conventual houses, only those mills directly held by the houses concerned are included in the tally.

The nine houses held 82 or more mills between them on well over 50 manors, vills and knights' fees in the late thirteenth and early fourteenth centuries, an average of just over nine mills per house. One of the most striking features of the data compiled in the table is the very low number of mills with suit which the Augustinians appear to have held, at only 32.3 per cent. Unlike most of the other houses examined so far, the Augustinians held a large number of non-seigneurial mills that were not in customary or hereditary tenure which they had almost invariably acquired from knights and a few other individuals of middling rank before the Statute of Mortmain was introduced. Of the nine Augustinian houses sampled, 61.3 per cent of their mills had non-seigneurial status, compared with 41.5 per cent of the Cistercian mills, 32 per cent of the episcopal mills and 18.8 per cent of the Benedictine mills. In other words, at the peak of the milling trade in medieval England, the majority of the mills held by the Augustinians were not owed suit and had no guaranteed custom. This lack of custom is clearly reflected in the very low rents which most of the canons drew from their mills.[252]

While there is a little uncertainty about these figures, they are based primarily on direct references to the mills concerned having held suit. However, it is important to note that only 21 per cent of the Augustinians' mills appear to have been held by customary and hereditary tenants, compared with 47.4 per cent for the five episcopal houses, 16.5 per cent for the four Benedictine houses and 3.9 per cent for the five Cistercian houses. In other words, two-thirds of the mills with non-seigneurial status that were held by the Augustinians were former fee mills, the additional category of non-seigneurial mill which I first flagged in Chapters 2 and 3.

Turning now to the mill management practices pursued by the various houses sampled, like the great Benedictine and episcopal houses, Cirencester appears to have followed a mixed policy of direct management and leasing of its 19 mills during the thirteenth century, at least four of seven mills leased in that period being for life. Such generous leases appear to have been due to the fact that it was unable to charge high rents for its mills, presumably as a result of competition from other mills and because it lacked suit on the majority of its own mills. Nevertheless, in those contexts where it clearly felt it was appropriate, Cirencester's efficient management of its estates extended to what might properly be regarded as coercive efforts to extract the maximum returns from its properties. As we will see more clearly in Chapter 9, Cirencester had a reputation for dealing harshly with uncooperative tenants, as attested by the destruction of illegal handmills by the abbot's men in the early fourteenth century and its refusal to allow the town of Cirencester burghal status. Although the rental data that is available records a three- to sixteen-fold increase in its mill rents from Domesday to the late thirteenth century, its overall mill revenues appear to be comparable to those of Chichester, which were about half the rates seen on the estates of the more extractive ecclesiastical lords and lords from the north: a source, perhaps, of the abbatial frustration which appears to have motivated the previously cited conflicts with tenants.

---

[252] See the tables compiled for each house which list any mill revenues recorded.

Table 6.10   Mill holdings of nine Augustinian houses in the late thirteenth/early fourteenth century

Name	No. of manors and/or vills	No. of mills	Mills with suit	Mills without suit	Mills in customary and hereditary tenure	Windmills	Industrial mills	Annual estate revenue
Bolton	20+	21+	11+	9	9	0	0	£445
Butley	3 (?)	1 (?)	?	?	0	0	0	£280
Cirencester	3	19	2	17 (?)	0	0	0	£242
Bradenstoke	9	9	2–3	6–7	3	1	0	£140
Blythburgh	1	5 1/4	2	3 1/4	0	2	0	£89
St Gregory's	6	5	0	5	0	0	0	£41
Burscough	1	13	7	5	4–5	4	0	£27
Lacock	5 1/2	2 1/2+	1 1/2–2 1/2	0–1	0	0	0	£24+
St Denys's	1	6 1/2	1–4 (?)	2 1/2–4 1/2	1	0	0	£24
TOTAL	**49 1/2**	**82+**	**26 1/2–30 1/2**	**50 1/4+**	**17–18**	**7**	**0**	**£1,312**

The almost universally low rents paid to Blythburgh, Bradenstoke, Burscough, Lacock and St Denys's for their mills demonstrates the marginal profitability of the mills held by these houses, all of which appear to have followed mixed practices of leasing and direct management of their mills throughout the period covered by the sample. Blythburgh in Suffolk, for example, was charging 14 shillings or less for four of its seven mills in the thirteenth century, while Bradenstoke in Wiltshire drew 10 shillings each in rents from two mills for which the rents only had been donated to it. Its own mills seem to have all been directly managed, but only two or three of them appear to have held suit, for which no revenues are recorded. During the same period, Burscough in Lancashire was renting five of its 13 mills for under three shillings each and another mill for £1 10s. In the second half of the thirteenth century, St Denys's in Southampton drew eight shillings from one of its town mills, £1 for the half share of a second mill, £2 13s 4d from a third mill in Tytherley, and £1 from a fourth mill between 1301 and 1410. It seems likely that the only reason St Denys's drew a relatively high rent from the Tytherley mill was because it had been managed by someone else before it was granted to the priory around 1280 and probably included suit. Only two rentals for c. 1260–80 are recorded for two of Lacock's three mills in Wiltshire, one of which drew £1 in rents, while a half share of the other rendered eight shillings. As we have seen, no rental information is contained in the charters for Butley or St Gregory's, although we do know that Butley had begun to favour a policy of leasing over direct management of its estates after 1300 (even if it held no mills of its own), while St Gregory's appears to have continued direct management of its mills throughout the period covered by its charters.

The black sheep of these Augustinian houses in terms of management and discipline was undoubtedly St Denys's in Southampton, which was both a poor manager of its estates and a poor disciplinarian of its brethren, with both tendencies appearing to mutually reinforce one another, and resulting in a fairly disastrous but somewhat predictable outcome, amongst which was the loss of some of its mills and their revenues for decades. This lack of discipline and low morale was undoubtedly related to its presence in a bustling port town in which the promiscuous behaviour of many of the inhabitants acted as a powerful disincentive to canons intending to follow the Rule.

The small northern house of Burscough in Lancashire is somewhat of an anomaly within the group, having been the third smallest house surveyed, but having held the third largest number of mills. More than half of the mills directly held by it appear to have been built by the canons, with most of these in the parish of Ormskirk which it held as a manor. Unlike any of the other houses in the north, the canons of Burscough were, like the southern canons of Chichester, pioneers in adopting windmill technology, building four windmills in the first quarter of the thirteenth century. The canons of Burscough appear to have been very conscious of what their southern brethren were doing, as their estate management practices also closely resembled those of the southern Augustinian houses. In the latter half of the twelfth century, its canons were farming out their possessions on similarly generous terms to those typically seen in the south in the first half of the twelfth century. By the second quarter of the thirteenth century, however, it was directly managing seven mills within the parish of Ormskirk from which it was presumably drawing significant revenues, a factor which may well have been a spur for the people of Ormskirk to seek their liberty from the canons in the late thirteenth century. When Ormskirk was subsequently granted the status of a free borough, it would seem that the canons retained suit on its seven mills. They also appear to have continued to directly manage these mills, as there are no records of any mill rents or leases for the Ormskirk mills. Unfortunately, the priory's surviving records do not give any clear indication of how many of its mills were directly managed in the late thirteenth and early fourteenth century, although the lack of documentation would suggest that they were all, with the exception of Cross Hall horse mill, in hand.

The evidence examined in this chapter clearly indicates that the highly extractive mill management practices of the larger episcopal and Benedictine houses were not, and indeed could not, be emulated by the Augustinians.

Even when Augustinian houses were able to secure mills with suit, there were limitations on their potential to extract high incomes from those mills, as we saw in relation to the mills of Adderbury and Cheltenham held by Cirencester, the mills of Bishopstrow and Heddington held by Lacock, and the mills of Henham and Darsham held by Blythburgh. All of these mills were located on manors in southern England with relatively small populations of villein tenants. Generally speaking, those houses in the south which held the majority of their mills without suit were only able to draw similar incomes to those from seigneurial mills in places with a high population density and/or little competition from other mills. Nevertheless, the Augustinians were clearly able to draw sufficient revenues from even their non-seigneurial mills to make it worthwhile to continue to invest in their maintenance and acquisition. Unfortunately, there is insufficient data available on most of them to determine how many of these mills survived the climatic, political and demographic shocks of the fourteenth and fifteenth centuries.

Chapter 7
The Cistercians

The Cistercians were the third largest monastic order in medieval England. Well known for their innovations in sheep breeding and wool growing,[1] the monks of the order also have a reputation within some scholarly circles for being enthusiastic mill builders and technological innovators with respect to the use of water power for industry. As we saw in the Introduction and in Chapter 3, a number of well-known historians of technology have argued that the Cistercians had a progressive attitude towards technological development that was pioneering for their age, and have remarked upon their 'humanizing' of technological processes.[2] To what extent this argument is well founded will be a focus for discussion in this and the concluding chapter.

Unlike the Benedictines and most of the other religious orders, the Cistercians did not generally decentralize their administration through the offices of obedientiaries, but instead entrusted responsibility for managing their financial affairs to a single cellarer.[3] Nor did the white monks tend to rely on the labour services of their tenants, as did the Benedictines and some of the other well-established houses. On the whole, the Cistercians developed their own system of direct farming through granges that were at least initially managed by lay brothers or *conversi*.[4]

Even though the popular mythology tends to portray the Cistercian grange as having been carved out of primeval waste, it was in fact a fairly common practice for the monks to repopulate or reclaim areas that had previously been abandoned. This enabled them to build up sufficient holdings in such areas to establish relatively compact land holdings that were directly cultivated and which possessed their own nuclei of farm buildings. Such holdings were often built up through the piecemeal acquisition of small parcels of land through grant, purchase and exchange, but sometimes also through the conversion of whole manors acquired via grants. The average grange size was between 300 and 400 acres, although they could range in size from less than 100 to around a thousand acres.[5] Most granges consisted of arable land, but some were almost exclusively pastoral.

Cistercian regulations dictated that granges were to be no more than a day's journey from the mother house, and should be at least two leagues apart (around 4.8 kilometres).[6] But a number of English Cistercian abbeys, including the majority of those sampled, had acquired property in either more distant or more compact locales, and consequently ignored these directives.[7] As we will see shortly in relation to the management of mills and prohibitions on wool broking, these were not the only ordinances of the General Chapter that were frequently violated for financial and/or practical reasons by the White Monks.

In chronological order of their dates of foundation, the five Cistercian estates in the sample belonged to the abbeys of Old Wardon (1136), Kirkstall (1147), Furness (1148), Sibton (1150) and Beaulieu (1204). These houses were located in Bedfordshire, Yorkshire, Lancashire, Suffolk and Hampshire, respectively. In terms of their origins, Old Wardon was founded by the great northern magnate, Walter Espec, while Kirkstall was founded by Henry de Lacy, grandson of one of the Conqueror's retinue. Furness was originally founded by King Stephen as a Savigniac house in 1127 and converted to Cistercian rule two decades later. Sibton was founded by monks from Old Wardon Abbey, and Beaulieu was the one and only royal foundation by King John.

---

[1]   For some detailed discussions of the Cistercian wool trade, see Power (1941) for the classic study, and Bell, Brooks and Dryburgh (2007) for a more limited update; also Knowles (1950), Ch. 7, and Donkin (1978), pp. 82–102, 135–53.

[2]   See, for example, White (1968). p. 67; Mumford (1967). p. 268. Also Gimpel (1988), pp. 3–6, 9, 46–8, 67–8, 229–30; Reynolds (1983), pp. 110–12, Reynolds (1984), p. 109.

[3]   As we will see below, Sibton Abbey was one example of an exception to this rule.

[4]   The grange as a form of land management was quickly adopted by a number of the other new monastic orders, such as the Premonstratensians and Gilbertines, but also occasionally by the Augustinians and Benedictines.

[5]   Bishop (1936), p. 209; Donkin (1978), p. 44.

[6]   The length of a league has been the subject of much debate. Recent research by John Langdon and David Harrison suggests that a league was about 2.4 km, or 1.5 miles (John Langdon, personal communication, March 2013).

[7]   Burton (1994), p. 253; Donkin (1978), p. 52.

Starting in the north-east and working south, most of Kirkstall's property was within a short distance of the abbey at Headingley, but it also held land in more distant locations, primarily in other parts of Yorkshire and in Lancashire. Also in the north, Furness held extensive properties in Lancashire, Cumberland, Yorkshire and Lincolnshire. Most of Sibton's property was in East Suffolk and Norfolk, although it also held some land in Sussex. Old Wardon held property in Bedfordshire, Huntingdonshire and Northamptonshire. Most of Beaulieu's property was in Hampshire, with other significant parcels of land in Gloucestershire, Berkshire, Oxfordshire, Devon, Cornwall and Suffolk. The sample thus covers the north-east and north-west, the East Midlands, East Anglia, the south and south-west.

Once a Cistercian house had acquired sufficient holdings within an area to form a home farm or grange, it was not uncommon for them to expel or gradually displace peasant farmers and even whole village communities that had occupied the lands which they acquired. Sometimes the previous inhabitants might be kept on in order to provide an additional workforce, or would be resettled elsewhere. In order to establish the granges of Barnoldswick, Roundhay and Acrington for example, Kirkstall Abbey was responsible for depopulating or reducing the size of a number of settlements in these areas. On the other hand, it was not unusual for Cistercian granges in previously uninhabited or abandoned areas to become hamlets or villages that were organised by the monks along manorial lines.[8] Most of this activity took place in England between the mid-twelfth and mid-thirteenth centuries.

Table 7.1   Relative wealth of five Cistercian houses in 1291 and 1539

1291	Revenue	1535	Revenue
Beaulieu	£263	Furness	£1,052
Furness	£223	Old Wardon	£428
Old Wardon	£200	Kirkstall	£329
Sibton	£144	Beaulieu	£326
Kirkstall	£68+	Sibton	£251

With respect to the relative valuations of the five houses' estates as they appear in the *Taxatio Nicholai IV* of 1291 and the various surveys conducted during the time of the Dissolution (including the *Valor Ecclesiasticus*), their incomes in descending order at the time of the *Taxatio* are set out in Table 7.1. In the *Taxatio*, Beaulieu's annual value was calculated at £244 6s 2d, although taking into account some additional spiritualities excluded from the papal assessment a more accurate figure of £263 9s 6d is rendered.[9] The *Valor*, on the other hand, assessed Beaulieu's net income in the mid-sixteenth century as being only about 25 per cent more valuable at just over £326.[10] It seems likely that this was a gross under-valuation, however. Furness's temporalities were assessed at £176 in the *Taxatio*, but if one takes into account its spiritualities, pensions and tithes, this figure increases to £223 8s 4d, or roughly comparable with Beaulieu.[11] By the time of the *Valor*, however, Furness's value had more than quadrupled, the net estimate being £1,052 2s 3 3/4d.[12] Old Wardon's temporal and spiritual possessions were valued at around £200 in the *Taxatio*.[13] By 1537, its net income had almost doubled at £389 16s 6 1/2d. Only two years later, this had increased to £428 6s 11 1/2d.[14] In 1291,

8   Donkin (1978), pp. 17–18, 39–40, 46, 60–1, 182–3. Perhaps unsurprisingly, the Cistercian practices of depopulation drew criticism at the time from a number of quarters, and active resistance from some of the tenants so affected. See Knowles (1940), Ch. 39, for a discussion of Gerald of Wales and his criticisms of the Cistercians and Cluniacs, as well as some other critics of the monks. Also Donkin (1978), pp. 39–51, esp. p. 46 on resistance to Kirkstall. Sibton Abbey was one Cistercian house that allowed its displaced peasants to become lay brothers, on which see Dugdale (1846), Vol. 5, p. 560.

9   See the discussion and footnote at the end of Section 6.0 on Beaulieu. It should also be noted that the Account-Book of 1269/70 renders a figure of £370 2. 8 1/2d., which is probably the most accurate reflection of its real value.

10   Knowles and Hadcock (1953), p. 105.

11   *Coucher Book of Furness Abbey*, Vol. I, Pt. III, ms. 409; *VCH Lancs.*, Vol. II, p. 128.

12   *VCH Lancs.*, Vol. II, p. 128. Knowles and Hadcock (1953), p. 109, give a *Valor* net income of just over £805, making it the second wealthiest Cistercian house at the Dissolution after Fountains.

13   *VCH Beds.*, Vol. I, p. 364.

14   Ibid., Vol. I, p. 365, Vol. III, pp. 253. Also Knowles and Hadcock (1953), p. 117.

Sibton's total income was £144 3s 4d, the bulk of which, at £132 16s, was for its temporalities. The *Valor* lists a valuation of £250 15s 7 1/2d, of which only £41 19s was for its spiritualities.[15] Kirkstall's temporalities were valued at £68 5s 8d in 1291. Although the entry for the abbey in the *Valor* is missing,[16] Knowles and Hadcock provide a net income for Kirkstall in 1535 of over £329,[17] almost identical to Beaulieu.

While Beaulieu was the wealthiest of the Cistercian houses sampled at the end of the thirteenth century, and Old Wardon only marginally less wealthy than Furness, by the time of the Dissolution, Furness had far surpassed its older sister and the house of Beaulieu in terms of wealth and status. Sibton's rise was similarly far less spectacular, with Kirkstall surpassing it in income by the time of the Dissolution.

Before entering into a detailed discussion of the five estates' mill holdings in the chapters to follow, it is first necessary to clarify some of the issues surrounding the Cistercians' ownership of mills. The initial Cistercian ordinances on mill ownership forbade monks of the order from owning or using mills other than for their own purposes. These were modified by the General Chapter in 1214 and 1215, which in turn forbade 'the purchase or acquisition of lands, vineyards, ovens or mills except those granted in pure alms as a gift, and if they were granted, they were not to be cultivated by the monks' hands or at their expense, but were to be sold or committed to others for cultivation'.[18] However, judging from the dates of acquisition and revenues drawn from their mills, most English Cistercian houses appear to have paid little or no attention to these ordinances, as most were granted mills during their foundations during the latter half of the twelfth century which were not for their own use but were directly held by them, and from which those in the sample drew significant revenues. There is also clear evidence that at least one of the houses concerned, Beaulieu, was involved in the purchase of mills during the thirteenth century, and that it drew very large revenues from its mills. Not only were its mills profitable, it was also drawing a significant proportion of its manorial income from its mills, in much the same fashion as many of the larger and more established Benedictine houses.

Given the profitability of milling for many Cistercian houses, it is perhaps not surprising to learn that those restrictions upon the order being involved in milling, or collecting revenues from land and mill rents, had been well and truly overturned by the 1250s.[19] By 1300 most Cistercians houses earned significant revenues from various sources, including mills, churches and markets that had originally been prohibited by the order. However, because the majority of the Cistercian houses in the sample directly managed their mills before the fourteenth century, and often recorded no revenues from their mills in surveys and rentals up to that time, it is difficult to determine exactly how much revenue they were drawing from their mills. The exception was Beaulieu Abbey, whose account book reveals that it was not only drawing tithes from a mill in Inglesham, Wiltshire, in the late 1260s,[20] but considerable income from 10 of its 12 other mills in Hampshire, Berkshire, Oxfordshire and Cornwall, most of which was from tollcorn that was then distributed to demesne servants. While Beaulieu did make some early concessions to Cistercian doctrine by letting its 'outside mills' (*molendini forensici*) at Little Faringdon from very early on, it was able to minimise its mill revenues by allocating tollcorn and large quantities of its own milled grain to *famuli* and other servants, as is witnessed by the many mill 'expenses' recorded in its account book. Furness Abbey in Lancashire also appears to have been engaged in such practices, as the nil valuation of its mills in Furness and the lack of any income recorded for any other mills in a survey of 1292 would suggest. There is also some strong evidence cited in the section on Sibton from its post-plague *compoti* that it was similarly engaged in minimising its surpluses in general through matching its revenues with its expenditure.[21] This is graphically illustrated through mapping its receipts against its expenses for the period 1363–72. Such behaviour clearly reveals

---

[15]   *VCH Suff.*, Vol. I, pp. 89–90.

[16]   *VCH Yorks.*, Vol. III, p. 145.

[17]   Knowles and Hadcock (1953), p. 110.

[18]   *Sibton Abbey Cartularies*, Pt. 1, p. 125.

[19]   Donkin (1978), p. 17.

[20]   *Account-Book of Beaulieu Abbey*, p. 68.

[21]   Holt (1988), p. 77 notes that it was common practice for lords to sell only a small proportion of tollcorn from mills in hand, and that most was used to feed *famuli*. However, it was not just tollcorn that was being allocated to demesne servants by these Cistercian houses, but their own milled grain as well.

the difference between the goals of monastic management practices and those of capitalist enterprises in the modern period.

Some other notable features of the relevant documents sampled include a brief reference to a tool-sharpening horse mill in Beaulieu Abbey's shoe shop and the details of millers' wages in the account-book of the same house. There are also details of the costs of construction and maintenance of mills held by Beaulieu in the late thirteenth century, and of mills held by Sibton in the wake of the Black Death, including a windmill. Other surviving records from Sibton indicate that a third of the grain mills which it held in East Anglia were windmills by the early 1360s. Furness's charters include references to the abbey's right to take millstones in Lancashire in the thirteenth century, and the multure rates which the abbey and other northern tenants paid during the same period.

Beaulieu Abbey

Beaulieu Abbey was the only religious house founded by King John during his reign, and was one of the larger Cistercian monasteries in England. Situated on the Beaulieu River in the New Forest, Hampshire, about 10 kilometres south-west of Southampton, it was originally intended that construction begin on the abbey in the royal manor of Faringdon in Berkshire in 1203, but possibly due to a lack of water at the Faringdon site, or the close proximity of other major religious houses with holdings in the same manor, the location was changed (Figure 7.1).[22] Construction was subsequently begun on the royal abbey near the king's hunting lodge in the New Forest in 1204. John's foundation grant consisted solely of the manor of Faringdon and the land around the abbey's new location (Figure 7.2).

Because of the poor quality of the soils in the area, Beaulieu had to acquire agricultural land further afield in order to sustain itself. The early years of the abbey were therefore dedicated to acquiring such land, usually through purchase. The majority of these early acquisitions were along the Avon and Breamore rivers to the abbey's west, as well as the Meon valley to the east of Southampton Water.[23]

Most of the abbey's granges were within 10 kilometres of the abbey itself, and included Sowley, St Leonard's, Beufre, Otterwood, Holbury and Hartford (Figure 7.2). It was these 'home' granges within the New Forest that supplied the monastery with food. At a slightly greater distance were more granges in and around Burgate on the river Avon (Figure 7.3),[24] while others were in Colbury,[25] Southampton[26] and Soberton on the river Meon (Figure 7.4),[27] as well as Norton and Shamblers on the Isle of Wight. It also held lands in Bristol and Little Yarmouth in Suffolk (now Norfolk), from where it purchased herring from the local fishery,[28] and in Ellingham, Blashford, Godshill, Buckland, Breamore and Burmore in Hampshire.[29] The abbey also owned a fish-drying facility on the Lizard Peninsula in Cornwall (Figure 7.5).[30] By the middle of the thirteenth century, Beaulieu held property in at least eight counties, including Hampshire, Berkshire, Cornwall, Devon, Gloucestershire, Oxfordshire, Suffolk and Wiltshire. By 1300, its holdings consisted of 14 granges and numerous other smaller properties (Figure 7.6).

The abbey had considerable difficulties in securing its rights to its Cornish properties, being involved in a number of expensive legal disputes over the years.[31] It was also involved in a long-running dispute with local graziers in the New Forest over its enclosure of over a thousand acres of uncultivated land between 1236

---

[22]   *Beaulieu Abbey Cartulary*, xxxiv. The other religious houses with holdings in Faringdon included Reading, Stanley, Thame, Bec, Cluny, Llanthony and Winchester.

[23]   Ibid., p. xxxv. One such purchase was the grange of Soberton, bought from Jordan de Walkerville in 1234–35. See ms. 46.

[24]   Ibid., mss. 173–212. This included land in Gorley.

[25]   Ibid., mss. 213–37. This included property in Eling, Lepe and Exbury.

[26]   Ibid., mss. 238–47.

[27]   Ibid., mss. 45–96.

[28]   Ibid., mss. 8–44. On the purchase of herring, see p. xliii.

[29]   Ibid., mss. 97–172.

[30]   Ibid., p. xliii.

[31]   Ibid., pp. liii–lvi.

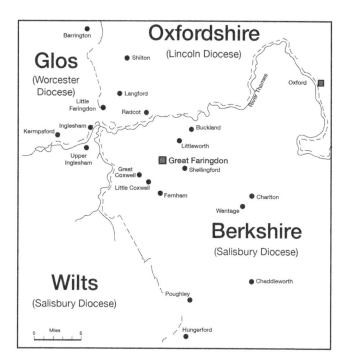

Fig. 7.1   Beaulieu Abbey's possessions in and around the manor of Faringdon. After *The Beaulieu Cartulary* (1974)

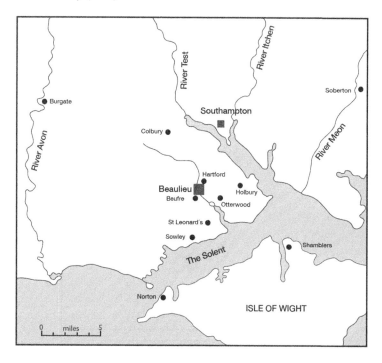

Fig. 7.2   Granges of Beaulieu Abbey After *The Beaulieu Cartulary* (1974)

Fig. 7.3   Beaulieu Abbey's possessions in the Avon valley. After Hockey (1974)

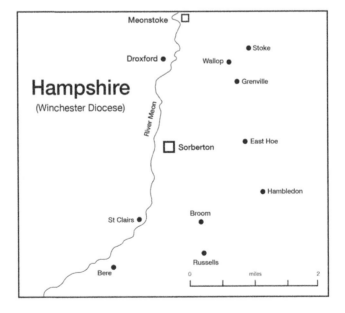

Fig. 7.4   Beaulieu's possessions in the Meon valley. After Hockey (1975)

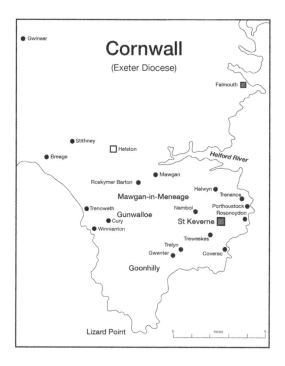

Fig. 7.5   Beaulieu Abbey's possessions in the Lizard Peninsula. After *The Beaulieu Cartulary* (1974)

Fig. 7.6   Beaulieu's possessions, c. 1300. After *The Beaulieu Cartulary* (1974)

and 1324,[32] and with a number of its tenants on its Faringdon manor, many of whom claimed during the mid-thirteenth century that they held their properties freely.[33]

Although the ownership of churches was contrary to the early principles of the Cistercians, in 1233 Beaulieu was given permission by Pope Gregory IX to appropriate the churches of Shilton and Inglesham, along with the chapel of Coxwell, and the church of St Keverne in Cornwall. The abbey also held grange chapels at St Leonard's, Boverey and Trougham, and had established three daughter houses within five decades of its own foundation. These were Netley in Hampshire (1239), Hailes in Gloucestershire (1246) and Newenham in Devon (1247).[34]

The abbey's patrons consisted of a number of prominent and notable figures, amongst whom were tenants-in-chief such as the earls of Cornwall and Hereford, members of the local gentry such as the Fleming, Foliot, Fortin, Punchardon and Sancto Laurencio families, and royal officials such as Nicholas de Moels, sometime sheriff of Hampshire and Yorkshire, and keeper of Winchester Castle, and Nicholas de Ponte Audemer, keeper of the salterns at Pennington.[35] The monks also spent some very large sums of money acquiring land in various areas, including £100 for houses in Southampton and more than £600 for land in Soberton, the Avon valley, Faringdon and Eling between 1205 and c. 1250.[36] It remains somewhat of a mystery as to how the monks were able to draw on such large cash reserves, as the abbey's gross receipts as recorded in the *Taxatio Nicholai IV* were only a little over £260, the majority of which were for its temporalities. Like many of the other valuations in the *Taxatio*, however, this was a gross under-valuation.[37]

The extant documents from the abbey's muniments include an account book of 1269–70 and two cartularies, one of which is a general collection of charters, while the second pertains only to the abbey's holdings in the manor of Faringdon. The general cartulary is arranged in nine parts, the first consisting of royal charters to the abbey, and the rest arranged geographically according to the areas in which the abbey's properties lay. It was drawn up sometime soon after 1250, with most of the subsequent additions entered during the 1320s. The second cartulary provides systematic notes on each of the abbey's properties that made up the manor of Faringdon, providing a custumal, table of rents, terriers of demesne arable and meadow, the amount of seed corn sown in a normal year and the wages paid to permanent demesne workers. This is followed by various miscellanea. It was probably drawn up between 1335 and 1349.[38]

The abbey's account book consists of two manuscripts, and is one of the most detailed to have survived the Middle Ages, containing annual accounts for each of the abbey's manors and granges, as well as each officer or servant who was entrusted with abbatial funds. These are interspersed with tables and rules for checking the veracity of the accounts and the honesty of the abbey's officials. The three collections of documents suggest that Beaulieu had instituted a systematic form of estate management by the last few decades of the thirteenth century.[39] Despite such diligence, however, the monks do not appear to have been very efficient at keeping their archives, as some of their muniments appear to have been kept on the manors to which they related. This resulted in at least one instance of theft of a large number of valuable documents. Furthermore, there is no evidence that the detailed accounting system set out in the account book was ever implemented on a yearly basis.[40]

While Beaulieu's mill holdings were not particularly large, it is unusual amongst the English Cistercian monasteries for having preserved not only detailed records within its account book of its mill revenues and expenses, but also of its monastic workshops, amongst which are included references to a tanning mill and a horse-driven tool-sharpening mill.[41] Its cartulary also contains a reference to the purchase of a watermill, which was bought with suit of the manor in which it was located sometime after 1230 for more than £16.[42]

[32] See *Cal. Pat. Rolls 1321–4*, p. 366; *Cal. Pat. Rolls 1324–7*, pp. 67, 281.

[33] *Beaulieu Abbey Cartulary*, pp. lviii–lx.

[34] Ibid., p. xxxviii. See ms. 249 for the grant of St Keverne from Richard, earl of Cornwall. Cf. ms. 304.

[35] Ibid., pp. xlviii–liii.

[36] Ibid., lxiii.

[37] See the discussion of Beaulieu's total revenues at the end of the case study.

[38] Ibid., pp. xv–xvii.

[39] Ibid., pp. xv–xvii.

[40] Ibid., p. xx.

[41] *Account Book of Beaulieu Abbey*, pp. 36, 210, and the discussion of industrial mills in Chapter 8.

[42] *Beaulieu Abbey Cartulary*, mss. 184–7, 209.

Only five mills are referred to in the abbey's cartulary, the relevant documents covering a fairly narrow time period from before 1218 to around 1243, while its account book covers the financial year of 1269–70. The only reference to Beaulieu's mills that post-date this period is a charter from the Faringdon Cartulary dated to 1335.[43] Of the five mills in the Beaulieu cartulary, one was not held by the abbey, while only three of the 12 recorded in the account book are mentioned in the cartulary. Nine of these 12 mills were dedicated to grinding grain, some of which also appear to have ground malted grains.

The earliest mill-related document from Beaulieu's cartulary is an agreement dated to sometime before 1218 between the Abbot of Beaulieu and Alexander son of Humphrey of Little Faringdon regarding the leasing of the mills of Little Faringdon in Oxfordshire. The lease included the pastures, meadows, fields, millpools, ditches, waters and fisheries that were appurtenant to the mills at a rent of four marks (£2 13s 4d) a year, as well as an initial payment or entry fee of three marks (£2). The agreement also states that the abbey's men at Little Faringdon and Langford were to continue following suit and services as if the abbey still directly held the mills, while Alexander was exempted from tolls and his servants from view of frankpledge.[44]

The next reference is to a single mill at Little Faringdon held by the abbey, and is dated to around 1225. The charter records a declaration by Walter son of William of Inglesham that all his men of Westbrook would henceforth grind their corn at the abbey's mill.[45] The fact that only one mill is mentioned may indicate the Little Faringdon mills were two mills in one house, or a double mill. It is not clear from the wording of the document whether the mill was still let to Alexander of Little Faringdon at this stage.[46]

Sometime between 1225 and 1269–70 when the abbey's account book was compiled, one of the mills of Little Faringdon was converted to a fulling mill, as a grain mill and fulling mill are recorded in the account book in relation to the manor, the former rendering £1 4d annually.[47] In a note to this entry, Hockey cites another document of the same time which states that Robert Acke held both mills for £2 a year.[48] In other words, the fulling mill was earning marginally less than the grain mill at this stage, a situation that appears to have been quite unusual. However, the total revenue from the two mills c. 1270 was significantly less than their earnings as grain mills before 1218, although the reasons for this are not clear, as they had returned to their early thirteenth-century levels by the mid-fourteenth century, as the following document testifies (see Table 7.2). The document in question is dated to 1335, and is reproduced in the Faringdon Cartulary.[49] It records the lease of the mills with two acres of ploughland and meadow for four marks annually, or the same rent paid by Alexander of Little Faringdon more than a century earlier. Unfortunately, it gives no indication of whether one of the mills was still operating as a fulling mill.

The only published manuscript references to the abbey's fulling mill are contained in the monastery's account book dated 1269–70.[50] While three manuscripts in the cartulary dated to sometime after 1218, c. 1225 and 1335 mention what are either two watermills or a double mill in the same manor,[51] it seems likely that one of these grain mills was converted to fulling cloth some time before the account book was written, as only one grain mill is discussed in the account. While the other two manuscripts both talk about Little Faringdon mills, neither specifies how many nor for what purpose were the mills being used.

The next series of documents from the cartulary refer to 'Clak' mill at Rockstead near Burgate in Hampshire. Although the term 'clak mill' was used on the Orkney Islands for a horizontal watermill, and this unusual name is not associated with the place where Beaulieu's mill was located, it seems fairly unlikely that this mill was a horizontal watermill.[52] The mill had originally belonged to nearby Breamore Priory, which held the lordship of Rockstead manor, which was located about five kilometres to the northwest of Fordingbridge

---

[43] *Beaulieu Abbey Cartulary*, p. lxvi.

[44] Ibid., ms. 22. Frankpledge was the compulsory mutual pledging of the tithing; members of the local tithing (i.e., the local area in which tithes were due) acted as sureties for each other if any were unable to pay fines or amercements.

[45] No doubt William of Inglesham's men of Westbrook regularly cursed their lord for this imposition, as Westbrook was more than 40 kilometres away from Little Faringdon!

[46] *Beaulieu Abbey Cartulary*, ms. 23. Cf. Ms. 22.

[47] *Account Book of Beaulieu Abbey*, p. 63.

[48] Ibid., n. 2, citing Cons. Bodl., fo. 70v.

[49] *Faringdon Cartulary*, ms. xliii.

[50] *Account Book of Beaulieu Abbey*, pp. 63, 219–20. Cf. Wilson (1957), p. 107, citing B.M. Add. Ms.48,978 f.42.

[51] *Beaulieu Cartulary*, p. lxvi, and mss. 22, 23. Cf. *Faringdon Cartulary*, ms. 43.

[52] See Rahtz and Bullough (1977), p. 31 on the Orkney mills.

outside the New Forest. As there are no other waterways nearby, the mill was probably on Sweatfords Water. Presumably the mill had fallen into hereditary tenure after being granted to Alice of Rockstead or her husband, who had bequeathed it to Breamore Priory in her will sometime in the early thirteenth century. Some kind of dispute subsequently arose between the priory and Alice's heirs, as around 1225 the priory quitclaimed the mill to Henry de Sancto Sampsone, who was Alice's brother-in-law, for which the priory received a fee of £2.[53] This must have been a blow to Breamore, as it was in financial straits at the time and had already sold land to Beaulieu to try to alleviate its troubles.[54]

Sometime soon after Breamore's quitclaim, Henry de Sancto Sampsone granted 'Clak' mill to William son of Henry de Wande, along with two crofts, a moor and curtilage for a rent of half a pound of cummin a year. By 1230, Henry had died, and Beatrice his widow confirmed the grant to William for the same rent in perpetuity.[55] Around the same time, William in turn sold the mill with its associated lands, as well as two men and suit of mill of the manor, to Beaulieu Abbey for 20 marks (£13 6s 8d) and a rent of half a pound of cummin a year for all secular services.[56] Although the earlier 'grant' from Henry to William does not mention an exchange of money, it probably did, as it is hard to imagine how William could have otherwise extracted such a hefty sum from Beaulieu. This was apparently to settle debts with Jewish moneylenders. It seems fairly likely that the same mill appears in the abbey's account book of 40 years later as 'Burgate mill', as Burgate is only a few kilometres south-east of Rockstead.

The first of only two other references to mills within the cartulary records the sale of two acres of land in Flexland in the manor of Soberton in Hampshire by Gocelin de Stoke to the abbey for two marks. The charter is dated to c. 1235. The land grant was located next to *la Bere* mill held by Thomas de Wemio'.[57] This may have been the Soberton mill recorded later in the abbey's account book, although there is no indication in any of the abbey's extant documents of how this mill was acquired by them.[58] The other reference is to a grant of one acre of meadow that was next to the Ilesham mill (i.e., Inglesham mill) in Wiltshire, by Albretha, the widow of Walter de Langeford, to the Vicar of Ellingham around 1243.[59] Beaulieu had acquired the tithes of this mill when it was granted the churches of Shilton, Inglesham and St Keverne in 1233, as the account-book registers that the abbey was collecting three shillings in tithes from Inglesham mill and its fishery, suggesting annual revenues of around £1 10s.[60]

At least two of the 12 mills held by the abbey in the late thirteenth century appear to have been purchased,[61] while at least three others were acquired through grants.[62] Only the windmill of Coxwell and the three industrial mills within the abbey's precincts appear to have been built by the monks, although it seems likely that it converted one of the watermills of Little Faringdon to a fulling mill sometime after the initial grant from King John. As will become clear from the discussion below, Beaulieu's revenues from its mills were extremely high, even when compared with the revenues of the more extractive lords from the north.

At least 12 mills are described in the abbey's accounts. These included windmills at Coxwell and Rydon, two fulling mills (one at Beaulieu and another at Little Faringdon) and two other industrial mills in the abbey's workshops (i.e., a water-powered tanning mill and a horse-powered tool-sharpening mill). It also held single water-powered grain mills at Nanclegy in Cornwall, Little Faringdon in Oxfordshire, Kyndlewere in Berkshire and Rockstead/Burgate and Soberton in Hampshire. There was also another mill whose location is unspecified, referred to only as 'the outside mill' (*molendinum forinsecum*), which was presumably located on Beaulieu's manor just outside the abbey's precincts. The abbey also collected tithes from a mill in Inglesham in Wiltshire. The only reference to the tanning mill is to repairs of 18 pence for the year, while the horse-powered tool-sharpening mill was attached to the smithy.[63]

---

[53]   *Beaulieu Abbey Cartulary*, mss. 185, 209.

[54]   Ibid., p. xlviii, mss. 154–5.

[55]   Ibid., mss. 186–7.

[56]   Ibid., ms. 184.

[57]   Ibid., ms. 86.

[58]   *Account-Book of Beaulieu Abbey*, pp. 116–18.

[59]   *Beaulieu Abbey Cartulary*, ms. 208.

[60]   *Account-Book of Beaulieu Abbey*, p. 68.

[61]   These were the mills of Soberton and Rockstead/Burgate (a.k.a. 'Clak' mill).

[62]   These were the mills of Little Faringdon and Nanclegy.

[63]   *Account-Book of Beaulieu Abbey*, pp. 210, 36.

Table 7.2   Fourteen mills in which Beaulieu Abbey held an interest before 1300

Name	Year acquired	Grantor	Grantee	Lessee/Tenant	Revenue
Little Faringdon mills (x2)*	1203	King John	Beaulieu Abbey	Alexander son of Humphrey of Little Faringdon (>1218)	2/13/4 (annual rent)
grain mill and fulling mill	1235–70 (fulling mill conversion)	n/a	n/a	Robert Acke (1269/70)	2/0/0 (annual rent)
"	"	"	"	?	3/6/8 (1335)
'Clak' mill, Rockstead*	c. 1230	William de Wande	Beaulieu Abbey		16/13/4 (purchase price) + 1/2 lb cummin (annual rent)
Soberton mill	1234–35	Jordan de Walkerville	Beaulieu Abbey (by purchase)		See Table 7.3
Inglesham mill and fishery	c. 1243	?	?	?	0/3/0 (tithes only)
Rydon windmill	>1250?	Built by abbey	n/a	n/a	See Table 7.3
Burgate mill	"	?	"	"	"
Kyndlewere mill	"	"	"	"	"
Nanclegy mill	"	"	"	"	"
Coxwell windmill	"	"	"	"	"
Outside mill, Beaulieu*	>1269–70	"	"	"	"
Beaulieu tanning mill	"	Built by abbey	"	"	In hand
Beaulieu tool-sharpening horse mill	"	"	"	"	"
Beaulieu fulling mill	"	"	"	"	"

* Mills stated to have held suit.

Before we examine the revenues and expenses of eight of the mills held by Beaulieu that are recorded in its account-book, it would seem instructive to look first at the year of acquisition, revenues, purchase prices and grantors of what appear to have been at least 12 different mills held by the abbey before 1300, the details for which are summarized in Table 7.2. The more detailed references to five of the mills mentioned in the abbey's cartulary are discussed in greater depth in Chapter 9.

All 12 of the mills held by Beaulieu by 1300 were acquired by the monks between 1203 and 1270, and at least four of them were built by the abbey, including the windmill of Rydon and the three industrial mills located within the abbey's precincts.

Nine of the mills appear to have been acquired by the monks before 1250, or three-quarters of them. Five out of 12, or more than one-third of the total, were not conventional grain mills; a significant finding and one which lends support to the claims made for Cistercian technological innovation made in the past by Mumford, White and Gille. At least two of the 12 mills were acquired by purchase from two local knights, but the origins of five mills are not recorded.

In Table 7.3, the incomes of eight of these mills for the financial year of 1269–70 have been translated into cash sums and compared with the costs of repairs for each mill, along with the sums of wages and cash translations of corn payments to the millers of each mill.[64] The average income and expenses for all eight mills are then provided, along with the percentage of expenses to income.

---

[64]   Holt (1987), pp. 16–17, performs a similar calculation for Rooks mill held by Glastonbury Abbey in the early fourteenth century.

Table 7.3   Incomes, expenses and millers' wages for eight mills held by Beaulieu Abbey, 1269–70 (£/s/d)*

Name	Income	Expenses	Exp./Inc. (%)	Millers' wages
Beaulieu fulling mill	4/14/0	2/5/8	48.6	0/14/0 (for 2 men)
Soberton mill	2/5/0	4/11/2	202.6	0/10/0
Rydon mill	5/11/8	4/14/2	84.3	0/6/0
Burgate mill	4/0/0	0/7/2	8.9	0/4/2
Kyndlewere mill	9/13/10	3/14/5	38.4	5/1/9
Nanclegy mill	1/4/0	0/14/0	58.1	-
Coxwell windmill	3/19/4	0/15/5	19.4	2/0/4
Outside mill	8/11/8	0/9/0	5.2	0/10/0
AVERAGE	**5/0/0**	**2/3/11**	**43.9**	**1/3/4**

* All halfpence rounded up to nearest penny.

A few preliminary observations need to be made about the figures reproduced in this table. First of all, the average income from Beaulieu's eight mills, at £5, was considerably higher than the average income from Bec's, Grove's and Hereford's mills, suggesting that Beaulieu's policy of collecting grain as income from its mills was more lucrative than the cash rents paid for the other ecclesiastical estates' mills at around the same time. Holt has argued that some lords at least appear to have been conscious of the fact that grain rents were more lucrative at times of high grain prices and therefore switched to grain rents when the opportunity arose.[65]

Apart from the bishop of Durham, the only ecclesiastical lord with an average mill revenue comparable to Beaulieu's was the Treasurer of St Peter's York, whose earnings from three mills as recorded in the *Taxatio Nicholai IV* averaged £6 3s 4d.[66] Beaulieu's average income from its mills was also more than double that of the average of £2 10s 8d recorded by Langdon for the mills of lay lords in the South based on the IPM material for 1307–27.[67]

What is most interesting about the 1269–70 accounts for eight of these mills is that their combined 'expenses' often came close to and sometimes exceeded their incomes in cash, multure grain and other associated revenues. The critical point here is that the mills' expenses do not simply consist of the costs of repairs and maintenance for the mills and wages for the millers. A significant proportion of what were counted as expenses for these eight mills were in fact food renders for servants not directly connected to the operation of the abbey's mills, including various obedientiaries, servants and retainers.[68]

For example, the Beaulieu fulling mill earned £4 14s for the year, but incurred expenses of £8 1½d. However, only £2 5s 8d of these expenses were repairs to the mill, most of the rest consisted of payments of cash, grain and beer to various servants. In other words, the mill's 'real' expenses for the year were about 48.6 per cent of its income.[69]

The Soberton mill was another of the mills whose expenses outstripped its earnings for the year, but this time purely owing to the amounts spent on repairs. The mill earned 13 quarters of barley in multure grain and 2 bushels of gruel, excluding 3 quarters of barley that was paid to the miller. As barley and gruel from the manor were sold respectively for 40d and 80d a quarter that year, its total earnings were the equivalent of £2 5s in cash, although the cost of repairs for the mill were £4 11s 2d, including £2 14s 2d for a new millstone and £1 14s for weatherboards. In this case, the cost of repairing the mill for the year was double its earnings.

In the case of Rydon windmill, its earnings exactly equalled its expenses, although again these expenses included costs other than those for repairing the mill, including a stipend of six shillings for the miller and 6s

[65]   See Holt (1988), pp. 72–4, 77, in relation to the bishoprics of Ely and Norwich, the estates of Ramsey Abbey and the earldom of Norfolk.

[66]   See Chapter 8.

[67]   Langdon (1994), p. 13. This figure takes into account Langdon's estimate that the manorial accounts tend to state revenues about double those of the IPM material.

[68]   This is a phenomenon which Holt (1988), p. 77, has also noted, but not the issue of recording such payments as 'mill expenses'.

[69]   *Account-Book of Beaulieu Abbey*, pp. 219, 221.

8d worth of 'mancorn' to the servants. Rydon's earnings for the year amounted to £5 11s 8d in grain sales, while the actual repair costs for the mill were £4 14s 1 1/2d, or about 84.3 per cent of its earnings for the year.

On the other hand, Burgate mill earned 24 quarters of barley as multure grain during the financial year, excluding 1 quarter 2 bushels paid to the miller and another four shillings a year paid to the abbey by the men of Gorley to run their own mill, i.e., as a licensed tenant mill. As barley from the manor was sold for 40d per quarter that year, these earnings amounted to £4 for the year, with an additional 50d worth of grain paid as a stipend to the miller. Repairs to the mill for the year amounted to only 7s 1 1/2d, or about 8.9 per cent of its income.[70]

The mill of Kyndlewere was one of the big earners for the abbey. Had it sold all of its multure grains that year it would have earned £9 13s 10d. The total includes rent from the 'old mill' (*veteri mola*), suggesting that an old demesne mill on the same property or adjacent had been replaced at some point by the abbey or a predecessor. Kyndlewere also earned an additional £2 10s for the sale of a pig, six gallons of honey and 8½ sticks of eels that were drawn from the mill's lands, and paid the miller 31 quarters 2 bushels of barley, which was worth £4 13s 9d, a very substantial wage for a miller, which probably indicates that it was he who had carried out some major repairs to the mill costing £3 14s 5d, or 38.4 per cent of its income for that year. However, the mill's expenses and liberties totalled £15 9s 11d, including the 31 quarters 2 bushels of barley and an additional eight shillings in wages for the miller. In this case, total expenditure exceeded total earnings by £3 6s 1d, clearly an unsustainable financial situation for Kyndlewere over the longer term.

The mill of Nanclegy in Cornwall was let at farm for three shillings a year, and paid an additional 14 quarters of dredge in multure grain. As dredge from the manor was sold for 18d a quarter that year, this amounted to an additional £1 1s, or £1 4s for the year in total. Repairs to the mill for that year totalled 13s 11 1/2d, or 57.8 per cent of its income. This consisted of 7 1/2d for mending and coopering, and 13s 4d for timber for 'the wheels' (*rotas*).[71]

The income from Coxwell windmill for the year was 5 quarters 2 bushels of barley and 23 1/2 quarters of malt.[72] The fact that the mill had such a large income of malt indicates that it was dedicated to milling malted grains, i.e., it was a 'malt' mill. Although no figures for grain sales are supplied for the manor, most of the sums paid for grain across the various manors were quite stable, allowing a rough calculation of their cash worth for Coxwell. The sum of the two amounts had these grains been sold would have been about £3 19s 3 1/2d, or very close to £4, while its expenses for the year amounted to 15s 5d, excluding a stipend of six shillings to the miller and an additional payment to him of 6½ quarters of wheat. The expenses, excluding the miller's wages, amounted to 19.4 per cent of its income.

Receipts for the 'Outside mill' totalled the very high sum of £8 11s 8d for sales of wheat, mancorn, malt and gruel, and another 17s 3d for the mill's fishery, 6s 9d for beer toll and another 10d pottage for the abbey's hospital. The grand total of £9 15s 8d was offset by expenses of £2 6s 2d, only nine shillings of which was spent on mill repairs. This included 5s 5d for timber, two shillings for ironwork and two shillings for dressing the millstones. The actual repair costs of the mill were therefore 5.2 per cent of its income.[73]

Based on three entries in the chamberlain's, bakehouse's and guest-house's accounts, it would seem that these three were drawing at least some of the rents of the mills outside the abbey, as the main treasury paid the abbot £7 3s 6 1/2d for their custody,[74] while the bakehouse paid 1 1/2 quarters and 4 pans of grain as well as 1s 6d for timber for one of the mills[75] and the guest-house 244 gallons of beer.[76] With respect to the treasury, this was probably for the mills of Faringdon, which included those of Kyndlewere, Rydon and Little Faringdon, while the payments by the bakehouse and guest-house were probably for revenues from the mills at Soberton and Burgate, providing some indication of how the abbey's mill revenues were split between various functions and obedientiaries.[77]

[70]   Ibid., pp. 109–12.

[71]   Ibid., pp. 102–4.

[72]   Ibid., pp. 93–4.

[73]   Ibid., p. 282.

[74]   Ibid., p. 314.

[75]   Ibid., p. 298.

[76]   Ibid., p. 279.

[77]   Ibid., pp. 14–15.

The high incomes from Beaulieu's mills were offset by their high maintenance costs during this year, which averaged out at £2 3s 11d per mill, or 43.9 per cent of their revenue. This compares with expenses of only 18 per cent of Bec's mill revenues for the period from 1272 to 1289, and 20.5 per cent of Durham's mill revenues in 1307. Because the account book provides a single 'snapshot' of Beaulieu's mill income and expenses, it is likely that this particular financial year was a particularly expensive one with regard to its mill repairs, an observation that is supported by the high sums paid for repairs to the mills of Soberton and Rydon, which in Soberton's case were double that of its income.

Kyndlewere was the only mill whose miller ran the establishment on his own, whereas Nanclegy was let out and Rydon and Soberton were in hand, but overseen by *conversi* (see Table 7.3).[78] The high sums paid to the miller of Kyndlewere indicate that he was a free man rather than a servant of the abbey, whereas the relatively low wages paid to the others reveals that they were demesne employees. Were it not for the fact that Kyndlewere is quite distant from Beaulieu's other mills, one would be tempted to think the man who ran it was the abbey's master miller, as the wage of over £4 which he was paid in the financial year of 1269 is comparable to that paid to John Berie, master miller for the Duryard mills in Exeter, who was paid over £5 per year in the 1380s.[79]

The wages for the miller servants are recorded in the account book as cash stipends and exclude any additional payments or liveries of grain, although it seems likely based on the evidence here and from Holt's work on the subject that grain renders for miller servants were paid as part of the grain liberties to the *famuli*, and not recorded as separate items, as it would have been almost impossible for any of these men to survive on such low stipends.[80] An admittedly crude indication of what the millers may have been earning on average in the equivalent of cash was calculated by summing and equally dividing the wages of the eight millers, providing a figure of around £1 3s a year (Table 7.3). This would have been a low wage for most labourers at the time, who could have expected anything from a penny to twopence a day.[81]

Finally, a rough idea of the proportion of Beaulieu's mill revenues to its total manorial revenues from its various estates can be determined by adding the sums of the revenues of its eight mills listed above with those of Little Faringdon and the tithes of Inglesham mill, and comparing them with its revenues from all of its estates as set out in the main treasury's receipts. Beaulieu's total revenues from temporalities for 1269/70 were £370 2s 8 1/2d,[82] while its mill revenues were £42 2s 5 1/2d, or 11.4 per cent of its income, which compares favourably with the revenues derived from mills by northern lords and the more extractive ecclesiastical lords.

Beaulieu was drawing revenue from at least four mills with suit and the tithes from another mill by the 1230s. These facts, combined with the low level of grain renders paid to its miller employees, its high average mill revenues and the high proportion of its total estate income derived from mills, all suggest that the Cistercian monks of Beaulieu were very much preoccupied with the efficient management of their estates during the 'high farming' period of the thirteenth century. However, it would seem that the monks of Beaulieu concealed the extractive nature of their milling enterprises (perhaps even from themselves!) by directly managing the vast majority of their mills, recording the revenues as grain rather than cash, and dispensing significant proportions of the tollcorn to monks and employees.

---

[78]   Hockey (1975), pp. 63–7.

[79]   Langdon (2004), p. 238, citing Maryanne Kowaleski, *Local Markets and Regional Trade in Medieval Exeter*, Cambridge, p. 141.

[80]   Holt (1988), pp. 92–5. See also Holt (1987), pp. 17, 19, where he provides some examples of Glastonbury Abbey paying *famuli* in tollcorn.

[81]   Ibid., p. 94, citing J.E. Thorold Rogers, *Six Centuries of Work and Wages*, London, 1884, p. 170. See also Langdon (2004), pp. 238–9.

[82]   *Account Book of Beaulieu Abbey*, p. 314. According to Hockey, Beaulieu's total revenues for 1291, as recorded in the *Taxatio Nicholai IV*, were £244 6s 2d (see *Beaulieu Abbey Cartulary*, pp. lxvii–lxviii). However, this figure does not include the spiritualities of Inglesham and Coxwell, and the temporalities of Inglesham and Kyndelwere in Berkshire (see Hockey [1976], p. 218). Adding the figures for the first three items (also provided by Hockey in his book on the abbey) gives the more accurate sum of £263 9s 6d, but still does not include the Kyndelwere revenues. This figure was undoubtedly an underestimation, however, as it is hard to imagine that the intervening 20 years saw a 29 per cent reduction in the abbey's revenues.

Sibton Abbey

The Abbey of the Blessed Virgin Mary at Sibton was one of the smaller Cistercian foundations. Located in East Suffolk about 10 kilometres north of the market town of Saxmundham just outside of Peasenhall, the abbey was colonized by 13 monks from Old Wardon Abbey, Bedfordshire, in 1150. It was the only Cistercian house in Suffolk, and was a sister house to Sawtry in Huntingdonshire (1149) and Tilty in Essex (1153). Like most of the religious houses in Suffolk, Sibton was overshadowed by the abbey of Bury St Edmunds, but nevertheless had extensive holdings in East Suffolk and Norfolk, including 10 parishes within the city of Norwich, as well as some property in Sussex and on the borders of Cambridgeshire. It also managed a hospital at its gate which was dedicated to St John the Baptist.[83]

The abbey played an important role in the agrarian economy of the region (Figure 7.7), which included the management of at least 14 granges in East Anglia, most of which had been built up through land acquisitions during the second half of the twelfth century (Figure 7.8). Its net income around 1535 was over £250,[84] although the abbey had been largely insolvent in the decades following the Black Death, a period for which some of its *compoti* have survived.[85]

The founding patron of Sibton was William de Chesney,[86] who was at the time High Sheriff of Norfolk and Suffolk, and reputedly the nephew of William Malet, the tenant-in-chief of the manor of Sibton during the Domesday survey. William's father Robert had married Sibilla, the daughter and heir of Ralph de Chesney. A wide variety of religious houses benefited from William's generosity during his lifetime, including grants of Newton mill in Norfolk to Castle Acre,[87] and tithes of Kilverstone mill, also in Norfolk, to the Cluniac priory of Thetford.[88] As we saw in Chapter 6, he also had a special relationship with the Augustinian priory of Blythburgh, being lord of the manor there and a major patron.[89] One of William's daughters and heirs, Margaret de Cressy, was also a substantial patron of Sibton, significantly augmenting her father's foundation grants.[90] Other major benefactors to the abbey included the related families of Cookley and Weston, and the family of Ralph of Peasenhall, which also granted property to the houses of Blythburgh and Leiston. William de Weston granted the abbey Darnford mill in Cookley, Suffolk, along with his own and his wife's body for burial around 1230.

While Sibton's charters have survived remarkably intact, there are few other extant records for the abbey, other than a series of court rolls and other documents from the fourteenth century to the early sixteenth century. These include the fragments of two registers of 1325, and an incomplete series of *compoti* extending from 1455 to 1525. Amongst this material are extents of demesne land for 1325, a rental of 1328, a rental of 1484 and *compoti* of 1363–72 and 1508–9. The *compoti* include some data of major interest in assessing Sibton's mill management practices in the wake of the Black Death. These include figures for the abbey's household and mill repairs, revenues for its grain sales and figures for its total profits and losses. The relevant figures are set out in Tables 7.4 to 7.7 and mapped in Charts 7.1 and 7.2. These data clearly reveal the difference between Cistercian management practices aimed at matching income to expenditure, thereby minimising profit, and those of capitalist enterprises in the modern period that are geared primarily towards profit making, accumulation and reinvestment. While this kind of behaviour by Cistercian houses has been suggested in some of the previous case studies, Chart 7.2 makes it very plain indeed.

Sibton's extent and rentals from the 1320s reveal that it was still engaged in a system of demesne farming at this time, which was abandoned after the Black Death for a system of cash rents, beginning in the early 1360s. By the late fifteenth and early sixteenth centuries, the abbey was almost entirely dependent upon rents, although the obedientiary system it had abandoned after the plague had been resumed.[91]

---

[83] *Sibton Abbey Estates*, p. 11.

[84] *Valor Ecclesiasticus*, Vol. III. 435.

[85] See Tables 5.8–5.10 and Charts 5.1 and 5.2 below.

[86] William was also known as William of Norwich and William son of Robert the Sheriff.

[87] B.L., Harley 2110 (Castle Acre cartulary), fo. 29v.

[88] Dugdale (1846), Vol. V. 142.

[89] *Sibton Abbey Cartularies*, Pt. I, pp. 16–17.

[90] *Sibton Abbey Estates*, p. 11.

[91] Ibid., pp. 11–12.

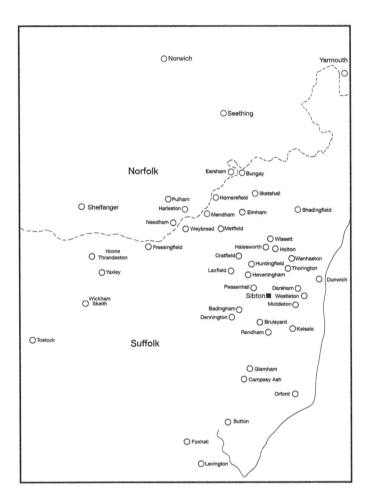

Fig. 7.7   Location of Sibton Abbey rents in Norfolk and Suffolk. After Denney (1960)

Despite the initial Cistercian ordinances prohibiting the ownership of mills that were not for the monks' own use, and subsequent ordinances of the early thirteenth century prohibiting the direct farming of mills granted to them in free alms, Sibton Abbey continued to acquire a number of watermills and windmills throughout the thirteenth and into the fourteenth centuries for these purposes. They included an early windmill at Tostock and others in Thwaite, Rendham and Cookley, and the watermills of Kennett, Walpole, Darnford, Instead and Weybread, as well as a share of the mill of Wenhaston and a grant of rents from two other mills held by Margaret de Cressy.[92] The abbey also held the site of a watermill at Dunwich that may have been operational when first granted to it, and a windmill that was built within the abbey's precincts in the financial year of 1363–64. More than 21 mills are mentioned in the abbey's extant documents. By the mid-fourteenth century, Sibton appears to have directly held at least 12 mills, although as we will see below, only a handful are mentioned in the abbey's extents or *compoti*.

The earliest reference to any mills held by Sibton is in a royal confirmation of William de Chesney's initial foundation grant by Henry II and dated to March 1163. Apart from the generic reference to 'lands, waters and mills', the charter records that part of these holdings included a watermill with meadows, waters and a

---

[92]   *Sibton Abbey Cartularies*, Pt. I, pp. 125–6. These were the *Calcmelnes* of Norwich.

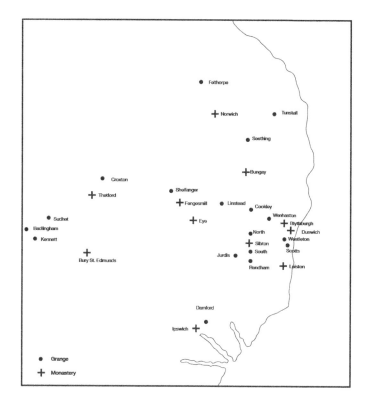

Fig. 7.8 Granges of Sibton Abbey. After Brown (1985)

millpond on the road between Kennet and Freckenham.[93] This would appear to have been the only mill which the abbey initially held, and was only ever intended to serve the needs of the monks, as the following grant makes very clear.

In 1161, Lord Nicholas of Kennett granted Sibton all of his land on the road which led to and from the mill of Kennett, along with the meadow and watercourse, for half a mark annually, as well as all his rights in common pasture on the other side of the river leading to the mill. Nicholas also gave them the right to use the land and watercourse however they saw fit, but were forbidden from grinding anyone's grain at their mill without his license. In return, the monks were to remit all moneys that he owed them, to pardon all past damages and suits, and to pay him £3 and one palfrey in consideration of the grant, with the half a mark in rent to be paid to his wife because he gave this land to his wife in dower.[94] Obviously, Nicholas as lord held suit of mill on the manor, and was keen to ensure that the monks did not undermine his seigneurial monopoly.

William de Chesney's initial foundation grant was confirmed by John of Oxford, bishop of Norwich, in 1178.[95] Another royal confirmation dated 22 May 1323 by Edward II lists all of the land which the abbey had acquired in the meantime, but only specifies a single windmill at Thwaite 'with its suit and other appurtenances'.[96] A mill within Sibton itself is mentioned as forming part of the boundary of some land exchanged by Hamon II of Sibton for other lands held by the abbey between 1201 and 1204, and a lease of

---

[93]   Ibid., Pt. II, ms. 29 (c). Presumably the mill in question was located on the stream just north of Kennett near Dane Hill Road, as there are still extensive dams to the east of Kennett. Alternatively, the mill could have been located west of Kennett on the stream that currently runs under Chappenham Road, the B1085.

[94]   *Sibton Abbey Cartularies*, Pt. IV, ms. 968. A 'palfrey' was a docile horse used for riding, especially by women.

[95]   Ibid., Pt. III, ms. 491.

[96]   Ibid., Pt. II, ms. 29 (j) (ii). Thwaite is about 32 kilometres west of Sibton.

land to the abbey by Sir Edmund de Sancto Mauro of 29 September 1335, but this mill appears to have been part of the knight's fee held in the first instance by Hamon and later by Sir Edmund.[97]

Around Easter in 1189, Margaret de Cressy granted Sibton £2 worth of annual rent of her mills called *Calcmelnes* in Norwich, which she specified was to be spent on 'wine, oblations, wax or necessities for the celebration of Mass'.[98] This was confirmed by her son Roger II in a document of 1205 to 1230.[99] A document dated 30 November 1258 records that the then tenant of these mills, Henry de Wittun' (Wetton) of Norwich, had been sued by the abbey for £4 worth of rental arrears. The document acknowledges Henry's debt to the monks and sets out a staged repayment over the subsequent months. Henry and his heirs were bound to pay the debt and to put up all their goods in surety, with the threat of interdiction and excommunication should they fail to meet this obligation.[100] The stipulation of such onerous conditions for repayment appears to indicate a somewhat harsh attitude amongst the monks towards their former tenant, as there is nothing comparable in any of the documents of other houses sampled, although there may well have been some justification for it.

Between the 1210s and 1230s, the abbey appears to have acquired a significant amount of property, including a windmill at Tostock about 40 kilometres to the west of the abbey, and watermills at Dunwich, Walpole, Cookley and Wenhaston.[101] A series of documents relating to each grant provides some interesting insights into the grantors and their motives. With the exception of the legal dispute over Darnford watermill in Cookley, which is discussed in detail in Chapter 9, the histories of the acquisition of these various mills and the others are set out below.

Around 1220, Roger II de Cressy granted the abbey all his rights in rents from 'homages, mills and the places where nets are stretched out to dry' in Heynhil in Dunwich, in return for an annual rent of two shillings, for which Roger agreed to acquit them to the king.[102] Sometime soon afterwards, Roger's son Richard effectively remitted 16 1/2d to Sibton of a number of rents, including fourpence 'for the site of a mill they hold outside Dunwich'.[103] Presumably, the watermill in question had fallen into ruin in the interim.

A mill called *Rottingesmilne* in the vill of Walpole along with an adjacent meadow was granted to the abbey some time during the 1220s by William fitz Roscelin in return for the monks' prayers for the salvation of his own soul and that of his wife, heirs and ancestors.[104] The grant is confirmed by William's nephew, Richard de Dagworth,[105] whose mother, Margaret de Rya, had granted and quitclaimed the same property to his uncle sometime between 1207 and the time of William's grant to Sibton. Margaret's grant of the mill and five shillings worth of annual rent to William were part of her marriage portion, and were in compensation 'for the heavy losses [her] brother [William] suffered at the hand of King John when Roger de Cressy married her daughter, Isabel'.[106] Sibton was still collecting only five shillings a year in rent from *Rottingesmilne* in 1413–14.[107]

The monks acquired a moiety of the watermill of Wenhaston between 1230 and 1235 when Robert Malet granted to the abbey all of his land in Wenhaston, held as a knight's fee from the Wenhaston family. In return, the abbey was to provide a mixture of cash and military services, including the provision of a quarter part of one knight annually, and 3s 2d to be paid for the castle-guard at Richmond. The monks were also expected to acquit all services to the chief lord if the donor or his heirs defaulted.[108]

---

[97]   Ibid., Pt. IV, mss. 1008, 1009 and 1114.

[98]   Ibid., ms. 243.

[99]   Ibid., ms. 244.

[100] Ibid., ms. 980.

[101] Dunwich is about 14 kilometres due east of Sibton only a few hundred metres from the coast, while Walpole and Cookley are about 6 km due north, and Wenhaston is about 12 km to the north-east.

[102] Ibid., ms. 192.

[103] Ibid., ms. 213.

[104] Ibid., ms. 157.

[105] Ibid., ms. 158.

[106] Ibid., ms. 159. On William's losses, see Pt. I, p. 92.

[107] Ibid., Pt. III, ms. 795.

[108] Ibid., Pt. II, mss. 304 and 305.

Sometime after 2 June 1252, Walter of Windsor granted Sibton a messuage with three acres of land in Mundham, Norfolk, as well as a number of tenements in Seething, Mundham, Thwaite St Mary, Sisland, Kirstead, Brooke, Langhale and Woodton, which included a windmill at Thwaite with its suit, all to be held of the lords of the fee and their heirs.[109] A notification from around the same time records that Sibton was to pay William of Seething, lord of the fee, £12 annually for all of these lands for William's lifetime only, and that it would not be held liable for any services that Walter or his heirs should fail to meet with regard to them.[110] The grant was confirmed by William of Seething, in return for which the monks gave him five marks (£3 6s 8d).[111] It would appear from the *Taxatio Nicholai IV* of 1291 that the rents of Brooke and Thwaite, including the windmill, amounted to £3 11s 6d, most of which was probably for the mill. Unfortunately, no mill rents are specifically mentioned.

A grant dated 24 May 1329 by Simon de Lytlehagh of Rendham to the abbey of a right of way over his lands to the monks' windmill in Rendham is the only reference to this mill in any of the abbey's documents.[112] A license by Robert de Ufford, earl of Suffolk, to grant the manor of Rendham to Sibton is dated 12 July 1355, but it is not clear whether this was simply a confirmation of an earlier grant.[113] The abbey appears to have held this windmill since at least the time of the *Taxatio* of 1291.[114]

The abbey also appears to have held at least three mills in its grange of Weybread, one of which was known as *Fengesmyll'* in Instead. *Fengesmyll'* is first mentioned in a charter of c. 1230 to c. 1240, which records a grant of marshland beside the mill,[115] while another grant and confirmation dated to sometime in the 1250s records the granting of a parcel of land to the west of the mill.[116]

The abbey's extent of 1325 records five mills, only one of which was held by the abbey and recorded in its cartularies and charters. The only mill rental that is recorded within the extent is for Cookley windmill, which is recorded as a gift from William of Cookley, and valued at £1 a year with right of pasturage.[117] This William of Cookley was presumably William de Weston's son, William II, who confirmed his father's grants to the abbey in Cookley sometime between 1250 and 1263,[118] although Cookley windmill is not mentioned in any of the documents relating to Darnford watermill in Cookley that are dated to between c. 1225 and the 1270s. The windmill was presumably constructed, therefore, sometime after 1280 and granted to the abbey between 1280 and 1325.

Five mills are also mentioned in the abbey's *compotus* roll of 1363–4, including a second mill in Instead (i.e., separate from *Fengesmyll*), which it presumably acquired sometime between the late thirteenth century and the date of the *compotus*, and a new windmill which the abbey constructed within its own precincts in that financial year. The rents that were collected from the other four mills varied wildly, from only two shillings a year for the abbey's third watermill in Weybread, which was held by Richard Wright of the bailiff,[119] to £5 13s 4d for the farm of *Fengesmelle*.[120] The rent roll for 1328 records that *Fengesmille* drew £4 9s 10d in revenue for that year, of which £1 4s 7 1/2d was rent, with the rest presumably issuing from tollcorn.[121] On the other hand, Darnford watermill and three meadows were rented for 15 shillings, although this rent was not collected,[122] presumably due to repairs of the mill that year, on which the abbey spent £1 13s 8d to mend its

---

109 Ibid., ms. 997.

110 Ibid., ms. 998.

111 Ibid., ms. 999.

112 Ibid., Pt. IV, ms. 994.

113 Ibid., ms. 995.

114 Ibid., Pt. I, p. 125.

115 Ibid., Pt. II, ms. 67.

116 Ibid., mss. 46 and 47.

117 Ibid., 'Cukeleye: Molendinum', p. 49.

118 See Table 7.4 below.

119 *Sibton Abbey Estates*, p. 134. Richard was presumably a millwright and fully responsible for the mill's maintenance and repairs.

120 Ibid., 'Firme', p. 111.

121 Ibid., 'Rent Roll 1328', p. 149.

122 Ibid., 'Firme', p. 111.

leat and milldam.[123] Instead the mill drew £1 2s a year in rent from Eye Priory, the sub-tenant of which was Simon Toppesfeld.[124]

Based on these figures, the only mill belonging to Sibton for which we have any details of more than one rental amount is for *Fengesmyll*, which drew rents of £4 9s 10d in 1328, and £5 13s 4d in 1363–64, and £3 10s in 1508, the last lease including 14 acres of land. These fluctuations would appear to be roughly consistent with the trends in Welsh fulling mill rents which have been documented in *ind, Water, Work* (2006) and which can be seen in the post-plague income for Battle Abbey's mill of *Peperynghey*, although the relatively high rent for *Fengesmyll* in the wake of the Black Death seems somewhat anomalous. It is nevertheless clear that this was one of the few mills held by Sibton that drew suit.

A number of details pertaining to the construction of the abbot's new windmill are also listed in the *compotus* rolls for 1363–64. The abbey paid £2 to John the carpenter 'for building the new mill inside the abbey's precincts', as well as two shillings from the curia for the same.[125] It also paid 14 shillings for 24 ells of cloth for the mill's sailcloths, £1 2s 4 1/2d for two millstones, 8s 8d for 8,000 laths, 18s 3d for 2,600 faggots, fourpence for the transportation of timber, and 4s 8d for making the mill's four sailcloths, which weighed 44 lbs.[126] The total listed costs for the mill were therefore £5 10s 3 1/2d, although it is clear that there are a number of other important components of the mill's costs which are not listed, including transport of some of the materials (which seem exceedingly low in this instance), and all of the ironwork and other metallic items used in the mill. It is possible that these costs were not paid directly, however, as the abbey may have prevailed upon some of its free tenants and sokemen in the area to provide cartage as part of their feudal obligations, and that a blacksmith in direct employ of the abbey provided the ironwork and other metal fittings. The low costs of the two millstones have also reduced the mill's overall cost. Taking these issues into account, therefore, one would imagine that the total cost of construction for the mill would have come close to the average of £10 that Holt found for East Anglia in the second half of the thirteenth century.

It is interesting to compare the sum paid for the construction of this new windmill with the 'consideration' paid by a local lord for a windmill in the first quarter of the thirteenth century that was later granted to Sibton. A series of four documents dated to between c. 1212 and 1229 record the granting in free alms and confirmation of Tostock windmill to Sibton Abbey. The first of these is a grant by William of Norton to Robert de Domno Martino, marshall of Boulogne, and his heirs, of William's windmill of Tostock and its site, in return for Robert's fealty, a consideration of four-and-a-half marks (£3), and a penny in annual rent.[127] Sometime soon afterwards, Robert then granted the same windmill with its site to Sibton, along with a tenement and the villein attached, both of which were held of William of Norton. In return, the monks were expected to pay a penny annually to William for the mill, and another threepence for the villein and his tenement.[128] Although this grant was subsequently confirmed by William,[129] a notification of the same period indicates that the abbey had re-granted the mill back to William for 12 shillings of annual rent, including the power of distraint in the event of non-payment, and William's obligation to keep the mill in good repair.[130] This arrangement freed the abbey from any responsibility to maintain the mill while guaranteeing it a regular income from it.

On 2 February 1354, the abbey leased the whole grange with its watermills for life to Thomas Schotinhayt of Rishangles for £10 a year. Based on the rents recorded in a rental of 1328 and the compotus roll of 1364–65, at least half of this amount was for the farm of *Fengesmyll*. The lessee was expected to maintain the grange at his own expense, including its 'embankments, causeways, dams, bridges and all appurtenances', and to return it to them at the end of his life in as good or better repair than when he acquired it. The abbey would in turn supply Thomas with 'good timber needed for planks, beams and the parts of the mill-wheel'. The abbey also reserved the right to enter and retain the premises if they were damaged in any way, even by accident,

---

[123]   Ibid., 'Minute', p. 123.

[124]   Ibid., p. 134. Philippa Brown confuses the mill of Instead recorded here with *Fengesmille*, which was also in Instead, and claims that it was held by Sibton from Eye Priory, rather than the reverse. The existence of three mills held by Sibton within the grange of Weybread is clearly indicated by this *compotus*.

[125]   Ibid., 'Custus domorum', p. 118.

[126]   Ibid., 'Minute', pp. 122–4.

[127]   *Sibton Abbey Cartularies*, Pt. II, ms. 70.

[128]   Ibid., ms. 72.

[129]   Ibid., ms. 73.

[130]   Ibid., ms. 75.

and that if the lessee defaulted on the agreement in any way, any goods found on the premises could be confiscated until the debt, waste or damage was made good.[131] This kind of agreement was very common in the wake of the Black Death. A document of 4 July 1508 records the granting of *Fengesmyll* (a.k.a. *Isted'* mill and *Fryersmyll'*) with 14 acres of land to three men, Richard Wright and Robert Ropere of Brockdish, and Thomas Wright of Syleham, for £3 10s and a single suit of the court at Instead, with all responsibilities for maintenance. The grant includes similar distraining clauses to the previous one.[132]

The abbey's extent of 1325 records five mills, only one of which was held by the abbey and recorded in its cartularies and charters. The four mills not held by the abbey which are described as forming parts of the boundaries of Sibton's lands are Falsham mill, which is said to be 'near the house of Horsman' between Burstherd and Falsham,[133] Huntyngfeld mill which was near one of the abbey's holdings in Linstede,[134] and two mills in Yokesford which were near lands over which the abbey had rights of pasturage.[135] I have not been able to determine who held these mills. A certain *Millemont* and *Maydenmyllemunt* are also mentioned in a number of places, which were presumably either ruined windmills or Iron Age barrows.[136]

To gain a better picture of the date of acquisition of the various mills acquired by Sibton between its foundation and the mid-fourteenth century, the data discussed in this section are set out in Table 7.4. At least eight and as many as 10 of the mills that were held by Sibton were acquired by it during the thirteenth century, with only one mill held at its foundation. At least two and as many as four mills were acquired by it during the fourteenth century. It held between nine and 11 mills by the early fourteenth century. Of the 13 mills that it held outright by 1364, five were windmills, at least one of which had been commissioned by the monks. Given that there is no information about the donors of the three watermills of Instead (i.e., Instead I and II, and Weybread) or of Rendham windmill, it is possible that the monks commissioned the construction of these four mills as well.

Table 7.4   Fifteen mills in which Sibton Abbey held an interest before 1364

Name	Year acquired	Grantor	Grantee
Kennett (?) watermill	1163	Henry II	Sibton Abbey
Calcmelnes (x2?) (rent only)	1189	Margaret de Cressy	"
Tostock windmill	<c.1212–29	Robert de Domno Martino	"
Dunwich watermill	c.1220	Roger II de Cressy	"
Rottingesmilne (Walpole watermill)	1220s	William fitz Roscelin	"
Darnford watermill	c.1230	William de Weston	"
Fengesmyll (Instead watermill I)	>c. 1230–c. 40	?	"
Wenhaston watermill*	1230–35	Robert Malet	"
Thwaite windmill	<2 June 1252	Walter of Windsor	"
Rendham windmill	>1291	?	"
Cookley windmill	c. 1280–1325	William of Cookley	"
Instead watermill II	c. 1290s–1363	?	"
Weybread watermill	>1363–64	?	"
Sibton windmill	1363–64	built by abbey	n/a

* Moiety only. Held of William of Seething for one lifetime, then held outright by Sibton.

Like the East Anglian Benedictines that Holt examined in detail in *The Mills of Medieval England*, therefore, the Cistercians of Sibton had a strong interest in building windmills on their water-deprived estates to fulfil the hitherto unmet demand for milled grain. Unlike Peterborough, Bury and Ramsey, however,

---

[131] Ibid., Pt. IV, ms. 1156.

[132] Ibid., ms. 1157.

[133] *Sibton Abbey Estates*, 'Burstherd', p. 43.

[134] Ibid., 'Linstede: Terre dominice', p. 51.

[135] Ibid., 'Yoxforde: Pastura seperabilis', p. 55.

[136] For example, pp. 43 and 60, as was presumably the 'mill hill' within *Milleclosse* recorded in Sibton's cartularies, e.g., ms. 1119.

Sibton was comparatively slow in committing to the new technology. This finding does not sit easily with the common picture of the Cistercians as great technological innovators. It should also be noted in this context that none of the abbey's mills were applied to industrial applications, while most of its mills appear to have come to it via donors who were either tenants-in-chief or members of the knightly class. The absence of any evidence for Sibton having been involved in water-powered industry on its estates provides more support for Holt's contention that English lords with limited water power would always prefer profitable grain milling over less-profitable industrial applications of water power. The majority of its mills having been acquired from members of the lay aristocracy (including the early Tostock windmill discussed previously) further undermine stereotypical notions of Cistercian milling innovation.

Tables 7.5 to 7.7 are based on figures provided in the abbey's aforementioned *compoti* for 1363 to 1372. The values for Tables 7.5 and 7.6 have also been plotted as a graph in Chart 7.1. The values for Table 7.7 have been plotted as Chart 7.2.

The data from 1363 to 1365 would seem to indicate that the abbey's grain income and expenditure on building repairs had been low in the 15 years or so following the first outbreak of the Black Death. However, the graphs and tables clearly demonstrate that Sibton took advantage of its high grain income between 1366 and 1369 by spending significant amounts of money on repairing its mills and conventual buildings, possibly with the prudent expectation that the good times might not last and that it should spend while the going was good.

Table 7.5   Sibton Abbey: Household and mill repairs 1363–72 (£/s/d)

1363	1364	1365	1366	1367	1368	1369	1370	1371	1372
12/14/11	9/12/3	15/19/11	39/17/0	34/19/6	42/2/8	45/12/9	25/15/3	19/0/7	5/4/7

Table 7.6   Sibton Abbey: Grain sales 1363–72 (£/s/d)

1363	1364	1365	1366	1367	1368	1369	1370	1371	1372
20/9/1	20/9/6	11/13/8	78/2/4	53/18/8	35/18/10	30/16/3	43/9/2	40/8/4	31/8/4

It is also very clear from the data plotted in Chart 6.2 that Sibton's receipts during the 10-year period covered by the *compoti* were matched almost exactly by their expenses, indicating that the monks were very consciously attempting to run their estates *without* making a profit. In fact, in terms of its overall receipts and expenses for this period, the abbey suffered a net loss of a little over £168, which was roughly the equivalent of a whole year of income over this 10-year period. We can thus see the difference in aims between Cistercian management practices and those of capitalist enterprises of the modern period that are primarily geared towards profit making. Many of the abbey's lands were let at farm during this time, with leases varying from three to 20 years, and occasionally, such as in the case of the grange of Weybread, for life. This strategy was a common one for lay and ecclesiastical lords to minimise their financial exposure to property maintenance in the wake of the plague.

Table 7.7   Sibton Abbey: Total profits and losses 1363–72, receipts minus expenses (£/s/d)

Year	1363	1364	1365	1366	1367	1368	1369	1370	1371	1372
Receipts	162/5/10	186/4/11	204/4/11	285/15/2	241/12/1	218/18/6	196/0/8	250/15/5	228/7/6	204/16/5
Expenses	188/2/2	183/9/1	199/12/11	293/12/10	262/2/11	224/5/11	229/7/10	288/12/9	264/4/11	213/10/10
Profit	-25/16/4	2/15/10	4/12/0	-7/17/8	-20/10/10	-5/7/5	-33/7/2	-37/17/4	-35/17/5	-8/14/5
TOTAL LOSSES 1363–72				£168 0s 7d						

Table 7.8 reproduces all those mill rents recorded in the abbey's cartulary, along with the years in which they were recorded. Despite having 11 separate records of mill revenues, and the six amounts listed for 1325–28, it is still difficult to get a sense of Sibton's overall mill revenues from the disjointed information supplied in its extant documents. The picture is further complicated by the fact that the abbey appears to have been drawing tollcorn from its mills at farm separately from the rented amounts, as is evidenced by the information supplied about *Fengesmille* in the 1328 rental. Apart from the low rent for the mill of Weybread, however, if Sibton was taking tollcorn from all of its mills at farm, its total revenue from each mill was

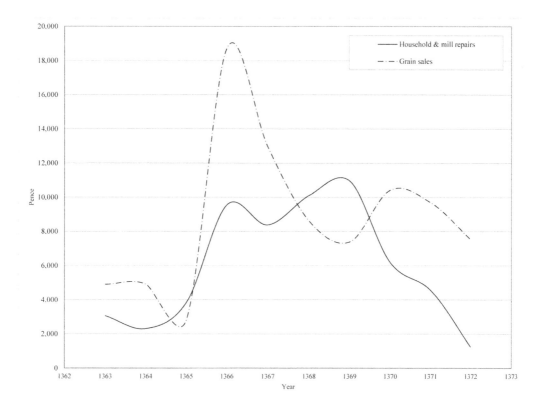

Chart 7.1   Sibton Abbey Grain sales mapped against household and mill expenses, 1363–72

presumably somewhere in the order of £3 to £4 per mill during the second and third quarters of the fourteenth century, a sum which is certainly comparable to the average mill revenues secured by the more extractive ecclesiastical lords of the south in the late thirteenth century and subsequently. One is also left with the impression from Sibton's mill-related documents that it was by no means soft on its tenants, and that it fought long and hard to secure its rights and privileges if the need arose.

There is wide variation in the revenues drawn from these mills, from only 13s 4d a year in 1328 for Weybread mill, to £4 9s for *Fengesmille* in the same year.[137] The low rent for the mill of Weybread, and of five shillings for *Rottingesmilne* in a rental of 1413–14, strongly suggest that both mills were in hereditary tenure at this stage, whereas *Fengesmille*, although it was at farm in 1328 for £1 4s 7d in rents, must have held suit, as the two other mills in the same vill were drawing nowhere near this income in the early fourteenth and early fifteenth centuries. The rents drawn from Sibton's other mills in the early fourteenth century were more modest at between 15 shillings and £1 2s a year, although as we have seen with *Fengesmille*, these amounts are not necessarily an accurate reflection of the total revenue being drawn from the mills concerned. It would seem, therefore, that only two of Sibton's nine mills in the early fourteenth century were owed suit, i.e. Thwaite windmill (£3 11s 6d p.a. with other land) and *Fengesmille*. Sibton's revenue from *Fengesmille* increased to £5 13s 4d in 1363–64,[138] but was only £3 10s in 1508,[139] indicating a 40 per cent loss in revenue that is in line with those experienced by most other mill owners in the fifteenth and sixteenth centuries in the wake of the Black Death. Furthermore, the terms of both leases made by Sibton to Thomas Schotinhayt after the Black Death were for life, whereas that for *Fengesmille* in the early sixteenth century was hereditary.

---

[137] *The Sibton Abbey Estates*, p. 149.
[138] Ibid., p. 111.
[139] *Sibton Abbey Cartulary and Charters*, Pt IV, ms. 1157.

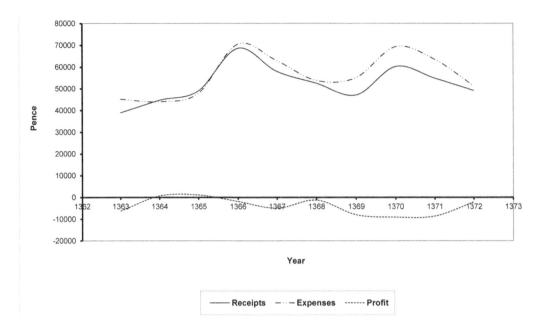

Chart 7.2   Sibton Abbey: Receipts mapped against expenses, 1363–72

Table 7.8   Mill rents and revenues for 14 mills in which Sibton Abbey held an interest between 1189 and 1508 (£/s/d)

Name	Year	Rent	Lord	Recipient
Calcmelnes (x2)	1189	2/0/0	Margaret de Cressy	Sibton Abbey
Heynhil mills, Dunwich (x2)	c. 1220	0/2/0	Roger II de Cressy	"
			Lord	**Tenant**
Rottingesmilne	<1207	0/5/0	William son of William son of Roscelin*	William Spekeman
Tostock windmill	c. 1212–29	0/12/0	Sibton Abbey	William, son of Robert of Tostock**
Thwaite windmill	1291	3/11/6 (with other land)	"	Margaret Seething (?)[+]
Cookley windmill	1325	1/0/0	"	Leased?
Weybread watermill	1328	0/13/4	"	"
Tostock windmill	1328	1/3/4	"	"
Instead watermill	1328	1/2/0	"	"
Darnford watermill	1328	0/15/0	"	"
		Revenue		**Tenant**
Fengesmille	1328	4/9/0 (1/4/7 in rent)	"	Richard Snow (?)
Weybread watermills	1354	10/0/0 (with other land)	"	Thomas Schotinhayt of Rishangles[++]
Fengesmille	1363–64	5/13/4	"	"
Rottingesmilne	1413–14	0/5/0	"	?
Fengesmille	1508	3/10/0	"	Richard Wright, Robert Ropere and Thomas Wright[†]

* Sibton *Abbey Cartulary and Charters*, Pt II, ms. 159.
** Ibid., ms. 75.
+ Ibid., Pt IV, ms. 997.
++ Ibid., ms. 1156.
† Ibid., ms. 1157.

These figures clearly reveal that Sibton sought to extract as much revenue as it could from its mills with suit, and that houses of the order were clearly ignoring earlier prohibitions on drawing seigneurial revenues from their mills, a point noted by Brown in her commentary on Sibton's charters, but not sufficiently appreciated by her.[140] An analysis of its post-plague *compoti* suggests that Sibton also made a very conscious effort to match its expenditure to its receipts in order to minimise any profits it made from its mills and other holdings. Perceptions of its wealth and profitability were clearly important for Sibton, but in virtually the opposite manner of a modern corporation.

Old Wardon Abbey, aka Warden Abbey

Situated about 12 kilometres to the south-east of Bedford, Old Wardon Abbey was the second Cistercian house to be established in England as a dependent house of Clairvaux.[141] Founded between 1135 and 1136 by the great northern magnate Walter Espec as a daughter house of his previous foundation at Rievaulx, the site of the abbey was newly broken land or assart, as a consequence of which the oldest charters in the cartulary refer to the abbey as 'de Sartis'. This was a practice that the monks of Old Wardon continued throughout their tenure, exemplifying one of the characteristics which made this pre-eminently agricultural fraternity the subject of both envy and admiration.[142]

By the end of the fourteenth century, Old Wardon held granges and other properties in Bedfordshire, Buckinghamshire, Cambridgeshire, Hertfordshire, Huntingdonshire, Middlesex, Norfolk, Northamptonshire and London, although most of its property was within a 14-kilometre radius of the abbey (Figures 7.9–7.11). The majority of grants to the abbey were made to it in the last quarter of the twelfth century, although it continued to be the recipient of local patronage until the second half of the thirteenth century. As was the case with most of the Cistercian houses in England, the well-spring of benefactions had mostly run dry by the end of the thirteenth century. Unlike the Benedictines and Augustinians, however, the Cistercians in general did not tend to acquire churches in order to augment their revenues, and in Old Wardon's case there is not a single instance of such an acquisition.[143]

Espec's foundation grant included all of the assarts of Wardon and Southill along with the woods there.[144] During the last few decades of the twelfth century, the monks acquired substantial parcels of additional land just to the south of the abbey, in and around Astwick, Broom, Chicksand, Clifton, Henlow, Meppershall, Southill and Stanford (Figure 7.9).[145] Between 1139 and 1153, King Stephen also granted the monks Ravenshoe wood that had belonged to Godmanchester, and confirmed Ramsey Abbey's grant to Old Wardon of Midloe wood in Huntingdonshire for a grange (Figure 7.10).[146]

The abbey's cartulary appears to have first been compiled during the thirteenth century, and rearranged during the fifteenth century. It contains entries from the second half of the twelfth century, the first quarter and the end of the thirteenth century, the late fourteenth and early fifteenth centuries, and the mid-fifteenth century. Its contents include papal privileges, grants, confirmations, quitclaims, leases and transcripts of legal proceedings, but not the abbey's foundation charter or the confirmations of the founder's kin or any successive royal confirmations. Some of the missing royal confirmations have been included from other sources at the back of the printed version of the cartulary.[147]

Because the holdings of the abbey have not been detailed elsewhere, their extent will be briefly outlined in the following few paragraphs. To the east of the abbey, the monks acquired lands in Caldecote, including

---

[140] Ibid., Pt. I, p. 126.

[141] Knowles (1950), p. 724.

[142] *Cartulary of Old Wardon Abbey*, p. 7.

[143] Ibid., p. 8.

[144] Ibid., ms. 344a, which is a confirmation charter of King Stephen dated to 1135.

[145] Ibid., mss. 22–7, 30–37, 39, 41, 43–64, 137, 143, 199, 214, 222, 248–68, 289, 324, 326, 344f, 335, 336g, q, 338d, f, v, y, 344a, e, f, 345 and 348–9.

[146] Ibid., ms. 344b.

[147] Ibid., pp. 1–7.

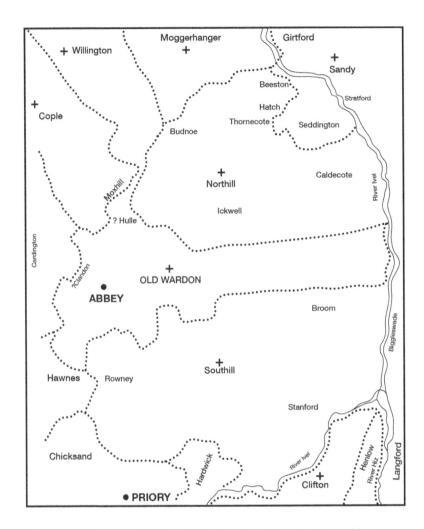

Fig. 7.9   Possessions of Old Wardon Abbey in Bedfordshire. After Fowler (1931)

two mills there,[148] as well as in Dunton,[149] Edworth,[150] Holme in Biggleswade[151] and Sutton.[152] To the north, the monks were granted land in Beeston,[153] Great Barford[154] and Sandy,[155] as well as the manor of Southmills in Charlton and Blunham, which was held from the Honour of Leicester.[156] To the west of the abbey in Bedfordshire, the monks acquired land in Hawnes and Houghton Conquest,[157] Priestley in Flitwick,[158]

148   Ibid., mss. 219, 269–72, 337q and 344f.
149   Ibid., mss. 87–8, 90, 96 and 344c.
150   Ibid., mss. 65 and 67.
151   Ibid., ms. 40, 114, 293, 323 and 344f.
152   Ibid., ms. 114.
153   Ibid., mss. 273, 287 and 324.
154   Ibid., ms. 335.
155   Ibid., mss. 215–20, 238, 325 and 328.
156   Ibid., mss. 42 and 341, also p. 302, n. 42.
157   Ibid., ms. 38, 240, 242 and 335.
158   Ibid., mss. 11, 98, 104, 106, 335, 336f, 337I and 344c.

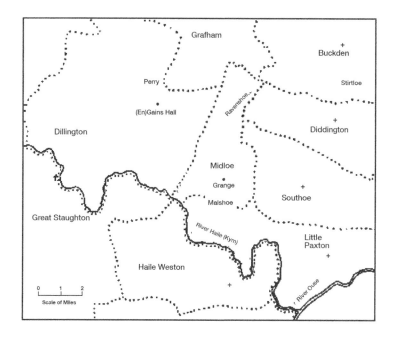

Fig. 7.10   Possessions of Old Wardon Abbey in Huntingdonshire. After Fowler (1931)

Ravensden,[159] Renhold,[160] Stagsden,[161] Steppingley[162] and a large amount of property in and around Goldington.[163] This included a significant number of acquisitions in Putnoe and Pertenhale.[164] It also acquired a small parcel of land, house and rents in the town of Bedford.[165]

In Northamptonshire, it acquired land in Aston,[166] Culworth,[167] Eydon,[168] Gayton,[169] Midloe,[170] Trafford[171] and a large number of grants in West Wardon[172] and in Farndon,[173] the latter being donated by various members of the Farendon family, which included a mill (Figure 7.11). In Cambridgeshire, it held the grange of *Burgheden* in Swaffham Bulbeck,[174] as well as land in Croydon[175] and Gaminglay.[176] In Hertfordshire, it held land in Ashwell,[177]

---

[159]   Ibid., mss. 11, 143, 182, 191–3, 195, 325, 328 and 335.

[160]   Ibid., mss. 190, 335, 340a, c, d, e, 344e and f.

[161]   Ibid., mss. 137, 219, 335 and 342.

[162]   Ibid., mss. 102, 204 and 337k.

[163]   Ibid., mss. 143, 151–81, 184–9, 194, 240 and 335.

[164]   Ibid., mss. 11, 140, 141, 145, 150, 151, 154, 188, 240, 335, 344e and f.

[165]   Ibid., mss. 144, 146 and 320.

[166]   Ibid., ms. 210.

[167]   Ibid., ms. 212.

[168]   Ibid., mss. 120–24, 127–9 and 134–5.

[169]   Ibid., ms. 244.

[170]   Ibid., mss. 70, 73, 205, 206, 344b, 344e and f.

[171]   Ibid., mss. 69 and 213.

[172]   Ibid., mss. 69, 109, 113, 115–19, 130–33, 209, 343, 344e and f.

[173]   Ibid., mss. 110–12, 124, 136 and 211m.

[174]   Ibid., mss. 1, 2 and 3.

[175]   Ibid., mss. 245–7.

[176]   Ibid., ms. 74.

[177]   Ibid., mss. 8, 77 and 89.

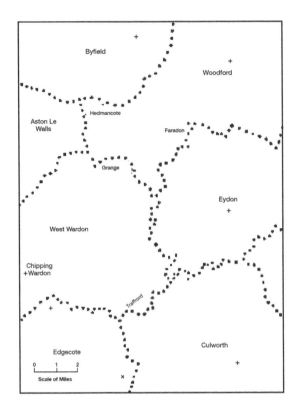

Fig. 7.11   Possessions of Old Wardon Abbey in Northamptonshire. After Fowler (1931)

Broadfield,[178] Hinxworth,[179] Hitchin,[180] Rushden[181] and Sandon.[182] In Buckinghamshire, it acquired land in Brickhill,[183] and in Middlesex, land in Haggerston.[184] In Huntingdonshire, it held land in Dillington,[185] as well as small holdings in Norwich[186] and London.[187]

At the more rarefied end of the scale, the social status of the abbey's patrons ranged from tenants-in-chief like Simon de Beauchamp and mid-ranking aristocrats such as Jordan Lenveise and Robert de Broi, to local knights such as the Farendons of Northamptonshire and the Harpers (*Citthariste*) of Southill, as well as local gentry such as the Goldingtons, Stanfords, Stoctons and Wardons. The abbey was also granted land by a number of local smallholders, such as Ralph of Southmills (*Sudmulin*), Osbert son of Maineri of Swaffham, and Geoffrey the fisherman.

Nine mills are mentioned in the abbey's charters in a number of grants, confirmations, agreements and notes dating from c. 1166 to 1297, but only seven of these appear to have been directly held by it. A single fulling mill is also recorded in the *Valor Ecclesiasticus* of 1535, but not in the abbey's cartulary.[188] The earliest

---

[178]   Ibid., mss. 79–81, 86, 89, 344c and f.
[179]   Ibid., mss. 65–7.
[180]   Ibid., mss. 314–17
[181]   Ibid., mss. 82–4 and 103.
[182]   Ibid., mss. 81, 86 and 89.
[183]   Ibid., ms. 107.
[184]   Ibid., mss. 309–10 and 322.
[185]   Ibid., ms. 71.
[186]   Ibid., mss. 306 and 307.
[187]   Ibid., mss. 277–8.
[188]   *VCH Bedfordshire*, Vol. 2, p. 283.

of the abbey's mill-related documents is a royal confirmation of the abbey's lands and liberties by Henry I, dated 1166–86, which includes a generic reference to the abbey's 'waters and mills and ponds and fisheries'. The same manuscript contains a later confirmation by Richard I, and includes extra privileges and immunities for the abbey.[189]

It would seem that the only mill which the abbey held at the time of its foundation was the so-called 'Monk's mill' which was probably located somewhere between Wardon and Southill (Beds.). The mill is mentioned in a confirmation by Joseph son of William Citthariste (i.e., Harper) of Southill of lands given to the abbey by his grandfather, Ailwin II. This included 'land in Flexland that is of my fee and is near the road that leads to the church of Southill next to the house of Walter of Stanford and also the road that leads to the abbey and the monk's mill.' The charter is dated to between c. 1180 and 1200.[190] It would seem that this same mill is also mentioned in a composition between Newnham Priory and Old Wardon over the payment by the abbey of four marks in lieu of tithes for lands which it held in parishes belonging to the priory in 1199. The agreement included one mark annually for tithes of hay and from their 'old mill' (*molendinis suis Antiqua*) in Southill, which suggests that these two assets were generating incomes in the vicinity of £6 13s annually, most of which was undoubtedly for the mill and strongly suggests it held suit. Any land which the abbey acquired in the area in future would also be subject to tithes, except for uncultivated land which it subsequently asserted.[191]

One of the earliest mills granted to the abbey is first mentioned in a confirmation dated to between c. 1190 and 1200. Apart from confirming a grant of 10 acres of land and meadow above *Charewelle* of his fee of *Stertes* in Northamptonshire, William de Farendon confirms to the abbey 'the watercourse near their mill that was at one time my father's above the land that is held of my fee and the same pond and ditch that leads to the aforesaid mill'. William warranted that the monks of Wardon should be able to make any necessary repairs to the mill while they held it, and that they should be free of any interference, deception or disturbance from himself or his heirs.[192] It would seem, therefore, that this mill was originally granted to the abbey by William's father Richard de Farendon shortly after the foundation of the abbey. The grant was again confirmed by William in another document of around the same time, which on this occasion refers to the mill as Aston or West Wardon mill, and specifies the monks' right to repair the mill's pond and leet.[193] William's son, Thomas, re-confirmed the grant sometime around 1270, which included the 10 acres of land mentioned in the earlier confirmation.[194]

The grant of Milton Earnest mill (Beds.) and its appurtenances were confirmed to the abbey in a grant by William de Bause of his land in the open field of Clopham pertaining to *Midiltonmill*, dated 1190 to 1200. It included a remission of sixpence of rent that was due from the land and mill and a standard warranty clause.[195] A grant of a millpond for this mill is confirmed in another charter of 1199 from Simon Basset. The charter states, 'I give our consent and assent with John's sons and my heirs to heighten and repair their millpool, giving them their share in the necessary measure [and state] that it is their mill of *Middeltone* [i.e., Milton Earnest] that was held of Robert de Hastinge and William Ursel, namely the millpond that pertains to his mill and that millpond which belongs to his highness in my lord [i.e., the abbot] there above my fee ... for twelvepence a year from me and my heirs.'[196] Presumably the John mentioned in Simon's confirmation was his brother.

A grant in perpetuity from Edwin de Goldington of half an acre of open field in Goldington (Beds.) was made to the abbey in exchange for 5s 4d rent from their mill in Risingho.[197] As this charter is dated to between c. 1170 and 1190, the monks had obviously acquired Risingho mill at some earlier date. An agreement from 1240 between William de Bello Campo (Beauchamp) and the abbey following a dispute over the same mill is discussed in more detail in Chapter 9.

---

[189]   *Cartulary of Old Wardon Abbey*, ms. 344.

[190]   *Cartulary of the Cistercian Abbey of Old Wardon, Bedfordshire*, ms. 37.

[191]   Ibid., ms. 143.

[192]   Ibid., ms. 112.

[193]   Ibid., ms. 209.

[194]   Ibid., ms. 211.

[195]   Ibid., ms. 147.

[196]   Ibid., ms. 142.

[197]   Ibid., ms. 153.

By 1210, the monks had built or acquired another mill, known as 'the North mill of the monks' at a place called *Thefurlange* in or near Henelaw (Henlow, Beds.), with regard to which the monks secured two grants of land between c. 1190 and 1210, the first of which involved a grant of land next to the mill's pond, and the second of land beside the mill. Both grants were from freeholders.[198]

The latest documents pertaining to grants of mills to the abbey are three charters dated c. 1205–10, regarding two mills in Caldecote (Herts.). The first records a grant by Richard the miller of Caldecote to the abbey of Caldecote mills, 'for the benefit of the poor' (*in usus pauperum*), along with lands, meadows and appurtenances in perpetuity for three marks annually (£2) to be paid to the lords of the manor, Hubert de Anesti and John de Birkin, which would suggest that both mills held suit.[199] The grant was confirmed at around the same time in two separate charters by Hubert and John, both of whom stated that the annual rent due to them and their heirs from the mills was £1 each.[200] Although it is not immediately clear to whom the other 10 shillings was being paid, the documents below shed some light on this anomaly.

The confirmation of Richard the miller's grant by his two mesne lords is followed by another confirmation by the heirs of Jordan Lenveise of the succession to Caldecote mills, which provides some insight into their complicated history. Jordan had been the tenant of an unnamed 'baron', who held Caldecote as half a knight's fee. Jordan had two daughters, Dionysia and Johanna, the former betrothed to Hubert de Anesti, lord of Beston, while the latter was betrothed to John de Birkin. John and Johanna gave birth to Thomas and Jacob, with Jacob inheriting the half fee of Caldecote. Jacob then granted his half fee to Old Wardon, with Richard the miller becoming the tenant of the mills at fee farm for £2 rent annually. Richard then gave up his lease of the mills to the monks, with the latter then obliged to pay the rent to lords Hubert and John, Jordan's sons-in-law and Jacob's father and uncle.

Jacob recorded that his uncle and aunt, Hubert and Dionysia, had given their half of this rent to the canons of the Holy Trinity in London, with nine shillings to be assigned by Holy Trinity as a pittance to Old Wardon. The canons of Holy Trinity subsequently quitclaimed this nine shillings to the monks for nine marks (£6), with a residual 11 shillings absolved of the monks and the heirs of Hubert. This 11 shilling residuum was then inherited through marriage by Thomas of Kent, knight, who was presumably Jacob's step-father, i.e., Johanna's second husband. Jacob and his heirs were thus to continue to be paid this 11 shillings, including his daughter who was betrothed to John de Carminho, a tenant of Edward I.[201] Unfortunately, these few details are the only firm information that we have about the revenues drawn from any of Old Wardon's mills, presumably because all the others were directly managed and their grain incomes were being consumed by the monks, *conversi* and servants; a strategy for which there is strong evidence in the cases of the other Cistercian houses of Beaulieu and Sibton.

Old Wardon's cartulary suggests that it was drawing rents from at least five grain mills long before adjustments were made to the Cistercian ordinances to allow such activities, thus suggesting that at least some English Cistercian houses appear to have paid little or no attention to them. Unfortunately, however, the only mill held by them for which there is any information about revenues is Risingho mill, which paid 5s 4d of its rent to Edwin de Goldington in the late twelfth century as part of an exchange of property. This part rent, along with the rent of £2 10s paid by the abbey for the two mills of Caldecote, is not sufficient evidence to draw any firm conclusions about revenues from the mills held by the abbey.

The relevant contents of the abbey's mill-related documents are summarized in Table 7.9. More detailed discussion of a water dispute in which the abbey was involved can be found in Chapter 9. The table makes it clear that unlike most of the other houses studied, Old Wardon acquired most of its mills during the twelfth century, but does not appear to have ever owned very many mills, despite its relative age and wealth.

---

[198] Ibid., ms. 49 and 57. The grantors were Wido de St Walerico of Henelaw and William son of Walter of Henelaw. Ms. 58 is a confirmation of ms. 57 by Agnes, daughter of Ailne de Henelaw, who was presumably a cousin or niece of Walter.

[199] Ibid., ms. 269.

[200] Ibid., mss. 270 and 272.

[201] Ibid., ms. 271.

Table 7.9   Seven mills in which Old Wardon Abbey held an interest before 1300

Name	Year acquired	Rent/Revenue	Grantor	Grantee
Monk's mill	c. 1135–36 (?)	13s 4d (1199, tithes only)	Walter Espec?	Old Wardon
Charewell mill (Aston or West Wardon)	c. 1135–36 (?)	no data	Richard de Farendon	"
Midiltone mill (Milton Earnest)	1190–1200	no data	William de Bause	"
Risingho mill	>c. 1170–90	5s 4d (c. 1170–90, part rent)	?	"
North mill (*Thefurlange*, Henlaw)	1210	no data	Built by abbey?	"
Caldecote mills (x2)	c. 1205–10	£2 10s (c. 1205/10)	Richard the miller Hubert de Anesti John de Birkin	"

The abbey appears to have only built one of its mills, with the rest granted or leased to it by members of the nobility or local knights. With respect to the revenues drawn from the various mills, the Monk's precinctual mill appears to have been earning a considerable sum of money as early as the second quarter of the twelfth century. The tithes of 13s 4d which the monks paid from this mill to Newnham Priory suggest that it was earning more than £6 13s annually, a princely sum by any standard at that time, and presumably indicative of the mill holding suit, as it was not in an urban centre. The part rent of 5s 4d paid for Risingho mill in the late twelfth century, and of £2 10s for the two mills of Caldecote in the early thirteenth century provide little in the way of reliable evidence about total revenues from these mills, although the rents from the mills of Caldecote are comparable to those being drawn from the mills held by knightly tenants of Cirencester Abbey at around the same time and suggest that they also held suit. Some further implications of these data will be discussed in the chapter's conclusion.

Furness Abbey

Furness Abbey was originally founded in 1127 as a Savigniac house by Stephen, who was at that time Count of Boulogne and Mortain and lord of Lancaster. During a visit to England by Vitalis, the Savigniac's founder, Stephen had offered Vitalis land at Tulketh on the Ribble just south of Preston for a new foundation. Several years later, in 1124, a colony of monks came from Savigny to establish themselves at Tulketh, only to move a few years later when Stephen granted them the forest of Furness. The new location was to prove very favourable, including as it did significant areas of wood, pasture and fisheries, as well as three or four mills, and large shares of the local salt works and iron and shale mines.

Stephen's foundation grant consisted of 'the whole of the forest and demesne of Furness, Walney Island, the manor of Ulverston, the land of Roger Bristwald, the count's fishery in the Lune by Lancaster, and Warin the Little with his land'.[202] A bull of Pope Eugenius III from 1154 confirms Stephen's original grant but also the gifts of Kirksanton and Harrum from Robert Bovill, as well as *Caldra* (aka *Caldram*) and its mill, and Bermerton and *Flolegate* from King David of Scotland, two saltworks in *Withoshd*, fisheries in the Derwent and Eggre, half of Foss, the vills of *Fordbotle*, *Crivelton* and *Ros* (Roose) with appurtenances, and four vills and other land on the Isle of Man. Eugenius' bull took the abbey under his special protection and also confirmed their exemption from tithes on lands worked by their own hands.[203]

Although several kilometres inland, the abbey was bounded by the Irish Sea on three sides, a situation which no doubt assisted it in its oversight of four Irish monasteries following an order of the Cistercian General Chapter in 1249, as well as its provision of senior clergy for the Isle of Man. Within eight years of its

---

[202] *VCH Lancs.*, Vol. II, p. 114.

[203] *Monumenta de Insula Manniae*, 'Bull of Pope Eugenius III to Furness Abbey, AD 1153', pp. 8–12. *Fordbotle*, *Crivelton* and *Ros* were in Amounderness Hundred within a few kilometres of the Abbey. They were held by Earl Tostig before the Conquest and valued at 95 geld units at Domesday. Only Roose still exists as a settlement.

foundation, it had established daughter houses in Calder near the Scottish border, as well as at Swineshead in Lincolnshire and Russyn (or Rushen) on the Isle of Man. However, it was not until 1148 that it converted with its sister houses to the Cistercian reform.

The abbey's growth in wealth and status during its first century was remarkable, primarily due to its special relationship with the Crown. Nearly every monarch from Henry I to Henry IV confirmed and enlarged its rights and privileges. By the end of the thirteenth century, Furness held lands in Lancashire, Cumbria, the Yorkshire Dales and Lincolnshire, including 17 granges, four vills and three churches. Two papal bulls from the late twelfth and mid-thirteenth centuries provide some insights into the rapidity with which it reorganised and added to its holdings during this period. The first was issued by Clement III and is dated to between 1187 and 1191. It confirms all of Furness's possessions, which by then included granges at *Roos, Neuton, Kilverdiswic, Irlid, Barrai, Wagneiam, Belli Montis, Lancastre, Winterburna* and *Nubi*, as well as the vills of Dalton, Ulverstone, Merton and Orgrave, the churches of Dalton and *Wrsewik*, and a carucate of land in *Fossa*.[204] The second is a bull of protection and privilege by Innocent IV (1243–54), which lists the abbey's granges as *Ros, Neutona, Irelid, Beumont, Winterburne, Neuby, Stalmine, Lindale, Soler, Caupland, Greneholme, Brutherulkil, Stubham, Northscale, Seleseth, Northend* and *Southend*, as well as a fishery in Lancaster.[205] This would suggest that Furness no longer held three of its 10 granges from the late twelfth century, but had acquired 11 additional ones by the middle of the thirteenth century, bringing its total number of granges to 17. The monks of Furness had obviously been involved in a great deal of activity in the land market in the interim, and not all of this property had been acquired through the generosity of wealthy benefactors.

A valuation of the abbey's temporalities from 1292, which is presumably related to the *Taxatio Nicholai IV*, lists holdings in Furness, *Coupland, Amunderness, Lonesdale, Wynterburne* and *Borcheredale*.[206] Eleven granges in Furness were said to comprise 10 and a half carucates of land in total, with each carucate valued at 3s 6d annually. Fifteen properties that can be identified as granges are recorded, five of which are not recorded in the bull of protection and privilege by Innocent IV (1243–54) cited above. The reasons for this are not clear.

The total temporal revenues listed in the valuation amount to only £38 19s 7 1/2d, although the total value of temporal properties is listed as almost five times as much in a document of the previous year, at £193 12s. The revenues from the abbey's mills, pastures, woods, ponds and fisheries, as well as from its lead mine and from heriot, royal fines and reliefs in Furness are listed as nothing for 1292. Nor are there any references to mill revenues from outside Furness in this document. This would seem to imply that the abbey was using its tollcorn to feed its monks, servants and retainers, while the cash revenues from the 13 or more mills in which it by then had an interest was presumably being used for their maintenance, much as Beaulieu was doing at around the same time. In other words, by consuming its mill revenues in various internal expenses, it was able to avoid listing any income from them.

Furness's spiritualities as valued in 1292 included the churches of Dalton and Ursewik, but also that of Millum, a portion of the custody of the altar of St Michael in the Church of York, and a pension of the church of Ulverstone (Cumb.), all of which amounted to £77 5s 4d, including £6 5s 4d for tithes.[207] The next manuscript in the coucher book is dated to 1291, and states that the 'sum of our temporal properties following the old tax' (*Summa bonorum nostrorum temporalium secundum antiquam taxam*) amounted to £176 and an additional £17 12s for tithes, while the 'sum of spiritual properties' (*Summa bonorum spiritualium*) amounted to £21 6s 8d and an additional £2 2s 8d for tithes, giving a grand total of £217 1s 4d, as opposed to the total of £116 4s 11 1/2d provided by the valuation for the *Taxatio*. It is not clear to which 'old tax' the charter is referring.[208] A valuation of the same spiritualities made in 1316 'after the ravages of the Scots' amounted to £31 13s 4d, and £3 3s 4d for tithes.[209]

The abbey's relative isolation combined with royal patronage and its control of a vast and fairly self-contained estate ensured that it exercised both independence and political power. Furness's abbot held the status of a feudal baron, and was often called upon to take his part in the ongoing conflicts between Scotland

---

[204]   *Coucher Book of Furness Abbey*, Vol. I, Pt. III, ms. 428.

[205]   Ibid., ms. 394.

[206]   Ibid., ms. 408.

[207]   Ibid.

[208]   Ibid., ms. 409.

[209]   Ibid., ms. 410.

and England. Although the proximity of the sea enabled the abbot to manage his estates further south in Lancashire by water as well as by land, the abbey's location was a definite disadvantage in lawsuits, as the abbot often received insufficient warning of suits brought against him, and even when he did, could not always reach the court in time to defend himself.

With regard to the abbey's extensive wool interests, it had established for itself by the late thirteenth century a cross-country network of lodgings, which included land in York and Boston in order to ship its produce directly to Flanders.[210] Earlier in the century, it appears to have been shipping its wool out of Beverley, presumably via Hull.[211] Between the early and mid-thirteenth century the monks of Furness also acquired the right to take millstones from the quarries of Kellet and Over Kellet.

While the many disputes and conflicts over precedence and territory in which Furness was involved have been detailed elsewhere,[212] it is perhaps not surprising to learn that the abbey's mining and fishing interests were the causes of some dispute with neighbours and competitors. Its interests in the rich Lune fishery were shared by Lancaster Priory, for example, which resulted in a number of disputes that were finally resolved in an agreement of 1315. When Lancaster was later dissolved and taken over by Syon, the abbess allowed the abbot of Furness to take control of the whole fishery.[213] The abbey was also involved in a dispute over who had rights to mine iron-ore and shale in Orgrave, with regard to which the monks made concerted efforts to consolidate their holdings in the area.[214] Some of these documents will be discussed in more detail in Chapter 9.

The coucher book provides some details of the abbey's mining activities, although it provides no indication of whether Furness was using water power to run its forges, bellows or furnaces. It records that in 1292, the abbey's revenue from sales of iron at its Furness ironworks, less expenses, was £6 13s 4d. This was by far the largest single source of revenue from its temporalities for that year, apart from its sales of cattle, horses and birds, which amounted to £25 across the various granges.[215] While details of the abbey's manufacturing of iron and salt are scant, the coucher book does provide some details of how the 'iron-stone' was mined and prepared for the furnace.

The editor of Furness's coucher book, J.C. Atkinson, believed that it was likely that the monks used the running water near their seven furnaces in the forest not just for washing the ore, but for powering the bellows for their furnaces.[216] Although it is possible that the monks may have operated a forge-mill and/or water-powered bellows at the site, there is no documentary evidence to support this. There does not appear to have been any archaeological work conducted on the area to test Atkinson's speculation. He also noted that, based on some royal hearings on behalf of the Queen's tenants of Low Furness made in 1652, 'about one ton of malleable iron, which they called livery iron, of the value of eightpence a stone (14lb), was bestowed yearly on certain tenants of the Abbey, for the reparation of their ploughs, etc.'[217] That the monks still had plenty of iron left to sell is borne out by the large sum recorded in the 1292 valuation. A valuation of lands in Cleveland held by the heirs of Peter de Brus III and dated to 1271–72, lists the value of five of their small furnaces at 10 shillings each annually, and another two nearby at £4 each. Based on these figures, Atkinson speculated that the abbey operated as many as 40 furnaces across its various holdings, although this figure is probably too high.[218]

While it is not possible to determine from the extant manuscripts if the monks of Furness operated any industrial mills, they do record that, by the end of the thirteenth century, they directly held or had interests in at least 16 mills. These were located in Furness and Ulverstone to the north-east (where they held two mills), Borrowdale in the Lake District, Newby south of Penrith, Forton and Stalmine just south of Lancaster and

---

[210] Ibid., ms. 217.

[211] Cited in Donkin (1978), p. 191.

[212] *VCH Lancs.*, Vol. 2, pp. 114–31.

[213] *Coucher Book of Furness Abbey*, Vol. II, mss. 217 and 219.

[214] Ibid., ms. Vol. I, Pt. I, ms. 114, etc. This was in the district of Cleveland, on which see Atkinson's note on pp. 238–9. See also the more detailed discussion of Furness's mining interests later in this section.

[215] Ibid., Vol. I, Pt. III, ms. 408.

[216] Ibid., Vol. I, Pt. I, pp. xi–xiv.

[217] Ibid., p. xv. Presumably the queen in question was Charles I's wife, Henrietta Maria, sister of Louis XIII of France.

[218] Ibid., pp. xvii–xix. Atkinson reached this figure based on the relative valuations of a carucate of land in Furness and in Danby in Cleveland, but there is little reason to suppose that these valuations were directly related to those of the furnaces located on them.

Stackhouse north of Skipton in the Yorkshire Dales. They also held a half share of nearby Rilleston (Rylstone) and Hetton mills, a third of the mill of Drogheda in northern Ireland, and a mill or mills in Orgrave (Cumbria) and in Grefholme and Driterum (Lancs.). Its lay brothers appear to have done suit at the mills of other lords at Flasby, Drigg, Kirksanton and Coupland, all of which were close to where they worked in cells managing their granges.

No mills are mentioned in any of Furness Abbey's foundation charters, although it seems likely that a precinctual mill was included in the new abbatial complex at Furness, and a number of papal bulls of immunity, privilege and confirmation make generic and occasionally specific references to mills held by the abbey. The earliest of these is the aforementioned special bull by Eugenius III from 1153, which specifically refers to a mill held by the monks at *Caldram*, but mentions no others. This mill does not appear elsewhere in the abbey's charters, although its actual donor was William, grandson of King David of Scotland.[219] It seems likely, therefore, that like the Drogheda mill in Ireland mentioned below, *Caldram* was one of those Scottish border possessions lost to the abbey during Edward I's campaign to re-impose English rule over the Scots from 1291 onwards. A list of privileges by Alexander III (1159–81) simply refers to the abbey's 'virgates (*virgultus*), meadows, fields and wastes (*nemoribus*), mills, saltpans and fisheries' as constituting its holdings.[220] A bull of papal privilege by Innocent IV (1243–54) refers to the abbey's 'mills for milling and its ovens for cooking' (*aut molentes in molendinis nostris, vel coquentes in furnis nostris*), and repeats the wording of Alexander III's generic list of the monastery's holdings.[221]

The earliest of the abbey's documents to record any references to specific mills is a grant dated to between 1150 and 1170, in which Adam son of Meldred gave the monks a carucate of land called Stackhouse (Yorkshire), along with timber from nearby Giggleswick, for which the monks were to pay Adam and his heirs 10 shillings annually. The grant included the mill of Stackhouse.[222] Between 1150 and 1170, William de Percy confirmed Adam's grant to the monks, a confirmation which was repeated by Henry de Puisat around 1180.[223] These men were presumably the successive chief lords of Adam's fee. Adam's grant was again confirmed by his son and grandson in two separate documents dated to 1180–90 and 1221, with his grandson Helias de Gicleswike releasing the monks from the obligation to pay the 10 shillings rent in the latter document.[224] Around 1194, the monks had demised to Helias the multure of their vill of Stackhouse, which consisted of the suit of all their free and servile men of the vill at a multure rate of 1/18, as well as free access to the millpond. In return, Helias was to pay a pound of cummin and twopence annually for all services.[225] In April 1221, a papal legate witnessed an agreement between Helias and the monks over the land of Stackhouse, which included a quitclaim from the monks to pay Helias and his heirs all of the tollcorn from Stackhouse mill at a multure rate of 1/18 for all free and servile secular tenants (*secularibus teneatur Stakhous*) who owed suit to the mill. Presumably then, the monks were free from having to pay multure on their own ground grain.[226] The monks were also to be quit of all secular services on the land for a pound of cummin and twopence annually.[227] In other words, this second agreement appears to be a re-negotiation of the original agreement following Helias's remission of the 10 shillings rent on the monks' holdings in Stackhouse.

The monks were granted the whole vill of Winterburn (Yorkshire), the wood and pasture of Flasby and additional lands in the Langlands of Thornhead by William of Graindeorge sometime before 1156, which was thrice confirmed by his son William between 1188 and 1216. The Winterburn land included a mill.[228] The original grant was also confirmed by Henry II between 1156 and 1166,[229] and by Roger archbishop of York, and

---

[219]   *Coucher Book of Furness Abbey*, Vol. II, Pt. III, pp. xvii–xviii.

[220]   Ibid., ms. 382. A farm called Caldra still exists on the Scottish border about 25km due west of Berwick-upon-Tweed.

[221]   Ibid., Vol. I, Pt. I, ms. 32.

[222]   Ibid., Vol. II, Pt. II, Stackhouse, ms. 1.

[223]   Ibid., mss. 5–6. Stackhouse consisted of three carucates at Domesday and was held by Roger of Poitou.

[224]   Ibid., mss. 2–3.

[225]   Ibid., ms. 12.

[226]   Ibid., Vol. II, Pt. III, pp. xxi–xxii. The second editor of the coucher book, John Brownbill, appears to have been confused on this matter.

[227]   Ibid., Vol. II, Pt. II, Stackhouse, ms. 4. The relevant phrase reads: *scilicet quod molent in ordine suo ad xviii vas sive sint servi sive liberi nec aliud molendinum frequentabunt sub certa pena.*

[228]   Ibid., Vol. II, Pt. II, Flasby, mss. 12–14.

[229]   Ibid., ms. 21.

Roger de Mowbray, chief lord of the fee, around the same time.[230] Roger also granted the monks the service of half a knight's fee in Winterburn, including scutage, Danegeld and tenmentale, free of all secular service, while his brother Nigel granted the monks the service of half a knight there.[231] William of Graindeorge the younger granted the monks an additional four bovates and more than three acres elsewhere in Flasby during the same period as his earlier cited confirmations reveal.[232] Sometime around 1320, John Graindeorge released all claim to the lands and rights granted to the monks by his ancestors after having consulted the appropriate charters.[233]

Between 1165 and 1177, Waltheof son of Edmund granted the monks the vill of Newby (Yorkshire) with all its appurtenances, including a mill and its waters.[234] This appears to have been in addition to a grant from Robert de Boivill and his wife Margaret of a moiety of Newby, which was confirmed by Waltheof (a.k.a. Waldeve) between 1160 and 1189.[235] Waltheof's grant was confirmed by Richard de Morevill, constable of the King of Scotland, and Avice his wife, who were presumably the heirs of Robert and Margaret de Boivill, sometime around 1177. The confirmation was made with the consent of their son and heir, William. Avice twice confirmed the original grant between c. 1177 and 1193. The 'waters and mills' which were a part of the grant are specifically mentioned in all three confirmations.[236] The same grant was again confirmed by Waltheof's son Richard around 1200, although on this occasion there is no reference to any mills.[237] Between 1210 and 1230, Waltheof's daughter Margaret released the monks from eight shillings in rent which they had customarily paid her for the carucate of land in Newby which her father had given them. The release does not mention the mill.[238] However, another release made in York county court dated 14 January 1241–42 by Sara, prioress of Arthington, acknowledges the monks' right in a messuage, mill-site and 20 acres of arable land in Newby, in return for a payment to the nuns of five marks (£3 6s 8d) and five cows.[239] It is not clear, however, how the nuns came into seisin of this land, and in particular the mill, when this appears to have been part of Waltheof's original grant, a grant which had, furthermore, been confirmed by Henry II between 1175 and 1180.[240] It is possible, however, that the mill-site was just that, and that the monks' mill lay elsewhere, although the value of the settlement between the two parties would suggest that there were at least waterworks for a mill on the site. Waltheof's original grant was again confirmed by Henry III around 1270.[241]

Sometime around 1170, Roger de Orgrave granted the abbey in free alms an appropriate site in Orgrave (Cumbria) for a mill to be built, to be chosen by them, with all of the associated lands and waters.[242] A confirmation of this grant was made after the site was chosen, which is described as being an acre of land below the road leading to their grange of *Ireleyth,* 'where the old stream is diverted near Orgrave around the mill'. Their free access to the watercourse is guaranteed in a series of warranty clauses.[243] A second confirmation was made after the mill had been constructed, but no details are given.[244] Presumably at the same time, Roger's brother William granted the monks the right to carry their watercourse through his land in free and perpetual alms.[245] The four sons of William and Roger all gave the abbey small parcels of Orgrave Common amounting to more than 17 acres some time later.[246]

---

230 Ibid., mss. 22–3 and 26.
231 Ibid., mss. 24–5.
232 Ibid., mss. 15–20.
233 Ibid., Winterburn, ms. 141.
234 Ibid., Vol. II, Pt. II, Newby, mss. 5 and 21.
235 Ibid., ms. 22.
236 Ibid., mss. 12, 16 and 23.
237 Ibid., ms. 14.
238 Ibid., ms. 6.
239 Ibid., ms. 8.
240 Ibid., ms. 24.
241 Ibid., ms. 20.
242 Ibid., Vol. I, Pt. I, ms. 94.
243 Ibid., ms. 95.
244 Ibid., ms. 96.
245 Ibid., ms. 99.
246 Ibid., mss. 101–4, 106–9.

At around the same time as Roger de Orgrave's grant of the millsite to the abbey, William de Lowick granted the abbey 30 acres of land in Lowick (Cumbria). Although the manuscript is damaged in the relevant section, it is likely that the fragments mentioning the mill of Lowick and its waterways referred to parts of the boundaries of the land, and that the grant probably did not include the mill, as no such mill is mentioned anywhere else in the coucher book.[247]

Between 1175 and 1194, William de Boivill granted the monks the pasture of the Meals of Kirksanton (Cumbria), 10 acres of land near the boundary between Millom and Kirksanton, and a moiety of the fishery of *Heleupool*, in free and perpetual alms. He also gave them access to his wood of Kirksanton and allowed them to grind their grain at his mill of Kirksanton free of multure.[248] Between 1190 and 1204, his son Robert confirmed all of the gifts granted to the monks by William.[249] Other members of the same family also gave the monks land in the area, including a carucate in Coupland and part of a forest.[250]

Aldred de Fortone granted the monks half of his land in *Modirsik* in Forton in exchange for another piece of land called *Muttunclincel* between 1200 and 1210. The grant included a mill or mills, although it does not appear to be referred to in any other documents in the coucher book, suggesting that the abbey's seisin of this property was not secure.[251]

Sometime around 1204, a series of grants were made by 10 different parties from the Boulton family to Adam son of Adam de Kellet (a.k.a. Adam de Grefholme) of moieties of the manors of Grefholme and Driterum in Bolton-le-Sands (Lancashire), which included a mill or mills. The various portions amounted to the whole, for which Adam paid a total of more than 40d in annual rents, and considerations totalling at least £3.[252] Around 1242, Adam granted the monks of Furness all of these lands, as well as additional land in Ramshead, all of which was confirmed by Ralph and Henry de Boulton, who were the heirs of the original grantors.[253]

Sometime after 1208, Walter de Lacy, lord of Meath and son of Hugh, granted in free alms to Furness all of his land that had been held by Christiana, namely the vill of Mariners in Scotland, and part of his land near Drogheda in Ireland. The latter included several messuages and a third part of Drogheda mill, a fishery, 90 acres of land with a turbary, and the right of carriage and transit to take timber from the forest of Trum. This is the one and only reference to the Drogheda mill in the abbey's coucher book, implying that it was lost to the abbey during the Scottish rebellion.[254]

Alice de Rumeli, daughter of William son of Duncan, granted the monks all of the vill of Borrowdale (Cumbria), as well as free passage through her barony of Allerdale and Coupland, between 1209 and 1210. The grant included a mill, although its name and location are not specified. This appears to be the only reference to the Borrowdale mill in the coucher book.[255]

In a series of documents from between 1210 and 1236, Gilbert de Kellet and his cousin Adam granted the monks the right to take millstones from their land in Kellet, as well as dead wood from their forest of Kellet, for the souls of their mothers and fathers.[256] Gilbert's brother William confirmed Gilbert's grant to the monks sometime between 1235 and 1245.[257] Thomas son of Adam de Coupmanwra also granted the monks millstones and dead wood from his part of Kellet between 1260 and 1269. In August 1269 he added to this a bovate of land in Over Kellet with a toft and croft, two acres of turbary, the right to take 10 oaks annually from his forest, pannage for 30 pigs, and confirmed the monks' right to take millstones sufficient for their purposes.[258]

A share of the mill of Hetton in Yorkshire was granted to the monks by Elias son of Harsqui de Heton around 1229. The grant was made for his own soul and that of his wife, ancestors and successors in pure and

[247] Ibid., Vol. I, Pt. II, ms. 264.

[248] Ibid., Vol. II, Pt. II, Meals/Kirksanton, mss. 3–6.

[249] Ibid., mss. 11–12.

[250] Ibid., mss. 13–14.

[251] Ibid., Vol. II, Pt. I, Forton, ms. 1.

[252] Ibid., Vol. II, Pt. I, Grefholme, mss. 9–15.

[253] Ibid., mss. 5–8.

[254] Ibid., Vol. I, Pt. 1, ms. 9.

[255] Ibid., Vol. II, Pt. II, Monkfoss/Borrowdale, ms. 2.

[256] Ibid., Vol. II, Pt. I, Kellet, mss. 1–3.

[257] Ibid., ms. 16.

[258] Ibid., mss. 4 and 5.

perpetual alms free of any secular services, saving for himself and his heirs £1 of rent annually. Interestingly, the grant is accompanied by a testimony from three Jews dated October 1229 that Elias was free of debt following a payment by the monks of Furness of 12 marks (£8) for a half share of the mill of Hetton.[259] In other words, the monks had purchased the half share from Elias by paying off his debts. He nevertheless did well out of the transaction, as he not only cleared his debts and secured the prayers of the monks for his family's souls, but managed to also extract a considerable annual rent for the mill.

A similar transaction is recorded in a release of 1237, in which two Jews of York released to the monks all claim in 10 bovates of land in Rilleston (Rylstone, Yorks.) near Hetton, along with the share of a mill and two bovates in Crathon (Crathorne, Yorks.) about 50 kilometres south-east of Durham. No exchange of money is recorded, nor is the amount of the debt specified. It is also not clear who originally held these properties.[260]

Sometime around 1230, Helias son of Peter granted to Gilbert Boyvill six acres of land in Arnaby (Cumbria) in hereditary fee farm for the homage and service of Gilbert and his heirs and assigns at an annual rent of sixpence. Gilbert and his heirs were also given the right to mill their grain at the lord's mill of Millom at a multure rate of 1/15, and in return for right of pannage were to supply the lord with their twentieth pig annually.[261] The next charter records a grant from Gilbert to Adam de Stokedale of the same land under the same conditions, which Gilbert said he purchased from Helias, although no purchase price is mentioned in the previous charter. In return for Gilbert's grant, Adam gave him in hand eight marks of silver (£5 6s 8d).[262] Adam then granted the same land to the monks of Furness for his own soul and those of his ancestors and successors. Although the details of the multure rate and pannage to be paid are not mentioned, it would seem that the monks were expected to pay the same rate as their predecessors.[263] Another grant dated 1183–1216 from Henry son of Arthur to William son of Waltheof consisted of a messuage and lands with free common in Millom as dower for marrying his daughter Aliz. The charter stipulates that William and Aliz and their heirs were to be quit of multure and pannage, an exemption which was obviously relevant to Furness's later possession of the Arnaby holding.[264]

Between 1227 and 1236, William son of Peter of Stalmyne granted the monks all his land in Stalmine (Lancashire), along with the bodies of himself, his wife and two sons. The grant included Stalmine mill.[265] Between 1236 and 1239, William's brother Robert granted the monks some additional land next to the mill for his soul and those of his ancestors and successors.[266] These properties were in addition to other land in Stalmine given to the monks by the same men and their father,[267] to which were added more small grants by their own sons in the following decades.[268] A series of further grants and disputes in relation to this mill are detailed in Chapter 9.

A charter of 1293 records the demise in fee-farm of the manor of Aldingham (Cumbria) by Furness to Robert, father of John de Harrington, who was then a minor and heir to the manor, pending John's minority. The manor included a mill or mills, and was demised to Robert for 65 marks (£43 6s 8d), to be paid in four instalments over the course of the following year.[269] Presumably due to Robert's death, the same manor was demised to William de Dacre during the abbacy of Hugh Skellar (1297–1303?) under the same conditions.[270] There is no record in the cartulary of whether John de Harrington eventually came into seisin.

---

[259] Ibid., Vol. II, Pt. II, Flasby/Hetton, mss. 120–21. This would suggest a total value for this mill of £20 8s around 1230, a value that is in line with those identified by Langdon (1996), pp. 42, 44–5; Langdon (2004), p. 179; Lucas (2006), pp. 133–5.

[260] Ibid., Rilston/Airton, ms. 123.

[261] Ibid., Millom/Arnaby, ms. 33. At Drigg nearby, the multure rate was 1/20. See ms. 61, dated to 1175–99.

[262] Ibid., ms. 34.

[263] Ibid., ms. 35.

[264] Ibid., ms. 56.

[265] Ibid., Vol. II, Pt. I, *Stalmine I*, ms. 4.

[266] Ibid., ms. 7.

[267] Ibid., mss. 1–3, 5 and 6.

[268] Ibid., mss. 8–11.

[269] Ibid., Vol. I, Pt. II, ms. 293.

[270] Ibid., ms. 294.

Sometime during the early fourteenth century, Benedict de Pennington granted Furness's daughter house of Russyn on the Isle of Man his land in Skeldou Moor near Bolton, which included its woods and plains, fields and pastures, moors, peat-bogs and marshes, saltpans and mills, roads and paths.[271] The next document in the coucher book records an acknowledgement by the abbot of Russyn that Skeldou Moor in Bretby belonged by hereditary right to Alan Fitz-Richard of Coupland and others, who appear to have granted substantial parcels of the moor to the monks of Furness, as a rent of one mark annually was granted by the abbot of Russyn to Furness from the revenues of the same place.[272]

The background to Furness's interest in this land is as follows. Sometime during the last two decades of the thirteenth century, Sir Alan de Coupland (a.k.a. Alan Fitz-Richard) had granted Richard Lombard and John Fegheser his manor of Bolton and Adgarlith, including its 'waters, ponds, mills, wastes, moors, meadows, pastures, and all of its produce (*commoditatibus*)'.[273] On 18 June 1299, Richard and John were given a royal license to grant Furness the manor of Bolton, while Thomas Skilhare was given license to grant the abbey Angerton Moss, all of which was given in perpetuity.[274] This document is followed in the coucher book by the original grant and confirmation of Bolton manor with Adgarlith by Richard and John.[275] Skeldou Moor in Bretby was presumably, therefore, a part of this grant. The mill of Bolton is mentioned as forming part of the boundaries of three acres of land granted to Gervase de Boulton by Adam de Boulton around 1240,[276] and again by Adam's son Ralph in a grant to the monks of land in Bolton townfields along with the right of turbary in a document dated to between 1240 and 1248, where the mill is described as being above *Thistelbrec*.[277]

Table 7.10   Eighteen mills in which Furness Abbey held an interest before 1300

Name	Year acquired	Grantor	Grantee	Suit of mill
Furness mill/s	1127?	Stephen, Count of Boulogne and Mortain (later king)	Furness Abbey	Y
Ulverstone mills (x 2)	"	"	"	Y
Lyttle mill	"	"	"	Y
Caldram mill	>1152	William, grandson of King David of Scotland	"	Y
Winterburn mill	>1156	William of Graindeorge	"	Y
Stackhouse mill	1150–70	Adam son of Meldred	"	Y
Newby mill	1165–77	Waltheof son of Edmund	"	Y
Orgrave mill	c. 1170	Roger de Orgrave (site only, mill built by abbey)	"	?
Forton mill	1200–10	Aldred de Fortone	"	?
Grefholme mill	c. 1204	Adam de Kellet (a.k.a. Grefholme)	"	?
Drogheda mill (1/3 moiety)	1208	Walter de Lacy	"	?
Borrowdale mill	1209–10	Alice de Rumeli	"	Y
Stalmine mill	1227–36	William son of Peter of Stalmyne	"	?
Hetton mill (1/2 moiety)	c. 1229	Elias son of Harsqui de Heton	"	Y
Rilleston mill (1/2 moiety)	1237	?	"	Y
Crathon mill (moiety)	1237	Two Jews of York	"	?
Bolton mill	1299	Richard Lombard and John Fegheser	"	Y

---

[271] Ibid., ms. 318.

[272] Ibid., ms. 319.

[273] Ibid., ms. 322.

[274] Ibid., ms. 323.

[275] Ibid., ms. 324.

[276] Ibid., Vol. II, Pt. I, *Wedholme*, ms. 1.

[277] Ibid., Bolton-le-Sands, ms. 7.

Table 7.11   Furness Abbey: Post-Dissolution mill revenues 1536–38 (£/s/d)

Name	Annual Rent/Revenue	Lessee	Lord
Furness mill/s	6/0/0 (incl. demesne lands)	n/a	Furness Abbey
Lyttle mill	7/0/0	John Barwyk (d.) Gabriel Proctor (c.)	"
Orgrave mill	6/13/4	"	"
Rowse mill	8/0/0	"	"
New mill	2/16/8	"	"
Hawkeshed mill	6/13/4 (incl. houses and land)	Giles and Elizabeth Kendall	"
Ulverstone mills (x3?)	1/10/0	Sir Robert Nevell	"
Newland mill	0/7/6	John Corker	"
Consey mill	0/12/0	William Sandes	"
Colton Beck mill	0/6/8	William Rawlinson	"
Grysdale (?) mill	0/16/0	James and Clement Banke	"
Dale Park fulling mill	0/1/0	William Walker	"
Soray Extra fulling mill	0/3/0	William, John and Edward Braythwayte	"
Newby mill	0/16/0	Humphrey Procter	"
Cartmell mills (x3)	0/10/0 (watercourse only)	James Newbye	Cartmell Priory
Wateryate mill	0/2/0 (watercourse only)	William Kyrkeby	?
TOTAL NO. OF MILLS HELD BY FURNESS ABBEY			**16+**
TOTAL MILL REVENUES			**£40 19s 6d**
AVERAGE MILL REVENUE			**£2 11s 2 1/2 d**

d. = deceased

c. = current lessee

The years of acquisition and grantors of 18 grain mills to Furness before 1300 are detailed in Table 7.10. The abbey appears to have come into possession of as many as five mills when it was first founded, although it only appears to have ever built a single mill of its own during this period. All of the other mills recorded in the coucher book were acquired through grant or purchase, which is certainly not compatible with Mumford's and White's thesis that the Cistercians were great mill builders. Furthermore, only seven of the 18 mills listed above can be unambiguously associated with the mills listed in the post-Dissolution rental. These are the mills of Furness, Ulverstone, Lyttle, Newby and Orgrave. It would also seem likely that Furness lost possession of the two mills it held in Scotland and Ireland (i.e., *Caldram* and Drogheda) within a short time of the beginning of Edward I's campaign against the Scottish rebellion in 1291, if not before. Considering that 16 mills are registered in the abbey's post-Dissolution rental, there would appear to have been virtually no growth in the number of mills held by the abbey in the intervening two centuries or so.

Furness's post-Dissolution mill revenues are detailed in Table 7.11. It is clear from this table that the mills of Furness, Lyttle, Orgrave, Roose and Hawkeshed were drawing by far the highest incomes of all the mills recorded in the survey. Five were drawing between £6 and £8 in rent, which is two to three times the average of £2 11s 2 1/2d. Ten other mills were drawing well under £1 in rents, including the fulling mills of Dale Park and Soray Extra, suggesting that they had almost certainly been sold off at some point since the Black Death and were held in customary or hereditary tenure.[278] Four other mills paid 12 shillings in total for access to watercourses.

Based on these data, it would appear that by the mid-sixteenth century, more than 62 per cent of the mills held by the abbey had slipped into customary or hereditary tenure, while only the mill (or mills) of Furness was in demesne. Five others were at farm drawing market rents. At what point this change in tenure occurred is not clear, but in the absence of any mill leases or rentals in the coucher book, it seems reasonable to conclude that the monks directly managed all of their mills until at least the 1360s, which is the latest date

[278] See Holt (1988), p. 55, who argues that such instances of very low mill rents indicate purchase or alienation.

for most of the documents therein, and that the transfer of the mills into customary and hereditary tenure occurred in the wake of the Black Death as a means of relinquishing ongoing responsibility for mills that were no longer drawing economic rents.

The average mill rent for the 16 mills, at £2 11s 2 1/2d, while not nearly so high as the averages for Beaulieu's mills in the late 1260s, is not so far below the average rents charged by many of the more extractive ecclesiastical lords from the south in the late thirteenth and early fourteenth centuries. In this context it is important to remember that mill revenues throughout England and Wales had experienced a marked and prolonged decline over the period between the Black Death and the Dissolution, with 30 per cent declines over this period being not at all unusual.[279] Given that this was the case, if we increase Furness's average mill revenues in the 1530s by 30 per cent, the resulting figure of £3 6s 7d is certainly comparable to those of the more extractive southern ecclesiastical lords of the late thirteenth and early fourteenth centuries, and of other lords in Lancashire in the late thirteenth and early fourteenth centuries. The very high rents paid to the Crown for five of the mills in the post-Dissolution account is probably an accurate reflection of how much revenue the monks had previously been earning from those mills. Those grain mills that were outside its control were not drawing market rents, and nor were the two low-rent paying fulling mills.

In the light of the monastic innovation thesis, it is especially interesting to note that there are no references to fulling mills held by the abbey prior to the post-Dissolution survey. The survey also makes it clear that at least one of the two fulling mills recorded in the survey had been built recently (i.e., Dale Park), and presumably by its lessee judging from the very low rent paid and the name of the lessee, William Walker. The two fulling mills' average revenue of two shillings was only a tiny fraction of the overall average rental, at 4 per cent. It would seem, therefore, that neither of them had been owned outright by Furness, as their nominal rents suggest the payment of license fees to operate them, as we have already seen in Chapters 5 and 6 with respect to several fulling mills on the estates of the archbishop of Canterbury in the late thirteenth century, the de Lacy family in the early fourteenth century, the bishop of Durham in the late fourteenth century, and of Glastonbury Abbey in the early sixteenth century.

Kirkstall Abbey

Located about four kilometres to the north-west of the city of Leeds, Kirkstall Abbey was founded by Henry de Lacy at Headingley in the West Riding of Yorkshire and established by a colony of monks from Fountains Abbey sometime between 1152 and 1153. *Hedingeleia* or *Hedingelei* is recorded as being held by Ilbert de Lacy in Domesday Book, and consisted of seven carucates (about 840 acres) of land. The vill was valued at only two shillings annually in 1086, down from £2 in 1066, presumably because only two households resided on the property by this stage. The vill was the administrative and military centre of a wapentake known as *Skyrack* under the Anglo-Saxons. Although the first settlement had been at Barnoldswick in Lancashire, the heavy rains and depredations of brigands in the area forced its relocation. The stay at Barnoldswick lasted for at least five years, but there is no evidence that the monks secured a single grant during their sojourn there.[280]

Unfortunately, Kirkstall's surviving charters are not a complete record of the grants made to the abbey during its history, with deeds from both its early and later years missing, so that any discussion of its mill holdings is compromised by the lack of extant documentation of its possessions. Furthermore, the abbey's scribes failed to enter the names of witnesses to many of the documents, making dating somewhat difficult, although some of these have been determined by the modern editors of the coucher book through cross-referencing with other records. The contents consist of four categories of documents: grants of property, privileges and protection; fines and final concords; copies of documents relating to legal disputes; and miscellanea. These were further grouped under territorial headings.

The first of the documents included under territorial headings relate to the five granges within Kirkstall's immediate neighbourhood, i.e., Horsforth, Cookridge, Brearey, Allerton and Roundhay. Except for Allerton

---

[279] See my discussion of the decline in Welsh fulling mill rentals in Lucas (2006a).

[280] *Coucher Book of Kirkstall Abbey*, pp. ix–xi. See also Donkin (1978), p. 33, who gives the duration of the stay at Barnoldswick as 1147–52.

on the western outskirts of modern Bradford, the other holdings were to the north, east and west of the town of Leeds, although it did not hold any land within the township itself until the late fifteenth century.[281] This group is followed by those possessions in more far-flung locations, including Clifford, Snydale, Bessacar and Cliveger, some of which were within Lancashire, although the abbey's scribes appear to have followed a convention whereby small grants in nearby vills were attached to a series of principle granges.

De Lacy's foundation grant of Headingley to the monks of Kirkstall was itself not without problems, as it soon transpired that Kirkstall's patron held the vill of Hugh Bigod, Earl of Norfolk, and had not been paying his rent for many years. Hugh brought a suit against de Lacy for recovery of the vill, which he won, and was subsequently persuaded by the abbot to re-grant it to the abbey on the condition that they continued to pay the rent which was due of de Lacy for the rest of Hugh's life. Furthermore, de Lacey never proved to be a large donor of land to the monastery, although he appears to have encouraged his vassals to assist the monks.[282] His son Robert added to Kirkstall's estates three carucates of land in Snydale south-east of Leeds, as well as the grange of Loscoe in Derbyshire and the vill of Rushton (now Riston Grange) north of Hull.[283] John de Lacy later granted the monks land in the Forest of Bowland, which was at that stage a sparsely inhabited and untamed district.[284]

The Allertons and the Reinevilles, both of whom were leading tenants of the Lacys, granted the monks large parcels of land in Allerton (and eventually the whole vill),[285] as well as the vill of Bramley north-east of Sheffield.[286] Other tenants of the Lacys who made grants to Kirkstall were the Peitivins, Longvillers and Woodlesfords, all of whom granted or leased significant parcels of land to the abbey, including mills and rents from mills.[287]

East of Leeds, the monks acquired lands in Seacroft of the Somerville and Wallis families, who were also local tenants of the Lacys, as well as land in Clifford of the Birdsall family.[288] The valuable estate of Micklethwaite, south of Wetherby, was granted to the monks soon after the abbey's foundation by Herbert de Moreville, who held the fee of Bardsey and Collingham under Roger de Mowbray. Due to the ill-feeling of Henry II towards de Mowbray, he was stripped of these fees and Micklethwaite was lost to the abbey. This resulted in a considerable loss of income for the monks, and even their temporary dispersal, but after repeated entreaties to the Crown, the grange was restored to the monks by King John at a yearly rent of £90, which was subsequently re-granted to them in free alms.[289]

To the north of Headingley within the great estate of the Paynels, Kirkstall acquired land in Adel, Cookridge and Eccup. The Mustel family, who held the first two vills under the Paynels, eventually granted these in their entirety to the abbey. The monks also acquired property in the nearby vills of Brearey and Burdon.[290] West of the fee of the Paynels, the monks acquired property in the vills of Bramhope and Horsforth of the Leathley or Lelay family, and an additional carucate of land in Horsforth from Haverholm Priory in Lincolnshire through the influence of Adam fitz Peter by the early 1160s.[291] Adam also appears to have been instrumental in securing Kirkstall's most southerly possession of Bessacar, near Doncaster, and granted them common rights in Horsforth.[292] His descendants, the Everinghams, did not share Adam's enthusiasm for Kirkstall, however, and were involved in several legal disputes with the monks over the lands which they held of Adam's fee in Horsforth and Keighley. The Bramhope family, who were tenants of the Percies, gave the mill of the village to the abbey in the mid-thirteenth century, which was subsequently leased to the Hospital of St Leonards for £2

---

[281] Ibid., pp. viii–ix, xxiii.

[282] Ibid., pp. x–xi.

[283] Ibid., p. xvii, mss. 206 and 212.

[284] Ibid., mss. 287 and 288.

[285] Ibid., mss. 67, 132 and 150. The village concerned is now known as Chapel Allerton, one of the northern suburbs of Leeds.

[286] Ibid., p. xii.

[287] Ibid., mss. 73–8 and 379.

[288] Ibid., p. xvi.

[289] Ibid., p. xxii, mss. 56, 314, 316 and 384.

[290] Ibid., p. xiv.

[291] Ibid., p. xv.

[292] Ibid., p. xvii, ms. 92.

a year; a sum which was still being paid at the time of the Dissolution.[293] The monks were also granted several bovates of land in the suburbs of Bradford, and additional land in the immediate neighbourhood, all of which were acquired from minor tenants of the Lacys.[294]

Like the monks of Furness, the monks of Kirkstall were involved in mining iron ore and producing iron. They were also involved in tanning leather and fulling cloth, although only their wool-growing activities are discussed in the coucher book. There is, however, firm evidence of the abbey having run a forge mill, tanning mill and fulling mill during the Middle Ages, all of which must have been commissioned by the monks. An archaeological dig on the abbey's precincts in the 1940s revealed the existence of a forge mill dating from as early as c. 1200 which is not recorded in any of the abbey's extant documents,[295] while an extent of 16 Edward I (1288) records that it held a tanning mill and a fulling mill at this time.[296] The fulling mill appears to have still been operating in 1459.[297]

No mills are mentioned in Kirkstall Abbey's foundation charter, although it seems likely that its mill in Kirkstall was probably within the abbey's precincts and was presumably built at the same time as the abbey's conventual buildings. One of the earliest mills granted to Kirkstall came to them by way of Adam fitz Peter through Haverholm Priory. Sometime before 1162, Adam granted the priory land in Horsforth and in Keighley, including a mill in the latter vill. Adam probably held these lands of Robert de Romille, lord of the estate of Harewood, who in turn held them of the barony of William Paynel.[298] This grant was later confirmed by Robert de Gaunt, husband of Paynel's daughter, Alice.[299] Haverholm subsequently made over this whole grant to Kirkstall, which included two carucates of land and the mill of Keighley, and an additional carucate in Horsforth, for £4 annually. However, in a final concord of 1246, it appears that Kirkstall had fallen £12 into arrears, but agreed to immediately pay £8 of the arrears to Haverholm, as well as keeping up their rent payments in future.[300] This arrangement was to be the cause of an almost century-long dispute with Adam fitz Peter's successors to this estate, the Everingham family.[301]

A grant of the vill of Adel to Kirkstall with all its appurtenances, including a mill, was made by another of Paynel's tenants, William Mustel, sometime before 1172. The vill was to be held by Kirkstall for three marks a year (£2). The same document also confirmed William's father Roger's grant to the abbey of the vill of Cookridge and the mill of *Scheneself*.[302] An agreement of 1198 records that tithes of these lands in Adel and Cookridge, amounting to £1 annually, were to be paid by Kirkstall to the Church of Adel in recompense for any losses it may have suffered as a result of the grants from the Mustels. This included tithes of the mill of Cookridge (i.e., *Scheneself*).[303]

A number of documents from the 1160s and 1170s record grants by another member of the minor gentry, William Peitivin, to Kirkstall of five and a half carucates in the hamlet of Headingley (i.e., most of the vill), as well as a wood and some other land in nearby Burley, for which Peitivin and his heirs received £2 8s annually from the abbey.[304] One of these grants, as well as a confirmation of them by Robert Peitivin (William's son) specifically includes amongst these holdings Headingley mill 'and the millstream as far as the boundary of Linley by the upper lane', which was the highway from Kirkstall to Burley.[305] However, it would appear that the chief lord of the manor and mill changed in the early fourteenth century, as another charter of 1311 records the grant by Thomas Peitivin (William's grandson) to John de Calverley of the manor and mill of Headingley,

---

[293] Ibid., pp. xv–xvi, ms.

[294] Ibid., p. xviii, mss. 239–47 and 270.

[295] On Kirkstall's forge mill, see the brief discussion in Chapter 8.

[296] See Carus-Wilson (1941), p. 45, citing PRO Ancient Extents 86 (1).

[297] On Kirkstall's fulling mill and weaving workshop, see Donkin (1978), pp. 136–7, 188. Also John Stansfield (ed.), 'A Rent Roll of Kirkstall Abbey', *Miscellanea*, Thoresby Society, Vol. 2, Leeds, 1891, p. 13.

[298] *Coucher Book of Kirkstall Abbey*, ms. 89 n. 4 and ms. 98.

[299] Ibid., ms. 98.

[300] Ibid., ms. 322.

[301] Ibid., p. xxiv, mss. 1, 55, 325 and 330.

[302] Ibid., ms. 104.

[303] Ibid., ms. 124.

[304] Ibid., pp. xi–xii, mss. 74, 75 and 78.

[305] Ibid., mss. 73. and 77.

which was subsequently re-granted to Kirkstall by John in 1324.[306] The monks had by this time established a grange in the vill, originally known as New Grange, and later as Kirkstall Grange.

A further series of documents from between 1172 and c. 1200 records a grant of 10 bovates of land in Burdon and Iverker by William de Witon, a subsequent confirmation by his son Hugh, and an agreement between Hugh and Kirkstall over the farm of the millpond of Tofthouse, above the tenement of Wyke. The agreement states that the monks should receive sixpence rent a year in order for Hugh to hold the farm of the millpond and to make the foundation of a milldam on the monks' land, and that they are distrained from taking any action against him or his heirs for any injury caused to their mill of Kirkstall which may have resulted.[307]

Two grants of mill rents to the abbey are contained in an assize of 1348. The first is from John de Longvillers of five shillings annual rent from his mill at Heton,[308] to which is added an additional one mark in a subsequent document, as well as another mark for rents from other land which John held in Heton. This is followed by an earlier grant in the same assize of an annual rent of £1 from Farnley mill by John de Woodlesford. The first mentioned grant is probably from around 1250, whereas the second is possibly as early as 1230.[309] An assize of 1356 confirms the rents to be paid from the vill and mill of Heton, but records the rent of Farnley mill as only seven shillings.[310] Presumably, this reduced rent was a direct result of the Black Death.

Another mill at Bramhope was granted to the monks in free alms sometime around the middle of the thirteenth century, and was subsequently leased to the Hospital of St Leonards at York in 1274 for £2 a year. This was still being paid at the time of the Dissolution.[311] As will be discussed in slightly more detail below, the abbey also constructed two mills with suit in Bramley within the vill of Allerton around 1220.

By the middle of the fourteenth century, Kirkstall held interests in at least 10 grain mills and three industrial mills. It collected rents from the mills of Heton and Farnley and paid at least three knightly patrons significant rents for mills and their associated vills in Keighley, Adel and Headingley. As many as six of the 11 mills which it held were built by the monks, but only the grain mills of Bramley in Allerton appear to have held suit. It is not clear whether the three mills of Adel, Cookridge and Headingley also held suit, although each of the respective mill holdings were attached to whole vills and a manor. It is also unclear whether the monastery's own precinctual mills held suit, or indeed, whether any of the other mills that it held had seigneurial privileges attached to them. The details of these various mills are listed in Tables 7.12.

As mentioned previously, the only rental amount for any of the four grain mills directly held by Kirkstall is for Bramhope mill, which was leased to St Leonard's Hospital for £2 annually, a sum that is more consistent with the medium to low mill rents charged by ecclesiastical houses in the south, rather than those from Yorkshire. The only other data on Kirkstall's revenues is contained in an agreement concerning tithes with the Convent of Trinity Priory, York, from around 1220. Kirkstall undertook to pay the priory an additional seven shillings in tithes from the vill of Allerton after it built the two mills of Bramley in the vill, indicating that the two mills with suit were earning around £3 10s annually in the early thirteenth century.[312] While these figures are not necessarily a reliable guide to the abbey's mill revenues, the rents paid by Kirkstall for the other mills and holdings in the mid-twelfth century and earlier suggest that Kirkstall's rents and revenues were in line with those of other lords throughout England at around the same time.

Considering that five of the seven mills which the monks directly held at the end of the thirteenth century were almost undoubtedly built by them, and three of the seven which they held outright were industrial mills, we appear to have some evidence in support of the claims made by Mumford and White that the Cistercians were technological innovators when it came to the application of water power to industry. However, the monks of Kirkstall appear to have taken a leaf from Furness's book and scrupulously avoided recording any revenue from their mills.

---

[306] Ibid., ms. 75, n.3. See Chapter 9 for a discussion of the dispute over seisin of Headingley mill between Kirkstall and another member of the Peitivin clan in 1337.

[307] Ibid., ms. 116.

[308] Ibid., ms. 379.

[309] Ibid.

[310] Ibid., ms. 390.

[311] Ibid., pp. xv–xvi.

[312] Ibid., ms. 348. An undated charter confirms the grant of a mill in Bramley to the abbey, along with suit of mill and land in Lingarth, by Adam de Reinville, which his grandfather Adam had earlier given the abbey. See ibid., ms. 355.

Table 7.12   Thirteen mills in which Kirkstall Abbey held an interest before 1300

Name	Year acquired	Grantor	Grantee	Rent/ Revenue	Assoc. holding
Kirkstall mill (precinctual)	1152–53?	Henry de Lacy? (built by abbey?)	Kirkstall Abbey	n/a	n/a
Keighley mill	>1162	Adam Fitz Peter (sub-tenant) Robert de Romille (tenant) William Paynel (tenant-in-chief)	"	?	Land in Horsforth and Keighley
"	>1246	Everingham family (sub-tenants) Haverholm Priory (tenant?)	"	£4	2 carucates in Keighley and 1 carucate in Horsforth
Adel mill	>1172	W. Mustel (tenant) William Paynel (tenant-in-chief)	"	£2 (whole vill)	vill of Adel
Scheneself mill (Cookridge)	>1172	R. Mustel (former tenant) William Paynel (tenant-in-chief)	"	?	vill of Cookridge
Headingley mill	1160s–70s	William Peitivin (tenant?)	"	£2 8s	5 1/2 carucates + wood, etc.
"	1324	John de Calverley (sub-tenant)	"	?	manor of Headingley
Kirkstall forge mill	c. 1200	built by abbey	n/a	"	
Bramley mills (x2), Allerton	c. 1220	built by abbey x 1	"	£3 10s (revenue)	
Farnley mill	c. 1230	J. de Woodlesford	"	£1 (7s in 1356)	part rent only
Heton mill	c. 1250	J. de Longvillers	"	5s (+ 13s 4d later)	part rent only
Bramhope mill	mid-13th c.	Bramhope family (tenants) Percy family (tenants-in-chief)	Kirkstall Abbey (sub-tenant: St Leonard's Hospital)	£2 (rent)	
Kirkstall tanning mill	>1288	built by abbey	n/a	n/a	
Kirkstall fulling mill	"	"	"	"	

Conclusion

Direct management of Cistercian mill holdings and the monks' apparent reticence to record mill revenues in their cartularies generally means that account books, extents and rentals are the only means of establishing the levels of income which they were drawing from their mills; such records have survived for only three of the five houses sampled. Nevertheless, for those Cistercian houses for which comparative revenue evidence is available, it is clear the monks from these houses were drawing economic rents from their tenants' mill leases whenever and wherever possible. It is also clear that the order was ignoring prohibitions on it holding suit on its mills from as early as the 1190s in the case of Furness with Stackhouse mill; the 1220s in the cases of Kirkstall and Beaulieu with the mills of Allerton, Beaulieu, Little Faringdon and Rockstead; and the 1250s in the case of Sibton with its windmill of Thwaite.

Beaulieu's average annual income from eight of its seigneurial mills in the financial year 1269–70 was £5, with individual revenues ranging from £1 4s for the mill of Nanclegy in Cornwall, to £9 13s 10d for its mill on the Thames of Kyndlewere, although of course most were drawing grain revenues used to feed *famuli*. The only reliable data for Sibton's seigneurial mill revenues relate to *Fengesmille*, which was drawing £4 9s in 1328, whereas Furness's post-Dissolution average income of £2 11s 2 1/2d from each of 16 of its mills converts to £3 6s 7d prior to the Black Death. The figure derived is comparable to the more extractive average mill revenues charged by ecclesiastical lords in the south and Midlands such as Bec, Hereford and Grove during the late thirteenth and early fourteenth centuries, but on the low side of those being drawn by other lords in the north.

Although there is no reliable data on the revenues drawn by Old Wardon and Kirkstall from their seigneurial mills, the fact that Old Wardon was paying 13s 4d to Newnham Priory in the late twelfth century for mill and hay tithes in Southill suggests it was drawing between £4 and £6 in annual revenue from its mill in Southill. The tithes of seven shillings that Kirkstall paid the Convent of Trinity Priory for its mills of Bramley in the early thirteenth century indicate that it was earning around £1 15s annually from each mill. The only two mills for which there is unambiguous information about rents paid by Old Wardon relate to the mills of Caldecote, for which it was paying £2 10s in the early thirteenth century. While there are rental amounts for five of the six grain mills that were donated to Kirkstall, three of these amounts were paid by Kirkstall to its donors and included very substantial parcels of land (up to 5 1/2 carucates or a vill). The other two amounts are shares that still indicate relatively modest rentals of £2 a year or less. Although this meagre information provides an insecure basis for drawing firm conclusions about the mill revenues earned by these two houses, it is nevertheless fairly clear from this case study that, like the Augustinian houses sampled, if we compare the relative incomes of each house to the number of mills which they held, there is no direct correlation between the two. However, as will be discussed in greater detail in the concluding chapter, there does appear to be a correlation between the number of mills held and whether or not the house concerned was a royal foundation.

Viewed in their totality, however, these data clearly indicate that romantic visions of Cistercian lordly beneficence should be treated with a good deal of scepticism, and are certainly not borne out by the empirical evidence. To the contrary, the Cistercians were, like other ecclesiastical lords with substantial holdings, not averse to ensuring that their tenants paid premium prices for the privilege of using monastic mills to grind their grain. As was the case with the other orders, the highest value mills held suit and were in areas of high population density, while the lower value mills held suit in manors with low populations, or did not hold suit, or were held by tenants in customary and hereditary tenure. At the same time, however, all of the Cistercian houses sampled seem to have been sensitive about recording the revenues from their mills, and either failed to record any income from them or did their best to minimize what income they did make by directly managing their mills and matching income to expenditure, while doling out their grain income to servants.

The origins of the 62 mills which the five houses held in whole or in part by 1364 are provided in Table 7.13. To some extent the results mirror those found for the Augustinians, although the Cistercians benefited more from magnate donations than did the Augustinians, whose initial foundations were mostly by kings and archbishops. However, the proportion of mill donations from knights to the two orders was very similar, at 36.5 per cent for the Augustinians and 38.7 per cent for the Cistercians. The size of the samples for both orders suggests that these figures are indicative. Magnate donations for the Cistercians constituted 14.5 per cent, compared to 5 per cent for the Augustinians, and just under 5 per cent from kings, compared to 11 per cent for the Augustinians. Around 19 per cent of the mills held by the Cistercians were built by them, while the origins of another 18 per cent were not recorded. The Cistercians' mill-building practices will be discussed in more detail below in relation to Table 7.14.

Table 7.13   Patterns of mill acquisition and investment for five Cistercian houses between 1135 and 1364

House/Patron	Sub-Total	Furness	Old Wardon	Kirkstall	Sibton	Beaulieu
Kings	3	1				2
Barons	9	6	1	1	1	
Knights	24	9	2	5	6	2xP
Peasants	2		2			
Other	1	1				
Built by house	12	1	1	5	1	4
Unknown	11	1	1		4	5
TOTAL MILLS	**62**	**19**	**7**	**11**	**12**	**13**

P = purchases

Table 7.14   Mill holdings and annual revenues of five Cistercian houses in the late thirteenth and early fourteenth century

Name	Total no. of mills	Mills with suit	Mills in customary and hereditary tenure	Windmills	Industrial mills	Annual estate revenue
Beaulieu	12	4–10	0	2	4	£263
Furness	16+	11+	0	0	0	£223
Old Wardon	7	1–3	0	0	0	£200
Sibton	9–11	2	1	4	0	£144
Kirkstall	11	2–6	0	0	3	£68+
TOTAL	**55–7**	**20–32**	**1**	**6**	**7**	**£898+**

NB: All estate revenues are taken from the Taxatio Nicolai IV. Kirkstall's figure is for temporalities only, whereas the other four also include spiritualities. Furness's temporalities were assessed at £176 in the Taxatio, and Sibton's at around £133, i.e. two to three times those of Kirkstall.

Examining each house in its turn, the donors to Furness were Stephen and King David of Scotland, and 12 knights, including a tenant-in-chief. Those to Kirkstall were two tenants-in-chief and one knight, with four mills leased to it in perpetuity by knightly donors as parts of subinfeudated knights' fees. Old Wardon's donors were a tenant-in-chief and two knights, while another two knights leased the abbey their shares in two more mills. Henry II, four tenants-in-chief and four knights donated Sibton its mills, while the only recorded mill donors to Beaulieu are King John and two local knights. The only mill that was let to or from other religious houses was a mill leased by Kirkstall from Haverholm Priory in the mid-thirteenth century that had in the previous century been let by the abbey from a knight. Thus we can see how all but one of the mill grantors and vendors to the Cistercians were royalty, tenants-in-chief or members of the knightly class. There is thus a somewhat more aristocratic basis to mill donations made to these Cistercian houses than is seen in those grants and sales made to the Augustinians. It should also be noted that the three royal foundations, i.e., Furness, Sibton and Beaulieu, held a disproportionately large number of mills between them, constituting more than three-quarters of the sample. It would therefore appear that although the relative wealth of the foundations does not appear to have affected the numbers of mills held by them, their royal status did.

With respect to the centuries of origin of these mills, at least 11 of the 62 were acquired by the five houses concerned at the time of their foundations, or almost 18 per cent of them. Four of the five houses acquired 20 mills during the twelfth century, or 32 per cent of the total. Most of the other mills were acquired during the thirteenth century, at 64.5 per cent of the total. Clearly, then, as with the other orders studied so far, the peak of monastic mill ownership was the late thirteenth and early fourteenth centuries, a finding that is consistent with Holt's and Langdon's earlier work and most of the previous scholarship on the medieval economy.

It is also worth noting that Old Wardon, which did not hold many of its own mills, and apparently few with suit, does not appear to have ever committed itself to a policy of mill acquisition. Like Beaulieu, Kirkstall held several industrial mills within its own precincts by 1300, all of which it had built. Five of its eight grain mills were acquired through grants, four of which were attached to significant parcels of land or whole vills. Three of these five paid significant annual rents to their donors, which were effectively perpetual leases of portions of knights' fees. As with Old Wardon, the lack of available land over which the monks of Kirkstall could build a sufficiently large estate to warrant claims of seigneurial rights seems to have encouraged the emergence of such mutually beneficial arrangements whereby the abbey could build up its granges and feed its own monks, retainers and *conversi* with the tollcorn from the mills it directly held and perpetually leased, while its knightly donors could draw reliable cash rents from their seigneurial and non-seigneurial mills without having to directly manage them.

Between 55 and 57 mills were directly held by the five houses at the end of the thirteenth century, six of which were windmills, and seven of which were industrial mills (Table 7.14). Unlike many of the grain mills that the Cistercians held, all of their industrial mills appear to have been built by the houses concerned. The seven industrial mills held by Beaulieu and Kirkstall constitute 12.7 per cent of the total, which is well over twice the percentage of industrial mills found by Langdon on lay lords' estates through his study of the IPM material for Edward II.[313] Even were we to ignore the possibility that Furness held forge mills and possibly water-powered bellows at this stage, this figure alone suggests that White's and Gille's claims for Cistercian technological innovation with respect to the use of industrial mills may well be true.[314] However, it should also be borne in mind that at least two of the five houses appear to have held no industrial mills.

Of the five houses studied, only Beaulieu and Kirkstall appear to have been engaged in any extensive mill building of their own. At least 38 per cent of Beaulieu's mills were built by the abbey before the end of the thirteenth century, while as many as 45 per cent of those mills held by Kirkstall were built by them. It is possible that Sibton may have built as many as five of the 15 mills it held by 1364, or around the same proportion as Beaulieu, but there is only strong evidence for it having built one mill (7 per cent). Likewise, Furness appears to have built only one of the 16 or more mills it held at the end of the thirteenth century (6 per cent), while there is some suggestion that Old Wardon may have built one of the seven mills that it held at this stage (14 per cent). The extent of mill-building activity by the various houses concerned appears to be related to the extent to which they held land in newly settled areas, or were involved in industrial activities.

Like most of the other ecclesiastical lords of the period, Furness, Sibton and Beaulieu seem to have directly managed most of their own mills throughout the thirteenth century. In 1269–70, Beaulieu was leasing only its mills of Little Faringdon and Nanclegy, all three of which were remote from the monastery, and was using miller servants to directly manage at least six of the other nine mills closer to home. Sibton only began to let out its mills at farm in the decades leading up to the Black Death, whereas Furness seems to have only begun to do so after the plague. None of Furness's 15 mills were in customary or hereditary tenure in 1360. In the wake of the plague and the related social and economic shocks, the number had grown radically to 60 per cent by 1530, a strategy that went against Langdon's observation that most lords after the plague tended to lease mills rather than allow them to slip into hereditary tenure.[315] Indeed, only one of the 55 or more Cistercian mills identified up to the early fourteenth century appears to have been an independent tenant mill, i.e., the mill of Weybread held by Sibton. At least 35 per cent of Cistercian mills in the sample held suit, although the proportion may have been as high as 58 per cent. The proportions held by the northern house of Furness and the southern house of Beaulieu ranged between 33 per cent and 75 per cent. As few as one-fifth of Kirkstall's, Sibton's and Old Wardon's mills appear to have held suit, which successive abbots and monks from both houses do not appear to have believed was an obstacle to their involvement in milling.

The records of the five houses' revenues in tollcorn and mill rents from this period indicate that while some of them may not have been drawing particularly large revenues from the majority of their mills, whenever the house concerned held suit, it drew a relatively high income from that mill. The evidence from Beaulieu in the late thirteenth century clearly bears this out, as does that from Sibton in the thirteenth and fourteenth century, and Furness in the mid-sixteenth century. This evidence also clearly demonstrates that the Cistercians were perfectly willing to extract as much revenue as they could from their tenants, and in the case of Beaulieu, were receiving very substantial returns from their mills, constituting more than a tenth of their total income in the late thirteenth century.

Despite the clear interest in mills and milling displayed by all five Cistercian houses sampled, several pieces of evidence suggest that the White Monks were somewhat nervous about their status regarding mill ownership in the twelfth and thirteenth centuries. The general lack of detail concerning mill revenues in the surviving mill records for three of the houses, as well as Kirkstall's policy of perpetually leasing several of its mills from other lords, combined with the efforts of Beaulieu and Sibton in their account books to minimize the high incomes they were clearly making from some of their mills, clearly attest to some continuing

---

[313] By the time of the Dissolution, Kirkstall and Old Wardon also held a single fulling mill each, and Furness, two.

[314] See Lucas (2005), in which I discuss the historical background to the IRMA thesis, and assess the empirical evidence used to support it. In the English translation to Bertrand Gille's *The History of Techniques*, Vol. 1 (1986), p. 84, he comments, 'It would be interesting ... to study Cistercian techniques in certain areas in order to discover how the diffusion of highly advanced techniques and their modification came about, and how these techniques themselves came about.' Indeed it would, but surely this is something which Gille, White and Mumford should have done *before* they began asserting that the Cistercians were leaders in medieval technological innovation.

[315] Langdon (2004), pp. 220–21. His computer sample of 330 manors found that only 16.2 per cent of mills recorded between 1530 and 1540 had independent tenant status. Although this was the highest proportion over the whole period from 1300 to 1540, almost 68 per cent of these mills were industrial.

discomfort within the order about being involved in milling, and in particular collecting revenues from mills that they owned and directly managed. As with its similar lack of enforcement of the prohibitions relating to commercial trafficking in the wool trade, the Cistercians clearly believed that milling and wool growing were far too profitable practices for them to relinquish or abandon.[316] Such issues have never, to the best of my knowledge, been raised by any of the historians of technology who have praised the Cistercians for their innovative attitudes to milling technology.

---

[316] See Knowles (1950), pp. 67–9, and Donkin (1978) for an overview of Cistercian involvement in the medieval wool trade; Bell, Brooks and Dryburgh (2007) for a case study of the Cistercian abbey of Pipewell.

Chapter 8
The Minor Orders

Amongst those minor orders which possessed mills or collected the revenues from mills were several kinds of houses: those established by some of the less influential monastic orders, such as the Premonstratensians; alien religious houses with holdings in England that were administered by either dependent cells or lay employees; and aristocratic family foundations with no specific clerical affiliation. Five such houses have been chosen for the sample, two of which were Premonstratensian, i.e. Cockersand Abbey and Leiston Priory, while the third was founded by an alien nunnery, i.e. Grove Priory by Fontevrault, and the fourth was an alien nunnery with holdings in England managed by laymen, i.e. Holy Trinity, Caen. The fifth was an aristocratic family foundation, i.e. the Wakebridge Chantries at Crich.

The Abbey of the Holy Trinity, Caen, was a ducal family foundation by William I and his wife Matilda shortly before the Conquest; Grove Priory was a royal foundation by Henry II as an alien dependency of Fontevrault that was established around 1164; Leiston and Cockersand Abbeys were Premonstratensian houses founded respectively by Ranulf de Glanville and Hugh the Hermit in the early 1180s; and the Wakebridge Chantries at Crich were knightly family foundations established in 1349 and 1367. The five houses were located in Poitou, Bedfordshire, Suffolk, Lancashire and Derbyshire. Most of Holy Trinity's English property was located in Norfolk, Essex, Dorset, Gloucestershire and Wiltshire, whereas Grove's holdings were in Bedfordshire and Buckinghamshire, and those of Leiston in Sussex and Yorkshire. Cockersand's estates were almost exclusively in Lancashire and those of the Wakebridge Chantries in Derbyshire.

Most of Holy Trinity's English lands were ancient demesne that had been granted to it by the king and queen in the late eleventh century, while most of the property that it subsequently acquired appears to have been almost exclusively by purchase. The vast majority of Grove Priory's lands were similarly acquired through the generosity of Henry I and Henry II, although the extant documents give no indication of how additional properties, if any, were secured. The Wakebridge Chantries, being an aristocratic family foundation without any connection to a particular monastic order, appear to have received most of their property through the efforts of William of Wakebridge, although several knights and Edward III were involved in granting, selling or licensing the alienation of the chantries' various lands. The patrons of the two Premonstratensian houses of Cockersand and Leiston consisted of a significant number of small freeholders and knightly families in the case of Cockersand, and knightly relatives and subordinates of the founding patron in the case of Leiston.

While their records provide few details of mill revenues, they do not suggest the order was any more or less oppressive towards its tenants than the other orders, although those who patronized both houses were generally of a lower rank than had been the norm for most religious houses in earlier years.

A number of female heirs and owners are recorded amongst the documents of all three houses, clearly indicating the importance of female descent in knightly tenure and its importance relative to patrilineality in establishing a family's noble lineage. The records of Holy Trinity, Grove and Wakebridge also demonstrate how important it was for newly founded houses to acquire mills through grant and purchase in order to raise their cash incomes. Unfortunately, there are no records of the valuations of any of these religious houses' estates in either the *Taxatio Nicholai IV* or the *Valor Ecclesiasticus*, although there are extensive records of mill revenues available for Holy Trinity and Grove, and to a lesser extent, Wakebridge, allowing some room for comparison across these three houses.

The Priory of Grove, a.k.a. Grovebury or La Grave Priory (alien dependency of Fontevrault Abbey)

Grove Priory, also known as Grovebury or La Grave Priory, was founded by Henry II sometime around 1164 as an alien dependency of the wealthy and influential abbey of Fontevrault in Anjou. In 1129, Henry I had endowed the nuns of Fontevrault with £100 of Rouen currency and another 50 marks in rents from the Farms of London and Winchester. This was later changed from a cash payment to a grant in 1164 by

Henry II. The latter's largesse consisted of £60 worth of land, i.e. the royal manor of Lecton (now Leighton Buzzard) in Bedfordshire for £56, and land in Radnage, Buckinghamshire, for £4.[1] As we saw in Chapter 1, both Henry and his queen were buried at Fontevrault, and this, perhaps, was part of their down-payment.

Situated on the Ousel or Lovent brook close to the south-west edge of the parish bounds between Leighton Buzzard in Bedfordshire and the Buckinghamshire parish of Grove, the alien priory of Grove was founded soon after the grant of the manor of Lecton by Henry II. The earliest extant manuscript reference to it dates to 1194, in which the prior is described as the 'Prior of Lecton'. By the time of the Bedford Eyre of 1227, the priory of Lecton had been renamed the Chapel of St John de Grava.[2] The chapel was apparently not connected to the vill of Grove or to the Church of Leighton or prebendal lands.[3]

The immediate surrounds and holdings of the priory are of some interest, as its farm buildings were organised around some large and very deep fishponds, while the mound of a windmill that was held by the priory could still be seen early in the twentieth century just north of the former chapel on the ancient road known as Thede Way.[4] Despite its relatively small size, the priory was earning over £180 a year in the mid-fourteenth century, including substantial revenues from five mills, of which two were windmills, while one of its three watermills was dedicated to malted grains.[5]

Apart from four hides of land within its boundaries that were held by the bishop of Lincoln, Leighton had been a royal manor up until the time it was granted to Fontevrault. Before the priory's foundation, Henry II had also granted 32 shillings worth of rents within the manor to Woburn Abbey. At the time of foundation, he gave the Woburn nuns an equivalent sum of rent on land elsewhere. An extent of 1154–57 indicates that in the decade before Grove's foundation, the king's constable, Henry of Essex, had been involved in restocking this and other royal manors in Bedfordshire and Buckinghamshire in the wake of the civil war between Stephen and Matilda.[6]

The documents relevant to Grove's mill holdings are an extent from around 1318, and a bailiff's account of 1341–42. The first makes clear reference to five mills that are all at farm, whereas the less specific entries pertaining to income of grain and cash from the later account book indicate that the same five mills were then operating, and were also still at farm, except that the malt mill appears to have been in hand at this time. At the time that the extent was taken, Edward II's sister, Mary of Woodstock, appears to have been the tenant-in-chief, whereas Lady Maud, Countess of Ulster, was tenant-in-chief when the bailiff's account was compiled.[7] Unfortunately, there appear to be no extant charters for any of Grove's holdings.

By the time that the early fourteenth century extent was taken, the priory held six manors and a handful of other properties in the vill of Radnage. The assessed land area was very substantial at 17 and a half carucates, or more than 2,000 acres. The original grant of the royal manor of Lecton/Grove consisted of six carucates, and more than one additional carucate held by customary tenants in demesne in the parish of Leighton. The total value for the two properties was £60 a year. Customary rents, farm of the market and perquisites of court were worth an extra £54 in a normal year.[8]

There were three mills on the manor in 1318, two of which were watermills in one house dedicated respectively to grinding corn and malted barley, and a windmill that held suit which had presumably been built by the priory. It also drew rents from two manors that were within Leighton parish, and three that were outside it. The former were the manors of Clipston, which consisted of two carucates, and Reach, which consisted of two and a half carucates. The latter were Stewkley, which consisted of three carucates with wood; Studham near Dunstable, which consisted of two carucates, a windmill and wood; and Northall which consisted of one

---

[1]   Ibid., pp. 17–18.

[2]   'Three Records of the Alien Priory of Grove', p. 15.

[3]   Ibid., p. 17.

[4]   Ibid., pp. 16–17.

[5]   Ibid., p. 25.

[6]   Ibid., pp. 15–18.

[7]   Ibid., pp. 19–21. Lady Maud was a Lancaster and the widow of William de Burgh, Earl of Ulster, who was murdered in Ireland in 1333. Their daughter Elizabeth married Edward's third son Lionel, and their great-great-great-grandson was Edward IV.

[8]   Ibid., 'Extent of the Manor of Grove', pp. 24–5. The customary rents were worth £6 annually, and were for Heuepanes, Giuepanes and St Peter's Pence. Farm of the market was worth £8 and perquisites of court £40. See Richmond's comments on p. 20 of the 'Introduction' regarding the likely nature and origins of the customary payments.

carucate and a watermill. The rents from these manors and its other holdings in Radnage amounted to another £69 a year.[9] Despite the priory's relative obscurity in the annals of English monasticism, it was obviously a comparatively wealthy house, holding more than 2,000 acres of land and paying over £180 in annual rents to the abbess of Fontevrault in the mid-fourteenth century, a sum that was certainly comparable to the revenues of some of the larger Cistercian houses of the time.

Unfortunately, the extent does not record the earnings from the double watermill at Leighton Grove or the windmill at Grove. On the other hand, although rents are provided for the manors on which the other two mills were situated, those manors consisted of a carucate of land or more, making it difficult to accurately assess what each individual mill was earning. The farm of Studham windmill with a wood and two carucates of land drew £8 a year, while Northall watermill with a carucate drew £6 a year.[10] While the windmill of Grove is clearly stated to have held suit, it seems likely that the manorial mills of Studham and Northall did also.

In the account book of 1341–42, although only one cash rent of 16 shillings is given for the farm of Northall mill,[11] the produce and tollcorn from the other mills is specified for this and the other four mills. Northall appears to have produced 10 quarters 2 bushels 2 perches of toll wheat,[12] whereas the malt mill of Leighton Grove produced 41 quarters 2 bushels of malt,[13] and the three other mills let to farm provided 89 quarters of toll wheat, the last of which was all fed to the priory's servants and free grainger.[14] Apart from similar information contained in the Beaulieu account-book, this is one of the few clear indications that we have encountered in this study of how much tollcorn was being consumed by servants and retainers as a proportion of total mill revenue for a single house. While the grainger's wages are not recorded, the nominal wages of 16 winter servants and 22 summer servants are listed, amounting to the lowly sum of £2 18s 4 1/2d.[15] It is therefore clear that the payment of tollcorn to these servants was an important supplement to their incomes.

If we combine the cash farm of Northall mill with the cash value of the malt and tollcorn produced by all five mills, a figure of £19 4s 5d can be calculated based on conservative sales figures for the priory's other grains.[16] It would appear on the basis of these figures that about 60 per cent of the mill's revenues were therefore paid as liveries to servants, which was about 70 per cent of their revenue in grain. This would make the average annual earnings for one of the priory's demesne servants around £1 3s 4d expressed as a cash sum, which was fairly typical for the period. It is not clear whether the remaining grain and malt was sold, stored or used by the prior's household, although the latter seems most likely.

A summary of the information contained in the extent of 1318 is set out below in Table 8.1. Although there are no charters relating to Grove's holdings, the double mill of Leighton Grove was probably acquired as part of the foundation grant from Henry II, whereas the windmills and Northall watermill were either later grants from other donors, or built by the priory itself.

Table 8.1   Five mills held by Grove Priory in 1318

	Name	Annual revenue
1.	Leighton Grove grain mill	no data
2.	Leighton Grove malt mill	no data
3.	Grove windmill	no data
4.	Studham windmill (with wood and 2 carucates)	£8
5.	Northall watermill (with 1 carucate)	£6

[9]   Ibid.

[10]   Ibid., p. 25.

[11]   Ibid., 'Bailiff's Accounts of the Manor of Grove, Michaelmas 1341 to Michaelmas 1342 [Receipts or 'Charge']: Farms', p. 27.

[12]   Ibid., 'First Schedule or Grain Account: Grove – Wheat [Receipts]', p. 34.

[13]   Ibid., 'First Schedule or Grain Account: Grove – Supply of Malt [Receipts]', p. 38.

[14]   Ibid., 'First Schedule or Grain Account: Grove – Payments to Servants [Receipts]', p. 37.

[15]   Ibid., 'Wages of Servants', p. 32.

[16]   This assumes a low figure relative to the priory's sales that year of 3s per quarter for malt (*brasei*), and 2s 8d per quarter for wheat, because the best grain was generally sold and the poorer quality grain kept for feeding servants.

While the 1318 extent provides the only information about cash revenues from the priory's mills, the later account book entries provide a fairly clear indication of total mill revenues as a proportion of total income. Total annual receipts for the priory for the financial year of 1341–42 amounted to £183 5s 0 1/8d, which is an almost identical amount to those earnings expressed in the earlier extent, suggesting that its income had remained static during the intervening three decades. Its outgoing payments were £117 0s 9 1/4d.

Assuming the mills' cash revenues for the year amounted to £19 4s 5d, around 10.5 per cent of Grove's revenues in 1341–42 were derived from its mills, while its average income per mill at that time was £3 16s 10 1/2d. Considering that the total revenues for the two records are virtually identical, it would seem safe to assume that the priory's mill revenues also remained relatively unchanged between 1318 and 1342. If we compare this figure with Langdon's findings regarding average mill incomes of £2 2s 10d for lay lords in the Home Counties in the period from 1307 to 1327 based on the Edward II IPMs (a figure which has been doubled in order to make a fair comparison with manorial account records), Grove's average mill revenues were almost 80 per cent higher than those of the average lay lord at around the same time.[17] It is clear, therefore, that the priory was drawing high revenues from its mills when compared with its lay counterparts. The most pertinent of this information is set out below in Table 8.2.

Table 8.2   Total and average revenues for five mills held by Grove Priory in 1318 and 1341–42

	1318	1341–42
Total mill revenues	£20	£19 4s 5d
Average mill revenue	£4	£3 16s 10 1/2d
Total revenue from all sources	-	£183 5s 0 1/2d
Proportion of total revenue derived from mills	**?**	**10.5%**

These data clearly indicate that Grove's average revenues from its mills were comparable to those of the more extractive southern lords and large Benedictine and Cistercian houses such as Hereford, Bec and Beaulieu. Its revenues also appear to have remained stable between 1318 and the early 1340s, suggesting that its manors in Bedfordshire and Buckinghamshire were relatively unaffected by the crop failures of 1314–15. It is clear from the high revenues from these mills that they almost certainly all held seigneurial status, ensuring that the priory maintained a close eye on their revenues, converting cash payments to payments in grain sometime between 1318 and 1341 in order to maintain or maximize their income. The proportion of manorial income which Grove appears to have derived from its mills at 10.5 per cent in 1341–42 was also 75 per cent higher than the average for lay lords in the Home Counties only a few decades earlier, which Langdon found derived an average of 6 per cent of their manorial income from mills.[18] While not as high a proportion of manorial income as that enjoyed by northern lords and the aforementioned ecclesiastical lords, it was still significant, and once again bears out my contention that ecclesiastical lords who held a high proportion of their mills with seigneurial status tended to extract higher revenues from their demesne tenants than most of their lay counterparts.

Leiston Abbey (Premonstratensian)

Leiston Abbey and the Augustinian priory of Butley were both founded by Ranulf de Glanville, once sheriff of Yorkshire and later chief justiciar of England. In 1171, while still but a minor royal servant, Ranulf founded Butley, whereas Leiston was not founded until 1183 when he had been elevated to the position of chief justiciar. The foundation grant for Leiston included the manor of Leiston with the neighbouring church of Knodishall, while many of its canons, including the first abbot, were 'borrowed' from the nearby abbey of Welbeck, as well as from Durford. Ranulf pursued this latter strategy because he wanted Leiston to be the greatest Premonstratensian foundation in England, and to thereby avoid the exactions of a mother house.

---

[17]   See Langdon (1994), p. 13.

[18]   Ibid.

After papal confirmation of its holdings in 1185, Leiston exchanged the church of Knodishall for the churches of Leiston and Aldringham which were then held by Butley. The exchange and foundation grants were confirmed later in the same year by Henry II, and two years later by the bishop of Norwich.[19] Gerald of Wales records that the house was founded for 26 canons, but by the late fifteenth century, there were only about 15, including novices.[20]

Like most Premonstratensian foundations, Leiston was established in a remote area, about three kilometres inland from the Suffolk coast and about 40 kilometres north-east of Ipswich. Its first site appears to have been an island or prominence within a marsh, but was a poor location from a number of perspectives, so was moved to within a few kilometres of the town of Leiston sometime between 1365 and 1380, just to the south of Blythburgh and Sibton. The first site had been inundated by the sea, probably in the early 1360s, with its buildings virtually ruined because their foundations had been undermined. After having already appropriated the church of Corton some years before, the abbey sought a license to alienate the church of Theberton in order to improve its financial situation.[21] However, Leiston was again struck by misfortune when its conventual buildings, with the exception of the church, were destroyed by a fire, and most of its lands made barren, presumably by flooding. After having been itself fined £50 for oppression when acting as a collector of subsidies in the 1330s and 1340s, the abbey had to plead poverty in 1380 in order to recover its sequestered goods because it could not pay its subsidy.[22]

A relatively small number of documents survive from Leiston, including a cartulary and an early thirteenth century register of deeds, but very little else, and few of these are original documents. About three-quarters of these consist of grants to the abbey, but there are also papal, royal, archiepiscopal and abbatial documents, grants from laymen to other laymen, confirmations, quitclaims, exchanges, leases, and purchases, amongst other things. As with many other monastic documents of the Middle Ages, the earlier ones are more concerned with who was in seisin, while the later ones are preoccupied with territorial borders and boundaries.[23] Leiston's history during the thirteenth century is particularly sketchy, although none of the material dealt with here post-dates the 1360s.

By the end of the thirteenth century, most of Leiston's property was within a 20-kilometre radius of the abbey in Suffolk, although it held several other properties in more far-flung areas. Its possessions were a mixture of manors and subinfeudated portions of knights' fees, and were mostly acquired during the late twelfth and thirteenth centuries. Its main possessions included eight churches in Corton, Kirkley, Middleton, Theberton, Leiston, Knodishall, Aldringham and Culpho, and land in 19 vills, including Chediston, Cookley, Yoxford, Dennington, Fordley, Kelsale, Rendham, Swefling, Sizewell, Friston, Farnham, Glevering, Grundisbergh, Hacheston, Orford, Tuddenham, Playford and Sutton (Figure 8.1). The priory's total revenue from its spiritualities and temporalities was valued at £147 in the *Taxatio* of 1291, the spiritualities being valued at over £56, and its temporalities at over £91. By 1535, the value of its spiritualities had dropped to £37, while those of its temporalities had increased to £145.[24]

Leiston appears to have held at least four mills, one or more of which were included in the manor of Leiston as part of its foundation, as well as a watermill at Langwade (Farnham), and two or more mills at Orford and Glevering, all of which were granted to it in the early thirteenth century. All four of its mills appear to have been directly managed. Two were earning relatively high incomes in the early thirteenth century.

[19]   *Leiston Abbey Cartulary and Butley Priory Charters*, pp. 1–3.

[20]   Giraldus Cambrensis, iv. 245.

[21]   The first church was appropriated from Adam de Cockfield and others, while the second was from Margaret, countess of Norfolk, in exchange for £2 rent and the provision of two chaplains to daily celebrate there. Adam was the same man who had sought to acquire the half-hundred of Cosford and the townships of Groton and Semer by hereditary right from Abbot Samson of Bury St Edmunds (see Butler's edition of *The Chronicle of Jocelin of Brakelond*, pp. 58–9, 138–9, also the discussion of Bury and Adam in Chapter 1), while Margaret was the countess who had proved such a troublesome neighbour to Sibton Abbey (see the discussion of Sibton's dispute with Margaret in Chapter 9). In 1382, Margaret released Leiston from the £2 rent and the provision of one of the chaplains in exchange for the advowson of Kirkley. Margaret was obviously more favourably disposed to the Premonstratensians than to the Cistercians!

[22]   *Leiston Abbey Cartulary and Butley Priory Charters*, pp. 6–7.

[23]   Ibid., pp. 29–41.

[24]   Ibid., p. 21.

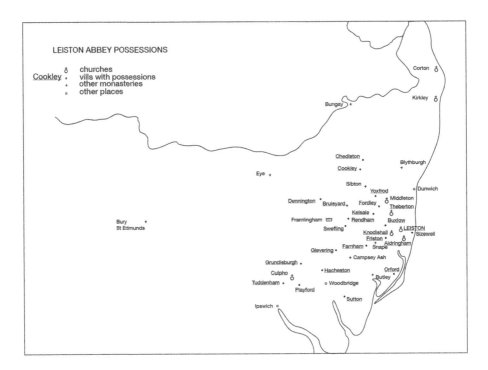

Fig. 8.1   Possessions of Leiston Abbey. After Mortimer (1979)

The earliest document recording any mention of mills is a grant from Henry II to Ranulf de Glanville of Leiston manor and some other property and rents dated to 1175–76,[25] which is followed by Ranulf's foundation grant to Leiston dated 1186–89,[26] and several other confirmations of the endowment by Henry II (December 1184–May 1185),[27] Richard I (14 October 1189),[28] and his brother John (October 1189–March 1190, and 14 May 1201),[29] as well as a charter of liberties from Henry II (May 1185–July 1189).[30] There are only six other charters which make any reference to mills, all of which are grants from the first half of the thirteenth century.

The first two of these latter documents is a grant dated to before 1212 from Rannulf de Onehouse and his brother-in-law Norman de Peasenhall to Leiston of the mill of *Lag Wade* (Langwade) in Farnham with suit, woods and a millpond, as well as another pond known as *Smithespol* and the woods and lands adjacent. Norman was either a knightly tenant of Ranulf de Glanville, or a former ward of Ranulf's while he was still a minor, and possibly a distant relative by marriage.[31] The grant does not include an annual pension of two marks that was the marriage portion of Rannulf's wife, Petronilla. Norman and Rannulf appear to have been joint owners of the mill prior to the two marks in rent from it being given by Norman as his sister's marriage portion. Rannulf was paid an additional 40 marks (£26 13s 4d) 'consideration' for the mill, ponds and woods.[32]

---

[25]   Ibid., ms. 26.

[26]   Ibid., ms. 27.

[27]   Ibid., ms. 24.

[28]   Ibid., ms. 23.

[29]   Ibid., mss. 29 and 28. The first of these was while John was still Count of Mortain.

[30]   Ibid., ms. 25.

[31]   Ibid., p. 15.

[32]   Ibid., mss. 63 and 64.

This grant and sale were not without subsequent difficulties, however. In Easter term 1221, the abbot of Leiston was sued by one William Russell who claimed that Langwade mill was his. The abbot requested that Rannulf warranty the original grant in court, which he did.[33] Two years later, William sued Rannulf for the mill, who in turn vouched his wife Petronilla to warrant, as well as her brother Norman.[34] In 1234 – presumably after Rannulf had died – Petronilla sued the abbot for the mill, arguing that it was hers as a marriage portion, and that the abbot had entry only through her husband. The mill had by this stage been taken into the king's hands, presumably because of its status as part of a knight's fee,[35] but the case is never referred to again. It would appear that this mill was very profitable, judging from the large sum paid to Rannulf by the canons for seisin.

Another grant dating from around the same time was made by Michael de Orford to the abbey of a meadow in Grundisburgh of his fee, which also mentions, and presumably thereby confirms, that his predecessors had given the canons a mill and messuage in the vill of Orford. All of these were given for the souls of himself and his ancestors and successors.[36] Nothing else is mentioned of this mill in the abbey's other documents. Presumably it was directly managed.

Sometime before 1225, Gerard 'Parker' of Dennington granted the abbey his mill-site of 'Holyoak' which Galfredus of Dennington had previously held of him. The grant was made in return for the prayers of the canons for his own soul and those of his ancestors and successors.[37] The Parkers of Dennington were a knightly family that were donors to both Leiston and Butley and were probably related to de Glanville's family by marriage.[38] It is not clear whether the canons ever took advantage of this grant by rebuilding Holyoak mill, although the absence of subsequent mentions of this site would suggest that it did not.

The only other references to mills granted or held by Leiston are in two documents of the early thirteenth century and from before 1235. The first of these is a grant from Jocelin de Hispania of all his land and a messuage in the vill of Glevering, including its 'waters and mills' ('*in aquis et molendinis*'), for two marks of rent annually and prayers for his own soul, that of Ranulf de Glanville, and also Jocelin's ancestors and successors.[39] The next document is more specific, repeating the terms of the other grant, but also mentioning specifically Jocelin's half share of the Glevering mill as being part of the grant. It does not, however, mention the two marks rent or the service of half a knight due from his fee.[40] It is possible that Jocelin continued to fulfil the latter obligations, however, as was the case with respect to Burscough Priory, for example.

Table 8.3   Four mills held by Leiston Abbey before 1250

Name	Year acquired	Grantor	Annual revenue
Leiston mill	1186–89	Ranulf de Glanville	no data
Langwade watermill (with ponds and woods)	>1212 £33 6s 8d 'consideration' to Rannulf de O.	Rannulf de Onehouse (kt.) and Norman de Peasenhall (kt.)	2 m (1/2 share)
Orford mill (with messuage)	early 13th c.	Michael de Orford's (kt.) predecessors	no data
Glevering mill (1/2 share with land, waters and messuage)	early 13th c.	Jocelin de Hispania (kt.)	2 m (+ 1/2 knight's service fulfilled by donor?)

A summary of the information contained in Leiston's mill-related charters is reproduced in Table 8.3. It is clear from these data that all of the mill grants to Leiston were from knights or knightly families, two of which were related to the Glanvilles (i.e. the Peasenhalls and Parkers), and one who directly served them (i.e. Jocelin

[33] *Curia Regis Rolls*, x. 46, c.f. 220.

[34] Ibid., xi. 39 and 996.

[35] Ibid., xv. 939.

[36] Ibid., ms. 77.

[37] Ibid., ms. 49.

[38] Ibid., p. 15.

[39] Ibid., ms. 93.

[40] Ibid., ms. 94.

de Hispania). The large consideration paid to Rannulf de Onehouse for Langwade mill and the subsequent disputes over its seisin by first William Russell and later Rannulf's wife Petronilla would appear to indicate that this was a very profitable mill. Petronilla had been drawing a two mark pension from a half share of the mill, which is the same amount which Jocelin de Hispania received from Leiston for a half share of Glevering mill. Although we have seen instances of similar fractional holdings of individual mills varying significantly in the revenues generated (such as one of Battle Abbey's mills in the manor of Wye in Kent which had fallen out of demesne control), it seems reasonable to assume that a doubling of the half share revenues of Langwade and Glevering mills probably gives a fair indication of their annual revenue. The figure rendered is £2 13s 4d.

Considering that lay lords in East Anglia in the early fourteenth century were only averaging £1 19s 2d from their mills,[41] Leiston appears to have been drawing well over 30 percent more revenue from its mills almost a century earlier. Because this sum is very much comparable to the revenues from other ecclesiastical mills with suit from the late thirteenth and early fourteenth century, there are strong grounds for concluding that all four mills held suit. The high revenues which Leiston appears to have been drawing from its mills in the early thirteenth century provides further evidence that ecclesiastical lords, no matter what their clerical affiliation, tended to extract far more revenue from their mills on average than did lay lords.

English lands of Holy Trinity Abbey, Caen (Aristocratic Family Foundation)

The abbeys of the Holy Trinity and St Stephen's in Caen were both founded by William I and his wife Matilda while the former was still duke of Normandy between 1059 and 1066. The nunnery of the Holy Trinity was dedicated on 18 June 1066 shortly before William's conquest of England, at which time he offered his daughter Cecilia as a child oblate. By the time of his wife's burial there in 1083, the abbey had been endowed with substantial holdings on both sides of the Channel. Most of the abbey's French endowments were given by Matilda and were situated around Caen, while William endowed the abbey early on with the tithes of six parishes on the Isle of Jersey.[42]

Because of its favoured status as a ducal abbey that was founded just prior to the Conquest, Holy Trinity was able to rapidly accumulate a number of generous donations from the royal family. Of the four English manors granted to the abbey in 1082, two were the special gifts of Queen Matilda, i.e., Felsted in Essex and Tarrant Launceston in Dorset, while Minchinhampton and Pinbury in Gloucestershire were probably gifts from the king. All were ancient demesne manors and included the liberties they had enjoyed during the reign of Edward the Confessor. Before the Conquest, Minchinhampton had been held by Countess Goda, Pinbury by the king, Felsted by the earls Edgar and Algar, and Tarrant Launceston by Brictric, sheriff of Wiltshire.[43] In 1083, the four manors were assigned to various obedientiaries, with Minchinhampton assigned to the nun's kitchen and for hospitality, while the other three were assigned to the abbey's wardrobe and for the provision of wood. The abbey's possessions are recorded in Domesday Book, and were held by it until the fifteenth century, when the war with France ended the abbey's relationship with England.[44]

By the end of the twelfth century, the abbey held seven manors. These were Horstead in Norfolk, Felsted in Essex, Pinbury, Minchinhampton and Avening in Gloucestershire, Tilshead on Salisbury Plain in Wiltshire, and Tarrant Launceston in Dorset (Figure 8.2). It also owned property in Lowesmore and Aston in Gloucestershire. These were two hamlets some distance away from Avening which made up a separate tithing group.[45] Avening appears to have been granted to the nuns by William I late in his reign as compensation to them for having lost the manors of Great Baddow in Essex and Umberleigh in Devon shortly after they were first granted in 1083. Tilshead and Horstead were the gifts of Henry I and his brother William Rufus, respectively.[46] The abbey also briefly held another manor known as *Dineslai* (probably Temple Dinsley in

---

[41]   Langdon (1994), p. 13. As previously noted, the figures from Langdon's table are doubled in order to reflect the difference between them and those of manorial account books.

[42]   *Charters and Custumals of the Abbey of Holy Trinity Caen*, p. xxi.

[43]   *Domesday Book*, Gloucestershire, Ch. 23, 166a; Essex, Ch. 15, 21b and 22a; Dorset, Ch. 21, 79a.

[44]   *Charters and Custumals of the Abbey of Holy Trinity Caen*, pp. xxiv–xxv.

[45]   Ibid., p. xxxiii.

[46]   Ibid., pp. xxv–xxvi.

Fig. 8.2   The English manors of the Abbey of Holy Trinity, Caen. After Chibnall (1982)

Hertfordshire) during Henry I's reign that was later held by the Templars, who had in turn acquired it from King Stephen and Bernard de Baliol.[47]

Holy Trinity appears to have held at least 18 mills throughout the twelfth century on at least five of its manors. There were at least 21 mills associated with these manors at Domesday, suggesting that the milling capacity of those that remained had been increased in the intervening period, as the populations of the various manors had undoubtedly risen during that time.[48] In the first half of the thirteenth century, the abbey acquired additional properties in the manor of Minchinhampton and Felsted by purchase, as well as in London.

While very few of the abbey's English charters and leases have survived, three detailed surveys of the abbey's estates were conducted during the twelfth century, the first between 1106 and 1127 (but probably before 1113), and the second and third between 1167 and 1176. Both these and later surveys included an outline of the abbey's property and stock holdings in each manor, the amount of corn sown and stored, their free and servile tenants, and the rents and some of the customary services due from them, along with statements of those holdings which owed regular works and any encroachments upon the demesne. The first was possibly stimulated by the depredations of powerful neighbours in France as the result of Robert Curthose's weak rule of Normandy and similar upheavals in England in the wake of William II's death. This was also the period during which William I's daughter, Cecilia, was abbess of the monastery. Cecilia was as able an administrator as her father and brother, Henry I, and this early survey under her abbacy shows many of the same criteria for structuring the entries as those conducted at the same time on the royal manors.[49] The second and third surveys

---

47   Ibid., pp. xxvi–xxvii.

48   *Domesday Book*, Gloucestershire, Ch. 1, 163d, Ch. 23, 166a; Essex, Ch. 15, 21b and 22a; Dorset, Ch. 21, 79a; Norfolk, Ch. 1, 140b and entry 235.

49   *Charters and Custumals of the Abbey of Holy Trinity Caen*, pp. xxvi–xxxi.

were conducted sometime between 1167 and 1176 (but probably before 1169) in the wake of the anarchy during Stephen's reign, when the abbey's holdings were seriously compromised by peasant assarts of wood and waste, as well as the unscrupulous behaviour of the abbess's principal representative in England, Simon of Felsted, of whom we will learn more shortly. This was a period during which many such investigations were conducted by great landholders throughout England, such as that undertaken by the king's chief steward of his royal manors in Buckinghamshire and Bedfordshire as already discussed in relation to Grove Priory's holdings. The manor of Tarrant Launceston was not included in these surveys. For convenience's sake and to avoid confusion, I will from henceforth refer to these two late twelfth century surveys as the second survey.

Two more surveys of Minchinhampton, Avening and Felsted were conducted sometime between 1183 and 1227 (but probably after 1192), at a time when direct exploitation of the demesne by bailiff farmers had just begun (Figure 8.3). While most of the Minchinhampton survey has been lost, all are notable for including details of demesne furlongs and woods, and contain much more detail on the customs and services owed than any of the previous surveys. Only one mill rental of 7s 6d is recorded, however, which is for the mill of Nailsworth (*Neylsworth*) in Avening with a quarter virgate leased to Roger de Neyls (wort). This is probably the mill simply labeled Avening mill I in the table of mills recorded from the 1167–76 survey. It was leased to a widow for a penny by the early fourteenth century.[50]

An additional, much more detailed, survey of the manor of Felsted was conducted in 1224–25, and is characteristic of the kinds of documentation conducted on estates where direct management of the demesne by bailiffs had replaced the previous custom of letting property to farmers. As with the previous two surveys, it therefore seems safe to assume that the reason why it contains no information about mill rents is that all three of the Felsted mills were directly managed at this time. The manor appears to have been kept in the demesne for about a century after the date of this survey.

Another custumal was drawn up around 1306–7 for the manor of Minchinhampton, and is much the same in form and content as the early thirteenth century survey of Felsted. Unlike the Felsted survey, however, all of the mills of Minchinhampton are recorded as having been let to free and customary tenants, suggesting a variation in the abbey's mill management practices which will be the subject of further scrutiny below. Four rentals of the fifteenth century, and sixteenth-century surveys of Felsted and Horstead remain unpublished. As Holy Trinity had lost control of its English possessions by this time, these documents fall outside the limits of this study.[51]

Holy Trinity never established a dependent cell of nuns in England, and does not appear to have ever intended to do so. Its estates were always administered through its agents in England. In the early twelfth century, the manors were all at farm, two of which were managed by groups of farmers, presumably with one or more agents collecting annual revenues and ensuring customary services were fulfilled. By the middle of the twelfth century, a single steward was directly responsible for all of the abbey's English manors. This was later developed into a system of direct management administered by three lawyer stewards who were accountable to a handful of priestly officials who reported directly to the abbey's chapter. The formal change in management practices was prompted by Simon of Felsted's appropriation of the abbey's property during his time as its chief steward in England.

Simon had begun his career as a free farmer who held a tenement of eight acres in Felsted of the abbess for eight pence and annual works. Through means that remain unclear, he was subsequently able to acquire additional property in London and in Felsted. It is around this time that he appears to have been appointed steward. A shrewd and ambitious man, he was able to curry favour with the king and secure a royal confirmation for all of his holdings, some of which had been held of Holy Trinity. He then proceeded to develop these properties in various ways and brought in new tenants of his own. When he was finally brought to heel by the nuns in 1176, he was forced to repay a hundred marks (£66 13s 4d) for rents and lands that he had illegally appropriated from the abbey during his administration.[52] This included the mills of Hereford (Hartford), *Apechildewude*, Suhalle, Melmore, and *Longaland*, all of which were in the manor of Felsted and drew well over £4 in annual rents.[53]

---

50   See ibid., pp. 48, 81, 133.

51   See ibid., pp. xxix–xl, for a detailed discussion of the surveys, their contents and manner of compilation.

52   Ibid., pp. xxxii, xl–xli.

53   Ibid., 'Depredations of Simon of Felstead', pp. 39–44.

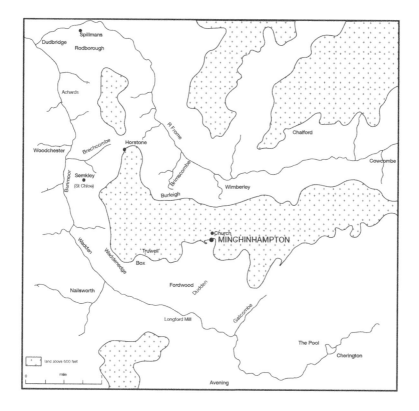

Fig. 8.3   Holy Trinity's possessions in Minchinhampton and surrounds. After Chibnall (1982)

But this was not the end of the abbey's problems with Simon and his kin. Upon Simon's death, his son William not only successfully took possession of all those lands which had been confirmed in hereditary fee-farm to his father by Henry II, but also held at farm all those properties which his father had managed for the nuns. The nuns paid William £100 in 1192 to ensure his renunciation of them, but nevertheless recognized his right to an extensive holding in Felsted with 20 free and servile tenants for an annual rent of 23s 1 1/2d. Simon's family still proved troublesome to the abbey unto the next generation, however, as William's son William had to be paid 25 marks (£16 13s 4d) and given land in Felsted to keep him from harassing the nuns with false suits. Simon and his descendants became men of means as a result of these various impositions. The nuns also became involved in a number of costly court cases during the thirteenth century to regain lost lands, including the manors of Felsted and Horstead which Aubrey de Vere, earl of Essex, had unjustly seized.[54]

It was in direct response to these various depredations that the abbey began appointing stewards to run its English properties for a fixed term and revocable at will from the early thirteenth century onwards. Three stewards, along with a handful of bailiffs and other officials, were based in the abbey's house in London. The stewards were university-trained lawyers, whereas most of the officials were priests who were directly accountable to the abbey's chapter.

It was around this time that the abbey began to make concerted efforts to draw its alienated lands back into the demesne and to clarify the nature of its various rights. This usually involved the expenditure of a great deal of money to buy out tenants who claimed to hold in hereditary fee-farm. The varying success of this strategy is well illustrated by the nuns' efforts to regain seisin of two of its mills in Norfolk and Essex in the early thirteenth century.

---

[54]   Ibid., pp. xl–xliii.

Seven tenants had claimed shares in the mill of Neford in Horstead. The nuns regained seisin by paying the six men and one woman involved individual amounts of compensation which totalled £2 4s, five quarters of barley and three-and-a-half acres of land to be held at a nominal rent.[55]

Far more expensive was the recovery of the abbey's mill of *Apechildewude* in Felsted, held by Robert Ostriciarius, his wife Basilia and Richard de Plesseto. Robert and his wife were paid out three and a half marks (£2 6s 8d), while Richard was paid 15 marks (£10) and half an acre of land at an annual rent of sixpence.[56] Marjorie Chibnall points out that as this charter 'was probably witnessed by the manor court of Felsted ... the action may have arisen from the general enquiries into the usurpation of tenants, both free and customary, that were being conducted in the courts at that time.'[57] As this mill was only earning £1 10s a year in the 1170s, the sum of well over £15 paid by the abbey to regain seisin was perhaps a little over-generous.[58] It may, however, have been the only way that the nuns could regain possession of the mill. Nevertheless, these experiences appear to have discouraged them from pursuing similar strategies against the many other free and customary tenants who had gained control of the abbey's mills since the early twelfth century.

Twelve mills held by Holy Trinity are recorded in Domesday Book for the manors of Minchinhampton, Felsted and Pinbury. With the acquisition of the manors of Avening and Horstead, the abbey acquired six additional mills, although seven are cited in Domesday Book. Eighteen mills are recorded in the surveys from the beginning and the end of the twelfth century, but it would appear that some of these fell out of use while others were newly built. While no details exist of the abbey's English possessions in the early fourteenth century, it probably held well over 20 mills by this time. The various changes in mill numbers on Holy Trinity's English manors and their varying status are set out below, beginning with Minchinhampton and working through to Avening, Felsted, Pinbury and Horstead. Neither of Holy Trinity's manors of Tarrant Launceston in Dorset nor Tilshead in Wiltshire appear to have possessed any mills, as none are recorded in any of the surveys, although Domesday Book records nine mills on the royal manor of Tilshead. This may have been because only half of the manor was later held by the nuns, i.e. the half without any mills.[59] The revenues from the abbey's English mills will be discussed shortly.

In the Domesday and early twelfth-century surveys, Holy Trinity held eight mills in Minchinhampton. While Domesday Book only records that all of these mills were in demesne, the second survey states that seven of them were directly managed by miller employees, while the eighth was ruined. Only six mills are described in the c. 1170 survey, all of which were held customarily. It seems likely that the other two were either ruined or completely out of the nuns' control by this time. Eleven mills are listed for the manor in the early fourteenth century survey, one of which was a fulling mill and the other a tool-sharpening mill. Six of these 11 mills appear to have been held freely and five customarily, although two of the latter were held on lifelong leases and a third was held by a lay lord. All three cases give some indication of the processes by which the other customary holdings had been converted into freehold between the late twelfth- and early fourteenth-century surveys. Because two of the mills recorded in the fourteenth century survey were industrial, it would seem that any increase in Minchinhampton's milling capacity between 1086 and c. 1320 must have resulted from larger and more efficient mills, as there was only a marginal increase in their numbers over this period.

Four mills are recorded in Avening in both the Domesday and early twelfth-century surveys, while five are recorded in the late twelfth century, indicating a slight increase in mill numbers by the end of the century.[60] Although the Avening mills were directly managed by miller employees in the early fourteenth century, had fallen into customary tenure by the end of the century and probably remained so subsequently.

Three mills are recorded in Felsted in the Domesday survey, but only two are listed in the early twelfth century. Their numbers had risen to five in the late twelfth century, indicating a much larger increase in milling capacity per capita in Felsted than on any of the other manors. This was probably related to the proportionally

---

[55]   Ibid., ms. 19, dated c. 1207 x 1230.

[56]   Ibid., mss. 20 and 21, dated to around the same time as ms. 19.

[57]   Ibid., p. xlv.

[58]   See Table 8.7 below.

[59]   *Charters and Custumals of the Abbey of Holy Trinity Caen*, pp. xxvi–xxvii, citing *Book of Fees*, ii, 742, for 1242–43. For the Domesday entry, see *Domesday Book, Wiltshire*, i, 65a.

[60]   The mills of Cleicumbe (?) and Lulle (?) are Avening IV and V, respectively, in the second survey.

larger increase in the manor's population as a result of the extensive assarting, reclamation and enclosure of woodlands and waste which occurred under Simon of Felsted's stewardship. From 1086 to 1176, there appears to have been a single mill on the small manor of Pinbury in Duntisbourne Rouse and three in Horstead. In both of the twelfth-century surveys, all of these mills appear to have been let at farm.

The mill information extracted from Domesday Book and Holy Trinity's three series of surveys is compiled in Tables 8.4 to 8.8 below. Based on the information in Tables 8.4 and 8.5 from Domesday Book, it would seem that Stanninghall was not included as part of the manor of Horstead when it was granted to Holy Trinity in the late eleventh century. Brictric, sheriff of Avening, held Avening at Domesday, while Roger of Poitou held Horstead.

Table 8.4   Twelve Domesday mills held by Holy Trinity Abbey, Caen

	Name	Rent (£/s/d)
1–3.	Felstead mills I–III	?
4.	Pinbury mill	0/3/4
5–12.	Minchinhampton mills (x8)	2/5/0
TOTAL OF MILL RENTALS (for 9 mills)		**£2 8s 4d**
AVERAGE REVENUE PER MILL		**5s 4 1/2d**

Table 8.5   Nine Domesday mills on two manors later held by Holy Trinity, Caen

	Name	Rent (£/s/d)
1–3.	Horstead mills I–III	?
4–5.	Stanninghall mills I and II (incl. as part of Horstead manor)	?
6–9.	Avening mills I–IV	0/19/2
TOTAL OF MILL RENTALS (for 4 mills)		**19s 2d**
AVERAGE REVENUE PER MILL		**4s 9 1/2d**

Table 8.6   Eighteen English mills held by Holy Trinity Abbey, Caen, 1106–13 (>1127)

Name	Holding	Rent (£/s/d)
Felstead mill I	n/a	0/10/0
Felstead mill II	n/a	0/5/0
Pinbury mill	n/a	0/2/9
Minchinhampton mills (x8)	7 with millers, 1 mill ruined	-
Horstead mills (x3)	+ fishpond @ 12d p.a.	3/0/0
Avening mills (x4)	4 with millers	-
TOTAL OF MILL RENTALS (for 6 mills)		**£3 17s 9d**
AVERAGE REVENUE PER MILL		**12s 10d**

Of the 18 mills recorded in the 1106–13 survey (Table 8.6), 11 were still operating in Minchinhampton and Avening and were directly managed with miller employees. No revenues are recorded against them. The two mills of Felsted were in villein tenure, having works and customary services attached to them, while the Pinbury mill was presumably held freely, as no customary services are recorded against it. All three were drawing low cash revenues in comparison to the three mills of Horstead, all of which appear to have been let at farm on fixed-term leases. The only manor for which mill rents can be directly compared in the Domesday and early twelfth-century surveys pertains to Pinbury, and these show a decrease in rent from 3s 4d to 2s 9d: 17.5 per cent less revenue over the course of 20 years or so. However, a comparison of the average revenues calculated from the two surveys suggests that this was in the context of a marked overall increase in Holy Trinity's income from its mills, which more than doubled in the intervening period.[61] It therefore seems likely

---

[61]   This issue will be discussed in greater detail below.

that by the time of the first abbatial survey, Pinbury mill had fallen into hereditary tenure and was thereafter outside the nuns' control, as it does not appear in any of the subsequent surveys.

Another possibility is that Pinbury mill had been acquired by Simon of Felsted during his stewardship and was still being illicitly withheld by him when the second survey was taken. That this may have been the case is supported by the fact that his son William sub-let the whole manor as if it were his own property to the Veim family in 1175–78. Protracted and expensive litigation eventually resulted in it being returned to the abbey's control in 1213. By 1286, an account roll records that the farm of the manor was £8, which was four times the sum that William had pocketed at the abbey's expense a little over a century earlier. This evidence is consistent with the mill having survived and contributed to the increased revenues from the manor.[62]

A comparison of the average revenues per mill between Tables 8.4 and 8.6 is, however, a more accurate reflection of the abbey's changing income from its mills between the late eleventh and early twelfth centuries. The two averages of 5s 4 1/2d and 4s 9 1/2d for nine and four mills respectively on the five manors recorded in Domesday Book are about 60 per cent below the average of 12s 10d for six mills recorded in the early twelfth-century survey. In other words, the nuns had more than doubled their average revenues from their mills in a little over two decades. Holt has found similar levels of increased revenues from 21 mills on 17 Peterborough Abbey manors between 1086 and 1125, i.e., from £14 4s 4d to £26 2s 4d, or an increase of around 84 per cent.[63] It should be noted that Holy Trinity's Domesday earnings from these Gloucestershire mills were low compared to the average mill value per year for the whole county, which John Ambler records as 6s 7d. Holy Trinity's average mill earnings were also only 11 pence higher than the lowest average, which was for Cheshire, and 18s 8d less than the highest, which was for Huntingdonshire.[64] It is therefore clear that the abbey's revenues from its Gloucestershire mills were starting from a relatively low base.

At the end of the twelfth century, Holy Trinity held 18 mills in total (Table 8.7). Five were in Felsted, four in Avening, three in Horstead and six in Minchinhampton. As just stated, the Pinbury mill does not appear in this survey, presumably because it had been either allowed to fall into ruin or had been taken out of the abbey's possession by Simon of Felsted. Eight of the mills recorded simply have cash rents recorded against them. These were the mills of Felsted and Horstead, all of which appear to have been earning over £1 each. At least five of these mills (mill numbers 1–5 in Felsted) had been directly held by Simon of Felsted, although he also had control of the revenues of all the others. The earnings from the Felsted mills suggest that they had been drawn back into the demesne since the last survey had been taken, and that they were, like the Horstead mills, either directly managed or rented on fixed-term leases at farm by that time. The other mills in Avening and Minchinhampton (mill numbers 6–9 and 13–18) were in customary tenure. Nine paid less than 10 shillings rent, while four paid five shillings or less. These amounts are comparable to the average mill rentals from Domesday, suggesting their rents had hardly changed since that time, despite inflation.

A comparison of the data in Domesday and the first two abbatial surveys reveals that its mill management practices had changed remarkably over that period. Of those 19 mills on Domesday manors that Holy Trinity was later to hold, six were directly managed and 13 were at farm. By 1106–13, it had doubled the number of those mills directly managed to 12, while the number at farm were cut by more than three-quarters to only three; two others had slipped into customary tenure and one was probably held freely. Here we can see clearly that only two decades after the Domesday survey, three out of 18 of Holy Trinity's mills, or almost 17 per cent, were no longer in demesne, with direct management replacing leases at farm as a preferred managerial method overall. By 1176–89, the situation had reversed in a number of ways, with only two mills being directly managed, or a sixth of the number at the beginning of the century, with six at farm, or double the number earlier in the century. The number of mills outside seigneurial control had more than tripled, however, with 10 mills held customarily, or almost 56 per cent of the total.

Unfortunately, there is little reliable comparative data for this period from other monastic estates to judge how typical this was, but Holt has done overall analyses of mill holdings by county in the Hundred Rolls which show that 45 per cent of Oxfordshire mills were in demesne at this time, while 55 per cent were outside

---

[62]   *Charters and Custumals of the Abbey of Holy Trinity Caen*, pp. xli–xlii. Chibnall cites the account roll of Minchinhampton, PRO SC 6/856/19 for the manor's revenue in 1286, but does not mention whether the mill still existed at this stage or how much it earned.

[63]   Holt (1988), p. 14.

[64]   Ambler (1994), p. 43.

(8 per cent in villein tenure and 47 per cent in hereditary tenure), while in Cambridgeshire, a little under half were outside seigneurial control in hereditary tenure, while the rest were in demesne.[65] Although Holy Trinity's own surveys do not allow a direct comparison of these figures with those from the Hundred Rolls, the same pattern of what appears to have been further alienation of mills from the demesne continued on its estate of Minchinhampton as recorded in the early fourteenth century, by which time only five of the 11 mills on the manor owed customary services, while the rest were apparently held freely.

Table 8.7   Eighteen English mills held by Holy Trinity Abbey, Caen, 1167–76

Name	Labour service/holding	Rent (£/s/d)	Tenant
Hereford mill (Hartford)	-	1/10/0	Simon of Felstead
Abachildewud mill	-	1/10/0	"
Suhalle mill	-	1/0/0	"
Melmore mill	-	-	"
Longland mill	-	-	"
Avening mill I	+ 1/4 virgate, biannual ploughservice and 2 measures (of grain)	0/7/6	Reginald of the forest (miller)
Avening mill II	1 terse, 4 hens, feudal aid for making and repairing doors, gates and houses of the church, money for pasture rights and ploughing and carrying services	0/3/4	Godricus
Avening mill III	9 annual ploughservices, 3 measures, 1 cartload (firewood) and payment for church host and candles	0/2/6	Hedricus
Cleicumbe mill	triannual ploughservice and 2 measures + all services as listed for Avening II, but no harvest service	0/3/0	Robert of Cleicumbe
Horstead mills (x3)	n/a	8/0/0	-
Lulle? mill	+ 1/2 virgate with all customary services as done by Adam	0/14/0	Eilaf son of Adam
Staford mill	+ 1/4 virgate with all customary services as above	0/5/0	Godard
Chaleford mill I	+ 1/2 virgate with all customary services as above	0/8/0	Radulf de Chaleford
Chaleford mill II	+ 3/4 virgate with all customary services as above	0/7/0	Roger de Chaleford
Gilbert canis' mill (Dudebrug')	+ 1/4 virgate with all customary services as above + prayer	0/10/0	Gilbert canis
Walter's widow's mill	+ 1/4 virgate with all customary services as above + prayer	0/6/0	Walter's widow
TOTAL MILL REVENUES (for 16 mills)			**£15 6s 4d**
AVERAGE REVENUE PER MILL			**19s 2d**

It is also interesting to note that both of the mills of Felsted that had been let customarily in the first abbatial survey were back in the demesne by the time that the second survey was taken, while the 10 mills of Avening and Minchinhampton had slipped into customary tenure after having been directly managed by miller employees earlier in the century. All 10 of the customary tenants who held these mills appear to have been smallholders. Four of the tenants held a quarter virgate, two held half a virgate, and one held three-quarters of a virgate. The other three mills do not appear to have had landholdings attached to them. All owed a variety of services, those on the Minchinhampton manors being fairly standardized, while those in Avening consisted variously of ploughing, carrying, repairing property and miscellaneous small payments of produce. Only Reginald of the forest, who held one of the Avening mills, is described as a miller.

It seems clear that the alienation of these mills from the demesne resulted in a dramatic loss of potential income for the nuns, as a comparison of the figures for Domesday Book and the first two abbatial surveys soon reveals. The three mills of Horstead that were directly managed had more than doubled in value between 1106 and 1167, from £3 a year to £8 (an increase of 167 per cent over six decades), while those in Felsted appear to have more than tripled their value, from 15 shillings for two mills in 1106 to £4 for three mills in 1167 (an

---

[65]   Holt (1988), p. 61.

increase, on average, of 266 per cent). The weighted average increase is therefore 207 per cent for the five mills between the beginning and the end of the twelfth century. This is considerably higher than comparable rises in mill revenue between 1086 and 1189 for 23 West Country manors held by Glastonbury Abbey (i.e., from £10 19s to £21 15s 4d), which experienced a 98 per cent increase in their revenues.[66] By way of contrast, Holy Trinity's eight mills in Minchinhampton were drawing £2 5s at Domesday, but only £2 6s in the 1167–76 survey for six mills. Even more stark is the contrast between the Domesday and late twelfth-century values of the four Avening mills, which recorded 19s 2d in rents at Domesday, but only 16s 4d in the 1167–76 survey. In other words, in the course of slightly less than a century, the Minchinhampton mills had gained only 2 per cent in revenues, while the Avening mills had actually lost about 17 per cent of their earlier income.

While Holt has argued that 'what twelfth century surveys show is that it was then nearly always the practice for mills to be let with peasant holdings, in return for a rent accompanied often by labour services',[67] the evidence presented for Holy Trinity so far demonstrates a rather more complicated situation. From no mills outside the demesne at Domesday, 17 per cent of the abbey's mills were outside seigneurial control by the second decade of the twelfth century, growing to 56 per cent by the eighth decade of the century. By the early fourteenth century, around 55 per cent of those independent tenant mills recorded in the late twelfth-century survey appear to have fallen into hereditary free tenure, suggesting a somewhat atypical trend in mill management during the thirteenth century.

The question which immediately arises is, how had this situation come about, and why did the nuns allow it to happen? Although Holt has argued that such policies were pursued to transfer costs of repair and maintenance and any potential losses onto tenants, and were therefore considered economically attractive to lords,[68] the process of mills being alienated from the demesne appears to follow no particular logic on Holy Trinity's manors. While the Avening mills' revenues had declined by 17 per cent between Domesday and the late twelfth-century survey, it is not clear whether this was the cause or the result of them having been let customarily. On the other hand, the relative profitability of the Minchinhampton mills before they were alienated is impossible to determine because no revenues are recorded for them in either Domesday Book or the early eleventh-century survey.

Because this slippage into customary tenure happened between the 1120s and the 1160s, it seems most likely that it occurred during the reign of Stephen (1135–54), and probably under the stewardship of Simon of Felsted. As we have seen, Simon was a law unto himself at a time when the rule of law was in abeyance as a result of the civil wars under Stephen. Had Simon summarily decided to reduce his own responsibilities by letting the Gloucestershire properties customarily so as to focus on more lucrative properties or, at least, those that were nearer to hand, there is probably very little that the nuns could have done to stop him, even had they known and were opposed to it. The nuns not only had a crooked chief steward managing their affairs, but would have found it difficult to dislodge him even had they wanted to during Stephen's reign. Once he had attained considerable wealth at the nuns' expense and ingratiated himself with Henry II, he was able to demonstrate just how difficult he would be to remove.

Even had the abbey's Gloucestershire mills been deemed worth recovering by the nuns, after having spent considerable amounts of money regaining seisin of all of their English properties from the Felsted and Veim families, as well as two mills in Norfolk and Essex, they were no doubt somewhat reluctant to further pursue their many customary tenants in Gloucestershire for additional revenues. Richard Holt's observation that '[s]uccessive abbesses of Holy Trinity of Caen seem to have been content to allow the mills of their Cotswold manors of Minchinhampton and Avening to remain in hereditary villein tenure, whilst they considered it worth recovering by outright purchase two of their own mills in Norfolk and Essex that had lapsed into hereditary fee-farm',[69] should therefore be slightly qualified. Rather than being content with the situation, the abbesses and their various chapters probably felt they had little choice other than to let the bulk of their mills remain outside the demesne unless they wanted to continue with a series of costly and protracted litigations.

---

[66]   Ibid., pp. 14–15.

[67]   Ibid., p. 56.

[68]   Ibid., pp. 63 and 66.

[69]   Ibid., p. 58.

Table 8.8   Eleven English mills held by Holy Trinity Abbey, Caen, on its manor of Minchinhampton, c. 1306–c. 1320

Name	Labour service/holding	Rent (£/s/d)	Tenant
? mill	1/4 virgate with assarts and customary services on a lifelong lease (*ad vitam suam*)	0/7/1	Robert the miller
Brechachre tool-sharpening mill	one plot on lifelong lease	0/0/6	Robert and wife
Bremescumbe fulling mill	messuage	0/4/3	Thomas de Rodebrec
William de Keem's mill (Bremescumbe)	n/a	0/1/6	Henry
Chalford mill I	+ 1/2 virgate with messuage and assarts and customary services	0/8/4	Richard Miblanc
Chalford mill II	+ 3/4 virgate + 1 virgate + 1/4 virgate with messuage and customary services	0/15/5	John de Chalford
Dodebrigge mill (Dudbridge)	2 1/2 virgates + 1/4 virgate + 1/2 virgate + 7 1/2 acres + 1 measure (of eels, skins, etc.) + 1 1/4 wild beasts (*ferend'*) and customary services	2/3/0	Lord John Matravers
Longford mill	+ 3/4 virgate and customary services	0/6/6	Mabilia de Longford
Nailsworth mill	n/a	0/0/1	unidentified widow
Stoford mill	+ 1/4 virgate with assarts	0/7/1	Richard de Stoford
Wymberle mill	1/2 share + 1/8 virgate with assarts	0/7/4	John Gille
	1/2 share + 1/8 virgate with assarts	0/6/2	Matilde Gille
TOTAL MILL REVENUES*		**£5 7s 3d**	
AVERAGE REVENUE PER MILL		**9s 9d**	

* For 9 mills, excluding Brechachre.

Turning now to the survey of Minchinhampton from c. 1306–20 (Table 8.8), six of the 11 mills recorded appear to have been held freely and five customarily, although as stated previously, two of the latter were held on lifelong leases and a third was held by a lay lord. This is an unusually high proportion of mills to have remained outside of seigneurial control for the early fourteenth century, as most lords had drawn the greater proportion of those mills that had been alienated during the twelfth century back into the demesne by this time.[70] None of Holy Trinity's mills were directly managed at this stage. Nine of the 11 mills were conventional grain mills, and two were industrial mills, including a fulling mill and a tool-sharpening mill. Only one mill appears to have been drawing an economic rent, i.e., Dudbridge mill at £2 3s, although it also owed customary services. It was being let to a lord named John Matravers, the descendant of a knight of the same name first mentioned in documents of the 1190s in relation to the family's seat, the manor of Lytchett Matravers in Dorset. It would seem that this John Matravers was the same man implicated in the murder of Edward II at Berkeley Castle in 1327. 'Sir John Maltravers' was brother-in-law to accused conspirator Lord Berkeley, and a long-standing supporter of Roger Mortimer, but like Berkeley escaped punishment from Edward III, acting on his behalf on business matters in Flanders subsequent to the murder.[71]

The early fourteenth century survey also reveals that by this time, a small number of mills that were independently held by small entrepreneurs or artisans had been allowed to emerge, such as William de Keem's mill in Brimscombe, which paid 18 pence rent, and the tool-sharpening mill of Brechachre, which paid only sixpence. The private tenants of both of these mills were undoubtedly responsible for their maintenance and repairs, and probably built them themselves. One of the three female tenants who held mills in Minchinhampton was partner with her husband in the tool-sharpening mill. The other two women respectively held a half share of Wimberley mill and Longford mill in their own rights.

---

[70]   Ibid., pp. 62–9.

[71]   See Mortimer (2005), for the latest analysis of the evidence surrounding Edward II's death and Matravers' role in it.

Two of the 12 leases registered in the survey were for life, one of which was for the tool-sharpening mill that had apparently been constructed by its tenant based on the nominal rent which it paid. Its rent was the second lowest recorded in the survey. Because it was the tenant who collected its revenue, there is no record of how much custom it drew *per annum*. The five mills in customary tenure had labour services attached to them. Two of the customary and three of the freely held mills included assarts, indicating that Holy Trinity had allowed the incorporation of earlier encroachments upon its lands into its customary tenants' holdings. Most of the mills were attached to substantial parcels of land. Three included messuages, another three were attached to a quarter-virgate holding, while single mills included a half virgate, three-quarters of a virgate and two virgates. The largest holding of three and a quarter virgates with other lands and obligations was attached to Dudbridge mill.[72] Interestingly, the fulling mill in Minchinhampton was attached only to a messuage, and the tool-sharpening mill to a plot of land, suggesting that they were, perhaps, urban or semi-urban establishments not tied to farm holdings. Consistent with the pattern recorded elsewhere, the abbey's fulling mill was drawing 43.5 per cent of the average revenue of the 11 mills recorded in the survey.

The highest annual rent for any of the Minchinhampton mills was for the mill of Dudbridge. It included a cash payment of £2 3s, customary services and the provision of various measures of eels, skins, and wild beasts. In stark contrast, the lowest rent for any of the seven grain mills that appear to have been in customary tenure was a penny for Nailsworth mill, while the highest was 15s 5d for the second mill of Chalford. The peppercorn rent for the Nailsworth mill suggests that it had probably been sold off at some stage to its tenant, as Holt has noted with respect to similar nominal mill rentals in Cambridgeshire and Oxfordshire that are recorded in the Hundred Rolls of 1279.[73] The same mill is recorded as having drawn 7s 6d with a quarter virgate in a late twelfth-/early thirteenth-century survey.[74]

The average income of the nine grain mills in free and customary tenure was 11s 4 1/2d. This is only 53 per cent more than the average revenues from nine mills in Minchinhampton and Pinbury that are recorded in Domesday Book more than two centuries earlier. A comparison of the revenues of £2 5s from its eight Minchinhampton mills at Domesday with the £5 7s 3d which it earned from 11 mills in the same manor in the early fourteenth century is probably a more accurate reflection of the earnings differential, however. This reveals that the abbey was earning 140 per cent more from its mills almost 250 years later. Alternatively, a comparison of the revenues of five of Minchinhampton's mills from the 1167–76 survey with the same five in the 1306–20 survey reveals that the average increase over that period was 123 per cent. In the case of the variations between the Chalford, Dodebrigge and Staford mills, there was a 60 per cent increase in the rentals of the two Chalford mills between 1170 and 1306, a 330 per cent increase in the rental of Dudbridge mill, and a 42 per cent increase in the rental of Staford mill. It is clear from all this that by the early fourteenth century, the Minchinhampton mills were collectively only drawing a little more than twice the income that they had enjoyed in the late eleventh and twelfth centuries, primarily because the vast majority of them had fallen into free or customary tenure in the interim and the rental returns from them had remained stagnant or only increased marginally.

The overall increase in mill revenues is far lower than that gained by many other ecclesiastical lords over the same period who were drawing four to six times the mill-rents which they had enjoyed during the late twelfth century in the early fourteenth century. For example, Glastonbury Abbey was drawing on average four times as much revenue from its mills by the early fourteenth century as it had in the late twelfth century,[75] whereas the bishop of Ely had experienced a six-fold increase in his mill revenues between the 1220s and 1298.[76] Although Holy Trinity's average revenue per mill appears to have increased by more than 150 per cent over

---

[72]   A quarter virgate in the region was rated at five to seven acres.

[73]   Holt (1988), p. 55.

[74]   This is the Avening D survey, dated to between 1183 and 1227, and probably shortly after 1192. The Nailsworth (*Neylswort*) mill is the only one to appear in this series of surveys of the three manors of Minchinhampton, Avening and Felsted. See *Charters and Custumals of the Abbey of Holy Trinity Caen*, pp. xxxvii and 81.

[75]   Based on data supplied by Holt (1987), p. 12, 12 manors containing mills held by Glastonbury Abbey experienced a 160 per cent increase in their mill revenues between 1086 and 1189, and rose by a further 400 per cent between 1189 and the early fourteenth century (see Holt (1987), p. 18).

[76]   Holt (1988), p. 85.

the 20 years or so between 1086 and c. 1106, and 76 per cent over the six decades or so between c. 1106 and c. 1170, by the early fourteenth century an 'average' mill of Minchinhampton was drawing only 27 per cent more rent than its late twelfth century counterpart, i.e., an average of 7s 8d for six mills in 1167–76, as compared with an average of 9s 9d for 11 mills c. 1306 to c. 1320. Indeed, if we ignore the revenues of the two industrial mills and Dudbridge mill from the early fourteenth-century survey, the average mill revenue for that time was actually slightly less than that for the late twelfth century. Clearly, then, most of Minchinhampton's mill earnings were going backwards, not forwards, and were certainly not even keeping up with inflation. Holt has found similar patterns of low rental increase between Domesday and the early sixteenth century with respect to customary mills held by Glastonbury Abbey in its manor of Nettleton in Wiltshire.[77]

A comparison of the average mill revenues in Minchinhampton with the overall averages being collected by other ecclesiastical lords such as the bishop of Hereford, the prior of Grove and the abbots of Bec and Beaulieu indicate that it was only drawing about a sixth as much revenue as those lords with comparable mill holdings on manorial lands. Even were we to take Holy Trinity's late twelfth-century average mill revenue of 19s 2d as a more reasonable benchmark of its average mill earnings across all of its manors and doubled them, in order to reflect what would appear to be a conservative rate of increase for the intervening period, the average produced, at £1 18s 4d, is still only half of the average revenue of the other religious houses' mills.

The only mill in Minchinhampton that appears to have been drawing anything approaching a market rent was Dudbridge mill. While it did include a much larger parcel of land than the other mills held customarily, the rent which the nuns collected from it was more than five times higher than the average revenue of the customarily held mills. It alone amounted to 55.7 per cent of the total revenue from mills in the manor. One is therefore left with the overwhelming impression that the nuns had decided that the only mill in customary tenure in Minchinhampton that could be charged a high rent was that held by a lord, and even perhaps, that the nuns had designated that Dudbridge mill was the only mill on the manor to which tenants owed suit.

As Holt has noted, mills held on customary leases were more desirable to lords than those held in hereditary tenure, as they allowed the renegotiation of rents and the recovery of lost profits through entry fines for new lessees.[78] The fact that the Dudbridge mill was no longer in villein tenure by the early fourteenth century gave the nuns room to renegotiate its rent over the years, as its revenues had increased by a massive 330 per cent between 1167 and 1306, as compared to an average of 27 per cent for all the mills on the manor, although this latter figure is, as already pointed out, itself largely an artefact of the huge increase in revenue from this single mill. That such renegotiations had also occurred on the three mills of Chalford and Staford that were in customary tenure is revealed by some of the earlier cited figures, although the average increase in revenue of only 54 per cent for these three mills over the same period clearly reveals that the margin for renegotiating the rents from those mills was far less than for the mill of Dudbridge.

It is therefore clear that although Holy Trinity had increased its mill rents across all of its manors over the 240 years covered by the various surveys, this increase was limited by the extent to which it was able to draw mills back into the demesne or charge market rents for them. While it was able to negotiate modest increases in rents of 40 to 60 per cent over the 150 years from the 1170s to 1310s for some of its customary mills, it appears to have lost or sold off mills that had formerly been held in hereditary tenure. The nuns' reluctance to assert seigneurial authority over their English tenants appears to have led to a more or less gradual erosion of the proportion of revenues which they received from the majority of their mills in customary and hereditary tenure, with the manor of Minchinhampton clearly demonstrating just how restricted the gains could be when the tenants of such mills were able to maintain these forms of tenure.

Although we have no way of knowing what sort of state of repair the various mills of Minchinhampton were in at this stage, the fact that assarts had been taken in relation to more than half of them suggests that the nuns' tenants had been appropriating timber from their woods, as well as land for cultivation from their waste, woods and common for some years. Although the tenants of these mills were undoubtedly responsible for their repairs and maintenance, it seems fairly clear that more than half of them had been doing so at the abbey's expense. It is therefore quite likely that the mills which these tenants held were well maintained and were potentially just as profitable as the mill held by Lord John Matravers, thus contributing far more

---

[77] Ibid., pp. 66–7.

[78] Ibid., p. 60.

to the wealth of the customary tenants than to the financial well-being of the abbess and her house, even if they did not hold suit. For all of Stephen's faults as a monarch, therefore, and Simon of Felsted's faults as an administrator, it would seem that the reign of the one and the employment of the other had a salutary effect on the fortunes of a number of Holy Trinity's villeins in Minchinhampton.

As there is only one mill rental contained in any of the abbey's surveys from the thirteenth century, Marjorie Chibnall's assessment that this was a period of 'prosperous and efficient administration' for the abbey is somewhat difficult to assess in the context of its mill ownership. While the nuns had certainly worked hard at regaining seisin of their mills and drawing as much revenue from them as possible, they obviously had limited success on this score with respect to more than half of their mills. Indeed, they were only able to regain seisin of two mills, those of *Apechildewude* and Neford, both of which were in Felsted, and these at a significant cost of almost £20 in cash plus some minor concessions on smallholdings. Such problems appear to have made it very difficult for the abbey to increase its average revenue from its mills at a similar rate to most of the larger English religious houses.

One is therefore drawn to conclude from this evidence that while Holy Trinity was charging higher rents for its 'town' mills from aristocrats like Lord John Matravers and *nouveau* gentry like Simon of Felsted and his successors, it generally had very limited success in drawing higher rents from its rural mills in hereditary and customary tenure. This is reflected in the relatively lower increases in the rents for three of the five Minchinhampton mills between the late twelfth and early fourteenth centuries, which were 60 per cent and 42 per cent as opposed to 330 per cent for one of the town mills. Although it is possible that these 'rural' mills drew far less custom than the town mills and therefore could not be charged higher rents, it seems more likely that it was the kind of tenure in which they were held that made it difficult for the nuns to increase their rents, although they may have been as profitable as the town mills. The only other ecclesiastical estate for which I have found any strong parallels in this study is with regard to Canterbury Cathedral Priory's holdings on its Sussex manors, many of which had also been in ancient demesne and had slipped into customary tenure during the twelfth century.[79]

Finally, if we compare Holy Trinity's revenues and the number of its mills in demesne at these various times, with those of comparably sized ecclesiastical estates, the initial parallels in the late eleventh and early twelfth centuries are overtaken by marked divergences later in the century that are far less typical. The somewhat inevitable conclusion that is suggested by all this is that remote oversight of its English estates proved to be seriously disadvantageous to Holy Trinity, and that despite adopting various reformist strategies in its management practices during the late twelfth and thirteenth centuries, it was unable to undo much of the damage to its mill revenues which had occurred during Stephen's reign and Simon's stewardship.

Wakebridge Chantries at Crich (Aristocratic Family Foundation)

The chantries of St Nicholas and St Catherine, and of St Mary, were founded by William of Wakebridge in 1349 and 1367 respectively, making them the latest foundations of any of the religious houses studied in the sample. Both chantries were set up by William in what was then a remote and heavily wooded part of Derbyshire after most of his family was taken by the Black Death. William was from a pious knightly family and held the position of commissioner and justice in various capacities in Nottinghamshire and Derbyshire.[80]

The first chantry was established partially as a means to 'succour the poor' and to provide assistance to the local vicar on holy days. The chantry of St Mary primarily performed the latter function. A chapel at Normanton was also established by William in a remote part of the parish of Southwell. All three survived almost 200 years until the time of the Dissolution in 1547.[81] The annual revenue for the properties associated with the chantries was £13 6s 8d in 1368, all of which was made over by William to the neighbouring Augustinian house of Thurgarton with the understanding that the latter would finance the chantries in perpetuity in return for a substantial share of the profits of the real estate.[82]

---

[79]   See Chapter 4.

[80]   *Cartulary of the Wakebridge Chantries*, pp. 4–5.

[81]   Ibid., pp. 1, 4, 6, 17.

[82]   Ibid., pp. 20–21.

William's family was originally from the manor of Wakebridge in the parish of Crich. Its members were descended by marriage from a daughter of Hubert FitzRalph (d. 1225), lord of Crich. The family appears to have held land in two main districts, the first being bounded by the rivers Amber and Derwent and the vills of Matlock and Wessington, while the second was several kilometres to the north-east in Palterton and Scarcliffe. It also held some other property just over the border in Nottinghamshire. Most of these lands were held of the barony of Crich.[83] The barony was passed on to the Freschevilles after the death of FitzRalph in 1225, and a hundred years later was enfeoffed to Roger Beler by Ralph II de Frescheville. Roger died in the same year, with his seven-year-old son of the same name inheriting in wardship.[84]

Only two mills are mentioned in the chantries' cartulary, both of which were held by one of the chantries, i.e., the Chantry of Sts Nicholas and Catherine. The complicated means by which these mills were secured by William of Wakebridge provides some intriguing insights into the acquisition and alienation of property in the late thirteenth and fourteenth centuries, and the extent to which knights' fees could be subinfeudated during that period.

The chantry's two mills were acquired through the purchase of land in the vill of Lea from John of Dethick sometime between 1349 and 1357, although one of them was ruined by this time, containing only the mill site and pond. The foundation grant of endowment to the chantry included nine messuages, nine cottages, four crofts, 13 bovates, 15 acres, two other pieces of land and one meadow, as well as 18s 10d of rents and the reversion of some other properties held by lifelong tenants.[85] The alienation in Mortmain of this grant and others were subsequently confirmed on 10 February 1362 by Edward III for a fee of £4 paid to the Crown.[86] However, as we will see below, the valuation upon which this fee was based was falsely given in order to minimize the fee paid, although to his credit, it was William of Wakebridge who pointed this out several years later.

A number of charters from the late thirteenth century are concerned with John of Dethick's acquisition of the mills of Lea, one of which dated c. 1290 provides a narrative account of their history. During the reign of King John, the vill or manor of Lea and two mills there were held by Robert de Alveley, who was a knight or member of the lesser gentry.[87] The vill and mills were subsequently inherited in severalty by his two daughters, Lettice and Sarra. Lettice married into the Ferrers family, and her son, Thomas de Ferrers, lord of Loxley (aka Lockesley), then inherited a half share of the mills with his share of the manor. Thomas's son Thomas sold his share of the mills to Lord Geoffrey of Dethick, who was a knight. Sarra was succeeded by her son Alexander de Lea, who in turn was succeeded by his son Alexander. This Alexander then sold his share of the mills to Geoffrey of Dethick's son Robert. Robert subsequently died in seisin of both mills and was succeeded by his son Geoffrey, who was in turn succeeded by his son John, who then enfeoffed William of Wakebridge, who gave the vill and mills to the cantarist of the Chantry of Sts Nicholas and Catherine.[88] A release dated 15 January 1360 by John to William confirms these grants, specifying that it included the site and millpond of a mill formerly known as *le Netherleemilne* and another mill called *le Overleemilne* with its appurtenances.[89] Another release by John's brother Henry confirms the grant.[90]

A number of other mill-related documents provide some details of the sums paid for purchase and rent of these mills in the process of being passed from one party to another. The first is from the late thirteenth century and records the grant by Thomas de Ferrers to Sir Geoffrey of Dethick of the share of two mills in Lea with the suit and labour services pertaining to them. In return, Geoffrey paid Thomas a 24 mark (£16) 'consideration'. Thomas and his house were also to be free of multure, and Geoffrey was to render the chief lord of the fee a half pound of cummin annually, as well as 11 bushels of tollcorn to the chaplain of Lea Chapel.[91] The mills'

---

[83] Ibid., pp. 2–4.

[84] Ibid., p. 4.

[85] Ibid., ms. 18.

[86] Ibid., ms. 111.

[87] Lysons and Lysons (1817), pp. 17–18.

[88] *Cartulary of the Wakebridge Chantries*, ms. 78.

[89] Ibid., ms. 105.

[90] Ibid., ms. 107.

[91] Ibid., ms. 79.

purchase price, as well as the ongoing rent to be paid to Thomas, clearly indicate both mills were earning relatively large sums at this stage.

Thomas's grant to Geoffrey is followed by another from his second cousin, Alexander de Lea, to Geoffrey's son Robert of the remaining share of the two mills. In return, Robert was to render two shillings annually to Alexander, and likewise give 11 bushels of tollcorn to the chaplain of Lea.[92] The additional payment of the cummin to the chief lord of the fee was due to the custom that the eldest daughter of an enfeoffed knight and her descendants were obliged to render any and all services to the chief lord.[93]

Another document from c. 1290 is worth mentioning in passing because of its significance as an example of a villein purchasing his (temporary) freedom through the commutation to a cash sum of suits and labour services owed by him. The document concerned is a release by Alexander de Lea to John son of Roger of Pinxton of half of the rent of six shillings payable to Alexander for a tenement held by John. The tenement consisted of a bovate in Wheatcroft with a toft and croft. In return, John paid Alexander a consideration of four marks (£2 13s 4d) and was exempted from suits of court and mill and other services. The exemption was for just under 18 years.[94] Presumably, the reason for the inclusion of this charter in the chantries' cartulary is that this same tenement had later come into the possession of William of Wakebridge as part of the lands granted to him by Alexander's son Alexander.

Sometime between the late thirteenth century and the foundation of the chantries, the lower mill of Lea (also known as *Netherleemilne* and the lower mill of Dethick), had fallen into ruin. A grant dated 19 August 1357 records that John son of Geoffrey of Dethick had leased the mill of Lea (singular) to Roger Beler, knight, for seven years beginning on 29 September 1356, and that Roger had in turn demised the mill to William of Wakebridge. The document records that John agreed to grant William the mill for his life. A final clause stipulates that if William died within 12 years of the expiry of the seven-year lease to Roger Beler, William's heirs should hold the mill until the expiry of that term. John also secured free suit of mill for himself while he was in residence at Dethick.[95]

A release dated 15 January 1360 by John of Dethick to William confirmed all of the above grants, specifying that they included the site and millpond of a mill formerly known as *le Netherleemilne* and another mill called *le Overleemilne* with its appurtenances.[96] Another release by John's brother Henry further confirmed these grants and several others to William and his wife and two other parties.[97]

A royal inquisition into William's grants to the chantry was declared on 1 October 1361, in which it was stated that the single mill held by William only milled oats, 'and is hardly worth ten shillings *per annum* after the deduction of charges'.[98] This is followed by a license dated 29 November 1361 from Roger Beler to William and two clerks named Roger of Chesterfield and Richard of Tissington to alienate in Mortmain to the chaplain of the church of Crich and his successors 'for the good estate of the said William of Wakebridge during his lifetime and for his soul and that of his wife, and all his ancestors and their parents and all the faithful now deceased' 14 messuages, one toft, one mill, five bovates and 100 acres of land, 40 acres of meadow and £2 in rents from Tansley, Matlock, Ashover, Clattercotes, Wheatcroft, Plaistow, Fritchley, Crich, Dethick and Lea.[99] Subsequent to this license from Roger Beler, and presumably in an effort to increase the chantry's cash revenues, William rebuilt *Netherleemilne* at his own expense for the benefit of the chantry some time before 1370.[100]

Further evidence of William's piety and honesty can be found in another charter from before 1370, in which the contents of the earlier cited narrative pertaining to the complicated manner in which Geoffrey of

---

92   Ibid., ms. 80.

93   Ibid., p. 100, n. 1.

94   Ibid., ms. 89.

95   Ibid., ms. 104.

96   Ibid., ms. 105.

97   Ibid., ms. 107.

98   Ibid., ms. 110.

99   Ibid., ms. 108.

100   Ibid., ms. 19.

Dethick gained seisin of the two mills of Lea is recapitulated, as are the details of the fees that were to be paid to the previous owners for securing the shares of the two mills. The charter is unusual because it records William's declaration that an earlier attempt to secure a license to alienate the foundation grants in Mortmain had provided a false valuation of the properties concerned in order to minimize the license fee, although it is not stated who made or endorsed the false valuation.[101]

The various details pertaining to these two mills are set out in Table 8.9. They present an interesting example of the degree to which subinfeudation could extend with regard to mill ownership in the mid-fourteenth century. Like the mill of Tarleton held by Cockersand Abbey, there are four levels of tenancy between John of Dethick as chief lord and the Wakebridge Chantries, with each man in between a member of the knightly class.

Table 8.9   Two mills held by the Wakebridge Chantries before 1365

Name	Year acquired	Grantor	Annual revenue
Netherleemilne (with suit and labour services)	1349–56	William of Wakebridge (sub-tenant) Roger Beler (tenant) John of Dethick (tenant-in-chief)	ruined (1348? <1362)
Overleemilne (with suit and labour services)	1349–56	As above	10s (1361)

It should be noted in conclusion that all of William's efforts, as costly and difficult as they may have been, appear to have been geared towards two main ends: other-worldly benefits for himself and his ancestors and successors, and the worldly provision of his chantries, which were the material vehicles for the realization of his other-worldly end. On this score, William's religious idealism may well have been leavened with a pragmatic sense of the future revenues that these mills might bring if the effects of the plague were eventually ameliorated. Because both mills held suit of the manor and had labour services attached to them, they were valuable assets for acquisition. William was presumably shrewd enough to have realized that although one of the mills was ruined and the other was only drawing 10 shillings in rent in the early 1360s, at the end of the thirteenth century, both mills must have been quite profitable, as the sum of £16 paid by Geoffrey of Dethick to Thomas de Ferrers for what was presumably a half share of the two mills would have otherwise been somewhat generous, especially when we consider the costs of rebuilding a ruined watermill, which would typically have been anywhere between £7 to £30 in the thirteenth century.[102]

If the high mortality in William's family as a result of the Black Death was a reflection of the wider mortality in the area, *Netherleemilne* was most likely allowed to fall into ruin in the wake of the plague and the deaths of a large number of manorial tenants. The low earnings from the other mill were undoubtedly for similar reasons. Because the income from both mills had collapsed, the release of this property to William for the use of his chantries at this time was obviously a far more attractive proposition for the tenant-in-chief, John of Dethick, and mesne lord, Roger Beler, than were William to have made the same request two or three decades earlier. Once again, therefore, we find that donors to religious houses were generally only prepared to grant out their mills if they were earning a low or a marginal income from them. In the case of the Wakebridge mills of Crich, the custom for the mills had collapsed when the plague took most of the manorial tenants. It was in this much-reduced condition that William secured a stream of revenue from what had become marginal mills to pray for the souls of his family. The chantries' mills would not regain the profitability they had enjoyed between the early thirteenth and early fourteenth centuries until the sixteenth century.[103]

---

[101] Ibid., ms. 7.

[102] See Lucas (2006a), pp. 137, 139–41.

[103] See Finley (1951), p. 154; Holt (1988), pp. 165–7.

Cockersand Abbey (Premonstratensian)

Cockersand Abbey was founded on the site of a hermitage and infirmary on the north coast of Lancashire that had been established by a pious recluse known as Hugh the Hermit in the early 1180s. The site is by the sea near the mouth of the river Lune, on a treeless, bleak and inhospitable stretch of coastline near the village of Thurnham about nine kilometres south-west of Lancaster. Like the Cistercians, the Premonstratensians favoured remote areas, and Cockersand was no exception. The foundation was secured by two grants, the first from William de Lancaster II and his wife Hawise de Stutevill around 1184, and the second by William de Furness, lord of Thurnham, in 1186. These initial grants were confirmed by a Papal Bull of Protection and Privilege by Clement III on 6 June 1190, which elevated the hospital to the status of a priory.[104] It also exempted the priory from any exactions by 'Archbishops, Bishops, Archdeacons, Deans or other ecclesiastical persons'.[105] As we have seen with regard to the Augustinians and Cistercians in previous chapters, such a privilege was greatly valued by the house concerned, as it effectively protected the house from any form of episcopal interference.

The early endowments of the Lancaster family were followed by additional grants by the statesman Theobald Walter sometime between 1194 and 1199 of Pilling Hay (now Pilling in Lancashire), and by King John of the demesne estate of Newbigging (near Singleton just to the south of the River Wyre) in 1204. John had in turn confirmed Cockersand's earlier grants and privileges a few years earlier. By this stage the priory had been further elevated to the status of an abbey.[106] A dispute arose during this period between Leicester Abbey and the Lancaster family over Cockersand's presence in the area, as William de Lancaster II had dispossessed Leicester Abbey of the manor and church of Cockerham (Lancs.) that had been granted to Leicester by his father in order to give it to Cockersand as the site for its new abbey. The dispute was settled by restricting Cockersand's liberties and commons to the areas of its land grants, and the granting of two fisheries to Cockersand by Leicester for twelvepence a year. Any further acquisitions of land in the manor were to pay tithes to Leicester, and Cockersand was prohibited from acquiring further property within the townfields of Cockerham. Cockersand was thus established as an extra-parochial property within the manor of Cockerham, an arrangement that received papal and royal confirmation, as well as subsequent reaffirmations by the two abbeys in 1230, 1242, c. 1242–45, 1340 and 1364.[107] As we will see, however, these documents did not prevent the two houses from entering into a series of acrimonious disputes, particularly during the mid-thirteenth century.

Between c. 1190 and 1282, shortly after the Statute of Mortmain came into play, Cockersand received as many as 40 or 50 land grants in the area, including several mills, such as Greenhalgh mill from Gilbert fitz Roger (c. 1190–1215),[108] and a grain mill in Garstang from Walter de Faulconberg (c. 1271–82).[109] Local gentry and knightly families who donated other property to the abbey included the Anglo-Norman Banastres, whose estates were based in Shropshire and Lancashire.

Cockersand was also the beneficiary of many grants from small freeholders who had risen in status from villeins during the twelfth and thirteenth centuries with the lordly commutation of labour services to cash rents.[110] None of Cockersand's mills appear to have come from such humble sources, however. By the end of the thirteenth century, the abbey's dispersed holdings covered an area bounded by the rivers Lune and Ribble, and what are now the towns of Preston, Blackpool, Fleetwood and Lancaster. In other words, the vast majority of its property lay in the western half of Lancashire.

---

[104]   *Chartulary of Cockersand Abbey*, pp. ix–xi.

[105]   Ibid., p. 8.

[106]   Ibid., pp. xi–xii.

[107]   Ibid., pp. xii–xiv. Another Papal Bull of 18 February 1218 exempted Cockersand from paying any tithes on newly acquired land which they had brought under cultivation, which obviously affected the terms of the agreement with Leicester Abbey (see ibid., pp. 24–5).

[108]   See ibid., pp. 46–7, for King John's confirmation of this and earlier grants to the abbey, and pp. 168–9 for the original grant from Gilbert.

[109]   Ibid., pp. 61–2. Walter's grant included the suit of mill of the parish.

[110]   Ibid., pp. xiv, xix. See Appendix A, section A.4.3.

It is difficult to determine from Cockersand's early documents just how many mills it initially possessed, although Greenhalgh mill is specifically mentioned in the grant of Medlar to the canons, while generic references to 'waters and pools, fisheries and mills' are made in the grants of Pilling Hay and Newbigging to Cockersand within a few years of its elevation to abbatial status.[111]

Apart from those mills mentioned in its foundation charters, the earliest mention of any other mills in Cockersand Abbey's charters is to two mills that were included in two separate grants to the abbey dated c. 1212 and 1230–50, both of which were included in the shares of knights' fees held by the grantors. The first of these was a carucate of land in the town of Tarleton, about eight kilometres to the west of Leyland south of the Ribble, which included a mill. The grantor was Gilbert de Notton, who held the fee of John Maleherbe, who in turn held it of Roger de Montbegon.[112] In other words, the mill was part of a heavily subinfeudated knight's fee. The second mill was included within a larger grant of the vill of Marton by Richard le Rous of Marton. The vill appears to have been somewhere near the river Wyre in the vicinity of Stalmine and Preesall. It had formerly been held by at least two tenants-in-chief who had fallen out of favour with their kings.[113]

The tithes of another mill near Westbrook were granted to the abbey by Thurstan Banastre sometime between 1213 and 1219. The grant in frankalmoin includes Thurstan's body, 'the tithe of the new mill in Walton-in-le-Dale, which [he] had erected, and of the fishery belonging to that mill'.[114] What is now called Walton-le-Dale is a few kilometres to the south-east of Preston. In another grant of around the same time, Thurstan states that the mill tithe was worth half a mark a year (6s 8d), indicating the mill was drawing over £3 6s in annual revenues, which would suggest that the mill held the suit of Walton-in-le-Dale.[115] Here we have a clear example of a minor lord with manorial rights apparently building a mill with the intention of donating some of its revenues to the local abbey for the salvation of his soul and those of his ancestors and successors.

Cockersand held a single fulling mill at Garstang halfway between Lancaster and Preston. Some contemporaneous documents from the 1270s indicate that it was distinct from the grain mill which Cockersand acquired from Walter de Faulconberg. The fulling mill of Garstang is first mentioned in a grant of 1246–56 by Richard le Boteler to the canons of Cockersand of the mill with its tenteryard and two perches of land, as well as free access to the mill and suit of the fee of Garstang. Here we have an unusual example of a fee mill with suit being granted to a religious house, whereas most of those we saw donated to the Augustinians in Chapter 6 had no seigneurial privileges attached to them. Richard also gives the abbey the right to take timber from his nearby wood for the repair and maintenance of the mill and millpool, 'and dead wood to store up for burning' without the interference of the foresters.[116] As proof of their legitimate right to seisin, the cartulary includes a copy of the original grant of the mill, its site and pool by William de Lancaster to Richard le Boteler, dated 1230–46.[117] It is interesting to note in the light of the Lancaster family's heavy involvement in the Welsh fulling industry later in the century that they had seemingly abandoned at least one such mill in Lancashire somewhat earlier.[118]

The next two documents are dated to sometime between 1268 and 1280. The first is a demise from the abbot and convent of the Garstang fulling mill and its suit to Richard le Boteler in return for a yearly rent of £2.[119] The second is a declaration by Richard that he would bind himself and his heirs to this payment, and

---

[111] For the initial grant of Pilling Hay from Theobald Walter, see ibid., p. 376; for Greenhalgh from Gilbert fitz Roger, see ibid., pp. 168–9; for Newbigging from King John, see ibid., p. 42. With regard to Greenhalgh mill, a notification by the monks of 1212–20 states that it serviced the vills of Greenhalgh, Medlar and Thistleton, and that the monks also held copies of the original grants which confirmed their seisin of this mill and the homage and service of Adam de Corney and his heirs (see ibid., p. 171).

[112] Ibid., p. 459, and n. 1.

[113] Ibid., p. 151, and n. 1 and 2. The first was Robert Ferrers for his involvement in the baron's rebellion, the second was Theobald Walter for being an appointee of King John's brother, Richard I.

[114] Ibid., p. 527.

[115] Ibid. As we saw earlier in the chapter, Cheshire appears to have been one of the counties in which both free and unfree tenants were required to perform suit.

[116] Ibid.. p. 357.

[117] Ibid., p. 358.

[118] See Lucas (2006a), Ch. 9.

[119] *Chartulary of Cockersand Abbey*, p. 246.

would also accept distraint from the sheriff of Lancaster in order to recover any unpaid rent.[120] Unfortunately, this is the last that we hear of this mill.

It should be noted that although a rent of £2 from a fulling mill is significantly higher than many that we have seen previously, the mill held suit and was probably drawing much lower revenues than the grain mills held by the abbey. If the half mark in tithes paid to the canons by Thurstan Banastre is taken as a tenth of the total mill revenue and a fair indication of the average revenue, a figure of £3 6s 8d for a grain mill held by them seems reasonable considering the kinds of rents that were typical of the north. A comparison of this hypothetical grain mill revenue with the fulling mill's rent reveals the same kind of relative value as seen elsewhere in the study, i.e. the latter is 48 per cent of the former, or just under half.

A series of charters from the first seven decades of the thirteenth century document Cockersand's attempts to acquire full seisin of Hutton mill, and provide some additional useful information about the value of mills in the north. A quarter share of Hutton mill – which served the townships of Howick and Hutton in the lordship of Howick – was granted to Cockersand by one of two daughters of the chief lord of the fee, Roger de Howick, sometime around the turn of the twelfth and thirteenth centuries. A second quarter share with three carucates was granted to the abbey by Roger's grandson, and the remaining two by local gentry, one of whom derived his own share from a member of the Banastre family, who were, apparently, one of Cockersand's more dedicated patrons, as the aforementioned grant by Thurstan Banastre of the tithes of his newly built mill of Walton-in-le-Dale indicate.

The content of the charters relating to Hutton mill and a dispute between Cockersand and a tenant over an illegally built mill in Garstang are discussed in detail in Chapter 9, although there is some important information pertaining to the value of Hutton mill in that material which should be cited here. Two quarter shares of the mill were valued at eight shillings in annual rent, implying the whole mill was valued at 16 shillings – a fairly low rent for the north which implies a concessionary rate. However, the fact that the canons paid £5 for another quarter share suggests a total value of £20 for this mill, a figure which is very much consistent with the price paid elsewhere in England in the thirteenth and fourteenth centuries for an existing watermill.[121]

Two independent tenant mills are explicitly exempted from grants to Cockersand. The first is dated 1220–50 and is from William de Tarnacre. Consisting of half a bovate of land in Upper Rawcliffe, the grant specifically exempts William's mill as well as his fisheries and nets.[122] In an earlier grant of 1200–1217, a millstream running into the Wyre is described as the boundaries of Alan de Tarnacre's land in Kirkcroft.[123] The millstream was probably for the same mill, as what is now called Out Rawcliffe is very close to the Wyre. The second mill is described in a grant from before 1268, in which William de Bispham gives the abbey a share of Dalebridgehead and four strips of ploughland in Newton, but exempts his 'fishery in Ribble and mill' (*salvo piscario meo in Ribbil et molendino*).[124] It is not clear whether the fishery of Ribble and the mill of Hutton described in the aforementioned series of documents from 1190 to 1268 are describing the same places as those being exempted in this charter.[125] Given that both parties appear to have held land and water rights, the Tarnacre and Bispham families were presumably minor gentry with manorial holdings in the area.

There is one mill described in the cartulary which was clearly held by a private or free tenant. It is mentioned in a grant to the abbey from Elias de Hutton dated 1199–1220 of a quarter of the town of Thistleton, along with another 12 acres of land by the dyke which presumably led to Greenhalgh mill. The grant exempts the abbey from multure at the same mill for all grain grown on the land granted, but excludes from the grant the land of a man named Esbreck and his mill.[126] Presumably, this grant was made to Cockersand before Gilbert fitz Roger's grant of Greenhalgh mill to the abbey, but the presence of an exempted mill within the town would suggest that it was a private tenant mill.

---

[120] Ibid., p. 247. Another grant from William le Boteler to Cockersand of 20 acres in the vill of Layton also describes a mill as lying just outside the boundaries of the grant (ibid., p. 157, dated 1252–68).

[121] Lucas (2006a), Ch. 4.

[122] *Chartulary of Cockersand Abbey*, p. 180.

[123] Ibid., p. 248.

[124] Ibid., p. 206.

[125] Ibid., pp. 412, 438–43.

[126] Ibid., p. 173.

A summary of the information contained in the various charters pertaining to Cockersand's mill holdings is set out in Table 8.10. By the end of the thirteenth century, the abbey's cartulary records that it had interests in at least nine mills. All of the documented mills were granted to the canons by members of the knightly class and aristocracy. We also know that the mill tithes granted to them by Thurstan Banastre were from a newly built mill. Like the Augustinians, therefore, the Premonstratensians appear to have acquired most of their mills from local lay lords and knights in the late twelfth and thirteenth centuries.

Table 8.10   Nine mills in which Cockersand Abbey held an interest before 1300

Name	Year acquired	Grantor	Annual revenue
Greenhalgh mill	c. 1190–1215	Gilbert fitz Roger	
Pilling Hay mill	1194–99	Theobald Walter	
Newbigging mill	1204	King John	
Tarleton mill	c. 1212	Gilbert de Notton (kt.)	
Walton-in-le-Dale mill (with 1/2 carucate)	1213–19	Thurston Banastre	6s 8d (tithes)
Hutton/Bradford mill (1/4 share)	1190–1218	Sapientia, wife of Elias de Hutton (kt.)	2s to grantor
	1212–32	Robert de Notesargh	
	1220–46	Robert de Howick	4s and 4 pairs of white gloves to four grantors
	1236–56	John and Alice de Clayton	£5 consideration to grantor
Marton mill (with vill of Marton)	1230–50	Richard le Rous of Marton (kt.)	
Garstang fulling mill (with suit of Garstang)	1246–56	Richard le Boteler	£2 (1268–80)
Garstang mill (with suit of parish)	c. 1271–82	Walter de Fauconberg	

With the exception of the fulling mill of Garstang and the tithes received for the mill of Walton-in-le-Dale, there is very little indication in the cartulary of how much these mills were earning. Thurstan Banastre's revenue from Walton-in-le-Dale mill was in the order of £4 3s, and is probably a reasonable indication of the kinds of revenues the canons were drawing from their mills with suit, which included those in Marton, Hutton and Garstang. It is possible, however, that the mills of Greenhalgh, Pilling Hay, Newbigging and Tarleton were also owed suit. It should be noted that this revenue was from the early, rather than the late, thirteenth century. Given that this was the case, it compares favourably with the average mill revenue for northern lay lords recorded in the Edward II IPMs a century later, which was £5 14s.[127] The Walton-in-le-Dale mill was therefore presumably drawing around the same amount by that time. As we saw in Chapter 3 in relation to the milling revenues of some of Lancaster's neighbouring lay lords, £3 6s is fairly typical of the kinds of mill income being enjoyed by Lancastrian lords in the early fourteenth century, although not, perhaps, in the first half of the thirteenth century.

Conclusion

There is a remarkable difference between the nature of the land and mill acquisitions of the late religious foundations studied in this chapter and those of the Augustinian houses, which they appear to have most closely resembled. Cockersand, Leiston, Grove and the Wakebridge Chantries all seem to have avoided the management problems that beset the Augustinians by ensuring that their holdings were within a relatively compact area, and by acquiring most if not all their mills with suit. How they managed to do so, however, remains far from clear, as there is no indication of whether this was pursued by them as a conscious strategy, or was instead simply the outcome of the particular patterns of patronage which they enjoyed. Holy Trinity, on the other hand, having been an early foundation with scattered manorial holdings of ancient demesne,

[127]   Langdon (1994), p. 13.

experienced similar problems with the management of its mills as those faced by both the Augustinians and the Benedictines. Although it was forced to accept low rents from many of its rural mills that had fallen into customary and hereditary tenure under Stephen, it was able to draw high custom to its town mills.

Like the Augustinians, all of the minor order houses in the sample acquired the vast majority of their mills through donation or purchase, and appear to have built few if any of their own. It would seem that as many as half of the 40 or more mills held by the five houses in the middle of the fourteenth century were acquired either at their foundation or within a short period of time afterwards. In order of their dates of establishment, Holy Trinity held 12 English mills within 17 years of it having been granted its first English lands just before the Conquest, while Leiston probably only acquired a single mill upon its foundation in the 1180s. Cockersand held at least three mills within 14 years of it having been elevated to abbatial status in 1190, while the Wakeford Chantries acquired both of their mills soon after the first chantry was established in the late 1340s or early 1350s, even though one of them was initially ruined. Although no records exist of Grove Priory's foundation, it seems likely that it held at least a single mill soon after it was established in the 1180s or 1190s.

Table 8.11   Mill holdings of five minor order houses in the late thirteenth to mid-fourteenth century

Name	Total no. of mills	Mills with suit	Mills in customary and hereditary tenure	Windmills	Industrial mills	Total estate revenue
Holy Trinity Abbey, Caen	20–23	5+	15+	0	2	no data
Cockersand Abbey	8	4–8	0–4	0	1	no data
Grove Priory	5	5	0	2	1	£183 5s (1341–42)
Leiston Abbey	4	4	0	0	0	no data
Wakebridge Chantries at Crich	2	2	0	0	0	no data
TOTAL	**39–42**	**20–24+**	**15–19+**	**2**	**4**	**-**

As with the Augustinian houses sampled, most of the mills donated to the houses of the minor orders were pious gifts, although unlike most of those mills donated to the Augustinians, many of these mills either held suit or were drawing fairly high incomes. Why this should have been the case is not at all clear.

Although most of these foundations were smaller than those established by the other orders, three of the five houses sampled held as many mills as the medium-sized abbeys and priories of the major orders; the alien abbey of Holy Trinity held as many mills as some of the largest English religious houses. By the early fourteenth century, Cockersand Abbey appears to have held at least eight mills, including a fulling mill, while Grove Priory possessed five mills, including two windmills. At the same time, Leiston Priory held at least four mills, and the Wakebridge Chantries two watermills. Although no complete records exist for this period for Holy Trinity, it probably held more than 20 mills by this time. The mill holdings of the five houses for the late thirteenth to mid-fourteenth century are set out in Table 8.11.

Based on their high incomes and/or their locations within whole manors or vills, by the mid-fourteenth century at least 20 of the 39 or more mills directly held by the five houses sampled were seigneurial mills, or 51 per cent of the total. The vast majority of the mills that did not hold suit were held by Holy Trinity, which had lost three-quarters of its mills to customary and free tenants by this stage (Table 8.12). Of the other estates, Cockersand appears to have held suit on half or more of its mills, Wakebridge on both of its mills, and Grove and Leiston on all of theirs. Although data on the revenues from these various mills is fairly thin, those for which there is data support the observation that those who held the majority of their mills with suit were drawing much higher revenues than those without.

In terms of their potential for revealing details of the operations and incomes of their mills, the best records relate to Holy Trinity and Grove. Holy Trinity in particular kept detailed records of its mill holdings, with its charters and custumals including three series of rentals of c. 1106, c. 1170 and c. 1306 to c. 1320, as well as details of its rents on several other mills. The records of Grove Priory also include a number of rentals and surveys, the most useful with regards to mills being an extent from around 1318, and a bailiff's account of 1341–42. The records of the other three houses are illuminating from other perspectives, however, especially in relation to the roles of patrons in the acquisition of ecclesiastical holdings.

The highest revenues recorded overall were for Grove Priory's five mills, most of which were acquired through an initial grant from Henry II in the late twelfth century, and were located on manors in an area of extensive woodlands and river-meadows geographically close to the priory. Based on their high incomes, it seems very likely that all of these mills were owed suit, as they had average annual revenues of slightly less than £4 in the early 1340s. The other northern house of Cockersand was probably drawing similar revenues from its grain mills with suit by this stage, but the evidence here is more inferential than substantial, as it appears to have directly managed all of its mills. Other mills that appear to have been drawing relatively high rents by the early to mid-fourteenth century were the mills of Langwade and Gleverill held by Leiston Abbey, and those of Felsted, Horstead and Dudbridge held by Holy Trinity. All of these mills appear to have owed suit.

Of the 40 or so mills directly held by the five houses sampled, at least four were acquired by purchase, or 10 per cent of them. The four mills concerned were Langwade watermill purchased by Leiston Abbey before 1212 for £33 6s 8d, the mill of Hutton/Bradford acquired in stages by Cockersand Abbey between 1190 and 1256 for a total sum of well over £11, and the two mills of Lea purchased by William of Wakebridge for the Chantry of Sts Nicholas and Catherine in the late 1340s or early 1350s for an undisclosed sum. The vast majority of the other mills were acquired by donation.

Holy Trinity's mill holdings were unique amongst the houses sampled in this chapter in that they were mostly inherited through its acquisition of ancient demesne lands from William I and his wife Matilda. A handful of others were acquired through later grants of manors post-Domesday and a few more from tenant mill-builders in the late thirteenth century. In addition to these acquisitions were two examples of alienated mills held by Holy Trinity that had to be bought from their tenants in the early thirteenth century in order to return them to the demesne. These were the mills of Neford in Norfolk and *Apechildewude* in Essex, the first of which cost the nuns £2 4s, five quarters of barley and three and a half acres of land to be held at a nominal rent, whereas the second cost them £15 8s 4d and half an acre of land at sixpence annually. As will be discussed in more detail in Chapter 9, the prolonged litigation and large sums which the nuns paid for regaining seisin of *Apechildewude* mill and other property held by the Felsted and Veim families acted as a powerful disincentive for them to attempt to regain seisin of their other alienated properties.

At least 14 of the 18 mills which Holy Trinity held in the twelfth century were acquired by it during the reign of William I, or about 78 per cent of them. Only 12 per cent were acquired during the twelfth century. Although it lost two or more of these mills over the subsequent decades, at least seven more mills were acquired by it during the thirteenth and early fourteenth centuries, most if not all of which seem to have been built by the tenants who held them. All of the abbey's English mills were attached to ancient manors that had been granted to them by members of the royal family.

Like many of the Augustinian houses in the sample, the Premonstratensian house of Cockersand acquired most of its mills from members of the lay élite in the late twelfth or thirteenth centuries. Six of the eight mills which it directly held were acquired during the thirteenth century, or 75 per cent of them. All of its mills were donated to it by the king, tenants-in-chief and members of the knightly class.

The Premonstratensian house of Leiston had acquired three of its four mills in the early thirteenth century, all of which had been donated to it from knightly tenants or relatives of its founder, Ranulf de Glanville, and most of which had been parts of knights' fees. Both of those mills held by the Wakebridge Chantries were acquired in the late 1340s or early 1350s via the purchase of a subinfeudated knight's fee by one knight from other knightly families. Unfortunately, it is not possible to determine when or from whom Grove Priory acquired its various mills, although it seems likely that it built at least one windmill close to its precinct during the thirteenth century.

The only clear evidence for newly built mills amongst the records of the houses sampled were for the mill of Walton-in-le-Dale built by Thurston Banastre in Lancashire between 1213 and 1219 for an undisclosed sum, the tithes of which were subsequently granted to Cockersand Abbey, and *Overleemilne* in Derbyshire which was completely rebuilt by William of Wakebridge in the late 1350s or early 1360s, also for an undisclosed sum. Apart from these two mills, however, it seems reasonable to conclude that Grove Priory built Grove windmill in Nottinghamshire sometime during the windmill-building boom of the thirteenth century, and that the fulling mill and grain mill of Brimscombe and the tool-sharpening mill of Brechacre on Holy Trinity's manor of Minchinhampton in Gloucestershire had been built by the abbey's tenants sometime between the late twelfth and early fourteenth centuries. If these assumptions are correct, six out of the 40 mills in which the five houses had interests had been newly built when they acquired those interests, or 15 per cent of them. However, only one of these six mills appears to have been built by the house concerned, rather than by donors or tenants. Once again, therefore, this evidence provides no succour for proponents of the monastic innovation thesis that religious houses were responsible for building most medieval mills. Less than 3 per cent of the mills held by the minor order houses in the early fourteenth century appear to have been built by the houses concerned.

The relatively unusual ways in which the various houses of the minor orders constituted their holdings provides valuable insights into the kinds of opportunities and constraints which such houses faced in their future development. A striking example is the alien abbey of the Holy Trinity, which acquired most of its English lands through royal patronage in the late eleventh century, including a large number of mills. During the thirteenth and fourteenth centuries, when most comparably sized religious houses had successfully managed to draw a large number of their alienated mills back into the demesne in order to exploit the higher profits that were then to be had from milling following a period of marked inflation, the nuns of Holy Trinity were singularly unsuccessful in following the lead of their English counterparts. This appears to have been largely due to the difficulties and expense of remotely managing their English estates, and in particular from having had a skilfully dishonest steward running their affairs for many years. On the other hand, however, such late foundations as Cockersand, Leiston, Grove and the Wakebridge Chantries managed to avoid the problems of mill management which beset Holy Trinity and the Augustinians by acquiring holdings that were within a relatively compact area close to home, as well as manorial mills with suit.

Most of the houses sampled appear to have developed and changed their mill management practices over the years, their interest in doing so appearing to be largely a function of the profitability and/or seigneurial status of their mills. With the exceptions of Grove and Holy Trinity, the mill management practices pursued by the other houses during the thirteenth century were fairly typical for that period. Cockersand appears to have directly managed all of its mills from the time of its foundation in the 1180s to the end of the thirteenth century, with the exception of its fulling mill of Garstang, although this single lease was to the noble who had first donated the mill to the abbey. Leiston also appears to have directly managed all four of its mills from the late twelfth to the end of the thirteenth century, as did the Wakebridge Chantries throughout the second half of the fourteenth century. Grove Priory seems to have let all five of its mills at farm on fixed-term leases for cash rents in the early fourteenth century, although by the middle of the century it had shifted its policy to collecting grain rather than cash rents.

The most detailed information on mill management for any of the houses sampled is for Holy Trinity. Its documents cover a period from the late eleventh century through to the early fourteenth century, and reveal some remarkable changes during that time. Of the 19 mills that are recorded on Domesday manors that Holy Trinity was later to hold, six appear to have been directly managed while 13 were at farm. By 1106–13, the number of mills that the abbey directly managed had doubled to 12, while those at farm had been reduced by more than 3/4 to only three. Two other mills had been allowed to slip into customary tenure while another was probably held freely. This evidence clearly demonstrates that the process of alienating mills from the demesne had already started on Holy Trinity's English manors only two decades after Domesday. Interestingly, however, direct management had also replaced leases at farm as a preferred managerial method overall as early as c. 1110, a phenomenon which is usually associated with the thirteenth century. By the end of the twelfth century, however, only two of Holy Trinity's English mills were being directly managed, or a sixth of the number at the beginning of the century, while six were at farm, or double the number earlier in the century, indicating that the intervening six or seven decades had seen a reversal in the abbey's mill management practices. What is most remarkable, however, is that the number of mills outside seigneurial control had more than tripled over the same period, with 10 mills held customarily at this stage, or almost 56 per cent of the total. By the early fourteenth century, all of the abbey's 11 mills of Minchinhampton remained outside the demesne, five of which continued in customary tenure but six of which appear to have been held freely. Furthermore, two of the mills that were held customarily were on lifelong leases while a third was held by a lord.

The chaos of Stephen's reign combined with the unscrupulous management of Holy Trinity's English holdings by its chief steward, Simon of Felsted, appear to have been the main factors responsible for the alienation and illegal assarting of much of its property during the twelfth century, including its mills. Despite vigorous efforts at reclaiming such property in the thirteenth century, including the creation of a more efficient system of direct management, Holy Trinity appears to have had limited success in increasing its mill profits. This was mainly due to its lack of success in regaining seisin of mills in free and customary tenure well into the fourteenth century.

Table 8.12   Average annual mill revenues and proportion of mills with suit of minor order houses in the late thirteenth to mid-fourteenth centuries

Name	Average annual mill revenue	Mills with suit	Mills in customary and hereditary tenure
Holy Trinity Abbey, Caen	19 s 2d (late 12th c.) 9s 9d (early 14th c.)	25%+	75%+
Cockersand Abbey	£4 3s (estimate only)	50–100%	0–50%
Grove Priory	£4	100%	0%
Leiston Abbey	£3 6s (early 13th c.)	100%	0%
Wakebridge Chantries at Crich	10s (1361)	100%	0%

It is therefore clear from these data and from the previous discussion that the seigneurial status of Holy Trinity's mills had enabled the development of systematic management practices, although the nuns had neither the financial resources nor the will to recover all of their alienated mills after they had been lost to them during the stewardship of Simon of Felsted, thus ensuring that their revenues from these mills remained low over the subsequent centuries. As a consequence, its average mill revenues across all of its manors in the early fourteenth century were probably around half of those of other large religious houses in England at the same time. However, the abbey's mill management practices were not shaped by beneficence towards their tenants, but the constraints placed on their ability to administer their properties due to their physical remoteness.

While Holy Trinity appears to have experienced some major difficulties in formulating a workable system for managing its English properties, the relatively compact nature of most of the other houses' holdings combined with the manorial status of many of their mills made direct management a straightforward and profitable option for them. For example, the temporal possessions of the Wakebridge Chantries at Crich were extensively subinfeudated portions of knights' fees within a relatively short distance of the houses concerned. The two mills which they acquired were also owed suit and had labour services attached to them. One of them had been rebuilt at the sub-tenant/founder's expense, and both were directly managed.

With respect to the mill revenues of the houses sampled, the clearest evidence pertains to Grove Priory, which held suit on all of its mills, and drew an average annual mill revenue of £4 from each of five mills on six Midlands manors in the early fourteenth century (Table 8.12). Most of Cockersand's holdings consisted of vills and manors in a relatively contained area in west Lancashire, and it likewise appears to have held suit on many if not most of its eight or nine mills, virtually all of which were directly managed. Although data for Cockersand's mill revenues are thin, they appear to have been as profitable as other northern mills, generating revenues in the vicinity of £3 6s in the early thirteenth century. What little evidence exists for Leiston's mill revenues from around the same time in East Anglia also suggests average annual earnings of around £3 6s from each of five watermills donated to it by knights related in some way to its founding patron. By way of contrast, the lowest revenues recorded were for Holy Trinity's Midlands mills in the early fourteenth century, all of which were held by tenants in customary and hereditary tenure, and drew an average of only 9s 9d for eight mills. A small number of these were former seigneurial mills that had been purchased by their tenants, while a number of others appear to have been built by their tenants and then let to them on lifelong leases for nominal rents. On the other hand, the low revenue of 10 shillings from the Wakebridge Chantries' *Overleemilne* with suit was undoubtedly the result of the devastation of the population on the Derbyshire manor on which the mill was located following the Black Death, as it had most likely drawn a much higher revenue earlier in the century based on the generous purchase price which had been paid by its previous owner to secure it.

Although the records of Cockersand and Wakebridge make few references to mill revenues, they do contain more detailed accounts of the broader social relations pertaining to their mill holdings. As we will see in the next chapter, these include legal disputes with lay folk of varying social status and other religious houses over property boundaries and land and water rights, the role played by female heirs in the inheritance of lay estates, and the entry of the lesser gentry and small freeholders into ecclesiastical patronage. Leiston's records, while not being rich in detail, provide an interesting counterpoint to Cockersand and Wakebridge with respect to their common acquisition of knightly grants of mills, and as we have seen, all three provide some details of the sums of money which each house was prepared to pay to gain the seisin of profitable mills.

Chapter 9
English Mill Law, Seigneurial Rights and Ecclesiastical Lordship

The legal status of mills and milling in medieval England is as difficult to disentangle as any of the more intractable problems in medieval history. Bennett and Elton, Holt and Langdon are virtually the only scholars to date to have conducted any detailed research on the topic.[1] Their respective discussions have ranged from suit of mill and mill lease agreements to disputes over possession, water rights, rental arrears and the behaviour of millers. The thorniest issue of all, however, remains suit of mill: how it first emerged as a customary obligation, under what conditions it could be claimed to exist and the extent to which it applied in different parts of England and to different strata of society. Because the answers to these questions are crucial to understanding how a commercial sector of the milling trade emerged during the twelfth century, as well as for understanding the tenurial status of the many mills without suit which were donated by knights to the Augustinians, Cistercians and Premonstratensians in the twelfth and thirteenth centuries, the discussion to follow focuses primarily on suit of mill, but also attempts to draw some broader conclusions about ecclesiastical disputes over mill possession, water rights and mill tithes. Prior to entering into these more detailed discussions, however, it is necessary to provide some background about how the laws relating to mills developed both before and after the Conquest.

Being valuable assets,[2] even when 'debilitated',[3] watermills and windmills had a special status in medieval English law, even though that status is difficult to definitively determine due to the paucity of statute law concerning mills and the complexity of the local customs surrounding them. Lords who possessed mills and the tenants who rented, leased or licensed them were very careful about specifying the conditions under which they were built, purchased, donated, exchanged, leased, tenanted and repaired.[4] Customary and statute law provided watermills with certain inalienable rights over access to water,[5] whereas windmills, as a new invention, required the development of new legal arguments to integrate them without disruption into existing practices.[6] The owners of mills with suit had certain rights over the unfree (and sometimes free) tenants covered by the obligation, albeit according to local custom and tradition, rather than common law.[7] All mills,

---

[1]   Bennett and Elton (1900); Holt (1987), pp. 8–9; Holt (1988), pp. 36–53, 56–69, 80–1, 98–105; Langdon (1994), pp. 22–4, 31; Langdon (2004), pp. 185–200, 209–18, 257–88. See also Bennett (1934), pp. 129–35; Loengard (2006); Sistrunk (2006).

[2]   As we have seen on some of the estates studied so far, mills were generating as much as 11 per cent of total annual revenues for religious houses, with 7–10 per cent being not at all unusual. Langdon has argued that 'those who built mills could normally expect them to contribute in excess of 5 per cent of manorial income' (2004, pp. 32, 34).

[3]   According to Langdon, mills that did not hold suit were considered to be under a 'severe financial handicap' and consequently often labelled 'debilitated' by jurors in the manorial courts, on which see Langdon (1991), p. 440. See also Langdon (1994), p. 36 n. 90, citing P.R.O., C134 54/3, m. 3; C134 41/1, m. 3 with respect to two cases in Little Weldon (Northants.) and Petworth (Sussex).

[4]   Langdon (2004), pp. 193–218.

[5]   *Henrici de Bracton de Legibus et Consuetudinibus Angliae*, Ch. LXII–XLV.

[6]   In response to the legal challenge to seigneurial rights presented by the new invention of the windmill, Tim Sistrunk describes how jurists sought to justify Celestine III's decision that novel devices such as windmills were still obliged to pay tithes to the Church. The argument ran as follows: even though windmills are reliant on a physically and legally unconstrained resource, i.e. the wind, and are a product of the ingenuity of men, they are as much guided by the hand of God as the water and the hands of men, all of which are a part of God's creation, and therefore subject to established canonical conventions. See Sistrunk (2006), pp. 154–5. This argument presumably did not hold for steam mills, as a legal ruling from Yorkshire in 1806 deemed that tenants who had traditionally done suit at two 'ancient watermills' and a horse mill on the manor of Selby did not have to do suit at a steam mill built to replace the watermills after the horse mill was also torn down. See Bennett and Elton (1900), pp. 213–14.

[7]   According to one justice serving under Edward II, '[the duty] to grind corn on certain lands at somebody's mill is not [imposed by] common law, but follows the usage of the country.' See *Year Books of Edward II, iii, 3 Edward II, A.D.*

along with the lands and waters associated with them, were subject to the laws of nuisance and damages, as were the millers who ran them and the tenants and lords who held them.[8] Disputes over suit of mill, nuisance, ownership, legal status, malicious damage, theft, rental arrears and labour services were heard in the secular courts, whereas disputes over payment and possession of tithes and other forms of ecclesiastical jurisdiction relating to mills were heard in the ecclesiastical courts.[9]

Before the Conquest, both laypeople and the clergy were subject to secular law through the hundred and shire courts.[10] Various kings had also granted some of the great landowners the right of private jurisdiction upon their estates as early as the eighth century. These lords subsequently had the right to create hall courts and manorial courts to hear cases concerning tenants with respect to all but the most serious of criminal offences.[11] William introduced two new kinds of court: borough courts and ecclesiastical courts. The borough courts were initially separated into courts for the 'English' and the 'French', while the ecclesiastical courts were set up specifically to hear spiritual matters that were subject to episcopal law rather than secular custom.[12]

The Normans subsequently introduced additional changes to the manorial courts, splitting their jurisdiction according to the status of the tenants concerned. The court of the honour was restricted to the manor's principal tenants or major landholders, especially those who performed knight service for the lord, and extended across the several manors that formed a lord's 'honour' or larger estate. The court baron was concerned with the resolution of disputes involving a manor's free tenants, including the enforcement of feudal dues, and the acquisition of land within the manor by new tenants. The court customary, or halmote court, performed much the same function as the court baron, but for the manor's unfree tenants. The court of the honour acted as a superior court of appeal within the lower manorial courts until the late thirteenth century. However, the halmote court became the predominant type of manorial court during the late Middle Ages, as the distinction between free and unfree tenants before the law declined.[13]

Despite efforts to clarify the respective jurisdictions of the various secular and ecclesiastical courts, there remained some ambiguity concerning which court was competent to hear which kinds of cases. The *curia regis* remained the ultimate court of appeal in secular matters, but became the preferred forum for many litigants who had little faith in the power of the lower courts to enforce their judgements.[14]

Until the late twelfth century when the English common law system was first established, the Normans utilized the terminology and institutional structures of Anglo-Saxon law – itself a mixture of royal writ, charter, custom and tradition – to legitimate the new power structures they created throughout the country.[15] In the process, as will be argued at greater length below, they fundamentally transformed the meanings of many of the legal instruments and customary obligations that had existed prior to the Conquest, albeit in a piecemeal fashion and over the course of many decades.

The common law system that emerged between the late twelfth and sixteenth centuries served the interests of both lords and peasants: it was at once a means of formalizing the network of principles and customs

---

1309–10, p. 201. The courts were generally adamant that if no such custom could be proven to exist, and especially if it could not be established to have existed before 1189 (see note 16), any lord who sought to argue a case on the basis of customary law was most likely to fail.

[8]   Langdon (2004), p. 262; Loengard (2006), pp. 130–31, 132–5, 141–2.

[9]   However, Van Caenegem (1988), p. 114, n. 37, notes that 'a bishop surrounded by his *curia episcopalis* ... could also hold pleas on feudal matters, surrounded by his vassals as in any other baronial *curia*, and the distinction is not always easy to make.'

[10]   See Vinogradoff (1908), pp. 90–93, 95–7, on the origins of the county court and its influence on the development of English law, and pp. 97–107 on the hundred court and the regional variations in the territories it covered. Cf. Chibnall (1986), pp. 166–8, on the functions and jurisdiction of the shire and hundred courts.

[11]   See Maitland (1987), pp. 80–150. These rights of private jurisdiction, known as 'soke and sake', and what they involved, will be discussed in more detail below with respect to the issue of suit of mill.

[12]   Van Caenegem (1988), pp. 12–13.

[13]   Mulholland (2002), pp. 65–6; (2003), p. 83. Cf. Vinogradoff (1908), pp. 214–15, on the origins of the halmote courts; Chibnall (1986), pp. 170–74, on the functions and jurisdiction of the honorial courts.

[14]   Van Caenegem (1988), pp. 15–16. However, only free men and women were allowed to have their cases heard in the king's court, and if litigants were unable to establish their free status, their cases would not be heard. See Holdsworth (1976), Vol. II, pp. 375–7, on the ambiguities surrounding distinctions of status in the courts. Cf. Faith (1999), pp. 259–61.

[15]   See Stenton (1910), pp. 51–2, for some interesting observations on this issue.

introduced by the Normans across England during the first century of their rule, and of challenging that rule on the basis of pre-Conquest custom and tradition. The notion that judicial precedent should be binding rather than simply persuasive was dependent on the reasons for the judgements being recorded and available for jurists to study (i.e., the *ratio decidendi*). However, it is more common than not to find that such reasons are not recorded in the medieval court rolls, nor are final judgements, making it difficult for historians to deduce the principles guiding many of the decisions made, and providing jurists of the time some latitude in forming their decisions. Until a formal body of law could be established, therefore, judicial authorities had to rely on a mixture of statute, common sense and precedent to build a body of internally consistent law.

Furthermore, due to the longstanding status of customary law in the English courts, they deemed it necessary in 1275 to declare a time before which there was no 'legal memory'. The first Statute of Westminster declared that any legal decision dating to before Richard I's accession to the throne on 6 July 1189 was deemed to have been in place since 'time immemorial'.[16] This development had profound implications for deeds of possession, tenancy, sale and purchase dated to before the late twelfth century, and is therefore important in understanding how mills and milling were treated as legal entities by religious houses, particularly during the thirteenth and fourteenth centuries.

As Langdon has previously noted, the legal ramifications of milling arose from the kinds of relationship that medieval people had with mills. On the one hand, there were those who possessed and used mills, or the land appurtenant to them, which included owners, lessees, tenants, neighbours and customers. On the other hand, there were those who made their living from building, operating, repairing or supplying mills, which included merchants, traders, workers, carpenters, masons and millwrights. Perhaps unsurprisingly, most of the records of legal cases pertaining to mills and milling relate to the first category of relationships.

Because the law is in many ways an expression of how power is mediated within any given society, when power structures change, so does the law to reinforce and legitimate them. After the Conquest, the English Crown sought to accumulate to itself the sole right to possess and disperse land and other fixed property, including mills. After the Statute of Mortmain was introduced, the only person who could legally do as he pleased with the mills he held was, of course, the king. But most lords had pretty much done as they pleased with their mills before the late thirteenth century,[17] and as long as they did not infringe on another lord's rights, they could build a mill wherever they pleased on land which they held both before and after the statute was introduced.[18]

Post-Conquest law nevertheless circumscribed the kinds of ownership rights lords had over mills. Of paramount importance was the fact that lords were entitled to lease and in some circumstances sell or grant their mills, or directly manage them for their own benefit. They could also specify the terms under which third parties could hold mills of them,[19] but they were also legally obligated to make good any damage that the mill and its associated workings caused to a neighbour's property, such as flooding by a broken milldam or a blocked weir.[20]

Mill tenants and farmers also had certain rights and responsibilities, depending on the kind of tenure in which they held the mill, and under what conditions. For example, mill lease agreements may or may not have included obligations on the tenant or lessee to maintain and repair the mill, depending on the rent charged and the level of custom to the mill. They were also obligated to pay their rent on time and to ensure that whoever was operating the mill dealt with customers fairly. Mill lease agreements from the post-Conquest period characteristically specified who possessed the mill and who was leasing the mill and for what period, how the revenues from the mill were to be directed, who was responsible for running and maintaining the mill, and who was responsible for any damage caused to a mill's 'appurtenances' i.e. its millhouse and machinery, access roads and footpaths, waterways and waterworks, etc. Distraining clauses concerning the consequences of illegal possession, rental arrears, misconduct by millers, malicious and accidental damage, and theft were also sometimes included. Such agreements might also mention who was obliged to grind their grain at the mill, inasmuch as it was considered necessary, and to the extent that lords were prepared to pass the privilege onto lessees.[21]

---

[16] *Statute of Westminster, The First*, 3 Edw. I, cap. 5.

[17] Holt (1987), pp. 9–10.

[18] *Henrici de Bracton*, Vol. III, Ch. XLV, fo. 234. Cf. notes 75 and 95 below.

[19] Langdon (2004), pp. 187–201.

[20] *Henrici de Bracton*, Vol. III, Ch. LXII–XLV.

[21] Langdon (2004), pp. 185–218.

As we have seen in earlier chapters, the level of custom drawn by any mill was of crucial importance in determining whether or not the mill was able to continue functioning. It therefore mattered a great deal to whoever owned or leased a mill how many customers were obliged to grind their grain at the mill, and if such obligations were not customarily associated with it, how many customers it could draw on a voluntary basis. The feudal obligation of suit of mill was clearly aimed at guaranteeing lords the custom of their tenants, but as noted in the introductory paragraph to this chapter, there continues to be some uncertainty about how and when suit of mill first emerged as a customary obligation, under what conditions it could be claimed to exist, and the extent to which it applied in different parts of England and to different strata of society. The following discussion attempts to resolve some of these issues.

The Diversity of Opinion on Suit of Mill

Bennett and Elton, Holt and Langdon are the only scholars to date to have delved in any depth into the issue of suit of mill. But although they all seem to agree that it was a pre-Norman phenomenon, none of them have explored the issue of how it came about in the first place and under what conditions. There is also some disagreement between them about what class of tenants were obliged to perform suit, and the circumstances in which tenants could be so obliged. It is therefore instructive to begin the discussion by reviewing their various positions on these issues.

In the third volume of their *History of Corn Milling* (1900), Bennett and Elton discuss suit of mill in terms of what they call 'milling soke', drawing on evidence from England, France, Scotland and Wales. They argue that although suit of mill was in place as early as the eighth century on at least one ecclesiastical estate, it was not until the eleventh century that it became commonplace, and remained in place in some parts of England until the nineteenth century.[22] The clear implication of many of the examples they cite is that suit of mill applied to all tenants, free and unfree, and that the Normans were primarily responsible for the custom's dissemination, if not its introduction.[23]

In 'Whose Were the Profits of Corn Milling?' (1987) and *The Mills of Medieval England* (1988), Holt argued against Bloch and others that suit of mill was a Norman imposition. He claimed that there is no evidence for the Normans having introduced suit of mill to England, or for the existence of a free market in milling before 1066. To the contrary, he felt that 'close seigneurial control of milling must have been a feature of English life before 1066',[24] and that 'the Domesday commissioners saw mills only as demesne assets under the control of the lord of each manor.'[25] Consequently, he concluded that all of the mills in Domesday are demesne mills, a position which Langdon also appears to endorse.[26] However, against Bennett and Elton, Holt suggested that suit of mill was a burden that applied only to villeins and people of servile status.[27]

---

[22]   Bennett and Elton (1900), pp. 202–46. The earliest case they cite relates to the monastery of Saints Peter and Paul in 762, whose mill of Cert Dover was said to hold soke rights over half the town of Hythe, 'the abbot to this extent being manorial lord of that part of Hythe by bequest or other gift from the original owner'.

[23]   Ibid., pp. 204–6, 209–12. Examples which they provide of freemen obliged to perform suit of mill included the burgesses of Salfordshire in the early thirteenth century, the burgesses of Stockport around 1206, the burgesses of Macclesfield in 1256, the burgesses of Altringham around 1290, and the burgesses of Manchester in 1301. However, according to the old county boundaries, all of these towns were in Cheshire or Lancashire, i.e., the north-west where stronger lordship prevailed. This is of some significance for the later discussion.

[24]   Holt (1988), p. 37.

[25]   Holt (1987), pp. 11–12.

[26]   Langdon (1994), p. 37, (2004), pp. 11, 14. Although I have not had the opportunity to systematically explore this issue, there is evidence from Cambridgeshire Domesday that there were at least half a dozen mills in that county which were almost undoubtedly *not* demesne mills, i.e., the three mills of (Steeple) Morden held by Bishop Walkelin of Winchester which were each drawing only 16d in revenues for the bishop; the mill of Whaddon held by Colswein, drawing 12d; and the mills of Kennett and Lolworth, each of which paid nothing. See *Domesday Book*, Vol. XVIII, fols. 190b, 194c, 196c, 201b. No such mills could be found in Huntingdonshire Domesday, which is perhaps not surprising given the history of strong lordship in that county.

[27]   Holt (1988), pp. 43–4 and 52, citing Bennett (1934), p. 130. Holt argues this is reflected in the 'economic' rate of multure generally paid by freeholders, as opposed to the 'extortionate' rate paid by villeins (ibid., pp. 50–51).

Langdon has characteristically undertaken the most systematic research on suit of mill to date, drawing on large-scale surveys of court records and the legal commentary and case law that subsequently arose. Central to Langdon's argument is the claim that obligations to perform suit of mill were based on the feudal status of both the tenant and the territory he or she held, obligations based on custom and contract which arose from the legal jurisdiction given to lords who held the soke and sake of a manor or vill. Essentially, these were the same rights of private justice or *ban* that Bloch argued lords appropriated for themselves and imposed on their demesne tenants from the ninth or tenth century onwards in France, and from the eleventh and twelfth centuries in England.[28] Langdon has also argued that the degree to which suit of mill applied to free tenants is unclear, as there is surviving evidence to show that both free and unfree tenants owed suit.[29]

Although Langdon has not explored the issue of the origins of suit of mill in any detail, perhaps because his later work has tended to focus on the late Middle Ages, he has made a few suggestive comments. For example, he indicates that a sizable share of the milling trade had already been cornered by lords by the time of the Domesday survey, and that '[m]uch of this was probably built upon the notable growth of a tenant population in the transition from slavery – or freedom – to serfdom.'[30] Slightly later in the same article, he adds that '[i]f a predominantly exploitative, *banalité*-driven phase of milling expansion ever did occur for England south of the Humber, it must have happened mostly in the later Anglo-Saxon period ... particularly as it could be tied to the late Anglo-Saxon nucleation of settlement and the development of English manorialism generally.'[31]

In what follows I will argue that, in terms of origins, all three of these positions are basically correct, but none take sufficient account of the profound changes which the Normans wrought upon Anglo-Saxon society within several decades of the Conquest, and the extent to which those changes provided a new legal framework within which mills and milling operated in post-Conquest England. Although there is little in the way of direct evidence to determine exactly how these changes were effected, there is plenty of indirect evidence that the Normans completely transformed the organisation and institutions of English society while maintaining the pretence that Anglo-Saxon customs and traditions were being broadly respected. The mechanized power represented by mills and milling provides one of the most instructive illustrations of the ways in which social power was dispersed and actualized in medieval England after 1066.[32]

The Transformation of Seigneurial Rights in Post-Conquest England

What is perhaps most significant about the transformation of political and legal structures introduced by the Normans after the Conquest is the systematic way in which they managed to elevate their own social positions at the expense of the majority of the people they conquered. There is no statute law which articulates how this was achieved, but the evidence from Domesday Book is unequivocal: many formerly free Anglo-Saxons were reduced to villein status and lost their security of tenure, or lost their land altogether, in the interests of the new ruling elite's goal of expanding demesne lands in places where their English predecessors had none.[33] In the words of Maitland, 'The work of the foreigners was done so completely that we can see but very little of the institutions that they swept away.'[34] Much of this transformation had occurred within 20 years of the Conquest and had a number of characteristic features which bear directly on the issue of mill seisin and suit of mill.

---

[28] Langdon (2004), pp. 64, 156, 183, 259–62, 270–72, 275–8, 283–90; Bloch (1967), pp. 152–3.

[29] Langdon (1994), p. 31, citing Langdon (1991), p. 440, where the mill of Tredington (Warks.) was held in customary tenure in 1379, along with the suit of both the free and customary tenants of the manor. This is the only reference of which I am aware which refers to freemen in the south being obliged to perform suit of mill.

[30] Langdon (1994), p. 37.

[31] Ibid., p. 39. This is not dissimilar to the position explored in the pages to follow.

[32] The main sources for my argument are Maitland (1987); Vinogradoff (1892), (1908), (1932); Stenton (1910); Seebohm (1915); Douglas (1939); Kapelle (1979); Faith (1999); Fleming (2004).

[33] Maitland (1987), pp. 135–9, 149–50; Vinogradoff (1908), pp. 219–62; Fleming (2004), pp. 107–8, 122–6; Faith (1999), pp. 215–18.

[34] Maitland (1987), p. 149.

One of the first tasks undertaken by William after the Conquest was his declaration that all land was from henceforth to be held from the king, including the rights of private jurisdiction or 'soke' which accompanied the many free holdings granted to tenants of varying status by his Anglo-Saxon predecessors.[35] As we have seen in earlier chapters, these sokelands existed before the Conquest but underwent what can only be described as a diminution in status in terms of the customary obligations due from them and the status of the tenants who held land on them.[36] What it also involved – which has not been sufficiently appreciated by earlier researchers – is a profound shift in the meaning of the concept of 'soke' and the social relations it delineated.

The Anglo-Saxon soke appears to have been primarily restricted to the delegation of territorial legal authority and revenues to lords which nevertheless incorporated the free men of the soke in witnessing and deciding on legal matters,[37] acknowledging their status and valuing their contribution to the communities of which they were a part.[38] As will be argued in more detail in the pages to follow, the Anglo-Norman soke was a different entity altogether, seemingly borrowing from French and Norman precedent.[39] In terms of its closest Anglo-Saxon equivalent, it involved an extension of the obligations due from bonded tenants and servants on the inland estates of royal and former royal demesnes to all current and former demesne, sokeland, assart and forest held of the king.[40]

As opposed to the obligations of free Anglo-Saxons to perform suit at the court of the lord, and military, bridge and fortification work for the king, the obligations that the Normans imposed on the recently made unfree retained to the king the *trinoda necessitas*, but stripped them of the right to perform suit at court, and transformed their obligations to provide royal *feorms* into the inland obligations of the demesne, just as their Anglo-Saxon predecessors appear to have done in the southern and western counties during the late tenth and eleventh centuries.[41] Noting the changes to free status wrought by the Normans, Stenton has remarked that '[t]he sokeman's tenure in 1086 had not the unmilitary characteristics which distinguished the socage of the thirteenth century.'[42] Vinogradoff likewise comments that although the terminological distinctions are not yet clear at Domesday, 'members of the soke ... are assumed to be merely under jurisdictional supremacy', whereas 'members of the village ... are taken to be under manorial authority'.[43]

The servile burdens imposed by the Normans on the recently unfree varied from county to county and manor to manor, the level of obligation being determined by what the local lord was capable of imposing through coercion, but tempered by the customs of the region, the landholder's status and/or the status of the holding. It is worth briefly describing how this process appears to have been effected.

---

[35] Ibid., pp. 80–107; Chibnall (1986), p. 29.

[36] Fleming (2004), pp. 122–3, 131–5.

[37] Maitland (1987), pp. 258–92.

[38] Vinogradoff (1908), pp. 194–5.

[39] Maitland (1987), p. 321.

[40] Stenton (1910), p. 11, notes that the meaning of 'inland' was extended during the eleventh century to 'cover not merely the lord's home farm, but also plots of land leased to cultivators out of the exempt demesne ... the term inland [was used by the compilers of Domesday] to cover the whole of that portion of an estate over which the lord had most immediate and direct control, the land of villeins and bordars in contrast to the land of sokemen.' My reason for assuming that after the Conquest, soke obligations customarily also extended to forest held of the king is that Henry III's 1218 confirmation of the Magna Carta (1215) makes an explicit reference to the milling soke of the king on his own estates, while granting to every freeman who held land directly of the king the right to 'erect in his portion of the forest or on the land he may have in the forest a mill, a pool, &c., provided such be not to the injury of his neighbours', cited in Bennett and Elton (1900), p. 209. Cf. *Henrici de Bracton*, Vol. III, Ch. XLV, fo. 234. Clearly, this clause implies that this right was not normally granted.

[41] Maitland (1987), pp. 318–24. Maitland (ibid., p. 115) explicitly contrasts the soke of the manor with its inland and with the berewicks, pointing out that the former encompassed justiciary rather than proprietary rights, unlike the latter two territorial categories. See also Stenton (1910), pp. 10–11, 30–31, and Fleming (2004), pp. 134–5, who clearly demonstrates that seigneurial rights over land were treated very differently to soke rights in legal disputes in the decades after the Conquest. Fleming points out that, according to the *Leges Henrici Primi*, 'soke did not automatically pass with the granting of the manor, but depended on 'personal arrangement', and that soke could be 'acquired by purchase, or exchange or in any other way.'

[42] Stenton (1910), p. 30.

[43] Vinogradoff (1932), p. 341.

One of William's first tasks was to appropriate in their totality the estates of vanquished Anglo-Saxon thegns, along with a significant proportion of those held by the ancient conventual and episcopal houses.[44] These were then split into smaller portions and enfeoffed to the king's military men through direct allocation, or by placing military burdens on their lay and ecclesiastical tenants-in-chief.[45] Numerous new manors were created out of these old estates, or combined from smaller manors and assart taken from woodland, heath, marsh and forest.[46] These manors were then leased to or tenanted by existing tenants and new settlers, who would often accept a diminished social status and even unfreedom in order to hold some land.[47] Villages were expanded and the surrounding commons and freeholdings turned into uniformly sized smallholdings (possibly including houses), the size of the holding depending on whether it was intended to be occupied by demesne servants, bonded tenants, customary tenants or so-called 'rustic knights'.[48] What had previously been a right to a portion of the shared resources of the village was transformed into the rights and obligations associated with a fixed area of arable land, together with its associated messuage and toft.[49]

More than a century ago, Stenton noted the 'marked general tendency towards the conversion of pre-Conquest sokeland into manorialized estates', portions of which were turned into discrete demesne holdings.[50] Many sokemen and other free men had their land expropriated by the Normans and were then turned into *nativi* or *rustici* or villeins, performing servile dues which had not been customary for them. Although this process had already begun by the late eleventh century,[51] it continued until well into the thirteenth century.[52] William's men from Normandy, France and Flanders were granted lordship over the dispossessed, displaced and landless, who were re-settled on existing manors and vills, such as in Oxfordshire, Leicestershire, Norfolk, Essex and Somerset,[53] and on new manors, such as in Yorkshire and Durham.[54] Some ecclesiastical lords who had lost property to *milites* responded by appropriating to the demesne ploughland from their

---

[44]   Faith (1999), pp. 178–80; Fleming (2004), Ch. 7.

[45]   As we have seen in earlier chapters, at the command of William, Glastonbury Abbey lost more than 100 hides to 40 knights from what had formerly been thegnland (Abrams (1996), pp. 311, 317), while the newly created estates of Battle Abbey were settled by William's former military retainers (Searle [1974]). See also Faith (1999), pp. 188–9, on Battle's *leuga*, and Douglas (1939), pp. 130–31, for examples of *miles* being enfeoffed by special command of the king on the estates of Bury St Edmunds and the bishop of Salisbury. Similar processes to those at Glastonbury were at work on the bishop of Lincoln's estates in Oxfordshire, who lost 64 hides to his *milites* in Dorchester, Great Milton and Cropredy. See Harvey (1970), pp. 14–23. Cf. Chibnall (1986), pp. 28–35; Fleming (2004), Ch. 4.

[46]   As we saw in Chapter 5 at Battle Abbey, where villein and customary tenants were given assarted and demesne land in return for a range of services (*Custumals of Battle Abbey*, pp. vi–vii). See also Vinogradoff (1932), pp. 299–303; Chibnall (1986), pp. 138–42; Faith (1999), pp. 179–80, 207–9.

[47]   Faith (1999), pp. 179, 222, the latter reference citing examples from the estates of St Albans and the bishop of Rochester. Cf. Kapelle (1979), p. 188, who cites Simeon of Durham on the imposition by Bishop Walcher of labour demands on newly created demesnes: 'many men sold themselves into perpetual servitude, provided that they could maintain a certain miserable life.'

[48]   Ibid., pp. 225–35. Faith has documented numerous instances of such processes at work drawing on primary and secondary sources.

[49]   Ibid., p. 235.

[50]   Stenton (1910), pp. 52–3.

[51]   For example, Stenton (1920), p. cviii, has noted that the village of Norton Disney (Lincs.), had no demesne in 1086. Its seven sokemen and 11 villeins with five ploughteams did soke to Countess Judith's manor of Stapleford; by the middle of the next century, the village was a manor consisting of 10 ploughlands in demesne. Kapelle (1979), pp. 182–90, has suggested that similar processes were at work on the former territories of northern Anglo-Saxon earls and the kings of Northumbria granted by William II to the bishop of Durham in the late eleventh century. Faith (1999), p. 188, notes that the bishops of Bayeux and Lincoln had also enlarged their demesnes at the expense of their warland tenants. See Faith (1999), pp. 215–8, 237, on the evidence for the reduction in status of many formerly free tenants throughout England after the Conquest. Cf. Maitland (1987), pp. 66–79, 141; Vinogradoff (1932), pp. 300, 340–43, 356–7, 367, 375; Fleming (2004), Ch. 4–7.

[52]   As Holt (1987), pp. 8–9, found on Glastonbury Abbey's manor of Brent, where two peasants 'described as *quasi liberos* and who had not hitherto performed labour services, were put under pressure to do so.' See also Hilton (1965) and Miller (1971), both of whom documented numerous cases of this kind.

[53]   Faith (1999), pp. 230–33.

[54]   As Kapelle (1979), pp. 183–6, 221–2, and Roberts (1987), pp. 196–201, found in Yorkshire and Durham after William's devastation of northern England.

tenants.[55] In other locations, new demesne was created in places where there had previously been none.[56] Faith has described the process through which Norman lords renegotiated the obligations of their tenants as 'the settlement', 'the establishment' or 'the great fixing'.[57]

During the twelfth century, members of the expanded servile class, consisting now of many formerly free men and women, were in some cases able to win customary tenure on their holdings on an individual or collective basis and rebuild some of the wealth which their ancestors had had taken from them.[58] By the late thirteenth century, most customary and freeholders had managed to convert their labour obligations to cash payments, enabling them to accumulate sufficient wealth by selling their surplus produce at local and regional markets to be able to reinvest in land and sometimes even equipment, such as mills, and improve their status.[59]

As these various processes unfolded, the recently installed knightly class played a number of important roles. On the one hand, those knights with small fees or manors (the so-called 'rustic knights') were under pressure to increase the size and profitability of their demesnes in order to make a living. They therefore tended to subject as many of their own tenants to villeinage or serfdom as they could manage,[60] which, as I will argue in the pages to follow, included where they could the imposition of suit of mill, just as many of their ecclesiastical predecessors had done before and after the Conquest. At the same time, as knights of varying status established themselves throughout England, they constituted a new class of consumers,[61] stimulating town, village and manorial economies. Knightly families who held in heredity became patrons of religious houses, contributing in important ways to monastic economies by providing rents and low- (or no-) cost sales and leases to those houses, including mills.[62]

These developments in social structure, exploitation of the land, and tenurial and settlement forms provide important context for the ways in which mills and milling were treated by English law in the second half of the Middle Ages.

'Milling Soke' and Suit of Mill

According to Vinogradoff, '[t]he absorption of Crown rights by privileged subjects is one of the most important and characteristic features of feudalism'.[63] Consistent with this observation, it has been argued that the origins of seigneurial monopolies in England were most likely a consequence of the extension of the royal privileges associated with inland estates to those lay and ecclesiastical lords who were the earliest beneficiaries of aristocratic largesse between the ninth and tenth centuries. It has also been suggested that previous discussions about seigneurial monopolies, and particularly suit of mill, have failed to adequately consider the evidence that although suit of mill certainly did exist during Anglo-Saxon times, it is a predominantly post-Conquest phenomenon. In what follows, I will attempt to describe how this situation came about.

---

[55]   For example, in response to having lost property to his knights after the Conquest, the bishop of Lincoln expanded his demesne ploughland at the expense of his peasants. See Faith (1998), p. 188.

[56]   For example, the demesne of the stud farm granted to Burton Abbey at Shobnall (Staffs.) 'seems to have been a post-Domesday creation.' See Faith (1999), p. 243, citing J.R. Birrell, 'Medieval Agriculture', *VCH Staffordshire*, Vol. VI, 1979, p. 15.

[57]   Faith (1999), pp. 217–21. Cf. Vinogradoff (1892), p. 335; Holdsworth (1973), pp. 266–7; Harvey (1977), p. 21; Fleming (2004), Ch. 7, amongst others, who similarly note that some kind of comprehensive, final settlement regarding peasant tenancies had taken place soon after the Conquest.

[58]   Ibid., pp. 218–23.

[59]   Hilton (1965), (1985); Faith (1999), pp. 236–7; Dyer (1989a), (2002), pp. 163–78. Cf. Biddick (1985) on the Crown's imposition in the late thirteenth and fourteenth centuries of lay subsidies on peasants whose wealth was over the minimum necessary for subsistence.

[60]   As did the sub-tenants of Robert d'Oilly in Oxfordshire at Domesday. See *Domesday Book*, Vol. I, 158a–c; Harvey (1988), p. 79. Cf. Kosminsky (1956), pp. 280–81. Faith (1999), pp. 169–70, cites several examples of cathedral clergy implementing similar policies on their smaller and poorer manors.

[61]   Chibnall (1986), p. 141; Faith (1999), pp. 198–9.

[62]   As we have seen in numerous different cases in Chapters 6, 7 and 8.

[63]   Vinogradoff (1908), p. 105.

Many scholars have previously noted that the possession of mills was an important marker of social status in feudal Europe, and that mills and milling were generally acknowledged to be a reliable source of cash or grain revenue, if there was sufficient custom from nearby suitors. A tenant's obligation to grind the grain grown on his or her holding, known in England as 'mill soken', *secta molendini* or suit of mill, was primarily aimed at guaranteeing that custom. For William and his great magnates, who had come from places where such rights had already become well-entrenched,[64] it would seem not unreasonable to assume that they would attempt to impose the same kinds of conditions on their English tenants as they had customarily imposed on their French and Norman ones. Having arrived in England to find that similar conditions already prevailed on some of the estates of the ancient religious houses and great magnates, they no doubt felt emboldened to encourage the extension of those rights to the many new lords whom they had enfeoffed.

As Bennett and Elton first noted well over a century ago, the legal obligation on the tenants of a manor to perform suit of mill – what they called 'milling soke' – was not established by statute law.[65] The lack of a definitive statement about suit of mill amongst any of the early legal commentators has proven to be an obstacle to gaining any clarity on the issue amongst contemporary historians. However, on one point there does appear to be agreement: that *secta molendini* was a form of 'soke right', and that it was closely connected to the rights of private jurisdiction granted by kings to their vassals from as early as the eighth century.[66] Two key issues have not been resolved, however. The first is whether suit of mill was one of those soke rights that from the very beginning was bound up with the right of a lord to hold courts and collect fines, taxes and amercements, and if it was not, how did it become one of the rights of private jurisdiction, when it clearly had no juridical basis? The second is to what extent and why were different strata of medieval (and early modern) society subject to suit of mill, and under what conditions could they be deemed to have that obligation? On the first issue, Bennett and Elton argue in one place that suit of mill was a Norman introduction, and in another that it was from the beginning an adjunct of the juridical rights of soke going back as early as the late seventh century.[67] Bloch dates the custom to the ninth and tenth centuries in France and the eleventh and twelfth centuries in England, after which he claims it became almost universal.[68] Holt and Langdon have both argued that milling soke rights were probably already commonplace by the late Anglo-Saxon period and not a Norman introduction.[69]

However, what has not been clarified in these discussions is what constituted a soke under the Anglo-Saxons, and whether there is any strong evidence that one of the rights of soke under the Anglo-Saxons was suit of mill. There are strong grounds for doubting that suit of mill was an automatic adjunct of suit of court from the time that this privilege was first conferred by kings in France and England. A sober assessment of the evidence suggests that it was, in fact, a later imposition by lords which in England required a change in meaning of the term 'soke' to encompass rights of private jurisdiction over both free and unfree tenants that extended well beyond collecting taxes and revenues and holding court for the king. Indeed, Maitland similarly suggests this was the case, arguing that by Domesday, 'the Norman lords are assuming a soke which their *antecessores* did not enjoy ... they are enlarging and consolidating their manors and thereby rendering a manorial justice possible and profitable.'[70] This extension involved imposing on tenants of a manor the lord's right to a monopoly on the ownership and usage of various pieces of manorial equipment, including mills, ovens, breweries and so on, that were essential for the subsistence of the people who held land within that manorial soke. And while Holt was undoubtedly correct in his assumption that 'close seigneurial control of

---

[64] Bennett and Elton (1900), p. 207, citing a complaint by Fulbert, Bishop of Chartres and Chancellor of France (1006–28), to Richard, Duke of Normandy, that 'Baldric our minister will have introduced a new trouble for our people, proclaiming that they shall go to the mill of St Andrews, five leagues distant from their homes.' Such 'proclamations' presumably played an important role in 'the great fixing' of the post-Conquest period.

[65] Ibid., p. 204. They also note that the eighteenth-century antiquarian, naturalist and jurist, Daines Barrington (1727–1800), commented in his *Observations upon the Statutes* (1774), p. 211, that 'less is to be found [on the topic of milling] in the laws of England than in those of perhaps any other country.'

[66] Bennett and Elton (1900), pp. 202–7, 209–15; Bloch (1967), pp. 149–59; Holt (1988), pp. 36–8, 40, 52; Langdon (2004), pp. 259–62.

[67] Bennett and Elton (1899), pp. 122–3, (1900), pp. 206–7.

[68] Bloch (1967), pp. 152–3.

[69] Holt (1988), p. 37; Langdon (1994), p. 39, (2004), p. 259.

[70] Maitland (1987), p. 94.

milling must have been a feature of English life before 1066', the available evidence suggests that it was not nearly so common then as it became after the Conquest.

My reasons for thinking this are several. First of all, there is no evidence from before the Conquest that the Anglo-Saxon concept of soke is anything other than a three-fold franchise from the king to a lord: the rights to hold court; to oblige the freemen of the soke to stand as judges, advocates, counsellors and witnesses; and to collect for oneself and the king the revenues of justice.[71] No other rights are described in association with soke in any of the early documentation, which, as Maitland noted, was a justiciary rather than a proprietary right.[72] The lords of the larger Anglo-Saxon estates who had been granted *saca* and *soca*, or sake and soke, had the right to hold court and to receive the proceeds of justice: *saca* was the privilege of exclusive jurisdiction over an estate, and *soca* was the area of jurisdiction over which the privilege extended.[73] The earl or lord of the estate retained 1/3 of the court revenues raised by fines, seizures, etc, and the remaining 2/3 were allocated to the king.[74] There is no indication that the Anglo-Saxon soke had anything to do with a lord's monopoly rights within the territory of the soke to own fixed (and formerly communal) assets such as mills, ovens and breweries, or to draw all of the custom of tenants under the lord's jurisdiction to those assets.

Second, under the Anglo-Saxons and in the Danelaw, sokelands were the domains of freemen, who performed lighter, 'non-servile' tasks for their lords than those performed by the bonded tenants who lived and worked the land of the lord's inland. The lord had jurisdiction over the men of the soke, but to do soke and to hold the associated responsibilities was a mark of freedom, not serfdom, and we know from Domesday Book that many of these men had been able to go wherever they pleased and to buy and sell their land to and from whoever they pleased.[75] It is not unreasonable on this basis alone to assume that many sokemen could similarly mill their grain wherever they pleased.

Third, soke rights usually covered a number of manors and estates (known as an 'honour') which need not have been contiguous, as it might include berewicks and sokelands of freemen located some distance from the caput or chief manor, i.e. the manor in which the lord normally resided. More rarely, a single manor had soke.[76] In the Danelaw, individual sokes were usually contained within the boundaries of a single wapentake or group of adjacent wapentakes, with the court being held in the chief manor.[77] However, not all manors had soke, because the size of manors varied enormously during Anglo-Saxon times.[78] Assuming for argument's sake that Anglo-Saxon soke rights included suit of mill, in the many documented cases of geographically dispersed sokes, it is difficult to imagine how free tenants located on distant manors or property could be expected to perform suit at the chief manor, especially if there were closer watermills at which to grind one's grain.

Fourth, in East Anglia and some other parts of southern England it was common to find that the *liberi homines* under the protection or commendation of one lord were under the soke of another lord. There is evidence from the Danelaw and southern England at Domesday that men who did not do soke to other lords

---

[71]   Ibid., pp. 82–3, 86–7, 89, 100. According to the *Leges Henrici Primi*, 20, art. 2, those who were entitled to receive this privilege under the Normans were restricted to 'archbishops, bishops, earls and other 'powers' [*potestates*]'. Under the Anglo-Saxons, however, any free man could be granted soke over his estates, even if it was generally restricted to larger landholders.

[72]   Maitland (1986), p. 115. Stenton (1910), p. 49, has remarked that 'even within the precincts of the manor, the sokemen were regarded as in some sense external to its organization ... the tenements which they occupied were their own property, subject to seigneurial exploitation, but co-ordinate with, rather than subordinate to, the lord's demesne.' However, Stenton simply assumes that seigneurial exploitation was an automatic implication of soke tenure, without demonstrating that it was so, or at what point in time it came into play.

[73]   Bennett and Elton (1900), p. 202. Cf. Maitland (1987), pp. 67–70, 84–6, 97, 102; Vinogradoff (1932), pp. 213–16, 280, 303, who describes soke as 'an outcome of protection, not of tenure'.

[74]   Maitland (1987), pp. 95–6. Except in special cases of royal plea where the king took all the revenue.

[75]   Maitland (1987), p. 123.

[76]   Ibid., pp. 107–28.

[77]   Stenton (1910), pp. 44–6.

[78]   Maitland (1987), p. 91. Also, as noted above, transfer of ownership of a manor did not necessarily include its soke. See note 41.

came under the jurisdiction of the king,[79] indicating that this category of freemen were subject solely to national jurisdiction.[80] Maitland cites an account of a situation that prevailed during Edward the Confessor's time that provides some insight into the legal ambiguities surrounding soke which the Normans appear to have already been prepared to exploit by Domesday. The lord of Wenham in Suffolk is described as only having soke over the four bordiers and one slave on his demesne lands, and not over his nine villeins, who performed suit at the hundred court in Bercolt.[81] Although Domesday describes the men concerned as 'villeins', the fact that they were doing suit at the king's court clearly indicates that they were, in fact, freemen. If we assume for argument's sake that suit of mill was automatically connected to socage tenure, and freemen were just as much subject to it as the unfree, there were clearly instances of individuals holding land on the manor of one lord who owed soke to another lord beyond the manor. They would therefore have to mill their grain at the soke lord's mill, clearly depriving their manorial lord of revenue, a situation which manorial lords would no doubt have found unacceptable had it existed, and which may well have involved for the sokemen concerned the need to travel a much greater distance than to the demesne mill to grind his household's grain: an onerous obligation that does not sit well with the concept of free tenure.

Fifth, unless freemen had improved their status to such an extent by the twelfth and thirteenth centuries that they could legitimately and convincingly claim in the English courts that they had the right to mill where they pleased on the basis of custom, it seems very unlikely indeed that freemen had ever been obliged to perform suit of mill as a customary obligation before the Conquest. The case law from the twelfth and thirteenth centuries in multiple jurisdictions strongly indicates that suit of mill 'was an obligation particularly associated with villeinage'.[82] There is strong evidence from many parts of England during this period that freemen were not generally obliged to perform suit of mill, and could therefore mill where they pleased,[83] just as many of the freemen described in Domesday could give and sell their land to whomever they pleased.[84] Because there were even some who could "go with their land to what lord they chose' and carry with them not merely their homage, but also their suit of court and their forfeitures',[85] it is difficult to imagine how any freeman before the Conquest could be obliged to perform suit of mill to a single lord. And if they were so obliged, was suit of mill owed to the lord to whom they owed homage, or the lord who held soke over them? Perhaps more importantly, because the obligation to perform suit of mill was primarily dictated by custom,[86] it stands to reason that there can never have been a time at which freemen or their ancestors had been obliged to perform suit of mill to any lord in those areas that claimed customary exemption from this obligation. And if, indeed, that is the case, it makes far more sense to think of suit of mill as an 'inland' obligation of demesne tenants which had always excluded freemen, in much the same way as Faith has conceptualized the diminution in status of peasants after the Conquest as an extension of inland-type obligations to a formerly free and significant segment of the peasantry. It follows from this that if formerly free Anglo-Saxons had lost their status either before or after the Conquest, and they continued to live on what was still or had been sokelands, they could be obliged to perform suit of mill to the soke lord on whatever estates the custom had been established.

While the obligation to perform suit may well have been ubiquitous for servile tenants on royal and formerly royal manors under the Anglo-Saxons, most scholars agree that the number of unfree peasants increased substantially after the Conquest, in which case the number of those obliged to perform suit of

---

[79]   Stenton (1910), p. 45.

[80]   Maitland (1987), pp. 90, 103–5. The fact that it was only freemen who were permitted to bring cases before the king's court after the Conquest would appear to support Maitland's observation.

[81]   Ibid., pp. 90–91, 97. The contemporary settlements of Great Wenham and East Bergholt are about three kilometres apart.

[82]   Langdon (2004), p. 265. Cf. Neilson (1910), pp. 86–7, 98–100.

[83]   Holt (1988), pp. 43–4; Langdon (2004), pp. 265–6, 268, 270. There are few exceptions to this rule in any of the surviving documentation, and virtually all of them are in the north or north-west, as we have already seen and as will be discussed further below.

[84]   Maitland (1987), p. 123.

[85]   Ibid., p. 101.

[86]   And occasionally by contract, but this required an agreement between the parties concerned (Langdon [2004], p. 265), which again has important implications that will be discussed at greater length below.

mill must also have substantially increased. By the time of Henry I (r. 1100–1135), the meaning of soke had already been extended to include 'all the customs' ('*cum omnibus consuetudinibus*') that fell within the territory of the soke,[87] and by the early thirteenth century, to any manorial district that was deemed to hold soke rights.[88] Suit of mill was, therefore, more often than not a recently introduced custom that was structurally embedded in the many new manorial holdings which the Normans and their successors created. In the words of Vinogradoff, the conquerors' purpose was 'not merely to collect the material for new impositions and a verification of the old, but to organise the country and to obtain a hold on its resources'.[89] The notion that suit of mill was a 'soke right' – an automatic right of manorial jurisdiction – enabled an extension of the obligation to all those places where it had not previously existed: an economic instrument for securing another source of reliable revenue from tenants dressed in the guise of an ancient custom.

There are strong grounds for concluding from all this that the Normans made a conscious effort to transform the concept of 'soke' after the Conquest, just as they transformed the status and holdings of many of the free and unfree. From a Kuhnian perspective, what we are seeing is a change in the legal paradigm under which land and power were held and tenant status assessed. It should not therefore be surprising to learn that, just as in scientific paradigms, the meanings of basic terms essential to the paradigmatic framework should also change, and indeed, that those meanings should be partially or even radically incommensurable.[90]

So what were the conditions under which a lord could establish that he or she held suit of mill as a customary right on his or her manor or vill? It has been noted above that legal decisions dating before 1189 were adduced by the courts to have been in place since 'time immemorial', a fact which undoubtedly explains why the former royal estates held by lay and ecclesiastical lords had unambiguous feudal obligations attached to them – including suit of mill – and why monkish forgeries of ancient charters were so commonplace in the thirteenth and fourteenth centuries. It was also noted above that a tenants' obligation to grind his or her grain at the manorial mill was a consequence of local custom and tradition, rather than common law. While this observation does lend weight to the previous argument about origins, the notion of 'custom' was a rather flexible concept in the Middle Ages. Whereas in France, the period required to establish customary obligations was stipulated in various charters to have been anywhere between 30 and 40 years,[91] several learned English jurists of the period argued that 10 years, or two legal precedents, were sufficient to establish a customary rule.[92] In other words, even recently established manorial practices which had commanded the assent of tenants could soon be argued to have attained customary status under Anglo-Norman law, a fact which may help to explain why it has proven so difficult to determine the exact circumstances under which suit of mill could be established.

---

[87]   A charter to London (*Liber Albus*, ii, 129) concedes that '*quod ecclesiae et barones et cives habeant et teneant bene et in pace* sokas *suas cum omnibus consuetudinibus*'.

[88]   Maitland (1987), p. 91.

[89]   Vinogradoff (1932), p. 301.

[90]   Kuhn (1962), p. 102. Cf. Feyerabend (1978), p. 70. For example, the meaning of 'soke', 'free', 'unfree', 'villein', 'manor', etc. Another way of thinking about these changes is in terms of a Foucauldian 'episteme': the historical set of assumptions that ground knowledge and its discourses and which delineate the circumstances in which they are realized within a particular epoch. According to Foucault, several epistemes may co-exist and interact at the same time, being the expressions of various power-knowledge systems. The fundamental assumptions upon which the episteme is based are generally invisible to the people operating within it, and, it would seem, to many historians as well. See Foucault (1970).

[91]   Bennett and Elton (1900), pp. 210–11, cite La Mare's compendium of French customary law, *Nivernois* (c. 18, arts. 1, 2), which states: 'To acquire *bannalité* of mill or oven, it is necessary to possess title or peaceable possession for 30 years on the part of the laity or 40 years on the part of the Church, and provided that the prescription has been preceded on the part of the lord by a prohibition to tenants to grind elsewhere than at his mill. Tenants subject to the *bannalité* cannot dispense with it and acquire their liberty by a custom of grinding or baking elsewhere unless such custom shall have peaceably continued for 30 years with regard to the laity and 40 years with regard to the Church.' They also cite the customs of Anjou (arts. 27, 28) and of Maine (arts. 31, 32), which stipulate a period of 30 years for tenants subject to both lay and clerical jurisdiction, adding that the lord must adequately maintain the mills and ovens on his manor, and that those tenants subject to suit must have resided on the manor throughout that time.

[92]   Van Caenegem (1988), p. 26.

Given what we have learnt so far, it would seem that the most likely explanation for how suit of mill had become the norm by the thirteenth century was because it had been established as a customary practice on many of the new manorial holdings created by William in the late eleventh century because most of these manors had only a single mill when they were first created, or had no mill at all. Indeed, it is possible that one of the criteria for establishing the boundaries of these new manors by William was that they contained at least one mill, or were at least adjacent to a manor or manors which contained one or more mills.[93] If the only choice for free and unfree tenants on a newly created manor was to handmill at home or use the single manorial watermill or windmill (or a mill held by the closest neighbouring lord), the simple fact of monopoly would be sufficient to create a customary obligation for tenants to mill their grain at the manorial mill if they lacked the time or resources to mill at home or outside the manor.

If, on the other hand, the villeins and free tenants on a manor were not already accustomed to milling their grain at the single mill on the manor (or a neighbouring manor), and that mill was in the demesne of the lord (bearing in mind that there was in the late eleventh and twelfth centuries quite some distance between manors, and therefore, manorial mills), it only took 10 years of continuous practice in the eyes of thirteenth century jurists (and, presumably, most lords) to establish that practice as customary and therefore legally binding on its tenants. On already established manors, it was a simple act of the chief lord nominating a demesne mill that would be sufficient to establish suit for its tenants, and that mill need not necessarily be on the lord's own manor if the soke lay elsewhere or there was no demesne mill on the manor.[94] If the manor had no mill when it was first acquired, and the lord later built a mill on his or her demesne, that mill could subsequently acquire suit of its villein (and possibly free) tenants.[95] A lordly proclamation to manorial tenants would be sufficient to establish that they were expected to perform suit at the lord's mill, and indeed there are examples of such proclamations in the charters of at least one of the religious houses.[96]

Thus was it possible, as a consequence of customary usage, to establish by the late twelfth century a legal monopoly on powered milling within a manor or vill where once there had been only a literal monopoly.[97] Lords who acquired their manorial holdings from the time of the Conquest onward could use

---

[93]   It is also possible that this strategy was borrowed from former royal estates and those of the great religious houses, such as Canterbury Cathedral Priory's estate of South Malling, which had one grain mill for each of its 10 borghs inside and outside the wood, although six of those borghs had no mill. See Table 4.2 in Chapter 4.

[94]   See, for example, Neilson (1910), p. 100.

[95]   Bennett and Elton (1900), pp. 212–14. However, it generally seems to have been the case that if there was no demesne mill on the manor, tenants could mill where they pleased. See, for example, ibid., p. 207, who cite a charter from Randolph (Ranulf), Earl of Chester (1170–1232), which explicitly exempts his burgesses from having to perform suit on his manorial holdings if there is no mill there. Holt (1988), p. 43, cites the case of the Abbey of Halesowen, where there had been no demesne mill before the foundation of the abbey in 1215 and for some time after, allowing the tenants to grind their grain wherever they pleased, and providing the basis for the later dispute between the abbey and its tenants, on which see Razi (1983).

[96]   For example, Bennett and Elton (1900), p. 236, cite a charter from Ramsey Abbey (*Cart. Ram.* i, 473) dated 1225 in relation to its mill on the manor of Pekesdene (Hunts.) which clearly included its free tenants:

> To this mill every tenant shall make suit with respect to all grain he shall produce. If on the first day the whole of the grain cannot be ground, then the mill shall grind as much as may be necessary for the tenant's family for that day. If on the same day this portion cannot be ground, then it shall be lawful for the tenant to claim his grain and take it elsewhere at his pleasure. It shall be lawful for everyone, if he buy his grain, to take it, without calumny, to the nearest mill he may come to. From the beginning of August until Michaelmas it shall be lawful for everyone to grind his grain where he shall please, if on the day he takes it to the lord's mill it cannot be ground there. At other times, also, if the lord's mill or pool be broken, so that the mill cannot grind at all, it shall be lawful for anyone, as above, to take his grain elsewhere. If any be convicted of not making suit to the mill of the lord in due and proper manner, he shall before trial pay sixpence; and if the trial sustain a conviction, then he shall pay twelvepence. Through the entire year the tenant shall grind his grain [at the lord's mill] at a certain multure rate, except for Christmas and Easter, when no toll is taken on grain.

This example supports earlier observations about Huntingdonshire being dominated by large and wealthy ecclesiastical estates that imposed their seigneurial rights on their tenants from very early on.

[97]   Such an interpretation helps to explain why Abbot Samson of Bury St Edmunds was so enraged by Herbert the Dean's construction of a windmill near the demesne watermill and ordered it to be torn down, because he knew that he would never be able to establish a customary obligation on his villein tenants to perform suit at his mill if there was more than one mill on the manor. See *The Chronicle of Jocelin of Brakelond*, pp. 59–60.

the fact that they held the only mill on the manor at the time of its acquisition to impose suit of mill on their tenants, and if custom allowed (or there had been no prior custom), it was not only the unfree but the free who could be so obliged. And even if a lord did not hold the only mill on the manor, or held no mill at all, Holt has demonstrated that the mere fact of holding the demesne of the manor was deemed sufficient by the early fourteenth century to establish the right to the custom: manors which held no demesne mill were by this time claiming suit of mill from their tenants, requiring them to pay a license fee in lieu of multure to the lord.[98]

Based on the well-documented customs of various French regions, including Anjou, Maine and Poitou, it seems likely that French precedents were increasingly influencing English custom by the thirteenth and fourteenth centuries.[99] For example, the customs of Poitou explicitly state:

> It is sufficient to establish a right of soke by the lord of a manor that he possess a sufficient mill, driven by either wind or water, provided that it be within his demesne or in some other place held by him in chief or as life tenant within the manor ... If the manorial lord have not a mill, the tenants shall be obliged to go to the mill of the baron, if he possess one in the barony; but if the manorial lord build a mill, he enters upon his rights, and the tenants shall grind with him.[100]

If suit of mill could be acquired through proclamation in France as early as the first half of the eleventh century (as the previously cited complaint from Bishop Fulbert of Chartres indicates),[101] there were French precedents for the Normans to similarly seek to declare to their English tenants that suit of mill was to be one of the obligations that they would have to perform on the many new manors which they had created.[102] The previously cited charter from Ramsey Abbey indicates that such proclamations were sufficiently common by the early thirteenth century to be included in cartularies.

With respect to the many mills granted by knights to the Augustinians, Cistercians and Premonstratensians during the twelfth and thirteenth centuries, almost all of them were located on fees within existing manors and vills, and could not, therefore, claim suit of the tenants within the fee. The only exception to this in any of the records sampled appears to have been the suit of the fee of Garstang in Lancashire granted to Cockersand Abbey by William le Boteler in the 1240s.[103] In this case, it would appear that the fee of Garstang did not lie within an existing manor, and therefore functioned by default as a manorial holding. The fact that suit of mill was indeed a territorial right that could be established through customary usage by manorial tenants of the demesne mill in those instances where a lord was in seisin of a whole manor or vill clearly delineates the circumstances in which suit of mill could be rightfully claimed. The custom of Poitou quoted above lends further weight to this supposition.

Tenurial Status and Suit of Mill

We have seen ample evidence throughout this book that the extent to which suit of mill applied to, and was enforced upon, the tenants of a manor or vill varied considerably throughout England. These variations can be attributed to a number of factors, including regional differences in the kinds of free and customary tenure that were permitted to persist in some parts of England after the Conquest, the extent to which tenants were able

---

[98]   Holt (1988), pp. 45–8, 53, citing examples from Suffolk, Norfolk, Somerset and Hampshire.

[99]   It is worth bearing in mind that Henry II (r. 1154–89) was Count of Maine, Nantes and Anjou, as well as Duke of Normandy and Aquitaine, and ruled more of France during his reign than did the King of France, providing the requisite political and administrative networks through which such influences could be brought to bear.

[100]   Bennett and Elton (1900), p. 211, citing *Poitou*, arts. 34, 38, 40, 51, 143.

[101]   See note 32, citing Bennett and Elton (1900), p. 207.

[102]   Indeed, Bennett and Elton (1900), p. 243, argue, with some justification it would seem, that 'milling soke depended in every case upon its establishment by special charter'.

[103]   *Chartulary of Cockersand Abbey*, p. 357. The implications of this case with respect to Cockersand's seigneurial rights on the fee are discussed in more detail below.

to avail themselves of milling alternatives,[104] and the ability of individual lords to either enforce customary obligations on their tenants,[105] or to win that custom on the basis of their moral rectitude.[106]

Clearly, there were parts of England in which such customary obligations to perform suit of mill could never be established due to the extent to which free tenures were the norm, such as in Kent, where suit of mill simply did not exist.[107] And if such customary obligations had only ever been applicable to unfree tenants, as was the case in East Anglia, the east Midlands and parts of the south-west, no lord could claim seigneurial rights over any of the free tenants who held property on his or her manors, unless that holding itself had villein status,[108] or the tenants themselves had only recently gained their freedom and had previously been accustomed to do suit at the manorial mill.[109]

In the frontier counties of the north, however, where powerful lords created customs and obligations upon a *tabula rasa*, the severity of the punishments meted out to transgressors of seigneurial privilege acted as a strong disincentive to disobey,[110] and even free tenants could be held obligated to perform suit of mill if custom had established that this was so.[111] Based on the evidence from the Bishopric of Hereford, it would also seem that at least some of the lords of the Marcher Counties were not only able to enforce suit of mill on the free and unfree tenants of their manors, they were able to extract most of the associated revenue from tenants who held mills of them in customary and hereditary tenure.[112]

All of these instances, and the individual cases which have been cited to support them, indicate that the obligation to perform suit of mill was not simply a function of a tenant's status; it was also a function of the tenurial status of the territory in which he or she held grain-growing land. Holt has argued that whether a tenant was obliged to perform suit at the manorial mill was determined by his or her villein status, rather than whether he or she was a manorial tenant. But the north and some pockets of strong lordship in the south were clearly more like France in the extent and severity of feudal compulsion. The examples already cited of free tenants being compelled to perform suit in Lancashire, Cheshire, Yorkshire and Huntingdonshire clearly demonstrate that the territorial component to suit of mill in the north and some parts of the south was the determining factor, rather than tenant status. Most free tenants in the south, to the extent that they survived the Conquest as a class of landholders and became more differentiated in the twelfth and thirteenth centuries, do indeed appear to have been free to grind their grain wherever they chose – as Holt was the first to emphasise – which explains why mills without suit were able to survive without seigneurial compulsion in many parts of England from the twelfth century onward.[113]

---

[104]   These alternatives included domestic and commercial handmills, and seigneurial and non-seigneurial horse mills, watermills and windmills within and outside the manor or vill of the tenants concerned.

[105]   As in the famous cases of Bury St Edmunds, St Albans, Peterborough, Halesowen, and Cirencester that have been canvassed in earlier chapters.

[106]   An example of the latter being the commitment by Walter son of William of Inglesham to have all his men of Westbrook do suit at Beaulieu Abbey's mill of Little Faringdon in the early thirteenth century; a quite onerous commitment considering that the mill was more than a day's riding journey from Westbrook. See *Beaulieu Cartulary*, ms. 23.

[107]   As we saw on St Gregory's estates in Chapter 6. See Vinogradoff (1908), pp. 92–4, on the unique body of customary law that characterised legal and social life in Kent.

[108]   As was clearly the import of the case concerning Martin and Agnes of Feltham who had been handmilling on their free tenement rather than doing suit at the mills of Staines (Midds.). See Langdon (2004), p. 268, citing *Curia Regis Rolls*, Vol. XVII, pp. 424–5.

[109]   As was found in the case of five tenants on the manor of Thrussington (Leics.) in 1242. See Langdon (2004), pp. 265–6, citing *Curia Regis Rolls*, Vol. XVII, pp. 88–9.

[110]   For example, Cecily de Rumilly's grant in perpetuity of the mills of Silsden and Harewood to Embsay (later Bolton) Priory was accompanied by the threat of confiscation of any illegally ground grain along with the horse that carried it, a much harsher penalty than the normal sixpence fine found in many of the court rolls. For de Rumilly's grant, see *Early Yorkshire Charters*, Vol. VIII, pp. 55–6, no. 4. On the level of fines imposed on violators of suit of mill, see Holt (1988), pp. 39, 45, 64–5 and Langdon (1994), pp. 24, 28 n. 68, 30 n. 78.

[111]   As in the vill of Stackhouse in the Yorkshire Dales that was held by Furness Abbey, at which all the free and servile tenants were obliged to do suit at a multure rate of 1/18. See *Coucher Book of Furness Abbey*, Vol. II, Pt. II, ms. 12. Cf. note 23 above, citing instances of burgesses in Lancashire and Cheshire being obliged to perform suit of mill in the thirteenth and fourteenth centuries.

[112]   See Chapter 4.

[113]   Holt (1988), pp. 43–4, 52–69.

If there was a significant number of freeholders who were not compelled to grind at the lord's mill, and there were no other mills nearby, the option of milling at home was still clearly available, if there were womenfolk in the household who were willing and able to perform the task. Handmills were not cheap pieces of equipment, however, so it is only the wealthier of peasant households who could afford to purchase them.[114] It therefore seems likely that, contrary to Langdon's claim that most of the domestic milling sector was probably illegal at Domesday and subsequently,[115] most of it was in fact legal, but as the wealth of villein tenants grew in the twelfth and thirteenth centuries, increasing numbers of unfree tenants were purchasing handmills and milling illegally at home, or taking their grain to be ground at establishments within or outside the manor (including commercial handmills).

Both Holt and Langdon have argued that manorial milling monopolies were not simply directed at compelling manorial tenants to grind their grain at the manorial mill, but to prevent other milling establishments from taking custom from that mill. Breaking suit could also encompass taking one's grain to an independent tenant's mill or the mill of a neighbouring manor, the most likely motivation being that the rate of multure taken by these mills was lower than that of one's own lord.[116] They argued, furthermore, that direct coercion of the tenantry was less of a concern to lords than preventing competition, and that the relatively low fines imposed on villeins for not obeying suit of mill indicate that it was considered more a misdemeanour than a crime because relatively few offenders were taken to court, and the fines imposed on them were consistent with what was then regarded as a minor offence.[117]

Nevertheless, the fines of sixpence that were typically imposed on tenants for disobeying suit amounted to a week's wages for a low-skilled labourer,[118] and if the penalty included confiscation of the household handmill (which appears to have been quite common), and in some jurisdictions, confiscation of the grain taken to be milled illegally (which went to the manorial miller) and the horse used to carry it (which went to the lord), the penalty was far from minor and certainly a strong incentive to comply.[119] Generally speaking, the penalties for transgression appear to have been harsher in the north than in the south, ensuring that high levels of compliance were maintained for centuries.[120] Furthermore, the fact that tenants were still being compelled

---

[114]   Colvin records the cost of a royal handmill 'built at task by Henry de Ryhull' at 11s 8d. See Colvin (1963), i, p. 381. Although the handmills of ordinary folk cost somewhat less, a new one would cost the equivalent of a few months' wages for a labourer. Langdon notes that among the debtor's effects of John Crook (Oxon.) in 1377 was a handmill valued at 40d. Other used handmills in debtors' extents were typically valued at 3s–5s per handmill. See Langdon (2004), pp. 127, 179, 230, citing PRO C131/25, no. 5, m. 3; PRO C131/56, no. 17, m. 2; PRO C131/57, no. 7, m. 2.

[115]   Langdon (1994), p. 6.

[116]   Holt (1988), p. 39, 43; Langdon (1994), p. 32, citing the instance of the bond tenants of Durham Cathedral Priory's manor of Hedworth, who were reported in 1365 and 1366 to have been avoiding the manorial mill for at least 20 years as they had been patronizing one belonging to Durham's sister cell at Jarrow, 'where their grain was milled at one-twentieth instead of the usual one-thirteenth.'

[117]   Holt (1988), pp. 38–9, 44–5, 65; Langdon (2004), pp. 258, 265–72, 275, 290.

[118]   Rogers (1894), p. 170. Marjorie Chibnall has commented in a different context that unfree tenants during the thirteenth century paid fines that were limited to sixpence before trial and twelvepence after trial for all but the most serious offences. See *Charters and Custumals of the Abbey of Holy Trinity Caen*, p. xlvii.

[119]   At St Albans and Cirencester, the offending tenants had their handmills confiscated, but so did two men running a commercial handmilling establishment in Ogbourne (Wilts.) in 1296, on which see Holt (1988), pp. 40–41. In 1278, a man caught on his way home from grinding his grain at the mill of neighbouring Frankley had both the sack of flour and the mare carrying it seized by the bailiff of the Abbot of Halesowen. See Holt (1988), p. 43, citing *Hales Court Rolls*, i, pp. 102–3, 136, iii, pp. 67, 68, 71. It is explicitly stated in a case brought by Cirencester against one of its tenants in 1302 that it was not only lawful for the abbot to confiscate from transgressing tenants the grain sack and horse on its way to a non-seigneurial mill, but for the seizure to take place outside the manor. See Bennett and Elton (1900), p. 221, citing *Year Books of Edward I*, 1302. Similar rights are claimed by Cecily de Rumilly in her grant in perpetuity of the mills of Silsden and Harewood to Embsay Priory (see note 110 above) and in a deed dated 1330 recording the settlement of a dispute between Pluscardyn Priory and the burgesses of Elgin in Scotland, on which see Bennett and Elton (1900), pp. 220–21, 237–40.

[120]   See Macadam (1856), p. 7, on the legal compulsion imposed on peasants to abandon handmills for watermills in Scotland in the late thirteenth century. He quotes a royal decree enacted during the reign of Alexander III in 1284 that: 'na man sall presume to grind quheit, maishlock, or rye, with hands mylne, except he be compelled be storm, or be lack of mills, quhilk sould grind the samen. And in this case, gif a man grinds at hand mylnes, he sall gif the thretten measure [1/13] as

to do suit at the manorial mill in many parts of England until the early nineteenth century, and were continuing to resist, surely indicates that it was not a popular custom.[121]

Although seigneurial monopolies on milling were a pre-Norman phenomenon, they only appear to have become widespread during the thirteenth century. It is only then that breaking suit of mill became a commonly recorded offence, particularly in southern England. Langdon has demonstrated through a systematic analysis of court rolls for 16 manors in 11 counties throughout England during the late thirteenth and early fourteenth centuries that the number of suit of mill violations brought by lords to the courts averaged only one case per year or less, suggesting that lords were generally aware of endemic violations of suit of mill but relatively unconcerned about the consequences. Their preferred strategy appears to have been to undertake occasional large-scale 'sweeps' of households to prosecute a number of offenders at a time, as seen at Cirencester and St Albans, for example.[122]

Of the 16 manors which he analysed in detail, Langdon found that eight were held by ecclesiastical lords, and of these, three brought cases of violation against their tenants during the 78 years covered by the relevant court rolls, i.e., Brancaster in Norfolk (1337–50), Halesowen in Worcestershire (1272–1307/1342–48) and Launton in Oxfordshire (1287–1303/1330–38).[123] Langdon found that by far the largest number of prosecutions occurred in three places: the towns of Wakefield in Yorkshire, Launton in Oxfordshire and Halesowen in Worcestershire, two out of three being held by ecclesiastical lords.[124] The highest level of enforcement was on Westminster Abbey's manor of Launton, where there were 49 prosecutions between 1287 and 1303, and 35 cases between 1330 and 1338, an average of around four people annually during the 24-year period covered by the court rolls. In Wakefield, there were at least 26 prosecutions over the period from 1274–98, 18 prosecutions over the period from 1306–17, and 34 prosecutions over the period from 1323–31. On the manor of Halesowen held by the Abbey of Halesowen, there were 17 prosecutions between 1287 and 1303, and 20 prosecutions between 1342 and 1348.

On the basis of these figures, it seems reasonable to conclude that suit of mill violations were generally only considered to be an important issue in the north, with the exception of some of the more despotic religious houses in the south. All of the evidence canvassed in this and previous chapters points to northern lords and the larger and more autocratic religious houses being the most concerned about enforcing suit of mill. Once again, this evidence does not support the benign view of the religious houses espoused by proponents of the monastic innovation thesis.

Just as they had done for other feudal obligations after the Conquest, by the fourteenth century, lords were increasingly prepared to commute suit of mill for individuals and even whole communities to a licence fee to be paid annually, a process which had of course been instigated by the lower orders. As previously noted, Holt records a number of instances where the lord concerned no longer owned a functioning mill on a manor but nevertheless insisted that a licence fee be paid.[125] He argues that such behaviour illustrates clearly that seigneurial mills were regarded by both users and owners 'as little more than a means of transferring wealth from the former to the latter'.[126] Both Holt and Langdon cite a number of similar cases from the fourteenth century in which manorial tenants were obliged to do suit at mills on neighbouring manors and managed to negotiate to pay fines to be free of the suit on those manors, including the payment of license fees to own

---

multer: and gif anie man contraveins this our prohibition, he sall tine his hand mylnes perpetuallie.' Macadam points out that by the nineteenth century, such prohibitions appear to have been largely ignored, at least in some parts of Scotland, as every house in St Kilda in 1819 was said to have a quern, while those in the parish of Sandsting in Shetland in 1845 were said to be so plentiful as to be 'without number'. No doubt the plague may have had something to do with the loosening up of such prohibitions in Scotland as it had done elsewhere.

[121] See Bennett and Elton (1900), pp. 244–8, who cite several such examples from the manor of Selby (Yorks.) in the early seventeenth, early eighteenth and early nineteenth centuries. As mentioned in Chapter 2, note 94, milling monopolies continued on the manor of Otterton in Devon until the early twentieth century, and in the Wakefield district in West Yorkshire until 1853. See Greenhow (1979), pp. 315–17, on Otterton, and Norman (1970), p. 176, on Wakefield.

[122] Langdon (1994), pp. 23–4.

[123] Ibid., p. 23.

[124] Ibid., pp. 22–3, esp. Table 3.

[125] Holt (1988), pp. 45–7.

[126] Ibid., p. 47.

and use handmills that were set at a similar level to the fines paid for breaking suit of mill.[127] While Langdon prefers to see such arrangements as compromises acceptable to both sides, the fact that such concessions were made at all indicates that lords in the fourteenth century had come under increasing pressure from both their free and unfree tenants to mill where they chose, as it was clearly not in the lords' financial interests to make such reforms voluntarily. As we have already seen, Augustinian, Cistercian and Premonstratensian houses that held non-seigneurial mills were undoubtedly among the beneficiaries of this type of custom.

Rather than being emblematic of peasant resistance to new technologies as Bloch maintained, suit of mill violations were a focus for peasant resistance to monopolistic behaviour by lords generally. Holt has argued that the disputes over handmilling were not so much due to a preference for the handmill by peasants, as Bloch had contended, but were symbolic of townsfolk's resentment at being forced to obey suit of mill by their lords (especially if they were freemen), and of not having the permission or right to build or own non-seigneurial grain mills.[128]

There are many records of disputes involving free peasants, townsfolk, lesser gentry and even monastic obedientiaries who built wind- and watermills without permission from their lords and then faced legal action or official pressure to either have the illicit mill destroyed, or ownership transferred to the lord.[129] With as much as 60 per cent of the milling trade outside demesne control by the early fourteenth century, and as many as a third of the watermills and windmills throughout England being held by peasants and freemen of varying status, this is hardly evidence in support of resistance to new technology on the part of the lower orders of society.[130]

It is very clear from the English evidence that no lord, no matter how powerful, could fully control their tenants' efforts to take their grain to be ground at a mill which did not owe them suit, or to use handmills to grind their grain at home and similarly avoid suit. Although lords could and did use coercion to enforce their rights, as was undoubtedly the case with St Albans, Halesowen, Cirencester and possibly Durham, this kind of behaviour appears to have been the exception rather than the rule.[131]

Although seigneurial power and French precedent do indeed appear to have been significant factors in the adoption of this customary obligation by post-Conquest lords, the evidence just canvassed undermines Bloch's

---

[127] Ibid., pp. 39–40, 44–7; Langdon (1994), pp. 6, 22; (2004), pp. 274–6. In the south, communities of manorial tenants paid £2 or less to be free from doing suit at the lord's mill in the thirteenth century, whereas communities in the north paid anywhere between 56s 8d and £4 for the same privilege. Langdon (2004), p. 276, reports that the *nativi* and *cotarii* of the village of Altofts (Yorks.) collectively paid 5s in 1356–57 to be free of suit and millpond repair obligations, whereas six *nativi* in Hertfordshire in 1388–89 paid 4d each year to be free of suit of mill. By way of contrast, Philip de Snaringes in 1225 paid 6s annually to the freemen of his lordship in Guist (Norf.) to follow the suit of his mill (Langdon [2004], p. 267).

[128] Holt (1988), p. 41.

[129] Probably the most famous case of such a dispute is from Bury St Edmunds, where Herbert the Dean built a windmill for his own use within the liberty of the town of Bury, only to have to tear it down when a furious Abbot Samson discovered its existence. See *The Chronicle of Jocelin of Brakelond*, pp. 59–60. Other examples include Worcester Cathedral Priory's reward in the late twelfth century of assarts and meadow in Wolverley (Worcs.) to Henry de Gaiwda 'in consideration of the service which Henry rendered them in throwing down the mill which Osbert of Astley and Walter of Kingsford had constructed, and Henry shall ... prevent the mill from being reconstructed.' See *Cartulary of Worcester Cathedral Priory*, p. 21, ms. 29. Another case from the late thirteenth century was the Cross Hall horse mill recorded in Burscough Priory's charter's, discussed in more detail below.

[130] Langdon has estimated that by the early fourteenth century, about 20 per cent of the population was illegally milling at home, while another 40 per cent of the industry was outside of demesne control in the borough and tenant sectors. See Langdon (1994), p. 37.

[131] The Cirencester case is often used to illustrate how freedom from feudal obligations – and especially suit of mill – was seen as a desirable and legitimate goal by many peasants and townsfolk throughout England, especially from the twelfth and thirteenth centuries onwards. According to this view, the efforts of free and bonded tenants to avoid suit of mill in the thirteenth and fourteenth centuries was part of a broader resistance in the towns and the larger manorial estates to the imposition of what were increasingly seen as unfair burdens lacking in historical legitimacy. See Holt (1988), Ch. 3, Fryde and Fryde (1991); Razi (2007). Holt argues the Cirencester case was merely a point of focus for a larger quarrel with the abbot about whether the townsfolk were entitled to be released from villein status and recognized as free tenants. He points out that by doing so, the abbot would have relinquished his rights to considerable revenues from this wealthy wool-town. See Holt (1988), pp. 41–2; also Ross's introduction from 1964 to Cirencester's cartulary, pp. xxxiv–xl, the *Calendar of Patent Rolls, 1292–1301*, and Fuller (1885).

and Dockès's thesis that the lower orders of medieval society were hostile to watermills and windmills, and would always prefer their handmills if given the choice. Clearly, 'small men' of varying backgrounds and wealth were all too ready to acquire and/or build watermills and windmills if the opportunity presented itself, and preferred to mill their grain at such a mill rather than continuing to require their womenfolk to mill at home. This is consistent with Langdon's suggestion that there was reduced use of handmills in the later Middle Ages and evidence of higher numbers of independent tenant mills, especially after the Black Death to 1440 and again from the 1490s onward.[132]

Ecclesiastical Land Tenure and Milling Law in Post-Conquest England

Having examined the legal context within which tenants were obligated to perform suit at the manorial mill, it is now appropriate to turn more specifically to the role of the Church in the development of milling law after the Conquest. Because both the Church and milling were a ubiquitous part of everyday life in the Middle Ages, it should not be surprising to learn that mill-related legal cases involving religious houses appear with great frequency in the English plea rolls, Year Books and manorial court records.[133]

Being major landholders, religious houses were often engaged in drafting legal agreements pertaining to the routine management of their estates, and in pursuing a variety of different forms of property-related litigation. The legal documents which medieval religious houses tended to preserve in their cartularies do not provide a comprehensive picture of the disputes and agreements in which they were involved and generally tend to place them in a reasonably positive light. For example, the cartularies routinely preserve records of disputes between religious houses and powerful lay lords concerning encroachments and depredations of their estates which subsequently proved difficult, if not impossible, to regain. There are likewise numerous records of unfriendly, uncooperative and even hostile neighbours refusing access to mills through their land, and interfering with the waterworks or waterways associated with, or leading to, watermills. Clerical officials and religious houses with overlapping jurisdiction frequently disagreed about who had the rights to rents and tithes, and tenants who were let ecclesiastical mills sometimes failed to pay their rent or meet their obligations to repair or maintain the properties they held. Occasionally, tenants and neighbours would build mills without the chief lord's permission, or took their grain to be milled at an establishment that was not the designated mill of the lord.

Previous chapters have revealed numerous examples of disputes and agreements concerning mills between religious houses, lay lords, tenants, sub-tenants, neighbours, servants and retainers. Several dozen legal cases were identified in the charters and cartularies of 21 of the religious houses examined in the main sample. The relevant cases were heard in the courts of most of the earlier cited jurisdictions.

The documents examined in the remainder of this chapter reveal the diversity of mill-related agreements and disputes between two or more religious houses; between conventual houses and episcopal authorities; between religious houses, patrons and lay lords; and between religious houses, lessees, tenants, sub-tenants and shareholders of parts of mills. While the legal status of suit of mill obligations and disputes concerning illicit mills built on manorial estates have already been discussed, the remainder of the chapter focuses on the following categories of cases:

- illicit mills built and/or operating on ecclesiastical property
- legal recognition for non-seigneurial mills
- rights to payment of mill tithes
- disputes and agreements over water flow and waterworks for mills
- disputes over possession of mills and associated lands
- acquisition of mills as an outcome of securing controlling shares.

---

[132] Langdon (2004), pp. 55–6, 230–31. Langdon cites Martin Biddle's *Object and Economy in Medieval Winchester* (1990) and his analysis of the archaeological remains of handmills at medieval Winchester, which suggests that there was a sharp decline in the use of handmills from the thirteenth century onward.

[133] See Langdon (1994), pp. 22–4, 31; Langdon (2004), pp. 257–88; Loengard (2006); Sistrunk (2006).

A systematic analysis of 40,000 cases in the *Curia Regis* Rolls undertaken by Langdon in the early 2000s revealed 223 cases related to mills. Of this sample, he found that more than 60 per cent involved ownership disputes. Many of these related to dowries and often included large parcels of land, while others were related to disputes over who was entitled to the grain taken as multure. Around one-quarter of the cases were related to suit of mill, while another 5 per cent concerned the status of mills, tithes or the labour services due to them. The remaining 8 per cent consisted of miscellaneous incidents ranging from malicious damage to rent defaults.[134]

If Bloch's thesis concerning seigneurial milling monopolies was correct, one would expect to find many instances of religious houses punishing tenants for defying their suit of mill obligations. However, with the exception of the well-documented case of Cirencester Abbey, there are very few records of disputes over suit of mill in the records of the houses examined, and most of the cases concerning suit of mill uncovered by Langdon were brought by a relatively small number of ecclesiastical and lay lords. By way of contrast, 13 cases of tithe disputes involving seven different houses were identified in the sample, five of which were Augustinian, two of which were Cistercian and one of which was Benedictine, or roughly the same proportion when sampling biases are taken into account.[135] More than 75 per cent of these cases are from the thirteenth century and the majority of the others from the fourteenth century.

Eleven houses were involved in nuisance cases surrounding damage caused by flooding or the obstruction of mill-related waterworks, sluices, dams, ponds and weirs. All five Cistercian houses were involved in one or more such disputes; three of the houses concerned were Augustinian. Of the 14 different mills involved, 80 per cent of the relevant documentation is from the thirteenth century, and almost 20 per cent from the fourteenth century.

Although many of the houses in the sample were involved in disputes over possession of mills and associated lands, only those relating to Battle, St Denys's and Kirkstall are documented in this chapter for the purposes of illustration, the first of which is from the twelfth century, while the other two are from the fourteenth century. Another three cases involved the patient efforts of Lancaster, Cockersand and Lacock to gain full possession of several mills through the acquisition of controlling shares, all of which are from the thirteenth century. These various categories provide the framework for the discussion to follow.

Illicit Mills Built and/or Operating on Ecclesiastical Property

There are several records of disputes over the construction and/or operation of non-seigneurial mills on ecclesiastical property amongst the houses sampled, which, as we saw earlier in the chapter, were of concern to lords wishing to maintain or establish a milling monopoly on their manors, and which could be judged illegal and torn down if they sought to draw suit from manorial tenants. Two cases, one involving a dispute between religious houses and the other between a religious house and its lay tenants, provide interesting counter-examples to the famous case of Abbot Samson's destruction of an early windmill on the estates of Bury St Edmunds in the 1180s.

The Premonstratensian Abbey of Cockersand in Lancashire was involved in a number of disputes over the years with Leicester Abbey over the manor of Cockerham, as well as other land and tithes nearby. This case is interesting from the perspective of 'nested lordship', wherein one religious house (Cockersand) was established as an extra-parochial property inside a manor (Cockerham) held by another religious house (Leicester). Leicester subsequently built a mill of some kind (presumably a watermill on the River Wyre) in the fee of Garstang about eight kilometres to the south-east of its manor on 40 acres of common land held by Cockersand which the latter had presumably acquired from its knightly benefactor, Richard le Boteler by way of William de Lancaster, in the mid-thirteenth century.[136]

---

[134] Langdon (2004), p. 262.

[135] The Cistercian houses concerned were paying tithes on land that they did not, presumably, cultivate themselves.

[136] It would appear that this was a different mill from the fulling mill with suit in Garstang which Cockersand later acquired from Walter de Faulconberg sometime between 1271 and 1282 (see Chapter 8). De Faulconberg was presumably a knightly retainer of the Lancaster family who had acquired the mill as part of a knight's fee in Garstang, as the abbey had also acquired a fulling mill with suit in the town in the 1240s from another knightly retainer of the Lancaster's, William le Boteler, in the 1240s.

Of most interest for our purposes is a composition of 1242 before the Dean of Nottingham, which records Cockersand had abandoned its case against Leicester on this score in the light of certain other agreements about who was allowed to be given spiritual succour by the canons, what was to happen to Leicester's pigs if they should enter into Cockersand's woods too often, which party was to pay and to keep which tithes, the re-measurement of a certain meadow, and Leicester's forgiveness to Cockersand for tearing down two of its houses![137] It would seem that the obedientiaries of Leicester were using the fact that Garstang was not a manor but a fee to indulge in some kind of payback by building this mill in Garstang. They clearly realized that they were pushing the envelope of acceptable practice by building a mill on common land in a fee where they had nothing but episcopal jurisdiction. However, the ambiguity of the law in this case meant that Cockersand had little choice but to accept that the mill built by Leicester on its land should remain, but only in exchange for certain other concessions. Obviously there was no love lost between the two houses.

Another brief mention of an illicitly built mill in Lancashire is contained in Burscough Priory's manuscripts. Sometime before 1290, Richard Waleys built a horse mill within Burscough's lands in Cross Hall, just outside what was soon to become the free borough of Ormskirk. The canons brought a case against Richard before the king's court at around this time, arguing that it was unjustly built to the injury of the prior. As we saw in Chapter 8, Burscough appears to have held suit of the parish of Ormskirk, in which there were at least seven mills by the late thirteenth century. Richard admitted in court that he had no right to build the mill without the consent of the priory, which in turn allowed him and his heirs to hold it of them for twelvepence rent for all service.[138] This clearly amounted to a license to operate within certain constraints, which presumably meant that Richard was not allowed to operate the horse mill as a commercial enterprise. As with the license fees paid by the operators of the many tenant-built fulling mills and grain mills we have encountered in earlier chapters, the canons of Burscough clearly saw no threat to their seigneurial rights from Richard's horse mill if he was not in direct competition with them for the suit of their tenants, which brings us to our next category of mill-related legal documents: those relating to legal recognition for non-seigneurial mills.

Legal Recognition for Non-seigneurial Mills

The period from the ninth through to the eleventh century witnessed the expansion of ecclesiastical holdings throughout southern England, together with an increasing tendency for significant holdings to be hived off to military retainers and lay officials of the Church and Crown. As we have seen, the first few decades of Norman rule involved a radical reorganization of feudal tenure throughout England. This included the imposition of serfdom on the majority of formerly free peasants, and the creation of numerous small manorial holdings from former Anglo-Saxon estates, sokelands and newly assarted land.

We have seen numerous examples in the previous pages of religious houses leasing property in the first half of the twelfth century on long-term and generous leases to tenants ranging in status from the more prominent of their patrons and lay officials to servants and retainers who had served them well. However, as the population grew and revenues increased during the last decades of the twelfth century and throughout the thirteenth century, these same lords attempted to regain seisin of alienated properties and to impose higher rents and labour obligations on their tenants. They also imposed entry fines on the heirs and successors of deceased hereditary tenants, and commuted customary tenancies into tenancies at will. In the case of some lay lords, as we will see below, another strategy was to renege on or ignore commitments to religious houses made by their ancestors or vassals.

Tenants, for their part, sought to maintain the gains in tenure they had acquired during the first half of the twelfth century. Such gains can in some respects be seen as a return to pre-Norman mores, and were perhaps in some cases successful attempts by tenants to have those pre-existing customs recognized. The large sums of money often paid by lords to regain control of mills granted in customary and hereditary tenure may not, therefore, be simply a recognition of the need to pay off a tenant in order to regain possession of a valuable, income-generating asset, but a recognition that the lessee had some kind of ancestral or customary rights of

---

[137] *Chartulary of Cockersand Abbey*, p. 383.

[138] Ibid., ms. 17. Richard Waleys also appears in Cockersand's charters.

ownership or possession of the mill they now held in tenancy. The latter observation might also be made with respect to those instances in which even well-established houses such as Canterbury Cathedral Priory, the Abbey of the Holy Trinity, Caen, and Battle Abbey were unable to regain seisin of some of their mills. For example, as we saw in Chapter 7, after paying out well over £17 to regain seisin of its mills of Neford and *Apechildewude*, Holy Trinity appears to have lost the will to pursue its other customary and hereditary tenants to regain possession of several of its other mills.

The temporalities of the archbishopric of Canterbury and the estates of Hereford, Battle and Lancaster were all encroached upon by acquisitive neighbours and tenants between the twelfth and fourteenth centuries. The ability of these houses to regain seisin of such property was primarily shaped by such considerations as how well connected they were to the king or a local magnate, and how much time and money they were prepared to spend in court to ensure that their case was won.

Throughout the documents analysed in the previous case studies were examples of independent tenant mills that were free to draw custom from within and outside the manors on which they were located, along with a small number of mills that appear to have been built and maintained by the tenants concerned and licensed to operate by their lords. These owner-operators were normally strictly forbidden from providing commercial services to bonded tenants of the manor.

Table 9.1 summarises this data with respect to the religious house concerned, the date/s of the record, the name of the tenant/s and the fee paid. Of those houses sampled, by far the largest numbers of independent tenant and private tenants mills were held by Holy Trinity, with three of its mills in the early twelfth century paying very low rents, a number that had increased to 10 mills in the late twelfth century, and which was maintained at that level until at least the early fourteenth century, although only three of the mills in the last survey appear to have been at the same sites as those in the late twelfth century. Four of Holy Trinity's 10 mills in the late twelfth century were held by free tenants and the remainder by customary tenants, a situation that appears to have been reversed by the time of the early fourteenth-century survey. A grain mill, tool-sharpening mill and fulling mill from the latter survey paid 1s 6d, 6d and 4s 3d, respectively. A horse mill illicitly built around the same time and held by a knight of Burscough Priory for personal use paid twice the fee of the tool-sharpening mill, at 12d, whereas two fulling mills built by free tenants that were held by Canterbury Cathedral Priory paid very similar amounts to that paid to Holy Trinity for its fulling mill, at 4s and 4s 2d in 1285. Eight of the 18 grain mills in the table whose records post-date 1200 paid four shillings or less in rent, suggesting that all of these mills had been built and were being fully maintained by their tenants. The only pertinent post-plague information relates to Furness Abbey, which, as we saw in Chapter 7, was drawing between £6 and £8 in rent from five of its mills in demesne just prior to the Dissolution, but well under £1 in rents from 10 other mills, including the fulling mills of Dale Park and Soray Extra, suggesting both mills had been alienated since the advent of the plague and were held in some form of independent tenure.[139] In other words, more than two-thirds of the abbey's mills were alienated between 1300 and 1536, which was not typical for religious houses of the period.

What appear to have been several other privately operated tenant mills are described as forming the boundaries to several other grants that were not discussed in earlier chapters. For example, one such mill is mentioned in a grant to Cockersand Abbey from Elias de Hutton dated 1199–1220, which consisted of a quarter of the town of Thistleton (Rutland), along with another 12 acres of land by the dyke which led to Greenhalgh mill, and the abbey's exemption from multure at the same mill for all grain grown on that land. Because the abbey is specifically exempted from having to do multure at the mill, the grant must have been made to Cockersand before Gilbert fitz Roger donated the mill to the abbey sometime between 1190 and 1215, narrowing the date of Elias's grant to 1199–1215.[140] Although Greenhalgh mill clearly held suit of the grain grown on the manor, the grant specifically excludes the land and mill of a man named Esbreck, which was adjacent to the holding and presumably privately operated.[141]

---

[139] See Holt (1988), p. 55, who has argued that such instances of very low mill rents indicate purchase or alienation.
[140] See Chapter 8.
[141] *Chartulary of Cockersand Abbey*, p. 173.

Table 9.1   Non-seigneurial mills recorded in the documents of nine religious houses, 1106–1538

Lord	Mill and Manor	Date	Tenant	Rent
Holy Trinity Abbey	Felstead mill I	1106-13	?	10s
	Felstead mill II	"	?	5s
	Pinbury mill	"	?	2s 9d
	Avening mill I	1167–76	Reginald of the forest, miller (f)	7s 6d
	Avening mill II	"	Godricus (f)	3s 4d
	Avening mill III	"	Hedricus (f)	2s 6d
	Cleicumbe mill	"	Robert of Cleicumbe (f)	3s
	Lulle? mill	"	Eilaf son of Adam (c)	14s
	Staford mill	"	Godard (c)	5s
	Chaleford mill I	"	Radulf de Chaleford (c)	8s
	Chaleford mill II	"	Roger de Chaleford (c)	7s
	Gilbert canis' mill (Dudebrug')	"	Gilbert canis (c)	10s
	Walter's widow's mill	"	Walter's widow (c)	6s
	? mill	c. 1306 – c. 1320	Robert the miller (c)	7s 1d
	Brechachre tool-sharpening mill	"	Robert and wife	6d
	Bremescumbe fulling mill	"	Thomas de Rodebrec	4s 3d
	William de Keem's mill (Bremescumbe)	"	Henry	1s 6d
	Chalford mill I	"	Richard Miblanc (c)	8s 4d
	Chalford mill II	"	John de Chalford (c)	15s 5d
	Longford mill	"	Mabilia de Longford (c)	6s 6d
	Nailsworth mill	"	unidentified widow	1d
	Stoford mill	"	Richard de Stoford	7s 1d
	Wymberle mill (1/2 share)	"	John Gille	7s 4d
	"	"	Matilde Gille	6s 2d
Burscough Priory	Knowsley mill	<1229	Richard of Lathom	2s
"	Tarbock mills	early 13th c.	Richard of Tarbock	3s
"	Cross Hall horse mill	<1290	Richard Waleys (kt)	12d
Cathedral Church of Hereford	Grendon watermill	1253-88	William de Wallecroft (f)	7s 6d
	Sevenhampton watermill	"	Galfridus of the mill (c)	9s
	Brocton mill	"	Philip Bode (c)	2s 6d
St Denys' Priory	Postern mill, Winchester	<1278–79	Robert le Bal (burgess)	8s
Canterbury Cathedral Priory	Andrew's fulling mill, Uckfield	1285	Andrew de Luddesham (f)	4s

Lord	Mill and Manor	Date	Tenant	Rent
	Helwis' fulling mill, Uckfield	"	Helwis' de Fullestr' (f)	4s 2d
	Crowherst mill, Wadhurst (1/2 share)	"	Simon at Breglonde (f)	2s
	"	"	Robert de Crowherst (f)	2s
	Pelle? mill, Wadhurst	"	Adam at Pelle (f)	1s 5d
William son of William son of Roscelin	*Rottingesmilne*	<1207	William Spekeman	5s
Sibton Abbey	"	1413–14	?	"
Furness Abbey	Newland mill	1536–38	John Corker	7s 6d
	Consey mill	"	William Sandes	12s
	Colton Beck mill	"	William Rawlinson	6s 8d
	Grysdale (?) mill	"	James and Clement Banke	16s
	Dale Park fulling mill	"	William Walker	1s
	Soray Extra fulling mill	"	William, John and Edward Braythwaite	3s
	Newby mill	"	Humphrey Procter	16s

Two other independent tenant mills are exempted from grants to Cockersand Abbey. The first is dated 1220–50 and is from William de Tarnacre. Consisting of half a bovate of land in Upper Rawcliffe (Lancs.), the grant specifically exempts William's mill, along with his fisheries and nets.[142] In an earlier grant of 1200–1217, a millstream running into the Wyre is described as the boundaries of Alan de Tarnacre's land in Kirkcroft.[143] The millstream was probably for the same mill, as what is now called Out Rawcliffe is very close to the Wyre. The second mill is described in a grant from before 1268. In this document, William de Bispham gives the abbey a share of Dalebridgehead and four strips of ploughland in Newton, but exempts his 'fishery in Ribble and mill' (*salvo piscario meo in Ribbil et molendino*).[144]

Eight mills are mentioned in the Augustinian priory of Bradenstoke's charters that were not held by it, several of which appear to have been independent tenant mills. The first of these is mentioned in a grant dated to before 1207 by Walter Crook (aka Cok) of a quarry in Hazelbury (Wilts.) 'which stretches from east to west from the road leading to his mill'. The priory acquired another two acres of land and a second quarry next to their existing holding in Hazelbury around 1255 from Samson, lord of la Boxe.[145] The second charter dated to around 24 June 1306 records a hundred-year lease from one of Walter Crook's descendants of an additional acre of land next to the first quarry and the road leading to what is here denoted as *Crookesmill*.[146] It would appear that Walter was the independent tenant who had built this mill, as it is referred to as Hasilbergh (i.e. Hazelbury) mill in an assize of *mort d'ancestor* in the Wiltshire county court in 1249. Walter Crook's nephew, Henry Crok', had brought the case in order to establish whether his uncle had died in seisin of the mill and half a virgate of land, which the prior of Farnlegh then held. The mill and land had presumably been granted to Farnlegh Priory at some earlier stage by Walter, as the court found in the prior's favour.[147]

All of the men who held these mills were freeholders, although it seems likely that not all of them were from knightly families (e.g. Esbreck), and there is no evidence or suggestion that any of them held suit. The

---

142   Ibid., p. 180.
143   Ibid., p. 248.
144   Ibid., p. 206.
145   *Cartulary of Bradenstoke Priory*, ms. 347.
146   Ibid., mss. 344 and 345.
147   *Civil Pleas of the Wiltshire Eyre, 1249*, ms. 241.

existence of such mills in Rutland, Lancashire and Wiltshire in the thirteenth century, which specifically name their lay owners without any reference to the jurisdiction of a lord, provides further support for my earlier contention that at least some of these mills were held on land that was not considered to be part of the lordship of the manor, and may have therefore been located on remnants of freely held warland or sokeland.

Rights to Payment of Mill Tithes

One of the most important reforms insisted upon by the new monastic orders of the eleventh and twelfth centuries was that lay owners should relinquish their ownership of parish churches to religious houses, including their tithes. The reformers also called for an end to the lordly privilege of bestowing tithes for demesne lands on favoured relatives and retainers.

The payment of tithes had initially been the prerogative of those churches where the sacrament was administered, and was intended to be dedicated to supplying alms for the poor and needy. The earliest English reference to the payment of tithes is from 687, when Eadberct, bishop of Lindisfarne and successor to Cuthbert, ordered that parishioners should, 'in accordance with the law give a tenth part to the poor every year not only of animals but also of all crops and fruits, and also of clothes'.[148] By the eighth century, many theologians and Church leaders were arguing that it was legitimate to spend these tithes on the upkeep of the clergy and places of worship, although this proved to be the subject of ongoing controversy.[149]

According to Constable, there was no place in Christendom where tithes were compulsory before the fourth century, although they had become well established in the Frankish and Italian kingdoms by the fifth and sixth centuries. He argues convincingly that it was not until the eighth century under the Carolingian rulers that tithes acquired the force of secular law, and that they had previously been enforced by religious sanction only as a moral and spiritual obligation.[150] In England, the earliest known civil enforcement of tithes was during the mid-tenth century,[151] by which time they had become 'in effect a seigneurial due and a rent on land'.[152] It was around this time that bishops began to usurp the right to collect and distribute tithes, while at the same time insisting that the monasteries had no business in collecting them.[153] In the late tenth century, the French bishops tried to strip the monks of the privilege, but failed miserably.[154]

Despite these efforts, both the monastic and lay possession of tithes became commonplace between the ninth and eleventh centuries, and had acquired the status of property that could be bought and sold. Both monks and lay lords had been able to secure this privilege for themselves as 'a result ... of usurpations, episcopal grants and sales, and the proprietary church system'.[155] The monks felt fully justified in having done so, firstly because many were by then performing the pastoral functions which had earlier been the sole province of regular and secular canons, and secondly because they had themselves (supposedly) renounced personal property and material possessions in order to take on their role as 'paupers of Christ'.

Bennett and Elton have argued that while the payment of tithes to lay and ecclesiastical lords may have existed in late Anglo-Saxon times – as is evidenced by what they claimed was the first reference in English law appearing during the reign of Edward the Confessor (1041–66) – it was not much in evidence in Domesday Book, and was only picked up again as a practice later in the twelfth century.[156] However, Constable has presented convincing evidence from *Domesday Book* and elsewhere to support his claims that

---

[148] Constable (1964), p. 23, citing Bede, *Historia ecclesiastica gentis Anglorum*, Vol. IV, 27 [29], ed. Charles Plummer, Oxford, 1896, I, 276.

[149] Ibid., p. 28.

[150] Ibid., pp. 19–20.

[151] Ibid., p. 31.

[152] Ibid., p. 64, quoting Imbart de la Tour, *Rev. Hist.*, LXIII, 30.

[153] Ibid., p. 61.

[154] Ibid., p. 80.

[155] Ibid., pp. 61–5.

[156] See Bennett and Elton (1899), p. 99.

'laymen in England had free possession of their tithes before 1066 ... [while] English monasteries held tithes at least a century before the Norman Conquest ... It is probable, however, that the number of tithes given to monasteries increased greatly after 1066, as the grants to Belvoir, Lewes, St Gregory's of Canterbury, Stoke-by-Clare, Lyre, and many other houses suggest.'[157] The evidence canvassed below indicates that disputes over the possession of tithes between religious houses and between ecclesiastical and lay lords were by far the most common during the thirteenth century, when their value increased significantly, supporting John Blair's observation that they were 'an expanding asset in an expanding economy' as a result of population growth and the increasing demands it placed on the exploitation of the land.[158] Twelve of the 14 tithe disputes and agreements identified in the charters of 21 houses occurred during the thirteenth century, two of which persisted well into the fourteenth century (see Appendix D).

By the twelfth century, many of the new monastic orders had successfully argued that they should be freed from paying tithes on goods they produced themselves, or those that were produced for their own sustenance. Some of them even went so far as to say that they would not collect them from their tenants or parishioners either. For example, the Cistercians obtained exemption from the payment of tithes on lands which they had cultivated themselves or at their own expense at the General Lateran Council held in 1215, although there were other circumstances in which they owed or could receive tithes. One example of a Cistercian house gaining a concession on tithes from a Benedictine neighbour is recorded in Furness Abbey's coucher book, in which the abbot of Furness and the prior of Lancaster signed a concord dated 17 June 1306 that the monks would pay two marks annually to the prior in lieu of tithes for their lands of Beaumont in Skerton as long as they continued to cultivate it themselves. This included the multure of the mills there. If the monks let the land out to others, the usual tithes were to be paid to the prior.[159]

However, as we saw in Chapter 7, although the Cistercians initially renounced their own ownership of tithes, this and other prohibitions on the order had been overturned by the 1250s; many Cistercian houses were collecting significant revenues from tithes by the fourteenth century. For example, Kirkstall Abbey entered into a number of agreements during the late twelfth and thirteenth centuries with churches in parishes where the abbey held lands which invariably involved some negotiation over the allocation of tithes. The most significant of Kirkstall's holdings in this respect was within the parish of Leeds, which was overseen by the Convent of Trinity Priory, York. An agreement over the payment of tithes within the vill of Allerton had been settled soon after the abbey was founded, whereby Kirkstall paid Trinity Priory £1 3s annually.[160] After the erection of the mills of Bramley within the vill c. 1220, this was increased to £1 10s, suggesting the mills were drawing £3 10s in annual revenues.[161] This modified agreement remained in place until 1236, when the priory surrendered to the abbey this same payment, as well as the priory's annual rents from its holdings in Adel, in return for recognition of its rightful claim to the advowson of Adel Church which had been in dispute between the two parties since the vill had first been granted to Kirkstall by the Mustel family. Although Kirkstall agreed, Trinity Priory was never able to appropriate the church of Adel.[162]

Most of the tithe disputes and agreements recorded in the surviving manuscripts of the other orders relate to various Augustinian houses. Five of the 11 Augustinian houses sampled were involved in disputes with ecclesiastical neighbours over which house had the right to collect mill tithes in lands over which they shared some jurisdiction. Cirencester was involved in five such cases, and won four of them. Bradenstoke was involved in four cases with lay and ecclesiastical neighbours and won all of them, while Chichester was involved in one dispute with a neighbouring house and two in which it acted as a mediator, and Blythburgh and St Denys were both involved in long-running tithe disputes with a single other religious house. By way of contrast, there are only two mill tithe disputes relating to other orders, both of which involved the Benedictine house of Lancaster, one of which was with Furness, as mentioned above. The other dispute involved a

---

[157] Constable (1964), p. 82, n.2.

[158] Blair (1988), p. 8.

[159] *Coucher Book of Furness Abbey*, Vol. II, Pt. I, *Beaumont*, ms. 14.

[160] *Coucher Book of the Cistercian Abbey of Kirkstall*, p. xxvi.

[161] Ibid., ms. 348. That is, the difference between the old and new rents multiplied by 10. An undated charter confirms the grant of a mill in Bramley to the abbey, along with suit of mill and land in Lingarth, by Adam de Reinville, which his grandfather Adam had earlier given the abbey (see ibid., ms. 355).

[162] Ibid., p. xxvi–xxvii, and the earlier discussion of Kirkstall in section 2.4.

longstanding legal tussle over the tithes of Bolton mill with the Archdeacon of Richmond, which was finally resolved in the early fourteenth century. The case provides an interesting insight into the complexities of the law surrounding tithes and how they could be remised for cash payments as early as the late twelfth century.

In an inquisition into the possession of the tithes of Bolton mill on the Lune River of 24 February 1320,[163] it was found that the parishioners of Bolton had customarily paid these tithes to Lancaster Priory. During Richard I's reign (1189–99), he had remised them in perpetuity to the parishioners for two marks. The parishioners subsequently built a new mill, from which the priory then collected the tithes. Between 1310 and 1317 at the latest, the vicar of Bolton Church had somehow appropriated them, while the priory was unable to regain them until sometime after 1317. Since 1317, a knight named Sir John de Heslerton had been collecting the mill tithes, although the charter does not specify how either party came into seisin.[164]

The exact nature of the dispute becomes clear in the next document. Dated 14 April 1320,[165] it is a declaration on behalf of Sir Roger de Northburgh, archdeacon of Richmond, that his sequestration of Bolton mill's tithes was not legitimately withheld from Lancaster Priory, although the wording of the document goes to extraordinary lengths to avoid an open admission of this, and gives some hint of the rancour which this dispute had obviously caused. It also makes no mention of the aforementioned Sir John being then in seisin.[166]

We learn from the next document dated 12 June 1322 that this same Sir John was the clerk for the aforesaid archdeacon, and that it was the archdeacon's official, Michael de Harcla, and Sir John who were the authors of his legal responses to the priory.[167] This declaration once again acknowledges legal possession of Bolton mill's tithes to Lancaster Priory, and orders all of the archdeacon's servants and others within the diocese to carry out the terms of the declaration.[168] Presumably Sir John had previously been collecting the Bolton mill tithes as part payment for providing clerical services for the archdeacon, which also goes some way to explain the wording of the archdeacon's declaration of 14 April 1320.

It would seem that the archdeacon's claim over the tithes of Bolton mill probably relate to the advowson of the Church of Bolton-le-Sands being surrendered to John le Romeyn, archdeacon of Richmond, in 1246, in exchange for the remaining share of the Church of Poulton and its chapel at Bispham. What is perhaps most interesting about this dispute, however, is the fact that it reveals the existence of a communally operated mill, run by the parishioners of Bolton from before the reign of Richard I. This is one of the earliest examples of such an arrangement that has so far been discovered in any of the detailed research on English milling to date.[169]

Rather than recounting all of the details of the remaining disputes, I have instead compiled a table which seeks to capture their most important elements, i.e. the dates, parties involved, and the basis for dispute and resolution, organized by order (Appendix D). To follow is a brief summary of their main elements.

Perhaps unsurprisingly given its stormy history with its tenants, the most extensive records of disputes over tithes amongst any of the houses recorded were between Cirencester Abbey and its ecclesiastical neighbours. Cirencester's charters record three disputes and two separate settlements with neighbouring religious houses over the allocation of mill tithes, most of which occurred in the period from 1235–38 under the abbacy of Hugh of Bampton (1230–50). In chronological order, the three disputes were with the rector of the church of Coates, the rectors of the church of Daglingworth and the vicar of the church of Shrivenham. The two settlements were with the bishop of Salisbury and the vicar of the church of Rothwell. In four out of five cases, the canons secured seisin of the mill tithes in question.

Another Augustinian house that appears to have involved itself in extensive litigation over mill tithes was Bradenstoke Priory. Over the course of the thirteenth century, Bradenstoke was involved in at least four mill-related tithe disputes. The first of these was in relation to unspecified tithes of a mill or mills somewhere in Wiltshire between the priory and a number of parties, which included Glastonbury Abbey and a number of clerks and laymen in the dioceses of Lincoln, Salisbury and Bath. The second was over the tithes of the mills

---

[163] VI Kal. Mar. 1320.

[164] *Materials for the history of the Church of Lancaster*, pp. 259–60.

[165] XVIII Kal. Mai. 1320.

[166] *Materials for the history of the Church of Lancaster*, p. 261.

[167] II Id. Jun. 1322.

[168] *Materials for the history of the Church of Lancaster*, pp. 261–3.

[169] My thanks to John Langdon for drawing my attention to the significance of this reference. See Langdon (2004), pp. 214–15, for similar examples from the later Middle Ages.

of North Aston with the miller who held those mills, which the priory won, while the third was over the tithes of some land in Costow with Stanley Abbey, for which Bradenstoke received the rents of several parcels of land, including those of the mill of Stratford, in exchange for abandoning its claim. The last was between Bradenstoke and the rector of Christian Malford over the tithes of two newly built mills in the parish, which the canons had been withholding for more than 20 years. The priory's claim to the tithes of the mill of North Aston was clearly based on its possession of the parish's advowson, whereas it did not hold the advowson of the parish of Christian Malford. It therefore seems rather churlish of the canons to have withheld tithes for its mills from the rector for such an extended period. Despite the large number of these disputes, most of which were initiated by Prior Simon in the first half of the thirteenth century, the canons were, on the whole, relatively slow to act against those who had wronged them, and most of those who had were quick to admit their liability once they appeared in court.

The canons of St Denys's Priory, Southampton, were involved in a series of tithe disputes with the church of St Mary, Southampton, which lasted for more than 30 years during the second quarter of the thirteenth century. St Denys's disputes with St Mary's indicate a level of acrimony which is not seen in St Denys's relations with God's House, another ecclesiastical neighbour, although the original basis for these poor relations is not clear. St Denys's ended up winning the dispute.

One thing is clear from these records, however, and that is that mill tithes were a valuable commodity, a fact with which Cirencester, Bradenstoke, Blythburgh and St Denys were all well apprised, and which John of Laund, prior of Bolton, also clearly understood when he pursued a strategy of ensuring that the tithes of his parishioners and dependent churches were paid in full in the late thirteenth century.[170] The fact that there were so many of these disputes and all were between religious houses again casts somewhat of a shadow over the images of benign lordship painted by proponents of the monastic innovation thesis.

Disputes and Agreements over Water Flow and Waterworks for Mills

Disputes about water flow to and waterworks for watermills were extremely common during the Middle Ages, and no less so for ecclesiastical lords. At least half of the houses sampled were involved in some kind of dispute with neighbouring lay and ecclesiastical lords over water flow to their mills, or the waterworks associated with their mills. Each of the Cistercian houses studied were involved in at least two or three mill-related water and land disputes with local lay lords, with Sibton involved in several. Three of the Augustinian houses were involved in mill-related water disputes, while three houses of the minor orders were involved in disputes over access to watercourses for mills or the lands pertaining to mills, some of which went on for decades. Almost all of the relevant documents are from the thirteenth century, many of which cluster around the 1240s to 1260s, a time when the population of England and the area of assarted and improved lands were growing rapidly. Some of the disputes involved improvements or expansions of the waterworks associated with existing mills, which often had a flow-on effect to tenants upstream and downstream. The absence of any records of such disputes amongst the Benedictine houses sampled is consistent with the fact that the grants of royal demesne of which most of their estates consisted automatically gave them priority water rights for their mills and fisheries.

As with the previous section on rights to payment of mill tithes, rather than recounting all of the details of the remaining disputes, I have instead compiled a table as an appendix which seeks to capture their most important elements, i.e. the dates, parties involved, and basis for dispute and resolution, organized by order (Appendix E). To follow is a brief summary of the contents and their implications. Readers are directed to the appendix for the relevant sources.

Perhaps unsurprisingly, most of the disputes concerning access to, and property damage caused by, watermills and their associated waterworks involved those which were located in urban and built-up areas, as well as areas in which many tenants and sub-tenants held small parcels of land adjacent to the mill or its waterworks. One way to obviate such disputes, which was increasingly practised by owners and tenants from the early thirteenth century onwards, was to negotiate the terms of a legal settlement with one's neighbours in order to guarantee unhindered right of way for the lord's servants, employees and customers. For example,

---

[170] See Chapter 6.

St Gregory's Priory, Canterbury, negotiated several such agreements with neighbours in the first quarter of the thirteenth century to secure water rights to and from its mill of Howfield (Kent), as did Lancaster Priory with respect to its mills of Catton (Lancs.) and the mill of Carleton (Yorks.) in the mid-thirteenth century, and Furness Abbey with respect to its mill of Stalmine (Lancs.) between 1260 and 1319. Likewise did the abbeys of Beaulieu and Holy Trinity and the Priory of St Denys negotiate with their ecclesiastical neighbours between 1222 and 1252 to grant or obtain water rights in relation to the mills of Eldee (Oxon.), Felsted (Essex), *Munekelond* (Hants.) and Stratford (Warks.).

Those houses which did not show the same level of foresight were perhaps inevitably drawn into conflict. The earliest record of such a dispute is between Kirkstall and Hugh de Witon from 1172 to c. 1200, concerning the millpond and milldam of Tofthouse belonging to Hugh. St Peter's, Lacock, Old Wardon, Beaulieu and Sibton were all involved in disputes with lay and ecclesiastical neighbours between the 1220s and 1280s involving the maintenance of weirs, milldams and bridges associated with their mills or the mills of their neighbours. Sibton was involved in a particularly acrimonious dispute with Margaret, countess of Norfolk, between 1342 and 1345, which resulted in Margaret extorting several unreasonable concessions from the abbey. Furness was similarly involved in such a dispute with two lay lords holding land adjacent to its mill of Stalmine between 1318 and 1337.

Because the water rights to and from demesne mills were well established in customary and statute law,[171] most of these disputes were settled relatively quickly and amicably. Those over whose land waterworks flowed were recompensed in one or more of several ways for the inconvenience. Some were paid cash 'considerations' in order for the house concerned to acquire the appurtenant land, while others had that land exchanged for land of an equivalent value, or were given the right to perpetual prayers from the monks and/ or were paid annual rents. In exchange, the relevant landholders were subject to various distraints. Most common were injunctions to not interfere with the waterworks of the mill and obligations to maintain any of the relevant boundaries between their own land and the relevant ecclesiastical property or right of way.

The longest running dispute in the sample was between the Treasurer of St Peter's, York, and St Mary's Abbey, York, concerning the Treasurer's mill and fishery on the river Foss in the manor of Clifton, which appears to have persisted for several decades, but was finally resolved in January 1250. The monks of St Mary's complained that the Treasurer's mill had been interfering with the water flow to their own mill not far downstream, near the bridge that led into the city of York. After it was established that there had been an almost century-long agreement about the co-existence of the mills, it was agreed that the Treasurer would not move his mill or millpond, that the monks would stop interfering with the Treasurer's fishery, and that he was entitled to the tithes of his mill plus a pension of three shillings annually from the monks 'for the good peace'.[172]

The only other documents of note relate to disputes involving the obstruction of navigable rivers by millworks which were interfering with the passage of ships and the loading and unloading of goods. In the case of Risingho mill held by Old Wardon Abbey, it had presumably raised the millpond leading to Risingho mill which had caused some kind of obstruction in the river Ouse, thereby reducing the water flow and making navigation of the river difficult for the ships of William de Bello Campo (aka Beauchamp). It was agreed in court that the mill and millpond should stand 'since the abbey already has sufficient warrant for using the site to their advantage', but that a weir should be built to return some of the reduced waterflow to the river and to presumably allow William's ships to pass over it.[173]

A similar dispute is recorded by Hockey in Beaulieu Abbey's *Faringdon Cartulary*. Sometime before 1250, Beaulieu acquired the mill of Kyndlewere on the River Thames near Radcot in Oxfordshire, about 30 kilometres west of Oxford. It was, in turn, only about seven kilometres east of the abbey's mills and its urban manor of Little Faringdon.[174] According to Hockey, the local lord of Radcot, Matthias de Besilles, appears to have had difficulty in accepting the presence of the monk's holding within his manor, as one charter records

---

[171] *Henrici de Bracton*, Vol. III, Ch. XLV, fo. 234.

[172] *Cartulary of the Treasurer of York Minster*, mss. 13, 14, 15. The memorandum of agreement is dated 12 January 1250/1.

[173] *Cartulary of Old Wardon Abbey*, ms. 240. See also Langdon (2007), pp. 115–16, on the use of mill-weir flashes or 'flash-locks' for the passage of shallow-drafted ships, 'many of which seem to have been equipped with a cable and winch system'.

[174] Blair (2007), p. 260.

an agreement on his part that he would no longer hunt game on their land, and would desist from impeding the abbey's men from free access to the mill and its pond so that they could keep it in good repair. The monks were granted a piece of embankment beside their mill by a local freeman soon afterwards in order for them to make improvements to the mill.[175]

Kyndlewere mill's location on the Thames also meant that Beaulieu's ships could dock beside it to load grain, which was a further bone of contention with the lord of Radcot. A concord was made between Beaulieu and Matthias de Besilles for him to desist from interfering with the shipping of their grain, which was later reaffirmed by his son Geoffrey, who also gave the monks permission to wash their sheep in the river, to embank their land against flooding, and to prevent their water-course from silting up by whatever means they thought fit.[176] Although Hockey provides no dates for any of these documents, Blair reports that those relating to Matthias de Besilles are from 1275–95, and for Geoffrey, from 1315–19.[177]

Taken together, all of these documents reveal that, unlike suit of mill, water rights pertaining to mills and the associated powers of distraint were fairly well codified by the law, leaving little room for ambiguity. Unlike the mills of Kyndlewere and Eldeya, most watermills were not built upon the main channels of streams and rivers, but on side channels or leats separate from the main watercourse, which, because they could be substantial in size and extent, often encroached upon the property of other landholders, especially in urban and densely populated areas. As we have seen in earlier chapters, these side channels might lead to a millpool, dam or weir which diverted water to the mill and allowed the water flow to be regulated with sluices.[178] In these circumstances, it was relatively commonplace for the lands of neighbours to be flooded, and for those neighbours to bring cases of nuisance against the mill owner. Preemptive agreements with neighbours could avoid such disputes, but as we have seen, even the most disgruntled of affected landholders were prepared to compromise, given the appropriate financial and/or spiritual incentives.

Disputes over Possession of Mills and Associated Lands

From the late twelfth century onward, it became more and more commonplace for both lay and ecclesiastical lords to directly manage their mills in order to benefit from the substantial increases in revenue which they were beginning to generate as the populations on their manors and neighbouring districts grew. This included building and acquiring more mills, and the pursuit of legal action to recover alienated mills from customary and hereditary tenants. Both activities became sites for legal disputation in the thirteenth and fourteenth centuries, as tenants sought to retain the tenurial gains they had made, and lords sought to re-establish and further entrench their seigneurial rights. Even though the king's law and the judiciary had become less favourably inclined towards the alienation of property, including mills, regaining seisin of such property remained an expensive exercise that required extraordinary tenacity and deep pockets.

It is nevertheless very clear from the records that to the extent that any house pursued managerial reforms, it usually benefited financially. Virtually all of the houses sampled adopted the new estate management practices of the monastic reform movement of the twelfth century, including policies of mill acquisition and/ or reacquisition. The Augustinian priory of St Denys appears to have been the only house in the sample to have made little or no effort to improve the accountability of its officials and the management of its estates, including regaining seisin of its alienated mills, while the Augustinian priory of Butley is the only house which appears to have had little or no interest in milling. By way of contrast, most of the houses studied were prepared to go to some lengths to acquire mills which they wanted to hold, to regain mills which they had at one stage held, or to retain mills which they had been granted.

---

[175] Hockey (1975), p. 80.

[176] Ibid. See also Blair (2007), pp. 260–61, 263, 264, 271, 282–3, who discusses the case of Kyndlewere mill at some length in the broader context of river transport on the Upper Thames. Thanks to John Langdon for drawing my attention to Blair's research on this issue.

[177] See Blair (2007), pp. 289–90, who discusses this and similar cases in some detail. He also reports that in 1261, it was specified that Kyndlewere's milldam 'should contain a weir at least 10 feet wide and 7 feet deep' (ibid., p. 263), indicating that it was a flash-lock (p. 264). Cf. note 172.

[178] See Hooke (2007), pp. 42–5 on Anglo-Saxon waterworks for mills, and Bond (2007), pp. 192–6, on Cistercian water-engineering.

As we saw in Chapters 6 and 7, the Augustinians acquired 36.5 per cent and the Cistercians 38.7 per cent of all their mills from knights and knightly families, so that it was inevitable that some of the descendants and lords of the original donors might not be so convinced that the agreement suited them. Because mills and the revenues which they generated were valuable assets, it should not be surprising that the descendants and superior lords of some patrons found cause to renege on their vassals' and forbears' commitments by disseising religious houses of mills they had been granted.

A number of cases brought by Glastonbury, Holy Trinity, St Denys's, Battle and Lancaster against lay lords, stewards, tenants and fellow clerics who sought to appropriate their mills and tithes have already been cited. The three cases cited below involve examples of lords and the descendants of patrons and donors attempting to regain seisin or some financial advantage from mills which their vassals or forebears had granted the houses concerned.

The Priory of St Denys' Dispute over Seisin of the Mill of King's Sombourne (Hants.)

As we saw in Chapter 6, St Denys's priory suffered from encroachments from neighbouring ecclesiastical lords, knightly tenants and the descendants of donors. In the case of the mill of King's Sombourne, the descendant of a lord of one of the major donors to the priory, a member of the Marisco or Marescallus family, had been withholding rents from the mill for more than five years in 1301, and was not required to pay his back rent in exchange for an undertaking to start paying. Thirty years later, the canons were still having difficulty drawing rent from the same mill – this time from a different knightly tenant – who was likewise forgiven back rents. Perhaps unsurprisingly, less than a century later, the canons had lost seisin of the mill to the Augustinian priory of Mottisfont, about 20 kilometres to its north-west.

When Michael de Columbariis granted all the tithes of his assarts and newly broken land of *Tederleia* to St Denys between 1184 and 1235, there does not appear to have been a mill on the land.[179] This property, along with a mill at *Mariscus* in the vill of *Kynessomburne* (King's Sombourne) on the river Test, seems to have been granted in fee to Michael in the late twelfth or early thirteenth century by William son of William Marescallus de la Lade.[180] A plea in the county court from 1301 between the canons and a direct descendant of William son of William, Nicholas de Marisco, records that he signed an agreement with the canons that they were entitled to an annual rent of 20 shillings from Nicholas which they customarily received from his mill at *Mariscus* (the mill of King's Sombourne), and that this sum should in future also be rendered from his meadow called Brodysmede, providing £2 in annual rents. In return for this agreement, the priory agreed to remise and quitclaim £5 10s in arrears on the mill which Nicholas owed them.[181]

The priory was back in court in the 1330s over the same rent from the same mill and meadow, this time in dispute with the knight in seisin, Sir Thomas de Weston. After mediation by John de Welynton and James de Ameneye, a settlement was reached on 12 March 1333 whereby Sir Thomas acknowledged that 20 shillings in yearly rent of the two properties had been withheld from the priory for many years, but that he would pay in future in return for the arrears being forgiven 'in view of benefits so far received and to come'.[182] There seems little doubt, however, that most of these benefits had flowed to he who held the mill! The reluctance of the canons to press their legitimate claims for back rents is one of the reasons for the priory's financial problems during the fourteenth and fifteenth centuries, and indicates a certain timidity when dealing with recalcitrant tenants.

The priory continued to have difficulties in maintaining seisin of the King's Sombourne mill at *Mariscus* until early next century. An inquisition of 10 January 1410 before William Overton and Thomas Emory records the names of 12 men who testified that five parcels of land held by St Denys's Priory were being unjustly withheld from them by 10 other individuals. The rents from them totalled £3 5s 2d, a not insignificant sum, considering that its total rents for Southampton in 1476 were just over £52.[183] Amongst the

---

[179] Ibid., ms. 428. Blake suggests that the most likely identity of this Michael was the elder rather than the younger, which certainly fits the charter evidence more convincingly.

[180] Ibid., ms. 430.

[181] Ibid., ms. 338.

[182] Ibid., ms. 339.

[183] Even at this late stage, it was unable to collect more than £7 owed.

five properties was the mill and meadow called *Brodysmede* at *Mariscus* in *Kengessomburne* parish, which was still paying 20 shillings rent annually. The mill had been in the hand of John the prior of Mottisfont and his predecessor John Netherhavene, implying that Mottisfont had somehow acquired an interest in the mill during the intervening period, a situation which had once again undermined St Denys's claim to any revenue whatsoever from the mill.[184]

Battle Abbey's Dispute over Its 'Excellent Mill' in the Marsh of Barnhorn (Suss.)

Battle Abbey was involved in a number of disputes over the years in relation to seisin of several of its mills, disputes that were at least in part a consequence of the complicated tenure in which the abbey held some of its mills during that period. One of the most interesting cases involves the construction by the abbey in the early twelfth century of what was probably a tide mill in an area of marshland in East Sussex that had been purchased from the vassal of a local knight.

In *The Chronicle of Battle Abbey*, the main chronicler, whose name is unknown, describes life at the abbey under the patronage of Henry I, 'when Abbot Ralph, of happy memory, had charge of the abbey'. The abbot to whom the chronicler was referring was Ralph of Caen (1107–24), described by Searle as '[t]he most active and effective administrator among the early abbots', who successfully recovered properties and enlarged the abbey's holdings during his abbacy.[185]

In this particular case, Ralph bought three wists of land in Barnhorn, East Sussex, from Ingelran, the vassal of a local knight named Withelard of Baillol, with the latter's knowledge and consent.[186] Withelard included with this sale a grant of a portion of the marsh adjoining the three wists, both transactions being later confirmed by the king, and Henry, Count of Eu, Withelard's lord. The land was then reclaimed, built upon and improved generally by the abbey, the improvements including the construction of what may have been a tide mill: 'An excellent mill was built in the marsh and it was expected to be very profitable, since it lay only five miles from the abbey.'[187]

Following Abbot Ralph's death, however, Withelard began making frequent and ongoing demands from Ralph's successor, Warner, for additional payments on the fief that was now so improved. After the abbot repeatedly refused to cooperate, Withelard reclaimed the entire property of Barnhorn, including the marshland with the mill that the abbey had built, 'and gave it in gage for money to Siward Hastings'. Despite repeated entreaties by the monks to various parties, nothing was done, as Henry I had died, and the reign of Stephen was a time during which 'he who was strongest prevailed'.[188] Finally, after much toing-and-froing between the monks and the new king Henry II, their complaint was heard and upheld by the king and the original grant and sale confirmed.[189] It would appear from all this that while Ingelran may have had good intentions with his original sale to the monks, his own lord, Withelard, was determined to extract additional value from the monks' entrepreneurship and was at least initially successful in doing so.

Kirkstall Abbey's Dispute over Seisin of Headingley Mill (Yorks.)

A more complicated and acrimonious dispute was settled in favour of Kirkstall Abbey at the King's Court before Edward III in 1337, concerning land in Headingley and Gledhow (Yorks.), which included the mill of

---

[184]   Ibid., ms. 299.

[185]   Searle (1974), p. 39.

[186]   A wist varied in size from about 9 to 12 acres. Hence this tract of land was between 27 and 36 acres in size.

[187]   *The Chronicle of Battle Abbey*, pp. 210–11. The manor of Barnhorn was located about 10 kilometres from Battle on the uplands surrounding Pevensey Level and the coastal marsh; the marshlands were at this stage still subject to tidal inundation. In a note to this passage, Searle comments that Barnhorn was 'throughout the Middle Ages a chief supplier of corn', and that '[a]t such an early date (1107–24) the mill, built in the sea marsh rather than on the windy coastal upland, would presumably have been a tidal mill.' See ibid., p. 211 n. 3. However, as we will see below, if this 'excellent mill' was indeed a tide mill, like most other tide mills, it had presumably been subject to destruction from flooding, and had been replaced with a windmill by 1240. Holt has noted a similar trend on some other estates held by the Earl of Norfolk and Christ Church, Canterbury, over the same period. See Holt (1988), pp. 88–9.

[188]   *The Chronicle of Battle Abbey*, pp. 212–13.

[189]   Ibid., pp. 210–19. See also Searle (1974), pp. 42–3.

Headingley that had been granted to Kirkstall by the Peitivin family in the twelfth century. The dispute was between one of the original donors' relatives, Alexander Peitivin, John de Calverley and Kirkstall Abbey.

As we saw in Chapter 8, the manor of Headingley, along with the mill, had been granted to John de Calverley sometime before 1312 by Alexander Peitivin's elder brother, Thomas. John had then re-granted the manor and mill to Kirkstall in 1324, after securing a quitclaim from Alexander, dated 27 May 1323. When Alexander later disputed the grant, John produced this quitclaim in court, which Alexander claimed was a forgery. The sheriff then summoned the witnesses to the deed. Those who were still living swore on oath that it was genuine, and judgement was made against Alexander, who was then committed to custody.[190]

More than 14 years later, in a court hearing at York in 1337, the matter was finally settled after the Abbot of Kirkstall produced another quitclaim from Alexander dated 15 November 1337, which guaranteed the abbey's seisin of the manor, along with the mill. The circumstances of Alexander's efforts to regain seisin of Headingley mill suggest that he was a man of fickle judgement who was prepared to perjure himself in order to achieve his goal. Perhaps he had been cooling his heels at the king's pleasure during the intervening period, but either way he had clearly had time to reflect on his own calumny and affirmed his original agreement to the grant.

Gaining Possession of Mills through the Acquisition of Controlling Shares

For religious houses with modest incomes, a potentially attractive way to gain possession of mills was to gradually acquire controlling shares from knightly and gentry families who were favourably inclined to the house concerned, or which were suffering from some form of financial or other hardship. Lancaster, Cockersand and Lacock were all involved in accumulating the shares of mills in the thirteenth century, sometimes with the payment of annual rents or 'up-front' cash sums, and at other times with exchanges of land or undertakings to provide perpetual prayers for the family of the donor. The relevant cases are outlined below.

Lancaster Priory's Acquisition of the Grain Mill and Fulling Mill of Caton (Lancs.)

A somewhat different dynamic to those seen above is captured in the documents pertaining to the possession of two mills in the extant documents for Lancaster Priory. These documents record a long and protracted conflict over shares of a grain mill and fulling mill in Lancashire granted to the priory in 1256 which lasted for more than 70 years. What was obviously a bitter dispute was only settled after repeated interventions from the king.

The earliest record relating to the first dispute is a charter dated December 1256, which records the grant of a share of 1/3 of Caton grain mill and Caton fulling mill by Roger, son of Vivian of Heysham, to the priory. This included 1/3 of the mill and its grain toll, 'and all my third part of the mill of Caton for fulling cloth, without any retention, with all its appurtenances, as in the site for the mill, the pond convenient, and the free water course to the said mills, and with free common in the wood of Caton [part of Quernmore Forest] for proper repairing and maintaining of the said mills without contradiction of any one, and in all other liberties and easements in land and in water pertaining to the said portion of the said mills'. A warranty clause guaranteed that if Roger or his heirs should fail in the conditions of the grant, that he or they would make an appropriate exchange for some of his land in Heysham. As this grant was to ensure perpetual prayers for his departed soul and that of his wife, his anxiety was perhaps understandable, as no money is mentioned in the grant, although this of course does not necessarily mean that none changed hands.[191] Caton is about eight kilometres east of Lancaster, and about 16 kilometres east of Heysham, so was not presumably in any way connected to the priory's 1/3 share of the vill of Heysham.

The next charter pertaining to Caton mill is dated 30 October 1329. It is an order made at Westminster by Edward III instructing the sheriff of Lancaster to command two laymen, William Wyther and William de Lancaster, as well as their wives and the sister of one of the wives, to immediately hand over the third part of

---

[190] *Coucher Book of Kirkstall Abbey*, ms. 397.

[191] *Materials for the history of the Church of Lancaster*, pp. 166–8.

a single mill in Caton with its appurtenances to Ralph, prior of the church of the Blessed Mary of Lancaster. Edward noted in the order that the five accused had 'no entry' (*non habent ingressum*) except on the basis of John de Caton's illegal possession of the mill when his great-grandfather King Henry 'first crossed into Gascony' (i.e., 1225) while John was prior of Lancaster. This John was presumably John de Alench, who was prior between 1207 and 1227. The king ordered that if the accused failed to carry out his order they would be summoned to appear before him at Westminster in three weeks' time.[192]

What the nature of the relationship was between the two Williams, their wives and sister-in-law and John de Caton is not made explicit, although it seems likely on the basis of some of the later records that the women were his descendants and heirs. Furthermore, although King Edward's reckoning of the date of John of Caton's illegal disseisin is consistent with John de Alench being prior at the time, as we have just seen, the share of the grain mill and fulling mill of Caton was not even granted to the priory until December 1256, a good 31 years after Henry's first expedition to Gascony, and 26 and 14 years before his second and third expeditions. It seems more likely that the significant date to which the king's faulty memory means to refer is 1259, the year of the signing of the Treaty of Paris with Louis IX of France, when Henry conceded Normandy, Anjou and Poitou to the French crown, and paid homage to Louis for Gascony.[193] As there is no record of anyone having inhabited the priorship between 1256 and 1266, it is possible that there was another John acting in the position during this time.

If this supposition is correct, it would imply that the grant by John of Hutton and John of Caton of Artlebeck watercourse for feeding John of Caton's and the priory's mills was made between 1256 and 1259 or soon after. Further support can be found in two writs dated 1251 and 1259 that are not amongst the priory's charters. The first records that Roger de Heysham held a third part of the fulling mill and the grain mill of Caton for £2 a year, while Roger Gernet, master forester, held another third for an additional £2 a year. The writ of 1259 contains the same information.[194]

As John of Caton is named as Roger Gernet's son in the earlier cited document pertaining to the watercourse of Artlebeck, and is said there to have held mills on the watercourse, as did the priory, we can clearly see how it was possible for John to establish a pretext for taking possession of one or both of the priory's mills during this period. Given that the two thirds of the mills were valued at £4 a year in the 1250s, we can also see that John of Caton's motivation for the illegal disseisin was probably monetary. It is important to note, however, that by 1329 only the third part of one mill of Caton is being disputed, a likely scenario being that the fulling mill had been allowed to fall into ruin in the interim due to its lack of profitability. The only inconsistency faced by this interpretation of the available evidence is that Roger de Heysham is still named as holding his shares of the two mills three years after they were supposedly granted to Lancaster Priory. This may, however, have simply been a bureaucratic error; hardly surprising in the circumstances.

The next document pertaining to the dispute over the seisin of the third part of Caton mill is a record of pleas from Westminster heard by the justices of the bench on 27 January 1330. It records that the accused had not appeared in court in either October or November of the previous year as they had been ordered by the king, nor had they handed over the third part of the mill to Ralph Courail, Prior of Lancaster. The king had also decreed that this share of the mill be taken into his hand, and again summoned the accused. As they had not turned up for this court case either, the court found against them once again, and again ordered that the share of the mill be taken into the king's hand, as there appears to have been some problem in executing the king's first order, although this is not made explicit.[195]

This record of the plea is followed by a decree by Edward III that was also made in Westminster and dated 18 February 1330. The king noted here that John of Caton's heirs had fraudulently acquired their share of Caton mill and that the Statute of Mortmain had thereby been broken. The king ordered once again that the third part of the mill be taken into his hands, and that all of the relevant parties be summoned to Westminster

---

[192]   Ibid., pp. 459–61; *VCH Lancashire*, Vol. II, p. 172.

[193]   Henry III made three expeditions to Gascony in 1225, 1230 and 1242. Gascony was the only one of the English crown's French territories to remain in English hands after 1224 (see Morgan (1997), p. 133).

[194]   *Lancaster Inquests and Extents*, Vol. I, pp. 184–5, 224. I thank Philip Hudson for drawing my attention to these documents.

[195]   *Materials for a History of the Church of Lancaster*, pp. 463–5.

on 22 April to settle the dispute.[196] It is important to note that such efforts by Edward were part of his general policy of becoming directly involved in the governance of the country that began around this time, and included efforts to quell baronial opposition to his rule, particularly in the north.

The last two documents pertaining to the dispute record a county court ruling dated to 6 December 1330, which re-states the findings of the Westminster court that full seisin of the mill share had been restored to Ralph, Prior of Lancaster, and that the fraudulent claimants should hand over the share of the mill with its appurtenances 'without delay'. It would seem that even a royal decree had been insufficient to restore the priory's seisin. The last document, which presumably dates to early the following year, records a sheriff's order against the same parties to hand over the share, which they presumably did subsequently, as nothing else is recorded of the matter.[197] It is worth noting that there are several other documents amongst the priory's muniments which record other troubles with tenants and neighbours in Poulton that were also heard by the king.[198] It would perhaps be an understatement to observe that this period was a difficult one for the canons of Lancaster Priory. A century later, the priory's mother house was transferred from Sées to Syon Abbey near London.

Cockersand Abbey's Acquisition of the Mill of Hutton (Lancs.)

Two series of grants, quitclaims and confirmations from the thirteenth century provide valuable insights into the complications that could arise when a single lord attempted to acquire controlling shares of a valuable mill in order to gain a milling monopoly on a manor. The first set of documents chart the extensive efforts of Cockersand Abbey to acquire full seisin of Hutton mill, which served the townships of Howick and Hutton. The mill was part of the lordship of Howick (Lancs.), and was probably located on a stream called the Mill Brook that separated the two towns. While Howick appears to no longer exist, Hutton is about four kilometres to the south-west of Preston.

The earliest document pertaining to Cockersand's acquisition of the Hutton mill is dated 1190 to 1218. It is a grant from Sapientia, the wife of Elias de Hutton to the abbey of a quarter share of the mill of Bradford, also known as the mill of Hutton. Sapientia (or Sabina) and Emma appear to have been the daughters and heirs of the former lord of the fee, Roger de Howick. In return for this share, Sapientia was to be paid two shillings annually.[199] However, her right to grant this share was somewhat complicated by the claims of the other heirs to Roger's estate. These appear to have been the four daughters of Sapientia, or one or more of her own daughters and likewise of Emma's. All four women made quitclaims regarding this portion of the mill between 1212 and 1220, with each of them agreeing that they should collectively receive four shillings and a pair of white gloves annually in return for this concession.[200] The same grant and quitclaims are acknowledged and confirmed by Sapientia's husband, Elias, around the same time.[201]

Another quarter share of Hutton mill was held by Roger de Howick's grandson, Robert, who was one of Sapientia's and Elias's sons. In a charter dated 1220–46, he quitclaimed three carucates of land and confirmed the grant and quitclaims of his father, as well as 'the share of the mill belonging to the town of Hutton', along with the 'whole fishery in Ribble'. This was all granted and confirmed in exchange for a half carucate of land in the town of Medlar, to be held in inheritance, in return for an annual payment of four shillings.[202]

A third quarter share of Hutton mill was granted and quitclaimed to the canons by Roger de Notesargh between 1212 and 1232. The grant included another site with water access within the bounds of Hutton for the construction of a second watermill.[203] It is not clear whether the canons ever took advantage of this site, as a later quitclaim by Roger dated 1236–68 confirms their right to 'the waters of Wimode and Bradford, wherever a mill might be built within the bounds of Hutton', and prohibits anyone from interfering with them,

---

[196] Ibid., pp. 461–3.

[197] Ibid., pp. 467–8.

[198] Ibid., pp. 468–70.

[199] *Chartulary of Cockersand Abbey*, p. 438.

[200] Ibid., pp. 439–40.

[201] Ibid., p. 440.

[202] Ibid., p. 412.

[203] Ibid., p. 441.

or whatever they built.[204] That the abbey was seeking to consolidate its holdings in the area is confirmed by several other leases, sales and quitclaims which it was able to secure at around the same time.[205]

Cockersand acquired the remaining quarter share of Hutton mill sometime between 1236 and 1256, when John de Clayton and Avice his wife quitclaimed their right in a fourth part of the mill to the abbey for a six mark 'consideration' (i.e., £4), which is roughly consistent with the £20 valuation for reconstructed watermills from around this time.[206] This document is followed by a quitclaim dated 1230 to 1268 by Warin de Walton of his interest in this portion of the mill, which he had already given to John and Avice de Clayton, Warin's daughter.[207] Warin had in turn derived his share from Richard Banastre of Breinerton, who was presumably a close relative of the previously mentioned Thurstan Banastre who had granted the canons tithes of his mill in Walton-in-le-Dale earlier in the century. Because Avice was Warin de Walton's daughter, the gift was probably part of her dowry.[208]

Having invested so much time and what would appear to have been a fair amount of money in securing the rights to this mill and the waters which fed it, the canons of Cockersand were obviously convinced that they could draw large revenues from a milling monopoly in the area. Unfortunately, there are no indications in the cartulary of how much mill revenue they eventually did draw from the people of Hutton, Howick and Bradford, although it would seem from the lack of further documentation that the mill was directly managed by the canons.

Lacock Abbey's Acquisition of the Mill of Bishopstrow (Wilts.)

The third example of an ecclesiastical lord attempting to acquire the shares of a valuable mill in order to gain a milling monopoly can be found in a series of documents relating to Lacock Abbey's acquisition of the mill of Bishopstrow (Wilts.) in the manor held by the abbey. Sometime before 1257, Thomas Arnold Sweyn of Westbury gave his nephew Adam of Westbury (a.k.a. Sweyn) all the land which had descended to him from his own uncle Ellis Serlon (a.k.a. Serle) in Bishopstrow, including 'lands, mills, and other things'. Adam was to hold of Thomas for a penny annually.[209] It would seem that this Thomas was the same Thomas, son of Cade, who brought a case of *mort d'ancestor* against Nicholas Bolevill' in the county court in 1249 for seisin of half a share of the Bishopstrow mill with nine acres of land which had been held by Thomas's uncle, Ellis Serle. The court found that Nicholas only held the share in wardship for the heir of John of Devis', leaving Thomas in the mercy of the court.[210] That Thomas was able to regain seisin of a share of Bishopstrow between 1249 and 1257 despite this ruling would suggest that the heir of John of Devis' had died in the interim. The identity of this heir is revealed in the following document.

In the same year that Thomas brought his case for seisin of a half share of the mill in the county court, i.e., 1249, Emma, a grand-daughter of Ellis Serle, brought another assize of *mort d'ancestor* before the court for the whole of the mill and 18 acres of land which the plea records had been held by Ellis son of Serle. In this case, the claim was against the same Nicholas Bouevill', but also Ela, daughter of John le Daveys (aka John of Devis') and her husband William son of Nicholas. William and Ela stated on oath that Ela's father John had died in seisin of the land, and that as she was under age, Nicholas Bouevill' held for her in wardship.[211] No judgement on the case is recorded for that year.

Between 1257 and 1283, Adam Sweyn 'granted' all of the land and a share of the mill of Bishopstrow which Thomas had given him to Lacock for six marks (£4). He also promised them any additional property which might have come his way following the death of Anastasia, the widow of Ellis Serle. Two and a half

---

[204] Ibid., p. 442.

[205] Ibid., pp. 442–4.

[206] Langdon (1996), pp. 42, 44–5, (2004), p. 179; Lucas (2006a), pp. 133–5.

[207] *Chartulary of Cockersand Abbey*, p. 441.

[208] See ibid., p. 438, n. 1. On Thurstan Banastre, see the section earlier in the chapter on 'Legal Recognition for Non-seigneurial Mills'.

[209] *Lacock Abbey Charters*, ms. 223.

[210] *Civil Pleas of the Wiltshire Eyre*, ms. 102.

[211] Ibid., ms. 323.

acres of land were excluded from the grant that had already been sold by Adam, for which the abbess was entitled to take 2 1/2d in rents per year.[212]

Adam's grant is followed by a quitclaim of 10 August 1259 by William de Smalebroke to Beatrice, abbess of Lacock, of his share of Bishopstrow mill and the surrounding meadow. The charter says that William had acquired the land from Ellis Serle, and the quitclaim includes any additional share of this property which he may have inherited from Anastasia Serle after her death, but excludes the land associated with the mill and any additional property which William may have inherited. William was obliged to pay five shillings a year to the abbess for this share until Anastasia's death, at which time it was to be increased to 6s 8d.[213] Presumably this William of Smalebroke was the husband of Ela, daughter of John le Daveys (or Devis'), and had inherited the share of the mill by marriage. The failure to mention Ela would seem to imply that she had indeed died sometime between 1249 and 1259, as previously speculated.

In the same year, Anastasia Serle quitclaimed to Lacock her own share of the mill in return for a quarter of wheat and a half quarter of barley every year, and was to be freed from paying multure and of having to pay any rent pertaining to her part of the mill.[214] Between 1259 and 1283, Emma, widow of Ellis Burgeys of Warminster, quitclaimed the same mill and a messuage in Bishopstrow to Lacock 'which Ellis Serle formerly held'. The quitclaim also included a tenement that Anastasia had formerly held as part of her dower, implying that Anastasia had died by this time.[215] This Emma was presumably the grand-daughter of Ellis Serle and second cousin of Adam Sweyn who had brought the earlier case against Nicholas, William and Ela. This complicated network of grants and quitclaims had put the canonesses in full seisin of Bishopstrow mill by the end of the thirteenth century. The whole process had cost Lacock at least £5, but as it was able to draw £1 a year in rents from the mill, it was clearly an investment that would soon pay itself off, even if there were repairs to be made to the mill over the coming years.

Conclusion

From the late twelfth century onward, mills and their incomes were increasingly regarded as valuable assets which needed to be protected from encroachment, alienation and competition. As suit of mill became entrenched as a customary right of manorial lords between the Conquest and the early thirteenth century, those who were subject to it, either theoretically or literally, sought and sometimes attained means for avoiding the obligation or minimizing its economic impact. Since the time of Edward the Confessor and possibly considerably earlier, lords had sought to extend what had initially been a royal obligation to as many of their manorial tenants as they could, including free tenants in many parts of the north and some of the ecclesiastically dominated counties such as Huntingdonshire. French precedents, of which many of the great magnates and obedientiaries of the religious houses were no doubt only too aware, had emboldened many of them to impose similar obligations on their English tenants: a simple act of proclamation, followed by a decade or two of customary usage, were sufficient to provide a legal justification for the imposition.

Suit of mill was not simply an irksome imposition for those people in medieval and early modern England who were subject to it. Although the fines imposed by the courts for disobeying suit were relatively modest, those affected were well aware that lords had the right to confiscate their household handmill, as well as any grain which they had milled at any establishment not belonging to the lord, along with the horse used to carry it, and there are many documented cases of lords doing precisely that. Clearly, these were very significant economic disincentives to non-compliance. Langdon's tendency to simply focus upon the fines imposed by the courts is therefore misleading. While it is certainly true that suit of mill does not appear to have ever been so widespread in England as it was in northern France, the ancient Benedictine and episcopal houses held suit on the vast majority of their mills and were therefore willing and able to enforce suit on their tenants. Where custom allowed, it was free as well as unfree tenants who were required to comply, and because it was the

---

212 *Lacock Abbey Charters*, ms. 224.

213 Ibid., ms. 225.

214 Ibid., ms. 226.

215 Ibid., ms. 227.

Benedictines and bishops who together held most of the ecclesiastical mills in England (see Chapter 10), it would not be unreasonable to conclude that the majority of unfree tenants who held land from religious houses were subject to suit of mill.

A very different picture is presented by those non-seigneurial mills granted by knights to the Augustinians, Cistercians and Premonstratensians between the twelfth and fourteenth centuries. These mills were almost invariably located on fees which lay outside the lord's demesne and could therefore not command the suit of the manors on which they lay. Although some of these mills may have existed before the Conquest on former sokeland or warland, and may even have been communally owned and operated, most had probably been built by the knightly families who held those fees for the exclusive use of their households (in cases where the chief lord held monopoly rights on the manor), or for any other freeholders on that fee or on neighbouring fees, manors and vills (in cases where the chief lord did not hold such monopoly rights).

The many disputes over mill tithes, water rights and mill seisin recorded in the case studies provide additional insights into just how important mills and mill income were to religious houses. At least a dozen of the disputes recorded in the charters of the houses sampled involved efforts on the parts of the religious houses concerned to regain seisin of alienated or illegally appropriated mills,[216] or efforts to fend off a disgruntled heir of a mill donor.[217] A few other disputes involved competition for access to water resources for purposes other than milling, such as navigation of rivers, as seen in Old Wardon's dispute with William de Bello Campo over the height of the millpond for the monk's mill of Risingho, which was occluding the water flow into the nearby river and making it difficult for William's ships to navigate. Another type of dispute was over access to watercourses where one party built a mill upstream from an earlier party's mill and thus deprived the older mill of sufficient water to properly run. One such a case was the dispute between the Treasurer of York Minster and St Mary's Abbey, York. Although such disputes could go on for years, and even decades, most were settled relatively quickly to the mutual benefit of the parties concerned.

The collection of mill tithes only became a significant issue for most religious houses in the thirteenth century, but they were obviously a significant source of revenue and therefore worth disputing in court if a question over seisin erupted.[218] The Augustinians were particularly preoccupied with securing mill tithes and maintaining them as an additional revenue stream. This appears to have been primarily due to the large number of appropriated churches which they inherited from lay lords in the twelfth century and subsequently, many of which had mill tithes attached to them. As we saw in the discussion of Bolton Priory's milling fortunes in Chapter 8, it does not appear to have even collected mill tithes until John of Laund's ascendancy to the priorship in the early fourteenth century. Once it had started to do so, however, the additional revenue stream was substantial and not lightly abandoned.

All of these cases highlight the importance which ecclesiastical estates attached to mills, not only as physical pieces of equipment which occupied diverse and sometimes contested landscapes, but as secure sources of both revenue and seigneurial power. Having long institutional memories and deep pockets, the wealthier religious houses were prepared to go to considerable lengths to secure and defend their customary, statute and contractual rights in relation to mills. Those of more modest means, such as St Gregory's, had to choose carefully which cases they were prepared to contest. For the most part, such houses appear to have been content with minor legal victories against other ecclesiastical lords, and seldom challenged lay lords who had disseised them or disadvantaged them in other ways.

---

[216] Such as the efforts of Battle to regain seisin of the mill of Barnhorn, and Holy Trinity's dispute with Simon of Felsted and his descendants over seisin of a number of mills and other lands.

[217] Such as Cirencester's dispute with Walter of Sherston over Sherston mill, Kirkstall's dispute with Alexander Peitivin over the manor and mill of Headingly, and Sibton's with the heirs of Robert II Malet over seisin of Wenhaston watermill.

[218] The small tithes and mill tithes owed to Lacock Abbey, for example, were worth £5 a year in 1337, which was a significant sum compared to the mill rents which it seems to have collected.

Chapter 10
Ecclesiastical Lordship and the
Commercialization of Medieval Milling

Historians of technology have argued for decades that the development of medieval milling is of crucial importance to understanding how the transition from feudalism to modernity occurred. While my own research and that of contemporaries working in the area tends to support this proposition, our research findings are generally at odds with two of the most widely accepted theories that have sought to explain why this is the case. As I have attempted to demonstrate throughout this book, neither the monastic innovation thesis first advanced by Lewis Mumford and Lynn White Jr., nor the seigneurial monopoly model first proposed by Marc Bloch, stand up to a trial of strength against the manuscript and archaeological evidence. Neither theory adequately captures the complexity of the processes which shaped ecclesiastical involvement in the development of the English milling trade. Furthermore, in attributing primary agency to the Benedictines in that development, neither theory takes sufficient account of the extent to which other social groups were able to shape milling technology according to their interests, and how wider processes of political conflict and diplomacy, social stratification and differentiation, environmental change and disease, and population growth and decline, shaped those interests in turn.

On the basis of the abundant ecclesiastical evidence of mill ownership and construction, proponents of the monastic innovation thesis, the seigneurial monopoly model and an industrial revolution in the Middle Ages have argued that it was the monasteries that led the way in medieval technological development, even though the scholars who advocated these theories have attributed different motivations to the monks for adopting powered milling, and drawn different conclusions about their role in shaping the direction of developments in the milling trade. As we have seen, the monasteries and episcopates played an important role in that development, and were undoubtedly one of the social groups that dominated the trade during the second half of the Middle Ages. However, their contribution to innovation with respect to milling technology appears to have been exaggerated.

While there was a favourable shift in attitudes towards the mechanical arts and invention amongst the Western European clergy from the middle of the thirteenth century onwards, neither the verbal enthusiasm of clergymen, nor the increased number of pictorial and literary representations of recent inventions by monkish artists and writers necessarily translated into active or financial support for technological innovation.[1] Furthermore, because such attitudes are not recorded in our sources from the tenth and eleventh centuries, they cannot be invoked as explanations for the growth in the number of monastic watermills or industrial mills which supposedly began at that time, despite White's efforts to do so.[2] If we add to this the fact that there is strong evidence for a steep decline in the number of windmills, and a revival of interest in horse mills and fulling mills at the expense of water-powered grain mills in the wake of the Black Death, it is clear that there was no inevitable progression and expansion of the use of 'new sources of power' during the Middle Ages, as White and others have contended.

Mumford's and White's idea that the promotion of manual labour as a legitimate form of activity for Benedictine monks somehow increased its status in medieval society is undermined by the abundant evidence which demonstrates that the monks themselves, especially from the eleventh century onwards, were seldom involved in any kind of manual work. Despite any later distinction which may have been made between 'degrading' and 'rewarding' forms of manual labour, the adoption of powered mills by monasteries as an alternative to hand-grinding was only partially to spare the monks from such tedium; it was also to protect them from the temptations of the outside world. Their acquisition of non-precinctual mills was primarily about ensuring a regular source of cash and grain income.

---

[1]   Ovitt (1986), (1987).

[2]   See, for example, White (1971), (1972).

On the one hand, the possession of mills by a religious house ensured its ability to provide for its brethren and servants. On the other, the donation of mills and other property to monasteries and priories helped legitimate feudal power relations and maintain the status quo. To be more specific, aristocrats founded religious houses to ensure the spiritual salvation of their ancestors and descendants, and as visible reminders to their vassals, dependents and tenants of their piety and temporal power. A viable house must have sufficient to provide for it, including a mill for its brethren and perhaps a handful of others to provide a cash income for the monks, or to feed the houses' servants and retainers. Knights of the founding lord could win favour with their lord, the monks and God by donating mills and other property on their subinfeudated lands to their preferred religious house. The monasteries and priories thus helped to legitimate the knight/warrior power base of medieval lords by providing knightly families with opportunities to publicly display their piety through donations and other forms of largesse. The fact that it was overwhelmingly individuals from the knightly class who donated mills to the Augustinians, Cistercians and minor orders clearly demonstrates this role.

As we have seen, free and bonded urban and rural workers, artisans and craftsmen, merchants, soldiers, clerks, lawyers, knights, nobles and kings all brushed shoulders with the clergy in the acquisition, management, operation and maintenance of mills. It is only through the kind of detailed examination of these networks of social interaction that we can come to appreciate the roles played by different social groups in the development of medieval milling, and how these groups transformed medieval milling from an activity based in the household or community to an important and profitable sector of the medieval economy.

Far from being benign and reasonable lords, as proponents of the monastic innovation thesis have argued, we have seen ample evidence throughout this book that most of the wealthy Benedictine and episcopal houses, as well as other powerful houses which sought to emulate them, did their best to extract as much revenue from their mills as they could, and jealously guarded their seigneurial privileges. There is, furthermore, no evidence that the increased mechanization of milling led to the diminution of slavery as an institution; miller slaves and unfree miller servants are recorded in Italy and England throughout the Middle Ages, and particularly on ecclesiastical estates.[3] During the thirteenth century, which was the period of highest growth in the number of mills throughout England, unfree status was imposed on a much larger number of peasants than ever before. Far from contributing to liberating peasants from the menial work of hand-grinding, as argued by White and his followers, the exploitative attitudes of the large religious houses in particular acted as a stimulant to the development of a non-seigneurial milling sector. As we saw in Chapter 3, Langdon has estimated that more than half of the powered milling undertaken throughout England in the early fourteenth century was outside seigneurial control, a proportion which grew in the wake of the Black Death. Further evidence in support of this estimate will be canvassed later in the chapter.

While there is no doubt that early scholars of church history and the history of technology have tended to exaggerate the philanthropic tendencies of the religious houses, we should be careful not to automatically endorse the opposite position. As the case studies in the previous chapters demonstrate, there were important differences in outlook and orientation, not just between lay and ecclesiastical lords and individual abbots and priors, but also between religious orders and small, medium and large foundations, all of which were further complicated by local custom, tradition, politics and geography.

Although grain milling was primarily a source of lordly profit making, and ecclesiastical lords were if anything more conscious of this than their lay counterparts, some of the smaller and medium houses appear to have been genuinely concerned with providing their own and neighbouring tenants with milling services that were not aimed at extracting from them as much revenue as possible. In the pages to follow, I wish to explore some of the reasons as to why this may have been so, and in the process, summarize the book's main findings.

The first section explores the issue of monastic philanthropy and innovation. It then moves onto an examination of the profitability of ecclesiastical milling for different orders and houses, followed by discussions of the differences in policy and orientation of the various houses with respect to mill management, the growth of non-seigneurial milling on ecclesiastical estates, mill acquisition through grant, purchase and construction, and ecclesiastical involvement in industrial milling. It concludes with a discussion of the range of factors which shaped the development of ecclesiastical milling in medieval England.

---

3   Britnell (1996), p. 35, reports that Domesday Book records the existence of 28,235 slaves throughout England in 1086, most of whom were employed in agricultural work managing the manorial demesnes and livestock of large estates in the south-west, west Midlands and the Marcher Counties. Eleven per cent of the population at Domesday were slaves, oxherds or swineherds (Britnell [1996], pp. 30–31).

Monastic Philanthropy and Innovation

Even were we to ignore the evidence presented in the previous case studies and focus exclusively on the evidence presented in the first few chapters, we would have strong grounds for being sceptical of the claims made by earlier historians of technology that the behaviour of medieval monks was characterized by a benign and philanthropic sense of mission towards the laity and a high regard for technological innovation. Most of the evidence pertaining to ecclesiastical mill revenues, including tithes, rates of multure and mill rents, as well as mill-related litigation and the enforcement of seigneurial rights by religious houses, clearly indicate that many religious houses were both ambitious and litigious. A number of powerful houses such as Hereford, Durham, Ramsey, Halesowen, Cirencester and St Albans were arguably both avaricious and authoritarian.

Indifference to the suffering of ordinary folk, a preoccupation with self-gratification and self-aggrandizement, and an authoritarian contempt towards the legitimate desires of free and bonded tenants to liberate themselves of irksome feudal obligations appears to have motivated the behaviour of a remarkable number of the abbots and priors who oversaw the larger religious houses. Such behaviour is clearly revealed in their mill management policies, which were aimed primarily at shifting costs onto tenants during hard times while maintaining maximum profits for themselves in good times and bad.

Generally speaking, the older a religious house, the wealthier and more powerful it tended to be, and the more it tended to rely on extractive rents and dues to maintain its status. However, as we saw with respect to several of the ancient houses, not all were successful in pursuing such practices, and some appear to have been prepared to accept the effective loss of control of many of their mills through either lack of managerial engagement, as in the case of Canterbury Cathedral Priory, or litigious exhaustion, as in the case of the Abbey of the Holy Trinity, Caen.

It is of course possible to interpret the rewarding of favoured servants with generous leases on mills and other property as philanthropy, and there is certainly some evidence for this amongst the religious houses sampled, such as Cirencester and Hereford. But the houses concerned could equally be argued to have been acting out of pragmatism, naivete or incompetence. When considering the records of such cases in isolation, it is difficult to distinguish unworldliness, incompetence and even corruption from cases of genuine philanthropy.

When considering claims of philanthropic clerical concern in the Middle Ages, the institutional role of the Latin Church during this period should be borne in mind. As the secular arm of the feudal state was relatively weak and decentralized, with no direct responsibility for maintaining citizens' welfare, the latter was almost invariably entrusted to the Church. Ecclesiastical authorities therefore had sound long-term reasons to act with some charity towards the poor, dispossessed, sick and needy in order to maintain its legitimacy, i.e. the trust and faith of the people. What may now seem like philanthropy to us in a secular welfare state was to them simply a matter of doing what was expected.[4]

Nevertheless, we have already seen a substantial body of evidence indicating that most of the wealthier religious houses were far from generous in their treatment of their tenants, and in the case of imposing additional feudal burdens on villein tenants and of refusing to grant liberties to the towns and villages under their control, they were generally harsher and more inflexible than their lay counterparts. This was presumably related to the long-term outlook of the bishoprics and monasteries, and their desire to retain as many valuable assets as they could for as long as they could.

A number of examples have been cited throughout the book of the destruction and confiscation of watermills, windmills, horse mills and handmills that infringed on their ecclesiastical lords' seigneurial rights, as well as the enforcement of suit of mill by the wealthier religious houses, and disputes over mill-related land and water rights between religious houses and lay lords. Although there is no evidence of the small and middling houses engaging in litigation with respect to suit of mill, they were not infrequently involved in tithe and water disputes, as well as disputes over possession of mills, shares of mills and mill rents. These disputes clearly reveal just how important were functioning mills and the revenues from mills in the affairs of the religious houses which possessed them, regardless of how they subsequently chose to manage them.

In those cases where it has been possible to determine who was responsible for the adoption of technological innovations in mill design and construction by religious houses, those innovations invariably

---

[4]   Chris Dyer, personal communication, October 2000.

appear to have been driven by abbots, canons, obedientiaries and even whole chapters who were, first and foremost, administrative innovators. With regard to the milling trade, any penchant which the medieval clergy may have had for technological entrepreneurship appears to have been primarily motivated by efforts to ensure that they got their share of the steadily growing market for flour upon their own and neighbouring estates. As we saw in the exemplary case of John of Laund, ecclesiastical lords could turn a tidy profit and cash money from well-managed milling assets. The milling accounts of houses such as Bolton Priory provide us with valuable insights into ecclesiastical management practices and general economic trends.

While it is clear that some religious houses were leaders in certain areas of what might be broadly termed 'technological innovation' – such as estate management, book-keeping, sheep breeding and the adoption of new milling technologies and applications – this leadership role was far from ubiquitous or universal. On the one hand, men like Henry of Eastry, Abbot Samson and John of Laund were fine administrators and visionary innovators. On the other, the monks of Battle, Beaulieu and Bury, as well as the canons of Bolton and Chichester, seem at times to have shared the commitment of their priors, abbots and bishops to technological innovation. But it was only those houses that possessed the capital for investment in new and sometimes risky technical practices which could afford to engage in such activities. It was rare for the smaller religious houses to involve themselves in any significant way in mill construction or innovation unless there was a significant unmet demand for millable commodities on their estates.

It was, therefore, not necessarily lordly wealth and power which determined whether milling innovation was encouraged or discouraged. Langdon has rightly noted that strong lordship in northern England discouraged mill innovation and growth in the number of powered mills, and that this flies in the face of the seigneurial monopoly model advanced by Bloch. However, it needs to be remembered that the north was a relatively poor and 'backward' area compared to other parts of England and Western Europe at the same time. Although it was an area in which similar modes of lordship existed to those that Bloch found in northern France, the two areas were very different in other ways. Northern France was a relatively wealthy and technologically advanced area, and although there were extensive lordly monopolies on milling throughout the region, its lords seem to have encouraged the use of industrial mills and milling innovation generally.[5]

What appear to be the most significant differences between the two regions are, therefore, their geography and demographics. While northern France consisted of a number of well-connected and densely populated regional centres with rich agricultural and industrial resources, the north of England consisted of sparsely populated and very large manorial holdings with reasonably well-developed agriculture, but little developed industry. The area was also poorly serviced by land and water transport. A crucial difference between the two areas was the former's ability to generate surpluses in key sectors of the economy, along with well-developed access to markets and finance.

Thus, it was not so much because northern English lords discouraged technological development in milling and other industries that northern England was less developed than other parts of England and Europe, but because the region lacked the population density, transport infrastructure and access to markets to make such activity more profitable, and therefore more attractive to lordly investors.

The reasons for the differences between northern England and northern France, despite strong lordship in both regions, can be further illustrated by contrasting the conditions which prevailed there with those of the east and south-east of England. The east and south-east had a large free peasantry and therefore far greater non-seigneurial ownership of mills compared to these two regions. Suit of mill was consequently much harder for lords to create or enforce. At the same time, because of the region's access to cross-channel and local markets, and being an area through which many goods passed, opportunities for economic and technological development were strong. Despite these regional advantages, however, eastern and south-eastern England did not develop a strong industrial milling sector during the latter half of the Middle Ages because there were insufficient water resources in the area to make industrial milling a viable alternative to grain milling, which remained the most profitable form of milling enterprise throughout England for many centuries.

With respect to the claims by proponents of both the monastic innovation and industrial revolution theses that the Cistercians were philanthropic and kind to their tenants, one would expect to find some evidence of this in their mill management practices, and especially the revenues they drew from their mills. However, in

---

those cases where there is unambiguous evidence regarding Cistercian mill revenues, as there is with Beaulieu and Furness, and to a lesser extent Sibton, what we find is that the monks were as extractive as the harshest and most authoritarian of ecclesiastical lords. Furthermore, in the case of Beaulieu, it was drawing 11.4 per cent of its seigneurial income from its mill revenues in the late thirteenth century, which compares more than favourably with northern lords and other extractive lords from elsewhere in the country. I will have more to say on this issue later in the chapter.

It would seem that for every innovative and perspicacious abbot, prior, obedientiary, prebend and chapter, there were half a dozen who were disinterested, lazy, reckless, venal or incompetent when it came to the management of their temporal affairs. Hereford, Battle, Holy Trinity and St Denys were among those houses that clearly suffered as the result of such behaviour, not to mention the numerous houses that lost revenues and lands during the twelfth century and subsequently because of the incompetence or corruption of their lay and/or ecclesiastical officials. And while it was the case that thrift, good sense and far-sighted thinking were encouraged and rewarded amongst the clerical leadership, wealth and power were as much a corrupting influence in the corridors of the abbeys, priories and ecclesiastical courts as they were in the halls of the lay aristocracy. Those who resisted prevailing mores were obliged to ensure they had powerful allies in high places if they wanted to survive, or face the often humiliating and even fatal consequences.

Those of the wealthier religious houses that were involved in mill innovation engaged themselves in the construction and operation of such novel contrivances as tide mills, windmills and industrial mills. Some of the senior clerics who were involved in these kinds of ventures seem to have been genuinely fired by an enthusiasm for new technology. However, few houses were prepared to continue their investment in such technology if it did not prove profitable in the longer term.

Tide mills were expensive to build and maintain, and were prone to serious damage by floods and storms, making their long-term viability marginal in most circumstances. Holt has documented how Henry of Eastry's expensive ventures in this area were abandoned by later priors of Christ Church, and there is some suggestion that the canons of Blythburgh and the monks of Battle similarly abandoned troubled tide mill ventures which they had entered into in East Anglia and East Sussex within two centuries of them having first been built.[6]

Windmills may have been cheaper to build than watermills, but they were just as expensive to maintain, and were only about half as profitable. Their utility was therefore largely restricted to areas with restricted supplies of running water and steady prevailing winds. Holt and Langdon had already established that this was the case with their work on East Anglia and the West Midlands, and additional evidence to support their claims with regard to Lancashire and Sussex has been discussed in previous chapters.[7] As we saw in Chapter 3, both scholars also found that during the extended social and economic hardships imposed by the plague, windmills were abandoned for horse mills and larger watermills on many estates, including those of religious houses such as Glastonbury.

Industrial mills, on the other hand, were only practical propositions where there was an abundance of running water, some existing expertise in industrial commodity production and ready access to local, regional or national markets. They were, furthermore, at best only around a third as profitable as grain mills. Again, Holt and Langdon had already argued that this was the case in their earlier research, and additional evidence to support their arguments has been cited in earlier chapters.

Nevertheless, as will be discussed in more detail below, there is some evidence that the Cistercians were indeed innovators in some industrial applications of milling technology, much as they were in water engineering more generally. James Bond has suggested that Cistercian technological prowess was an outcome of the strength of the order's centralized organization, which provided Cistercian houses with 'access to technical expertise on a scale unavailable to older, more autonomous houses'.[8] Nevertheless,

---

[6] See Holt (1988), pp. 136–7, on the history and fate of Henry's tide mill. See Chapter 6 on what appears to have been a tide mill at Blythburgh's original location on the Suffolk coast that was replaced by a windmill some time before 1240, and Chapter 5 on what appears to have been a tide mill built by Battle at Barnhorn that was similarly replaced by a windmill by 1307.

[7] See Chapter 4 for a discussion of the Sussex windmills of Chichester and Chapter 6 for a discussion of the Lancashire windmills of Burscough.

[8] Bond (2007), pp. 192–7.

a considerable amount of work remains to be done to determine how extensive were the networks of technical knowledge upon which the Cistercians drew, as well as the range of technical activities which that expertise entailed.

The Profits of Ecclesiastical Milling

Although the profitability of medieval milling was shaped by a number of factors, including the seigneurial status of the mill concerned, the level of competition from other mills in the locality, the amount of grain being grown and/or consumed in the district, the costs of maintenance and repair, and the multure rate that customers were charged, the primary driver remained demand fuelled by population growth and decline. In the absence of competition, manors with growing populations generated more milling revenue, and those with declining populations, less. If the level of milling custom dropped below the threshold required to consistently cover the costs of operation, maintenance and repair, it was only those lords with deep pockets, or resourceful and enterprising tenants, who could keep them functioning.

As we have seen in earlier chapters, milling revenues more than doubled in many parts of England between the middle of the twelfth and thirteenth centuries, a process which was primarily driven by increased consumption due to population growth.[9] Milling generally remained a profitable enterprise until the second half of the fourteenth century, when revenues again experienced a marked and prolonged decline in the wake of the Black Death. Ramsey, Glastonbury, Westminster, Battle, Sibton, Bolton and Durham all experienced substantial declines in the income from their mills, although Durham appears to be one of the few English houses to maintain a reasonable level of post-plague income from its mills overall.[10]

A key indicator of the extent to which milling contributed to the wealth of individual houses is the proportion of their total revenues that were generated by it. As we have seen, a number of the religious houses in the sample were drawing a consistently higher proportion of their total revenues from mills than the average lay lord at the same time. Whereas Langdon found that lay lords throughout England were drawing on average between 5 per cent and 7 per cent of their manorial income from mill revenues by the early fourteenth century,[11] most of the religious houses in the sample for which comparable data were available were drawing considerably higher proportions of their total revenues from mills. For example, Bec's mills in southern England were responsible for producing 7.7 per cent of its temporal income, while Grove Priory was drawing 10.5 per cent of its total income from its mills. Even higher as a proportion of its total income were Beaulieu's mill revenues, at 11.4 per cent. In the Midlands, Hereford generated a comparable proportion of between 8.3 per cent and 11.5 per cent of its temporal income from its mills, whereas in the north, Bolton produced around 8.7 per cent of its total income from its mills, and Durham, around 10 per cent. This compares with Holt's and Langdon's findings that in some parts of northern England at the same time mills contributed as much as one third of a lord's rental income, with the average in the north being around 14 per cent.[12]

The main contributor to the high proportion of mill revenues enjoyed by these houses appears to have been the high proportion of their mills that were located on whole manors and vills, which, as I argued in Chapter 9, directly correlated with their ability to hold milling monopolies and/or enforce seigneurial rights on those manors and vills. The extent to which suit of mill and multure rates contributed to the revenues of the houses sampled provides the framework for the discussion to follow.

---

[9]   See Langdon (1994), (2004), pp. 237, 291–2.

[10]   See the discussion in Chapter 8. Also Holt (1987), pp. 12, 18; (1988), p, 14, Ch. 5 and 10; (1990), p. 57.

[11]   Langdon (1994), p. 5.

[12]   Holt (1988), pp. 79–86, Langdon (1994), p. 13. Durham's mill revenues constituted one-quarter of its rental income in the late thirteenth century. Lords in some other parts of England were also able to extract high incomes from their mills, such as in East Anglia, where the Earl of Norfolk earned more than 15 per cent of his total revenues in the late thirteenth century from mills, although the average proportion for the whole region in the early fourteenth century was only 6.1 per cent. See Holt (1988), pp. 83–4.

Suit of Mill

What made suit of mill such a desirable characteristic for lords and tenants who operated mills was that, saving some natural disaster such as extended drought, violent storms or the plague, it generally guaranteed the lord (and in certain circumstances, the tenant) an income well in excess of the mill's operating costs. As we have seen throughout this study, mills with suit that were either directly managed or held on short-term leases almost invariably drew the highest revenues. If this was combined with high custom and/or a high multure rate, the profit margin for the lord concerned could be considerable. Bec, Durham, St Peter's and Hereford all appear to have followed such strategies in the late thirteenth and early fourteenth centuries, all of which held suit on more than three-quarters of their mills. On the other hand, those mills without seigneurial rights attached to them were far more marginal because they had no dependable source of custom and therefore income. This included seigneurial mills that had fallen out of the demesne after having acquired customary or hereditary status, such as Canterbury's Sussex mills, none of which held seigneurial status in 1285. Nonetheless, a considerable number of non-seigneurial mills managed to survive the thirteenth and much of the fourteenth centuries, and were clearly drawing enough custom from the districts in which they were located to cover their costs and presumably provide a modest income for their tenants and owners.

Mills that were held in customary and hereditary tenure were by definition no longer part of the demesne, although as we have seen they were sometimes permitted to retain the suit of manorial tenants. Because this would normally result in most of the profits from the mill flowing to an independent tenant during periods of economic prosperity, in such circumstances lords tended to respond in one of several ways: litigation to regain seisin of the alienated mill (which often involved cash compensation to the former tenant), construction of a new demesne mill or mills (thus replacing those that were no longer controlled by the lord), or renegotiation of the terms of the lease to include entry fines and rent increases for new tenants. We have seen how Glastonbury and Holy Trinity pursued the first strategy with respect to several of their mills, while Holt has documented how one of the mills on the bishop of Ely's manor of Bridgeham (Norf.) was allowed to remain on a tenancy at will during the thirteenth century, although its revenues declined against the demesne mill on the manor after the latter was declared to have the suit of its tenants.[13] A clear example of the third strategy was in evidence at Hereford, where a number of mills held in customary and hereditary tenure that undoubtedly held suit of the manors on which they were located were paying economic rents. As Hereford had a reputation for being an authoritarian landlord, the most likely explanation for this is that the annual rents were being increased and entry fines charged whenever the leases on these mills expired or a new tenant took up the lease (whether customary or hereditary).[14]

However, we have also seen that suit of mill was not necessarily a guarantee of high revenues from manorial tenants. If a mill held suit on a manor with a small population, the amount of revenue that could be extracted from manorial tenants was obviously far more limited. For example, although half of Battle's mills appear to have held suit in the late thirteenth century, because the population of unfree tenants on a number of its manors was quite small, it was drawing relatively low revenues from the seigneurial windmills and watermills on those manors, even in the early fourteenth century. The same appears to have been true of Cirencester Abbey's mill of Adderbury, which held suit but only paid eight shillings a year in rent in the late thirteenth century.

Multure Rates

Holt has argued that one of the key factors affecting the profitability of milling assets was the multure rate charged by the lord concerned.[15] The more authoritarian forms of lordship that were the norm in northern England in the twelfth and thirteenth centuries assisted lords in controlling their tenants' milling habits.

---

[13]   Holt (1988), pp. 64–5, citing Brit. Lib., Cotton MS Claud. Cxi, fol. 241. The fact that the demesne mill 'was said to have the suit of its tenants' in 1252, 30 years after there appears to have been no such custom, provides further support for my argument about the conditions under which suit of mill could be established.

[14]   See Langdon (1992), pp. 56–7, Langdon (1994), p. 6, for some other examples of lords starving former demesne mills of custom by building new demesne mills, and of allowing tenants to retain suit of mill on leased mills.

[15]   Holt (1988), p. 80.

Their virtual stranglehold on the ownership of mills enabled them to set multure rates that were at least 23 per cent higher than that which prevailed in the rest of the country.[16] It is clear from the behaviour of northern lords, as well as those lords whose estates dominated the regions in which they were located, that they well appreciated the economic principle that once a market has been cornered, the price can be raised accordingly.

The Statute of Bakers (*Statutum Pistoribus*) from c. 1270 stipulated that the rate of tollcorn charged should be 1/20 or 1/24, depending on local custom and the strength of the watercourse driving the mill.[17] Throughout most of southern England, the rate ranged from as low as 1/32 to 1/16, whereas in the north, most unfree tenants were paying between 1/13 and 1/18 of the grain ground at the mill.[18] While freeholders generally paid less than their villein counterparts, Holt has noted that the multure rate set for freeholders on the manors of Durham in the 1370s was one 1/24, whereas during the twelfth century they had been obliged to pay as much as 1/16.[19] This is roughly consistent with two of the charters discussed in Chapter 8, which stated that Furness was obliged by the grantor of Stackhouse mill (W. Yorks.) to charge both free and servile men a multure rate of 1/18 in the late twelfth century,[20] while one of its Cumbrian neighbours charged one of his free tenants a multure rate of 1/15.[21]

Holt has argued that whereas the northern rates were considered onerous by those subjected to them, the rates paid by most southerners were probably only regarded as irksome. He has also noted that landless labourers and small households could purchase bread or grain and were in these cases generally not obliged to obey suit of mill.[22] However, as I argued in Chapter 9, it was not so much the multure rates that lords charged which tenants in many parts of England found problematic, but the fact that because many of them were obliged to use the manorial mill, and lords were within their rights to punish them severely for non-compliance, they had little or no choice but to pay whatever rate the lord charged. There is, furthermore, a considerable body of evidence which suggests that 'bought corn' was subject to suit and multure in much of northern England and in Scotland,[23] in which case the absence of evidence for the practice in the south is not necessarily evidence of the custom's absence there also.

It is nevertheless clear from these and many other cases that most lords sought to extract as high a rate of multure as they could, the rate paid by free tenants being determined mainly by the amount of competition from other mills in the district and their relative proximity.[24] Ecclesiastical lords appear to have been no less enthusiastic than lay lords at pursuing such strategies, although Langdon has discovered an interesting example of a competitive multure rate being adopted by one northern house to the detriment of at least one of its more extractive neighbours. He found that Durham Cathedral Priory had been losing the mill custom of its bonded tenants to its sister cell of Jarrow for at least 20 years, because the multure rate charged by Jarrow was only 1/20 as opposed to the rate of 1/13 charged by Durham, clearly demonstrating his contention that most lords were not too concerned about who it was that patronized their mills, or whether their customers were breaking the suit of their lordly neighbours.[25]

---

[16]   Langdon (1994), p. 19.

[17]   Ibid., p. 49.

[18]   On rates of multure charged for different statuses of tenants in different parts of England, cf. Bennett & Elton (1900), pp. 207–9, 221–3, 240–42; Bennett (1934), p. 133; Holt (1988), pp. 49–51, 80–82; Langdon (1994), pp. 18, 19, 22, 29, 31, 32, 35, 37, 38; (2004), pp. 261, 265, 277–80, 330–33. Bennett's assertion that the average in England was around one-sixteenth is based almost exclusively on evidence from northern England, a point also made by Holt (1988), p. 81.

[19]   Holt (1988), p. 50.

[20]   *Coucher Book of Furness Abbey*, Vol. II, Pt. II, ms. 12; Vol. II, Pt. III, pp. xxi–xxii.

[21]   Ibid., Vol. II, Pt. II, Millom/Arnaby, ms. 33. In the late twelfth century, the multure rate was 1/20 at neighbording Drigg (ms. 61)

[22]   Holt (1988), pp. 49–51.

[23]   Cf. Bennett & Elton (1900), pp. 236–49, and Langdon (2004), pp. 277–8, on bought grain.

[24]   Holt (1988), p. 50.

[25]   Langdon (1994), p. 32.

Although there is no evidence for it in any of the documents cited, it seems likely that those Augustinian, Cistercian and Premonstratensian houses which held fee mills were similarly charging lower multure rates than their neighbours to secure custom for them, as it is unlikely that they were solely reliant on the customer 'overflow' from nearby demesne mills.[26] In the absence of any evidence for their systematic management of such mills, this would appear to be the most likely explanation for their ongoing financial viability.

Mill Revenues

Although there are always difficulties in calculating the profitability of medieval ventures, and especially those relating to milling, the available data for the late thirteenth and early fourteenth centuries allows some direct comparisons to be made between 17 of the 28 houses in the sample. This data has been compiled in Table 10.1, which lists the name and order of each religious house, the number of mills which it held at the time, the percentage of its mills which held suit, and its average annual mill revenue.

A comparison of the data pertaining to the Benedictine and episcopal houses sampled supports the observation that seigneurial status and multure rates were two of the key determinants of a mill's revenue. The lowest earning mills were in the south, while the highest earning mills were in the north, with the Midlands somewhere in between. The lowest by far was for Canterbury's 14 Sussex mills, all of which were held in customary and hereditary tenure, and drew an average of only 12s 5d in 1285. Less than three decades later, Battle's average revenues from four of its seigneurial mills were more than double that at £1 7s 6d, while those of Glastonbury were a little over £2 per mill for 40 mills, one-quarter of which were in customary and hereditary tenure. All three of these houses had seen many of their mills alienated in the twelfth century, with Canterbury being the least successful at regaining seisin. In the West Midlands, with 76 per cent of his 21 mills holding suit, the bishop of Hereford was drawing an average revenue of between £3 5s 3d and £3 14s 4d in the late thirteenth century, while the abbot of Bec drew an average of £3 13s 7d from 23 of his English mills at around the same time, 87 per cent of which held suit. With exactly the same proportion of seigneurial mills as Bec, the bishop of Durham was drawing four times as much in average mill revenues, at £14 4s per mill for 38 or 39 mills in the early fourteenth century. The only northern Benedictine lord in the sample – the prior of Lancaster – appears to have been drawing an average of around £3 13s per mill at the same time, with all of his mills holding suit.

The extant manuscripts of the Augustinian houses sampled list the revenues for less than 20 per cent of their seigneurial mills. Of the 17 mills concerned, only those held by the northern house of Bolton were drawing the high revenues recorded on comparable Benedictine and Cistercian estates. The prior of Bolton, John of Laund, was drawing an average of between £2 18s and £4 7s from each of his eight to 12 seigneurial mills in 1305. The average revenue for all of Bolton's mills in the late 1280s, at around £2 12s, is comparable to the average mill revenues of southern lords at the same time. There are only three other Augustinian mills with suit for which rents or tithes are recorded, i.e. the two mills of Christian Malford in Wiltshire held by Bradenstoke Priory, and the mill of Adderbury in Oxfordshire held by Cirencester Abbey. However, the evidence from these three is far from consistent. While the Adderbury mill drew only eight shillings in rent in the second half of the thirteenth century, the Christian Malford mills paid 16 shillings for tithes only in 1229. In the first instance, even though those who owed suit to the Adderbury mill were described as 'the abbot's men of Adderbury and Milton', the most likely explanations for the low rent paid on this mill is that the number of people who owed suit to it was small, and/or that the abbot's men were charged a comparably low rate of multure for services rendered. On the other hand, revenues from the two mills of Christian Malford must have amounted to about £8, or £4 each. These amounts are certainly comparable to those for mills with suit held by the larger Benedictine and Cistercian houses, as well as northern houses such as Bolton, Lancaster and St Peter's York.

Nevertheless, based on the evidence of the low value of the vast majority of the Augustinians' mills, it seems very clear that their profitability, as well as Augustinian attitudes to mill investment and development,

---

[26]   A point made by Holt. He also noted an example from 1301 of a windmill on the manor of Tilney in Norfolk held by Bury St Edmunds which was said to be worth £2 annually, even though the only two villeins on the manor paid 6d each per year to be free of suit (1988, p. 53, note 52).

were primarily shaped by three factors: the feudal status of their mill holdings, the value of the feudal obligations tied to those holdings, and the number of people who were so obligated. Because more than 60 per cent of the mills held by the Augustinian houses in the sample were non-seigneurial (Table 10.2), it is not surprising that their average rents should have been so low.

Generally speaking, the highest revenue mills in the south were in areas of relatively high population density, such as Chichester's mills in Bishopstone, and Cirencester's mills in Winchester, Cirencester and some other towns. Although the breaking of handmills by the abbot of Cirencester's men in 1305 was part of an effort to enforce 'the ancient custom of suit of mill', it is not clear whether the aforementioned mills of Chichester and Winchester held suit, in which case the major determinant of their high income was simply the population density of the towns concerned.

Table 10.1   Suit of mill and average mill revenues for 17 religious houses in the late thirteenth/early fourteenth century

Name and order of religious house	Number of mills held	% of mills with suit	Average annual mill revenue
Episcopal houses			
Durham Cathedral Priory	38–9	87%	£14 4s
Treasury of St Peter's Church, York	5	80%	£6 3s 4d
Hereford Cathedral Priory	21	76%	£3 14s 4d
Canterbury Cathedral Priory *Sussex manors only*	14	0%	12s 5d
Benedictine houses			
Lancaster Priory	2 1/3–3 1/3	100%	£3 13s
Battle Abbey	19+	89%	£1 7s 6d
Abbey of Bec *English manors only*	23	87%	£3 13s 7d
Glastonbury Abbey	40	75%+	£2
Augustinian houses			
Lacock Priory	2 1/2	60–100%	18s
Bolton Priory	21+	52%	£2 12s
Bradenstoke Priory	9	22–33%	£3 2s 7d
St Denys Priory	6 1/2	15–62%	£1 10s 1d
Cirencester Abbey	19	11%	£1 13s
Cistercian houses			
Beaulieu Abbey	12	33–83%	£5
Sibton Abbey	9–11	18–22%	£1 7s
Minor order houses			
Grove Priory (French dependency)	5	100%	£4
Holy Trinity Abbey, Caen (French foundation)	20–23	25%+	9s 9d

These data suggest that average annual mill revenues in the last quarter of the thirteenth century and the first half of the fourteenth century were in the vicinity of 10 shillings to £4 in southern England and East Anglia (depending on the extent to which non-seigneurial tenure had established itself), £3 6s to £4 in the Midlands, £3 6s to £6 in northern England, and twice that or more in the far north. By the late thirteenth century, annual revenues of £4 to £8 from a seigneurial mill in the north were not at all unusual. The low revenues collected by houses such as Canterbury and Holy Trinity, and the high revenues collected by Beaulieu and Durham, appear to have been outliers that largely reflected the geographic locations and tenurial status of their mills. While the average revenues of only £2 11s from Furness's mills just before the Dissolution were probably a reflection of post-plague recession, some parts of the north were still thriving, as the Treasurer of York was drawing £8 from Alne windmill in 1542.

The much higher average for mill revenues in the north is something that Kosminsky, Miller, Holt and Langdon have all noted in the past.[27] This difference in rental incomes is even more profound when we consider that northern mills processed a far greater proportion of lower-valued grains than did the southern mills.[28]

Like their French counterparts, northern lords were most jealous of maintaining their milling monopolies, and restricted as far as possible the establishment of rival mills, including the slippage of demesne mills into customary or hereditary tenure. Their overall strategies included the construction of large, centrally located mills, the enforcement of bans on handmills, and the rigorous enforcement of suit of mill on their tenants, which even went so far as extracting suit of mill from subinfeudated holdings in order to minimize the opportunities for the tenants of such holdings to exempt themselves from this lordly obligation. As we have already seen, northern lords also charged communities that sought to exempt themselves from suit of mill about twice as much as their southern counterparts.[29]

Langdon has argued against Hodgen that the reason northern lords were able to extract such high revenues from their tenants has more to do with the 'particular conditions in the region rather than ... [being] typical of regions first obtaining their mills.'[30] He adds that rather than the northerners 'learning' such patterns of exploitation from southerners, these patterns appear to have been exported in the opposite direction, as there is evidence from Derbyshire that at least one manor tried to change its multure rate from 1/20 to 1/14 in an apparent effort to emulate its neighbours further to the north, while relatively high mill values occur fairly frequently in the north-west midland counties of Cheshire, Derbyshire and Staffordshire.[31]

Although Bloch's model of seigneurial control does, on the face of it, fit the data in the far north and for the more extractive and authoritarian of the religious houses, it is less than helpful when trying to understand the situation elsewhere in England. As we have seen, Bloch argued that it was the application of strong lordship throughout England and France which encouraged the growth in the number of watermills and windmills in both countries, whereas Langdon has argued that strong lordship actually inhibited the more widespread distribution of mills in the north of England. He argues this was just as true of industrial mills as it was of grain mills, where any impulse to build these mills by the lower orders of society was seriously curtailed by the stranglehold that lords had over investment. Langdon concludes, therefore, that 'large-scale milling spread despite the forces implicit in the Bloch model, rather than because of them.'[32] Nevertheless, I have already argued that it seems unlikely that strong lordship was primarily to blame for this situation, and that it had probably more to do with the low population density of the region combined with a lack of transport infrastructure and access to markets. Furthermore, we have seen some evidence in the previous pages that several of the northern Cistercian, Augustinian and Premonstratensian houses in Lancashire, Cumberland and Yorkshire were not only interested in building mills, including windmills and industrial mills, they were quite happy to take milling custom from their lordly neighbours where and when they could. As we have seen, this included charging lower multure rates to win custom from their ecclesiastical neighbours.

Mill Management

Generally speaking, the strategies which individual religious houses deployed to manage their mills were a function of broader policies of estate management. These policies were an outcome of the administrative and decision-making structures which existed within the house concerned, which were in turn shaped by canonical, archiepiscopal and papal directives, as well as the administrative competence, honesty and loyalty

---

[27]   Kosminsky (1956), p. 182; Miller (1988), pp. 693–4; Holt (1988), pp. 79–81; Langdon (1994), p. 18.

[28]   Langdon (1994), p. 18, note 43, found that the range between the lowest average mill value per manor per year and the highest was even more extreme, with the lowest in Worcester at 181d and the highest in Durham at 2853d, the latter being more than 15 times higher than the former.

[29]   Ibid., pp. 22, 38.

[30]   Langdon (1994), pp. 34–5. See also my discussion of the possible reasons for Durham's extremely high milling revenues in Chapter 8.

[31]   Ibid., p. 35. We also saw evidence in Chapter 9 of these shires imposing suit on free as well as unfree tenants.

[32]   Ibid., p. 38.

of its estate managers, and the geographical dispersion and seigneurial status of the property from which it drew revenues. These factors in turn had a profound influence on the kind of custom its mills could draw and the revenues it could expect to earn.

Other exogenous and endogenous factors played important roles in shaping ecclesiastical mill management practices in different contexts. For example, population growth and decline, the quantity of arable land and consumer preferences drove the demand for milled grain and shaped the maintenance and investment decisions of both lay and ecclesiastical lords.[33] Rainfall, water resources, prevailing winds, topography, soil types and local building materials determined the types of mill that could be successfully deployed in different localities.[34] Natural disasters such as the floods, crop failures and livestock murrains of the 1310s and 1320s, compounded by the successive waves of bubonic plague that hit England between the late 1340s and 1490s, produced long-term structural changes in the medieval economy and society which profoundly curtailed milling custom and opened the milling trade to more independent and private tenants, as well as a greater diversity of industrial applications.[35]

It is interesting to note that in her recent comprehensive review of the development of alternative agricultural practices in England, Joan Thirsk has found that during periods of agrarian recession, new crops and animals were substituted for staples, and new agricultural techniques were developed. She also found that most periods of innovation coincided with either population decline or stagnation.[36] Given the extensive nature of her research, it would not be too long a bow to draw with respect to milling technology to argue that the same kinds of stimuli were at work in the milling trade after 1348.

The general principle that ongoing or seemingly intractable problems stimulate innovation is also in evidence with respect to the monastic reforms of the thirteenth century. As we saw in Chapters 1 and 2, because many religious houses had fallen prey to the unscrupulous and opportunistic during the eleventh and twelfth centuries, the religious orders attempted to establish more transparent and accountable forms of bookkeeping and decision-making in the thirteenth and fourteenth centuries. These reforms required of obedientiaries and chapters some level of competent management and long-term planning to implement: skills which were often not possessed by the lay and ecclesiastical officials charged with those responsibilities. Both issues had a significant impact on how mills and milling fitted into the management strategies of the different religious houses. However, it would seem that the dates of foundation of the various houses and the kinds of property they acquired were the most significant influences on their attitudes to mill investment and development, leading to a number of variations in the ways in which different religious houses, and orders, managed their mills.

For example, because the Benedictines' and episcopal houses' property consisted primarily of former royal demesnes with seigneurial privileges attached to them, most were able to extract relatively high returns from their mills. Because of their later dates of establishment, the Augustinians and Cistercians did not benefit nearly so much as their predecessors from large grants of ancient demesne. While the Cistercians, Premonstratensians and some other minor orders were able to compensate for this disadvantage to some extent by founding their houses in relatively isolated areas and subsequently consolidating their holdings nearby, the Augustinians tended to acquire their property in a far more piecemeal way, with most of their estates consisting of widely scattered non-seigneurial holdings which most houses found difficult to effectively manage. The Cistercians, by way of contrast, appear to have pursued a conscious strategy of property acquisition aimed at acquiring manors which held the suit of their tenants, and/or building their equivalent on granges on which they had established milling monopolies. To the extent that individual Cistercian houses were successful at implementing this strategy, they were able to emulate the Benedictines' mill management techniques. Furthermore, through reproducing where they could the more innovative industrial milling practices of their French mother and sister houses, they were able to process and manufacture a number of other commodities for local and regional markets or their own consumption, including wool, leather and iron.

---

33   Holt (1988), pp. 10–11, 13–16; Ambler (1994), pp. 44–5; Langdon (1991), p. 433, (1994), pp. 26, 36, 41–2.

34   Holt (1988), pp. 13–16, 115–16; Langdon (1994), pp. 9–12, (2004), Ch. 3; Lucas (2006a), Ch. 4 and 6–9.

35   Holt (1988), pp. 159–70; Langdon (1994), pp. 26–7, (2004), pp. 26–31, 34–64, 224–6, 236; Lucas (2006a), Ch. 9.

36   See Thirsk (1997). Her preoccupation with changing consumer tastes and fashions as drivers of innovation is also worth noting.

These differences in management strategy meant that most of the episcopal and Benedictine houses, along with some of the Cistercian houses and most of the houses of minor orders, were able to draw higher average mill revenues from their tenants than were the Augustinians, even in cases where they had not been granted whole manors or mills with suit. Comparison of the data contained in Tables 10.1 and 10.2 generally bears this out. Table 10.2 represents the proportion of different kinds and tenurial categories of mills held by the 28 conventual and episcopal houses sampled in the late thirteenth/early fourteenth century.

Table 10.2   Proportion of mills per order for 28 episcopal and conventual houses in the late thirteenth/ early fourteenth century

Type/Order	Total no. of mills in seisin	Mills built by house	Mills with suit	Mills without suit	Mills in customary and hereditary tenure	Windmills	Industrial mills
Episcopal	78+	-	74%	26%	47%	4%	6%
Benedictine	85+	-	81%	19%	16%	19%	6%
Augustinian	82+	16%	32–7%	61%	21%	7%	0%
Cistercian	55–7	19%	35–56%	44–65%	2%	11%	12–13%
Minor Orders	40	-	46–57%	38–52%	36–49%	5%	10%

With respect to the data contained in Table 10.2, by the early fourteenth century, the nine Augustinian houses sampled held suit on only 32 per cent to 37 per cent of the 82 or more mills in their possession, whereas the five Cistercians houses held suit on between 35 per cent and 56 per cent of their 55 or more mills, and the five minor order houses, between 46 per cent and 57 per cent of their 40 mills. By way of contrast, the four Benedictine houses sampled held suit on 81 per cent of their mills, and the five episcopal houses, 74 per cent of their mills, even though almost half were in customary and hereditary tenure, indicating that at least some of the latter houses appear to have been comfortable with allowing their mills with suit to fall out of their direct control.[37]

The scattered nature of most Augustinian holdings and the large number of fee mills they were granted generally precluded the Augustinians from exercising lordly control over their tenants with respect to milling, whereas the Benedictine and episcopal houses, with their large and consolidated manorial holdings and longer established wealth and power, were able to impose their will far more easily on their tenants. Falling somewhere in between these two extremes, the Cistercians and minor orders exercised their lordly authority to the extent that they were able to consolidate their holdings. As will be discussed in more detail in the next section, a significant proportion of the mills held by the Augustinians, Cistercians and minor orders were non-seigneurial fee mills, and therefore performed a different function to the seigneurial mills of the Benedictines and episcopates for a different clientele.

Turning now to the data compiled in Table 10.1, we can see the strong correlation between houses which enjoyed higher average mill revenues and their greater proportions of mills with suit. Generally speaking, the northern and 'frontier' houses had the highest proportions of mills with suit and the highest average mill revenues, i.e. Durham, St Peter's, Hereford, Lancaster and Bec, whereas those houses with few or no mills with suit generally had the lowest average mill revenues, i.e. Canterbury, Cirencester, Sibton and Holy Trinity. The only exceptions to this rule were the abbeys of Battle and Lacock, and the priories of Bradenstoke and St Denys. In the cases of Battle and Lacock, although both houses possessed high proportions of mills with suit, their lower average mill revenues were a consequence of the relatively low number of tenants on those estates who were obliged to do suit at their mills. In the case of Bradenstoke, on the other hand, although only one-third of its mills held suit, the data on its mill revenues are from its mills with suit. With respect to St Denys's, there is some uncertainty about the number of mills with suit which it held, and how much of their revenue it was able to keep for itself due to the unscrupulous behaviour of its knightly tenants.

---

[37]   A rough calculation of the (mostly East Anglian) Benedictine houses studied by Holt came to around 57 per cent. For the episcopal estates studied in detail, the percentages ranged wildly from 0 per cent for Canterbury's Sussex mills, to 87 per cent for Durham's mills (see Chapter 4, Table 4.9), and for the Benedictines, from 78 per cent for Glastonbury to 100 per cent for Lancaster (see Chapter 5, Table 5.9).

Those houses which held mills that drew lower average mill revenues had almost invariably allowed the majority of their mills to fall out of the demesne in the twelfth century or earlier, and had failed to recover all or most of them from customary or hereditary tenure, as in the cases of Canterbury and Holy Trinity. The only exceptions to this were windmills and watermills lying in manors with low populations, such as those held by Battle in Barnhorn, Limpsfield and Brodeham. The highest value mills were either demesne mills with suit in relatively densely populated manors, or mills without suit located close to population centres.

Furthermore, in those counties where religious houses were able to dominate the milling trade because of their extensive landholdings, such as Ramsey Abbey in Huntingdonshire, Beaulieu in and around the New Forest, and the bishoprics of Hereford and Durham on the Welsh border and in the far north of England, they tended to extract higher mill rents and/or rates of multure from their tenants than did ecclesiastical lords in counties with more mixed ownership. As we have seen, it was also the larger and more despotic religious houses (most of which were Benedictine or episcopal houses) that tended to enforce suit of mill on their tenants during the thirteenth and fourteenth centuries.

The low incomes that were generally a corollary of the non-seigneurial status of most Augustinian mills, combined with the fragmented nature of most of their holdings, appears to have acted as a strong disincentive to those houses without many seigneurial mills to develop any systematic policies on mill investment and development. Mills let on long leases for very little money were not at all unusual amongst the holdings of the Augustinian houses sampled, at a time when the other major religious orders were systematically re-examining and rationalizing their estate management practices. For the majority of the houses concerned, this was partially a function of their lack of financial resources, but even the larger Augustinian houses studied appear to have had few opportunities to acquire sufficient property in the areas where they were donated non-seigneurial mills to also acquire the suit of local tenants, thus enabling them to draw higher revenues or charge higher rents. There is also some evidence from several of the Augustinian houses that they were leasing mills on generous terms to their lay servants and retainers in the twelfth and thirteenth centuries (i.e. Cirencester and Blythburgh), as well as re-letting mills to the individuals and families that had first granted them (i.e. Blythburgh, Burscough and Bradenstoke). Given that more than half of the houses sampled were engaged in such practices, it would seem that they were not at all unusual.

The most common mill management strategy pursued by the more entrepreneurial houses was to maximize their incomes from their mills through direct management or short-term leases. As we have seen, this need not have necessitated the establishment or maintenance of a monopoly, as was the case with Durham. Peterborough, Glastonbury and Holy Trinity were able to double their milling revenues between 1086 and 1130 through direct management and fixed-term leasing, while Glastonbury and Ely experienced four- to six-fold increases in mill revenues between 1086 and the early 1300s by employing similar strategies.[38] Starting from a much higher base, Durham was able to increase its average mill revenues by three or four times between 1183 and 1307 by taking the same approach.

In the twelfth century, the Benedictine and episcopal houses of Battle, Bec, Canterbury and Hereford let their mills to free and customary tenants, including knights, together with fractions of virgates and substantial acreages for low rents accompanied by labour services, as did the alien abbey of Holy Trinity; something which Holt also found in his research. At the same time, the Cistercian, Augustinian and Premonstratensian houses were being granted fee mills with messuages and sometimes larger landholdings by knights throughout the kingdom. On the one hand, therefore, some knights were benefiting from acquiring mills on hereditary and customary leases from the Benedictine and episcopal houses, while many others were donating mills in perpetuity to the Augustinians, Cistercians and Premonstratensians. The only evidence from the sample that any of these fee mills might have once been in the possession of another religious house is with respect to one of the mills of Christian Malford (Wilts.) held by Bradenstoke Priory, which was at one time almost certainly in the possession of Glastonbury Abbey.[39]

---

[38]   Glastonbury Abbey's policies of imposing economic rents, direct management and the construction of windmills in areas without mills in 1189 meant that by the early fourteenth century they had more than quadrupled their income from mills over a little more than a century, from less than £20 to over £80. See Holt (1987), pp. 6–8, 18.

[39]   See the discussion of these mills in Chapters 5 and 6.

With the notable exception of Canterbury's Sussex manors, which remained outside the demesne for centuries, most of the southern Benedictine and episcopal houses appear to have let the majority of their mills at farm by the late thirteenth and early fourteenth centuries (sometimes with labour services still attached). By way of contrast, the northern houses of Lancaster, St Peter's York and Durham seem to have mostly favoured direct management of their mills by this time, as did the Cistercian houses of Furness, Sibton and Beaulieu, although it would appear from the fourteenth-century surveys that customary services had all but disappeared in favour of cash commutations by this stage. By the late fourteenth century, most southern lords were letting their mills at farm on short-term (and sometimes generous) leases. Although the evidence from Durham suggests that similar strategies were beginning to be pursued in the far north as well, Furness appears to have been an exception (see Table 9.1).

In those cases where a Benedictine or episcopal house with ancient demesne did not seek to reform its management practices in the thirteenth century, or to recover property alienated from it in the twelfth century, it could expect its mills to remain outside its direct control. Those that did pursue these twin strategies tended to develop systematic mill management practices, e.g., Bec and Battle, whereas those that failed to pursue them could presumably see no benefit in doing so, e.g. Canterbury. Some variety in the kinds of tenure and forms of management pursued by the more entrepreneurial houses was still in evidence, however, with the northern houses appearing to generally favour cash rents throughout the periods covered, while those in the south appear to have favoured cash or grain rents depending on what was likely to provide them with the most revenue at the time.

By way of contrast, Cirencester and Chichester appear to have pursued a mixed policy of leasing and direct management of their mills in the late twelfth and thirteenth centuries. But whereas Cirencester acquired most of its mills from knights, administrative officials and gentry, and only ever appears to have built one of its own mills, Chichester invested quite heavily in windmill building long before many of its ecclesiastical counterparts, building three windmills between the 1180s and the early 1200s. However, unlike any of the other houses surveyed, it granted out all of these mills and two others within a relatively short period of time, although two had soon returned to the bishop's hand. By the early fourteenth century, Chichester's mill revenues were derived from a mixture of tithes (four mills), mill rents granted by knights (three mills), and leases and direct management (three mills). The fact that it did not build watermills on two sites donated to it for that purpose between 1204 and 1256 would suggest that Chichester's canons had realized by this time that investment in the construction of mills without suit was not likely to be profitable.

Due to the fragmented nature of many of the sources, it is difficult to get a clear idea of how all of the houses managed their mills over the centuries. However, it is very clear that the Benedictine and episcopal houses that sought to bring as many of their mills back into demesne control as possible sought at the same time to maximize their mill revenues through leasing their mills on short terms and high rents, and/or by imposing high multure rates. What might be described as extractive mill rents were charged by these houses, while the little evidence that we have of longer-term mill management practices for Battle and Lancaster demonstrates that both houses frequently engaged in litigation against laypeople and other religious houses in order to secure the seisin of alienated, appropriated or threatened properties. As with many of the other disputes that we saw recorded in Chapter 9, persistence, royal connections and abundant financial reserves were usually the most advantageous characteristics in settling to one's favour.

With the exception of the bishops of Durham and treasurers of York Minster, all of the evidence canvassed in previous chapters indicates that the general attitude amongst the larger ecclesiastical lords was to maximize the income from the mills on their manors, rather than to ensure monopolistic control of them. The Cistercian monks of Furness, for example, may well have been extracting high revenues from their seigneurial mills prior to the Black Death, but it would not only appear that the abbey's mills were all in hand at this stage; the monks of Furness, like the monks of Sibton and Beaulieu, were careful to disperse any income as grain allowances to obedientiaries and abbatial servants so as to not have to declare them to papal authorities. Kirkstall likewise appears to have directly managed its seigneurial mills at Bramley and Bramhope, and effectively leased in perpetuity four other mills with significant parcels of land in the twelfth and thirteenth centuries at rates which were typical of the north at that time.

The Growth of Non-seigneurial Milling on Ecclesiastical Estates

It has been argued that the number of mills with suit which lords held was determined by two factors: the extent to which they held former royal estates, and the extent to which they were able to establish this customary obligation on any whole manors which they held, usually because a literal monopoly on milling already existed on the manor. This situation created what we might now call a structural distortion in the medieval economy which favoured lords with manorial holdings and consolidated property.[40] The religious houses which held the largest number of manors and the most consolidated property – consisting primarily of former royal estates – were the ancient Benedictine and episcopal houses. It is therefore not surprising to see that they almost invariably held the largest number and proportion of mills with suit of all the religious orders, as well as the highest value mills (Tables 10.1 and 10.2).

With relatively few manorial holdings and scattered properties, most Augustinian houses had fewer mills with suit and lower mill revenues, whereas the Cistercians were the most successful of the later orders to acquire whole manors and vills, and to consolidate their other properties to create seigneurial rights on their granges. Consequently, the number of mills with suit which the Cistercians held per capita and the revenues they enjoyed were somewhat higher than the Augustinians, but somewhat lower than those of the great Benedictine and episcopal houses. As has already been discussed, however, the correlation is not always quite so neat (see Table 10.1).

Holt and Langdon have demonstrated that ecclesiastical lords played a significant role in the growth of demesne milling during the latter half of the Middle Ages. My own research has confirmed this picture, but has also revealed that ecclesiastical lords played a significant role in the growth of commercial milling in many parts of England as well. Whereas the wealthy episcopal and Benedictine houses were the main ecclesiastical players in the demesne milling sector, and continued to be up until the time of the Dissolution, the Augustinians, Cistercians and Premonstratensians played a more minor but nevertheless significant role in the growth of the non-seigneurial milling sector, and hence, the growth of a commercial trade in milling services.

As stated previously, one of the most striking features of the mill-related data pertaining to the nine Augustinian houses sampled is the low number of seigneurial mills held by them in the late thirteenth and early fourteenth centuries. Between 26 and 30 of the 82 or more mills directly held by the houses concerned unambiguously held suit, constituting 32 to 37 per cent of the total (Table 10.2). Eleven or more of these mills were held by Bolton, seven by Burscough, and two or more each by Blythburgh, Bradenstoke and Cirencester, indicating that 2/5 of the total were held by Bolton and 1/2 by Burscough, both of which were northern houses (see Table 6.10). Burscough's seigneurial mills appear to have maintained their status after the priory granted free burghal status to the vill in which they were located, suggesting that the canons were loath to abandon their interest in what were presumably quite profitable mills.

A significant number of the mills without suit held by the Augustinians, Cistercians and Premonstratensians were donated to them by knights and members of the lesser gentry, administrative and curial classes. Over 60 per cent of the mills held by the Augustinians were non-seigneurial, and of these around 2/3 were fee mills donated by knights. The fact that only 17 or 18 of the more than 50 mills without suit held by the Augustinians were held in customary or hereditary tenure indicates that 40 per cent of Augustinian mills in the late thirteenth and early fourteenth centuries were being operated by the canons themselves as commercial, non-seigneurial ventures, i.e. they drew custom from whomever in the district chose to mill at them.

A similar overall proportion of fee mills was held by the Cistercians, indicating that both orders maintained their interests in fee mills from the time they were first acquired, and almost undoubtedly operated such mills on a commercial basis (Charts 10.1 and 10.2). Only 4 per cent of the mills recorded for the five houses were unambiguously held in customary and hereditary tenure, indicating that around 1/2 to 2/3 of Cistercian mills were being operated by the monks as commercial, non-seigneurial ventures. Of the 55 or more mills held by the houses sampled in the late thirteenth and early fourteenth centuries, between 35 per cent and 58 per cent of them held suit (Table 10.1). The lower figure for suit represents those mills whose suit is confirmed in the

---

[40]   William I and his administrators clearly understood these principles, as Fleming (2004), Ch. 5–6, has found that great care was taken by them in allocating property and redrawing tenurial boundaries to create estates for favoured magnates which had both features.

relevant houses' documents, whereas the higher figure is inferred from available mill revenues and whether the mill concerned was part of a manorial demesne holding.

Drawing on the data contained in Table 7.15, the relative numbers of mills with suit held by each of the five Cistercian houses before 1300 were as follows. Of the 16 or more mills held by Furness, at least 11 of them held suit.[41] Of the 11 mills directly held by Kirkstall, between two and six held suit.[42] Between one and three of Old Wardon's seven mills held suit,[43] and only two of Sibton's nine or more mills.[44] At least four and as many as 10 of the 12 mills held by Beaulieu before 1300 held suit.[45] Only one of its mills was leased at this stage, with the other two being industrial mills within the abbey's workshops that recorded no income.

Drawing on the data contained in Table 8.11, the houses of the minor orders also held a significant number of non-seigneurial mills, although many of those in the sample were mills in customary and hereditary tenure in the nominal possession of Holy Trinity. Between 36 per cent and 49 per cent of the 40 mills held by the five houses were in customary or hereditary tenure, with between 46 per cent and 57 per cent holding suit. Once again, half or more of the minor orders' mills overall did not hold suit. However, all of the mills held by Grove Priory, Leiston Abbey and the Wakebridge Chantries did, whereas 1/2 or more of Cockersand's mills held suit, but only 1/4 of those held by Holy Trinity. Of all those mills for which revenues and suit of mill are recorded, there is a direct correlation between the seigneurial status of those mills and their revenues, once again supporting the observation that, with the exception of urban mills, seigneurial mills were generally more profitable than those which did not hold suit (Table 10.2).

We have also seen some evidence in earlier chapters of privately and even communally operated mills that paid their lords a license fee to operate (see Table 9.1). While the overall number of such mills throughout England was probably initially fairly small, as mill tenures and customs freed up in the wake of the Black Death, a growing proportion of industrial mills in particular appear to have been built and held on such terms.[46]

Such arrangements appear to have first emerged as early as the late twelfth century, as can be seen in the case of William, a tenant of Durham's at Oxenhall, who was allowed to operate his own private horse mill for a fixed rent while being freed from suit and customary work at the manorial mills.[47] Such agreements had become well entrenched by the early fourteenth century, as we saw with a number of mills paying nominal rents to the nuns of Holy Trinity,[48] as well as the significant number of private operators who entered the Welsh fulling industry at around the same time. Indeed, although such 'small men' appear to have held only 10 per cent of Welsh fulling mills in the fourteenth century, they held almost 40 per cent of the newly built mills in the fifteenth century.[49] This and other evidence already canvassed suggests that by the end of the thirteenth century, freemen of varying status were already building mills in significant numbers, and in some cases donating and selling them to religious houses (see Table 10.4).

The license fee to privately operate a non-seigneurial grain mill or fulling mill in the late twelfth and thirteenth centuries appears to have been around four shillings, whereas the typical rental for a customarily or freely held mill was between six and 10 shillings (Table 9.1). For example, Andrew de Luddesham and

---

[41]   These were the mills of Furness, Ulverstone (2), Lyttle, Winterburne, Stackhouse, Newby, Borrowdale and Bolton, and shares of Hetton and Crathon. It may also have held suit on the mills of Grefholme, Driterum and Stalmine.

[42]   The mills held by Kirkstall which held suit were the two mills of Bramley, which were probably clearing about £3 10s in revenue in the early thirteenth century. It is also likely that Keighley, Adel, Cookridge and Headingley held suit. Kirkstall's fulling mill, tanning mill and forge mill were almost undoubtedly for the exclusive use of the monks.

[43]   The mills with suit held by Old Wardon included the Monks' mill in Southill and the two mills of Caldecote. The grants of Milton Earnest and West Wardon mills to Old Wardon were parts of knight's fees and make no reference to suit of mill, while it is not at all clear what was the seigneurial status of Risingho and North mills.

[44]   The mills with suit held by Sibton before 1300 were *Fengesmyll* and the windmill of Thwaite.

[45]   These were the mills of Beaulieu (a.k.a. the 'Outside' mill), Little Faringdon (x2) and Rockstead, but possibly also included Soberton, Rydon, Burgate, Kyndlewere, Coxwell, and the fulling mill of Beaulieu.

[46]   For example, see my discussion of this issue with respect to the Welsh fulling industry in Lucas (2006a), Ch. 9.

[47]   See Appendix C.

[48]   These were: Brimscombe fulling mill held by Thomas de Rodebrec for 4s 3d, William de Keem's grain mill at Brimscombe which Henry held for 1s 6d and the tool-sharpening mill of *Brechachre* held by Robert and his wife for 6d.

[49]   See Lucas (2006a), p. 300.

Helwis' de Fullestr' held two fulling mills for annual rents of four shillings from the Archbishop of Canterbury in 1285,[50] while the men of Gorley paid Beaulieu Abbey four shillings a year for a license to communally run their own mill in 1269–70.[51] Holt has similarly found evidence for three shilling, four shilling and six shilling rents being paid in 1189 to Glastonbury by free and customary tenants for the mills of Shapwick, Buckland Newton, Pucklechurch and High Ham, and of a four shilling license fee being paid by a free tenant holding one of Glastonbury's mills of Wrington in 1250.[52] A variation on this theme can be seen in the case of Blythburgh Priory, which charged the son of the donor of the mill of Henham watermill only four shillings in annual rent in the early thirteenth century, even though the mill retained the suit of the manor.[53] It is possible that the other mills cited were similarly licensed to their tenants on the basis of some long-standing familial relationship with that holding, whereby the tenant bore the full costs of maintenance and repair, but also retained most of the mill's revenue. In the case of Darsham windmill, leased to Turgild and Anastasia by Blythburgh Priory in the early thirteenth century for 15d annually and a half-mark consideration, it seems most likely that the lessees were either acting in an official capacity for the priory, or were relatives or military retainers of the original donor, Roger de Chesney.

The relatively large number of non-seigneurial mills held by the Augustinians, Cistercians and Holy Trinity suggests that Bloch's emphasis on seigneurial monopolies being the provenance of English ecclesiastical lords is in need of serious modification. Of the 15 houses concerned, only Furness, Beaulieu and Lacock appear to have attained any extensive milling monopoly over their tenants. Nevertheless, both Furness and Beaulieu were large and powerful royal foundations, and certainly comparable in wealth and status to many of the older and more established episcopal, Benedictine and Augustinian houses with whom they shared such monopolistic behaviour. The less wealthy and powerful Cistercian houses, like their Augustinian and Premonstratensian cousins, appear to have been perfectly willing to accept, maintain and operate the less profitable non-seigneurial mills.

The very large number of mills donated by knights and nobles to the Augustinians, Cistercians and Premonstratensians during the twelfth and thirteenth centuries clearly demonstrates that most of the mills acquired by these three orders during this time were not built by them. However, some important questions remain as to the status and origins of the mills donated to these religious orders by knights throughout England. For example, where did these mills come from? Why did many of them not hold suit? And how did the knights who donated these mills acquire such mills in the first place? Several possibilities present themselves.

Although it is not possible to determine from whence these donated mills originated from the extant documents, it seems most likely that they had multiple origins, including:

- seigneurial mills granted to the knight as part of a fee to solely serve his household and/or retinue;
- mills that had at some point been seigneurial, but were replaced with larger and/or more powerful mills outside the knight's fee;
- mills built by the knight with the permission of the tenant-in-chief which exclusively served the knight's household and retinue, or which served or contributed to a religious house which they supported;
- mills that had been built by the knight or others without the permission of the tenant-in-chief, and subsequently granted to religious houses to avoid their destruction; and
- mills that had been freely held by the knight's family since time immemorial, which held customary or hereditary status within the manor, and may or may not have been recorded in Domesday Book.

It is possible that there were other sources for these mills, but those outlined above appear the most likely given the documentation discussed in previous chapters.

While some may have been recently built on property where they were not owed suit, such as a knight's fee, or in an urban setting, or on former common land, sokeland or woodland, it seems very unlikely that such non-seigneurial mills would have been built in order for them to be donated or sold. In such cases, although their lack of profitability may have made them suitable as pious gifts, one would imagine that any donor

---

50 *Custumals of the Sussex Manors of the Archbishop of Canterbury*, 'Borgh of Uckefeud: [free tenants]', p. 75.

51 *Account-Book of Beaulieu Abbey*, pp. 109.

52 Holt (1987), pp. 10, 12.

53 *Blythburgh Priory Cartulary*, Pt. I, mss. 304 and 314.

would at least try to recoup his or her costs before parting with such a valuable asset. The fact that a number of mill donations to religious houses appear to have been made not long before the donor's death confirms this observation, as does the fact that there is little manuscript evidence to suggest that lay lords or other laypeople of stature granted newly built mills to an ecclesiastical institution.[54]

It is also possible that some of these mills were either independent tenant mills that had been acquired as investments, or were old seigneurial mills (possibly ruined in some cases) that either had so little custom associated with them as to justify giving them away, or were on ancient manors where most of the holdings had fallen into hereditary or customary tenure at some point in the past. Another possibility is that the mills concerned had remained in free tenure since Anglo-Saxon times, and had not changed status since then.

Some evidence for the first and third possibilities is the large number of lordly confirmations that accompany many of these non-seigneurial mill grants, indicating that many of the mills concerned were on small parcels of subinfeudated lands in manors and vills that were not held by the party who possessed the mill. In other words, these mills had the status of independent tenant mills, and therefore provide valuable insights into the revenues of such mills which are not available from most other medieval documents that tend to record only demesne lands and seigneurial mills. Particularly in Lancashire, however, mill donations appear to have been included in larger grants of a whole or large part of a vill or manor, even though such grants did not always include suit of mill.

While Canterbury, Glastonbury and Battle saw varying but significant percentages of their mills alienated to free and customary tenants during the twelfth century on very low rents and seem never to have regained them, the abbots of Bec-Hellouin managed to retain control of the majority of their mills on short-term and lucrative leases throughout the twelfth century and subsequently. The bishops of Hereford, on the other hand, appear to have been able to increase to economic rates the rents of several of its mills held in customary and hereditary tenure; an unusual situation that does not appear to have been emulated by any of the other houses in the sample. Even more successful in the milling business were the bishops of Durham, who only ever allowed a few of the many mills which they held to fall out of direct control, and were extracting what appears to have been the highest average mill revenue in the country by the early fourteenth century.

Mill Acquisition through Grant and Purchase

All nine of the Benedictine and episcopal houses sampled were established in England in the late eleventh century or earlier, as were the three East Anglian Benedictine houses studied by Holt. However, the only houses for which there is clear evidence for the number of their mill holdings at Domesday are Ramsey, Glastonbury and Battle, all of which experienced significant growth in their mill numbers over the subsequent two centuries. Ramsey, for example, held 14 mills in 1086 and 35 by 1279, while Glastonbury held 21 mills in 1086, and 40 by the early fourteenth century. Battle appears to have held as many as 10 mills by 1100, and more than 20 by the early fourteenth century. In the cases of Glastonbury and Battle, therefore, their mill numbers doubled in 200 years, whereas those for Ramsey increased by 150 per cent. This was due to the fact that by the late thirteenth century Ramsey was able to fulfil what had been unmet demand for milled grain on its East Anglian estates by constructing a large number of windmills.

With regard to the dates of acquisition of the various mills held by the five Cistercian houses, only 10 or 11 of them were acquired at the foundation of the houses concerned, or around 20 per cent of those held by 1300. Excluding Bolton, only 14 of the 62 mills held by the other eight Augustinian houses by the late fourteenth century were part of foundation endowments, or a little under 1/4 of them. By way of contrast, the minor ecclesiastical orders held about half of the mills at their foundation compared to those which they had acquired by 1300.

---

[54]   Three exceptions to this general rule were found in the sample, the first being William of Wakebridge's foundation of his family's chantry at Crich, where he rebuilt a mill at his own expense on a fee held by his lord in order to grant it to his fledgling house (see Chapter 8). The second is the case of Robert de Domno Martino, marshall of Boulogne, who granted Sibton Abbey the recently built Tostock windmill soon after he purchased it from William of Norton (see Chapter 7). A less generous case involved Thurstan Banastre granting Cockersand Abbey the mill tithes of his newly built mill at Walton-in-le-Dale (see Chapter 8).

Almost all of the houses sampled acquired the majority of their mills through grants and purchases in the twelfth and thirteenth centuries, by far the greatest number occurring during the thirteenth century (Table 10.3). Only 18 of the Augustinian mills were granted, purchased or built before the thirteenth century, or just under 30 per cent of them. Forty-two of these mills were acquired during the thirteenth century, or 68 per cent of the total. Likewise, only 1/3 of Cistercian and Premonstratensian mills were acquired during the twelfth century and 2/3 during the thirteenth century. Another way of expressing these figures is to say that the number of Augustinian and Cistercian mills doubled between the beginning and the end of the thirteenth century, an observation that roughly conforms with earlier findings by Holt and Langdon.

Table 10.3	Periods of mill acquisition and investment for five Cistercian, eight Augustinian and two Premonstratensian houses, 1084–1364

Century	Cistercian	Augustinian	Premonstratensian	Total
11th	0	3	o	3
12th	20	15	3	38
13th	38–40	42	10	90–92
14th	2–4	2	0	4–6
TOTAL MILLS	**62**	**62**	**13**	**137**

Between four and six mills of the total are recorded as having been acquired during the fourteenth century, although there is insufficient data from the fourteenth century to draw any firm conclusions about mill acquisition for most of the houses concerned. Nevertheless, these data indicate that the period during which the houses concerned acquired most of their mills, either through grant, purchase or construction, was the thirteenth century, a period of general prosperity and economic expansion.

Turning now to the question of how these various mills were acquired, Table 10.4 gives us a very clear idea of the social status of those who granted or sold mills to the three orders. The sample reveals that at least 41 of the 62 mills that were directly held in the late fourteenth century by eight of the Augustinian houses sampled were donated or sold to them, i.e., roughly 2/3 of them, a figure almost exactly mirrored by that for the Cistercians. By far the largest number of mills acquired by all three orders were donated or sold to them by knights, constituting almost 40 per cent of the total, a figure that was roughly consistent across all three orders. Although the Cistercians benefited most from baronial grants, and the Augustinians from royal as well as archiepiscopal grants (the latter to the exclusion of the other two orders), 8 per cent of the total mills recorded were royal in origin, 8 per cent of baronial origin and 3 per cent of archiepiscopal origin. In other words, kings, archbishops, nobles and knights were the donors and possibly in some cases the builders of almost 60 per cent of the mills which the three orders held. These mills amounted to almost 90 per cent of those donated. Of the remaining 10 per cent or so, only two of the donors can be unambiguously identified as members of the administrative classes, although of course many men of the knightly class at this time also served as royal or ecclesiastical officials. Members of the gentry were responsible for donating six mills, burgesses, one mill, and peasants, two mills. The 'other' category involved a single mill donated by the huntsman of a lord.

Only five of the Augustinians' mill acquisitions and two by the Cistercians are recorded as sales, or just over 5 per cent of the total (see Tables 6.9 and 7.14). It is of course possible that more were acquired through sale or exchange but were not recorded as such. Bradenstoke's and Lacock's charters record their purchases of single mills as part of larger holdings, while Cirencester's record the purchase of three mills, and Beaulieu's, two mills. Most of the mills concerned cost as much to buy as it would to construct them (Table 10.5).

The Cistercian house with the largest number of mills at its foundation was undoubtedly Furness, which held as many as five mills within a few years of its establishment. Kirkstall and Sibton only appear to have held a single mill of their own when first founded, while Old Wardon and Beaulieu held two. It seems likely, however, that in Beaulieu's case it had acquired a significant number of additional mills within 10 to 15 years of its relocation.

Table 10.4   Patterns of mill acquisition and investment for five Cistercian, eight Augustinian and two Premonstratensian houses, 1084–1364

Order/Patron	Cistercian	Augustinian	Premonstratensian	Total
Kings	3	7	1	11
Archbishops		4		4
Magnates	9	2	1	12
Knights	24	23	6	53
Gentry		1	5	6
Admin. and curial		2		2
Burgesses		1		1
Peasants	2			2
Other	1	1		1
Built by house	12	10		22
Unknown	11	11		22
TOTAL MILLS	**62**	**62**	**13**	**137**

What is perhaps most surprising about these data is the low proportion of mills that appear to have been built by the houses concerned. In the cases of both the Cistercians and the Augustinians, it was not possible to determine the origins of 18 per cent of the mills recorded, but only 16 per cent of the total could be unambiguously attributed to construction by the houses concerned. Even if it was the case that all of those mills in the 'unknown' category were built by the Augustinian and Cistercian houses concerned, it would still only amount to one-third of the total. Nevertheless, the evidence strongly indicates that it was a minority of the Augustinian and Cistercian houses that were prepared to build their own mills, Burscough being an exception amongst the Augustinians, and Kirkstall and Beaulieu amongst the Cistercians (see Tables 6.9 and 7.14). The relative proportions of these various patterns of acquisition are represented as pie charts in Charts 10.1 to 10.3.

These figures are therefore far from a ringing endorsement of the claims made for more than 80 years by various historians of technology that the Church was primarily responsible for building the many mills that have been documented to exist in the latter half of the Middle Ages. Almost 70 per cent of the mills held by the Augustinians, Cistercians and Premonstratensians by the beginning of the fourteenth century had been acquired from nobles and knights who had either built the mills themselves or acquired them from lay tenants of varying status who had built them at some point in the recent to distant past. These mills were subsequently granted to the monks and canons in exchange for cash, or for the health of their own souls and those of their ancestors, successors, and lords. While this latter motivation usually only started to become explicit in charters of the thirteenth century, the earliest of those recorded in the sample is a confirmation of the grant of Goldmill in 1195 to St Gregory's.[55] The charters of Bradenstoke, Chichester and Lacock all record single instances of such mill grants,[56] while St Gregory's and St Denys's both record two mills each that were granted to them on such terms.[57]

With the exception of Bishop Seffrid II of Chichester donating the windmills he commissioned to his dean and chapter and dependent churches, there is no evidence that any of the mills that were held by the three orders in the early fourteenth century had been built by other religious houses in the more distant past. The evidence for 'religious attitudes' being a motivation for the construction and development of watermills and windmills as part of a widespread but diffuse technological system is even less apparent in the case of the Augustinian, Cistercian and Premonstratensian houses than in those of the Benedictine and episcopal houses.

---

[55]   St Gregory's, ms. 104.

[56]   Bradenstoke, ms 510 (1249–50); Chichester, ms. 750 (1244–53); Lacock, ms. 49, (1264–70).

[57]   St Gregory's, mss. 104 (1195, but a confirmation of a document of the 1140s or 1150s), 131 (c. 1213–14); St Denys's, mss. 441 (1228–33), 368 (1282).

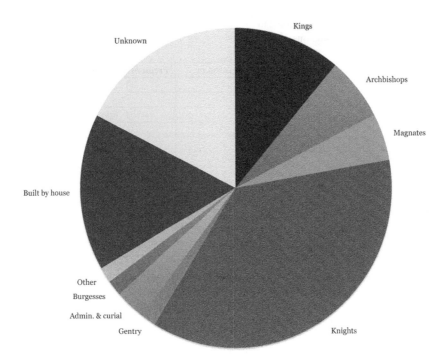

Chart 10.1   Proportion of Augustinian mills acquired from different sources, 1084–1320

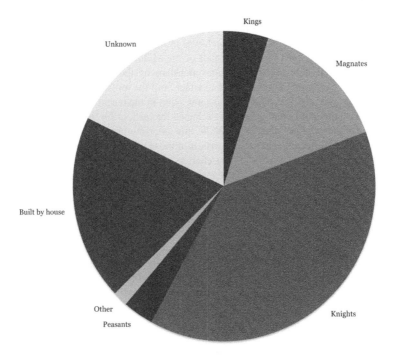

Chart 10.2   Proportion of Cistercian mills acquired from different sources, 1135–1364

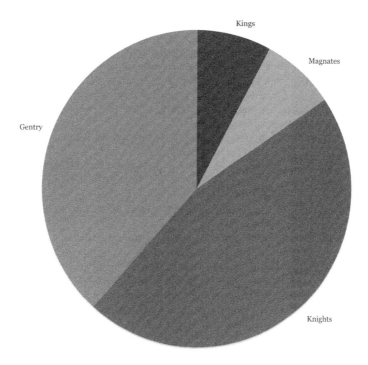

Chart 10.3   Proportion of Premonstratensian mills acquired from different sources, 1186–1282

Mill Construction by Religious Houses

Although we do not know exactly who was responsible for building most of the watermills that existed in England at the time of the Conquest, Langdon and Ambler have found evidence that the larger Benedictine and episcopal houses in southern England and the West Midlands had already exploited the watermilling capacity on their estates by Domesday.[58] We do know, however, that the Church held a quarter of all the fixed property at Domesday,[59] and that the Benedictines held a sixth of all the property south of the Humber at that time.[60] We also know that Anglo-Saxon kings had granted ancient demesne lands to the Benedictines and bishops as early as the seventh century, while thegns and sokemen had been selling manorial holdings to and purchasing them from the Benedictines as early as the ninth century.[61]

Although firm evidence is lacking, it seems likely that the Benedictines were responsible for building at least some of the mills which they held at Domesday in the century or so leading up to the survey as part of an effort to take full advantage of their seigneurial privileges. The evidence for a second phase of mill construction by houses of the order during the thirteenth century is, however, much stronger; a period during which mill profitability was at an all-time high and the English population was booming. Most of this second phase of mill-building activity involved the construction of windmills, however, and most of these were built in areas where there were insufficient supplies of running water to meet local demand for milled grain with watermills.

With respect to the attitudes of the Benedictine and episcopal houses sampled to the construction and acquisition of mills, the available data do not allow an accurate assessment for Canterbury, Hereford and

---

[58] See Langdon (1991), pp. 431–2; Langdon (1994), p. 8, n. 17; Ambler (1994), p. 44.

[59] Hallam (1986), p. 19; Goody (1983), pp. 125–7; Hudson (1994), p. 230.

[60] Burton (1994), p. 9.

[61] See Cownie (1998).

Bec, as they consist of rentals and compotus rolls covering relatively short time spans which do not allow any temporal analysis of mill ownership, whether by purchase, grant or construction. The episcopates of Canterbury and Hereford probably acquired the majority of their mills as part of their initial royal grants of ancient demesne. Although it is likely that they built some new mills on their manorial estates, limits of time and space have prevented fuller studies of these houses.

The Benedictine house of Lancaster does not appear to have been engaged in any mill building whatsoever. While it appears to have received all of its three or four mills by donation from local knights, it was undoubtedly responsible for rebuilding some or all of its mills over the course of its seisin of them. These mills were all attached to manorial holdings, and all of them appear to have been directly managed.

The monks of Battle were responsible for building a tide mill, a horse mill, two windmills and a tanning mill, or around a quarter of all those mills which it held by the middle of the fourteenth century, all of which were built over the 200-year period between c. 1185 and 1385. Battle may also have built a handful of grain mills, as there was roughly a doubling in the number of mills held by the abbey between c. 1100 and c. 1350, and there are only two records in the abbey's documents of grants relating to any of these mills, both of which are from the first half of the fourteenth century.[62]

The evidence from the Benedictine and episcopal houses in the sample does not, however, tend to support the idea that they were enthusiastic mill builders. While seven out of nine of them held industrial mills of some kind and had probably built them themselves,[63] none but Battle and Glastonbury appear to have been engaged in any significant mill-building activity, most of which occurred during the thirteenth century.[64] Whereas Battle demonstrated a clear interest in technological innovation with regard to its mills within a few decades of its establishment,[65] it was not until the fifteenth century that Glastonbury appears to have begun to display any interest in diversifying its milling assets, replacing two windmills and three water-powered grain mills with five industrial mills and four horse mills by 1520.[66]

While as many as 3/4 of the mills held by Battle in the late thirteenth century were probably acquired through grants by William I, William II, and various knights and tenants-in-chief, those held by Lancaster were all acquired by donation from local knights of various means. Those held by Bec were similarly acquired via grants from knights and members of the nobility, whereas most if not all of the mills which Glastonbury acquired after 1086 appear to have been built by the monastery.

A closer inspection of the data for the four Benedictine and five episcopal houses sampled gives a clearer picture of the difference between them and the three East Anglian Benedictine houses examined by Holt. For example, the number of windmills held by the four Benedictine houses sampled in the late thirteenth and early fourteenth centuries constituted 19 per cent of all the mills which they held (16 of 85 or more mills), suggesting that outside East Anglia, local demand was already well served by watermills in those areas in which the Benedictines held manorial estates. This is in contrast to the East Anglian Benedictines studied by Holt, whose tenants' unmet demand for milled grain appears to have been the spur for many an ambitious windmill-building program. By the end of the thirteenth century, almost half of the mills held by the East Anglian Benedictines were windmills.[67] The proportion of windmills held by the five episcopal houses was tiny in comparison, at only 4 per cent (three of 78 or more mills), although it should be noted that Chichester had built and given away two windmills in the early thirteenth century which are therefore not recorded here. The fact that these houses held prime real estate on major waterways goes some way to explaining their general lack of enthusiasm for building windmills.

---

[62]   Battle acquired a watermill in West Greenwich or Lewisham (Kent) as part of a parcel of urban properties c. 1323, as well as a mill in Southwark near London sometime before 1346. See Chapter 5. Both were high-earning seigneurial mills, one of which was donated by a local knight in order to provide for the upkeep of a chapel for his family.

[63]   The only houses which did not hold industrial mills by the early fourteenth century were Chichester Cathedral Priory and the Treasury of St Peter's York. See Chapter 4, Table 4.8, and Chapter 5, Table 5.8.

[64]   Glastonbury's mill building during the thirteenth century coincided with some ambitious river diversion projects. See Hollinrake and Hollinrake (2007), p. 241.

[65]   See Chapter 5, Table 5.6.

[66]   See Chapter 5, Table 5.3.

[67]   Holt (1988), pp. 23–4, 26, 32. For example, in 1279, Ramsey held 13 watermills and 21 windmills, whereas Bury St Edmunds held 34 windmills and 65 watermills.

On the other hand, around 6 per cent of the total number of mills held by the episcopal and Benedictine houses sampled in the late thirteenth and early fourteenth centuries were used for industrial applications. While the proportion of industrial mills to grain mills is higher than that found by Langdon in his analysis of lay estates recorded in the Edward II IPMs, it is half the proportion held by the Cistercians and significantly less than that of the minor orders. The Augustinians, on the other hand, held no industrial mills by the beginning of the fourteenth century. It seems fairly clear from this that while the Benedictines and Cistercians may not have been quite so ready to apply watermills to industrial applications as historians of technology have tended to claim, they do seem to have been far more willing to do so than the Augustinians, and possibly more so than lay lords and free men, at least up until the early fourteenth century, as will be discussed in more detail below.

Judging from the small number of mills taken over by the Augustinians from minster estates after the Conquest, it seems clear that the secular canons had little or no interest in mill-building, as any mills associated with their churches would have been built by the lay lords who held their estates prior to the Conquest. While most of the small to medium Augustinian houses in the sample appear to have been quite capable estate managers, only Burscough appears to have been interested in any kind of policy of mill construction and investment, and probably did so in order to take advantage of the suit which it was owed by its tenants within the parish of Ormskirk, as its non-seigneurial mills were drawing very low rents. Chichester's spate of windmill building at around the same time appears to have been purely related to the enthusiasm of a handful of bishops and obedientiaries.

With regard to the Cistercians' involvement in mill building before 1300, as pointed out earlier, most of those mills for which there is clear evidence of this were industrial mills, i.e., four out of nine of the total that were definitely built by the houses concerned. However, these mills were built by only two of five houses. While Furness does not seem to have built any of the more than 16 mills which it held before 1300, perhaps as many as six of the seven mills held outright by Kirkstall by the late thirteenth century were built by the monks, although there is only clear evidence for five of these, and three of them were industrial mills, one of which was a forge mill not recorded in any of its documents. With regard to Old Wardon, it may have built two or three of the five mills that it held before 1300, but there is no clear evidence for this in its cartulary. There is, however, clear evidence that Sibton built one of the four windmills which it held before 1364, although it is not clear who or what was the source of four of the 14 grain mills which it held by that time. Beaulieu built at least four of the 12 mills that it held by this time, three of which were industrial mills built sometime between its foundation in 1204 and the financial year of 1269–70, and one of which was a windmill probably built before 1250.

Of the 55 or more mills which the five Cistercian houses held by the early fourteenth century, seven were industrial mills, or 12.7 per cent of the total. It would therefore seem that while the Cistercians were indeed far more involved in mechanized fulling and industrial milling than the other orders, providing some support for the assertions of earlier historians of technology, in most other respects the evidence suggests a pragmatic approach to mill management. There is only clear evidence for 12 of the 62 mills which the order held by the late fourteenth century having been built by the houses concerned, or a little over 19 per cent of them. As stated previously, this is only slightly higher than that found for the Augustinians (16 per cent), providing little support for the claims by an earlier generation of historians of technology that the Cistercians were great mill builders. The previously cited evidence suggests that commercial and practical considerations, rather than 'religious attitudes', were the primary motivating factors for Cistercian mill building.

The evidence is thus fairly clear that the White Monks built mills only when they needed to process their own produce – whether grain, iron, wool or leather – and there were available waterways to site their mills. When they were unable to build or acquire mills of their own, they leased them from knights and tenants-in-chief to provide for their *conversi* and servants, some of which were included in leases of whole vills, or they used the mills of donors on neighbouring manors and vills, as was the case with Furness, which was granted the right of free multure at its Cumbrian mill of Kirksanton, and a reduced rate at Millom (also in Cumberland).

All in all, therefore, the only clear evidence of active involvement in mill building by any of the houses studied relates to only one-quarter of the houses in the sample, i.e. Battle, Beaulieu, Burscough, Chichester, Durham, Glastonbury and Kirkstall, as well as the East Anglian houses studied by Holt. With the exceptions of Battle's early construction of a tide mill in Barnhorn and Chichester's construction of three early windmills, this evidence strongly indicates that mill building was pursued as a strategy for financial reasons, rather than any particular interest in technological innovation or a desire to reduce the manual burden of over-worked peasants. The evidence we have for periods of mill construction by the various orders is primarily correlated with population increases on their manorial holdings, and a desire to tap into unmet demand on their own and neighbouring estates. Most of the houses studied regarded their mills as valuable assets which required care and attention in their management. While they do not appear to have been particularly entrepreneurial in their construction of mills, ecclesiastical lords clearly appreciated the value of mills with suit, and did their best to maintain a reasonable level of income from such mills for as long as possible.

It should also be borne in mind that those who built these mills were not those who owned them. Feudal élites selectively appropriated the milling innovations and skills of craftsmen, artisans and husbandmen from the lower orders of society which they perceived would further their own economic interests. They did so by providing them with regular employment on a relatively high wage, thus ensuring their ongoing cooperation and loyalty through social elevation.[68] At the same time, however, the élites marginalized or suppressed those innovations which they perceived to be against their interests. By acting in this way, lay and ecclesiastical lords were simply ensuring that they gained what they considered their share of the profits from various agricultural and industrial activities.

This situation only began to change in the thirteenth and fourteenth centuries, with the entrance of larger numbers of small entrepreneurs into the milling trade. These 'self-made men', or 'small men', were artisans, craftsmen, merchants and traders. As we have seen, they built mills for their own use or for specific purposes which did not infringe upon the seigneurial rights of their lords, and paid their lords a nominal rent for the privilege.

Ecclesiastical Involvement in Industrial Milling

The invention (or perhaps, rediscovery) of various industrial applications of the watermill and horse mill in the second half of the Middle Ages provided lords with the opportunity to mechanically process a growing range of manufactured products. In England, the main industrial applications of water power occurred between the late twelfth and sixteenth centuries and involved fulling woollen cloth and forging iron.[69] Mills which ground bark to produce tannin for curing leather, and water-powered grinding wheels for tool sharpening were much rarer.[70]

Although the archaeological evidence indicates that lay and ecclesiastical lords were far from scrupulous about documenting all of the industrial mills which existed on their estates, the surviving manuscript sources reveal the limited extent to which water power was applied to industrial purposes in England and Wales during the latter half of the Middle Ages when compared with contemporaneous France and Italy.[71] The main reason

---

[68]   The issue of millers' wages is discussed in detail by Holt (1988), Ch. 6; Langdon (1996), pp. 46–7; Langdon (2004), pp. 238–48; Lucas (2006a), pp. 137–9. See also Chapter 7 on Beaulieu Abbey's millers.

[69]   See: Holt (1990), pp. 56–7; Langdon (1994), pp. 13–17. On the English and Welsh fulling industries see: Scott (1931–32); Carus-Wilson (1941), (1944), (1950); Lennard (1947), (1951); Miller (1965); Donkin (1978), pp. 53, 135–8, 172–3, 188–90; Jack (1981); Hall & Russell (1981); Beamish (1983); Holt (1988), Ch. 9; Herlihy (1990); Langdon (1991), pp. 434–6.

[70]   The earliest reference to any kind of industrial mill in England is a bark-crushing or tanning mill (*I. molend' tanerez*) from Cumberland, dated to 1164–65. See Langdon (1991), p. 434, citing *Great Roll of the Pipe*, 1164–65, p. 54. Three of the five other references to tanning mills in England have been discussed in earlier chapters, including one at Beaulieu Abbey in 1269–70 (*Account Book of Beaulieu Abbey*, p. 210), at Kirkstall Abbey in 1288 (*Pipe Roll, 11 Henry II*, Pipe Roll Society, 1887, p. 54), and at Battle Abbey in 1384–85 (see Searle (1974), p. 301). The other two references are from Truro, Cornwall, in 1337 (see Holt (1988), p. 148, citing *Caption of Seisin*, p. 73), and Tavistock Abbey, where two tanning mills were converted to fulling mills in the fifteenth century (see Finberg (1951), pp. 153–4). Such mills nevertheless remained both rare and relatively unprofitable, most of them being held on peppercorn rents from their lords by craftsmen or workshop proprietors, as we saw on the estates of Holy Trinity, where the tool-sharpening mill of *Brechachre* paid only sixpence. As stated previously, the private tenants of such mills were undoubtedly responsible for their maintenance and repairs, and probably built them themselves.

[71]   See Lucas (2005), (2006a), Ch. 6–9 and Appendix A.

for this difference appears to have been the lower profitability of English industrial mills when compared with grain mills, and the conservatism of English lords.[72]

Like lay lords, ecclesiastical lords were primarily involved in milling for profit, and were generally reluctant to invest in milling ventures which did not guarantee a decent income. The most evidence that we have for the profitability of English industrial mills relates to the fulling industry, and this evidence clearly indicates that English fulling mills were not as profitable as grain mills. The majority were earning on average around 1/4 to 1/3 as much as the average income from grain mills.[73] This meant that they were usually only built in places where there were either plentiful supplies of running water, or they could be guaranteed a handsome profit.[74] The fulling mills of Durham, Hereford and Canterbury fell into the former category, while the tanning mill of Battle and the fulling mill of Ramsey fell into the latter.

On the basis of my own previous research and that of John Muendel and Ian Jack, there are strong grounds for believing that although ecclesiastical lords may have been 'early adopters' of a number of industrial milling technologies, it does not appear that they ever dominated the growth of industrial milling. For example, my analysis of the Welsh fulling industry in Chapter 9 of *Wind, Water, Work* (2006) suggests that although ecclesiastical lords probably held as many as 1/3 of all the fulling mills in Wales in the late thirteenth century, the ecclesiastical sector comprised only about 20 per cent of the industry in the fourteenth and fifteenth centuries.[75] In other words, during the period of the greatest expansion in the Welsh industry, i.e., the fourteenth century, ecclesiastical estates appear to have been the least committed to expansion of all the various players. However, these findings contrast with those of John Langdon in his 1993 and 2004 studies, which suggest that ecclesiastical lords were investing far more heavily than lay lords in converting water-powered grain mills to fulling mills, and in building new fulling mills in the late thirteenth, fourteenth and fifteenth centuries.[76] Although Langdon has not specifically commented on the motivations for this difference, it would appear that pragmatic considerations were the primary motivating factor here, with ecclesiastical lords attempting to maintain the financial viability of their watermills by changing their function in a declining (or collapsing) market for milled grain. Not only was it relatively cheap to make such conversions, the costs of ongoing maintenance for fulling mills were considerably lower than for grain mills.[77]

Of the 12 English religious houses sampled whose documents mention fulling mills before the 1320s, 16 individual mills are cited. Three of these mills do not appear to have provided revenue for the religious house concerned and were probably private tenant mills, as may have been another fulling mill from which tithes only were collected. The estates concerned include Bec, Beaulieu, Canterbury, Hereford, Durham, Cockersand, Glastonbury, Grove, Holy Trinity, Kirkstall, Lacock and Lancaster. It should also be noted that two of the abbeys concerned were nunneries, i.e., Lacock and Holy Trinity. Only one of these houses was Augustinian, i.e., Lacock.

While there is no evidence that any of the houses studied were heavily involved in mechanized fulling, all but one of the Benedictine houses sampled held one or more fulling mills in the thirteenth and fourteenth centuries. Nevertheless, only 6 per cent of the total number of mills held by the Benedictine and episcopal houses sampled were fulling mills. With respect to the five episcopal houses, Canterbury's Sussex mills represented the highest proportion, with two out of 14 being fulling mills (14 per cent), followed by Hereford, with two out of 21 of its

---

[72] See Langdon (1997).

[73] See Holt (1988), pp. 155–8; Langdon (1994), pp. 13–15. Similar evidence has been uncovered in the previous case study chapters. By way of contrast, although John Muendel has not discussed the income from medieval Italian industrial mills in his published papers to date, the government tax on fulling mills in Pistoia and Firenze at the end of the thirteenth century was the same as or more than that for grain mills. See Muendel (1981), p. 89.

[74] Holt (1988), p. 158.

[75] Furthermore, it was the wealthiest quarter of Welsh religious houses that dominated half of the ecclesiastical sector of the Welsh industry. With respect to mechanized fulling in northern Italy, Muendel similarly found that religious houses held no more than about a fifth of the fulling mills during the thirteenth and fourteenth centuries. See Muendel (1981), p. 99. While the social groups in possession of fulling mills in early fifteenth century Firenze were different from those in Wales, comparable figures for ecclesiastical ownership of fulling mills have been compiled by Muendel. He found that of 60 fulling mills held in Firenze between 1407 and 1416, 20 per cent were held by ecclesiastical authorities, 22 per cent by communes, 35 per cent by individuals, 14 per cent by families and 9 per cent by consortia. Muendel does not discuss the social status of the individuals who owned these mills.

[76] Langdon (1991), pp. 434–5 and Table 2.2, (1994), p. 14, (2004), pp. 47–8.

[77] See Lucas (2006a), Ch. 4.

mills (10 per cent). Only 2.5 per cent of Durham's mill holdings in 1301 were fulling mills (one out of 38 or 39), whereas Chichester Cathedral Priory and the Treasury of York Minster held none. Of the four Benedictine houses sampled, Lancaster's one-third share of the fulling mill of Caton constituted the highest proportion overall, at around 10 to 14 per cent of the 2 1/3–3 1/3 mills it held in the early fourteenth century. Glastonbury had interests in three fulling mills out of the 40 which it held by the early fourteenth century, or 7.5 per cent of the total, while Bec held only one fulling mill of the 23 mills it held at the same time, amounting to 4.3 per cent of its total. Although Battle does not appear to have ever held any fulling mills, by the middle of the fourteenth century it held a horse-powered precinctual grain mill converted to a cider mill and a tanning mill within its factory complex at Iltonsbath, which amounted to about 10 per cent of the mills which it held at that time.

By way of contrast, Holt's analysis of fulling mill ownership by the wealthy Benedictine lords of Bury, Peterborough and Ramsey revealed that they were far less enthusiastic about turning watermills to industrial applications. Bury St Edmunds, Peterborough and Ramsey held only two fulling mills between them (Bury had none), out of well over 150 mills which they held in total.[78] The very much lower proportion of industrial mills held by the East Anglian houses was undoubtedly due to the lack of availability of adequate watercourses upon which to site watermills, and the higher revenues obtained from water-powered grain mills versus fulling mills and other industrial mills.

Around 12 to 13 per cent, or more than one in seven of the mills held by the five Cistercian houses in the sample, were industrial mills, which was a significantly higher proportion than that found for any of the other categories apart from the minor orders. This figure is almost four times higher than the rate identified by Langdon for lay lords in the IPMs for Edward II covering the period from 1307 to 1327 (i.e. 3.5 per cent).[79] The percentage of industrial mills that were not fulling mills is also much higher at just over 8 per cent of the total, as opposed to none found by Langdon in his IPM study of lay lords.[80] The proportion of fulling mills held by the Cistercians was much the same as the Benedictine and episcopal houses, at 6 per cent of the total.

In addition to their interest in mechanically fulling cloth, there is strong evidence that the Cistercians were pioneers in the application of water power to iron processing in Western Europe, harnessing water power to run hammer-forges and blast furnaces. The evidence from England indicates that the northern Cistercian houses with iron deposits on their estates were engaged in such industrial activities from a very early date. The earliest evidence for medieval English forge mills is from Kirkstall and Bordesley abbeys, and dates to c. 1200, while recent archaeological work on Rievaulx's iron-working sites reveals that it was using water-powered blast furnaces earlier in the fifteenth century than had previously been accepted.[81]

Several points need to be kept in mind when drawing attention to these data, however. First of all, two of the five Cistercian houses studied here showed no signs whatsoever of having been involved in industrial milling at any time during their existence, and only one of the five houses' charters made a single reference to an industrial mill before 1300. Documentation of the four industrial mills held by Beaulieu came mostly from its account-book, while the forge mill held by Kirkstall was only revealed by an archaeological dig; references to its tanning and fulling mills were contained in an extent of the late thirteenth century. These findings strongly suggest that ecclesiastical charters are a poor source of evidence for Cistercian industrial milling activities in England.

Second, while it is possible that all of the Cistercian houses studied here possessed industrial mills of some kind before the Dissolution, Donkin's study of the English Cistercian houses revealed that 14 of the 75 which he identified held fulling mills before 1300, including Beaulieu and Kirkstall, or about 19 per cent of them. By the time of the Dissolution, the number had doubled to 28 (including Old Wardon), or slightly over 37 per cent of them (Figure 10.1).[82] Factoring in the two fulling mills identified in Furness's post-Dissolution survey that Donkin appears to have missed, the percentage increases to about 38.5 per cent. While this is clearly significant and a greater involvement in mechanized fulling than can be seen amongst the other orders, one must keep in mind the two major constraints on the expansion of mechanized fulling in England first identified by Holt, i.e., the availability of surplus water power and the relatively low profits to be made from

---

[78]   See Holt (1988), pp. 156–7.

[79]   See Langdon (1994), p. 12.

[80]   Ibid., p. 14.

[81]   'Henry Snuffed Out Fires of Industry', *Sydney Morning Herald*, 25 June 2002, p. 9. The relevant work is being conducted by Dr Gerry McDonnell and a team of archaeologists from Bradford University.

[82]   Donkin (1978), p. 188 (Appendix 5).

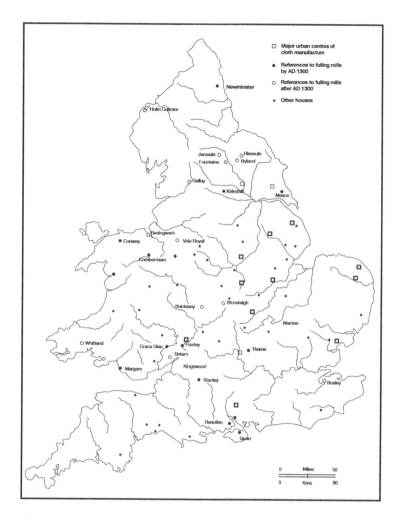

Fig. 10.1   Cistercian houses with fulling mills and the distribution of the major urban centres of cloth
manufacture. After Donkin (1978)

fulling mills as opposed to grain mills. These two issues were clearly a factor in the lack of involvement in
industrial milling of Sibton and Old Wardon, which did not have abundant water power available to them,
whereas Furness, Kirkstall and Beaulieu did. These three houses also had extensive wool and/or mining
interests, providing them with additional incentives to mechanically process their own wool and iron ore. It
is also perhaps significant that while only Furness and Kirkstall had toll exemptions and/or were transporting
wool (Figure 10.2), all three of the five houses that owned fulling mills also had wool surpluses (Figure 10.3).

Thirdly, while Donkin notes that 17 Cistercian houses possessed tanneries before the Dissolution,[83] only
Beaulieu and Kirkstall have so far been discovered to have held tanning mills, and, other than brief mentions
of Beaulieu's tanning mill by Hockey in the introduction to the published cartulary and by me in *Wind, Water,
Work* (2006), its existence was first discussed in detail in this book. Of the five houses studied here, Beaulieu,
Furness and Sibton are included in Donkin's list of Cistercian houses that held tanneries, although Kirkstall
is omitted. If the surviving documentation can be trusted, the shoemaking workshop at Beaulieu was unique
amongst English Cistercian houses.

---

[83]   Ibid., p. 187 (Appendix 4).

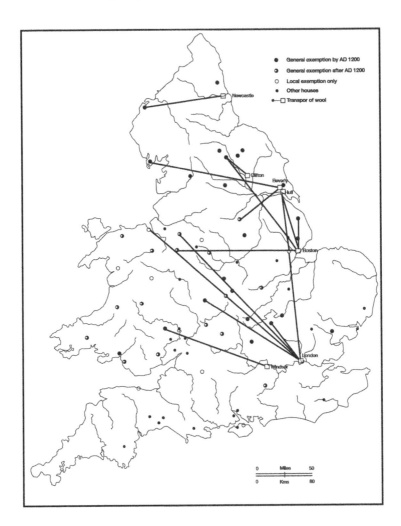

Fig. 10.2   Cistercian houses with toll exemptions. After Donkin (1978)

On the other hand, although Furness was one of those Cistercian houses with an ongoing and extensive interest in mining and producing iron, there is no manuscript evidence of it having ever applied water power to these activities. As the archaeological find of the water-powered forge at Kirkstall demonstrates, however, the absence of manuscript evidence for water-powered industry at Furness is not a reliable indication of whether it did in fact apply water power to its iron production activities.

Another important point to keep in mind, which appears to have been completely overlooked by proponents of the monastic innovation thesis, is that there were general prohibitions on the Cistercians receiving revenues from land, mills and markets that were not officially overturned until the first half of the thirteenth century. Unless they were flagrantly disobeying canon law, their initial involvement in water-powered industry cannot have been geared towards commercial production. It was only towards the end of the thirteenth century and subsequently that Cistercian production began to be geared towards market consumption, and this primarily in grinding grain and woollen cloth production, and to a lesser extent in iron mining and leather making.[84]

---

[84]   For case studies including discussions of Cistercian iron mining, see, for example, Waites (1964), Courtney (1981), Astill and O'Meara (2013).

A: Towns with merchants licensed to export wool, 1273 and/or 1277-8

B: Other towns with wool merchants, 1327

C: Cistercian houses with more than the average quantity of wool for sale

D: Cistercian houses with 'best' and/or 'middle' wool exceeding the average price difference between Cistercian (c. 1300) and county (1337) wool

E: Other Cistercian houses

Fig. 10.3   Cistercian houses with wool surpluses (after F.B. Pegolotti) and the distribution of towns
with wool merchants. After Donkin (1978)

It was during the thirteenth century that the Cistercians responded to an increasing demand for English
wool by marketing their own both locally and overseas, occasionally with disastrous results.[85] In this instance
at least, we can see that the Cistercians' involvement in mechanized milling for the fulling of cloth led to their
greater involvement in trade and even usury.[86] Any contribution which the Cistercian use of water power may
have made to the general productivity of the handicrafts was therefore largely restricted to the manufacture
of woollen cloth in England and most other parts of Europe until the growth of industrial milling throughout
Europe in the fifteenth century, simply because what few products that were produced using water power in
these areas were, on the whole, not geared towards a market trade or external consumption.[87]

Only one of the Augustinian houses in the sample, i.e., Lacock Abbey, owned a fulling mill or any other
kind of industrial mill, whether self-built or acquired through grant or purchase. Even this single example of a

---

[85]   See Donkin's more lengthy discussion of this issue in Donkin (1980), pp. 135–8, 172–3.

[86]   See ibid., and Appendixes 7–10.

[87]   See my discussion of Furness Abbey's involvement in iron working in Chapter 8 as a partial exception.

fulling mill on Lacock's estates is not documented until after the Dissolution.[88] The fact that no industrial mills are evident amongst these Augustinian holdings before 1350 would suggest that the order was generally not in the least bit interested in industrial activities in general and industrial milling in particular.[89]

While some of the figures just cited do indicate a far greater interest in industrial milling amongst ecclesiastical lords than that found by Langdon for lay lords throughout England in the early fourteenth century,[90] they still do not support the assertions of White, for example, that all of the so-called 'basic industries' had been converted to water power by that time.[91] Those Benedictine houses for which there is evidence of substantial involvement in industrial milling appear to have become involved primarily because they had an abundance of water resources to draw upon, and, in the case of Battle, because several generations of its monks and abbots were perhaps genuinely interested in technological innovation.[92]

Shaping Factors in the Development of Ecclesiastical Milling

There were three main reasons for lordly interest in grain milling during the Middle Ages. Foremost amongst them was that mills were not only valuable labour-saving machines for large households; they were a means of generating revenue from anyone outside the household who chose, or was compelled, to grind their grain there. Because it included the lucrative privilege of suit of mill, the extension of 'inland' rights to religious houses, military retainers and royal officials from the ninth century onward provided lords who held a former royal manor or vill with the possibility of securing from their demesne tenants a reliable source of cash or grain income from whatever mills he or she held, as well as other resources such as hay, honey, eels and fish from the meadows and waters appurtenant to those mills. After the Conquest, the notion gradually took hold that any lord in seisin of a whole manor or vill could acquire for themselves this customary obligation from their tenants. If a lord held the only mill on the manor, a simple act of proclamation followed by a decade or so of customary usage would be sufficient to establish the claim's legitimacy.

The second reason for lordly interest in milling was that a growing population combined with changing tastes in bread and cereals meant that an ever larger proportion of harvested grain was being ground by watermills and windmills. Lay and ecclesiastical lords with entrepreneurial skills soon recognized that milling was one sector of the economy in which substantial profits could be made, particularly during the thirteenth and fourteenth centuries. New management and accounting techniques, together with advances in milling technology, enabled the more acquisitive of lords to exploit territories and custom that had previously been out of their reach. This included the widespread introduction during the thirteenth and early fourteenth centuries of the postmill and more powerful watermills in regions with poor water resources. However, the success of these strategies was to be relatively short lived, demonstrating that the growth in commercial milling throughout the Middle Ages was anything but inevitable and inexorable. As successive waves of the plague denuded the English population between the late 1340s and 1490s, rendering windmills a less attractive option for ongoing maintenance and investment, cash-strapped lords allowed some to fall into ruin and substituted others with horse mills, while similarly marginal watermills were increasingly converted to fulling cloth and other industrial uses.

The third reason for lordly interest in milling was that mill ownership was a marker of social status. The extent to which a lord held mills with suit was an indicator of his or her wealth and power in the feudal hierarchy. The bestowal of tithes, rents and the lands associated with mills therefore became a focus for the patronage of religious houses by the nobility, gentry and peasantry. Mill ownership also became a focus for

---

[88]   In 1553. See Appendix E.

[89]   The Augustinian chantry of Edington which was also in Wiltshire did hold a single fulling mill in 1225, Bolton Priory probably held a tanning mill in its tannery in the fourteenth century, but such holdings appear to have been very unusual amongst Augustinian houses.

[90]   See Chapter 3.

[91]   See White (1964), p. 88.

[92]   On this point, Searle's concluding remarks on Battle's tannery are worth quoting at length: 'Battle Abbey regarded the local leather industry as sufficiently important to invest in what was evidently a large barkmill and tannery – which it found profitable. That tannery, like so much at Battle, tied abbey and town together in a symbiotic economic relationship. The monks' capital and the crafts of their burgesses were linked.' See Searle (1974), pp. 299–303.

peasant unrest between the late thirteenth and sixteenth centuries as lords sought to impose higher rents and heavier feudal burdens on their tenants, supporting Bloch's observation that juridical opinion of the time sought to develop the new ideas of servitude encapsulated in the notion of villeinage.[93]

The participation of lords and tenants in the ownership and operation of mills was therefore in large part motivated by the social status which mills conferred and the recognition of their potential to generate significant revenues, revenues which could be further enhanced with the introduction of new milling technologies and new management techniques. Most lords from the late twelfth century onward appear to have been very much aware that several factors determined the level of income which could be expected from a mill: its seigneurial and/or monopoly status, the amount of competition from other mills in the region, the quantities of grain being grown and/or consumed on the manorial estate, the number of free and servile tenants who were obliged (or not) to frequent the mill, and the reliability of water supply for watermills and of prevailing winds for windmills.

We have seen clear evidence throughout the book that structures of ecclesiastical lordship and patterns of mill acquisition and innovation were shaped not only by the size, wealth and distribution of a house's estates, but also by environmental and demographic factors; changing cultural attitudes and legal conventions; prevailing and emergent technical traditions; the personal relations of a house with its patrons, tenants, servants and neighbours; and the entrepreneurial and administrative flair of bishops, abbots, priors and other ecclesiastical officials. Religious houses and episcopal authorities were no different from lay lords in recognizing and exploiting the revenue-raising potential of watermills and windmills on their estates. Any involvement which they had in the construction and acquisition of mills between the ninth and fifteenth centuries was therefore primarily geared toward protecting or enhancing their share of those revenues.

As we have seen, any mill which enjoyed seigneurial status provided its lord with a strong incentive to closely monitor that mill and to change its management policies if this was deemed to be financially advantageous. But despite the enthusiasm for acquiring mills which appears to have characterized most of the houses concerned, they were almost invariably more interested in doing so through donations and purchase than through building their own mills.

Although one exception to the self-interest that characterized most of these houses' behaviour was that of William of Wakebridge, his behaviour appears to have been rare indeed. As we have seen, Holy Trinity's seemingly liberal management of its estates appears to have been more the result of financial and litigious exhaustion than any conscious philanthropic strategy, whereas the management of the estates of Hereford, Cirencester and Grove generally conforms with the more extractive and autocratic approaches of the larger religious houses first examined in detail by Holt and Langdon.

Both lay and ecclesiastical lords were very conscious that if they did not attempt to meet the growing rural and urban flour market by providing more milling facilities for their tenants, others would find a way to meet that demand which would not necessarily provide any benefit to them. This is indeed what happened as the population grew as a result of more arable coming under cultivation and incremental improvements in agriculture and transport more generally.[94] As I will argue in more detail below, the Benedictine and episcopal houses, who appear to have dominated mechanized milling with as much as a quarter of the total market at Domesday, probably held no more than 1/5 of all the watermills and windmills in England by the early fourteenth century, and less than 1/6 of the overall market for milling. These estimates, as rough and ready as they are, suggest that the role of ecclesiastical lords in the milling trade was diminishing as more varied forms of mill tenure and ownership emerged, particularly from the second quarter of the fourteenth century, when most lords again began to lease out their demesne assets.[95]

The growing dissatisfaction of the peasantry and townsfolk with the feudal burdens imposed on them by the nobility expressed itself in one form as a desire to share with their lords the advantages conferred by mill ownership. As Hilton and many other scholars have noted before me, the rights and obligations associated with different forms of tenure became a site of contestation and negotiation between lords and peasants from the mid-twelfth century onward. Postan and Lennard were amongst the first scholars to demonstrate that it

---

[93]   Bloch (1961), p. 273.

[94]   See Astill and Langdon (1997), Campbell (2007), pp. 10–15.

[95]   On the latter issue, see Campbell (2007), p. 3.

was during the late twelfth century that the great landowners sought to restore the direct exploitation of their demesne lands – which had in many cases been leased to free and customary tenants on generous leases earlier in the century – thereby securing their share of rising crop prices. This included the re-implementation of what had earlier been compulsory labour services and the introduction of hired labour, although as we have seen, Hilton, Miller and others argued that lords were not just re-implementing customary services during this period, but creating new and additional services as well. Nor was it just the Cistercians and Premonstratensians who pursued such reactionary policies on their newly formed estates, but most of the wealthier religious houses and lay lords. In attempting to claw back control of the profits from their demesne holdings, most lay and ecclesiastical lords sought to replace free and customary tenures with tenancies at will and for fixed terms.

As we have seen, the main beneficiaries of mill acquisition by hereditary tenure during the twelfth century were free men and their descendants who were military or legal retainers of the lord they served, whereas peasants who served a lord in some capacity, or whose families had once held in socage or some other form of free tenure under the Anglo-Saxons, seem to have been the main beneficiaries of customary tenure in mills. The effective ownership of mills held by tenants of lower rank in customary and hereditary tenure, or which were licensed to serve their own households or workshops, enabled men and women of varied status to improve their social position during the course of their tenancies. We know this because some of the wealthier peasants, military retainers and administrative and curial officials donated or sold mills to religious houses both with and without suit. I have argued that the mills without suit served a similar function in the milling trade to the non-seigneurial mills held by customary and hereditary tenants, i.e. they provided a non-coercive alternative to customers who chose to grind their grain there.

Langdon's generalization that it was lords who were the crucial decision-makers when it came to mill investment in the early fourteenth century, and generally acted very conservatively, nevertheless still holds true. English lords in the thirteenth and fourteenth centuries expected most of their profits from milling to issue from the agricultural sector, and had far more experience in controlling this sector than they had in speculative, and certainly less profitable, industrial milling ventures. In those instances where they did invest in industrial mills, this invariably appears to have been due to local demand from a local industry. It is clear from the English evidence examined by Langdon, as well as the Welsh evidence examined in *Wind, Water, Work* (2006), that it is not until investment activity shifted decisively into non-seigneurial hands in the fifteenth century and subsequently that milling resources began to be shifted to non-agricultural uses.

However, the lack of lordly investment in industrial mills should be contrasted with the use of waterwheel technology in the workshops of fourteenth and fifteenth century craftsmen and artisans, as the examples of privately operated tool-sharpening and fulling mills cited in previous chapters suggests. Generally speaking, the existence of such mills was recorded in reeves' accounts and manorial surveys, even if those mills had been built by small entrepreneurs who simply leased the water rights or the site on which the mill was located.

Bearing in mind the limitations of the sample, a rough idea of the relative numbers of mills held by the four categories of religious house in the early fourteenth century can be gained by calculating the average numbers of different kinds of mill per house. The five episcopal houses sampled held 78 or more mills between them; the four Benedictine houses, 85 or more mills; the nine Augustinian houses, 82 or more mills; the five Cistercian houses, between 55 and 57 mills; and the five houses of minor orders, 40 mills (Table 10.5). This gives us an average of 21 mills per house in the case of the Benedictines, 16 mills per house for the episcopal houses (even when Canterbury is removed as it held more mills outside Sussex), 11 mills per house for the Cistercians, nine mills per house for the Augustinians, and eight mills per house for the minor orders. Although the sample is fairly representative for the bishops, Augustinians, Cistercians and minor orders, there is a sampling bias with respect to the Benedictines, with two out of the four houses earning over £1,000 annually in the late thirteenth century. The fact that the four Benedictine houses held roughly twice as many mills on average as the Augustinians, Cistercians and minor orders per capita and around one-third more than the bishops is therefore probably a reflection of that bias, but it is nevertheless probable that the Benedictine houses held more mills on average than all but their episcopal brethren. Because there are no eastern Benedictine houses in the sample, the figures probably do reflect wider trends with respect to windmill numbers. They suggest that the Benedictines held four times as many windmills as the Cistercians and Augustinians per capita, and eight times as many as the bishops and minor orders. Likewise we can be reasonably confident that the sample accurately reflects the fact that all but the Augustinians had a minor interest in industrial milling by the early fourteenth century, but the Cistercians were slightly more engaged.

Table 10.5   Average numbers of mills per order for 28 episcopal and conventual houses in the late thirteenth/early fourteenth century

Type/Order	Total no. of houses	Total no. of mills in seisin	Average no. of mills per house	Average no. of mills with suit per house	Average no. of windmills per house	Average no. of industrial mills per house
Episcopal	5	78+	16	11	½	1
Benedictine	4	85+	21	17	4	1
Augustinian	9	82+	9	3	1	0
Cistercian	5	55–7	11	4–6	1	1 1/2
Minor Orders	5	40	8	4–5	1/2	1

It is also possible on the basis of these figures to calculate the proportion of the powered milling sector which was held by different orders and categories of religious house in the late eleventh and early fourteenth centuries. With the Church holding 25 per cent of all the fixed property in England at Domesday, but as many as one-third of demesne properties, it would appear that by the late eleventh century, the Church (i.e. predominantly episcopal and Benedictine houses) held between 36 per cent and 40 per cent of all the demesne mills throughout England, and around 18–20 per cent of the total market for milled grain.[96] In order to make an estimate of the total number of mills held by religious houses in 1300, the Benedictine houses' average mill numbers would need to be reduced in line with their episcopal brethren. However, the other sample sizes are arguably sufficiently representative to provide reliable figures.

If the average number of mills per house is multiplied by the number of such houses at the Dissolution (bearing in mind that the figures for the episcopal and Cistercian houses remained static from 1300 to 1540, and that most of the Benedictine and Augustinian houses that did not survive to the Dissolution are unlikely to have possessed many mills), the following figures can be calculated. Around 270 mills were held by the 17 dioceses and archdioceses (16 x 17 houses), and around 840 by the Cistercians (11 x 76 houses). The Augustinians held around 1,500 mills (9 x 170 houses), and the Benedictines perhaps 2,300 mills (16 x 142 houses). Allowing for a few hundred more that were probably held by the minor orders, we get a figure of around 5,200 throughout England.

If we compare these numbers with recently revised estimates by Langdon of 10–12,000 mills throughout England by 1300,[97] the figure of 5,200 ecclesiastical mills seems more consistent with the higher estimate of 12,000, suggesting that the Church held around 43 per cent of all the powered mills in early fourteenth-century England, i.e. a slightly larger proportion than it held at Domesday. This finding is consistent with Langdon's 1991 and 2004 research which suggested that ecclesiastical lords between 1086 and 1400 were acquiring mills at a higher rate than their lay counterparts. These figures suggest that by the early fourteenth century, religious houses still retained around 17 per cent of the total market for milled grain throughout England, indicating that their share of the milling trade had kept up with population growth over the two centuries following Domesday.[98]

If these estimates are accepted as reasonably accurate, the Benedictines controlled around 45 per cent of all ecclesiastical mills, and the Augustinians, around 30 per cent. If we apply the other calculations concerning the proportion of seigneurial and non-seigneurial mills held by the different categories of religious house, we find that the Augustinians held around 900 non-seigneurial mills, of which around 600 were fee mills, whereas the Cistercians held between 370 and 550 non-seigneurial mills, virtually all of which were fee mills. About 370 of the mills held by the Benedictines were in customary and hereditary tenure and perhaps as many as 250 of those held by the episcopal and minor order houses. These figures suggest that around 1,900 to 2,000

---

[96]   The estimate of 36–40 per cent of demesne mills is based on earlier cited observations by Langdon and Ambler that ecclesiastical lords were quicker at building mills on their seigneurial estates than were lay lords. The estimate of their share of the total market is based on Langdon's estimate that half of the milled grain in England at Domesday was being processed by handmills. See Langdon (1994), p. 37, n. 93.

[97]   Langdon (2004), pp. 14–15.

[98]   This figure is based on the estimates provided by Langdon of the proportion of milling custom processed by the demesne and independent tenant sectors in 1300. See Langdon (1994), pp. 27–8, 30–31.

of the 12,000 or so mills throughout England in the early fourteenth century were non-seigneurial mills, or 16 per cent of the total, a figure which is consistent with Langdon's estimate that less than 20 per cent of millable grains were being processed by tenant mills in the early fourteenth century.[99] It is also significant to note that perhaps as many as 1,000 of these mills had been donated by knights to religious houses, or as many as half of them. This suggests that around 8 per cent of all the mills in England c. 1300 were non-seigneurial mills under the direct control of religious houses, i.e. around half of the non-seigneurial sector; a significant finding which casts considerable doubt on the Bloch model and further clarifies and supports Langdon's earlier research on the topic.

A long-standing debate in medieval studies continues to focus on the extent to which class structure, commercialization or demographic factors were the main drivers of social and economic change in the Middle Ages, the various positions owing their pedigrees in turn to Marx, Pirenne, and Malthus and Ricardo.[100] The Dobb-Sweezy and Brenner debates between the 1940s and 1980s provided the framework for much of the discussion that subsequently emerged.[101]

Generally speaking, there appears to have been a rapprochement between these views, with each factor accorded a more or less important role depending on context, an observation that was made by Britnell more than 20 years ago,[102] and one which I have attempted to emulate in this book. However, there are still some unresolved tensions, one of which involves the role that differentials in social, political and economic power played in the development of later medieval society, and to what extent those differences were based in class structures, ethnicity, kinship ties or occupational affiliations.

Leaving aside for the moment the influence of the last three factors and focusing upon the classic concerns of Marxist scholars, the evidence from medieval France suggests that seigneurial lordship throughout much of the country was strong, pervasive and enduring,[103] whereas class structures in medieval England do not appear to have been quite so constricting and determining. I have argued that the persistence of some Anglo-Saxon conceptions of land tenure after the Conquest enabled the development of forms of non-seigneurial tenure that were harnessed to the social and economic advantage of people from the lower and middle strata of English society from the twelfth century onwards.

There has nevertheless been a tendency amongst English medievalists during the latter half of the twentieth century to be dismissive of claims that the Normans completely transformed socio-property relations in the wake of the Conquest. These views have now to be re-evaluated in the context of the detailed studies of scholars such as Robin Fleming and Rosamond Faith. The evidence from Domesday Book is clear: 'the Norman yoke' was both real and pervasive. It was a complex web of new tenurial relations and new customary obligations which maintained the pretence of closely following pre-existing relationships, but which in fact was primarily motivated by the desire to simplify, consolidate and where possible, monetize a whole raft of difficult or impossible to maintain services, fees, renders and dues.

In one respect at least it would seem that Bloch was correct: one of the economic platforms upon which was built the Norman transformation of land tenure and customary obligations was the imposition of suit of mill. One of the great successes of the Conquest was the establishment throughout England of a pervasive demesne sector of powered milling which compulsorily acquired the custom of manorial tenants, a custom which extended even to free tenants in the north and some other parts of England where pre-Conquest tenures had been largely or completely erased. The extension of suit of mill to large sections of the population which had not previously fallen under its yoke had important implications for how mills and milling fitted into

---

[99]   Langdon (1994), p. 31. This also suggests that relatively few non-seigneurial mills were held by or from lay lords.

[100]   For overviews of these theories and the accompanying debates, see Hatcher & Bailey (2001); Verhulst (1997). On the influence of Marx on various medievalists and the debate in general, see: Dobb (1946); Kosminsky (1956), pp. xvi–xvii, 319–20; Brenner (1976); Hilton (1976); Holton (1981); Katz (1993); Razi (2007); Epstein (2007). On the influence of Pirenne, see: Bois (1992), pp. 74–5; Thoen and Vanhaute (2011). On the influence of Malthus and Ricardo, see Postan and Hatcher (1978), pp. 28–30.

[101]   See Hilton (1976); Aston and Philpin (1987).

[102]   Britnell (1991), p. xv. It is also worth noting that similar eclecticism is a feature of recent scholarship in the history of science.

[103]   See, for example, Croot and Parker (1978), pp. 41–6.

English society and England's economy, not only with respect to the forms of mill tenure that emerged during the twelfth century and subsequently, but with respect to the levels and proportions of revenue that lords and tenants could expect from their mills and the kinds of milling establishments to which they could take their grain and process other materials.

However, it is important in this context to remember Michel Foucault's axiom that social power is not merely negative in the sense of being coercive and restrictive, it is also positive, creative and productive. With this point in mind, at the other end of the temporal spectrum covered by the book, it is worth noting that in recent years, the pessimism of the neo-Malthusians/neo-Ricardians and neo-Marxists concerning late medieval agricultural productivity and proficiency has given way to a more optimistic view which acknowledges that advances in agricultural technology did take place during the thirteenth and fourteenth centuries.

As Britnell, Campbell and others have argued in several major publications over the last two decades, technological changes with respect to such issues as livestock breeding, crop types, manuring and horse transport increased productivity and yields in many parts of England, while the growing recognition of the role played by peasant production for market and export has demonstrated the role of the non-seigneurial sector in broader processes of commercialization, monetization and agrarian specialisation. Likewise, recent archaeological research has revealed the limitations of manuscript sources. Throughout this book, we have encountered evidence which supports or directly arises from all these lines of inquiry. By drawing on this research to inform my own conclusions, I hope to have demonstrated its efficacy in illuminating the role played by the Church in the commercialization of the medieval milling trade.

Conclusion

It should now be clear that the 'top-down' conception of technological development advocated by proponents of both the monastic innovation thesis and the seigneurial monopoly model fails to take into account the 'pull-factors' of growing urban and rural populations with an increasing demand for milled grain and other processed commodities, the interests of lay lords and others of middling rank with the necessary economic clout to profit from this growth, and the opposing interests of members of the lower classes to mill their grain, full their cloth and so on without being economically exploited by their lords. Any attempt to explain these processes must also take sufficient account of the varieties of milling tenure, how those forms of tenure arose, and how widespread they were at different stages and in different regions. As I have tried to demonstrate throughout this book, changing notions of tenure, property and ownership were amongst the most important factors shaping the development of the medieval milling trade, and had profound implications for the emergence of market capitalism in the late medieval and early modern periods.

While my findings are to some extent negative, in that they clearly demonstrate the fallacious nature of most aspects of the monastic innovation thesis and the seigneurial monopoly model, I have also sought to demonstrate that many of the previous assumptions about the role of the Latin Church and monasticism in the development of English milling need to be thoroughly revised. Ecclesiastical authorities were not, on the whole, just like other lords. The wealthier houses were in most cases more rapacious and oppressive than their lay counterparts, and were not, on the whole, great mill builders. Rather than being the most benign and philanthropic, the Benedictines and Cistercians appear to have been the most oppressive and extractive of all the orders. If any of the orders deserve praise for their beneficence, it was clearly the Augustinians, who, along with the Cistercians, were far more involved in the non-seigneurial milling sector than previous researchers have realized, and appear to have been more than willing to continue operating mills that were only marginally profitable (or not profitable at all) for the benefit of their own and neighbouring tenants.

Some of those working in the history of medieval technology have in the past spurned empirical study of the kind undertaken here as being too difficult and insufficiently rewarding to warrant the effort. However, such studies, while at times onerous for the researcher, clearly reveal important insights into medieval technology which could not have been discovered any other way. Because there are a number of other important questions relating to medieval milling which remain to be answered, such as the origin of the 6,000 mills that existed in Domesday England, the distribution of tide mills and windmills throughout Western Europe, and the extent to which industrial mills were utilized and profitable in what we now call Spain, southern Italy, France, the Low Countries and Germany, it is hoped that my research, like that of John Muendel, Richard Holt, Colin Rynne,

Paul Benoit, Catherine Verna, Miquel Barcelo, John Langdon, Thomas Glick, Paolo Squatriti and many others before me, will inspire others to adopt similar research methods in future. Although my own work is by no means the last word on the subject of ecclesiastical involvement in the development of milling in medieval England, it should at the very least provide a sound basis for future research on the topic.

Abbey of Bec Computus Rolls, 1272–89

The letter 'F' next to an entry indicates that the mill concerned is recorded as being at farm for that year.

The acronym SVR stands for *Sede Vacante* Rolls, which are the rolls prepared by the Royal Exchequer during an abbatial vacancy.

Where an amount of grain is listed in brackets beneath a cash entry, the cash amount is the figure received for that amount of grain.

All halfpennies rounded up to nearest penny.

Name/Location	Year	Rent per six month term (£/s/d)	Expenses (£/s/d)
Atherstone mill F	1272–73	1/7/0	
	"	"	
	1276–77	"	
	"	"	
	1281–82	2/14/0	
	"	0/13/4 (SVR)	
F	1287–88	2/14/0	
Anna mill	1272–73	2/3/0	
	"	0/14/0	
	1276–77	2/14/6	2/10/0
		11 1/2 quart'	
	"	1/16/6	
		7 1/2 quart'	
	1281–82	0/17/10	1/12/10
	"	1/17/6	
	"	0/2/7 (SVR) (1/2 quart' frumenti)	
	"	0/14/3 (SVR) (4 quart' ordei et brasii)	
	1283–84	3/15/2	1/16/5
	"	21 quart' 1 bus'	
	1287–88	1/4/10	0/13/5
Blakenham watermill	1272–73	4/9/2	3/9/1
	1276–77	3/10/2	2/1/8
	"	17 quart' and 4 quart' 2 bus	
	1281–82	2/1/11	1/10/11 (incl. fulling mill)
	"	0/18/0	
	1283–84	1/19/0	1/8/9 (incl. fulling mill)
	"	10 quart' and 2 1/2 bus'	
Blakenham fulling mill	1276–77	0/17/0	
	1281–82	0/17/0	
	"	0/17/0 (SVR)	
	1283–84	0/17/0	
Bledlow mill	1272–73	4/6/10	
	"	1/17/9	
	"	24 quart'	
	"	10 quart' 6 bus'	
	1276–77	2/4/0	

Name/Location	Year	Rent per six month term (£/s/d)	Expenses (£/s/d)
	"	3/0/6	
	"	12 quart' 7 bus'	
	"	14 quart' 2 bus'	
	1281–82	3/8/6	
	"	0/6/2 (SVR 1)	
	"	0/11/8 (SVR 2)	
	1283–84	4/6/8	
	1287–88	2/3/3	
	"	4/16/5	
	"	1 quart'	
Chisenbury mill	1272–73	1/11/10	0/5/4
	"	1/6/9	
	1276–77	1/18/12	0/2/6
	"	2/19/3	1/6/11
	"	8 1/2 quart' and 3 quart'	
	1281–82	19 quart' 1 bus'	
	"	1/1/1 (SVR)	
	1283–84	3/17/4	
	"	20 quart'	
	1287–88	2/1/5	1/12/2
Combe mill	1276–77	1/2/6	
	"	0/15/0	
	1281–82	9 1/2 quart'	
	"	0/11/8 (SVR)	
	"	0/4/8 (SVR) (1 quart' 3 bus' frum.)	
	1283–84	1/14/6	0/7/0
	1287–88	0/14/10	0/8/1
Cottisford mill	1281–82	1/3/0	
	"	0/8/6 (SVR)	
	1283–84	1/12/0	
	1287–88	0/10/0	
Deverill mill	1281–82	0/2/0 (SVR)	
Garing' mill, Swyncombe	1272–73	1/0/11	
	"	14 quart'	
	1276–77	1/8/0	
	"	1/12/5	
	"	8 quart' and 5 bus'	
	1281–82	0/13/4	
	"	0/13/4 (SVR)	
	"	18 quart' and 1 bus'	
	1287–88	2/0/6	0/11/2
Hooe mill	1272–73	0/15/10	
	1276–77	0/15/3	
	"	4 quart' and 3 bus'	
F	1281–82	1/13/4	0/1/6
F	1283–84	1/5/0	
F	1287–88	1/10/0	0/0/13
F	1288–89	1/6/8	
Lessingeham mill	1272–73	2/19/4	
	"	13 quart' and 6 bus'	

Name/Location	Year	Rent per six month term (£/s/d)	Expenses (£/s/d)
	1276–77	2/4/1	0/8/5
	"	11 1/2 quart'	
	1281–82	2/1/8	1/16/8
	"	0/11/0 (SVR)	
		15 quart' and 2 bus'	
	1283–84	2/9/14	0/10/11
	"	16 quart' and 2 bus'	
	1287–88	1/11/4	
Ogbourne major mill	1272–73	1/1/11	
	1276–77	2/3/9	
	"	1/4/11	
	"	9 quart' 6 bus'	
	1281–82	19 quart'	
	"	0/16/0 [SVR]	
Ogbourne major windmill	1272–73	0/18/0	
	1281–82	2/8/11	
F	1287–88	2/13/4	
Ogbourne minor mill F	1281–82	4/0/0	
F	1283–84	5/6/8	
F	1287–88	4/13/4	
F	1288–89	4/13/4	
Preston mill/s	1272–73	2/15/0	
F	1276–77	1/13/4	
F	"	1/13/4	
F	"	1/13/4	
F	1281–82	3/13/4	0/7/1
F	1283–84	3/13/4	
F	1287–88	3/13/4	0/4/3
F	"	3/13/4	
Ruislip mill	1272–73	0/16/6	
	"	0/1/6	
	1276–77	0/4/10	
	"	0/2/1	
	1281–82	0/0/12 (SVR)	
	1283–84	1/8/10	
	1287–88	0/17/0	
Stowe mill, Weedon F	1180	0/12/0	
F	"	1/0/0	
	1272–73	0/5/0	
	1276–77	1/2/4	
	1281–82	0/5/0	
	"	0/5/0	
F	"	0/6/8 (SVR)	
(not received)	"	0/8/0 (SVR)	
	1283–84	0/8/0	
	1287–88	1/0/0	
Wantage mill	1272–73	4/0/0	
	1276–77	3/6/0	0/1/0
	"	3/2/3	

Name/Location	Year	Rent per six month term (£/s/d)	Expenses (£/s/d)
	"	15 quart' 2 bus'	
	1281–82	4/7/8	0/3/0
	"	0/2/6 (SVR)	
	1283–84	6/15/4	
	"	29 quart' 3 bus'	
	1287–88	2/12/6	
Warham mill, Povington	1287–88	2/10/0	
Weedon mill	1272–73	2/5/10	0/4/0
	'	3/0/0	
	1276–77	6/2/8	0/13/8 (also for Stowe)
(for granary grain)	1281–82	1/7/0	0/14/5 (also for Stowe)
(*duro blado*)	"	0/17/6 (SVR)	
(*brasio*)	"	0/6/0 (SVR)	
(*per idem tempus*)	"	0/9/0 (SVR)	
	1283–84	4/19/10	0/2/0 (also for Stowe)
	1287–88	2/2/2	29/18/2
	"	4 bus' (from the miller)	
Wretham mill	1272–73	3/0/0	1/19/6
	"	12 quart'	
	1276–77	2/19/0	1/8/1
	"	16 quart'	
	1281–82	3/15/0	1/16/4
	"	0/12/0 (SVR1 and 2)	
	1283–84	3/4/10	0/9/1
	"	18 1/2 quart'	
Chelegrave mill tithes	1287–88	0/1/6	
Glynde mill tithes	1281–82	22 quart' 2 bus'	
Hungerford mill tithes	1272–73	0/10/6	
	1276–77	0/8/1	
	1281–82	0/2/4	
	1287–88	0/7/8	
Waddesdon mill tithes	1276–77	0/4/8	

Note: Italics differentiate mill tithes from general mill revenues.

Appendix B:
Leases for 12 Mills on 11 Manors Held by Ramsey Abbey, 1398–1450

Source: *The* Liber Gersumarum *of Ramsey Abbey*, Edwin Brezette Dewindt (ed.), PIMS, Toronto, 1976.

Name/Location	Year	Rent *per annum*	Term	Lessee
WINDMILLS				
Elsworth	1411–12	16 s	20 years	John Howesson
	1432–33	8 s	20 years	John Howysson Sr. and Jr.
Holywell	1398–99	20 s	7 years	William Prykke
	1413–14	13 s 4d	10 years	William Prykke
Warboys	1400–1401	40 s	10 years	John Hygh Sr.
	1410–11	"	10 years	William Ravene and John Miller
	1422–23	"	10 years	John (?) Covyngton
	1438–39	"	10 years	William Pynder of Houghton, miller
	1443–44	30 s	10 years	John Pomeys, a.k.a. Miller
	1448–49	26 s 8 d	20 years	John Caton Sr. and Jr., William Bonde, John Plombe and John Horwode
Wistow	1409–10	20 s	12 years	Radulph Pelle, miller
	1413–14	8 s	for life	Thomas Breselaunce
	1433–34	13 s 4 d	13 years	Richard Pope and John Pegge Jr. of Somersham
	1439–40	20 s	?	William Pyndon of Houghton, miller
	1443–44	22 s	12 years	Richard Miller, a.k.a. Covynton and son William
Wistow & Raveley	1449–50	20 s	?	John Morton
WATERMILLS				
Burwell (milldam & ponds)	1398–99	11s 4d	10 years	William Taillor a.k.a. W. Poket and John Toys
Elton (x 2)	1425–26	10 m	10 years	John Whytyng
Houghton & Hemingford (x 1)	1399–1400	20 m	10 years	William, son of Gelfridus Smyth of Houghton, and Stephen Fuller of Hemingford Abbot's
FULLING MILL				
Houghton	1406–7	24 m	7 years	Thomas Styward
HORSE MILL				
Chatteris	1440–41	4s 3 1/2d	for life	Richard Smyth
Muslake (Chatteris)	1447–48	2s 10d (ruined)	for life	Laurence Hykkeson (son of tenant prior to Smyth?)

Appendix C:
Mills Held by the Bishops of Durham – Bishops Pudsey, Beck and Hatfield Rentals

The rentals for 1307 are quarterly figures (i.e., quadruple them for the annual figure). Underlining of rental amounts indicates that substantial landholdings were included with the mill rental. Figures in brackets indicate the customary rent of a holding prior to the Black Death.

Name/Location	1183	1307 (quarterly)	1377–80
Auklandshire mills	£20 0s 0d[1]	-	-
Auklandshire fulling mill	-	£1 0s 0d	5s 0d
Bedlingtonshire mills	£20 0s 0d[2]	£5 0s 0d[3]	-
Benefeldside mill/s	-	£1 3s 4d	3s 4d[4] (£1 13s 4d)
Biscopley mill	-	£1 0s 10d	-
Boldon mill/s	£4 11s 8d	£8 16s 8d[5]	£17 13s 4d[6]
Brunhop' mill	-	£1 0s 10d	-
Burdon mill	16s 8d[7]	-	13s 7 1/4d[8]
Carlton mill	20 skeps of wheat	£1 10s 0d	
Chester mill/s	£20 0s 0d[9]	£6 13s 4d	£16 6s 8d[10] (£22 0s 0d)
Cokirton mill	-	-	£4 13s 4d
Cornforth fulling mill	-	-	RUINED (£1 13s 4d)
Cothome Amundvill mill	-	-	18s 7d + 1 lb pepper
Crawcrook mill	£9 11s 8d[11]	-	-
Darlington, Houghton, Ketton and Blakewell mills	£25 0s 0d[12]	£16 0s 14d[13]	£90 0s 0d[15]
	-	£2 13s 4d[14]	£5 13s 4d[16]
Dunelm mill	-	(not let at farm)	-
Durham and Quaringtonshire mills	£30 0s 0d	£1 1s 8d	-
Easington amd Shotton mills	£6 13s 4d[17]	£5 3s 4d[18]	£6 13s 4d[20] (£13 6s 8d)
		£3 6s 8d[19]	
Gateshead mills	£50 0s 0d[21]	£6 13s 4d	£16 13s 4d[22] (£22 0s 0d)
Great Usworth mill	10s 0d	-	-
Halughton mill	-	£1 1s 8d	0d[23] (£2 13s 4d)
Hameldon windmill	-	-	£5 13s 4d (£6 13s 4d)
Hamsterley mill	-	3s 4d	
Heighintonshire mills	£10 0s 0d	£6 13s 4d	-
Hertilpole windmill	-	-	-[24] (£3 17s 8d)
Knycheley mill	-	-	£2 13s 4d
Kyblesworth mill	-	-	6d
Kyllyrby mill	-	-	£2 0s 0d
Lanchester mill/s	£6 13s 4d[25]	£3 6s 8d[26]	£6 6s 8d[27] (£13 6s 8d)
Lynesak mill	-	9s	13s 4d[28] (£3 6s 8d)
Middleham and Cornforth mill	£8 6s 8d	£5 0s 0d	
Newbottle and Biddick mills	£12 10s 0d[29]	£4 6s 8d[30]	£8 13s 4d[31]
Norhamshire and Islandshire mills	£36 13s 4d[32]	-	-
North Aukland mill	-	£10 0s 0d	-
North Aukland fulling mill I	-	(£1 0s 0d)	5s[33]

Name/Location	1183	1307 (quarterly)	1377–80
Norton mill/s	£16 12s 16d[34]	3s 4d £6 13s 4d	£26 13s 4d[35]
Oxenhall horsemill[36]	£3 0s 0d	-	-
Pencher or Middleham mill	£1 12s 16d	-	-
Quicham mill	-	£6 16s 8d	-
Rouley mill	-	16s 8d	-
Rughsyde mill[37]	-	-	£1 0s 0d
Ryhope mills	-	-	9s 6d[38] 9s 0d[39]
Ryton mill	£14 0s 0d[40]	£2 3s 4d	£5 16s 8d[41]
Sateley mill	-	-	RUINED (6s 8d)
Sedgfield mill/s	£5 0s 0d	£4 15s 0d	£13 6s 8d[42]
Southbedburn watermill	-	-	£2 0s 0d
Southbedburn fulling mill	-	-	2s 0d (site only)
Stanhope and Wolsingham mills	£8 6s 8d[43]	£6 0s 20d £4 6s 8d	£6 0s 0d £8 0s 0d[44]
Tunstall windmill	-	-	13s 7 1/4d
Tursdale mill (in Bishop's hand)	-	-	-
Urpath mill at farm	£3 5s 12d	£1 3s 4d	-
Wearmouth mill	£20 0s 0d[45]	£8 6s 8d	19d[46]
West Aukland mill	-	£5 6s 8d	£6 6s 8d (£10 13s 4d)
Westow mill (Whessoe)	£10 16s 8d[47]	15s 6d	-
Whickham mill/s	£2 10s 0d[48]	-	2s 0d[49] 13s 4d[50] £20 0s 0d[51] (£38 0s 0d)
Whitburn mill	-	-	£56 0s 0d[52]
Wilton and Fulforth mill	£1 13s 4d	-	-
Winlaton and Barlow mill	£4 11s 8d	-	-
Wotton mill	-	-	13s 4d

Endnotes

[1]   This amount probably represents the income from four or five mills.

[2]   Idem.

[3]   Rent for one mill only.

[4]   This amount was for the Bishop's mill-site on a lifelong lease. The survey records that the original mill was ruined, but a new mill had been built on the site (presumably at the lessee's expense) and was held on the same lease at the same rent. The customary rent for the old mill is listed below the current rent.

[5]   This amount includes the rents for Clivedon and Wyteburne mills also.

[6]   This amount was for a windmill and a watermill, but it isn't clear whether this included one of the Clivedon or Wyteburne mills.

[7]   This mill initially served the manor of Ryhope as well.

[8]   This amount included payment of beer toll.

[9]   This amount included all of the rents paid by villeins for the demesne without stock, as well as for fisheries, and the mill.

[10]   The rent for two mills for that financial year.

[11]   This amount included the town at farm with its demesne, one mill, one plough and one harrow.

[12]   Rent for the Darlington, Houghton and Ketton mills.

[13]   This amount was for the Darlington mill.

[14] Rent for the Houghton mill.

[15] Rent for the Darlington, Houghton and Blakewell mills. Why Ketton has been substituted for Blakewell in this survey is not clear.

[16] Rent for a half share of Houghton mill. It also is not clear from the rental whether the £90 of rent for the Darlington, Houghton and Blakewell mills included this half share.

[17] This amount was for both mills.

[18] Rent for Easington millshare

[19] Rent for Shotton mill.

[20] Rent for Easington windmill for that financial year.

[21] This amount included the rent for the borough, fisheries, mills, bakehouses and three parts of the town's arable.

[22] Rent for two watermills and one windmill.

[23] This mill was presumably ruined by this stage.

[24] The manuscript is damaged at this point.

[25] Two mills are referred to in this rental, but judging from the subsequent surveys it was probably a double mill, i.e., a single waterwheel powering two sets of millstones.

[26] Only a single mill is referred to here.

[27] One (double?) mill appears to be serving the vills of Lanchester and Burnhop at this stage.

[28] This mill was earning £10 17s 1d in the fifteenth or sixteenth century.

[29] This was the rent for both Newbottle and Biddick mills, plus a share of Rainton mill.

[30] Rent for Newbottle mill only.

[31] Rent for Newbottle mill only.

[32] There may have been as many as eight mills serving these two vills.

[33] Rent for old fulling mill site.

[34] The lease included eight acres of land and a 'meadow near the mill'.

[35] This was the rent for Norton, Stokton and Hertburn mills.

[36] The lease included the land appurtenant to the mill plus free multure for its lessee and no customary work at the mills.

[37] This was known as Aleynforth mill and was located in West Rouley.

[38] Rent for Smythland mill with nine acres of land.

[39] Rent for Punderland mill.

[40] The lease included the town at farm with demesne, assize-rent, works, 20 chalders oats, one plough, one harrow and fisheries)

[41] This included 10 shillings of beer service.

[42] Rent for one windmill, one watermill and beer toll.

[43] Rent for both mills.

[44] This was the rent for a fulling mill and a grain mill.

[45] This included the demesne at farm with 20 oxen, 200 sheep, one mill and two harrows, and covered the vill of Tunstall also.

[46] This was for the farm of Wearmouth windmill with beer toll.

[47] The lease included the manor at farm with demesne, villains, works, one mill, two ploughs and two harrows.

[48] The rental says 'formerly' rented for this amount, which presumably meant that it was ruined by this stage.

[49] Rent for the site only of a mill in the village of Asshels.

[50] Rent for Creswellcrok mill.

[51] Rent for Smalwels mill.

[52] The lease was to 28 tenants who held 336 acres, 56 bovates in bondage, a mill, moorland and superior pasture.

Appendix D:
Tithe disputes between religious houses, 1200–1400

Date	Plaintiff/party	Defendant/party	Presiding papal delegate/ curial court	Issue	Details of resolution
Kirkstall Abbey and Trinity Priory, York: Allerton (W. Yorks.)					
<1153[1]	Kirkstall Abbey	Convent of Trinity Priory, York		Payment of tithes within the vill of Allerton.	Kirkstall to pay Trinity Priory £1 3s annually.
c. 1220[2]	"	"		Payment of tithes within the vill of Allerton following erection of two mills.	Kirkstall to pay Trinity Priory £1 10s annually.
1236[3]	"	"		Advowson of Adel Church, in dispute between parties since vill first granted to Kirkstall by the Mustel family.	Priory surrendered to abbey tithe payment from Allerton, as well as priory's annual rents from its holdings in Adel, in return for recognition of Trinity's rightful claim to advowson of Adel Church.
Furness Abbey and Lancaster Priory: Beaumont in Skerton (Lancs.)					
1306[4]	Abbot of Furness	Prior of Lancaster		Payment of tithes from monks' lands of Beaumont in Skerton, incl. multure of mills there.	Monks to pay 2m *per annum* to prior in lieu of tithes for their lands of Beaumont in Skerton as long as they continued to cultivate it themselves, incl. multure of mills. If monks let same land to others, the usual tithes were to be paid to the prior.
Lancaster Priory and Church of Bolton: Bolton (Lancs.)					
1320[5]	Prior of Lancaster	Archdeacon of Richmond and vicar, church of Bolton		Tithes of Bolton mill, remised in perpetuity to parishioners for 2m *per annum* by Richard I, now claimed by church of Bolton.	Legal possession of Bolton mill's tithes to Lancaster Priory. Archdeacon's servants and others within diocese to carry out terms of declaration.
Cirencester Abbey: Coates and Daglingworth (Gloucs.)					
1235[6]	Rector, church of Coates	Hugh of Bampton (1230-50), Abbot of Cirencester	Archdeacon, chancellor and subdeacon of Hereford	Tithes of Trewsbury and demesne of Elias Cockerel in Coates, incl. mill, belong to church of Coates.	Greater and lesser tithes of Trewsbury to Coates. Tithes of Elias Cockerel and mill to Cirencester.
1235[7]	Hugh of Bampton, Abbot of Cirencester	Rector, church of Daglingworth	Abbot and prior of Winchcombe Mandated by Pope Gregory IX	Tithes of mill, house, arable and meadow of Osbert Brain, plus oblations of church, all within parish of Cirencester, unjustly withheld by rectors of Daglingworth.	All major and minor tithes of mill, house, arable and meadow, as well as fishery, income and mortuary rights pertaining to parish church, to abbot of Cirencester. Canons gave rector of Daglingworth £2 'for the good peace'.

Date	Plaintiff/party	Defendant/party	Presiding papal delegate/curial court	Issue	Details of resolution
Cirencester Abbey: Shrivenham (Oxon.)					
1236[8]	Vicar, church of Shrivenham	Hugh of Bampton, Abbot of Cirencester	Abbot and prior of Winchcombe	Tithes of hay and mills of Shrivenham.	Tithes of hay and mills of Shrivenham to abbot of Cirencester. Canons to pay vicar 17 shillings 'for the good peace'.
1326[9]	Vicar, church of Shrivenham	"	Dean of Cricklade	Tithes of hay, mills and market of Shrivenham confirmed to vicar, with other specified tithes added.	Tithes of hay, mills, market and c. of Shrivenham to vicar of Shrivenham. Vicar to render £3 annually to the abbot. Vicar to bear all burdens of church.
1237[10]	Bishop of Salisbury	"		Various tithes in Shrivenham including those of merchant's mill and curtilage.	Stated tithes to be released by abbot to bishop of Salisbury. Bishop to pay 20s annually to abbot of Cirencester.
Cirencester Abbey: Rothwell (Northants.)					
1234[11]	Hugh of Bampton, Abbot of Cirencester	Vicar, church of Rothwell		Vicar of Rothwell to renounce all right in tithes of all mills in parish of Rothwell to abbot and convent of Cirencester.	All small tithes of Rothwell not assigned to vicarage, incl. mill tithes, granted by abbot and convent of Cirencester to chaplain of Rothwell for 5 years: value 10m *per annum*
1326[12]	Abbot Richard and convent of Cirencester	Sacrist, church of Rothwell		Tithes of Rothwell.	Tithes of Rothwell assigned to sacrist, incl. all tithes of mill, to be allocated to poorhouse.
Bradenstoke Priory: Wells diocese (Soms.) and North Aston (Oxon.)					
1216-27[13]	Prior and convent of Bradenstoke	Abbot of Glastonbury and several clerks and laymen in dioceses of Lincoln, Salisbury and Bath	Three papal appointees from Ivychurch and Salisbury	Defendants 'injured them in regard to tithes, possessions, rents, and other matters', incl. 'long-disputed tithes of mill'.	Roger Tyrel and successors 'pay the tithes to the canons without dispute, or diminution, and without deduction of rent or expenses''. Subdean of Wells to 'put the canons into full possession of the tithes'.

Date	Plaintiff/party	Defendant/party	Presiding papal delegate/ curial court	Issue	Details of resolution
1226[14]	Canons of Bradenstoke	Simon Gamboun, miller of North Aston	Prior and dean of Malmesbury and dean of Farleigh	Tithes of hay, mills and fishponds due to the church of North Aston.	Simon conceded he owed and wished to pay tithes. Judgement made that he should pay both tithes in arrears and priory's expenses in bringing case against him. Simon agreed to conditions and that failure to comply would result in court compelling him to do so.
Bradenstoke Priory: Costow, Stratford and Christian Malford (Wilts.)					
1247[15]	Canons of Bradenstoke	Stanley Abbey	Court of Westminster	Tithes of sheaves from 4 hides of land in Costow and 10s rent from Stratford mill, which the prior claimed were being unjustly withheld by the abbot of Stanley.	Prior quitclaimed all right to sheaves in exchange for 10s rent from Stratford mill and other rents amounting in total to 2m *per annum*
1229	"	Rector, church of Christian Malford		Tithes of two newly constructed mills, 2 meadows, feed and 1 virgate in parish of Christian Malford.	Canons should pay rector 16s *per annum* for all tithes.
1236	Rector, church of Christian Malford	Canons of Bradenstoke		Tithes of 16s *per annum* not paid by Bradenstoke to rector of Christian Malford.	Rector withdrew action 'for the sake of peace'. Canons agreed to pay rector arrears and legal expenses of £2 10s, less eightpence, 1/2 to be paid that day and other 1/2 within 15 days. Penalty of 2 besants for any further infringement.
1252[16]	"	"	Bishop of Bath and Wells, prior of Bath, and dean and chapter of Wells	Tithes of 16 acres *per annum* still not paid by Bradenstoke to rector of Christian Malford.	Original fine upheld. 5m 16s should be paid by canons to rector.

Date	Plaintiff/party	Defendamt/party	Presiding papal delegate/ curial court	Issue	Details of resolution
Blythburgh Priory: Claxton (Norf.)					
1266[17]	Blythburgh Priory	Vicar Robert de Scholtisnelle, church of Claxton	Court of Official sede vacante	All tithes to go to vicar except grain, peas and beans, plus a marsh with its windmills and watermills and 2a. near churchyard.	Vicar agreed to pay rectors all homage free and servile owing to church, with tenements and revenues. Priory conceded to vicar all tithes except those for chickens and piglets. Parties agreed not to diminish portion of tithes in priory's case, and vicar to not let any of church's lands to tenants who may be hostile to priory. Fine of £5 to be imposed on either party should they transgress.
St Denys's Priory: Southampton (Hants.)					
1225[18]	St Mary's Southampton	St Denys's Priory	R. chancellor of Salisbury and William archdeacon of Berkshire	Parochial rights of St Mary's as mother church of chapels of St Michael, Holy Rood, St Lawrence, All Saints, Holy Trinity and St Andrew.	Parochial rights assigned to St Mary's, incl. tithes of fishery and 2 windmills between town of Southampton and house of the lepers, plus tithes of pigs in the marsh of Southampton. Prior and canons in seisin of 'tithes of a watermill that is next to the court just to its north and a garden between seven houses', plus mortuary rights.
1258[19]	"	"	Winchester Court	Tithes of mills of Aldinton, plus fishery pertaining to mill which both parties claimed by common law (*iuri communi*).	St Mary's renounced all right in tithes of Aldinton. St Denys's to pay St Mary's ¼ grain *per annum*

Endnotes

1   *Coucher Book of Kirkstall Abbey*, p. xxvi.

2   Ibid., ms. 348.

3   Ibid., p. xxvi–xxvii, and the earlier discussion of Kirkstall in section 2.4.

4   *Coucher Book of Furness Abbey*, Vol. II, Pt. I, *Beaumont*, ms. 14.

5   *Materials for the history of the Church of Lancaster*, pp. 261–3, VI Kal. Mar. 1320.

6   *The Cartulary of Cirencester Abbey*, Vol. 1, ms. 911. The agreement is dated 23 April 1235.

7   Ibid., ms. 271/127. The agreement is dated 1235 or shortly thereafter.

8   Ibid., ms. 498/775.

9   Ibid., Vol. 2, ms. 757, 5 Nov. 1326.

10   Ibid., Vol. 1, ms. 507/756.

11   Ibid., ms. 684, 10 June 1234; cf. ms. 685/862., c. 1231–46.

12   Ibid., ms. 757.

13   *Cartulary of Bradenstoke Priory*, ms. 388.

14   Ibid., ms. 12. See also B.M., Cott. MS. Vit. A. XI, 147a, and idem., ms. 11.

15   Ibid., mss. 363, 541. The gift of the rent from Stratford mill was to the Church of St Mary in Stanley from William earl of Salisbury between 1168 and 1179.

16   Ibid., ms. 155.

17   *Blythburgh Priory Cartulary*, Pt. I, pp. 18-19.

18   *Cartulary of the Priory of St Denys*, mss. 283, 284, 285.

19   Ibid., pp. 6–7, n. 1a) and b). The priory had been granted five shillings rent from a mill in Aldinton by William Alis and his mother in 1204, which presumably constituted the tithes in question. The priory justified its possession by adding to its legal claim in 1258 that it held the mill tithes 'by just title and peacefully possessed by them for a very long time' (*dicti vero prior et conventus dicebant eas se iusto titulo adeptos ac per longissima tempora pacifice possedisse*).

Appendix E:
Water rights and disputes between religious houses, 1200–1400

Date	Plaintiff/party	Defendant/Party	Issue	Obligations and Distraints
Priory of St Gregory's, Canterbury: mill of Howfield (Kent)				
c. 1200[1]	Robert of Sevanz	Priory of St Gregory	Grant by Robert of Sevanz of 'all of my part of the water that divides my meadow from the land of St Gregory of Canterbury', to be diverted through the canons' meadow to their mill of Tunford, Howfield.	Robert's land should not be damaged in any way. Canons to pay Robert 4m 'consideration' and 4s *per annum* rent for himself and his heirs.
>1222[2]	Robert, son of Robert of Sevanz	"	Grant from Robert to the priory in gavelkind of 1/2 acre of land in Howfield with alder grove.	Canons to pay Robert 1m 'consideration' and 8d *per annum* rent. Priory to close the ditch between their meadow and the brook which Robert's father had allowed them.
c. 1213–14[3]	Giles of Badlesmere	"	Grant from Giles to the priory of a piece of water which divided his land in Horton from that of the canons in Howfield, as well as a pool there.	Giles' tenants obliged to maintain boundary between their land and that of the canons. If the latter suffered any damage due to the neglect of Giles' tenants, he agreed to make restitution.
c. 1215[4]	"	"	Grant from Giles to the priory of the aforementioned pool and 1 1/2 acres of marshland with the alder grove in Howfield.	Neither Giles nor his men to prevent the canons from enclosing the stream which flowed through the grove.
Abbey of the Holy Trinity, Caen: mill of Felsted (Essex)				
1227–28[5]	Abbess of Holy Trinity, Caen	Prior William of Leighs	Dispute between abbess and prior over watercourse to the abbess' mill of Felsted.	Prior to pay 10s *per annum* rent to the abbess for 1/2 virgate of land in Felsted. 'It is acknowledged that we are not to divert or cut off the watercourse of the abbess' mill …Nor that we make any demands over old boundaries with regard to the pond.'
Treasurer of St Peter's, York: mills of Alne (Yorks.)				
1250–51[6]	Treasurer of St Peter's, York	Delantoft, Abbey of St Mary's, York	Treasurer's mill and fishery on the river Foss in the manor of Clifton, was located not far upstream from the monks' mill near the bridge that led into the city of York. Mill and fishery were interfering with the water flow to the monk's mill. Treasurer made repeated requests to monks to move their mill further downstream, which they did not want to do. Monks argued doing so would threaten their monastery and was against the original agreement about the mills which the two parties had signed in 1154–61, long pre-dating the construction of the Treasurer's milldam above the fishery.	Treasurer's mill and fishery predated the monks' mill. Mill agreement between parties of 1154–61 long pre-dated construction of treasurer's milldam above the fishery. Agreement confirmed by Archbishop of York c. 1161 and Pope Alexander III on 30 June 1163. In return for prohibition on Treasurer altering or moving the site of his mill or its millpond, monks required to stop interfering with Treasurer's fishery near their mill and the bridge. Monks agreed to pay Treasurer 3s pension *per annum* and agreed Treasurer was entitled to tithes of his mill.

Date	Plaintiff/party	Defendant/Party	Issue	Obligations and Distraints
St Denys' Priory: mill of Stratford (Warks.) and Munekelond mill, Southampton (Hants.)				
1240[7]	Dean of Salisbury Cathedral Priory	St Denys's Priory	Construction of sluices and watercourse for the canons' mill in Stratford on the river Avon across land belonging to the dean of Salisbury, thereby damaging his property.	Exchange of land between dean and canons, whereby the priory granted the dean 'two profitable acres' in the fields of Stratford for the dean's piece of land lying between their mill and the river, as well as a strip of land six feet wide from the river bank to the mill (presumably encompassing the watercourse to the mill) with the dean and his men reserving the right of passage across this strip.
1252[8]	St Denys's Priory	Church of St Mary Southampton	Right of way through St Mary's land in Munekelond, as well as a watercourse leading to a mill in Munekelond held by St Mary's which it claimed was on the highway, but which the canons claimed was on their land of Kingeslond.	Canons allowed right of way in return for warrant that they would not interfere with the watercourse of the priests of St Mary's, and that the latter would be able to repair and maintain the watercourse.
			Canons required right of way in order to get to their barn and land on the other side.	St Mary's to make appropriate restitution to the canons if watercourse were to cause any damage.
				Both parties agreed to forgive all injurious actions and quarrels which they had previously entered into.
Lacock Abbey: Abbess' mill, town of Lacock (Wilts.)				
1241[9]	Roger Bloet, parson of Lacock	Ela, abbess of Lacock	Inadequate maintenance of a mill with its pond and a bridge held by the abbess in the town of Lacock on the south side of the abbey.	Roger to let the mill and pond stand without further molestation. Roger and his successors must not build anything which might compromise mill's operation.
				Abbess to ensure bridge properly maintained, and to make any necessary repairs to it 'as speedily and serviceably' as possible.
				If Roger were to suffer any damages as a result of her default, she was to compensate him.
				Ela to find an alternative path for Roger to conduct his business to the south of the graveyard if she were not to let him pass through it, and to pay Robert 4s per annum from one of her tenants 'for having good peace'.

Date	Plaintiff/party	Defendant/Party	Issue	Obligations and Distraints
c. 1264[10]	Sir William Bluet of Lacham	Beatrice, abbess of Lacock	Conflict over 'the cutting off of the watercourse to the mill standing within the close of the abbey and … turning back the water as far as William's free tenement, and about the damage of the whole path called Churigwe across Snailesmede and of the street extending from the abbey as far as Bewley'.	Sir William quitclaimed any right to damages against the abbess for having cut off the watercourse and that he would not disturb or implead the abbess further, even if the water inundated the aforementioned properties and rights of way. Abbess gave William 2 1/2 acres of land in the area.
1264–70[11]	"	"	Sir William gave Abbess permission to 'freely make and mend the watercourse or aqueduct so that the aqueduct and watercourse continue in the same place and state … upon his fee of Lacham, and freely carry water … as far as the abbey of Lacock.	William, his wife and heirs were to be admitted 'into the benefits' of the abbey, i.e. burial within the abbey's cemetery along with the prayers of the canonesses for the salvation of their souls.
1280–8[12]	"	"	Grant by Sir William to allow the abbess 'free and quiet passage for her conduit from Bouedone to their church of Lacock through the middle of the land of William and [his] men of Bewley, with right to erect and repair the conduit when necessary.	Abbess bound to make reasonable amends to Sir William or his men should the waters from the conduit cause any damage.
1258–80[13]	Robert de Holta	"	Grant of 'free power to dig and conduct her water across or beneath the land [Robert held] of the fee of Sir William Bluet, and to repair her conduit wheresoever and whensoever she wishes without hindrance forever.'	As above.

Old Wardon Abbey: mill of Risingho (Beds.)

Date	Plaintiff/party	Defendant/Party	Issue	Obligations and Distraints
1240[14]	Old Wardon Abbey	William de Bello Campo (aka Beauchamp)	Modifications to the millpond adjacent to the river (Ouse?) on which their mill of Risingho was located, which interfered with passage of ships along the river.	William conceded to abbey that: 'the buildings erected at Risingho mill are to stand, notwithstanding the obstruction of the river, since the abbey already has sufficient warrant for using the site to their advantage' 'the millpond there is to remain as heightened, but a weir is to be opened at its head towards Cardington and Cole Meadows'. Any further disagreements to be heard in the appropriate court.

Beaulieu Abbey: mills of Eldee and Kyndelwere, Radcot (Oxon.)

Date	Plaintiff/party	Defendant/Party	Issue	Obligations and Distraints
1222[15]	Beaulieu Abbey	Stanley Abbey	Five-year dispute over which house was responsible for maintenance of weirs upstream from two abbeys' mills of Eldee and Kyndelwere on the Thames, which had caused flooding of Beaulieu's mill and land.	Monks of Stanley ordered to make repairs to weir and maintain water-level behind it through the construction of a sluice. Both parties also agreed that Stanley would indemnify Beaulieu against any flooding of its land, and that both houses would permanently expel any monk who broke the agreement.

Date	Plaintiff/ party	Defendant/ Party	Issue	Obligations and Distraints
mid-14th c.[16]	"	Matthias de Besilles, lord of Radcot	Matthias to desist from impeding abbey's men from gaining access to its mill of Kyndelwere on the River Thames near Radcot and hunting game on their land.	Matthias agreed to no longer hunt game on abbey land, and to desist from impeding abbey's men from free access to the mill and its pond so they could keep it in good repair.
				Monks also granted a piece of embankment beside their mill by a local freeman soon afterwards to make improvements to the mill.
mid-14th c.[17]	"	Matthias de Besilles, lord of Radcot	Matthias de Besilles to desist from interfering with the shipping of the abbey's grain from its mill of Kyndelwere.	Matthias agreed to desist from interfering with shipping of grain.
				Agreement later reaffirmed by his son Geoffrey, who also gave the monks permission to wash their sheep in the river, to embank their land against flooding, and to prevent their watercourse from silting up by whatever means they thought fit.
Lancaster Priory: mills of Caton (Lancs.) and mill of Carleton (N. Yorks.)				
1256–59[18]	Lancaster Priory	John of Hutton	Grant by John of Hutton to priory and John Gernet of the watercourse of Artlebeck (near River Lune) which leads to the mills of Caton, held by John Gernet and the priory.	Grantees given permission to rebuild the watercourse if it was damaged by floods, and the right to make a new course on grantor's land and enclose it if need arose.
				John of H. and his heirs to receive 6d *per annum* for every secular service due to them.
mid-13th c.[19]	John, prior of Lancaster	Henry of Carleton	Water rights pertaining to a mill in Carleton held by Henry.	Henry and his heirs to be given divine celebration in the chapel of Carleton, as well as right to clear any obstructions from the waterway leading from Henry's mill to a place called Lamepot located on land held by the priory.
				Henry to pay the priory 4s *per annum* in perpetuity, with the mill and 1 bovate of land placed as surety.
				Priory allowed to take possession of the mill if rent not paid on time, and released Henry and his heirs of this obligation if the waterway was obstructed.
Kirkstall Abbey: mill of Kirkstall, Tofthouse millpond (Yorks.)				
1172–c. 1200[20]	Hugh de Witon	Kirkstall Abbey	Dispute concerning Tofthouse millpond, above the tenement of Wyke, held by Hugh de Witon.	Hugh and monks agree the latter should receive 6d rent *per annum* in order for Hugh to hold the farm of Tofthouse millpond and to make the foundation of a milldam on the monks' land.
			Monks accuse millpond and milldam of causing injury to their mill of Kirkstall.	Monks distrained from taking any action against him or his heirs for any injury caused to their mill of Kirkstall which may have resulted.

Date	Plaintiff/ party	Defendant/ Party	Issue	Obligations and Distraints
Furness Abbey: mill of Stalmine and Lune River fishery (Lancs.)				
1220–40[21]	Furness Abbey	Geoffrey the crossbowman	Grant from Geoffrey to the monks of the marsh of Horestepul and 1/2 share of the waters of Horestepul, including water for their mill of Stalmine.	
1220–40[22]	"	"	Grant from Geoffrey to the monks of various parcels of land in the townfields of Preesall (Lancs.), which was located on each side of the bridge of Horestepul, 'with sufficient water for all their mills there'.	
1260–90[23]	"	John, son of Adam de Stalmyne	Release and confirmation of Geoffrey's grants by John, together with 3 acres of land in Stalmine, the remaining 1/2 share of the waters of Horestepul, and another pool on the east side of Stalmine moss.	John's confirmation and release allows the monks to make and maintain a watercourse as far as Horestepul.
1318–19[24]	"	Nicholas de Oxclyf	Dispute concerning rights over the mill of Stalmine and the waters which led to it.	Nicholas acknowledged monks' claim to the mill and millpool near their grange, as well as 5 acres from the waste of Stalmine. Monks acknowledge his right to a messuage and salthouse situated in the waste held by Nicholas near the vill of Stalmine.
1337[25]	"	Thomas de Gosenarghe (a.k.a. Thomas Schilehare of Dalton), lord of Stalmine	Dispute concerning rights over the mill of Stalmine and the waters which led to it.	Thomas confirmed to the monks the lands and rights which had been given to them by various grants, incl. Horestepul and the mill of Stalmine. Thomas agreed to do suit to the county and wapentake courts and to pay 5s *per annum* due to the earl of Lancaster. Monks allowed Thomas sites for a sheepfold and 2 salthouses, along with the rights of way to them.
1460[26]	Abbot John of Furness	Elizabeth, abbess of Syon	Possession of the Lune fishery and access to mill of Neuton, which Elizabeth, the abbess of Syon, had recently acquired from the estate of the priory of Lancaster.	Elizabeth demised the fishery of the Lune to Abbot John for 60 years at 10s *per annum* Furness agreed the abbess should continue to operate, access and repair her mill and its watercourses in the vill of Neuton without impediment from the monks of Furness.

Date	Plaintiff/ party	Defendant/ Party	Issue	Obligations and Distraints
Sibton Abbey: mill of Darnford (Suff.)				
1230[27]	Sibton Abbey	William de Weston	Grant from William to the abbey of his own body and that of his wife, along with the mill of Darnford in Cookley, incl. fishing rights in its waters and the outlet of water over his fee, a small marsh and other land east of the mill, and free transit over William's land to the mill.	William also granted abbey the right to raise the causeway or millpond, to take soil from the neighbouring meadows of one of William's tenants in order to repair breaches in the causeway, and to do as it would with the causeway, mill and waters
c. 1230[28]	"	John Umfrey	John granted the abbey a parcel of meadow beside the mill and the right to repair the bridge of Darnford or raise the water level or causeway on either side of the bridge should they need to.	In return for the first release, John was conceded right of burial in abbey cemetery. For the second grant, he and his heirs reserved the right to fish in the waters of the bridge and free drovage to his meadows.
1260s and 70s[29]	"	"	John granted the abbey 3 additional parcels of land by the mill, pond and causeway to enable the monks to 'dig out and construct bays in the millpond so that water from this pond can flow in perpetuity by these bays to the stream running under the bridge near his garden to the south'.	
First half 13th c.[30]	"	Thomas Tyrel	Thomas T. granted the abbey an additional rood of land beside the millpond.	
1245[31]	Abbot Henry I of Sibton	Robert, son of Hugh of Darnford	Dispute over the size of the millpool of Darnford watermill and the height of its milldam.	Monks were not to raise the millpond or increase its size, in return for which Robert confirmed their right to all of their other holdings in the area. Abbot allowed Robert and his heirs the right to drove his animals through the marsh which the monks held as part of a grant from Robert's father, as well as the right to water his animals at the millpond of Darnford which they held of Butley Priory.
1270s[32]	Sibton Abbey	Robert, son of John Umfrey	Robert granted the monks additional lands beside the mill-site and watercourse.	Robert bound himself, his wife and heirs to honour the terms of the grant or pay the monks 5m 'to make good all damages and expenses'.
1270s[33]	"	Thomas Brown of Walpole	Thomas B. granted the abbey another parcel of meadow beside the bank of the mill.	

Date	Plaintiff/party	Defendant/Party	Issue	Obligations and Distraints
Sibton Abbey: mill of Kennett (Cambs.)				
1342–1345[34]	Margaret, countess of Norfolk	Abbot Ralph de Bradenham of Sibton	Monks of Sibton altered watercourse leading to their watermill in Kennett, and failed to maintain a bridge between Badlingham (in Chippenham, Cambs.) and Kennett.	Petition from Abbot Ralph to Countess Margaret argues Nicholas, former lord of Kennett, had granted Sibton the lands, tenements, waters and pastures concerned 'to be made use of to their profit', according to the original terms of the grant.
				Abbot claims countess wrongfully brought repeated suits against abbey's men in her court for blocking the watercourse, and appealed to her to instruct her steward that these various suits were illegitimate.
				Subsequent inquisition established Lord Nicholas and his descendants were in lawful seisin of Kennett when grant issued to Sibton, and had 'used and enjoyed' liberty of the manor in view of frankpledge.
				Although three of Margaret's stewards agreed this was the case and that the monks should be left alone until the terms of the original grant were established, Margaret removed and replaced one of them with another man, Thomas of Felsham.
1342[35]	"	"	Thomas of Felsham charged that Sibton had failed to keep up repairs on the aforementioned bridge.	Sibton amerced 20s, which it duly paid.
				Abbot Roger paid Margaret's chief steward, Ralph de Bockinge, another 40s, and retained Thomas at livery.
				Thomas extracted another 2m *per annum* from the abbey in return for a quitclaim regarding the grant of the manor of Peasenhall.
				Although Thomas agreed on settlement, he failed to stand surety in court, and the matter dragged on until it was heard again in the manorial court in 1345.
1345[36]	Sibton Abbey	Margaret, countess of Norfolk	Wrongful amercement of 40s from abbey to Countess Margaret.	Abbot agreed he was obliged to pay 20s for the bridge repairs, but another 40s which the countess obtained from him was wrongfully amerced.
				Transcripts of the abbey's relevant charters and muniments to be made and presented to the countess's council in London in order to establish whether the abbot's claims were legitimate.

Endnotes

[1] Cartulary of the Priory of St Gregory, Canterbury, ms. 129.

[2] Ibid., ms. 130.

[3] Ibid., ms. 131.

[4] Ibid., mss. 132 andand 161.

[5] Charters and Custumals of the Abbey of Holy Trinity Caen, ms. 18.

[6] Cartulary of the Treasurer of York Minster, mss. 13, 14, 15. The memorandum of agreement is dated 12 January 1250–51.

[7] bid., ms. 405. This mill does not appear to have been the same mill from which Stanley Abbey was granted 10 shillings rent from William, earl of Salisbury, in the late twelfth century, and which was then demised to Bradenstoke Priory in 1247 as part of the settlement of a dispute between the two houses, about which see Chapter 6.

[8] Cartulary of the Priory of St Denys, ms. 282.

[9] Lacock Abbey Charters, ms. 168.

[10] Ibid., ms. 169.

[11] Ibid., ms. 49.

[12] Ibid., ms. 51.

[13] Ibid., ms. 50.

[14] Cartulary of Old Wardon Abbey, ms. 240.

[15] Hockey (1975), p. 79.

[16] Ibid., p. 80.

[17] Ibid.

[18] Materials for a History of the Church of Lancaster, pp. 170–72. Based on the analysis of the documents pertaining to the mills of Caton discussed in Chapter 5, the grant of Artlebeck watercourse by John of Hutton to John of Caton and the priory was made between 1256 and 1259.

[19] Ibid., pp. 432–3. The charter is not dated, but the witness list includes Sir William le Botiler and Thomas Banaster, both of whom appear in Cockersand's documents from around this time.

[20] Coucher Book of Kirkstall Abbey, ms. 116.

[21] Coucher Book of Furness Abbey, Vol. II, Pt. I, Stalmyne, ms. 22, p. 24. The mill of Stalmine was granted to the monks by William de Stalmyne between 1227 and 1236 (see ms. 4, p. 233).

[22] Ibid., mss. 23-6, p. 24.

[23] Ibid., Stalmine II, mss. 33, 44 andand 45.

[24] Ibid., Preesall/Stalmine, ms. 50, p. 26. It would seem that Nicholas's claim to this land had been based upon a grant from his father William to Furness 'of all my lands in Stalmine and Staynall ... with the homages and services of my free tenants ... and [those] of the abbot of Furness, with services and rents of eight shillings from Stalmine Grange', including 'waters, ponds, and mills' (see ibid., Stalmine/Claughton, ms. 63.

[25] Ibid., Vol. II, Pt. I, Preesall/Stalmine, ms. 53. Thomas's claim to the monks' lands and waters appears to be related to a grant to him from Clarice daughter of Robert de Wath dated to 1284–85 of all the land which her father had given her in Stalmine, including its 'mills and ponds' (molendinis et stangnis), in return for a penny annually (see ms. 58). It is not at all clear, however, what was the status of Clarice's claim to this land via her father.

[26] Ibid., Vol. IV, Pt. I, ms. 30, dated 24 November 1460.

[27] Sibton Abbey Cartularies and Charters, Pt. II, ms. 147. This grant was confirmed by William's son, William III, sometime between 1250 and 1263, see ibid., Pt. III, ms. 799. The mill of Darnford is first mentioned in a document from around 1225, in which Adam Rusteyn quitclaimed to Sibton his rights in all the tenements which his family held in Darnford, but it would seem that this grant did not include the mill of Darnford itself, see Pt. II, ms. 260.

[28] Ibid., Pt. II, mss. 148 andand 149.

[29] Ibid., Pt. III, mss. 807–9.

[30] Ibid., Pt. II, ms. 264.

[31] Ibid., mss. 255 andand 257. Robert's son, Alan, negotiated a similar agreement with the monks some time during the 1260s, in which they similarly conceded not to raise the height of the millpond and to allow the overflow into the northern marsh held by Alan, in return for which he agreed not to plant or build anything or in any way interfere with the waterway or millpond as already agreed with Alan's father. See ms. 259.

[32]   Ibid., ms. 805.

[33]   Ibid., ms. 810.

[34]   *Sibton Abbey Cartularies*, Pt. II, ms. 5. Margaret, countess of Norfolk (c. 1320–99), daughter of Thomas Plantagenet and Alice de Hales, was the only woman to have ever served as Lord Marshall. She appears to have been a strong-willed woman who was accustomed to getting her way. Fryde describes her as a 'mean, harsh and grasping' landowner. See Fryde (1995), pp. 26, 42, 248–9.

[35]   Ibid.

[36]   Ibid.

Bibliography

List of Abbreviations for Publishers

BA	British Academy
BAS	Buckinghamshire Archaeological Society
BIHR	Borthwick Institute of Historical Research
BHRS	Bedfordshire Historical Record Society
BuRS	Buckinghamshire Record Society
CaS	Camden Society
CS	Chetham Society
DAS	Derbyshire Archaeological Society
HMSO	Her Majesty's Stationery Office
LUP	Leicester University Press
NLW	National Library of Wales
MUP	Manchester University Press
NRS	Norfolk Record Society
NSRS	Northamptonshire Record Society
OHS	Oxford Historical Society
OUP	Oxford University Press
PIMS	Pontifical Institute of Mediaeval Studies
PRS	Pipe Roll Society
RHS	Royal Historical Society
SomRS	Somerset Record Society
SoRS	Southampton Records Society
SRS	Suffolk Records Society
SuRS	Surrey Record Society
SusRS	Sussex Record Society
SS	Surtees Society
SUP	Southampton University Press
ThS	Thoresby Society
TS	Thoroton Society
WRS	Wiltshire Record Society
YAS	Yorkshire Archaeological Society

Primary Sources

NB: 1. Numbers next to the publishers' abbreviations indicate the volume or number in the series;
2. Where a title begins with 'A', 'An', or 'The', the work is listed alphabetically according to the first noun in the title.

Pre-Conquest – General Charters

Anglo-Saxon Charters, P.H. Sawyer (ed.), RHS, London, 1968.
Anglo-Saxon Charters, c. 450 - 1100, A.J. Robertson (ed. and trans.), W.W. Gaunt, Holmes Beach (FL), 1986.
Cartularium Saxonicum: A Collection of Charters Relating to Anglo-Saxon History, Vols. I–IV, W. de Gray Birch (ed.), Johnson Reprints, New York, 1965 (1st pub. 1885–99).
Facsimiles of Anglo-Saxon Charters, Simon Keynes (ed.), Oxford University Press, Oxford, c.1991.

Pre-Conquest – Regional and Manorial Charters

Early Yorkshire Charters: Being a Collection of Documents Anterior to the Thirteenth Century Made from the Public Records, Monastic Chartularies, Roger Dodsworth's Manuscripts and Other Available Sources, Vols. I–III, William Farrer (ed.), Ballantyne, Hanson and Co., Edinburgh, 1914–16.

Early Yorkshire Charters: Based on the Manuscripts of the Late William Farrer, Vols. IV–XII, Charles Travis Clay (ed.), YAS, Leeds, 1935–65.

Post-Conquest – Regional and Manorial Charters

An Edition of the Cartulary of Burscough Priory, A.N. Webb (ed.), CS, Manchester, 1970.

The Beaulieu Cartulary, P.D.A. Harvey and S.F. Hockey (eds.), SUP, Southampton, 1974.

Blythburgh Priory Cartulary, Parts I and II, C. Harper-Bill (ed.), SRS, Trowbridge and Earls Barton, 1980 and 1981.

Cartulary of Bradenstoke Priory, Vera C.M London (ed.), WRS 35, Devizes, 1979.

The Cartulary of Cirencester Abbey, Gloucestershire, Vols. I and II, C.D. Ross (ed.), OUP, London, 1964.

The Cartulary of Cirencester Abbey, Gloucestershire, Vol. III, Mary Devine (ed.), OUP, London, 1977.

The Cartulary of the Cistercian Abbey of Old Wardon, Bedfordshire, G.H. Fowler (ed.), BHRS/MUP, Manchester, 1931.

The Cartulary of Daventry Priory, M.J. Franklin (ed.), NSRS 35, Northampton, 1988.

Cartulary of God's House, Southampton, Vols. I and II, J.M. Kaye (ed.), SUP, Southampton, 1976.

The Cartulary of Missenden Abbey, Parts I and II, J.G. Jenkins (ed.), BAS 2 and 10, London and Jordans, 1938 and 1955.

The Cartulary of Missenden Abbey, Part III, J.G. Jenkins (ed.), HMSO/BuRS 1, London, 1962.

The Cartulary of the Priory of St. Denys near Southampton, Vols. I and II, E.O. Blake (ed.), SUP/SoRS 24 and 25, Southampton, 1981.

Cartulary of the Priory of St. Gregory, Canterbury, Audrey M. Woodcock (ed.), RHS/CaS 88, London, 1956.

The Cartulary of the Treasurer of York Minster and Related Documents, Janet E. Burton (ed.), BIHR, York, 1978.

The Cartulary of the Wakebridge Chantries at Crich, Avrom Saltman (ed.), DAS, Ripley, 1976.

The Cartulary of Worcester Cathedral Priory, R.R. Darlington (ed.), PRS 76/38, London, 1968.

Charters and Custumals of the Abbey of Holy Trinity Caen, M. Chibnall (ed.), BA/OUP, London, 1982.

The Chartulary of Cockersand Abbey of the Premonstratensian Order, Vol. I, Pts. I and II, Vol. II, Pts. I and II , William Farrer (ed.), CS 38, 39, 40, Manchester, 1898.

The Chartulary of the High Church of Chichester, W.D. Peckham (ed.), SusRS 46, Lewes, 1942–43.

The Coucher Book of the Cistercian Abbey of Kirkstall in the West Riding of the County of York, W.T. Lancaster and W. Paley Baildon (eds.), ThS 8, Leeds, 1904.

The Coucher Book of Furness Abbey, (Vol. I), Pts. I–III, J.C. Atkinson (ed.), CS 9, 11 and 14, Manchester, 1886 and 1887.

The Coucher Book of Furness Abbey, Vol. II, Pts. I–III, John Brownbill (ed.), CS 74, 76 and 78, Manchester, 1915, 1916 and 1919.

'The Customs of Four Manors of the Abbey of Lacock', W.G. Clark-Maxwell, *Wiltshire Archaeological and Natural History Magazine* 32, no. 98 (December 1902), pp. 311–46.

Lacock Abbey Charters, Kenneth H. Rogers (ed.), WRS 34, Devizes, 1979.

Leiston Abbey Cartulary and Butley Priory Charters, Richard Mortimer (ed.), SRS, Ipswich, 1979.

The Lost Cartulary of Bolton Priory, Katrina Legg (ed.), YAS/Boydell Press, Woodbridge, 2009.

Materials for the history of the Church of Lancaster, Vols. I and II, William Oliver Roper (ed.), CS 26 and 31, Manchester, 1892 and 1894.

Reading Abbey Cartularies, Berkshire, Vols. I and II, B.R. Kemp (ed.), RHS/CaS 4/31 and 4/33, London, 1986 and 1987.

Sibton Abbey Cartularies and Charters, Pts. I–IV, Philippa Brown (ed.), SRS/Boydell and Brewer, Woodbridge, 1985, 1986, 1987, 1988.

Two Cartularies of Abingdon Abbey, Vols. I and II, C.F. Slade and Gabrielle Lambrick (eds.), OHS 32 and 33, Oxford, 1990 and 1992.

Post-Conquest – Account Books, Custumals, Registers, Rentals, Surveys, Terriers

The Account-Book of Beaulieu Abbey, S.F. Hockey (ed.), CaS 4/16, London, 1975.
Account Rolls of the Obedientiaries of Peterborough, Joan Greatrex (ed.), NSRS 33, Northampton, 1984.
Accounts of the Cellarers of Battle Abbey, Eleanor Searle and Barbara Ross (eds.), Sydney University Press, Sydney, 1967.
Accounts of the Obedientiars of Abingdon Abbey, R.E.G. Kirk (ed.), CaS, 1892.
Bishop Hatfield's Survey (1377–80): A Record of the Possessions of the See of Durham, made by Order of Thomas de Hatfield, Bishop of Durham, William Greenwell (ed.), SS 32, Durham, 1857.
Boldon Buke, A Survey of the Possessions of the See of Durham made by Order of Bishop Hugh Pudsey in the Year 1183, William Greenwell (ed.), SS 25, Durham, 1852.
The Bolton Priory Compotus, 1286–1325: Together with a Priory Account Roll for 1377–1378, Ian Kershaw and David M. Smith (eds.), YAS/Boydell Press, Woodbridge, 2000.
Bolton Priory Rentals and Ministers' Accounts, 1473–1539, Ian Kershaw (ed.), YAS Record Series, Woodbridge, 1970.
'Computus Rolls of the English Lands of the Abbey of Bec (1272–1289)', Marjorie Chibnall (ed.), in *Camden Miscellany Vol. XXIV*, RHS/CaS 4/34, London, 1987.
Custumals of Battle Abbey in the Reign of Edward I and Edward II (1283–1312), S.R. Scargill-Bird (ed.), CaS 41, Westminster, 1887.
Custumals of the Sussex Manors of the Archbishop of Canterbury, B.C. Redwood and A.E. Wilson (eds.), SusRS 57, Lewes, 1958.
The Liber Gersumarum *of Ramsey Abbey*, Edwin Brezette Dewindt (ed.), PIMS, Toronto, 1976.
The Sibton Abbey Estates: Select Documents 1325–1509, A.H. Denney (ed.), SRS 11, Ipswich, 1960.
Surveys of the Estates of Glastonbury Abbey, c. 1135–1201, N.E. Stacy (ed.), British Academy and Oxford University Press, Oxford, 2001.
'Three Records of the Alien Priory of Grove and the Manor of Leighton Buzzard', Robert Richmond (ed.), in *The Publications of the Bedfordshire Historical Record Society Vol. VIII*, Aspley Guise, 1924.
'A Transcript of "The Red Book," a Detailed Account of the Hereford Bishopric Estates in the Thirteenth Century', A.T. Bannister (ed.), in *Camden Miscellany Vol. XV*, CaS 3/41, London, 1929.

Post-Conquest – Chronicles

The Chronicle of Battle Abbey, Eleanor Searle (ed. and trans.), Clarendon Press, Oxford, 1980.
The Chronicle of Jocelin of Brakelond, Concerning the Acts of Samson, Abbot of the Monastery of St. Edmund, H.E. Butler (ed. and trans.), Thomas Nelson and Sons, London, 1949.
'The Hexham Chronicle', in J. Raine (ed.), *Priory of Hexham*, SS 44, Durham, 1864.

Post-Conquest – Court Rolls, Year Books and Legal Treatises

Civil Pleas of the Wiltshire Eyre, 1249, M.T. Clanchy (ed.), WRS 26, Devizes, 1971.
Henrici de Bracton de Legibus et Consuetudinibus Angliae, Vols. 1–5, Sir Travers Twiss (ed.), William S. Hein and Co., Buffalo (NY), 1990 (1st pub. 1880).
Leges Henrici Primi, L.J. Downer (ed.), Oxford University Press, Oxford, 1972.
Liber Albus: The White Book of the City of London, Compiled A.D. 1419, By John Carpenter & Richard Whitington, Mayor, trans. by Henry Thomas Riley, Ulan Press, 2012.
'Roll of the Justices in Eyre at Bedford, 1227', in G. Herbert Fowler (ed.), *The Publications of the Bedfordshire Historical Record Society Vol. III*, Aspley Guise, 1916.
Year Books of Edward II, iii, 3 Edward II, A.D. 1309–10, F.W. Maitland (ed.), Selden Society, London, 1905.

Post-Conquest – Taxation Records

Domesday Book, John Morris (gen. ed.), 35 vols., Phillimore, Chichester, 1973–1992 (1st pub. Winchester, 1086).

Taxatio Ecclesiastica Angliae et Walliae Auctoritate Patris P. Nicolai IV, Circa A.D. 1291, Printed by Command of His Majesty King George III in Persuance of an Address to the House of Commons of Great Britain, John Caley and S. Ayscough (eds.), Eyre, 1802.

Valor ecclesiasticus temp. Henr. VIII. Auctoritate regia institutes, Vol. I–VI, Printed by Command of His Majesty King George III in Persuance of an Address to the House of Commons of Great Britain, John Caley (ed.), Eyre and Strahan, 1810–1825 (Vols. I–V), Eyre and Spottiswoode, 1833 (Vol. VI).

Secondary Sources

Abrams, Lesley. 1996. *Anglo-Saxon Glastonbury: Church and Endowment*, Boydell Press, Woodbridge.

Abrams, Lesley, and Carley, James P. 1991. *The Archaeology and History of Glastonbury Abbey: Essays in Honour of the Ninetieth Birthday of C.A. Ralegh Radford*, Boydell Press, Woodbridge.

Abrams, Philip. 1978. 'Towns and Economic Growth: Some Theories and Problems', in Abrams and Wrigley, pp. 9–34.

Abrams, Philip, and Wrigley, E.A. (eds.). 1978. *Towns in Societies: Essays in Economic History and Historical Sociology*, Cambridge University Press, Cambridge.

Adams, William Henry Davenport. 1856. *The History, Topography, and Antiquities of the Isle of Wight*, Smith, Elder and Co., London.

Adas, Michael. 1990. *Machines as the Measure of Men: Science, Technology, and Ideologies of Western Dominance*, Cornell University Press, Ithaca, NY.

Ambler, John. 1994. 'Mill Values at Domesday', *Past and Present*, no. 145 (November), pp. 43–6 [this article forms an appendix to Langdon (1994)].

Arvanigian, Mark. 2009. 'A County Community or the Politics of the Nation? Border Service and Baronial Influence in the Palatinate of Durham, 1377–1413', *Historical Research* 82, no. 215, pp. 41–61.

Astill, Grenville. 1989. 'Monastic Research Designs: Bordesley and the Avon Valley', in Gilchrist and Mytum, pp. 277–94.

———. 1993. *A Medieval Industrial Complex and its Landscape: The Metalworking Watermills and Workshops of Bordesley Abbey, Bordesley Abby III*. Council for British Archaeology, York.

———. 1997. 'An Archaeological Approach to the Development of Agricultural Technologies in Medieval England', in Astill and Langdon, pp. 193–224.

Astill, Grenville, and Langdon, John (eds.). 1997. *Medieval Farming and Technology: The Impact of Agricultural Change in Northwest Europe*, Brill, Leiden.

Aston, Mick. 2000. *Monasteries in the Landscape*, Casemate, London.

Aston, T.H., Coss, P.R., Dyer, Christopher, and Thirsk, Joan (eds.). 1983. *Social Relations and Ideas: Essays in Honour of R.H. Hilton*, Cambridge University Press, Cambridge.

Aston, T.H., and Philpin, C.H.E. (eds.). 1987. *The Brenner Debate: Agrarian Class Structure and Economic Development in Pre-Industrial Europe*, Cambridge University Press, Cambridge.

Barceló, Miquel. 2004. 'The Missing Water-Mill: A Question of Technological Diffusion in the High Middle Ages', in Barceló and Sigaut, pp. 255–314.

Barceló, Miquel, and Sigaut, François (eds.). 2004. *The Making of Feudal Agricultures?*, Brill, Leiden.

Barrington, Daines. 1774. *Observations upon the statutes: Chiefly the more Ancient, from Magna Charta*, Bowyer and Nichols, London (4th edition).

Basalla, George. 1998. *The Evolution of Technology*, Cambridge University Press, Cambridge.

Bautier, Anne-Marie. 1960. 'Les Plus Anciennes Mentions de Moulins Hydrauliques Industriels et de Moulins à Vent', *Bulletin Philologique et Historique* 2, pp. 567–626.

Beamish, C.J.M. 1983. 'The Fulling Mill – One of the Oldest Mechanised Industries in Britain', *Industrial Archaeology* 18, pp. 78–82.

Bean, J.M.W. 1991. 'Chapter Six: Landlords', in Miller, pp. 526–586.

Beckwith, Ian S. 1971. 'Londonthorpe Mill', *Industrial Archaeology* 8, no. 1, pp. 25–8.

Bedwin, Owen. 1976. 'The Excavation of Ardingley Fulling Mill and Forge 1975–76', *Post-Medieval Archaeology* 10, pp. 34–64.

———. 1980. 'The Excavation of Batsford Mill, Warbleton, East Sussex, 1978', *Medieval Archaeology* 24, pp. 187–201.

Bell, Adrian H., Brooks, Chris, and Dryburgh, Paul R. 2007. *The English Wool Market, c. 1230–1327*, Cambridge University Press, Cambridge.

Bellairs, George C. 1905. 'Wooden Cross Found under a Mound at Higham-On-the-Hill, Leicestershire', *Transactions of the Leicestershire Architectural and Archaeological Society* 9, pp. 18–19.

Bennett, H.S. 1937. *Life on the English Manor: A Study of Peasant Condition, 1150–1400*, Cambridge University Press, Cambridge.

Bennett, J., Jones, J.H.T., and Vyner, B.E. 1980. 'A Medieval and Later Water Mill at Norton-on-Tees, Cleveland', *Industrial Archaeology Review* 4, no. 2 (Spring), pp. 171–6.

Bennett, P., Riddler, I. and Sparey-Green, C. (eds.). 2010. *The Roman Watermills and Settlement at Ickham, Kent*, Archaeology of Canterbury Monograph Series 5, Canterbury Archaeological Trust Ltd, Canterbury.

Bennett, Richard, and Elton, John. 1898. *History of Corn Milling, Vol. I: Handstones, Slave and Cattle Mills*, Burt Franklin, New York.

———. 1899. *History of Corn Milling, Vol. II: Watermills and Windmills*, Burt Franklin, New York.

———. 1900. *History of Corn Milling, Vol. III: Feudal Laws and Customs*, Burt Franklin, New York.

———. 1904. *History of Corn Milling, Vol. IV: Some Feudal Mills*, Burt Franklin, New York.

Benoit, Paul, and Rouillard, Joséphine. 2000. 'Medieval Hydraulics in France,' in Squatriti, pp. 161–216.

Biddick, Kathleen. 1985. 'Medieval English Peasants and Market Involvement', *Journal of Economic History* 45, no. 4, pp. 823–31.

Biddle, M., Lambrick, T.H., and Myres, J.N.L. 1967. 'The Early History of Abingdon, Berkshire and its Abbey', *Medieval Archaeology* 11, pp. 26–69.

Birch, William de Gray (ed.). 1965. *Cartularium Saxonicum: A Collection of Charters Relating to Anglo-Saxon History, Vols. I–IV*, Johnson Reprints, New York (1st pub. 1885–99).

Bishop, T.A.M. 1936. 'Assarting and the Growth of Open Fields', *Economic History Review* 6, pp. 13–29.

Blair, John. 1988. 'Introduction: From Minsters to Parish Churches', in J. Blair (ed.), *Minsters and Parish Churches: The Local Church in Transition, 950–1200*, Oxford University Committee for Archaeology Monograph 17, Oxford University Press, Oxford, pp. 1–19.

———. 2007a. 'Transport and Canal-Building on the Upper Thames, 1000–1300', in Blair (2007b), pp. 254–94.

———, (ed.) 2007b. *Waterways and Canal-Building in Medieval England*, Oxford University Press, Oxford.

Blaine, Bradford. 1966. *The Application of Water Power to Industry During the Middle Ages*, Phd. diss., University of California, Los Angeles.

Blanchard, I.S.W. 1973. 'Seigneurial Entrepreneurship: The Bishops of Durham and the Weardale Lead Industry 1406–1529', *Business History* 15, no. 2, pp. 97–111.

Bloch, Marc 1935. 'Avènement et Conquêtes du Moulin à Eau', *Annales Économique, Sociale et Culturelle* 7, pp. 538–63.

———. 1961. *Feudal Society*, 2 vols., University of Chicago Press, Chicago.

———. 1967. *Land and Work in Medieval Europe*, trans. J.E. Anderson, Routledge and Kegan Paul, London.

Bois, Guy. 2002. *The Transformation of the Year One Thousand: The Village of Lournand from Antiquity to Feudalism*, trans. Jean Birrell, Manchester University Press, Manchester (1st English pub. 1992, 1st French pub. 1989).

Bond, C.J. 1989. 'Water Management in the Rural Monastery', in Gilchrist and Mytum, pp. 83–111.

———. 2000. 'Landscapes of Monasticism', in Hooke, pp. 63–74.

Bond, James. 2007. 'Canal Construction: An Introductory Review', in Blair (2007b), pp. 153–206.

Boucher, C.T.G. 1987–88. 'The Restoration of Two Water Mills in Greater Manchester', *Manchester Memoirs* 127, pp. 18–28.

Brenner, Robert. 1976. 'Agrarian Class Structure and Economic Development in Pre-industrial Europe', *Past and Present*, no. 70, pp. 30–75.

Bridbury, A.R. 1977. 'Before the Black Death', *Economic History Review* 30, pp. 393–410.
———. 1978. 'The Farming Out of Manors', *Economic History Review* 31, pp. 503–20.
Britnell, R.H. 1981. 'The Proliferation of Markets in England, 1200–1349', *Economic History Review* 34, pp. 209–21.
———. 1990. 'Feudal Reaction after the Black Death in the Palatinate of Durham', *Past and Present*, no. 128, pp. 28–47.
———. 1996. *The Commercialisation of English Society, 1000–1500*, Cambridge University Press, Cambridge (1st pub. 1993).
British Library. 1980. *The Benedictines in Britain*, British Library, London.
Brooke, Christopher. 1975. *Europe in the Central Middle Ages 962–115*, Longman, London (rev. ed., 1st pub. 1964).
Brooks, Nicholas. 1984. *The Early History of the Church of Canterbury: Christ Church from 597–1066*, Leicester University Press, Leicester.
Buchsenschutz, O., Jacottey, L., Jodry, F., and Blanchard, J-L. 2011. Évolution typologique et technique des meules et technique des meules du Néolithique à l'an mille, Actes des IIIe Rencontres Archéologiques de l'Archéosite gaulois, Aquitania Supplément 23, Bordeaux.
Burton, Janet. 1994. *Monastic and Religious Orders in Britain 1000–1300*, Cambridge University Press, Cambridge.
———. 1999. *The Monastic Order in Yorkshire, 1069–1215*, Cambridge University Press, Cambridge.
Butler, L.A.S. 1988. 'Rural Building in England and Wales: Wales', in Hallam (1988b), pp. 933–65.
Butler, Rodney F. 1945. *The History of Kirkstall Forge: 1200–1945 AD*, Henry Jenkinson, Kirkstall.
Campbell, Bruce M.S. 2000. *English Seigniorial Agriculture, 1250–1450*, Cambridge University Press, Cambridge.
Campbell, Bruce M.S., Galloway, James A., and Murphy, Margaret. 1992. 'Rural Land-use in the Metropolitan Hinterland, 1270–1339: The Evidence of *Inquisitiones Post Mortem*', *Agricultural History Review* 40, no. 1, pp. 1–22.
Campbell, Bruce M.S., Galloway, James A., Keene, Derek, and Murphy, Margaret. 1993. *A Medieval Capital and Its Grain Supply: Agrarian Production and Distribution in the London Region c. 1300*, Historical Geography Research Series, 30, Institute of British Geographers, Cheltenham.
Carley, James P. 1985. *The Chronicle of Glastonbury Abbey: An Edition, Translation and Study of John of Glastonbury's* Cronica sive Antiquitates Glastoniensis Ecclesie, trans. David Townsend, Boydell Press, Woodbridge.
Carus-Wilson, Eleanora Mary. 1941. 'An Industrial Revolution of the Thirteenth Century', *Economic History Review* 11, pp. 39–60.
———. 1957. 'The Significance of the Sculptures in the Lane Chapel', *Medieval Archaeology* 1, pp. 107–17.
———. 1959. 'Evidences of Industrial Growth on Some Fifteenth-Century Manors', *Economic History Review* 12, no. 2, pp. 190–205.
Chibnall, Marjorie. 1986. *Anglo-Norman England, 1066–1166*, Basil Blackwell, Oxford.
———. 1987. 'Introduction', in 'Computus Rolls of the English Lands of the Abbey of Bec (1272–1289)', pp. 5–16.
Cipolla, C.M. (ed.). 1976. *The Fontana Economic History of Europe, Vol. I: The Middle Ages*, Harvester Press/Barnes and Noble, Hassocks (1st pub. 1972).
Clemoes, Peter (ed.). 1977. *Anglo-Saxon England*, Vol. 6, Cambridge University Press, Cambridge.
Coates, S.D., and Tucker, D.G. 1978. *Water-Mills of the Monnow and Trothy and Their Tributaries*, Monmouth.
Collinson, Patrick, Ramsay, Nigel, and Sparks, Margaret (eds.). 1995. *A History of Canterbury Cathedral*, Oxford University Press, Oxford.
Colvin, H.M. 1951. *The White Canons in England*, Clarendon Press, Oxford.
Colvin, H.M. (ed.). 1963. *The History of the King's Works, Vols. I and II: The Middle Ages*, HMSO, London.
Constable, Giles. 1964. *Monastic Tithes: From Their Origins to the Twelfth Century*, Cambridge University Press, Cambridge.
Cook, G.H. 1961. *English Monasteries in the Middle Ages*, Phoenix House, London.
Cooper, Alan. 2006. *Bridges, Law and Power in Medieval England, 700–1400*, Boydell Press, Woodbridge.
Costen, Michael D. 1991. '"Some Evidence for New Settlements and Field Systems in Late Anglo-Saxon Somerset', in Abrams and Carley, pp. 39–56.

Cownie, Emma. 1998. *Religious Patronage in Anglo-Norman England 1066–1135*, Royal Historical Society/Boydell Press, Woodbridge.

Croot, Patricia, and Parker, David. 1978. 'Agrarian Class Structure and Economic Development', *Past and Present*, no. 78, pp. 37–47.

Crosby, Everett U. 1994. *Bishop and Chapter in Twelfth-Century England: A Study of the Mensa Episcopalis*, Cambridge University Press, Cambridge.

Crossley, D.W. (ed.). 1981. *Medieval Industry*, Council for British Archaeology Research Report 40, London.

Courtney, Paul. 1981. 'The Monastic Granges of Leicestershire', available for download at: https://www.le.ac.uk/lahs/downloads/grangesPagesfromvolumeLVI-5.pdf

Darby, H.C. 1952. *The Domesday Geography of Eastern England*, Cambridge University Press, Cambridge.

———. 1977. *Domesday England*, Cambridge University Press, Cambridge.

Darby, H.C., and Terrett, I.B. (eds.). 1954. *The Domesday Geography of Midland England*, Cambridge University Press, Cambridge.

Darby, H.C., and Welldon Finn, R. (eds.). 2009. *The Domesday Geography of South-West England*, Cambridge University Press, Cambridge (1st pub. 1967).

Daumas, Maurice (ed.). 1969. *A History of Technology and Invention: Progress Through the Ages*, vol. I: *The Origins of Technological Civilization*, trans. Eileen B. Hennessy, Crown Publishers, New York.

Davis, G.R.C. 1958. *Medieval Cartularies of Great Britain: A Short Catalogue*, Longman Green, London.

Day, John. 1987. *The Medieval Market Economy*, Basil Blackwell, London.

Dickinson, John Compton. 1950. 'Early Suppressions of English Houses of Austin Canons', in V. Ruffer and A.J. Taylor (eds.), *Medieval Studies Presented to Rose Graham*, Oxford University Press, Oxford.

———. 1961. *Monastic Life in Medieval England*, Adam and Charles Black, London.

Dobb, Maurice. 1946. *Studies in the Development of Capitalism*, Routledge and Kegan Paul, London.

Dockès, Pierre. 1982. *Medieval Slavery and Liberation*, trans. Arthur Goldhammer, Methuen, London.

Dodds, Ben, and Britnell, Richard (eds.). 2008. *Agriculture and Rural Society after the Black Death: Common Themes and Regional Variations*, University of Hertfordshire Press, Hatfield.

Donkin, R.A. 1978. *The Cistercians: Studies in the Geography of Medieval England and Wales*, Pontifical Institute of Medieval Studies, Toronto.

Douglas, David C. 1939. 'The Norman Conquest and Feudalism', *Economic History Review* 9, no. 2, pp. 128–43.

Du Boulay, F.R.H. 1966. *The Lordship of Canterbury: An Essay on Medieval Society*, Nelson, London.

Duby, Georges. 1968. *Rural Economy and Country Life in the Medieval West*, Arnold, London (1st pub. Paris, 1962).

Du Cange, Charles. 1954. *Glossarium Mediae et Infimae Latinitatis, Vols. I–IV*, Akademische Druck and Universitat Verlagsanstalt, Graz (1st pub. 1883–87).

Dugdale, William. 1846. *Monasticon Anglicanum: a history of the abbies and other monasteries, hospitals, frieries, and cathedral and collegiate churches, with their dependencies, in England and Wales: also of all such Scotch, Irish, and French monasteries, as were in any manner connected with religious houses in England*, 4 vols., J. Bohn, London.

Dyer, Christopher C. 1980. *Lords and Peasants in a Changing Society: The Estates of the Bishopric of Worcester, 680–1540*, Cambridge University Press, Cambridge.

———. 1989a. *Standards of Living in the Later Middle Ages*, Cambridge University Press, Cambridge.

———. 1989b. 'The Consumer and the Market in the Later Middle Ages', *Economic History Review* 42, no. 3, pp. 305–27.

———. 2002. *Making a Living in the Middle Ages: The People of Britain, 850–1520*, Yale University Press, New Haven and London.

Epstein, S.R. 2007. 'Rodney Hilton, Marxism and the Transition from Feudalism to Capitalism', *Past and Present*, no. 195, Supplement 2, pp. 248–69.

Faith, Rosamond. 1999 (1st pub. 1997). *The English Peasantry and the Growth of Lordship*, Leicester University Press, London.

Feyerabend, Paul. 1978. *Science in a Free Society*, New Left Books, London.

Finberg, H.P.R. 1951. *Tavistock Abbey: A Study in the Social and Economic History of Devon*, Cambridge University Press, Cambridge.

Finberg, H.P.R. (ed.). 1957. *Gloucestershire Studies*, Leicester University Press, Leicester.

Fleming, Robin. 2004. *Kings and Lords in Conquest England*, Cambridge University Press, Cambridge (1st pub. 1991)

Flete, John. 1909. *The History of Westminster Abbey by John Flete*, ed. J. Armitage, Cambridge University Press, Cambridge.

Foucault, Michel. 1970. *The Order of Things: An Archaeology of the Human Sciences*, Tavistock, London (1st pub. 1966).

Forbes, Robert J. 'Power', in Singer, Hall and Williams, pp. 589–622.

Fraser, C.M. 1958. *A History of Antony Bek, Bishop of Durham, 1283–1311*, Oxford University Press, Oxford.

Fryde, E.B. 1995. *Peasants and Landlords in Later Medieval England, c.1380–c.1525*, St Martin's Press, New York.

Fryde, E.B., and Fryde, Natalie. 1991. 'Chapter Eight: Peasant Rebellion and Peasant Discontents', in Miller, pp. 744–819.

Fuller, E.A. 1885. 'Cirencester – Its Manor and Town', *Transactions of the Bristol and Gloucestershire Archaeological Society* 9, pp. 298–344.

Fuller, Steve. 2000. *The Governance of Science: Ideology and the Future of the Open Society*, Open University Press, Buckingham.

Fumagilli, Vito. 1976. *Terra e società nell'Italia padana. I secoli IX e X*, Einaudi, Turin.

Gelling, Margaret (ed.). 1979. *The Early Charters of the Thames Valley*, Leicester University Press, Leicester.

Gilchrist, Roberta, and Mytum, Harold (eds.). 1989. *The Archaeology of Rural Monasteries*, B.A.R. British Series 203, Oxford.

Gille, Bertrand. 1969a. 'Toward a Technological Evolution', in Daumas, pp. 425–30.

———. 1969b. 'The Problems of Power and Mechanization', in Daumas, pp. 44–59.

———. 1986. *The History of Techniques, Vols. I and II*, trans. P. Southgate and T. Williamson with A. Keller, Gordon and Breach, New York (1st pub. 1978).

Gimpel, Jean. 1988. *The Medieval Machine: The Industrial Revolution of the Middle Ages*, Wildwood House, London, 2nd. edn., 1st pub. 1976.

Glick, Thomas F., and Kirchner, Helena. 2000. 'Hydraulic Systems and Technologies of Islamic Spain: History and Archaeology,' in Squatriti, pp. 267–330.

Goddard, Richard. 2007. 'Church Lords and English Urban Investment in the Later Middle Ages', *Past and Present*, no. 195, Supplement 2, pp. 148–65.

Goody, Jack. 1983. *The Development of the Family and Marriage in Europe*, Cambridge University Press, Cambridge.

Graham, Alan H. 1986. 'The Old Malthouse, Abbotsbury, Dorset: The Medieval Watermill of the Benedictine Abbey', *Dorset Natural History and Archaeological Society* 108, pp. 103–25.

Greenhow, Desna. 1979. 'More Water by the Mill: The Restoration, Machinery and History of Otterton Mill, Devon', *Industrial Archaeology* 14, no. 4 (Winter), pp. 309–25.

Haddan, Arthur West, and Stubbs, William (eds.). 1871. *Councils and Ecclesiastical Documents relating to Great Britain and Ireland*, Vol. III, Oxford at the Clarendon Press, Oxford.

Hale, William (ed.). 1865. *Registrum Sive Liber Irrotularius et Consuetudinarius Prioratus Beatae Mariae Wigorniensis*, Camden Society Publications, Vol. 91, Westminster.

Hall, Bert S. 1989. 'Lynn Townsend White, Jr. (1907–1987)', *Technology and Culture* 30, no. 1 (January), pp. 194–213.

Hall, Bert S., and West, Delno C. (eds.). 1976. *On Pre-Modern Technology and Science: A Volume of Studies in Honor of Lynn White Jr.*, Undena, Malibu (CA).

Hallam, Elizabeth M. 1986. *Domesday Book Through Nine Centuries*, Thames and Hudson, London.

Hallam, H.E. 1965. *Settlement and Society: A Study of the Early Agrarian History of South Lincolnshire*, Cambridge University Press, London.

———. 1988a. 'Social Structure: Eastern England' and 'South Eastern England', in Hallam (1988b), pp. 594–634.

———, (ed.). 1988b. *The Agrarian History of England and Wales, Vol. II: 1042–1350*, Cambridge University Press, Cambridge.

Hardy, Alan, Watts, Martin, and Goodburn, Damian. 2011. 'The Mid-Saxon Mill at Northfleet', in Phil Andrews, et al. (eds.), *Settling the Ebbsfleet Valley*, Wessex Archaeology, Salisbury, pp. 307–29.

Hart, C.R. (ed.). 1975. *The Early Charters of Northern England and the North Midlands*, Leicester University Press, Leicester.

Harvey, Barbara F. 1966. 'The Population Trend in England between 1300 and 1348', *Transactions of the Royal Historical Society* 16, 5th series, pp. 23–42.

———. 1977. *Westminster Abbey and Its Estates in the Middle Ages*, Oxford at the Clarendon Press.

Harvey, Sally. 1970. 'The Knight and the Knight's Fee in England', *Past and Present*, no. 49, pp. 3–43.

———. 1988. 'Domesday England', in Hallam, pp. 45–165.

Hatcher, John. 1977. *Plague, Population and the English Economy 1348–1530*, Macmillan, London.

Hatcher, John, and Bailey, Mark. 2001. *Modelling the Middle Ages: The History and Theory of England's Economic Development*, Oxford University Press, Oxford.

Herlihy, David. 1990. *Opera Muliebria: Women and Work in Medieval Europe*, Temple University Press, Philadelphia.

Hibbert, A.B. 1953. 'The Origins of the Medieval Town Patriciate', *Past and Present*, no. 3, pp. 15–26.

———. 1978. 'The Origins of the Medieval Town Patriciate', in Abrams, Philip, and Wrigley, E.A. (eds.), *Towns in Societies: Essays in Economic History and Historical Sociology*, Cambridge University Press, Cambridge, pp. 9–34.

Hill, David. 1981. *An Atlas of Anglo-Saxon England*, University of Toronto Press, Toronto.

Hill, Geoffry. 1900. *English Dioceses: A History of the Their Limits from the Earliest Times to the Present Day*, Elliot Stock, London.

Hilton, R.H. 1965. 'Freedom and Villeinage in England', *Past and Present*, no. 31 (July), pp. 3–19.

———. 1984. 'Small Town Society in England before the Black Death', *Past and Present*, no. 105, pp. 53–78.

———. 1985. 'Medieval Market Towns and Simple Commodity Production', *Past and Present*, no. 109 (November), pp. 3–23.

———. 1992. *English and French Towns in Feudal Society*, Cambridge University Press, Cambridge.

Hilton, R.H. (ed.). 1976. *The Transition from Feudalism to Capitalism*, New Left Books, London.

Hilton, R.H., and Sawyer, P.H. 1963. 'Technical Determinism: The Stirrup and the Plough', *Past and Present*, no. 24, pp. 90–100.

Hockey, S.F. 1970. *Quarr Abbey and Its Lands 1132–1631*, Leicester University Press, Leicester.

———. 1976. *Beaulieu, King John's Abbey: A History of Beaulieu Abbey Hampshire 1204–1538*, Pioneer Publications, London.

Hockey, S.F. (ed.). 1975. *The Account-Book of Beaulieu Abbey*, RHS, London.

Hodgen, Margaret T. 1939. 'Domesday Water Mills', *Antiquity* 13, no. 51 (September), pp. 261–77.

Holdsworth, Sir William. 1973. *A History of English Law, Vol. III*, Methuen, Sweet and Maxwell, London (1st pub. 1908, rev. 1923).

———. 1976. *A History of English Law, Vol. II*, Methuen, Sweet and Maxwell, London (1st pub. 1908, rev. 1923).

Hollinrake, Charles, and Hollinrake, Nancy. 2007. 'Glastonbury's Anglo-Saxon Canal and Dunstan's Dyke', in Blair (2007b), pp. 235–43.

Hollister, C. Warren. 1962. 'The Knights of Peterborough and the Anglo-Norman Fyrd', *English Historical Review* 77, no. 304, pp. 417–36.

Holt, Richard. 1987. 'Whose Were the Profits of Corn Milling? An Aspect of the Changing Relationship between the Abbots of Glastonbury and Their Tenants 1086–1350', *Past and Present*, no. 116, pp. 3–23.

———. 1988. *The Mills of Medieval England*, Basil Blackwell, Oxford.

———. 1989. 'The Medieval Mill – a Productivity Breakthrough?', *History Today* 39, no. 7, pp. 26–31.

———. 1990. 'Milling Technology in the Middle Ages: The Direction of Recent Research', *Industrial Archaeology Review* 13, no. 1, pp. 50–58.

———. 1996. 'Medieval Technology and the Historians: The Evidence for the Mill', in Robert Fox (ed.), *Technological Change: Methods and Themes in the History of Technology*, Routledge, Abingdon, pp. 103–22.

———. 1997. 'Mechanization and the Medieval English Economy', in Smith and Wolfe, pp. 139–57.

———. 2000. 'Medieval England's Water-Related Technologies', in Squatriti, pp. 51–100.

Holton, Robert J. 1981. 'Marxist Theories of Social Change and the Transition from Feudalism to Dapitalism', *Theory and Society* 10, no. 6, pp. 833–67.

Homans, George Caspar. 1953. 'The Rural Sociology of Medieval England', *Past and Present*, no. 4, pp. 32–42.

———. 1969. 'The Explanation of English Regional Differences', *Past and Present*, no. 42, pp. 18–34.

Hooke, Della. 2007. 'Uses of Waterways in Anglo-Saxon England', in Blair (2007b), pp. 37–54.

Hooke, Della (ed.). 2000. *Landscape: The Richest Historical Record*, Supplementary Series 1, Society for Landscape Studies, Westbury.

Hopkins, Keith. 1978. 'Economic Growth and Towns in Classical Antiquity', in Abrams and Wrigley, pp. 35–78.

Hudson, John 1994. *Land, Law, and Lordship in Anglo-Norman England*, Clarendon Press, Oxford.

Hurst, J.G. 1984. 'The Wharram Research Project: Results to 1983', *Medieval Archaeology* 28, pp. 77–111.

———. 1988. 'Rural Building in England and Wales: England', in Hallam, pp. 854–930.

Jack, R. Ian. 1963. 'The Cloth Industry in Medieval Ruthin', *Transactions of Denbighshire Historical Society* 12, pp. 10–25.

———. 1981. 'Fulling-Mills in Wales and the March before 1547', *Archaeologia Cambrensis* 130, pp. 70–130.

Jarrett, Jonathan. 2010. 'Settling the King's Lands: *Aprisio* in Catalonia in Perspective', *Early Medieval Europe* 18, no. 3, pp. 320–42.

Kapelle, William E. 1979. *The Norman Conquest of the North: The Region and Its Transformation, 1000–1135*, University of North Carolina Press, Chapel Hill.

Kealey, Edward J. 1987. *Harvesting the Air: Windmill Pioneers in Twelfth Century England*, University of California Press, Berkeley.

Keene, Derek. 1985. *Survey of Medieval Winchester, Vols. I and II*, Winchester Studies 2, Oxford University Press, Oxford.

Kershaw, Ian. 1973a. '"The Great Famine and Agrarian Crisis in England 1315–1322', *Past and Present*, no. 59, pp. 3–50.

———. 1973b. *Bolton Priory: The Economy of a Northern Monastery 1286–1325*, Oxford University Press, Oxford.

Kershaw, Ian (ed.). 1970. *Bolton Priory Rentals and Ministers' Accounts, 1473–1539*, YAS Record Series Vol. 132, YAS, Leeds.

Kershaw, Ian, and Smith, David M. (eds.). 2000. The *Bolton Priory Compotus, 1286–1325: Together with a Priory Account Roll for 1377–1378*, YAS/Boydell Press, Woodbridge.

King, Edmund. 1973. *Peterborough Abbey 1086–1310: A Study in the Land Market*, Cambridge University Press, Cambridge.

Kirk, R.E.G. (ed.). 1892. *Accounts of the Obedientiars of Abingdon Abbey*, CaS.

Klemm, Friedrich. 1959. *A History of Western Technology*, trans. Dorothea Waley Singer, George Allen and Unwin, London.

Knowles, David. 1940a. *The Monastic Order in England: A History of Its Development from the Times of St Dunstan to the Fourth Lateran Council, 943–1216*, Cambridge University Press, Cambridge.

———. 1940b. *The Religious Houses of Medieval England*, Sheed and Ward, London.

———. 1948. *The Religious Orders in England*, Cambridge University Press, Cambridge.

Knowles, David, and Hadcock, R. Neville. 1953. *Medieval Religious Houses: England and Wales*, Longmans Green, London.

Kosminsky, E.A. 1956. *Studies in the Agrarian History of England in the Thirteenth Century*, trans. Ruth Kisch, Basil Blackwell, Oxford.

Kuhn, Thomas 1962. *The Structure of Scientific Revolutions*, University of Chicago Press, Chicago.

Langdon, John. 1986. *Horses, Oxen and Technological Innovation: The Use of Draught Animals in English Farming from 1066 to 1500*, Cambridge University Press, Cambridge.

———. 1989. 'A Quiet Revolution – The Horse in Agriculture, 1100–1500', *History Today* 39, no. 7, pp. 26–31.

———. 1991. 'Water-Mills and Windmills in the West Midlands, 1086–1500', *Economic History Review* 44, no. 3, pp. 424–4.

———. 1992. 'The Birth and Demise of a Medieval Windmill', *History of Technology* 14, pp. 54–76.

———. 1994. 'Lordship and Peasant Consumerism in the Milling Industry of Early Fourteenth-Century England', *Past and Present*, no. 145, pp. 3–46.

———. 1996. 'The Mobilization of Labour in the Milling Industry of Thirteenth- and Early Fourteenth-Century England', *Canadian Journal of History* 31, pp. 37–58.

———. 1997. 'Was England a Technological Backwater in the Middle Ages?', in Astill and Langdon, pp. 275–92.

———. 2004. *Mills in the Medieval Economy: England 1300–1540*, Oxford University Press, Oxford.

———. 2007. 'The Efficiency of Inland Water Transport in Medieval England', in Blair (2007b), pp. 110–30.

Larking, Lambert B. (ed.). 1869. *Domesday Book of Kent*, James Toovey, London.

Latham, R.E. 1999. *Revised Medieval Latin Word-List from British and Irish Sources*, Oxford University Press, Oxford (rev. edn., 1st pub. 1965).

Legg, Katrina. 2004. *Bolton Priory: Its Patrons and Benefactors, 1120–1293*, Borthwick Paper 106, University of York/Borthwick Institute, Heslington.

Lennard, Reginald. 1947. 'An Early Fulling-Mill', *Economic History Review* 17, p. 150.

———. 1951. 'Early English Fulling Mills: Additional Examples', *Economic History Review* 3, no. 3, pp. 342–3.

———. 1956. 'The Demesnes of Glastonbury Abbey in the Eleventh and Twelfth Centuries', *Economic History Review* 8, no. 3, pp. 355–63.

Lennard, R. V., Harvey, B. F., and Stone, E. 1975. 'The Glastonbury Estates: A Rejoinder', *Economic History Review* 28, no. 3, pp. 517–23.

Levesque, R., Bessonet, J-F., and Boureau, J. 2002. 'L'Art de Fouler en Vendée: Le Moulin de Gaumier à Cugand'. *303: Arts, Recherches et Creations* 73, pp. 16–33.

Liddy, Christian D. 2008. *The Bishopric of Durham in the Late Middle Ages: Lordship, Community and the Cult of St Cuthbert*, Boydell Press, Woodbridge.

Lindberg, David C., and Shank, Michael H. (eds.). 2013. *The Cambridge History of Science, Vol. 2 – Medieval Science*, Cambridge, Cambridge University Press.

Loengard, Janet S. 2006. 'Lord's Rights and Neighbours' Nuisances: Mills and Medieval English Law', in Walton, pp. 129–52.

Long, Pamela. 1997. 'Power, Patronage, and the Authorship of *Ars*: From Mechanical Know-How to Mechanical Knowledge in the Last Scribal Age', *Isis* 88, pp. 1–41.

———. 2000. *Technology, Society and Culture in Late Medieval and Renaissance Europe, 1300–1600*, Society for the History of Technology and American Historical Association, Washington, DC.

———. 2001. *Openness, Secrecy, Authorship: Technical Arts and the Culture of Knowledge from Antiquity to the Renaissance*, Johns Hopkins University Press, Baltimore.

Lucas, Adam. 2005. 'Industrial Milling in the Ancient and Medieval Worlds: A Survey of the Evidence for an Industrial Revolution in Medieval Europe', *Technology and Culture* 46, no. 1, pp. 1–30.

———. 2006a. *Wind, Water, Work: Ancient and Medieval Milling Technology*, Brill, Leiden.

———. 2006b. 'The Role of the Monasteries in the Development of Medieval Milling', in Walton, pp. 89–128.

———. 2010. 'Narratives of Technological Revolution in the Middle Ages', in Albrecht Classen (ed.), *Handbook of Medieval Studies: Terms, Methods, Trends*, vol. 2, De Gruyter, Berlin, pp. 967–90.

Luckhurst, David. 1975. *Monastic Watermills: A Study of the Mills within English Monastic Precincts*, Society for the Protection of Ancient Buildings, London.

Lysons, D., and Lysons, S. 1817. 'Parishes: Alfreton – Aston-on-Trent', *Magna Britannia, Vol. 5: Derbyshire*, Cadell, London.

MacKenzie, Donald, and Wacjman, Judy (eds.). 1985. *The Social Shaping of Technology: How the Refrigerator Got Its Hum*, Open University Press, Milton Keynes.

Magnusson, Roberta. 2001. *Water Technology in the Middle Ages: Cities, Monasteries, and Waterworks after the Roman Empire*, Johns Hopkins University Press, Baltimore and London.

Maitland, Frederic William. 1987. *Domesday Book and Beyond: Three Essays in the Early History of England*, Cambridge University Press, Cambridge (1st pub. 1897).

Manby, T.G., Moorhouse, S., and Ottaway, P. (eds.). 2003. *The Archaeology of Yorkshire: An Assessment at the Beginning of the 21st Century*, Yorkshire Archaeological Society Occasional Paper No. 3, Yorkshire Archaeological Society.

McGregor, Patricia. 1983. *Odiham Castle 1200–1500: Castle and Community*, Alan Sutton, Gloucester.

McNamara, Colin. 1997. *The Wars of the Bruces: Scotland, England and Ireland, 1306–1328*, Tuckwell Press, East Linton.

Miller, Edward. 1951. *The Abbey and Bishopric of Ely*, Cambridge University Press, Cambridge.

———. 1965. 'The Fortunes of the English Textile Industry during the Thirteenth Century', *Economic History Review* 18, no. 1, pp. 64–82.

———. 1971. 'England in the Twelfth and Thirteenth Centuries: An Economic Contrast?', *Economic History Review* 24, no. 1 (2nd series), pp. 1–14.

———. 1988. 'Social Structure: Northern England' in Hallam, pp. 685–98.

Miller, Edward (ed.). 1991. *The Agrarian History of England and Wales: Vol. III 1348–1500*, Cambridge University Press, Cambridge.

Miller, Edward, and Hatcher, John. 1978. *Medieval England: Rural Society and Economic Change 1086–1348*, Longman, London.

———. 1995. *Medieval England: Towns, Commerce and Crafts*, Longman, London.

Moorhouse, David. 1989. 'Monastic Estates: Their Composition and Development', in Gilchrist and Mytum, pp. 29–81.

Moorhouse, Stephen. 2003a. 'Medieval Corn Mills in the Manor of Rothwell', in Wrathmel, pp. 18–28.

———. 2003b. 'Medieval Yorkshire: A Rural Landscape for the Future', in Manby, Moorhouse and Ottaway, pp. 181–214.

———. 2003c. 'The Anatomy of the Yorkshire Dales: Deciphering the Medieval Landscape', in Manby, Moorhouse and Ottaway, pp. 293–362.

Morgan, Kenneth O. 1997. *The Oxford Illustrated History of Britain*, Oxford University Press, Oxford (1st pub. 1984).

Morgan, Marjorie. 1946. *The English Lands of the Abbey of Bec*, Oxford University Press, London.

———. 1968. *The English Lands of the Abbey of Bec*, rev. edn., Oxford University Press, London.

Mortimer, Ian. 2005. 'The Death of Edward II in Berkeley Castle', *English Historical Review* 120, pp. 1175–224.

Muendel, John. 1972. 'The Grain Mills of Pistoia in 1350', *Bollettino Storico Pistoiese* 7 (3rd series), pp. 39–64.

———. 1974. 'The Horizontal Mills of Pistoia', *Technology and Culture* 15, no. 2 (April), pp. 194–225.

———. 1981. 'The Distribution of Mills in the Florentine Countryside during the Late Middle Ages', in Raftis, pp. 83–115.

———. 1990. 'Book Review: Richard Holt, *The Mills of Medieval England*', *Technology and Culture* 31, no. 3 (July), pp. 508–12.

———. 1991. 'The Internal Functions of a 14th-Century Florentine Flour Factory', *Technology and Culture* 32, no. 3 (July), pp. 498–520.

Mulholland, Maureen. 2002. 'The Jury in English Manorial Courts', in John Cairns and Grant McLeod (eds.), *The Dearest Birth Right of the People of England: The Jury in the History of the Common Law*, Hart Publishing, Oxford, pp. 63–74.

———. 2003. 'Trials in Manorial Courts in Late Medieval England', in Maureen Mulholland and Brian Pullan (eds.), *The Trial in History: England and Europe from the Thirteenth to the Seventeenth Century*, Manchester University Press, Manchester, pp. 81–101.

Mullens, E.L.C. 1958. *Texts and Calendars: An Analytical Guide to Serial Publications*, RHS, London.

Mumford, Lewis. 1963. *Technics and Civilization*, Harcourt Brace, Orlando (FA) (1st pub. 1934).

———. 1964. 'Democratic and Authoritarian Technics', *Technology and Culture* 5, no. 1, pp. 1–8.

———. 1967. *The Myth of the Machine: Technics and Human Development*, Secker and Warburg, London (1st pub. 1966).

———. 1969. *The Pentagon of Power*, Secker and Warburg, London.

Neilson, N. 1910. 'Customary Rents', in Stenton.

Newman, Christine M. 2000. 'Employment on the Priory of Durham Estates, 1494–1519: The Priory as an Employer', *Northern History* 36, no. 1, pp. 43–58.

Norman, W.L. 1970. 'The Wakefield Soke Mills to 1853', *Industrial Archaeology* 7, pp. 176–83.

O'Meara, Don. 2013. 'Scant Evidence of Great Surplus: Research at the Rural Cistercian Monastery of Holme Cultram, Northwest England', in M. Groot, D. Lentjes and J. Zeiler (eds.), *Barely Surviving or More Than Enough? The Environmental Archaeology of Subsistence, Specialisation and Surplus Food Production*, Sidestone Press, Leiden, pp. 279–96.

Ovitt, George Jr. 1986. 'The Cultural Context of Western Technology: Early Christian Attitudes toward Manual Labor', *Technology and Culture* 27, no. 3, pp. 477–500.

———. 1987. *The Restoration of Perfection: Labour and Technology in Medieval Culture*, Rutgers University Press, New Brunswick, NJ.

Page, Frances Mary. 1934. *The Estates of Crowland Abbey: A Study in Manorial Organization*, Cambridge University Press, Cambridge.

Parry, M.L. 1978. *Climatic Change, Agriculture, and Settlement*, Dawson, Folkestone.

Pelteret, David A.E. 1995. *Slavery in Early Medieval England: from the Reign of Alfred until the Twelfth Century*, Boydell Press, Woodbridge/Rochester, NY.

Pestell, Tim. 2004. *Landscapes of Monastic Foundation: The Establishment of Religious Houses in East Anglia c.650–1200*, Boydell Press, Woodbridge/Rochester, NY.

Pierce, S.V. 1966. 'A Medieval Windmill, Honey Hill, Dogsthorpe', *Proceedings of the Cambridgeshire Antiquarian Society* 59, pp. 95–103.

Pirenne, Henri. 1893. 'L'origine des constitutions urbaines au Moyen-âge', *Revue Historique* 53, pp. 1–32.

———. 1898. 'Villes, marchés et marchands au Moyen Age', *Revue Historique* 67, in Henri Pirenne, *Les villes et les institutions urbaines*, Alcan-Nouvelle société éditions, Paris-Bruxelles, 1939, Vol. 1, pp. 111–22.

———. 1925. *Medieval Cities: Their Origins and the Revival of Trade*, trans. Frank D. Halsey, Princeton University Press, Princeton.

Platt, Colin. 1984. *The Abbeys and Priories of Medieval England*, Secker and Warburg, London.

Podmore, Colin. 2008. *Dioceses and Episcopal Sees in England: A Background Report for the Dioceses Commission*, Dioceses Commission, London, DC/R3.

Posnansky, M. 1956. 'The Lamport Postmill', *Northamptonshire Natural History Society and Field Club* 33, no. 239, pp. 66–79.

Postan, Michael M. 1950. 'Histoire économique: Moyen Age', *IXe Congrès International des Science Historiques, Vol. I: Rapports*, Paris, 150.

———. 1953. 'Glastonbury Estates in the Twelfth Century', *Economic History Review* 5, no. 3, pp. 358–67.

———. 1956. 'Glastonbury Estates in the Twelfth Century: A Reply', *Economic History Review* 9, no. 1, pp. 106–18.

———. 1966a. 'Medieval Agrarian Society in Its Prime: England', in Postan (1966b), pp. 548–632.

———. 1966b. *The Cambridge Economic History of Europe, Vol. 1: The Agrarian Life of the Middle Ages*, Cambridge University Press, Cambridge.

———. 1975. 'The Glastonbury Estates: A Restatement', *Economic History Review* 28, no. 3, pp. 524–7.

———. 1993. *The Medieval Economy and Society: An Economic History of Britain in the Middle Ages*, Penguin, London (1st pub. 1972).

Postan, M.M., and Hatcher, John. 1978. 'Population and Class Relations in Feudal Society', *Past and Present*, no. 78, pp. 24–37.

Power, Eileen. 1941. *The Wool Trade in English Medieval History*, Oxford University Press, Oxford.

Raban, Sandra. 1977. *The Estates of Thorney and Crowland: A Study in Medieval Monastic Land Tenure*, Department of Land Economy, Occasional Paper No. 7, Cambridge, University of Cambridge.

Raftis, J.A. (ed.) 1981. *Pathways to Medieval Peasants*, Papers in Medieval Studies 2, Pontifical Institute of Medieval Studies, Toronto.

Rahtz, P.A. 1981. 'Medieval Milling', in Crossley, pp. 1–15.

Rahtz, P.A., and Bullough, Donald. 1977. 'The Parts of an Anglo-Saxon Mill', in Clemoes, pp. 15–37.

Raine, James. 1833. *A brief account of Durham cathedral, with notices of the castle, university, city churches, & c.*, Blackwell and Co., Newcastle.

Razi, Zvi. 1983. 'The Struggles between the Abbots of Halesowen and Their Tenants in the Thirteenth and Fourteenth Centuries', in Aston et al., pp. 151–68.

———. 2007. 'Serfdom and Freedom in Medieval England: A Reply to the Revisionists', *Past and Present*, no. 195, Supplement 2, pp. 182–7.

Reynolds, Terry. 1983. *Stronger than a Hundred Men: A History of the Vertical Water Wheel*, Johns Hopkins University Press, Baltimore, MD.

———. 1984. 'Medieval Roots of the Industrial Revolution', *Scientific American* 251, pp. 109–16.

Roberts, Brian K. 1987. *The Making of the English Village: A Study in Historical Geography*, Longman, London.

Robinson, David M. 1980. *The Geography of Augustinian Settlement in Medieval England and Wales, Parts I and II*, BAR British Series 80 (I), Oxford.

Rogers, James E. Thorold. 1894. *Six Centuries of Work and Wages: the history of English labour*, Swann Sonnenschein, London (1st pub. 1884).

Roland, Alex. 2003. 'Once More into the Stirrups: Lynn White Jr., Medieval Technology and Social Change', *Technology and Culture* 44, no. 3 (July), pp. 574–85.

Rollins, J.G. 1981. 'Forge Mills, Redditch, Worcestershire: From Abbey Metalworks to Museum of the Needlemaking Industry', *Industrial Archaeology* 16, no. 2 (Summer), pp. 158–69.

Russell, J.C. 1966. 'The Pre-Plague Population of England', *Journal of British Studies* 5, pp. 1–21.

Rynne, Colin Bernard. 1988. 'The Archaeology and Technology of the Horizontal-Wheeled Watermill, with Special Reference to Ireland, Vols. I and II', unpub. PhD diss., National University of Ireland, University College Cork.

———. 1989a. 'Archaeology and the Early Irish Watermill', *Archaeology Ireland* 3, no. 3, pp. 110–14.

———. 1989b. 'The Introduction of the Vertical Watermill into Ireland: Some Recent Archaeological Evidence', *Medieval Archaeology* 33, pp. 21–31.

———. 2000. 'Waterpower in Medieval Ireland', in Squatriti, pp. 1–50.

———. 2011. 'Technological Continuity, Technological "Survival": The Use of Horizontal Mills in Western Ireland, c. 1632–1940', *Industrial Archaeology Review* 33, no. 2, pp. 94–103.

Salmon, J. 1940. 'Erection of a Windmill at Newborough (Anglesey) in 1303', *Archaeologia Cambrensis* 95, pp. 250–52.

———. 1941. 'The Windmill in English Medieval Art', *Journal of the British Archaeological Association* 6, 3rd ser., pp. 88–102.

Salzman, L.F. 1964. *English Industries of the Middle Ages*, new edn., H. Pordes, London (1st pub. 1913).

Savine, A.N. 1909. *English Monasteries on the Eve of the Dissolution*, Oxford Studies in Social and Legal History, Vol. I, Clarendon Press, Oxford.

Sawyer, P.H. (ed.) 1968. *Anglo-Saxon Charters*, Royal Historical Society, London.

Scammell, Jean. 1966. 'The Origin and Limitations of the Liberty of Durham', *English Historical Review* 81, no. 320, pp. 449–73.

Scott, E. Kilburn. 1931–32. 'Early Cloth Fulling and its Machinery', *Transactions of the Newcomen Society* 12, pp. 31–52.

Searle, Eleanor. 1974. *Lordship and Community: Battle Abbey and Its Banlieu 1066–1538*, Pontifical Institute of Medieval Studies, Toronto.

Seebohm, Frederic. 1915. *The English Village Community: Examined in Its Relations to the Manorial and Tribal Systems and to the Common or Open Field System of Husbandry*, Longmans Green, London.

Seymour, Deryck (ed.). 1977. *Torre Abbey: An Account of Its History, Buildings, Cartularies and Land*, pub. by the author, Torquay.

Singer, Charles, Holmyard, E.J., Hall, A.R., and Williams, Trevor (eds.) 1956. *A History of Technology Vol. II: The Mediterranean Civilizations and the Middle Ages, c. 700 BC–c. A.D. 1500*, Oxford at the Clarendon Press, London.

Sistrunk, Tim. 2006. 'The Right to the Wind in the Later Middle Ages', in Walton, pp. 153–70.

Smith, E., and Wolfe, M. (eds.). 1997. *Technology and Resource Use in Medieval Europe*, Ashgate, Aldershot.

Smith, R.A.L. 1969. *Canterbury Cathedral Priory: A Study in Monastic Administration*, Cambridge University Press, Cambridge.

Southgate, Michael. 1999. *The Old Tide Mill at Eling*, Hampshire Mills Group, Southampton.

Spain, R.J. 1984. 'Romano-British Watermills', *Archaeologia Cantiana*, 101–28.

———. 1992. 'Roman Water-Power: A New Look at Old Problems', Imperial College of Science and Technology, unpublished Doctorate thesis.

Squatriti, Paolo. 1997. 'Advent and Conquests of the Water Mill in Italy', in Smith and Wolfe, pp. 125–38.

———. 1998. *Water and Society in Early Medieval Italy, AD 400–1000*, Cambridge University Press, Cambridge.

Squatriti, Paolo (ed.). 2000. *Working with Water in Medieval Europe: Technology and Resource-Use*, Brill, Leiden.

Stacy, N.E. (ed.). 2001. *Surveys of the Estates of Glastonbury Abbey, c. 1135–1201*, British Academy/Oxford University Press, Oxford.

Staudenmaier, John M. 1989. *Technology's Storytellers: Reweaving the Human Fabric*, MIT Press, Cambridge, MA.

Stenton, Frank M. 1910. *Types of Manorial Structure in the Northern Danelaw*, Oxford Studies in Social and Legal History, Vol. 2, Clarendon Press, Oxford.

Stenton, F.M. (ed.). 1920. *Documents Illustrative of the Social and Economic History of the Danelaw*, Records of Social and Economic History, Vol. 5, British Academy/Oxford University Press, London.

Stöber, Karen. 2007. *Late Medieval Monasteries and their Patrons: England and Wales, c. 1300–1540*, Boydell Press, Woodbridge.

Stockdale, Rachel. 1980a. 'A School of the Lord's Service', in British Library, pp. 24–39.

———. 1980b. 'Benedictine Libraries and Writers', in British Library, pp. 62–81.

———. 1980c. 'Dissolution', in British Library, pp. 82–91.

Sweezy, Paul. 1976. 'A Rejoinder', in Hilton, pp. 102–8.

Tann, Jennifer. 1967. 'Multiple Mills', *Medieval Archaeology* 11, pp. 253–4.

Thirsk, Joan. 1997. *Alternative Agriculture: A History From the Black Death to the Present Day*, Oxford University Press, Oxford.

Thoen, Erik, and Vanhaute, Eric. 2011. 'Pirenne and Economic and Social Theory: Influences, Methods and Reception', *Belgisch Tijdschrift Voor* 61, nos. 3–4, pp. 323–53.

Thomson, Rodney M. 1983. 'England and the Twelfth Century Renaissance', *Past and Present*, no. 101 (November), pp. 3–21.

Titow, Jan. 1978. 'Book Review: *Plague, Population and the English Economy 1348–1530*, by John Hatcher', *Economic History Review* 31, no. 3 (August), pp. 466–77.

Trovò, R. 1996. 'Canalizzazioni lignee e ruota idraulica di età romana ad Oderzo (Treviso)', *Quaderni di archeologia del Veneto* 12, pp. 119–34.

Turner, D.H. 1980a. '"This Little Rule for Beginners"', in British Library, pp. 10–23.

———. 1980b. 'Guests Who Are Never Lacking in a Monastery', in British Library, pp. 54–61.

Van Caenegem, R.C. 1988. *The Birth of the English Common Law*, Cambridge University Press, Cambridge (1st pub. 1973).

Vaughn, Sally N. 1981. *The Abbey of Bec and the Anglo-Norman State 1034–1136*, Boydell Press, Woodbridge (Suffolk).

Verhulst, Adriaan 1991. 'The Decline of Slavery and the Economic Expansion of the Early Middle Ages', *Past and Present*, no. 133 (November), pp. 195–203.

———. 1997. 'Medieval Socio-economic Historiography in Western Europe: Towards an Integrated Approach', *Journal of Medieval History* 23, no. 1, pp. 89–101.

Verna, Catherine. 1995. *Les mines et les forges des Cisterciens en Champagne méridionale et un Bourgogne du Nord, XIIe–XV e siècle*, Association pour l'Edition et la Diffusion de Etudes Historiques/Vulcain, Paris.

———. 2002. *Le Temps des moulines: Fer, technique et société dans les Pyrénées centrales (XIIIᵉ–XVIᵉ siècles)*, Publications de la Sorbonne, Paris.

Vinogradoff, Paul. 1892. *Villainage in England: Essays in English Medieval History*, Cambridge University Press, Cambridge.

———. 1908. *English Society in the Eleventh Century: Essays in English Medieval History*, Oxford at the Clarendon Press, Oxford.

———. 1932. *The Growth of the Manor*, George Allen and Unwin, London (1st pub. 1904, rev. edn. 1911).

Wagstaff, J.M. 1970. 'The Economy of Dieulacres Abbey, 1214–1539', *North Staffordshire Journal of Field Studies* 10, pp. 83–101.

Waites, B. 1964. 'Medieval Iron Working in Northeast Yorkshire', *Geography* 49, no. 1, pp. 33–43.

Walton, Steven A. (ed.). 2006. *Wind and Water in the Middle Ages: Fluid Technologies from Antiquity to the Renaissance*, University of Arizona Press, Phoenix.

Westell, W. Percival. 1934. 'Sandon Mount, Hertfordshire: Its Site, Excavation and Problems', *St Albans and Hertfordshire Architectural and Archaeological Society Transactions*, pp. 173–83.

White, Lynn Jr. 1940. 'Technology and Invention in the Middle Ages', *Speculum* 15, pp. 141–59; repr. in White (1978), pp. 1–22.

———. 1962. 'The Act of Invention: Causes, Contexts, Continuities, and Consequences', *Technology and Culture* 3, no. 4 (Fall), pp. 486–500.

———. 1964. *Medieval Technology and Social Change*, Oxford University Press, Oxford (1st pub. 1962).

———. 1967. 'Technology in the Middle Ages', in Melvin Kranzberg and Carroll W. Pursell (eds.), *Technology in Western Civilization*, Oxford University Press, New York, pp. 66–78.

———. 1968. *Dynamo and Virgin Reconsidered: Essays in the Dynamism of Western Culture*, MIT Press, Cambridge, MA.

———. 1971. 'Cultural Climates and Technological Advance in the Middle Ages', *Viator* 2, pp. 171–201, repr. in White (1978), pp. 217–54.

———. 1972a. 'The Expansion of Technology 500–1500', in Cipolla (1976), pp. 143–74.

———. 1972b. 'The Historical Roots of Our Ecologic Crisis', in Carl Mitcham and Robert Mackey (eds.), *Philosophy and Technology: Readings in the Philosophical Problems of Technology*, Free Press, New York, pp. 259–65.

———. 1975. 'The Study of Medieval Technology, 1924–1974', in White (1978), pp. xi–xxiv.

———. 1978. *Medieval Religion and Technology: Collected Essays*, University of California Press, Berkeley, CA.

———. 1979. 'Technological Development in the Transition from Antiquity to the Middle Ages', in *Tecnologia, economia e società nel mondo romano*, Atti del convegno di Como, 27–29 September, Como, pp. 235–51.

Wickham, Chris. 2006. *Framing the Early Middle Ages: Europe and the Mediterranean, 400–800*, Oxford University Press, Oxford (1st pub. 2005).

Wikander, Örjan. 1984. *Exploitation of Water-Power or Technological Stagnation? A Reappraisal of the Productive Forces in the Roman Empire*, Scripta Minora Regiae Societatis Humaniorum Litterarum Lundensis, Lund.

———. 2000a. 'The Watermill', in Wikander (2000c), pp. 371–400.

———. 2000b. 'Industrial Applications of Water-Power', in Wikander (2000c), pp. 401–12.

———, (ed.). 2000c. *Handbook of Ancient Water Technology*, Brill, Leiden.

Williams, Brian. 2000. 'Nendrum Monastery, Northern Ireland', unpub. paper presented at *Archaeology, Heritage and Tourism*, Australian Institute for Maritime Archaeology/Australasian Society for Historical Archaeology Conference, 27 November–2 December 2000, Adelaide, South Australia.

Williams, G. 1962. *The Welsh Church from Conquest to Reformation*, University of Wales, Cardiff.

Wilson, Andrew. 2002a. 'Machines, Power and the Ancient Economy', *Journal of Roman Studies* 92, pp. 1–32.

———. 2002b. 'The Water-Mills on the Janiculum', *Memoirs of the American Academy in Rome* 45, pp. 219–46.

Wood, Michael. 1986. *Domesday: A Search for the Roots of England*, BBC Books, London.

Wood, Susan. 1955. *English Monasteries and Their Patrons in the Thirteenth Century*, Oxford University Press, London.

Wrathmel, S. 2003. *Rothwell: The Medieval Manor and Manorial Mills*, West Yorkshire Archaeology Service, Leeds.

Zeepvat, R. J. 1980. 'Post Mills and Archaeology', *Current Archaeology* 6, pp. 375–7.

Index

For Product Safety Concerns and Information please contact our EU
representative GPSR@taylorandfrancis.com Taylor & Francis Verlag GmbH,
Kaufingerstraße 24, 80331 München, Germany

Printed and bound by CPI Group (UK) Ltd, Croydon, CR0 4YY
01/05/2025
01858440-0001